T3-BNX-770
BETHANY
COLLEGE
LIBRARY
DISCARD

Sports Films: A Complete Reference

Sports Films
A Complete Reference

Compiled by
Harvey Marc Zucker
and
Lawrence J. Babich

McFarland & Company, Inc., Publishers
Jefferson, North Carolina, and London

Library of Congress Cataloguing-in-Publication Data

Zucker, Harvey Marc, 1949–
Sports films.

Bibliography: p. 495
Includes indexes.
1. Sports films – Catalogs. 2. Actors – Biography.
3. Athletes – Biography. I. Babich, Lawrence J.,
1935– . II. Title.
PN1995.9.S67Z83 1987 016.79143'09'09355 86-21090

ISBN 0-89950-227-X (acid-free natural paper) 

Printed in the United States of America.

McFarland Box 611 Jefferson NC 28640

Acknowledgments

We gratefully acknowledge the assistance of Herman Zucker, Kevin Scretchin, Rory Babich and Marc Babich for helping with the research for this book.

We would also like to express gratitude to these fine individuals and organizations:

National Baseball Hall of Fame, Elinor Babich, Ricky Babich, Steve Newhouse, Library of Performing Arts at Lincoln Center, Dave Szen and Kip Ingle of the New York Yankees Publications Department, the Cosmos team, Donnell Library, Library of Congress, Troma Film Productions, Inc., Muhammad Ali, Glenn Davis, the Film Forum, Bernard Hassan, Stewart Benedict, the University of California Media Extension, Chuck Connors, Elroy Hirsch, O.J. Simpson, Alex Karras, Vera Ralston, Bob Smith of the Rutgers University Public Relations Office, the American Film Institute, Monte Irvin, the **Jersey Journal**, the sports information office at the United States Military Academy, and Columbia Pictures International Corp.

Also, Bill Apter of **Inside Wrestling**, Yosh Kawana, Lou Thesz, the public relations office of the National Football League, Tim Brown, Werner Roth, Mike Mazurki, Screen Actor's Guild, Tony Ferrara, the Museum of Modern Art, Michael Hogan, Michael Rowan, Wayne Witkowski, George Korologos, Rick Tosches, Herbert Goldman of **Ring Magazine**, Guenter Schack of United Artists/MGM, Peacock Publications and the public relations office of the New York Knicks.

Table of Contents

How to Use This Book

In the main listings of sports films under the individual chapters, we have listed first the title of the film. Any title variants we have put in parentheses immediately following the main title and preceded it with "aka" (also known as).

We next list the year of release, which sometimes gets pretty sticky inasmuch as some films opened on the West Coast in one year and on the East Coast the next. Then there's the problem of foreign-made films, which often take at least a year or two to reach the United States. We have tried to note the variants on release dates.

Immediately after the release date, we have indicated whenever the film was not made in the United States; in the golf chapter, for instance, we have the listing: "**The Long Hole**, 1924, British."

We then give the distributor of the film and the running time. If the film is in color, we note that as well. We have found huge discrepancies between sources on running times of many films. On one film alone, the running time listed in the company's "presskit" varied more than 10 minutes from the time listed in other company publicity materials. Those times, in turn, differed from the length listed in Library of Congress records, which, in turn, differed from the three different lengths given in three separate reviews of the film! And all those differed from the length of the print we screened (thus: seven different running times).

Some of this can be explained by the fact that companies often preview a film before audiences, and, judging from the film's reception, re-edit the film, thus altering its length.

Then, too, sometimes a film will be recalled by the distributor after it opens and then re-released in a different length. The classic example of this is the all-time bomb **Heaven's Gate**, which ran more than three and one-half hours when it opened, was initially cut by more than an hour and was finally released in a version little more than an hour and one-half long.

Then there's also the matter of television prints. As in the case of **Two Minute Warning**, footage is sometimes added for a theatrical film's television release. And sometimes prints are drastically cut for TV viewing.

What we have done here is list a film's "length range" for theatrical releases only, when major discrepancies exist. For example "80-103 minutes" would mean the shortest theatrical version of the film we found was 80 minutes long while the longest was 103 minutes.

For silent films, because of the difference between silent running speed and sound speed, we list the actual footage as the length of the film. There are about 60 feet per minute at silent speed and 90 feet per minute at sound speed.

Next comes the matter of where to find a film listed in this reference book. Many films involve more than one sport. **The Social Lion**, for example, is about a polo-playing boxer—or is it about a boxing polo player? Then there's **My Way**, which involves swimming, auto racing and track and field; and, of course, **Pat and Mike**, which includes tennis and golf.

We have sometimes had to make arbitrary decisions on where to place these, based on what we believe is the dominant sport in each film.

The film may also be part of a series like **The Leather Pushers** and be listed under that series rather than the individual episode's title.

We believe we have made this book as easy as possible to use. One should always check the index at the back.

We have included films released through December 31, 1984.

An Overview

Willa Cather once wrote: "There are only two or three human stories and they go on repeating themselves as if they had never happened before." For the most part, that's certainly true about the plots of sports movies. Practically all of them can be sorted into three categories: the triumph of the underdog, the fall (and sometimes resurrection) of the mighty and the sporting event as a pretext.

There are exceptions, of course. The gentle Scottish soccer comedy **Gregory's Girl** is hard to categorize. The Mexican wrestling films such as **Samson and the Vampire Women** and **The Wrestling Women vs. the Aztec Mummy** are similarly hard to hang a label on, but in their case, why would you want to? Basically, however, it's the same plots over and over again in new forms.

Most sports films fall into the "triumph of the underdog" category, with good reason. Nearly everyone can identify with—and therefore cheer on—someone who triumphs over the greatest of odds and who can think of a better genre to play on these emotions than sports films?

Nowhere is this more evident than in sports comedies in which a perennial loser becomes champ through some sort of deus ex machina (which basically means an unusual, even extraordinary or supernatural event more or less out of the blue). In Walt Disney's **Gus**, it's a field goal-kicking mule that turns the team around. The **Bad News Bears** are transformed by the arrival of a star pitcher who happens to be a girl, while in its ripoff, **Here Come the Tigers**, the catalyst is a deaf lad.

In **The Fish That Saved Pittsburgh**, it's astrology which helps a basketball team while **Blackbeard's Ghost** is the savior of a track team and **Angels in the Outfield** come to the rescue of the Pittsburgh Pirates.

Two of the most famous and popular sports films of all times rely heavily on the underdog theme. In **Pride of the Yankees**, Hall of Famer Lou Gehrig, portrayed by Gary Cooper, endears himself to the audience by falling over a stack of bats in an early major league appearance. By thus humanizing the superstar, making him appear like any ordinary Joe, more sympathy is evoked for Gehrig's later losing battle against disease.

Rocky is the ultimate underdog. A nothing club fighter, a loser in everything he does, he suddenly and unexpectedly gets the opportunity to fight for the heavyweight championship of the world. That he loses the big fight doesn't really matter, because by then he's won the hearts of the world and set the stage for **Rocky II.**

Sylvester Stallone, as writer-director-actor of **Rocky II**, gives himself an added handicap aimed at getting the audience's sympathy. He's told that if he fights again, he's likely to suffer permanent damage to his already battered eye. That Rocky does fight, and the matter of the eye doesn't come up again, somehow gets lost in the shuffle of Rocky besting Apollo Creed. Audiences didn't seem to mind.

Rocky III, in which the new champ must defend his title, fits more into the "fall of the mighty" category.

There's nothing in the **Rocky** films that's really new except the freshness of the telling. There have been literally dozens of boy-from-the-slums boxing films dating to the silent days. Once again, it's the same themes over and over again.

The blinded fighter theme of **Rocky II** recalls James Cagney in **City for Conquest** and is akin to the blinded Olympic skater in **Ice Castles,** the one-legged pitcher of **The Stratton Story,** the crippled skier of **The Other Side of the Mountain** and the hearing-impaired football player of **Choices,** just to mention a few. And let's not forget the blind racehorse of **Chorus Lady** and the 1939 version of **Pride of the Blue Grass.**

The hero doesn't even have to be a "good guy" to become the underdog. In **Coup de Tête (The Hothead),** he's a totally unsavory and disagreeable fringe soccer player who's the perfect patsy for the team's management to frame when its star player commits a rape. When through a series of circumstances the team is forced to spring him from prison for a big game, he becomes the unlikely hero and wreaks a comic vengeance upon the entire town.

Getting to the top is hard enough, but staying there is even tougher, which is why "fall of the mighty" is another favorite theme of sports movies. The most poignant moment of **The Guy Who Came Back** is when ex-grid star Paul Douglas tries to tell jokes at a banquet only to learn that what people found funny when he was on top isn't funny coming from a has-been. Similarly, Charlton Heston finds that being **Number One** won't prevent advancing age from eroding his skills as a quarterback, while **Saturday's Hero** discovers there are six other days of the week.

Then there are those with the shady pasts who get a new lease on life and thus fit into this category under the "resurrection of the mighty" subsection. Robert Mitchum as the boxer in **Second Chance** and Wallace Beery as a drunken racetrack vet in **Stablemates** come to mind quickly, but the all-time champ in this category is just that: **The Champ.**

The 1931 Wallace Beery vehicle about a boxer who makes a comeback through the love of his son was so popular it spawned two direct remakes (**The Clown,** a 1953 non-sports film with Red Skelton, and **The Champ,** which starred Jon Voight in 1979) and countless imitations.

The theme of young children affecting a personality change in either fallen or seedy personalities pops up often in films such as **Little Miss Marker, Sorrowful Jones, King of the Turf, Stablemates, Little Miss Thoroughbred, Fast Companions** and **You Can't Buy Luck,** to name a few.

Then there are those films which fit into the "sporting event as a pretext." In Stanley Kubrick's **The Killing,** the murder of a horse in the middle of a race is to serve as a diversion for a heist of the racetrack receipts. Similarly, in **The Split,** it's football receipts at stake; and in **Fiasco in Milan,** it's soccer money.

Sure, **The Arsenal Stadium Mystery** has lots of soccer action, but it's basically a murder story, just as **Death on the Diamond** deals with just that and one of its descendants, **Girls Can Play,** is about murder on a women's softball team.

In **Victory,** a soccer game between the Nazis and a team of prisoners of war serves as a cover for an escape plot; and although it was hailed as fresh when the film was released, you will see later in this book that its roots can be traced to no fewer than six earlier films.

WHAT'S A SPORTS FILM?

It's necessary now for us to define just what we consider a sports film and what we don't. Naturally, there'll be the obvious films such as

The Babe Ruth Story and **Knute Rockne, All American.** No one can argue about that. However, we have limited this book to spectator sports, so that leaves out hunting and fishing (although a 1960's comedy, **Man's Favorite Sport?** concerned a fishing tournament) and mountain climbing, although we have included **The Man Who Skied Down Everest** because of the crossover in sports. We may get some arguments from areas of the world where bullfighting is popular, but we feel those films should be treated separately and again, we haven't included them.

Now, how about those movies in which the central plot doesn't concern sports? If sports plays an **integral** part in the film, even if it's not basically about sports, that film will be included. Our selections may sometimes seem arbitrary; and there will probably be those who will disagree with some of them, but if we included every film with a sports segment you might mistake this book for Webster's Dictionary.

For example, Nagise Oshima's **The Ceremony** deals with the disintegration of a powerful Japanese family after World War II. In one segment, a college baseball player returns home to find his mother committed harakiri because he dropped a pop fly in a championship game. He then takes his bat and glove to the top of the hill and burns them. As the segment, in our opinion, has important meaning in a film which can in no way otherwise be called a sports film, it will be included.

Very few people would consider **The Notorious Gentleman** with Rex Harrison a sports film, but you will find it in the Wheels chapter. That's because the playboy protagonist begins to undergo a personality change when he meets a Jewish girl during an auto race in Europe shortly after Hitler's takeover.

Any reference on sports films would certainly be incomplete without Abbott and Costello's famous "Who's on First" routine, yet that appears in a non-sports film, as does Red Skelton's baseball pitching segment of **Whistling in Brooklyn.** You'll find them both discussed in the Baseball chapter.

What you won't find here is every film in which, for example, one of the major characters attends or plays in a ball game or goes to the racetrack. Major cameo appearances by sports stars, such as those in **The Geisha Boy** and **That Touch of Mink,** will be noted at the beginning of each chapter.

WHAT'S NOT HERE

We have not included films made for television or cable, television shows or specials, industrial or educational films, promotional films with the exception of 1942's **The Ninth Inning,** newsreels (except for feature length or exceptional ones) or porno films.

We have included only those cartoons we feel are of special interest; and although we list hundreds of short films, we have limited those to what we consider to be significant or of some special interest.

WHAT MAKES A GREAT SPORTS FILM

Of the approximately 2,000 sports films discussed in this book, we have discovered one key element which distinguishes the top films from the mediocre and the bad ones. The great movies all have what we'll call a "conflict from within," as opposed to the films which have a conflict imposed from without. In both **Pride of the Yankees** and **Knute Rockne,**

All American, two famous examples, the conflict from within exists in the struggle to maintain dignity as well as personal standards in the face of serious disease.

Sure, in **Body and Soul** there's a gangster imposing a crisis upon John Garfield; but it's his betrayal of his loved ones and all they stand for and his ultimate decision not to throw a fight that makes it great. In **They Made Me a Criminal,** Garfield's other boxing movie, the inner struggle is whether to box his natural way and expose his identity, or face a terrible beating, or worse, the scorn of his loved ones if he decides not to fight at all.

Even the great sports comedies contain this vital element. In Harold Lloyd's **The Freshman,** it's the hero's inability to see that he's the school laughing stock. Once he does, he goes on to become the hero of the big game. In contrast, Buster Keaton's character in **College** knows he's a laugh-ing stock, but his struggle is to become an athlete when all his life he's hated sports.

It will be easy to tell most of the mediocre and just plain bad sports films from the listings in this book. Just look for those with the same old tired plots and gimmicks.

There will be endless kidnappings of the hero or one of his loved ones by the villain when the filmmakers can't think of any other way to keep the plot going.

There will be gangsters aplenty to threaten and bribe the star, who we'll call Our Hero; and when that gimmick isn't used, there's the vamp, to lure him away from his true love and his training. And, when all seems totally hopeless for Our Hero, let's not forget the ringside pleas, or the sudden appearance at the big game by the sweetheart to suddenly make him superman and win.

TREATMENT OF MINORITIES

Surprisingly, while countless westerns in the silent film era were portraying the American Indian as a bloodthirsty savage, he fared better than any other minority group in the sports films of the era.

The early baseball film **His Last Game** portrayed an Indian as being framed and otherwise abused by evil whites; and the Indian in general was generally sympathetic in these films, with **Braveheart** and **Strongheart,** among others, quickly coming to mind. The Indian generally disappeared from sports films during the sound era, however, except for the caricature of the rich football player in the Ritz Brothers comedy **Life Begins in College** and for the screen biographies of Jim Thorpe and Billy Mills (**Jim Thorpe—All American** and **Running Brave**, respectively).

Hispanics? Until the portrayals of Mexican boxers in 1950's **Right Cross** and 1952's **The Fighter** and **The Ring,** they were virtually nonexistent although a South American fighter does appear in one of Monogram's Joe Palooka films. At least 1942's **Moonlight in Havana** acknowledged that baseball was played south of the border.

Until the kung fu films (which incidentally we feel belong in a separate genre and don't include here) became popular in the United States, Asians fared worst of all; and their only appearances in sports films were for comic relief.

The exceptions are few and far between. The Yellow Man who stands up to the brutal boxer in **Broken Blossoms** (1919) is probably the prime example and detectives Charlie Chan and Mr. Moto are others. Mr. Moto's jiujitsu was often displayed in his films.

The treatment of blacks in sports films is something different, because dating to the silent era, there were movies geared for black audiences, many of them starring sports heroes such as Jack Johnson and Joe Louis. Johnson, incidentally, inspired many "black vs. white" boxing films in the early 1900's.

However, until the 1950's, their treatment in the "mainstream" cinema was, for the most part, abysmal at best. In the sports films of the 20's, 30's and 40's, when they appeared at all, it was as a horse trainer, a water boy or some other trivial character in the film mainly as so-called comic relief. Every now and then, there'd be a black boxer, such as Canada Lee in **Body and Soul.**

Just as Jackie Robinson broke major league baseball's color barrier, 1950's **The Jackie Robinson Story** marked the emergence of black athletes into the mainstream of motion pictures. Its success was soon followed by **The Harlem Globetrotters** in 1951, **The Joe Louis Story** in 1953 and another Globetrotters movie, **Go Man Go** in 1954.

WOMEN

If Martians tried to find out what Earth women are like by watching the majority of sports movies, they would see them as selfish, vain, fickle, greedy, talkative and laughing stocks when they try to play sports. With films like **Golden Girl, Personal Best, The Other Side of the Mountain** and many others of the past decade, that screen image is changing. For the most part, however, women have come off poorly in sports movies, with few memorable roles or performances.

The portrayal of women in sports films up to the 1960's can basically be broken down into several categories:

1. "Fickle Flora"—Again and again and yet again, Flora appears in sports movies. She shows her fickle face whenever there's a plot—which is quite often—where the two leads in the film are both in love with her. And how does she decide between the two in 90 percent of these films? You guessed it. The winner. The he-man. The loser loses the girl.

2. "Sweet Susie"—This is the frail young thing who covers her eyes at the boxing ring or at the football field whenever there's physical contact and who runs out on Our Hero for having such a nasty occupation, leaving him to the clutches of the vamp. But, never fear, she's back there at ringside when Our Hero is being beaten to a pulp to tell him she forgives him, and to spur him to victory.

3. "Vicki the Vamp"—Her appearance is an absolute must in any grade "B" boxing movie. Who else is going to sap the otherwise unbeatable hero of his strength (not to mention his money) and to make life miserable for Sweet Susie? She gets hers, in the end, most of the time.

4. "Window Dresser Wanda"—Why she's in the film at all, except for box office purposes, is a mystery except perhaps so the hero won't have to talk to himself when he goes home after the game. She's made more lackluster screen appearances than any other actress.

5. "Bungling Bertha"—Ho, ho, ho. Look at her try her hand at a man's sport. If she'd close her mouth once in a while, maybe the ball wouldn't land in it.

6. "Noble Nellie"—No matter how often hubby beats her or how often he cheats on her, she stands by her man and is the epitome of American womanhood.

There are exceptions to all these stereotypes; but until the 1970's, the stereotypes outnumber the exceptions by at least ten to one.

One of the most notable early exceptions is the little-known **Sidewalks of New York,** made in 1923. A woman is kicked out of the house by her father for refusing to marry the man of his choice, and she becomes a boxing champ, bailing her dad out of deep financial trouble. Lilli Palmer in **Body and Soul** and Audrey Totter in **The Set-Up** have meaty roles, and so their performances are memorable.

The first semblance of a real breakthrough was June Allyson's 1950 performance in **Right Cross,** in which she becomes the manager of a Mexican-American boxer. Not only is she portrayed as capable, but in a twist on the usual boxing cliché it's the fighter who believes he has to keep winning to retain her love. Female managers of athletes were not new to the movies but the handling was.

Pat and Mike, made in 1952, is the landmark film for women's equality in sports movies. Although a comedy in form, there's no question of the proficiency of the female athletes shown in the movie; and, ultimately, the heroine rescues her manager from being beaten by two thugs. With a top cast headed by Katharine Hepburn and Spencer Tracy and its excellent reception by the public, one would think the old stereotypes would have died forever. But change sometimes comes slowly, and it wasn't until the late 1960's and early 70's that women in sports films could share the winner's circle on an equal footing with men.

Baseball

In the early part of the 20th century, there was little doubt that baseball was the dominant sport in the United States. Soccer was all but nonexistent, and basketball and hockey would be a long time growing to the business sports they are today. The only real rival was football, running a distant second.

When Babe Ruth came along and captured the imagination of an entire nation with his mammoth home runs, baseball's position as The Great American Pastime was cemented. There's little mystery, therefore, why the heyday of baseball movies was during the era up to about 1935.

Although there had been a filmed dramatization of **Casey at the Bat** as early as 1899, most of the earliest baseball movies were newsreels of actual events, such as the 1909 **Detroit-Pittsburgh Baseball Series,** produced by the Essanay Co. The film era for baseball legitimately begins in 1909 with **His Last Game,** a cowboys-and-Indians diamond drama.

Filmmakers were quick to realize the added box office potential of the day's baseball stars, so it wasn't long before some of them began appearing, usually as themselves, in dramatized films as well as newsreels.

Hal Chase in 1911's **Hal Chase's Home Run** (not to be confused with Home Run Baker in **Home Run Baker's Double** which would follow in a couple of years) led the parade. The same year, Chief Bender, Jack Coombs and Rube Olding had major roles in **The Baseball Bug.** They would be followed by a whole host of players over the next few years, including Christy Mathewson in **Love and Baseball** and Mike Donlin, whose **Right Off the Bat** in 1915 launched him on a respectably long, if not spectacular movie career. Famed manager John McGraw also had a role in **Right Off the Bat,** as well as **The Universal Boy.**

Baseball great Ty Cobb had a role in **Somewhere in Georgia** (1916) in which he's kidnapped and must ride to the big game on a mule. One critic called it "absolutely the worst movie I've ever seen."

By the time sound was firmly established in films in the 1930's, dramatic baseball films had seemingly run their course, with comedy now king. Joe E. Brown, for example, starred in three slapstick baseball comedies within a three-year span: **Fireman, Save My Child, Elmer the Great** and **Alibi Ike.**

Knute Rockne, All American, a football film about the great Notre Dame coach, marked a general renaissance for sports films in general. Its box office success helped inspire **Pride of the Yankees,** about baseball star Lou Gehrig, and the two movies ushered in what we'll call the biographical era of sports movies, which lasted until the mid 1950's.

During the 1940's and 50's, baseball biographical films included **Pride of St. Louis, The Winning Team, The Jackie Robinson Story** and **Fear Strikes Out.**

One problem filmmakers had with baseball movies was that they were box office poison outside the United States; and during the post-World War II era with growing European markets, this particularly began to hit home.

If you think about it a bit, when was the last time you saw the British cricket films **The Final Test** or **It's Not Cricket** on television? That's how baseball movies were received abroad, in general. Therefore, the studios began changing the titles for foreign consumption to try to hide the fact they were baseball movies. Thus **Take Me Out to the Ball Game** became **Everybody's Cheering** in England.

With the exception of **Bang the Drum Slowly** in 1973, baseball movies hit the doldrums until, believe it or not, **The Bad News Bears** proved in 1976 the genre was still capable of producing a box office hit.

There are a number of films we could have included in the listings of baseball movies that follow, but which we felt would have been stretching it a bit to call them sports films. Nevertheless, some of them deserve at the very least passing mention.

At the top of the list is 1936's **The Black Legion** with Humphrey Bogart joining a Ku Klux Klan-type organization. When we first see the baddies, they're playing catch to emphasize that they're ordinary American Joes. Later, when Bogie's wife is leaving him after she learns of his activities, his baseball-playing little boy is reading aloud one of the Merriwell baseball stories, this time emphasizing the American values his father has betrayed.

Other footnotes to baseball film history include Jerry Lewis' **Geisha Boy,** with its look at Japanese baseball and appearances by members of the Dodgers (notably Gil Hodges); **Touch of Class,** with its opening softball sequence in London's Hyde Park the only acknowledgment on screen that baseball is played in Europe; **That Touch of Mink,** in which Cary Grant, trying to impress Doris Day, introduces her to several members of the New York Yankees; and **Speedy,** in which Harold Lloyd as a taxi driver scares the wits out of Babe Ruth while driving him to the ballpark and who gets a seat directly behind his boss when he should be on the job. Then there's Tony Randall preventing sportswriter pal Walter Matthau from seeing a triple play in **The Odd Couple,** and the East Side kids in **Block Busters.**

As we'll try to do in each chapter when a pattern of cliches has been established, we'll list the cliche and how often it's been used.

In baseball films, there have been at least 18 homers in the ninth inning to win the game.

The hero, who's either been kidnapped, suspended or otherwise waylaid, must rush to the ballpark to get there on time in 11 films.

1 Abner the Baseball

1961, Paramount Pictures, 13 minutes, Color. Director: Seymour Kneitel. Story and Narration: Eddie Lawrence.

A cartoon which traces the "life" of a baseball named Abner from his humble beginnings in the ball bag to a display case in the Baseball Hall of Fame. After seeing his pal socked out of the park by Yogi Berra, Abner quivers at the thought of being pitched to Mickey Mantle, but after being socked 987 feet and becoming a celebrity, all turns out well for our hero.

2 About Face

1952, Warner Brothers, 93 minutes, Color. Director: Roy Del Ruth. Producer: William Jacobs. Screenplay: Peter Milne, based on a play by John Monks Jr. and Fred Finklehoffe. Cameraman: Bert Glennon. Editor: Thomas Reilly.

Cast: Gordon MacRae, Dick Wesson, Eddie Bracken, Virginia Gibson, Phyllis Kirk, Aileen Stanley Jr., Joel Grey, Larry Keating, Cliffe Ferre, John Baer.

Brother Rat, which starred Ronald Reagan, Eddie Albert and Wayne Morris, was such a big hit in 1938 that Warner Brothers decided to film it again, this time with music and in color. It's the same shenanigans at the good ol' Southern Military Institute, as three seniors try to play baseball, hide a marriage and keep from being expelled, all at the same time.

3 Adventures of Frank Merriwell

1936, Universal, 12 chapters. Director: Louis Friedlander (Lew Landers). NOTE: (Some sources list the director as Cliff Smith). Producer: Henry McRae. Screenplay: George Plympton, Ella O'Neill, Basil Dickey, Maurice Geraghty; based on stories by Burt L. Standish.

Cast: Don Briggs, Jean Rogers, John King, Carla Laemmle, Sumner Getchell, Wallace Reid Jr., House Peters Jr., Allan Hershot, Monte Montague, Edward Arnold Jr., Bryant Washburn Jr.

Chapter One: The College Hero; Chapter Two: The Death Plunge; Chapter Three: Death at the Crossroads; Chapter Four: Wreck of the Vikings; Chapter Five: Capsized at the Cataract; Chapter Six: Descending Doom; Chapter Seven: Monster of the Deep; Chapter Eight: The Tragic Victor; Chapter Nine: Between Savage Foes; Chapter Ten: Imprisoned in a Dungeon; Chapter Eleven: The Crash in the Chasm; Chapter Twelve: The Winning Play.

One of the few sports film serials, it has enough action for at least six films. Briggs portrays Frank Merriwell, Farsdale High School's star pitcher, but that's just the beginning. He becomes involved with a mysterious old ring that carries the secret to buried Spanish gold, is attacked by Indians, kidnapped by the villain but escapes in the nick of time and gets to the ballpark to find Farsdale losing the big game 19-6. Singlehandedly, he wins the game 20-19 in time for the final fadeout.

4 Alibi Ike

1935, Warner Brothers, 73 minutes. Director: Ray Enright. Producer: Edward Chodorov. Screenplay: William Wister Haines. Story: Ring Lardner.

Cast: Joe E. Brown, Olivia DeHavilland, Ruth Donnelly, Roscoe Karns, William Frawley, Eddie Shubert, Paul Harvey, Joseph King, Joseph Crehan.

America's favorite comic sports "hero" of the 1930's, Brown again portrays a major league ballplayer as he did in **Fireman, Save My Child** (1932) and **Elmer the Great** (1933). This time he's Frank X. Farrell, a Chicago Cubs player who always has a ready excuse every time something goes wrong. As happens again and again and again (and then some) in sports films, Our Hero is waylaid by evil gamblers on the day of the big game, but we don't have to tell you who arrives at the ballpark in his pajamas in the nick of time, do we?

Angels and the Pirates--see **Angels in the Outfield.**

5 Angels in the Outfield (British title: **Angels and the Pirates**)

1951, Metro Goldwyn Mayer, 99 minutes. Producer and Director: Clarence Brown. Screenplay: George Wells, Dorothy Kingsley. Story: Richard Conlin. Cameraman: Paul C. Vogel. Editor: Robert J. Kern.

Cast: Paul Douglas, Janet Leigh, Keenan Wynn, Donna Corcoran, Lewis Stone, Spring Byington, Bruce Bennett, Marvin Kaplan, Ellen Corby, Jeff Richards, John Gallaudet.

The Pittsburgh Pirates are baseball's most hopelessly inept team, managed by Guffy McGovern, whose chief talent is setting a major league record for blaspheming and cursing. If you know anything at all about sports comedies, you just know something is miraculously going to turn them into pennant contenders. This time, it's the prayers of a little girl, portrayed by Corcoran, whom MGM had hoped would make it big as a new Shirley Temple. The orphan's prayers are answered by the Angel Gabriel, who sends the spirits of baseball greats past down onto the field to help out the Pirates. Byington and Corby portray nuns and Wynn is a baseball announcer out to get Douglas' scalp.

6 As the World Rolls On

1921, Elk Photo Plays, 5,600 feet. Cameraman: W.A. Andlauer.

Cast: Jack Johnson, Blanche Thompson.

That's right! Black boxing great Jack Johnson stars in a baseball movie which also features the Kansas City Monarchs. Sure there's some boxing as Johnson rescues a youth being beaten up by a gang led by the boy's rival for the love of a girl. Johnson teaches the lad how to box and to play baseball and, naturally, he becomes adept at both, helping to win a big game and later beats up the bully and gets the girl.

7 Babe Comes Home

1927, First National Pictures, 5,761 feet. Director: Ted Wilde. Producer: Wid Gunning. Scenario: Louis Stevens. Cameraman: Karl Struss.

Cast: Babe Ruth, Anna Q. Nilsson, Louise Fazenda, Ethel Shannon, Arthur Stone, Lou Archer, Tom McGuire, Mickey Bennett, James Bradbury, Big Boy Williams.

The Babe portrays Babe Dugan, the Angels' star player, who meets his Delilah in the form of laundress Nilsson. Tired of washing tobacco stains out of his uniform every week, she convinces him to give up chewing, but as soon as he does, he goes into a horrible batting slump. But as this is a 1920's Hollywood film, Babe's fiancee gives him some tobacco during the big game; he wins it with a homer.

8 Babe Ruth Series

In the early 1930s, Universal Pictures released a series of shorts ranging in length from seven to 10 minutes and featuring the baseball immortal. Titles include **Fancy Curves, Just Pals** and **Slide, Babe, Slide.** They include a very slim plot, providing Babe with the opportunity to show kids how to play baseball.

9 Babe Ruth Story

1948, Monogram Pictures, 106 minutes. Producer and Director: Roy Del Ruth. Screenplay: Bob Considine, George Callahan. Based on the book by Considine. Cameraman: Philip Tannura. Editor: Richard Herrmance.

Cast: William Bendix, Claire Trevor, Charles Bickford, Sam Levene, William Frawley, Gertrude Niesen, Stanley Clements, Lloyd Gough, Bobby Ellis, Fred Lightner, Mel Allen, Matt Briggs, Mark Koenig, Knox Manning.

If we have to tell you who Babe Ruth was, you really shouldn't be reading this book. Suffice to say that if you want a definitive biography of baseball's home run champ, read the book instead, although it's an enjoyable movie.

The film traces Ruth's life from his days at St. Mary's Industrial School for Boys and a waterfront saloon in Baltimore to his superstar days with the Red Sox and Yankees and to his final playing days with the Boston Braves. Much of the latter part of the film is devoted to Ruth's illness (he died shortly after the release of the film).

10 Bad News Bears

1976, Paramount Pictures, 102 minutes, Color. Director: Michael Ritchie. Producer: Stanley R. Jaffe. Screenplay: Bill Lancaster. Cameraman: John A. Alonzo. Editor: Richard A. Harris.

Cast: Walter Matthau, Tatum O'Neal, Vic Morrow, Joyce Van Patten, Ben Piazza, Jackie Earle Haley, Alfred W. Lutter, Brandon Cruz, Shari Summers, Joe Brooks.

William Bendix, right, greets Babe Ruth as he gets off the train in California to assist during the filming of The Babe Ruth Story. Also joining Bendix at the station are Claire Trevor and little Charley Dunsmoor. (Courtesy National Baseball Hall of Fame.)

This comedy about a ragtag foul-mouthed bunch of Little Leaguers proved so popular it spawned two direct sequels, a direct ripoff (**Here Come the Tigers**), several other imitations, including **Manny's Orphans** and **Swim Team** and even a Korean version. Not even the sequels, however, could come close to Matthau's portrayal of the coach, an alcoholic ex-minor leaguer, now reduced to cleaning swimming pools. He leads, however reluctantly, a motley bunch of losers in a WASP league, to be contenders for the title. The arrival of a new ace pitcher, who happens to be a girl (Tatum O'Neal), speeds the team's transformation.

11 Bad News Bears Go to Japan

1978, Paramount, 91 minutes. Director: John Berry. Producer: Michael Ritchie. Screenplay: Bill Lancaster. Cameraman: Gene Polito. Editor: Richard A. Harris.

Cast: Tony Curtis, Jackie Earle Haley, Tomisaburo Wakayama, Hatsune Ishihara, Matthew Douglas Anton, Erin Blount, George Gonzalez, Brett Marx, David Pollock, David Stambaugh.

When no other baseball team in America wants to go, the Bears volunteer to take on the Japanese national Little League champs, in the third and last of the series.

Taking them on the trip--and for a ride--is an unscrupulous promoter (Curtis) who's in trouble with loan sharks and is out only to make a bundle on the boys. When they're all stranded in Japan without a cent, Curtis somehow manages to promote a wrestling match between Antonio Inoki and a stooge, but the kids wind up in the ring and defeat the champ.

At the big game between the two teams, Curtis is persuaded to take on three ringers, who end the game by starting a fight, but the kids all go to an empty lot and complete the game by themselves without commercial pressure.

Samurai fans will recognize the Japanese baseball coach (Wakayama) as the stern-faced assassin of the popular Baby Cart series.

12 Bad News Bears in Breaking Training

1977, Paramount Pictures, 99 minutes, Color. Director: Michael Pressman. Producer: Leonard Goldberg. Screenplay: Paul Brickman. Cameraman: Fred J. Koenekamp. Editor: John W. Wheeler.

Cast: William Devane, Clifton James, Jackie Earle Haley, Chris Barnes, Erin Blount, Jaime Escobedo, George Gonzalez, Alfred Lutter, Brett Marx, David Pollock, David Stambaugh.

In this first sequel, streetwise biker Jackie Earle Haley talks his estranged dad (Devane) into coaching those lovable Little Leaguers as they head for a big game in the Astrodome; eventually father and son reconcile.

13 Ball Game

May 20, 1896. Producer: Thomas A. Edison.

Probably the first baseball film ever, this "peep show" was photographed from a single position behind home plate and shows some action from a game in which at least one of the teams is from Newark, New Jersey.

14 Bang the Drum Slowly

1973, Paramount Pictures, 98 minutes, Color. Director: John Hancock. Producer: Maurice and Lois Rosenfield. Screenplay: Mark Harris, based on his novel. Cameraman: Richard Shore. Editor: Richard Marks.

Cast: Michael Moriarty, Robert DeNiro, Vincent Gardenia, Phil Foster, Ann Wedgeworth, Patrick McVey, Tom Ligon, Heather Macrae, Selma Diamond, Barbara Babcock, Maurice Rosenfield.

Although Harris' story was made into a television special starring Paul Newman and Albert Salmi in the 1950s, it bounced around for a long time before finally hitting the big screen.

Much of the action was filmed at New York's Shea Stadium, with Moriarty portraying a Tom Seaver-like pitcher named Henry Wiggen who insists that fringe catcher Bruce Pearson (DeNiro) be kept on the roster after he learns that his batterymate is dying of Hodgkin's Disease.

Coming on the heels of **Love Story**'s phenomenal box office success, the time was right for this male tearjerker distinguished by believable characters and by humor. Particularly memorable is the unusual card game played by Foster.

15 Baseball, An Analysis of Motion

1919. No credits available.

While slow motion replay is old hat to anyone who has watched baseball on television, it was a novelty in 1919 as the **New York Times** review of this short attests:

"While the picture, because of its novelty, was received yesterday with the laughter of surprise, the process by which it was made will certainly be of value in the serious study of motion." Truer words were never spoken.

16 Baseball Bill

1916, Universal, 1 reel each. Director-Producer-Scenario: Bill Mason.

Titles in this series of shorts include **Broadway Bill, Flirting with Marriage, The Black Nine, Box of Tricks** and **Strike One!**

17 The Baseball Bug

1911, Thanhouser.

Cast: John W. Noble, Florence La Badie, Chief Bender, Jack Coombs, Rube Olding.

A young clerk is a small town baseball hero and thinks he's the greatest player who ever lived. When he's on the verge of being fired for neglecting his job, his wife contacts her cousin, Philadelphia A's pitcher Chief Bender. Bender and teammates Jack Coombs and Rube Olding visit the town and play a game with the clerk. When the clerk sees how good they are compared to him, he burns his baseball equipment and the "bug" is cured.

18 Baseball Bugs

1946, Warner Brothers. Director: I. Freleng. Story: Michael Maltese. Animation: Manual Perez, Ken Champin, Virgil Ross, Gerry Chinquy.

Everyone's favorite wabbit, Bugs Bunny, tries to play all nine positions against the Gas House Gorillas even though they cheat in this Looney Tunes cartoon.

19 Baseball Fan

1908, Essanay, 10 minutes. Director-Scenario: G.M. Anderson. No credits available.

An avid fan tells his wife he has urgent business. That turns out to be a game between the White Sox and Highlanders at Comiskey Park. Finding the park sold out, he peeks through a knothole before being chased away.

20 The Baseball Star from Bingville

1911, Essanay, 1,000 feet. No credits available.

Bim McGuffrey is discovered by a National League scout and given a hero's sendoff by his hometown. Arriving in the major league camp, he's told he's a top prospect, but too fat and the team physician recommends a steam bath. The doctor goes to the ballgame with a friend, forgetting he's left Bim in the steam bath, but suddenly remembers. When he lets Bim out, the player is down to 92 pounds.

21 Baseball, That's All!

1910, Méliès, 950 feet. Director-Producer: Gaston Méliès.

The American-based company of French film pioneer George Méliès' brother made this comedy short about an avid baseball fan who begs off the job with a toothache so he can attend a game. Unfortunately for him, his boss decides to go to the game that day, too; and when the fan is involved in a ruckus in the stands, he's found out and fired.

22 Battling Orioles

1924, Hal Roach Studios for Pathe Exchange, 5,600 feet. Directors: Ted Wilde, Fred Guiol. Producer: Hal Roach. Story: Roach. Cameramen: Floyd Jackman, George Stevens.

Cast: Glenn Tryon, Blanche Mehaffey, John T. Prince, Noah Young, Sam Lufkin, Robert Page.

No, this isn't about the Baltimore Orioles, but about an 1870 team known as the Battling Orioles. Fifty-four years later, they're the crotchety old members of the National Club, living a life of ease. They come out of retirement briefly to help the son of a former pal get his sweetheart out of the clutches of the villain.

23 Big League Glory

1948, Paramount, 10 minutes. Directors: Russell T. Ervin, Rod Warren. Narrator: Ted Husing.

A short which illustrates how players are developed in the New York Giants' farm system.

24 Big Leaguer

1953, Metro Goldwyn Mayer, 70 minutes. Director: Robert Aldrich. Producer: Matthew Rapf. Screenplay: Herbert Baker. Story: John McNulty, Louis Marheim. Cameraman: William Mellor. Editor: Ben Lewis.

Cast: Edward G. Robinson, Vera-Ellen, Jeff Richards, Richard Jaeckel, William Campbell, Paul Langton, Lalo Rios, Bill Crandall, Frank Ferguson, John McKee, Mario Siletti, Carl Hubbell, Al Campanis, Tony Ravish.

About 200 big league hopefuls attend a two-week tryout camp under Coach Lobert (Robinson), chief among them Adam Polachuk (Richards), who's trying to get out of his mining town and land a $150-a-month minor league contract.

Although it's a generally undistinguished film, it offers one of Hollywood's rare glimpses at life in the bush leagues.

25 Bingo Long Travelling All-Stars and Motor Kings

1976, Universal Pictures, 111 minutes, Color. Director: John Badham. Producer: Rob Cohen. Screenplay: Hal Barwood, Matthew Robbins. Director of Photography: Bill Butler.

Cast: Billy Dee Williams, James Earl Jones, Richard Pryor, Rico Dawson, Stan Shaw, Tony Burton, Ted Ross, Mabel King, Leon Wagner.

Fed up with cheapskate owner Ross, Williams quits and forms his own Negro League barnstorming team in the late 1930's. It eventually boils down to one showdown game between the two teams. If Bingo's team wins, it gets a place in the league, but if they lose...

Pryor steals the show (what else is new?) as a black player who tries posing as a Cuban and then as an Indian to try to break baseball's color barrier and get into the big leagues. That honor, in the film at least, eventually goes to teammate Shaw.

26 Blue Skies Again

1983, Warner Brothers, 96 minutes, Color. Director: Richard Michaels. Producers: Alex Winitsky, Arlene Sellers. Screenplay: Kevin Sellers. Photography: Don McAlpine. Editor: Danford B. Greene.

Cast: Robyn Barto, Mimi Rogers, Harry Hamlin, Kenneth McMillan, Dana Elcar, Marcos Gonzales, Cilk Cozart, Gerry Coleman.

The major leaguers in this film all seem to have nicknames such as "Wall Street" and "Brush-back". The starting pitchers each hurl complete games in the first game of spring training. The minor leagues apparently don't exist. And the new candidate for the Devils' second base position is a woman.

If you can buy all that, there's still much to be enjoyed in **Blue Skies Again,** although it was an unqualified box office bust.

A scene in which Barto, as a woman softball player trying to crack the big leagues, tries to learn how to chew tobacco, is particularly effective.

McMillan, as the harried manager, proves a capable foil for Hamlin, the owner, who comes across as a hybrid of Ted Turner and George Steinbrenner.

What dilutes whatever impact the film might have had is the over-importance given to the first game of spring training in which Barto will either win the starting second base job for the Devils or go back to softball. There's never even any mention of her going to the minor leagues.

27 Boulevardier from the Bronx

1936, Warner Brothers. Supervisor: I. Freleng. Animation: Cal Dalton and Paul Smith.

In this Merry Melodies cartoon, featuring an all-bird cast, the good guys beat a baseball team composed of city slickers.

28 Brother Rat

1938, Warner Brothers, 90 minutes. Director: William Keighley. Screenplay: Richard Macaulay, Jerry Wald, from the play by John Monks Jr. and Fred F. Finklehoffe. Editor: William Holmes.

Cast: Ronald Reagan, Eddie Albert, Wayne Morris, Priscilla Lane, Johnnie Davis, Jane Bryan, Jane Wyman, Henry O'Neill.

This comedy about three seniors at the Virginia Military Institute was so popular, it was remade in 1952 as a musical, **About Face.**

All key members of the school's baseball team, pitcher Albert's mind is more on his secret wife's pregnancy than on baseball and he promptly gets knocked out. And with the big game coming up, his pals Reagan and Morris find themselves suspended for staying out after hours.

29 Buddy's Bearcats

1934, Warner Brothers. Supervised by Jack King. Animation: Ben Clopton.

A caricature of Joe E. Brown is the announcer of the big baseball game between Buddy's Bearcats and the Battling Bruisers in this Looney Tunes cartoon.

30 Bush Leaguer

1927, Warner Brothers, 6,281 feet. Director: Howard Bretherton. Scenario: Harvey Gates. Story: Charles G. Saxton. Camera: Norbert Brodin.

Cast: Monte Blue, Clyde Cook, Leila Hyams, William Demarest, Richard Tucker, Bud Marshall, Wilfred North, William Wilson, Violet Palmer, Rodney Hildebrand.

An Idaho garage owner becomes a big league pitcher and falls for the woman owner of the club (Hyams). He suffers from stage fright in front of a large crowd, but later in the season proves his worth by hitting a big home run.

31 The Busher

1919, Paramount Pictures, 5 reels. Director: Jerome Storm. Screenplay: R. Cecil Smith. Photography: Chester Lyons.

Cast: Charles Ray, Colleen Moore, Jack Gilbert, Jay Morley, Otto Hoffman.

It was fresh in 1919, although it seems trite now. A small-town pitcher gets a swelled head after some early success in the big leagues and eventually winds up back home. He returns to the team a changed man and hits a homer in the ninth inning to win the game. If the plot sounds similar to **Slide, Kelly, Slide,** you've done your homework.

32 Cannery Row

1982, United Artists, 120 minutes, Color. Director-Screenplay: David S. Ward. Producer: Michael Philips. Based on "Cannery Row" and "Sweet Thursday" by John Steinbeck. Photography: Sven Nykvist. Editor: David Bretherton.

Cast: Nick Nolte, Debra Winger, Audra Lindley, Frank McRae, M. Emmet Walsh, Tom Mahoney, John Malloy, James Keane, Sunshine Parker, Santos Morales, Ellen Blake.

Drifter Winger, in the role Raquel Welch was fired from, wanders onto the scene at California's famous Cannery Row in the 1940's and meets Steinbeck's odd assortment of characters. Chief among them is Doc, a secretive marine biologist. It turns out he's a former big league pitcher haunted by his memories of beaning an opposing player, who suffered permanent brain damage and is now a fellow resident of the Row.

In the film's only ballplaying scene, the injured hitter, who has been the butt of many jokes, amazes everyone by hitting a tremendous drive.

33 Casey at the Bat

1899, Edison Co.

This is the first known film version of the famous poem and in all likelihood, the earliest fiction baseball film.

34 Casey at the Bat

1916, Triangle-Fine Arts. Scenario: William Everett Wing.

Cast: DeWolf Hopper (Casey), Kate Toncray, May Garcia, Carl Stockdale, William H. Brown, Marguerite Marsh, Frank Bennett, Robert Lawler, Bert Hadley, Hal Wilson, Frank Hughes.

Here's another version, described by Variety as "a cheap mushy heart thriller."

35 Casey at the Bat

1927, Paramount Pictures, 6,040 feet. Director: Monte Brice. Producer-Story: Hector Turnbull. Screenplay: Jules Furthman. Photography: Barney McGill.

Cast: Wallace Beery, Ford Sterling, ZaSu Pitts, Sterling Holloway, Spec O'Donnell, Iris Stuart, Sidney Jarvis, Lotus Thompson, Rosalind Byrne, Ann Sheridan, Doris Hill.

Casey strikes out, but much of the action takes place in Centerville instead of Mudville, at around the turn of the century, as the Mighty Casey, a junk dealer by trade and baseball slugger as well, travels to New York under the impression he's been signed by the New York Giants.

36 Catch-As-Catch-Can

1927, Lumas Film Corp., 5,000 feet. Director: Charles Hutchison. Scenario: L.V. Jefferson. Cameraman: James Brown.

Cast: William Fairbanks, Jack Blossom, Rose Blossom, Larry Shannon, Walt Shumway, George Kotsonaros, George Chapman.

The star pitcher of a small town baseball team is the son of the mayor and brother of the manager's girlfriend. A crooked political figure bribes the pitcher (Blossom) to throw the big game and throws the blame on the poor manager (Fairbanks), who becomes a newspaper reporter and eventually exposes the villains, who include a heavyweight wrestler.

37 The Ceremony

1971, Japanese, Shibati Organization, 122 minutes, Color. Director: Nagisa Oshima. Screenplay: Oshima, Tsutomu Tamura, Memoru Sasaki. Cinematography: Toichiro Narushima. Editor: Keichiro Uracka.

Cast: Kenzo Kawarazaki, Atsuko Kaku, Atsuo Nakamura, Kei Sato, Kiyoshi Tsuchiya.

Baseball becomes symbolic of the disintegration of traditional Japanese culture in this work by one of that nation's top directors.

It's the story of the downfall of a powerful family ruled by a harsh partriarch. When a youth's fiancée fails to show at the wedding altar, he orders the ceremony to take place anyway.

One of the film's main characters is a lad who's a top college baseball player. When he drops a routine pop fly that causes his team to lose the big game, his mother commits hara-kiri. The lad, returning home, goes to the top of the nearest hill and burns his baseball bat and glove, never to play the game again.

38 The Chosen

1982, Analysis, 108 minutes, Color. Director: Jeremy Paul Kagan. Producers: Edie and Ely Landau. Screenplay: Edwin Gordon, based on the novel by Chaim Potok. Cinematography: Arthur Ornitz. Editor: David Garfield.

Cast: Robby Benson, Barry Miller, Maximilian Schell, Rod Steiger.

We're including this film about the friendship between two Jewish youths of completely different backgrounds because of the memorable softball game scene at the film's opening which brings Benson and Miller together. Benson rips a line drive into Miller's face.

39 Clancy at the Bat

1929, Educational Films, 20 minutes. Director: Earle Rodney. Producer: Mack Sennett.

Cast: Andy Clyde, Harry Gribbon, Marjorie Beebe, Bert Swor, Wade Boteler, Patsy O'Leary.

This early talkie two-reel comedy features Gribbon as an over-the-hill ballplayer.

40 College

1927, United Artists, 5,916 feet. Director: James W. Horne. Screenplay: Carl Harbaugh, Bryan Foy. Photography: Dev Jennings, Bert Haines. Editor: J.S. Kell.

Cast: Buster Keaton, Anne Cornwall, Flora Bramley, Harold Goodwin, Buddy Mason, Grant Withers, Snitz Edwards, Carl Harbaugh, Sam Crawford, the University of Southern California Baseball Team.

Keaton, the great stone-faced comedian, tries his hand at more sports than you can shake a bat at.

He portrays Ronald, the high school valedictorian, who gives a graduation speech on "The Curse of Athletics". The only problem is that his clothes have been soaked by a heavy rainfall and are shrinking so badly the buttons are popping off. Girlfriend Mary (Cornwall) calls him a sissy after the speech, opting instead for the school jock, Jeff (Goodwin), who has taken seven years to graduate.

All three attend Clayton College together and Ronald, hoping to impress Mary, tries out for the baseball team, but he becomes a total laughing stock because he doesn't know the first thing about it. While playing the infield, he wears catcher's equipment, and he keeps on bumping into other players.

He tries out for the track team next, with similar results, and similar ridicule from the other students; but Mary, seeing how hard he's trying, changes her mind about him.

The college dean takes sympathy on Ronald and lands him on the crew squad. On the day of the big meet, Ronald is coxswain but puts his feet through the bottom of the boat, and the rudder of the next boat the team tries breaks off.

Ronald saves the day by attaching the rudder to his body and leads Clayton to victory. He then puts on an incredible athletic display to knock out Jeff, who has been making indecent advances at Mary after being expelled because of poor grades.

41 Damn Yankees (British title: **What Lola Wants**)

1958, Warner Brothers, 110 minutes, Color. Directors and Producers: George Abbott, Stanley Donen. Cinematography: Harold Lipstein. Editor: Frank Bracht. Screenplay: Abbott, from the novel "The Year the Yankees Lost the Pennant" by Douglass Wallop. Choreography: Bob Fosse, Pat Ferrier.

Cast: Tab Hunter, Ray Walston, Gwen Verdon, Russ Brown, Shannon Bolin, Nathaniel Frey, Jimmy Komack, Rae Allen, Robert Shafer, Jean Stapleton, Albert Linville.

A smash hit on Broadway for three seasons, this musical comedy features the songs "Whatever Lola Wants," "Heart" and "Shoeless Jo from Hannibal, Mo."

An avid Washington Senators' fan, tired of seeing his team lose to the Yankees every year, sells his soul to Walston and is changed into a 22-year old slugger named Joe Hardy who turns them into winners. The Devil, however, sends temptress Verdon to lure the slugger (Hunter) and complications begin when he tries to back out of the deal.

42 Death on the Diamond

1934, Metro Goldwyn Mayer, 69 minutes. Director: Edward Sedgwick. Adaptation by: Harvey Thew, Joseph Sherman, Ralph Spence, from the book by Cortland Fitzsimmons. Photography: Milton Krasma.

Cast: Robert Young, Madge Evans, Nat Pendleton, Ted Healy, Henry Gordon, Paul Kelly, David Landau, DeWitt Jennings, Edward Brophy, Willard Robertson, Mickey Rooney.

Who is murdering members of the St. Louis Cardinals? Who

poisoned the mustard one of the players put on his hot dog? Three players bite the dust before the ending; but don't worry, we won't tell you who the culprit is even though you should figure it out by the end of the second reel. What you may find hard to believe, however, is the throw the hero pitcher makes to conk out the villain.

43 Elmer the Great

1933, Warner Brothers, 64 minutes. Director: Mervyn LeRoy. Adaptation: Tom Geraghty, based on a play by Ring Lardner. Photography: Arthur Todd. Editor: Thomas Pratt.

Cast: Joe E. Brown, Patricia Ellis, Frank McHugh, Claire Dodd, Preston Foster, Russell Hepton, Sterling Holloway, Emma Dunn.

Although this typical Joe E. Brown sports vehicle didn't set any records at the box office, it may have set an all-time record for the quickest remake in sports movie history, coming only four years after the original--**Fast Company**--the 1929 Jack Oakie vehicle.

As usual, Brown portrays an egomaniacal bumbler who makes good despite himself. Here, he's a small town baseball star who becomes a hero in the World Series between the Cubs and the Yankees. The best scene is Brown trying to see the pitcher during a rainstorm.

44 Experiment in Terror

1962, Columbia, 123 minutes. Producer-Director: Blake Edwards. Screenplay: Mildred and Gordon Gordon. Cinematography: Philip Lathrop. Editor: Patrick McCormack.

Cast: Glenn Ford, Lee Remick, Stefanie Powers, Ross Martin, Roy Poole, Ned Glass, Anita Loo, Patricia Huston, Gilbert Green, Clifton James, Al Avalon, William Bryant.

A bank teller is forced to steal $100,000, but she tells the FBI and the villain is shot down on the playing field at Candlestick Park just as the Giants' game is ending.

45 Fast Company

1929, Paramount Famous Lasky Corp., 6,459-6,863 feet. Director: A. Edward Sutherland. Screenplay: Florence Ryerson, Patrick Kearney, Walton Butterfield. Adaptation: Kearney, Butterfield. Photography: Edward Cronjager. Editor: Jane Loring.

Cast: Jack Oakie, Evelyn Brent, Richard "Skeets" Gallagher, Sam Hardy, Arthur Housman, Gwen Lee, Chester Conklin, E.H. Calvert, Eugenie Besserer, Bert Rome and a number of major league baseball players.

Elmer Kane (Oakie) is a small-town baseball hero turned major leaguer with the Yankees. He's hopelessly in love with a vaudeville star (Brent) who won't give him a tumble.

Throw in the usual crooked gamblers during the World Series with the Pittsburgh Pirates and the girl discovering she really loves Elmer, and you have all the ingredients which made the film popular enough to be remade four years later with Joe E. Brown as **Elmer the Great.**

The two different lengths are because this was an early talkie, and as many theaters around the country weren't set up yet in 1929 for sound films, it was common at this time to also release a silent version (the shorter one).

46 Fear Strikes Out

1957, Paramount, 100 minutes. Director: Robert Mulligan. Producer: Alan Pakula. Screenplay: Ted Berkman, Raphael Blau. Story: James A Piersall, Albert S. Hirschberg. Cinematography: Haskell Boggs. Editor: Aaron Stell.

Cast: Anthony Perkins, Karl Malden, Norma Moore, Adam Williams, Perry Wilson, Dennis

Actor Jack Oakie, right, gets together with major leaguer Jack Adams, left, and technical adviser Mike Donlin prior to the filming of the 1929 baseball comedy Fast Company. Donlin, a former big leaguer himself, also had a respectably long film career. (Courtesy National Baseball Hall of Fame.)

McMullen, Gail Land, Brian Hutton, Peter J. Votrian, Bart Burns.

Baseball and psychiatry are successfully mixed in Mulligan's directorial debut dealing with the real-life story of Jimmy Piersall.

Malden plays the Red Sox outfielder's dad, who puts too much pressure on his son to be a star. The elder Piersall is portrayed as a former semipro player eager to see his son do what he himself couldn't do and who gives criticism without ever a word of encouragement to his boy. When he's among the top hitters in the league, he tells his son he should be the best.

By the time Piersall makes the big leagues, he's already halfway to a breakdown. Nervous at the prospect of the Red Sox switching him to third base from the outfield, his father tells him: "You want them to call you yellow? If that's what you want, then you're no son of mine."

The breakdown finally comes when Piersall hits a home run and, after crossing home plate, clings to the backstop and screams "I showed them".

After extensive treatment at Westborough State Hospital, including electric shock, Piersall makes a comeback and has a reconciliation with his sadder, but wiser, dad.

Perkins' portrayal of the Red Sox star shot him to movie fame.

47 Fireman, Save My Child

1932, Warner Brothers, 67 minutes. Director: Lloyd Bacon. Story and Adaptation: Robert Lord, Ray Enright, Arthur Caesar. Photography: Sol Polito. Editor: George Marks.

Cast: Joe E. Brown, Evalyn Knapp, Lillian Bond, George Meeker, Guy Kibbee, George Ernest, Ben Hendricks Jr., Virginia Sale, Frank Shallenbach, Richard Carle, Louis Robinson, Curtis Benton.

Here's yet another Brown sports vehicle. He's a Kansas

fireman who in his spare time pitches for the St. Louis Cardinals--or maybe he's a pitcher who in his spare time fights fires, while trying to raise enough money to complete a new fire extinguisher project.

Much to the chagrin of his baseball manager (Kibbee), he spends more time putting out real fires than blazing the ball past opposing batters, but guess who arrives at the ballpark in the nick of time to win the World Series?

48 Giants vs. Yanks

1923, Pathe, 2 reels. Director: Robert F. McGowan. Writer-Producer: Hal Roach.

A baseball game is at the core in this early Our Gang comedy short, although there's extremely little action.

Several of the boys are stuck at home doing chores while umpire Farina and the rest of the Gang await their arrival so they can start the big game. When they finally do arrive and get the game started, the man who owns the lot where they're playing chases them away.

49 Girls Can Play

1937, Columbia, 59 minutes. Director: Lambert Hillyer. Screenplay: Hillyer. Story: Albert DeMond. Cameraman: Lucien Ballard.

Cast: Jacqueline Wells, Charles Quigley, Rita Hayworth, John Gallaudet, George McKay, Gene Morgan, Patricia Farr, Guinn Williams, Joseph Crehan.

Production-wise, this virtually forgotten film is just another low-budget, bottom-of-the-bill programmer. Historically, however, there's much that's worth noting.

With the exception of a female jockey or so, it's the first sound era **feature** film dealing primarily with women in sports. What's also noteworthy is that it's basically a murder mystery and not a comedy, as virtually all films about women athletes would be up until the 1970's.

Although there had been some comedy shorts about some women's teams, this is also the first feature-length movie about softball.

Plot-wise, it falls into the "sporting event as a pretext" category and traces its roots directly to the 1934 MGM film, **Death on the Diamond.**

Reporter Quigley and ace pitcher-hitter Wells team up to thwart the baddies who poisoned the team's catcher. The team is sponsored by an ex-convict drug store owner, but you might want to look closely at the labels or you could get drunk.

Guess who his "moll" is? None other than Rita Hayworth. And if you think the camerawork is exceptional for a routine Grade B programmer, note that it's by Lucien Ballard, who would develop into one of the greats.

50 Goodbye, Franklin High

1979, Cal-Am Artists, 90 minutes, Color. Producer-Director: Mike McFarland. Screenplay: Stu Krieger. Cinematography: Dean Cunday. Editor: Peter Parasheles.

Cast: Lane Caudell, Julie Adams, William Windom, Darby Hinton, Myron Healy, Ann Dusenberry, Ron Lombard, Stu Krieger, Virginia Gregg, Kenneth Tobey, Loren Ewing.

It would be amazing to learn whether anyone connected with **Goodbye, Franklin High** ever played or even saw a baseball game before making the film. The most merciful thing that can be said for the baseball scenes is that they're sloppy. What else can you say when during a couple of big high school baseball games:

1. None of the hitters wear batting helmets.

2. There are no coaches on the bench or on the basepaths.

3. The players guzzle beer on the bench.

4. The pitcher winds up with men on base and pitches from the stretch otherwise.

5. The public address announcer at the field, who prattles ceaselessly like he's broadcasting over the radio, says a ball is hit to centerfield, while the camera clearly shows the third baseman catching the ball.

The plot concerns a high school pitching sensation (Caudell--who also wrote and sings the songs) who is torn between a scholarship to Stanford and a career with the California Angels. Principal Healy, who apparently saw the film footage showing Caudell's awkward pitching motion, tries to push him toward a college education.

The lad's relationship with his parents (Adams and Windom) is the film's lone redeeming factor as he discovers his mom is reluctantly cheating on his terminally-ill dad.

51 Gracie at the Bat

1937, Columbia, 20 minutes. Director: Del Lord.

Cast: Andy Clyde, Leora Thatcher, Ann Doran, Bud Jamison, Vernon Dent, Eddie Fetherstone, Bess Flowers, William Irving.

Made in the same year as Columbia's **Girls Can Play**, this is strictly slapstick nonsense as Clyde takes over the helm of a girl's softball team.

52 Great American Pastime

1956, Metro Goldwyn Mayer, 89 minutes, Color. Director: Herman Hoffman. Producer: Henry Berman. Screenplay: Nathaniel Benchley. Photography: Arthur E. Arling. Editor: Gene Ruggiero.

Cast: Tom Ewell, Anne Francis, Ann Miller, Dean Jones, Rudy Lee, Judson Pratt, Raymond Bailey, Wolfred Knapp, Bob Jellison, Todd Ferrell, Raymond Winston, Paul Engel.

Twenty years before the birth of **The Bad News Bears**, there was **The Great American Pastime.**

Pity poor Tom Ewell. His wife hates baseball with a passion, yet he decides to become a Little League coach so he can be closer to his son. That's when his troubles really begin.

He's faced with all kinds of pressures from the kids' parents, even to the point where widow Ann Miller flirts with him to get him to play her son.

The kids, of course, are the most inept crew ever assembled; but as this is 1956 and not 1976, they at least don't curse in front of the camera like the Bears. When the losses mount up, Ewell finds himself an outcast in the community, but, surprise, surprise, he eventually leads them to victory.

53 Hal Chase's Home Run

1911, Kalem, 1,000 feet. No credits available.

Cast: Hal Chase.

When Tom pays more attention to baseball than to her, Grace registers her objections. Tom urges her to attend a baseball game with him so she can see what the fuss is all about. She does and he gets more than he bargained for: She won't marry him unless the home team wins the pennant.

Tom asks his pal, real-life major leaguer Hal Chase, to help out and Chase promises to do so. In the bottom of the ninth, with the home team trailing 2-0, Chase belts a three-run homer to win the pennant.

54 The Heckler

1940, Columbia, 20 minutes. Director: Del Lord.

Cast: Charley Chase, Bruce Bennett, Richard Fiske, Stanley Brown, Don Beddoe, Robert Sterling, Bud Jamison.

Comic chaos results when a loudmouth disrupts everyone in the stands as well as the baseball team on the field.

55 Here Come the Tigers

1978, American-International, 90 minutes, Color. Director: Sean Cunningham. Producers: Cunningham and Stephen Miner. Screenplay: Arch McCoy. Photography: Barry Abrams. Editor: Miner.

Cast: Richard Lincoln, Samantha Grey, Xavier Rodrigo, Kathy Bell, Sean Griffin, Ted Oyama, Aloysius Kerry.

An unabashed imitation of **The Bad News Bears** by the makers of **Friday the 13th**, this received very limited distribution.

The police officer coach of the Tigers dons a headdress, climbs to the top of the Little League stadium, beats his tom-tom and threatens to jump unless his cop pal agrees to take his place as coach. The young officer agrees, but when he and his bumblebrained assistant see the material they have to work with, they feel like jumping too.

However, with the addition to the starting lineup of a juvenile delinquent, a karate-chopping Japanese boy who sends balls flying over the fence with his bare fists and a deaf pitcher, the team begins to win despite the dirty tricks of the nasty opposing teams.

The film's setting is Westport, Connecticut.

56 His Last Game

1909, Imp. Presented by Carl Laemmle. No other credits available.

The first major baseball feature is a real collector's item—a cowboy and Indians sports film!

Set in Arizona, it's about an ace pitcher for an Indian baseball team who refuses a bribe from two cowboy gamblers to throw the game.

When a plot to murder him with poison whiskey fails, they get into a fight with him and one of the gamblers is killed. Sentenced to death for the slaying, the Indian is allowed out of jail to play in the big game, which he wins with a grand slam homer.

However, in true silent movie style, he's executed just moments before his reprieve reaches the sheriff.

57 Hit and Run

1924, Universal Pictures, 5,508 feet. Director: Edward Sedgwick. Story-Scenario: Sedgwick, Raymond L. Schrock. Photography: Virgil Miller.

Cast: Hoot Gibson, Marion Harlan, Cyril Ring, Harold Goodwin, DeWitt Jennings, Mike Donlin, William A. Steele.

You're going to read this plot over and over again in this book. Slugger Swat Anderson, portrayed by cowboy star Hoot Gibson, is kidnapped by gamblers, but Our Hero escapes in time to win the big game.

You might want to keep a scorecard on how many times in sports films the hero is kidnapped by villains.

58 Home Run Ambrose

1918, L-Ko, 2 reels. Director: W.S. Fredericks. An early two-reel baseball short for which we have been unable to find much information on.

59 Home Run Baker's Double

1914, Kalem, 2 reels. Director-Screenplay: Kerean Buel.

Cast: Home Run Baker, Marguerite Courtot, Henry Hallam, Ben Ross, Helen Lindroth.

Hall of Famer Frank "Home Run" Baker was among the first major league baseball stars to have a starring role in a narrative film.

60 Home Run on the Keys

1937, Vitaphone, 1 reel. Director: Roy Mack.

A baseball short, with music, starring the one and only King of Swat, Babe Ruth.

61 Horizontal Lieutenant

1962, MGM, 90 minutes,

Color. Director: Richard Thorpe. Producer: Joe Pasternak. Screenplay: George Wells. Photography: Robert Bronner. Editor: Richard Farrell.

Cast: Jim Hutton, Paula Prentiss, Jack Carter, Jim Backus, Charles McGraw, Miyoshi Umeki, Yoshido Yoda, Marty Ingels, Lloyd Kino, Yuki Shimoda, Linda Wong.

Hutton incurs his superior's wrath by his ineptitude on the interservice baseball team during World War II, so he's assigned to the most remote island the brass can find and ordered to capture a lone Japanese who's been stealing Army food.

62 In Hot Curves

1930, Tiffany Productions, 7,893 feet. Director: Norman Taurog. Screenplay: Earle Snell. Story: A.P. Younger, Frank Mortimer. Photography: Max Dupont. Editor: Clarence Kolster.

Cast: Benny Rubin, Rex Lease, Alice Day, Bert Kelton, John Ince, Mary Carr, Mike Donlin, Natalie Moorhead.

Until the 1970's, women in sports films generally fit into one of three categories: The Vamp, who causes the hero's downfall; The Homebody, who suffers with the athlete and wants him to quit; and The Upstart, who dares to enter the world of sports and is ridiculed for her efforts.

In this early talkie, it's The Vamp, the most prevalent of the three, who turns the head of the baseball star Jim Dolan (Lease). Soda jerk Rubin, who becomes one of the key players for the Pittsburgh Cougars, helps bring his pal to his senses in time to win the big game.

63 I'll Buy You

Japanese, 1956, Schochiku, 113 minutes. Director: Maseki Kobayashi. Screenplay: Zenzo Matsuyama. Story: Minoru Ono. Photography: Yuharu Atsuta.

Cast: Keiji Sata, Keiko Kishi, Minoru Oki, Yunosuke Ito, Mitsuko Mito.

An early film by the director of **Hara-Kiri** and **Kwaidan,** this is an exposé of corruption in the world of Japanese baseball.

An unscrupulous scout stops at nothing to sign a high school baseball star. When the youth turns him down, the scout wrecks the lad's relationship with his girl friend, disrupts his family life and seeks out the youth's friends in efforts to make him sign, which he eventually does.

64 I'll Fix It

1934, Columbia, 68 minutes. Director: Roy William Neill. Screenplay: Dorothy Howell, Ethel Hill. Photography: Benjamin Kline.

Cast: Jack Holt, Mona Barrie, Winnie Lightner, Jimmy Butler, Edward Brophy, Nedda Harrigan, Charles Moore.

Here's another Columbia Grade B programmer which is more interesting subject-wise than production-wise, and which has been virtually forgotten since its initial release.

The matter of good grades vs. school sports is examined, but it's at the grade school level rather than at some big-time college.

A boy is good enough to make his school's baseball team, but when bad grades threaten to keep him benched, his meddling father arranges for him to get another test. When he's caught cheating on the new test, the father has the teacher fired. It's the other teachers and the town newspaper to the rescue of the fired teacher.

65 It Happened in Flatbush

1942, 20th Century-Fox, 80 minutes. Director: Ray McCarey. Producer: Walter Morosco. Screenplay: Harold Buchman and Lee Loeb. Photography: Charles Clarke. Editor: J. Watson Webb.

Cast: Lloyd Nolan, Carole Landis, Sara Allgood, William

A slightly battered Benny Rubin embraces pal and teammate Rex Lease in Tiffany Productions' 1930 film Hot Curves. (The Museum of Modern Art/Film Stills Archive.)

Frawley, Robert Armstrong, Jane Darwell, George Holmes, Scotty Beckett, Jed Prouty, Joseph Allen Jr.

The manager of the Brooklyn Dodgers has to fight his past as well as his own players and the opposition in this wartime programmer.

The manager (Nolan) as a player had made an error in a crucial game. Now buried in the bush leagues, he's hired for the big club and builds up a romance with top stockholder Landis.

As the pressures of the pennant race heat up, the team petitions for Nolan's removal, but he manages to rally them together in time.

66 It Happens Every Spring

1949, 20th Century-Fox, 87 minutes. Director: Lloyd Bacon. Producer: William Perlberg. Screenplay: Valentine Davies. Story: Shirley W. Smith. Photography: Joe MacDonald.

Cast: Ray Milland, Jean Peters, Paul Douglas, Ed Begley, Ted deCorsia, Ray Collins, Jessie R. Landis, Alan Hale Jr., Bill Murphy, Gene Evans.

College professor Vernon Simpson (Milland), while trying to come up with a bug repellent for trees, instead discovers a wood repellent and becomes a pitching star for the St. Louis Cardinals, winning 38 games in his rookie season.

Much to the bafflement of catcher Monk Lanigan (Douglas) and Manager Dolan (deCorsia), let alone opposing hitters, the ball, when doused with the substance, goes through all kinds of gyrations to avoid making contact with a wooden bat.

67 It's My Turn

1980, Columbia, 91 minutes. Color. Director: Claudia Weill. Producer: Martin Elfand. Screenplay: Eleanor Begstein. Photography: Bill Butler. Editor: Byron Brandt, Marjorie Fowler.

Cast: Jill Clayburgh, Michael Douglas, Charles Grodin, Beverly Garland, Steven Hill, Teresa Baxter, Joan Copeland, Jennifer Salt.

Major league baseball star Douglas woos Clayburgh away from her live-in boyfriend Grodin.

68 The Jackie Robinson Story

1950, Eagle Lion Films, 76 minutes. Director: Alfred Green. Producer: Mort Briskin. Screenplay: Lawrence Taylor, Arthur Mann. Photography: Ernest Laszlo. Editor: Arthur H. Nadel.

Cast: Jackie Robinson, Ruby Dee, Louise Beavers, Joel Fluellen, Billy Wayne, Bernie Hamilton, Kenny Washington, Minor Watson, Richard Lane, Bill Spaulding, Howard Louis MacNeely.

Robinson portrays himself in this workmanlike biography of the man who broke major league baseball's color barrier. There's a lot of emphasis on the jeers and insults the Dodger great had to endure from fans and players alike after he was signed by Rickey and sent to play minor league ball for Montreal, and how he eventually turned them to cheers.

69 Just the Beginning

Korean, 1977, Yung Bang Films, 105 minutes, Color. Director: Jong In Yup. Producer: Choi Chun Ji. Screenplay: Suh Yoon Sung. Photography: Paing Jung Moon. Editor: Chang Kil Sang.

Cast: Jin Yoo Young, Ha Myoung Jung, Kang Juttee, Doh Kum Bong, Han Se Hun.

It didn't take long for the Koreans to come up with their own version of **The Bad News Bears.** An ex-star turns a team of losers into the champs despite a number of roadblocks, including a mishap involving their star pitcher.

70 Kid from Cleveland

1949, Republic, 89 minutes. Director: Herbert Kline. Producer: Walter Colmes. Screenplay: John Bright. Photography: Jack Marta. Editor: Jason H. Bernie.

Cast: George Brent, Lynn Bari, Rusty Tamblyn, Tommy Cook, Ann Doran, Louis Jean Heydt, K. Elmo Lowe, Johnny Berardino and the 1948 World Championship Cleveland Indians.

A popular John Wayne film the year this was made was **Three Godfathers,** in which three cowboys adopt a waif. Publicity material for this film dubbed it **30 Godfathers.**

A teenager who loves baseball is persuaded to go straight by the entire Indians team. Maverick owner Bill Veeck has a major role and his performance was praised by the critics. Also appearing are Lou Boudreau and Tris Speaker. Meanwhile, the Indians' fortunes on the field rise as they and the youngster get closer.

71 Kid from Left Field

1953, 20th Century-Fox, 80 minutes. Director: Harmon Jones. Producer: Leonard Goldstein. Screenplay: Jack Sher. Photography: Harry Jackson. Editor: William Reynolds.

Cast: Dan Dailey, Anne Bancroft, Billy Chapin, Lloyd Bridges, Ray Collins, Richard Egan, Bob Hopkins, John Berardino, Leo Cleary, Fess Parker, George Phelps, John Gallaudet.

Former ballplayer Dailey is reduced to being a peanut vender at the ballpark, but his 9-year-old son Chapin is the team's batboy.

When Dad passes on some tips to his son on how slugger Bridges can get out of his batting slump and how the team can improve, the boy relays them to the team and suddenly the last place team starts winning. Chapin becomes manager of the team until he gets ill and admits that it's been Dad all along who's responsible for the team's upswing.

A popular and unpretentious little feature, it was remade as a made-for-television movie with Gary Coleman and the San Diego Padres.

72 Kill the Umpire

1950, Columbia Pictures, 77 minutes. Director: Lloyd Bacon. Producer: John Beck. Screenplay: Frank Tashlin. Photography: Charles Lawton Jr. Editor: Charles Nelson.

Cast: William Bendix, Una Merkel, Ray Collins, Gloria Henry, Alan Hale Jr., Richard Taylor, Connie Marshall, William Frawley, Tom D'Andrea, Luther Crockett, Jeff York, Glenn Thompson.

Just call this one **The Life of Riley at the Ballpark.** Chances are if you enjoyed Bendix in that popular TV series, you'll enjoy this baseball comedy, noteworthy in the fact that it's the only feature film to focus on the lives of the Men in Blue.

Films about sports officials in general are rarer than hen's teeth; in fact, with the exception of this and **The Referee**, you really have to start thinking hard.

Bendix portrays a baseball fan who is merciless on the umpires until he's forced by circumstances to become one himself. Some of the funniest scenes are those of Bendix trying to get into shape at the umpire's school and then putting in some eyedrops which make him see double.

Thus earning the nickname of Two-Call Johnson, he makes a controversial "safe, safe" call at home plate during a big game and finds the whole town is out to tar and feather him.

73 Ladies Day

1943, RKO Radio Pictures, 62 minutes. Director: Leslie Goodwins. Producer: Bert Gilroy. Screenplay: Charles E. Roberts and Dane Lussier, based on a play by Robert Considine, Edward Clark Lilley and Bertrand Robinson. Photography: Jack Mackenzie. Editor: Harry Marker.

Cast: Lupe Velez, Eddie Albert, Patsy Kelly, Max Baer, Jerome Cowan, Iris Adrian, Joan Barclay, Cliff Clark, Carmen Morales, George Cleveland, Jack Briggs, Russ Clark.

Velez, who gained fame in the Mexican Spitfire comedy series, this time is a wacky flirt who singlehandedly manages to mess up a major league team's pennant drive.

Star pitcher Albert, who became totally useless in **Brother Rat** when his mind was on his pregnant wife, repeats his role, this time because he's in love with Velez.

It's Albert's teammates and their wives to the rescue by pulling a switch on the usual sports film plots. Instead of the hero being kidnapped for the big game, the wives kidnap Velez and keep her away from Albert during the World Series.

74 Life's Greatest Game

1924, Emory Johnson Productions, 7,010 feet. Director-Story-Scenario: Harry Revier. Presented by George H. Davis.

Cast: Tom Santschi, Jane Thomas, Dicky Brandon, Johnnie Walker, David Kirby, Gertrude Olmstead.

An evil gambler gets revenge on Chicago Cubs' star pitcher Jack Donovan (Santschi), who refused his offer to throw the big game, by breaking up his family. Donovan, thinking his wife and

Tom Santschi and Johnny Walker are father and son in Life's Greatest Game (1924). (The Museum of Modern Art/Film Stills Archive.)

son are long dead, becomes manager of the New York Giants when guess who joins the team? None other than Jack Jr., who plans to get even with Pop for deserting Mom by blowing the World Series against the Yankees.

If you don't know how this one comes out, you've been hibernating in the North Pole for the past 75 years.

75 Little League Baseball

1949, Little League Baseball Association, 20 minutes. Narrator: Joseph Hasel. Produced with the cooperation of the U.S. Rubber Co. Director: Emerson Yorke. Photography: Burgi Conter, Russell Carrier.

The development of the Little League is traced, with the highlight being a play-by-play (announced by Ted Husing) of the 1948 Little League World Series.

76 The Loud Mouth

1932, Paramount Pictures, 19 minutes. Director: Del Lord.

Cast: Mat McHugh, Ray Cooke, Franklin Pangborn.

A two-reel comedy in which gamblers hire a loudmouth fan to rattle a team's star player. The plan backfires when the heckler gets a sore throat.

77 Lovable Trouble

1941, Columbia, 20 minutes. Director: Del Lord.

Cast: Andy Clyde, Esther Howard, Ann Doran, Luana Walters, Vernon Dent.

When a group of showgirls take on Clyde as their coach, marital problems ensue in this two-reeler.

78 Love and Base Ball

1914, 101 Bison, 2 reels.

Cast: Christy Matthewson.

A slim romantic subplot provides an excuse for baseball Hall-of-Famer Matthewson to perform pitching and batting heroics.

79 Make Mine Music

1946, Disney-RKO Radio Pictures, 74 minutes, Color. Directors: Jack Kinney, Clyde Geronimi, Hamilton Luske, Robert Cormack, Joshua Meador.

Story: Homer Brightman, Dick Huemer, Dick Kinney, John Walbridge, Tom Oreb, Dick Shaw, Eric Gurney, Sylvia Holland, T. Hee, Dick Kelsey, Jesse Marsh, Roy Williams, Ed Penner, James Bodrero, Cap Palmer, Erwin Graham.

A Walt Disney animated feature which describes itself as "a music fantasy in ten parts," one of the segments is a musical version of "Casey at the Bat," featuring the voice of Jerry Colonna.

Set in the Gay 90's, when Casey takes his mighty swing at strike three, "the force of Casey's blow" causes a miniature hurricane in the stadium.

80 Max Dugan Returns

1983, 20th Century-Fox, 98 minutes, Color. Director: Herbert Ross. Producer: Ross, Neil Simon. Screenplay: Simon. Photography: David M. Walsh. Editor: Richard Marks.

Cast: Marsha Mason, Jason Robards, Donald Sutherland, Matthew Broderick, Dody Goodman, Sal Viscuso, Panchito Gomez.

The late great batting coach Charlie Lau—then of the Chicago White Sox—has a major supporting role in this Neil Simon comedy about a widowed teacher whose shadowy father suddenly materializes years after he abandoned her.

The father (Robards), wanting to make up for lost time, buys his daughter (Mason) and grandson (Broderick) everything they could ever hope for, but is it with stolen money? That's what detective boyfriend Sutherland wants to know.

When Robards sees that his grandson always strikes out in the clutch for his high school team, he hires Lau to give him personal instruction and voila! the kid hits a homer in the big game.

81 Moonlight in Havana

1942, Universal Pictures, 63 minutes. Director: Anthony Mann. Producer: Bernard W. Burton. Screenplay: Oscar Brodney. Photography: Charles Van Enger. Editor: Russell Schoengarth.

Cast: Allan Jones, Jane Frazee, Marjorie Lord, William Frawley, Don Terry, Sergio Orta, Wade Boteler, Hugh O'Connell, Jack Norton.

A big league catcher (Jones) who can sing only when he has a cold, manages to antagonize his teammates during spring training in Havana when he takes a job in Frawley's nightclub and becomes torn between the two careers.

82 Mr. Dynamite

1941, Universal Pictures, 63 minutes. Director: John Rawlins. Producer: Marshall Grant. Screenplay: Stanley Crea Rubin. Photography: John Boyle. Editor: Ted Kent.

Cast: Lloyd Nolan, Irene Hervey, J. Carrol Naish, Robert Armstrong, Ann Gillis, Frank Gaby, Elisabeth Risdon, Shemp Howard, Cliff Nazarro, Monte Brewer.

No relation to the 1935 Universal film of the same name, this concerns baseball and sabotage.

Nolan portrays a World Series pitching hero who romances a British spy who is working at a carnival ball-tossing concession in New York. The two become entangled in the murder of a man who had information about sabotage at munitions plants and with a ventriloquist's dummy which gives out secret messages.

83 The Natural

1984, Tri Star Pictures, 134 minutes, Color. Director: Barry Levinson. Producer: Mark Johnson. Screenplay: Roger Towne, Phil Dusenberry, based on the novel

Tony Ferrara, right, a batting practice pitcher for the Yankees and a member of the Screen Actors Guild, enjoys a lighter moment with Robert Redford during a break in the filming of The Natural. Ferrara portrays a member of Redford's team in the film. (Courtesy Tony Ferrara.)

by Bernard Malamud. Photography: Caleb Deschanel. Editor: Stu Linder.

Cast: Robert Redford, Robert Duvall, Glenn Close, Kim Basinger, Wilford Brimley, Barbara Hershey, Robert Prosky, Richard Farnsworth, Joe Don Baker, John Finnegan, Alan Fudge, Paul Sullivan Jr., Rachel Hall, Robert Rich III.

A film made in 1984, set in 1924 and 1939 and with all the basic plot elements of a silent-era sports film, many film critics just couldn't get caught up with **The Natural**'s magical-mythical atmosphere.

There's the typical hero of the 1920's sports film—a confident but naive farmboy (Redford) who's on his way to try out for the Cubs.

There's the bragging established star Whammer (Joe Don Baker) a Babe Ruth-type hero even though he bats righthanded.

There's the girl back home (Close), a lass in white of such purity that her mere presence in the stands is enough to cure our hero, Roy Hobbs, of a dreadful batting slump.

And, of course, there are the typical supporting characters such as the grumpy manager (Brimley) Pop Fisher and the fatherly coach Red Blow (Farnsworth).

Then there are the villains: Vamp Memo Paris, who robs Hobbs of his virtue and his strength, the crooked gambler McGavin and Prosky, the part-owner who's betting against his own team.

The film opens in 1924 as Hobbs, on a bet, strikes out the Whammer on three pitches at a small prairie-town carnival. He's made a celebrity by a cartoon by newspaperman Max Mercy (Duvall), but before he can reach the Cubs' tryout, he's shot with a silver bullet by a mysterious femme fatale (Hershey).

Sixteen years later, Hobbs turns up one night in the dugout of the New York Knights, a pitiful excuse for a last place team which draws more flies than fans to the ballpark (War Memorial Stadium) in Buffalo was used for scenes to represent both the Knights' home park and Wrigley Field in Chicago. For the Wrigley Field scenes, ivy was put in front of the fences.

Unwilling to talk about his past and without any real professional experience, Hobbs finds manager Fisher unwilling to use him until in desperation he's sent up as a pinch hitter and literally knocks the cover off the ball as the fielders find themselves with a handful of thread.

Later, when Hobbs hits a big home run, the ball hits a light tower, causing a massive fireworks-like display.

Former Cleveland Indians outfielder Joe Charboneau has a bit role in the film, while veteran ballplayer and coach Sibby Sisti portrays the Pittsburgh manager.

84 Naughty Nineties

1945, Universal Pictures, 76 minutes. Director: Jean Yarbrough. Producers: Edmund L. Hartmann and John Grant. Screenplay: Hartmann, Grant, Edmund Joseph and Hal Fimberg. Photography: George Robinson. Editor: Arthur Hilton.

Cast: Bud Abbott, Lou Costello, Alan Curtis, Rita Johnson, Henry Travers, Lois Collier, Joe Sawyer, Joe Kirk, Barbara Pepper, Jack Norton, The Rainbow Four, John Hamilton, Ed Gargan, Ben Johnson, John Indrisano, Rex Lease.

This Abbott and Costello comedy has absolutely nothing to do with sports plot-wise, as it's set on a Gay 90's showboat and has the comedy duo trying to help the boat's captain from losing it to gamblers. This is the film in which Abbott and Costello's famous "Who's on First" routine appears. Abbot appears in the skit wearing the uniform of the

St. Louis Wolves.

Although Abbott and Costello didn't create the "Who's on First?" sketch, their version is certainly the most famous. In their original burlesque version of it, Costello's last line was "I don't give a damn", but for radio it was changed to "I don't care".

Shorter versions of the skit popped up in other Abbott and Costello films, not to mention their television series. They once performed it with Joe DiMaggio on **The Colgate Comedy Hour** on television.

85 The New Klondike

1926, Paramount Pictures, 7,445 feet. Director: Lewis Milestone. Presented by Adolph Zukor, Jesse L. Lasky. Scenario: Thomas J. Geraghty. Story: Ring Lardner. Photography: Alvin Wyckoff.

Cast: Thomas Meighan, Lila Lee, Paul Kelly, Hallie Manning, Robert Craig, George De Carlton, J.W. Johnston, Brenda Lane, Tefft Johnson, Danny Hayes.

Well, here's a baseball film that's truly different as its emphasis is on making a living after one's playing days are over.

Tom Kelly (Meighan) is cut during spring training because his manager, Joe Cooley (Johnston), is jealous of his knowledge of the game and fearful he may eventually lose his job to him.

Kelly, however, becomes a huge success in the real estate business and gets his ex-teammates to invest their money with him. Re-enter the villain Cooley! He gets his pal Morgan West (Craig), to sell Kelly some worthless real estate.

As this film fits into the "triumph of the underdog" mold, it shouldn't surprise anyone that eventually Cooley's worst fears are realized and guess who becomes the new manager?

86 Ninth Inning

1942, Presented by the American League. Screenplay and direction: Lew Fonseca. Narration: Bob Elson.

Normally, we are not including team or league promotional films in this volume, but we're making an exception here. This is the eighth official American League film, and it's dedicated to the memory of Yankees' great Lou Gehrig and opens with some shots of him in action.

Other highlights include Joe DiMaggio's 56-game hitting streak, Ted Williams' homer in the ninth inning of the All-Star game and Mickey Owens' passed ball on a third strike in the ninth inning during the World Series. It also brings together Babe Ruth, Ty Cobb and Tris Speaker for a few shots, so with so much baseball history here, **The Ninth Inning** must stand out as the most noteworthy of promotional films.

87 One Run Elmer

1935, Educational Films, 27 minutes. Director: Charles Lamont.

Cast: Buster Keaton, Lona Andre, Harold Goodwin.

When business gets slow at comedian Keaton's desert gas station—and that seems to be most of the time—he plays baseball.

His rival for his sweetheart is also a rival gas station owner, and the two decide to play a ballgame with the winner getting the girl.

Here's another example of the early treatment of women in sports films, with the femmes either being vamps or merely objects. Time and time again in the early sports films (and to a lesser degree in later films), the women were portrayed as fickle beings who are only attracted to winners and the films revolved around a contest to see who would get the girl.

88 One Strike You're Out

1981, Akita Pictures.

There's no evidence we can find that this ever saw the light of day in the United States outside of a few private screening rooms. Pre-release publicity states "An old man and a kid risk all to help their club and find each other".

89 Opening Day

1938, Metro Goldwyn Mayer, 1 reel. Director: Roy Rowland.

Cast: Robert Benchley, Harland Briggs, John Butler.

One of the one-reel comedies in the Robert Benchley series, he's to throw out the first ball of the baseball season in this one.

90 Out of the West

1926, R-C Pictures, 4,609 feet. Director: Robert DeLacy. Story: Frederick Arthur Mindlin. Photography: John Leezer.

Cast: Tom Tyler, Bernice Welch, L.J. O'Connor, Ethan Laidlaw, Alfred Hewston, Frankie Darro, Gertrude Claire, Barney Furey.

Yup, partner, here's a rootin', tootin' baseball western.

Tom Hanley (Tyler) and his grandmother settle on the ranch of John O'Connor (Hewston) and joins the ranch's baseball team as its ace pitcher.

This riles rival ranchman Rollins (L.J. O'Connor), who's used to his own baseball team winning by crooked means. Hanley and O'Connor's daughter Bernice (Bernice Welch) are kidnapped, but as is usual in this sort of thing, Our Hero escapes in time to win the big game and then uses his cowboy skills to capture the villain.

91 Over-Under, Sideways-Down

1977, Steve Wax/Cine Manifest, 86 minutes, Color. Directors: Eugene Corr, Steve Wax, Peter Gessner. Screenplay: Corr, Gessner. Photography: Stephen Lighthill. Editor: David Schickele, Corr.

Cast: Robert Viharo, Sharon Goldman, Roy Andrews, Robert A. Behling, Michael Cavanaugh, Lonnie Ford, Fran Furey, Esteban Oropreza, Larry Patterson.

A man nearing 30 slowly begins to realize his lifelong dream of becoming a major league ballplayer will never come true and his subsequent depression affects his factory job and his relationship with his wife.

92 Peerless Leader

1913, Patheplay, 2 reels.

Cast: Frank Chance, Gwendolyn Pates, Ned Burton.

An early baseball film with major leaguer Frank Chance.

93 Pinch Hitter

1917, Triangle-Ince-Kay Bee, 5 reels. Director: Victor L. Schlesinger. Screenplay: C. Gardner Sullivan.

Cast: Charles Ray, Sylvia Bremer, Joseph J. Dowling, Jerome Storm, Darrel Foss, Louis Durham.

An early prototype "triumph of the underdog" concerns a shy boy at a small college who becomes the butt of pranks and jokes at the school.

The baseball coach takes him on the team only as a mascot, but when he runs out of players, is forced to send the boy into the game. Lo and behold, the kid hits the game winning homer and becomes the campus hero.

The Pinch Hitter was re-edited and re-released in 1923 and then re-made just two years after that. It's practically forgotten nowadays, although its storyline is almost identical to Harold Lloyd's **The Freshman,** which is considered a silent comedy classic (see Football Films chapter).

94 Pinch Hitter

1925, Associated Exhibitors, 6,259 feet. Director: Joseph Henabery. Story: C. Gardner Sullivan. Photography: Jules Cronjager.

Cast: Glenn Hunter, Constance Bennett, Jack Drumier, Reginald Sheffield, Antrim Short, George

Cline, Mary Foy, James E. Sullivan, Joseph Burke.

A remake of the 1917 film described earlier.

95 Play Ball

1925, Pathe, 10 chapters. Director: Spencer G. Bennet. Story: Frank Leon Smith.

Cast: Walter Miller, Allene Ray, J. Barney Sherry, Harry Semels, Mary Milnor, Wally Oettel.

Chapter One: To the Rescue; Chapter Two: The Flaming Float; Chapter Three: Betrayed; Chapter Four: The Decoy Wire; Chapter Five: Face to Face; Chapter 6: The Showdown; Chapter Seven: A Mission of Hate; Chapter 8: Double Peril; Chapter 9: Into Segundo's Hands; Chapter 10: A Home Plate Wedding.

This baseball serial finds a senator's son as a rookie in the big leagues and becoming involved with a millionaire's daughter and an exiled nobleman who's plotting a revolution in his homeland.

96 Pride of St. Louis

1952, 20th Century-Fox, 93 minutes. Director: Harmon Jones. Producer: Jules Schermer. Screenplay: Herman Mankiewicz. Story: Guy Trosper. Photography: Leo Tover. Editor: Robert Simpson.

Cast: Dan Dailey, Joanne Dru, Richard Hilton, Hugh Sanders, James Brown, Chet Huntley, John Doucette, Richard Crenna, Leo T. Cleary, Stuart Randall.

The real-life story of pitcher Dizzy Dean, from his beginnings as an Ozark hillbilly to his days as a sportscaster when he used his own unique version of the English language.

Dailey convincingly portrays the baseball great who rises from poverty to stardom and joins his brother Paul Dean in beating the Detroit Tigers to give the Cardinals the World Championship.

The film also covers Dean's career-ending injury and the star's battle with himself before he realizes it's all over.

97 Pride of the Yankees

1942, RKO Radio Pictures, 128 minutes. Director: Sam Wood. Producer: Samuel Goldwyn. Screenplay: Joe Swerling, Herman J. Mankiewicz. Story: Paul Gallico. Photography: Rudolph Mate. Editor: Daniel Mandell.

Cast: Gary Cooper, Teresa Wright, Ludwig Stossel, Elsa Janssen, Walter Brennan, Dan Duryea, Virginia Gilmore, Pierre Watkin, Addison Richards, Hardie Albright, Douglas Croft, Ernie Adams, Harry Harvey, George McDonald, Babe Ruth, Bill Dickey, Bob Meusel, Mark Koenig, Bill Stern, Fay Thomas, David Manley.

The most famous of all baseball movies, **Pride of the Yankees** won Oscar nominations for Cooper as Yankee great Lou Gehrig and for Wright as Eleanor Gehrig. Daniel Mandell won the Oscar for Best Editing, while the film also received a nomination for Best Picture.

It also features the song "Always" by Irving Berlin, which was the real-life love song of Lou and Eleanor.

Cooper was 41 years old when he was called upon to play baseball's Iron Man, who still holds the major league record for most consecutive games played. Not only that, but he had never played baseball in his life.

Lefty O'Doul was assigned the herculean task of coaching Cooper to the point where audiences could believe he was a ballplayer, but O'Doul couldn't overcome certain obstacles.

The major one was that while Gehrig was lefthanded, Cooper was a righty and getting him to throw and swing his natural way was hard enough. The filmmakers overcame this by having Cooper swing the bat his natural way—righty—and run to third base. The negative was flip-flopped so that in the film it appears that Cooper is hitting left-handed and running to first.

Mr. and Mrs. Babe Ruth give their opinions of The Pride of the Yankees after attending its premiere. (Courtesy National Baseball Hall of Fame.)

In long shots, real-life baseball star Babe Herman doubled for Cooper.

The story itself traces Gehrig from his early days to the time when the Iron Man, now wracked by disease, gives his famous farewell speech at Yankee Stadium in which he calls himself "the luckiest man in the world." It was Gehrig's farewell speech which reportedly convinced Goldwyn, who wasn't too keen on doing a baseball film, to make **Pride of the Yankees.**

Brennan portrays a sports writer who brings Gehrig, then a Columbia University star, to the Yankees attention.

When Gehrig goes up to hit for the Yankees as a rookie, he trips over a pile of bats, earning him the nickname "Tanglefoot" and humanizing the superstar to the film audience.

One of the film's most poignant moments occurs when Gehrig topples over while attempting to tie his shoelaces and Dickey motions to his teammates to let Gehrig get up by himself.

98 Rhubarb

1951, Paramount Pictures, 94 minutes. Director: Arthur Lubin. Producers: William Perlberg, George Seaton. Screenplay: Dorothy Reid, Francis Cockrell, based on the novel by H. Allen Smith. Photography: Lionel Linden. Editor: Alma Macrorie.

Cast: Ray Milland, Jan Sterling, Gene Lockhart, Elsie Holmes, Taylor Holmes, William Frawley, Willard Waterman, Henry Slate, James Hayward, Leonard Nimoy, Strother Martin.

A few new twists and a few old twists add up to one of the most popular baseball comedies.

The major new twist is that the major character, Rhubarb, is a cat who winds up as owner of the Brooklyn Dodgers. Just another alley cat, Rhubarb likes to steal golf balls and attracts the attention of millionaire Lockhart, who leaves him $30 million.

The major old twist is that Rhubarb, who has been built up by press agent Milland as the Dodgers' lucky mascot, is kidnapped but manages to escape in time for the big game. The Dodgers had managed to delay the game by means of an artificial rainstorm on the field.

Rhubarb must also prove his identity to lawyers who have been told by greedy relatives of Lockhart who want the estate for themselves that the real cat is dead. Fortunately for the Dodgers, Milland's girlfriend (Sterling) is allergic to Rhubarb and that proves his identity.

99 Right Off the Bat

1915, Donlin Productions, 5 reels.

Cast: Mike Donlin, John McGraw, Henry Grady, Fan Bourke, Claire Mercereau, George Henry, Mabel Wright, Rita Ross Donlin, George Sullivan, Doris Farrington.

Major leaguer Donlin began a fairly active acting career with this feature about his own life, but how much of it is true is a matter for debate.

All the typical silent-era melodramatics are present: Donlin rescues the pretty maiden from a boat and later again from a runaway horse, he becomes the star pitcher for a factory team but an evil gambler kidnaps him but he escapes just in time to win the big game and be signed for the big leagues, etc. etc.

Legendary major league manager John McGraw has a role in the film as himself.

100 Roogie's Bump

1954, Republic, 71 minutes. Director: Harold Young. Producers: John Bash, Elizabeth Dickenson. Screenplay: Jack Hanley, Dan Totheroh. Story: Frank Warren, Joyce Selznick. Photography: Burgi J. Contner.

Cast: Robert Marriot, Ruth Warrick, Olive Blakeny, Robert Simon, William Harrigan, David Winters, Michael Mann, Archie Robbins, Louise Troy, Guy Rennie, Michael Keene, Tedd Lawrence, and Roy Campanella, Billy Loes, Carl Erskine, and Russ Meyer as themselves.

Roogie's Bump is probably the most well-known sports film that nobody has ever seen. It would seem that nearly everybody in film and baseball circles has heard about this movie, but because the film was so poorly received upon its release, not many people have had the chance to see it and to our knowledge it has never appeared on television.

Remington "Roogie" Rigsby (Marriot) finds it hard to adjust to life in his new neighborhood because the kids won't let him play ball with them.

As in most "triumph of the underdog" comedies and fantasies, to the rescue comes the deus ex machina, this time in the form of the ghost of baseball star Red O'Malley (Harrigan). It turns out that O'Malley once loved Roogie's grandmother, so he wants to help him.

O'Malley puts a bump on Roogie's arm that allows him to throw a baseball at the speed of light.

À la **It Happens Every Spring**, Roogie is an instant sensation and becomes the youngest major leaguer ever when he joins the Brooklyn Dodgers.

Exploited by the team and by the media, Roogie's manager (Simon) is one of the few people to really care about him.

Although the film contains a good amount of footage of the Dodgers, many baseball fans will find it disappointing as it's generally lifeless and in some cases doesn't really match what's supposed to be happening. In one instance, a Dodger batter grounds out and then comes right back up and hits again.

Mickey Mantle and Roger Maris of the Yankees chat with their young costar in Safe at Home. (Courtesy New York Yankees.)

Members of the New York Yankees are mobbed by youngsters and photographers during a break in the filming of Safe at Home. (Courtesy New York Yankees.)

101 Safe at Home

1962, Columbia Pictures, 83 minutes. Director: Walter Doniger. Producer: Tom Naud. Screenplay: Robert Dillon. Story: Naud, Steve Ritch. Photography: Irving Lippman. Editor: Frank P. Keller.

Cast: William Frawley, Patricia Barry, Don Collier, Bryan Russell, Eugene Iglesias, Flip Mark, Scott Lane, Fred A. Schwarb, Charles G. Martin, Desiree Sumarra and Roger Maris, Mickey Mantle, Ralph Houk, and Whitey Ford as themselves.

Suffice to say that Mantle and Maris never starred in another film after this feature, made to capitalize on the two Yankee sluggers' assault on Babe Ruth's home run record in 1961.

A young boy who has just moved to Florida from New York boasts to his Little League pals that his widower charter boat captain dad is friends with Mantle and Maris. He gets hooked into promising they'll show up at a Little League dinner and hitchhikes to the Yanks' training camp to try and get the sluggers to come.

Unsuccessful, he makes a confession to his teammates, but it's the Yanks to the rescue at the very end (you didn't think the Yankees would cooperate in making a film that didn't show them in a good light, did you?).

102 The Short-Stop's Double

1913, Selig Polyscope, 1,000 feet. Producer: Charles H. France. Scenario: Arthur P. Hankins.

An early silent starring major leaguer Frank "Home Run" Baker.

103 Slide, Kelly, Slide

1927, Metro Goldwyn Mayer, 7,856 feet. Director: Edward Sedgwick. Screenplay: A.B. Younger. Photography: Henry Sharp. Editor: Frank Sullivan.

Cast: William Haines, Sally O'Neil, Harry Carey, Junior Coghlan, Warner Richmond, Paul Kelly, Karl Dane and Mike Donlin, Irish Meusel, Bob Meusel, and Tony Lazzeri as themselves.

All the melodramatic stops are pulled out in this one. Bush leaguer Jim Kelly (Haines) signs with the Yankees and becomes an instant success until he gets a swelled head. When told he's suspended, he retorts "So's the Brooklyn Bridge". It takes an accident to the team's mascot to turn things around as the kid is wheeled to the big game from the hospital and spurs Kelly on to be the big hero.

104 Slide, Nelly, Slide!

1936, Vitaphone, 20 minutes. Director: Murray Roth. Story: Bert Granet.

Cast: Joe Cunningham, Herman Bing, Al Shean, Marie Wilson.

The rivalry between two women's softball teams—one sponsored by a hot dog firm and the other by a mustard factory—highlights this two-reel comedy which features members of the California champion softball team in the cast.

105 A Soldier's Story

1984, Columbia, 102 minutes, Color. Director: Norman Jewison. Producers: Jewison, Ronald L. Schway, Patrick Palmer. Screenplay: Charles Fuller, based on his play.

Cast: Howard E. Rollins, Jr., Adolph Caesar, Denzel Washington, Larry Riley.

Set in a Deep South military base during World War II, this murder mystery finds Rollins cast as the first black officer any of the men on the base—black or white—had ever seen. He's been assigned by Washington to investigate the shooting death of a black sergeant, a killing many people have attributed to the Ku Klux Klan.

Although there are only two to three minutes of actual baseball action footage in the film, sports is an integral part of the plot as the major characters spend a long amount of time either in uniform or talking about baseball.

The dear old sarge was also the manager of the platoon's baseball team. The team's members are all former Negro League players and they're practically unbeatable. In fact, all they needed was a few more wins and they'd get to play the Yankees in an exhibition game.

Dear old Sarge (Caesar), however, possesses an unnatural hatred for stereotypes of his own race and drives the team's star player to suicide after framing him.

Rollins learns that the team, in protest, loses their final game of the season and also the chance to play the Yanks. He also discovers the Sarge was shot by one of his own men.

106 Squeeze Play!

1979, Troma, Inc., 92 minutes, Color. Director: Samuel Weil. Producers: Lloyd Kaufman, Michael Herz. Screenplay: Haim Pekelis. Photography: Kaufman. Editor: George T. Norris.

Cast: Jim Harris, Jenni Hetrick, Rick Gitlin, Helen Campitelli, Rick Kahn, Diana Valentien, Alford Corley, Melissa Michaels, Michael P. Moran, Sonya Jennings.

"It's the World Series of Laughs" read the ads for this "screwball" sex comedy, which was the first feature length softball film since **Girls Can Play.**

This low-budget film, loaded with visual gags, proved so popular at the box office that Troma, Inc. kept the same format in subsequent films (**Waitress, Stuck on You,** etc.).

The boys from the Beavers team in the Mattress Companies Softball League seem to be more interested in playing ball and drinking beer than paying attention to their women, so the battle of the sexes is on.

When Mary Lou Whatley (Michaels), Georgia's top woman softball pitcher, arrives in Springtown, the girls decide to form their own team and take on an alcoholic coach to show them the ropes.

The battle of the sexes culminates on the diamond in a game between the Beavers and the Beaverettes.

107 Stealin' Home

1932, RKO Radio Pictures, 20 minutes. Director: Harry Sweet. Screenplay: Ralph Ceder, from the Rufftown stories by Arthur "Bugs" Baer. Editor: Fred Maguire.

Cast: James Gleason, Eddie Gribbon, Mae Busch.

Gleason, who made an entire career out of playing managers and trainers, this time runs a team which features ace pitcher "Smoky Joe." However, the villainous barber pours hair tonic down his throat while he's sleeping, and he arrives at the big game drunk.

108 The Stratton Story

1949, Metro Goldwyn Mayer, 106 minutes. Director: Sam Wood. Producer: Jack Cummings. Screenplay: Douglas Morrow, Guy Trosper, based on a story by Morrow. Photography: Harold Rosson.

Cast: James Stewart, June Allyson, Frank Morgan, Agnes Moorehead, Bill Williams, Bruce Cowling, Eugene Bearden, Cliff Clark, Mary Lawrence, Robert Gist, Dean White, Florence Lake and Bill Dickey, Jimmy Dykes, and Mervyn Shea as themselves.

MGM tried to pull off another **Pride of the Yankees** here, even hiring that film's director, Sam Wood, and while the results were quite successful, they didn't quite measure up to the great Cooper films.

It's the real-life story of White Sox pitcher Monty Stratton who refused to call it quits after his leg was amputated following a hunting accident.

Squeeze Play was the first feature-length film to focus on women's softball since the 1937 Girls Can Play. (Courtesy Troma, Inc.) Top: Al Corley (left) and Jim Harris are featured as softball fanatics. Bottom: the team.

The story by Douglas Morrow, who won an Academy Award for his efforts, traces the Texas farm boy's career from his initial failures in the big leagues, through the times of self-pity following the accident to his eventual triumph over adversity.

109 Take Me Out to the Ball Game

1910, Essanay, 990 feet. Director-Scenario: G.M. Anderson.

An early baseball comedy by the man who would go on to fame as Bronco Billy Anderson.

110 Take Me Out to the Ball Game (British title: **Everybody's Cheering**)

1949, Metro Goldwyn Mayer, 93 minutes, Color. Director: Busby Berkeley. Producer: Arthur Freed. Screenplay: Harry Tugend, George Wells. Photography: George Folsey. Story: Gene Kelly, Stanley Donen.

Cast: Frank Sinatra, Esther Williams, Gene Kelly, Betty Garrett, Edward Arnold, Jules Munshin, Richard Dane, Tom Dugan, Murray Alper, Wilton Graff, Mack Gray, Douglas Fowley, Gordon Jones, Dick Wessel, Si Jenks, James Burke.

The old-time baseball setting is merely an excuse for lots of singing and dancing as shortstop Sinatra and second baseman Kelly becomes involved with woman owner Williams and some gamblers.

111 They Learned About Women

1930, Metro Goldwyn Mayer, 11 reels. Directors: Sam Wood, Jack Conway. Scenario: Sarah Y. Mason. Story: A.P. Younger. Dialogue: Arthur "Bugs" Baer. Photography: Leonard Smith. Editors: James McKay, Thomas Held.

Cast: Joseph T. Schenck, Gus Van, Bessie Love, Mary Doran, J.C. Nugent, Benny Rubin, Tom Dugan, Eddie Gribbon, Francis X. Bushman, Jr.

Jack (Schenck) and Jerry (Van) are torn between careers in baseball and in vaudeville in this early talkie which features as much music as baseball action.

They're baseball stars who enter the stage after a World Series and become a success there.

As is usual in this sort of thing, they meet one virtuous girl (Love) and a vamp (Doran) and their friendship is broken up. However, they're reunited and play in another World Series.

112 Trifling with Honor

1923, Universal Pictures, 7,785 feet. Director: Harry A. Pollard. Scenario: Frank Beresford, Raymond L. Schrock. Photography: Jack Brown.

Cast: Rockliffe Fellowes, Fritzi Ridgeway, Buddy Messinger, Hayden Stevenson, William Robert Daly, Jim Farley, Emmett King, William Welsh, Frederick Stanton, Sidney De Grey.

The Gas-Pipe Kid (Fellowes) is released from prison only to find his mother dead and his father evicted from their home. He beats up the slumlord and is re-arrested but escapes and becomes Bat Shugrue, a baseball star. Widely idolized by youngsters, he refuses to cave in to blackmailers who threaten to reveal his past unless he throws a game. Guess who wins out?

113 Two Mugs from Brooklyn

1940, Favorite Films. Director: Kurt Neumann. Screenplay: Earle Snell, Clarence Marks. Photography: Robert Pittack. Editor: Richard Currie.

Cast: William Bendix, Max Baer, Sheldon Leonard, Marjorie Woodworth, Joe Sawyer, Arline Judge, Frank Faylen, Mike Mazurki, J. Farrell MacDonald, Grace Bradley, Sig Arno.

Bendix falls for burlesque star Bradley, who happens to be the "property" of gangster Leonard. The jealous mobster schemes to get rid of his foe during a sandlot baseball game during which Bendix is the pitcher and

Sawyer the catcher for the Flatbush team.

During the game, which winds up in a free-for-all, Leonard has some bootleg liquor planted in the heroes' cab and conveniently calls the cops.

After some wild adventures, the pair gets a reward for bringing Leonard to justice, but that's not the end. They wind up on a crazy health farm where Baer gets to join in the nonsense.

114 Up the River

1930, Fox Film Corp., 8,280 feet. Director: John Ford. Screenplay: Maurine Watkins. Photography: Joseph August. Editor: Frank E. Hull.

Cast: Spencer Tracy, Warren Hymer, Humphrey Bogart, Claire Luce, Joan Lawes, Sharon Lynn, Morgan Wallace, George MacFarlane, Gaylord Pendleton, Robert E. O'Connor, Goodee Montgomery.

One of the most popular and imitated sports comedies features Tracy as a character called St. Louis and Hymer as Dannemora Dan, the star battery for their prison baseball team, which even has its own marching band. They break out of prison to help their pal Steve (Bogard), but return in time to help win the big game.

Up the River inspired a 1939 remake, this time featuring a football team, and numerous imitations. Even the 1970's football film, **The Longest Yard**, traces its roots to this early talkie.

115 Warming Up

1928, Paramount Famous Lasky Corp., 6,509 feet. Director: Fred Newmeyer. Screenplay: Ray Harris. Story: Sam Mintz. Photography: Edward Cronjager. Editor: Otto Lovering.

Cast: Richard Dix, Jean Arthur, Claude King, Mike Donlin, Philo McCullough, Billy Kent Schaefer, Roscoe Karns, James Dugan and Wally Hood, Truck Hannah, Joe Pirrone, Bob Murray, Mike Ready, and Chet Thomas as themselves.

The Green Sox—that's right, green—win the World Series through the efforts of star pitcher Bert Tulliver (Dix), but not before the usual silent-era trials and tribulations.

As usual, the hero is just a small town star at the opening of the film; and as usual, he arouses the jealousy of the team's star (McCullough) when he arrives in the big leagues.

He also falls for the star's girlfriend, who happens to be the daughter of the team's owner. The rival winds up on another ballclub, which, of course meets the Green Sox in the World Series, setting the stage for a final confrontation between the two. We don't think we ruined the film by telling you who wins.

116 Whistling in Brooklyn

1943, Metro Goldwyn Mayer, 87 minutes. Director: S. Sylvan Simon. Producer: George Haight. Screenplay: Nat Perrin. Photography: Lester White. Editor: Ben Lewis.

Cast: Red Skelton, Ann Rutherford, Jean Rogers, Rags Ragland, Ray Collins, Henry O'Neill, William Frawley, Sam Levene and members of the Brooklyn Dodgers.

Comedian Skelton starred as the radio detective "The Wolf" in the 1940's in this film, **Whistling in the Dark** and **Whistling in Dixie.**

Whistling in Brooklyn is by no means a sports movie—it's plot has The Wolf tracking down a cop killer—but it features a sequence in which Skelton portrays a bearded pitcher in a game with the Dodgers, so it's included here.

117 The Winning Team

1952, Warner Brothers, 97 minutes. Director: Lewis Seller. Producer: Bryan Foy. Screenplay: Ted Sherdeman, Seelag Lester, Merwin Gerard. Photography: Sid Hickox. Editor: Alan Crosland.

Cast: Ronald Reagan, Doris Day, Frank Lovejoy, Eve Miller, James Millican, Rusty Tamblyn, Gordon Jones, Hugh Sanders, Irv Noren, Hank Bauer, Gene Mauch, Bob Lemon, Peanuts Lowrey, Jerry Priddy, Hank Sauer, Al Zarilla.

Our future president doesn't match the success he had starring in **Knute Rockne, All-American** in his portrayal of baseball-great pitcher Grover Cleveland Alexander.

Major leaguers Jerry Priddy and Arnold Statz, technical advisers for this somewhat whitewashed account of Alexander's life, worked with our future president on his pitching form. Whitewashed, we say, because while the film deals with Alexander's rapid rise, fall and comeback, his disease is never identified as epilepsy.

The Winning Team traces the Hall of Famer's career from his days as a telephone lineman to stardom with Philadelphia until he is struck in the head. The resultant spells of dizziness are worsened during his military hitch, and he begins to drink heavily.

He's eventually cut by Philadelphia after his epileptic fits are mistaken for drunkenness and he becomes a circus attraction until bouncing back with the St. Louis Cardinals.

118 Youth

1968, Japanese, Toho, Color. Director-Screenplay: Kon Ichikawa. Producer: Asahi Shimbunsha.

From the director of **Tokyo Olympiad, Harp of Burma** and **Fires on the Plain** comes this documentary about high school baseball. Starting with winter practice, it follows the season up to the 50th annual Japanese High School All-Star game.

119 Zapped!

1982, Embassy, 96 minutes, Color. Director: Robert J. Rosenthal. Producer: Jeffrey D. Apple. Screenplay: Bruce Rubin, Rosenthal. Photography: Daniel Pearl. Editor: Robert Ferrelli.

Cast: Scott Baio, Willie Aames, Felice Schacter, Robert Mandan, Heather Thomas, Scatman Crothers.

Baio portrays a scientific whiz who's a flop for his high school baseball team until he develops telekinetic powers and presto! not only can he alter the path of baseballs (shades of **It Happens Every Spring**), but he can strip girls and defeat his tormentors with his new-found powers.

Basketball

There really haven't been enough basketball features made to determine any kind of real pattern. In the early days of filmmaking, basketball wasn't the big-money sport it is now so few films were made.

The lack of wide open spaces, such as those offered in baseball and football films, also proved a deterrent as did basketball's former rule that there be a jump ball after each basket. Filmwise, this tended to slow the action, although in **Angels with Dirty Faces** it proved no handicap.

Coincidence or not, the only two major features dealing with basketball in the silent era were **The Fair Co-ed** and **High School Hero,** which were released practically simultaneously in 1927.

Basketball features were few and far between until a spate of them in the 1970's included **Maurie, The Fish That Saved Pittsburgh, Mixed Company, Fire Sale, One on One, Drive, He Said** and **Fast Break.**

The one advantage filmwise that basketball holds over baseball is the time clock, which can be used to much greater cinematic advantage than the innings of baseball. Therefore, the only real basketball film cliche is the race against time to score the winning basket in the final second.

Until the 1970's, the only cage films of any kind of note were **The Harlem Globetrotters** in 1951 and **Go, Man, Go** in 1954, which, as we mentioned earlier, were landmarks so far as breaking the sports film color barrier.

Of the numerous films not listed here which include basketball sequences, the only one we feel worth mentioning is that in **The Great Santini,** in which Robert Duvall uses his prowess at basketball as a tool to continue to dominate his son.

120 Absent-Minded Professor

1961, Buena Vista, 97 minutes. Director: Robert Stevenson. Producer: Walt Disney. Screenplay: Bill Walsh, based on a story by Samuel W. Taylor. Photography: Edward Colman. Editor: Cotton Warburton.

Cast: Fred MacMurray, Keenan Wynn, Ed Wynn, Nancy Olson, Tommy Kirk, Leon Ames, Wally Brown, Alan Carney, Elliott Reid, Edward Andrews, Ned Wynn.

Medfield College professor Ned Brainard (MacMurray) invents "flubber"—short for flying rubber, a gooey gook that floats. When he puts it on his car, it makes his car fly.

Medfield's basketball team, in the meantime, is hopelessly inept. Watching the team being humilated by a rival team literally twice Medfield's size, Brainard irons flubber onto his home team's sneakers during half-time; and suddenly the players can jump high over the basket and perform all kinds of comic acrobatic feats.

A popular comedy from the Disney studio, with special effects by Peter Ellenshaw and Eustace Lycett, it inspired a sequel, **Son of Flubber,** in which some similar gags were used during a football game (see Football Films section).

121 All-American Blondes

1939, Columbia, ca. 20 minutes. Director: Del Lord.

Cast: Andy Clyde, Dick Curtis.

Comedian Clyde, who piloted a women's softball team in 1937's **Gracie at the Bat,** tries his hand this time at the helm of a female basketball team.

122 The American Game

1979, World Northal, 89 minutes, Color. Writer-Directors: Jay Freund, David Wolfe. Producer: Anthony Jones. Editors: Freund, Nancy Baker. Photography: Robert Elfstrom, Peter Powell.

Here's an interesting feature-length documentary for cage fans which never received wide distribution. It juxtaposes the lives of two highly sought-after high school basketball stars who come from completely different backgrounds.

Brian Walker is from a white middle class family, while the film's other "star", Stretch Graham, is black and from Brooklyn.

123 Angels with Dirty Faces

1938, Warner Brothers, 97 minutes. Director: Michael Curtiz. Producer: Sam Bischoff. Screenplay: John Wexley, Warren Duff. Story: Rowland Brown. Photography: Sol Polito.

Cast: James Cagney, Pat O'Brien, Humphrey Bogart, Ann Sheridan, George Bancroft, Billy Halop, Bobby Jordan, Leo Gorcey, Bernard Punsley, Gabriel Dell, Huntz Hall, Frankie Burke.

One of Warner Brothers' most famous gangster movies of the 1930's, **Angels with Dirty Faces** is included here because it contains the most memorable basketball sequence in film history.

Cagney was nominated for best actor for his portrayal of Rocky Sullivan, a career criminal who is idolized by the Dead End Kids (who would later, as the East Side Kids and the Bowery Boys, make a number of sports films themselves).

The Rev. Jerry Connolly (O'Brien), Sullivan's lifelong pal who but for a twist of fate and fleetness of foot could well have taken the same criminal route as Sullivan, runs a gymnasium for the neighborhood slum kids. He talks Sullivan and the delinquent Dead End Kids into coming down to see what's going on.

When Sullivan sees the Dead End Kids roughhousing a neighborhood team during a basketball game, he decides to referee, street style. Every time a Dead End Kid fouls one of the neighborhood boys, Sullivan decks a Dead End Kid until finally, they start playing basketball cleanly.

In the film's most memorable sequence, Rev. Connolly pleads with Sullivan, who is on his way to the electric chair, to feign fear, so the kids would no longer idolize him and follow his criminal footsteps. Sullivan refuses, but as he's strapped into the chair, starts screaming.

Bogart, as usual, plays the heavy—this time a shady lawyer—while Ann Sheridan is the love interest.

124 The Basketball Fix (also known as **The Big Decision)**

1951, Realart Films, 68 minutes. Director: Felix Feist. Producer: Edward Leven. Screenplay: Peter R. Brooke, Charles K. Peck, Jr. Photography: Stanley Cortez. Editor: Francis D. Lyon.

Cast: John Ireland, Marshall Thompson, Vanessa Brown, William Bishop, Hazel Brooks, John Sands, Bobby Hyatt, Ted Pierson.

Here's a low-budget film based on the college basketball scandals of the day.

Ireland, who also serves as the film's narrator, portrays a sports columnist who follows the career of cage star Thompson, who gets a scholarship to a major college.

Economics, however, eventually induce him and Sands to listen to the overtures of wicked gambler Bishop to shave points. As you might expect in a 1950's B-film, the two eventually are caught by the law and learn their lesson.

125 Basketball Stars

1974, Filipino, HPS, 90 minutes, Color. Writer-Director: Abraham Cruz Gregorio.

Cast: Tembon Melencio, Ramon Fernandez, Yoyung Martinez, Francis Arnaiz, Bogs Adornado, Rosanna Ortiz, Tina Revilla, Leila Hermosa, Marilou Destreza, Aline Samson, Coach Tito Eduque, Trainer Juan Cutillas.

Made with the cooperation of the Basketball Association of the Philippines, **Basketball Stars** deals with the real-life stories, on and off the court, of the Filipino national cage team. It includes a lot of scenes of their training, as well as dealing with their off-court romantic lives.

126 Big Town Scandal

1948, Paramount Pictures, 61 minutes. Director: William C. Thomas. Producers: Thomas, William Pine. Screenplay: Milton Ralston. Photography: Ellis W. Carter. Editor: Howard Smith.

Cast: Philip Reed, Hillary Brooke, Stanley Clements, Darryl Hickman, Carl "Alfalfa" Switzer, Roland Dupree, Tommy Bond, Vince Barnett.

Big Town was a popular radio series which also inspired a number of films starring Reed as Steve Wilson of the Illustrated Press.

In this episode, the crusading editor sets up a youth center for troubled kids. Naturally there's one kid (Clements) who's still mixed up with bad elements and nearly ruins it for everyone.

Clements is not only involved in hiding stolen goods, but places bets on the youths' cage games. When a youngster is killed by the crooked gamblers, however, Clements undergoes a change of character.

127 Campus Confessions

1938, Paramount Pictures, 65 minutes. Director: George Archainbaud. Screenplay: Lloyd Corrigan, Edwin Gelsey. Photography: Henry Sharpe. Editor: Stuart Gilmore.

Cast: Betty Grable, Eleanore Whitney, William Henry, Fritz Feld, John Arledge, Thurston Hall, Roy Gordon, Lane Chandler, Richard Denning, Matty Gemp, Sumner Getchell, Hank Luisetti.

Henry, the son of a college's main patron, enrolls at the school and finds that practically no one wants to associate with him until he makes the college basketball team despite his dad's hatred of sports.

He joins with real-life All-American Hank Luisetti to make the team a winner, but his father manages to keep him out of the big game. As is the norm in this kind of sports comedy, Henry gets into the game at the end to lead the team to victory.

Ex-cowboy star Lane Chandler portrays the coach.

128 Coach

1978, Crown International, 100 minutes, Color. Director: Bud Townsend. Producer: Mark Tenser. Screenplay: Stephen Bruce Rose, Nancy Larson. Photography: Mike Murphy. Editor: Bob Gordon.

Cast: Cathy Lee Crosby, Michael Biehn, Keenan Wynn, Channing Clarkson, Jack David Walker, Meredith Baer.

A computer picks the new coach of a high school basketball team after Wynn, whose grandson is on the squad, fires the previous coach.

The computer's choice, "Randy," turns out to be a woman (Crosby) and the usual comic complications ensue with the team, of course, eventually becoming a winner.

The film received extremely limited distribution.

129 Cornbread, Earl and Me

1975, American-International, 95 minutes, Color. Director-Producer: Joe Manduke. Writer-executive producer: Leonard Lamensdorf. Photography: Jules Brenner. Editor: Aaron Stell.

Cast: Keith Wilkes, Tierre Turner, Moses Gunn, Rosalind Cash, Bernie Casey, Madge Sinclair, Antonio Fargas (One-Eye), Vincent Mortorano, Charles Lampkin.

Made during the height of the black exploitation film era, this stands out for its sincerity and lack of stereotypes in its portrayal of the lives of three young ghetto dwellers.

Cornbread, portrayed by NBA star Wilkes, represents the hopes of his two young companions as well as the entire community as a rising basketball star. These hopes are dashed when Cornbread is mistakenly killed by a white policeman.

130 Drive, He Said

1971, Columbia, 95 minutes. Color. Director: Jack Nicholson. Producers: Nicholson, Steve Blauner, William Topper. Screenplay: Nicholson, Jeremy Larner. Photography: Bill Butler. Editors: Pat Somerset, Donn Cambern, Christopher Holmes, Robert L. Wolfe.

Cast: William Topper, Karen Black, Bruce Dern, Michael Margotta, Robert Towne, Henry Jaglom, Mike Warren, June Fairchild.

When you see four editors, it's usually a sure sign that a film's in trouble. Even they couldn't save Nicholson's first directorial effort from being a box office flop.

College basketball star Topper has an anti-Vietnam war roommate (Margotta) who shows increasingly unstable behavior. Margotta and some pals in guerilla uniforms stage a raid on a basketball game.

131 The Explosive Generation

1961, United Artists, 89 minutes. Director: Buzz Kulik. Producer: Stanley Colbert. Screenplay: Joseph Landon. Photography: Floyd Crosby. Editor: Melvin Shapiro.

Cast: William Shatner, Patty McCormack, Lee Kinsolving, Billy Gray, Steve Dunne, Arch Johnson, Virginia Field, Beau Bridges.

A much unheralded film centering on sex education, **The Explosive Generation** nevertheless has one of the most memorable basketball game sequences this side of **Angels with Dirty Faces.**

A teacher is suspended for having his class write an essay on the taboo subject. The kids, in retaliation for the suspension, go on a silence strike.

At the school basketball game, the only sounds are the ball dribbling and the whistle of the referee. Eventually, the parents see the wisdom of sex education.

132 The Fair Co-Ed

1927, Metro Goldwyn Mayer, 6,408 feet. Director: Sam Wood. Adaptation-Continuity: Byron Morgan. Photography: John Seitz. Editor: Conrad A. Nervig.

Cast: Marion Davies, Johnny Mack Brown, Jane Winton, Thelma Hill, Lillian Leighton, Gene Stone.

Silent-era basketball features are rarer than hen's teeth. That's why it's noteworthy to mention that **The Fair Co-Ed** was released just one day before **High School Hero,** a Fox basketball comedy. Coincidence?

Based on a 1909 play by George Ade, the movie concerns a girl who enrolls at college only after meeting the handsome coach (Brown) of the women's basketball team.

The girl (Davies) becomes one of the team's key players but deserts the team after a spat with the coach. Scorned by the other students for jumping the team, she naturally rejoins her teammates and wins the game at the last minute.

The Fair Co-Ed is also noteworthy inasmuch as it's the only feature-length film about women's basketball, until 1979's **Scoring.**

133 Fast Break

1979, Columbia, 107-117 minutes, Color. Director: Jack Smight. Producer: Stephen Friedman. Screenplay: Sandor Stern. Story: Marc Kaplan. Photography: Charles Correll. Editor: Frank J. Urioste.

Cast: Gabe Kaplan, Harold Sylvester, Michael Warren, Bernard King, Reb Brown, Mavis Washington, Bert Remsen, Randee Heller, Jack Smight.

Delicatessen clerk Gabe Kaplan somehow becomes basketball coach at hopelessly inept Cadwalader College in Nevada, but there's a catch: his salary is dependent upon how many victories he gets.

Knowing that he needs a deus ex machina to succeed in a "triumph of the underdog" comedy, Kaplan recruits players straight off New York City streets to play for the college team (never mind academic standards, of course).

Mavis Washington strikes a blow for women's lib as a basketball player disguised as a man who arouses the rest of the team's suspicions when she never showers with them.

You can guess the outcome unless the only film you've ever seen in your life is **Rebecca of Sunnybrook Farm.**

134 Fire Sale

1977, 20th Century-Fox, 88 minutes, Color. Director: Alan Arkin. Producer: Marvin Worth. Screenplay: Robert Klane. Photography: Ralph Woolsey. Editor: Richard Halsey.

Cast: Alan Arkin, Anjanette Comer, Rob Reiner, Byron Stewart, Vincent Gardenia, Kay Medford, Barbara Dana, Sid Caesar, Alex Rocco.

A lunatic family includes Gardenia, the owner of a department store who wants to burn it down for the insurance; Reiner, as a timid assistant store manager; and Arkin, a total flop as a basketball coach.

Arkin adopts a black basketball star (Stewart).

135 The Fish That Saved Pittsburgh

1979, United Artists, 104 minutes, Color. Director: Gilbert Moses. Producers: Gary Stromberg, David D. Ashev. Screenplay: Jaison Starkes, Edmond Stevens. Photography: Frank Stanley. Editors: Frank Mazolla, Arthur Schmidt, Bud Friedgen, Jr.

Cast: Jonathan Winter, Julius Erving, Meadowlark Lemon, Kareem Abdul Jabbar, Margaret Avery, James Bond III, Michael V. Gazzo, Flip Wilson, Stockard Channing, M. Emmet Walsh.

Pittsburgh's basketball team is awful and coach Delaney (Wilson) just as bad. Eventually, only Moses Guthrie (Erving) is left and the team must rebuild.

The team's water boy (James Bond III) steers the team to astrologer Channing, who advises the team to sign only players born under the sign of Pisces. Naturally, the team is transformed overnight into a winner.

There's some sloppy filmmaking involved in the basketball sequences—in one scene, announcer Marv Albert says there's a capacity crowd while the players run in front of a bunch of empty seats—but if you're not too picky, there's enough to be enjoyed.

136 Girls Demand Excitement

1931, Fox, 64 minutes. Director: Seymour Felix. Story: Harlan Thompson. Photography: Charles Clarke.

Cast: John Wayne, Virginia Cherrill, Marguerite Churchill, Helen Jerome Eddy, Marion Byron, Addie McPhail.

Before the Duke became

an international celebrity, he starred in this lightweight film about the rivalry between a school's boys and girls basketball teams.

Besides Wayne's appearance, the only thing really noteworthy is the acknowledgment of women as athletes.

137 Go Man Go

1954, United Artists, 82 minutes. Director: James Wong Howe. Producer: Anton M. Leader. Screenplay: Arnold Becker. Photography: Bill Steiner. Editor: Faith Elliott.

Cast: Dane Clark, Pat Breslin, Sidney Poitier, Edmon Ryan, Bram Nossem, Anatol Winogradoff, Celia Brodkin, Ruby Dee, Marty Glickman, Bill Stern.

It's always been the rule in Hollywood if that at first you **do** succeed, try and try again. Columbia Pictures had success in 1951 with its film version about the Harlem Globetrotters, so in 1954 came another one.

Go Man Go concentrates on Abe Saperstein's long struggle through years of barnstorming and opposition from the big leagues to establish a niche for his team in basketball.

Much of the basketball action is played to the all-black team's theme song of "Sweet Georgia Brown," and there's a typical whirlwind finish with the Globetrotters winning out. But there's enough basketball wizardry shown to dazzle even the non-fan.

138 Halls of Anger

1970, United Artists, 98 minutes, Color. Director: Paul Bogart. Producer: Herbert Hirschman. Screenplay: John Shaner, Al Ramrus. Photography: Burnett Guffey. Editor: Bud Molin.

Cast: Calvin Lockhart, Janet MacLachlan, James A. Watson, Jr., Jeff Bridges, Rob Reiner, Dewayne Jesse, Patricia Stich, Roy Jensen, John McLiam, Edward Asner, Lou Frizzell.

In a switch on the usual school busing issue, 60 whites are sent to a mostly black urban high school, causing tension between militants on both sides, particularly between Reiner and Watson.

Assistant principal Lockhart must defuse a really explosive situation after white basketball player Bridges is beaten up during tryouts.

139 Harlem Globetrotters

1951, Columbia, 75 minutes. Director: Phil Brown. Producer: Buddy Adler. Screenplay: Alfred Palca. Photography: Philip Tannura. Editor: James Sweeney.

Cast: Thomas Gomez, Dorothy Dandridge, Bill Walker, Angela Clarke, Peter Thompson, Steve Roberts, Peter Virgo, Ray Walker, Reese "Goose" Tatum and the Harlem Globetrotters.

The sounds of "Sweet Georgia Brown" hit the basketball court as a black college athlete quits school to join the Globetrotters.

Using the same plot as in numerous football films of an earlier era, the new kid has no real feeling for the team and is only out for the money until his girlfriend and the Globetrotters set him right.

140 High School Hero

1927, Fox Film Corp., 5,498 feet. Director: David Butler. Scenario: Seton I. Miller. Story: Butler, William M. Conselman. Photography: Ernest Palmer.

Cast: Nick Stuart, Sally Phipps, William N. Bailey, John Darrow, Wade Boteler, Brandon Hurst, David Rollins, Charles Paddock.

Stuart (Pete Greer) and Darrow (Bill Merrill) have been at each other's throats since they were young whippersnappers, and it gets even worse in high school when they're both cage stars in love with the same girl (Phipps).

School spirit eventually prevails when the boys' rivalry eventually spills over onto the basketball court in this silent-era comedy.

141 Inside Moves

1980, Associated Film Distributors 113 minutes, Color. Director: Richard Donner. Screenplay: Valerie Curtin, Barry Levinson, based on a novel by Todd Walton. Producers: Mark M. Tanz, R.W. Goodwin. Photography: Laszlo Kovacs. Editor: Frank Morriss.

Cast: John Savage, David Morse, Diana Scarwid, Amy Wright, Tony Burton, Bill Henderson, Harold Sylvester, Bert Remsen, Pepe Serna.

Savage, crippled during a suicide attempt, tries to begin life anew by running a bar patronized mostly by the handicapped.

Morse portrays a basketball player who frequents the bar and whose career is boosted after he undergoes a knee operation.

142 A Man Betrayed

1941, Republic Pictures, 82 minutes. Director: John Aver. Producer: Armand Schaefer. Screenplay: Isabel Dawn. Story: Jack Moffit. Adaptation: Tom Kilpatrick. Photography: Jack Marta. Editor: Charles Craft.

Cast: John Wayne, Francis Dee, Edward Ellis, Wallace Ford, Ward Bond, Harry Hayden, Russell Hicks, Pierre Watkin.

A young small-town basketball player is murdered while visiting a big city and the political bigwigs call it suicide.

Enter John Wayne as the murdered player's lawyer pal, who smashes the corrupt political machine and gets the big shot's daughter in the bargain.

143 Maurie (also known as **Big Mo**)

1973, National General, 112 minutes, Color. Director: Daniel Mann. Producers: Frank Ross, Douglas Morrow. Screenplay: Morrow. Photography: John Hors. Editor: Walter A. Hennemann.

Cast: Bernie Casey, Bo Swenson, Janet MacLechian, Stephanie Edwards, Paulene Myers, Bill Walker, Curt Conway, Jitu Cumbuka, Chris Schenkel.

Douglas Morrow, who won an Academy Award for the screenplay of **The Stratton Story**, which was about the efforts of baseball pitcher Monty Stratton to come back after a leg amputation, tries the same formula here in the real-life story of Cincinnati Royals player Maurice Stokes' attempts at rehabilitation after a crippling stroke.

There's very little on-court action, as the story focuses on the friendship between Stokes (Bernie Casey) and Jack Twyman (Swenson), who becomes his teammate's caretaker at an immense personal cost for reasons even he doesn't fully comprehend.

The film covers a 10-year span as Twyman makes Stokes a member of the family and arranges for fund raisers to help his stricken friend.

144 Mixed Company

1974, United Artists, 109 minutes, Color. Director-Producer: Melville Shavelson. Screenplay: Shavelson, Mort Lachman. Photography: Stan Lazan. Editors: Walter Thompson, Ralph James Hall.

Cast: Joseph Bologna, Barbara Harris, Lisa Gerritsen, Arieanne Heller, Ron McIlwain, Al McCoy, Stephen Honanie, Haywood Nelson, Eric Olson, Jina Tan and members of the Phoenix Suns basketball team.

Pity poor coach Bologna. Not only is his team a loser on the court, but he can't get along with the team's black star (McIlwain). To boot, with three kids of his own he can't have a fourth, so the family takes on a black kid, a Vietnamese girl and an Indian boy and then must cope with bigoted townspeople.

145 One on One

1977, Warner Brothers, 96-98 minutes, Color. Director: Lamont

Johnson. Screenplay: Robby Benson, Jerry Segal. Photography: Donald M. Morgan. Editor: Robbe Roberts.

Cast: Robby Benson, Annette O'Toole, G.D. Spradlin, Gail Strickland, Melanie Griffith, James G. Richardson, Hector Morales, Cory Faucher.

UCLA and USC refused to cooperate in this exposé of big time basketball, so it was filmed at Colorado State University. Benson, who portrays basketball player Henry Steele, co-authored the screenplay with his dad, Jerry Segal. Steele is a small but talented high school star who finds himself in danger of losing his college scholarship when he can't fit into the style of play dictated by Coach Smith (Spradlin).

What's worse, his lovely tutor (O'Toole) won't give him a tumble (only at first, of course), and he must bear the scorn of non-athletes. When he starts telling O'Toole's boyfriend his opinion on something, he begins with "I think..." only to be interrupted by the rival, who retorts "No, you don't."

Just when things appear darkest for our hero, he gets into the game and...need we say more?

146 Palm Springs Weekend

1963, Warner Brothers, 100 minutes, Color. Director: Norman Taurog. Producer: Michael A. Hoey. Screenplay: Earl Hamner, Jr. Photography: Harold Lipstein. Editor: Folmar Blangsted.

Cast: Troy Donahue, Connie Stevens, Ty Hardin, Stefanie Powers, Robert Conrad, Andrew Duggan, Jack Weston, Carole Cook, Jerry Van Dyke, Bill Mumy.

During their Easter vacation, a basketball team heads for some fun in the sun at Palm Springs. It's basically just inconsequential teenage shenanigans.

147 Rabbit, Run

1970, Warner Brothers, 94 minutes, Color. Director: Jack Smight. Screenplay-Producer: Howard B. Kreitsek, based on the novel by John Updike. Photography: Philip Lathrop. Editor: Archie Marsnek.

Cast: James Caan, Anjanette Comer, Carrie Snodgress, Arthur Hill, Jack Albertson, Melodie Johnson, Henry Johnson.

Set in Reading, Pa., this total box office bust opened in that city and almost no place else and was sold to television without ever going into general distribution.

Ex-basketball star Caan is now married to an alcoholic and has suffered from a lack of success in his career. His former coach (Albertson) is still a source of inspiration.

148 Rah, Rah, Rah

1928, Educational, 2 reels. Director: Norman Taurog.

Cast: Dorothy Devore, Babe London, Wallace Lupino, Jack Miller.

A hick girl (Devore) undergoes the hazing treatment at a snooty college but makes the girls' cage team.

Comedy situation arises when the petite girl is matched against a giant fat girl.

149 Revenge of the Cheerleaders

1976, Monarch, 86 minutes. Color. Director: Richard Lerner. Producers: Lerner, Nathaniel Dorsky. Screenplay: Dorsky, Ted Greenwald, Ace Baandage. Photography: Dorsky. Editors: Richard S. Brummer, Joseph Ancore, Jr.

Cast: Carl Ballantine, Jerii Woods, Rainbeaux Smith, Helen Lang, Patrice Rohmer, Susie Elene, Eddra Gale, William Branley, Norman Thomas Marshall.

Sex-oriented nonsense in which the cheerleaders help their basketball team to victory while also triumphing over a greedy real estate developer who wants to shut down their school.

150 Scoring

1979, Intermedia Artists, 91 minutes, Color. Director-Screenplay: Michael de Gaetano. Producers: de Gaetano, Nicholas Nizich. Photography: William E. Hines. Editor: Oliver B. Katz.

Cast: Myra Taylor, Charles Fatone, Gregg Perrie, Freya Crane, Pete Maravich, Nina Scotti, Paunita Nichols, Joseph Hardin, Gary Moss, Dick Hardiman.

Scoring tries to do for women's basketball what **Squeeze Play** did to softball, but it lacks the comic talents involved in the latter film.

The Des Moines Vixens are the worst professional women's team in the Central Division. Their manager has run off with their money, their bus has been blown up and the city is kicking them out for being a laughing stock, even though no one attends their games anyway.

They convince a loony florist and his druggie son to take over as coaches, raise money for the team by selling marijuana cultivated in the rear of the flower shop and begin to turn things around.

The city gives them one last chance: beat a men's team from the Army, including Pistol Pete Maravich, and they can stay in Des Moines.

151 The Slumber Party Massacre

1982, New World Pictures, 77-78 minutes, Color. Director: Amy Jones. Producers: Jones, Aaron Lipstadt. Screenplay: Rita Mae Brown. Photography: Steve Posey. Editor: Wendy Green.

Cast: Michele Michaelis, Robin Stille, Michael Villela, Andre Honore, Debra Deliso, Gina Mari, David Millbern, Joe Johnson, Pamela Roylance, Brinke Stevens.

This might have passed through local theaters without too much notice if it hadn't been directed by a woman and written by Brown, a feminist novelist noted for her **Rubyfruit Jungle.** Otherwise, it fits right into the mad slasher genre of **Halloween** and **Friday the 13th,** although it has a little more humor than most.

Members of a girls' basketball team get done in by a psycho during the party of the title.

152 Tall Story

1960, Warner Brothers, 91 minutes. Director-Producer: Joshua Logan. Screenplay: Julius Epstein from the play by Howard Lindsay and Russel Crouse from the novel "The Homecoming Game" by Howard Nemerov. Photography: Ellsworth Fredericks. Editor: Philip W. Anderson.

Cast: Anthony Perkins, Jane Fonda, Marc Connelly, Anne Jackson, Murray Hamilton, Bob Wright, Karl Lukas, Elizabeth Patterson, Tom Laughlin.

The most noteworthy thing in this college basketball comedy is that it's Jane Fonda's screen debut.

Otherwise, it's a basically routine story of cage star Perkins involved with the inevitable gamblers who want him to help lose the game with a team of visiting Russians—if he ever gets to play, that is. It seems his love affair with Fonda has affected his grades, and he must first pass a big exam.

153 That Championship Season

1982, Cannon, 110 minutes, Color. Director-Writer: Jason Miller, based on his Pulitzer Prize-winning play. Photography: John Bailey. Producers: Menahem Golan, Yoram Globus. Editor: Richard Halsey.

Cast: Bruce Dern, Stacy Keach, Robert Mitchum, Martin Sheen, Paul Sorvino, Arthur Franz, Michael Bernosky, Joseph Kelly, James M. Langan, Tony Santaniello, Barry Weiner.

The members of the 1957 Pennsylvania state basketball champions get together for a

25th anniversary reunion, and they're sorry they do.

Dern is a shady politician hoping for re-election, Keach is a dissatisfied school principal, Sheen an alcoholic and Sorvino a greedy contractor. The fifth member of the starting team is the lucky one as he can't be found by the rest of the team and doesn't have to sit through this talkathon, which was a successful play which simply didn't transfer well to the screen.

Mitchum is their still strong-willed coach, who must endure all his former players' sob stories about how unhappy they are.

There's no on-screen cage action—just a recorded radio broadcast of the team's moment of glory in 1957.

Boxing

From the start, filmmakers have had a love affair with boxing. For one thing, they can be filmed on a relatively low budget since most of the action can take place in the tiny boxing ring.

Secondly, if they don't really have a first class plot, the action can take care of itself. Just let two guys stand there and beat each other to a pulp and that provides enough action for a lot of film fans, although of course there is a limit.

And third, if you have a lot of action outside the ring, it comes in handy for your hero to know how to use his fists on the baddies when necessary.

Even before the turn of the century, fight films were popular with the Corbett-Fitzsimmons bout in 1897 and the Jeffries-Sharkey fight in 1899 clicking at the box office. That started a tradition in which virtually every major bout up until the Ali-Foreman fight was screened theatrically at one point or another.

Many of the early "newsreel" fight films were fakes in which hired hands would impersonate the real-life boxers and recreate the fight.

Variety described one of these reproductions in its review of the film of the Burns-Palmer fight in 1908: "The arena and ring are poorly contrived and at a first glance, the film shows upon its face that it is a fake pure and simple. About a dozen tiers of benches hold a gathering of observers who have been very poorly rehearsed in their duties and their enthusiasm over the fake is vastly greater than that of the audience which witnesses the picture. There are knock downs galore, many times when no blow is shown to have been delivered, and the final knockout is a ridiculous piece of fakery."

The early boxing newsreels were hindered also by a federal law which forbade the importation of fight pictures. The **New York Times** described how, in 1916, clever film distributors circumvented the law to show films of the Jack Johnson-Jess Willard classic bout in Havana of April 5, 1915.

According to the **Times**, the film was delivered to Canada, where it was screened outdoors at Rouse Point, a few inches north of the U.S. border. A camera was placed a foot away on American soil and re-filmed the action off the screen.

When the Brown Bomber himself, Joe Louis, rose to boxing prominence, newsreel operators found themselves with a new obstacle because most places in the South refused to show his victory films.

From the beginning of the 20th century, filmmakers were quick to realize the drawing power of big name boxers so even before baseball stars were drafted for the big screen there were a number of boxers. Jim Corbett, Jess Willard, Jack Johnson, Joe Louis, Billy Conn, Muhammad Ali—the list of boxers who have acted on screen is almost like reading **Ring Magazine**'s boxing encyclopedia.

Most of the plots of boxing films are the same thing over and over again. A slum boy rises to be a contender, but he either loses his virtue to a vamp or is corrupted by gangsters and falls, only to make a comeback at the end aided by the pleas at ringside of the sweetheart he's left behind. Oh yes, there's often a kidnapping plot thrown in for good measure.

The formula had been used so often, that by the mid 1940s, the boxing film genre had hit rock bottom. Then came **Body and Soul** in 1947 to usher in what we'll call the Golden Gloves Decade (1947-1957) of the boxing movie. It's during these 10 years that the overwhelming majority of top boxing films were made. Besides **Body and Soul**, there were **The Set-Up, Right Cross, The Ring, Monkey on My Back** and **The Harder They Fall**, among others. Notable exceptions are, of course, **The Champ** from 1931, **Requiem for a Heavyweight** in 1962 and **Rocky** in 1976.

Films which we have not included in the main listings, but which deserve historical footnotes in the history of boxing films include **Son of a Sailor** (1933) with Joe E. Brown; **Sailor, Beware** (1951) with Dean Martin and Jerry Lewis; **The Mighty McGurk** (1946), in which Wallace Beery portrays a bragging ex-champ; **The Nickel Ride**, in which a fighter refuses to take a dive; **The Great American Broadcast** (1940), which incorporates footage from the Dempsey-Willard bout; **Boys Town** (1938), where Mickey Rooney's defeat in the boxing ring is one of the keys to getting him to reform; **The Bells of St. Mary's** (1946), in which nun Ingrid Bergman teaches a boy how to defend himself; **Diamond Jim** (1935), in which Bill Houlihan portrays the great John L. Sullivan; **Alias the Deacon** and **To Sir with Love** 1967) with Sidney Poitier, in which one of the tough student leaders must be outboxed before the class gains respect for the teacher.

In **From Here to Eternity** (1953), Montgomery Clift portrays a soldier who refuses to box for his company because he blinded an opponent in the ring.

And, finally, in MGM's **The Big City** (1937), cabbie Spencer Tracy runs into Jack Dempsey's restaurant to get help for the big fight against a rival owner. Joining in the chase are the likes of Jim Thorpe, Maxie Rosenbloom, James J. Jeffries, Bull Montana, Jimmy McLarnin and a whole host of sports celebrities.

At last count, we totalled 58 boxing films in which gangsters try to rig the big bout, 22 in which the hero becomes a boxer by accident and another 22 in which the hero, because of something in his past, can't or won't fight—until the end that is.

154 Abbott and Costello Meet the Invisible Man

1951, Universal-International, 82 minutes. Director: Charles Lamont. Producer: Howard Christie. Screenplay: Robert Lees, Frederic I. Rinaldo, John Grant. Story: Hugh Wedlock, Jr., Howard Snyder, suggested by a story by H.G. Wells. Photography: George Robinson. Editor: Virgil Vogel.

Cast: Bud Abbott, Lou Costello, Arthur Franz, Nancy Guild, Adele Jergens, Sheldon Leonard, William Frawley, Gavin Muir, Sam Balter, John Day, Paul Maxet, Ed Gargan.

The boys are bungling private detectives in this one. They take on boxer Franz as a client after he's accused of murdering his manager.

To escape the cops, Franz takes an invisibility serum and the fun begins. The best sequence finds Lou in the boxing ring with the invisible Franz throwing his punches for him as the crooked gamblers try to figure out what's going on.

155 The Abysmal Brute

1923, Universal, 7,373 feet. Director: Hobart Henley. Scenario: A.P. Younger, from a story by Jack London. Photography: Charles Stumac.

Cast: Reginald Denny, Mabel Julienne Scott, Hayden Stevenson,

David Torrence, George Stewart, Charles French.

Prizefighter Denny keeps his vocation a secret from socialite Scott and with good reason--she dumps him when she finds out. But as this is 1920's Hollywood, there's a happy ending.

156 Ace of Aces

1982, French-German, Gaumont, 100 minutes, Color. Director: Gerard Oury. Producer: Alain Poire. Screenplay: Oury, Daniele Thompson. Photography: Xavor Schwazenberger.

Cast: Jean-Paul Belmondo, Marie-France Pisier, Rachid Ferrache, Frank Hoffman, Gunther Meisner.

It's 1936 and ex-World War I fighter pilot Belmondo finds himself at the Berlin Olympics as head of the French boxing team.

He meets a young orphan who happens to be Jewish and becomes involved in an attempt to get the whole family out of Germany. Meisner portrays both Hitler and his sister (that's right) in this strange film.

157 Adventures of Bullwhip Griffin

1967, Buena Vista, 110 minutes, Color. Director: James Neilson. Screenplay: Lowell S. Hawley, based on the novel "By the Great Horn Spoon" by Sid Fleischman. Photography: Edward Colman. Editor: Marsh Hendry.

Cast: Roddy McDowell, Suzanne Pleshette, Karl Malden, Harry Guardino, Richard Haydn, Hermione Baddeley, Bryan Russell, Liam Redmond, Cecil Kellaway, Joby Baker, Mike Mazurki, Alan Carney, Dub Taylor, Pedro Gonzalez-Gonzalez.

When a young Boston rich kid (Russell) gets gold fever during the California gold rush, he takes his butler Griffin (McDowell) with him.

Landing a lucky punch on a San Francisco saloon bouncer named Mountain Ox, the butler earns the nickname Bullwhip and accepts a challenge to a boxing match to earn enough money to get Russell's sister out of the saloon where she works. The milquetoast butler uses his wits and quick footwork to defeat his giant opponent, played by Mazurki.

158 The Adversary

1970, Belle-Kay International, 75 minutes. Director-Writer: Larry Klein. Producer: Lee Franklin. Photography: Stephen R. Winsten. Editor: Sam Raleigh.

Cast: Howard Lawrence, Vic Campos, Frank Mangiapane, Stephanie Waxman, Brian Roberts, Marvin Davis, Chris Assini.

Boxer Lawrence gives up his ring career and becomes Campos' manager in this obscure homosexually-oriented film.

159 Afraid to Fight

1922, Universal, 4,600 feet. Director: William Worthington. Scenario: Charles Sarver. Story: Leete Renick. Photography: Arthur Reeves.

Cast: Frank Mayo, Lillian Rich, Wade Boteler, Peggy Cartwright, Lydia Knott, W.S. McDunnough, Tom McGuire, Harry Mann, Roscoe Karns, Tom Kennedy, Al Kaufman.

Gassed during World War I, Tom Harper (Mayo), who was the boxing champ of the American Expeditionary Force, goes to the fresh mountain air to recuperate and is given strict orders by his doctor to rest.

Needing money for an operation for his crippled sister, he's got to take it on the chin when a town ruffian picks on him.

He who laughs last laughs best, however, as Harper regains his health, goes back home to win the boxing crown and get enough money for the operation, and then returns to beat up his tormentor and win the girl.

160 A.K.A. Cassius Clay

1970, United Artists, 79 minutes. Director: Jim Jacobs. Producer: William Cayton. Screenplay-Associate Director: Bernard Euslin. Photography: Izzy Mankovsky. Editor: Edward Bartsch.

Narrator: Richard Kiley.

One of the numerous film biographies of Muhammad Ali (nee Cassius Clay as the title indicates) you'll be reading about in this chapter, this one covers his career from his days in the Olympics to his fights with Sonny Liston.

Much emphasis is placed on the influence of Muslim leader Malcolm X on Ali's life, and the film covers Ali's refusal to be inducted in the armed services and his eventually being stripped of his boxing title.

161 Ali the Man: Ali the Fighter

1975, CinAmerica, 142 minutes, Color. Directors: Rick Baxter, William Greaves. Producers: Shintaro Katsu, William Greaves. Music: Simon Stokes, performed by Richie Havens.

Two short feature films were packaged together for showings in theaters as a single long film. Besides that novelty, the most noteworthy aspect of this double documentary is that one of the segments was produced by Shintaro Katsu, the man who portrays Zatoichi, the blind swordsman, in Japanese samurai films.

Ali the Man concentrates on the fighter's life outside the ring and on his training.

Ali the Fighter incorporates a lot of footage from **The Fighters** and has scenes from his fights with Joe Frazier and George Foreman.

162 All-American Boy

1973, Warner Brothers, 118 minutes, Color. Director: Charles Eastman. Producers: Joseph T. Naar, Saul J. Krugman. Screenplay: Eastman. Photography: Philip Lathrop. Editors: Christopher Holmes, Ralph Winters, Bill Neel.

Cast: Jon Voight, Carol Androsky, Anne Archer, Gene Borkan, Ron Burns, Rosalind Cash, Jeanne Cooper, Peggy Cowles, Leigh French, Ned Glass, Bob Hastings.

Released four years and three film editors after it was shot, and then receiving only a very limited release, **All-American Boy** did nothing to further the career of Voight, who had scored big in **Midnight Cowboy.**

Voight portrays a small-time boxer named Vic, who's a real cad outside the ring and walks out on girlfriend Archer.

The only thing of real interest in the film, which very few people have seen, is the division of the story into six "rounds," each preceded by a title card.

163 All for Mabel

1930, Pathe, 2 reels. Director: Harry Delmar. Producer: John C. Flinn. Photography: Bobby Carney. Adaptation: Charles Diltz. Editor: Fred Allen.

Cast: Sally Starr.

A short gag film in which the rough tough college boxing champ is decked by his rival for a girl's love; he is a little runt.

164 The Amateur Gentleman

1935, British, United Artists, 102 minutes. Director: Thornton Freeland. Producers: Marcel Hellman, Douglas Fairbanks, Jr. Screenplay: Clemence Dane, Edward Knoblock, Sergei Nolbandov, based on a novel by Jeffrey Farnol. Photography: Gunther Krampf.

Cast: Douglas Fairbanks, Jr., Elissa Landi, Gordon Harker, Basil Sydney, Hugh Williams, Irene Browne, Coral Brown, Athole Stewart, Margaret Lockwood, Frank Pettingell.

One of Fairbanks' top swashbucklers as he portrays a son who must rescue his father from hanging by exposing the real villain.

Although born a commoner, he works his way through London society by his prowess as a boxer and wrestler and by romancing a fashionable lady.

165 American Pluck

1925, Chadwick Pictures, 5,900 feet. Director: Richard Stanton. Scenario: Ralph Spence. Photography: Lyman Broening.

Cast: George Walsh, Wanda Hawley, Sidney DeGrey, Frank Leigh, Tom Wilson, Leo White, Dan Mason.

Cowboys, hoboes, boxing and royalty all mix in this busy silent melodrama based on a novel by Eugene P. Lyle, Jr.

The son of a cattle baron is evicted by dad with orders not to return until he's made at least $5,000 on his own.

The youth, Blaze Derringer (what a name!), played by George Walsh, rides the rails with some hoboes until one of them, Lord Raleigh (Leo White), discovers Blaze's prowess with his fists.

He beats his ring opponent, Hard Boiled Perry, so badly the crowd wants his scalp, but he's rescued by the Princess of Bargonia (Wanda Hawley), who's trying to avoid a forced marriage to the evil Count Verensky. Needless to say, Our Hero wins the girl and the throne.

166 And the Same to You

1959, British, Eros, 70 minutes. Director: George Pollock. Producer: William Gell. Screenplay: John Paddy Carstairs, John Junkin, Terry Nation. Photography: Stan Pavey.

Cast: Leo Franklyn, Dick Bentley, Brian Rix, John Robinson, Tony Wright, William Hartnell, Sidney James.

A new vicar discovers he must share the church hall with a boxing promoter; but when his nephew knocks out the promoter's boxer, the clergyman seizes upon the chance to raise funds for a new roof by staging boxing matches.

Members of the "Carry On" crew join in the antics as the archdeacon tries to stop the bouts.

167 Any Old Port

1932, Metro Goldwyn Mayer, 21 minutes. Director: James Horne.

Cast: Stan Laurel, Oliver Hardy, Jacqueline Wells, Walter Long, Harry Bernard, Arthur Houseman, Robert Burns, Charlie Hall, Sam Lufkin, Dick Gilbert.

Laurel and Hardy play a couple of sailors who run afoul of a real tough hombre while trying to rescue a girl. He's so tough, in fact, that the billiard balls they throw just bounce off his head.

Later, Hardy promotes Stan as a fighter so they can get some meal money. Surprise, surprise! Guess who Stan's opponent is?

168 Any Which Way You Can

1980, Warner Brothers, 115 minutes, Color. Director: Buddy Van Horn. Producer: Fritz Manes. Screenplay: Stanford Sherman, based on characters created by Jeremy Joe Kroneberg. Photography: David Worth. Editors: Ferris Webster, Ron Spang.

Cast: Clint Eastwood, Sondra Locke, Geoffrey Lewis, William Smith, Harry Guardino, Ruth Gordon, Michael Cavanaugh, Barry Corbin, Roy Jensen, Dan Vadis, Glen Campbell (himself).

The sequel to **Every Which Way but Loose** turns into a ripoff of John Ford's classic, **The Quiet Man**, but proved popular nonetheless.

Barefist fighter-trucker Eastwood and his faithful orangutan give up their roving fighting life after a good victory. Also back is the gang of motorcycle creeps Eastwood handled in the original.

Eastwood goes back on his vow not to fight when he gets an offer he can't refuse to fight the West's other great bare knuckles fighter (Smith).

With orangutan Clyde and feisty mom, Ruth Gordon, providing most of the comic relief, the climactic fist fight through most of a Wyoming town is reminiscent of the sprawling fight between John Wayne and Victor McLaglen toward the end of **The Quiet Man.**

169 April Showers

1923, Preferred Pictures, 6,350 feet. Director: Tom Forman. Presented by B.P. Schulberg. Screenplay: Hope Loring, Louis D. Lighton. Photography: Harry Perry.

Cast: Colleen Moore, Kenneth Harland, Ruth Clifford, Priscilla Bonner, Myrtle Vane, James Corrigan, Jack Byron, Ralph Faulkner, Tom McGuire, Kid McCoy, Danny Goodman.

Dan O'Rourke (Harland) hopes to follow his hero dad's footsteps on the police force, but fails the final test. To boot, his sister is caught shoplifting, and to save her from prison, he enters a boxing contest.

Danny's luck isn't all bad—he loses the fight, but it's discovered there was a clerical error on the policeman's test and that he passed after all.

170 Around the Corner

1930, Columbia Pictures, 64 minutes. Director: Bert Glennon. Producer: Harry Cohn. Scenario-Continuity-Dialogue: Joe Swerling. Photography: Joe Walker. Editor: Gene Milford.

Cast: George Sidney, Charlie Murray, Joan Peers, Harry Strang, Jess Devorska, Fred Sullivan.

An Irish cop and a Jewish pawnbroker bring up a baby girl who was left on their doorstep. When she grows up, the two "fathers" object to her affections to a boxer and to a young rich man's attentions to her. The blueblood arranges a fight with the boxer and wins over the objections of her guardians.

171 Auld Lang Syne

1929, British, Famous-Lasky, 75 minutes. Director-Producer: George Pearson. Screenplay: Pearson, Hugh E. Wright, Patrick L. Mannock. Photography: Bernard Knowles.

Cast: Sir Harry Lauder, Pat Aherne, Dodo Watts, Dorothy Boyd, Hugh E. Wright.

Legendary performer Lauder is a farmer who comes to the big city to visit his son, a boxer, he believes is studying chemistry, and his daughter, a dancer, he believes is a nurse.

172 Bachelor's Paradise

1928, Tiffany-Stahl, 6,147 feet. Director: George Archainbaud. Story: Curtis Benton. Photography: Chester A. Lyons. Editor: Robert J. Kern.

Cast: Sally O'Neill, Ralph Graves, Eddie Gribbon, Jimmy Finlayson, Sylvia Ashton, Jean Laverty.

It's old-time melodrama to the hilt here. After a young woman takes in a boxer who's injured in a street fight, he leaves her standing at the altar.

When he's knocked down in the ring and is taking the count, lo and behold, he sees a vision of his beloved and gets up and wins.

173 Bad Girl

1931, Fox, 90 minutes. Director: Frank Borzage. Photography: Chester Lyons.

Cast: Sally Eilers, James Dunn, Minna Gombell, William Payley, Frank Darien.

Based on a novel by Vina Delmar, it concerns a youth (Dunn) who gives up his ambition to own a radio shop when he marries a girl he meets in Coney Island.

With a baby on the way, he enters the boxing ring to earn some money, and finding himself outclassed in the ring, tells his foe all his problems. The result:

the rest of the fight is more like a waltz than a boxing match.

174 Baddest Daddy in the Whole World

1972, New York Films, 52 minutes, Color. Director: Fred Haines.

Another documentary about Muhammad Ali, this one filmed in Switzerland as he prepares for his fight with Jurgin Blin. It shows his practice sessions and Ali with his family and the boxer entertaining the fans outside the ring.

175 The Ballyhoo Buster

1928, Action Pictures, 4,805 feet. Director: Richard Thorpe. Story: Robert Wallace. Photography: Ray Reis.

Cast: Buffalo Bill, Jr., Peggy Shaw, Nancy Nash, Albert Hart, George Magrill, Walter Brennan.

A cattleman (Buffalo Bill, Jr.) who is robbed during a sale by two men becomes a barker in a traveling medicine show and also offers cash to anyone who can last three rounds in the boxing ring with him.

During one of the boxing matches, who should show up in the audience but the two hombres who robbed him. Not only does he knock out his ring foe, but he whips the thieves as well.

176 Barocco

1978, French, LaBoetie-Sarah Films, 102 minutes, Color. Director: Andre Techine. Producer: Andre Genoves. Screenplay: Techine, Marylin Goldin. Photography: Bruno Nyutten. Editor: Claudine Merline.

Cast: Gerard Depardieu, Isabelle Adjani, Marie-France Pisier, Jean-Claude Briarly, Claude Brasseur, Julien Guiomar, Helene Surgere.

Here's a strange one with Depardieu in a dual role as a boxer who's paid off to say he had a homosexual affair with a politician and as the hit man who kills him to keep him quiet.

177 Battling Bookworm

1928, Balshofer Productions-Biltmore Pictures, 4,800 feet.

Except for the fact that it's about boxing and stars William Barrymore, little is known about this film, which seems to be one of those old films for which no prints exist today.

178 Battling Brown of Birmingham

1914, British, Regent, 3,000 feet. Director: Charles Weston. Producers: Weston, Arthur Finn.

Cast: Rowland Moore, Alisia Lean.

The old ringside plea by the girlfriend works again, but with a slight twist. In this one, she has to pose as a man to enter her lover's corner in the ring and persuade him to win.

179 Battling Bunyon

1925, Associated Exhibitors, 4,900 feet. Director: Paul Hurst. Scenario: Jefferson Moffitt, based on the story "Battling Bunyon Ceases to Be Funny" by Raymond Leslie Goldman in the **Saturday Evening Post.** Photography: Frank Cotner. Editor: Fred Burnworth.

Cast: Wesley Barry, Molly Malone, Frank Campeau, Harry Mann, Johnny Relasco, Chester Conklin, Jackie Fields, Pat Kemp.

Garage mechanic Aiken Bunyon (Barry) makes a fool of himself when he tries to fight off the lightweight boxing champ who tries to woo his girl.

He's signed up for laughs by a fight promoter (Campeau) and will get $200 for each round he can stay in the ring with the champ. If he goes five rounds, he will earn enough money to buy a partnership in the garage.

Badly beaten in the ring after lasting only four rounds, Bunyon watches the champ make another pass at his girlfriend and gathers up the strength to beat him.

180 Battling Butler

1926, Metro Goldwyn Mayer,

6,970 feet. Director: Buster Keaton. Adaptation: Paul Gerard Smith, Al Boasberg, Charles Smith, Lex Neal, from a play by Stanley Brightman, Austin Melford, Douglas Furber, Philip Brabham.

Cast: Buster Keaton, Sally O'Neil, Snitz Edwards, Francis McDonald, Mary O'Brien, Tom Wilson, Eddie Borden, Walter James.

One of the great stone-faced comedian's least-seen films today has him as a lazy rich man named Alfred Butler who meets the girl of his dreams while on a camping trip.

His marriage proposal meets with the strong disapproval of the girl's family until Butler's faithful valet (Edwards) tells them that the suitor is, in reality, the boxing champ, Battling Butler.

Of course, who should show up later than the real Battling Butler (McDonald), who's infuriated by the masquerade and sets out to teach Keaton a lesson.

The rest of the film follows the traditional Keaton pattern—he suffers humiliating defeat only to wind up triumphant in the end.

181 Battling Fool

1924, Perfection Pictures, 4,978 feet. Director: Willard S. Van Dyke.

Cast: William Fairbanks, Eva Novak, Fred J. Butler, Laura Winston, Mark Fenton, Catherine Craig, Jack Byron, Pat Harmon, Ed Kennedy, Andy Waldron.

The son of a minister rises to become a champion boxer, but must also thwart an embezzlement plot and save his beloved from a fire.

182 Battling Kelly

1912, British, Brittania Films, 1,055 feet. Director: A.E. Coleby.

When a boxer fails to show up for a match, an ex-champ gets another chance and wins the bout.

183 Battling King

1922, Clark-Cornelius Corp., 4,809 feet. Director: P.D. Sargent.

Cast: William J. Otts, Nevada Grey.

More of a western than a boxing film, this one finds Our Hero, a boxer, stranded in a town after his manager runs out on him.

He becomes a state policeman and singlehandedly rids the town of the evil gang that controls it.

184 Battling Mason

1924, Bud Barsky Corp., 4,800 feet. Screenplay: William E. Wing.

Cast: Frank Merrill, Eva Novak, Billy Elmer, Dick Sutherland, Milburn Morante.

Politics mix with boxing in this comedy, which was directed either by Jack Nelson or by William James Craft, depending upon which source you believe.

A candidate for public office vows not to fight during the campaign and must bear the worst of humiliations keeping that pledge.

When his girlfriend gets into trouble, however, that's the limit, and Our Hero defeats the villains and wins the election to boot.

185 Be Yourself!

1930, United Artists, 69 minutes. Director: Thornton Freeland. Adaptation: Freeland, Max Marcin. Story: Joseph Jackson. Photography: Karl Struss, Robert H. Planck. Editor: Robert J. Kern.

Cast: Fanny Brice, Robert Armstrong, Harry Green, G. Pat Collins, Gertrude Astor, Budd Fine, Marjorie Kane, Rita Flynn, Jimmy Tolson.

Could this have been the inspiration for the Barbra Streisand film, **The Main Event**? The roots of it are certainly here.

In **The Main Event**, Ms. Streisand becomes the manager of a broken-down prize fighter.

In **Be Yourself**, Fanny Brice, whose own career was portrayed by Streisand in **Funny Girl**, is a nightclub gal who becomes the manager for Jerry Moore (Armstrong), an aspiring pugilist who's decked in the club by the heavyweight champion, McCloskey (Collins).

The fact that 49 years after **Be Yourself!** the idea of a woman manager for a prizefighter could still be considered fresh gives some indication of how little the portrayal of women on screen has changed over the years.

186 Beau Broadway

1928, Metro Goldwyn Mayer, 6,037 feet. Director-Story: Malcolm St. Clair. Adaptation: F. Hugh Herbert. Photography: Andre Barlatier. Editor: Harry Reynolds.

Cast: Lew Cody, Aileen Pringle, Sue Carol, Hugh Trevor, Heinie Conklin, Kit Guard, James J. Jeffries.

A hard-drinking, womanizing, gambling fight promoter (Cody) grants a man his dying wish to care for a granddaughter, who turns out to be a gorgeous woman (Carol).

The promoter changes his personality overnight to care for her. Complications ensue when one of the promoter's fighters falls for the girl, but it's really Cody she loves.

187 Because of a Hat

1914, Biograph. Director: Edward Dillon. Writer: E. Middleton.

Have you ever had the desire to snatch that huge hat from the woman sitting in front of you in the theater so you can see what's going on? The hero of this short comedy does just that and winds up in the boxing ring with her boyfriend.

188 The Bermondsey Kid

1933, British, First National Pictures, 75 minutes. Director: Ralph Dawson. Producer: Irving Asher. Screenplay: W. Scott Darling. Story: Bill Evans.

Cast: Esmond Knight, Pat Patterson, Ellis Irving, Ernest Sefton, Clifford McLagen, Eve Gray, Syd Crossley, Winifred Oughton, Len Harvey.

A newsboy who also boxes is forced by circumstances to fight a friend in the ring. The kid knocks out his friend only to discover that his fight manager used the ever-present vamp to make sure his foe would be out of shape. After properly disposing of the crooked manager, the two pals meet again in the ring.

189 The Better Man

1921, Aywon Film Corp., 5 reels. Director: Wilfred Lucas.

Cast: Snowy Baker, Brownie Vernon, Charles Villiers, Wilfred Lucas.

Filmed in Australia, this is a strange mix of western action, religion and whatever.

Baker portrays a former boxer, now a minister, who's transferred from his congregation for his unorthodox methods and who meets a beautiful woman (Vernon) at his new parish.

He won't fight the town bully (played by the film's director), who is also a cattle thief, and this gets him into hot water with his gal, but he wins her in the end.

190 The Big Chance

1933, Eagle, 63 minutes. Director: Al Herman.

Cast: John Darrow, Mickey Rooney, Merna Kennedy, Natalie Moorehead, J. Carroll Naish, Matthew Betz, Hank Mann, Eleanor True Boardman.

Young Rooney, here even before his days as Andy Hardy, idolizes boxer Darrow, who's mixed up with a crooked fight racket.

191 Big Dan

1923, Fox Film Corp., 5,934 feet. Director: William Wellman. Screenplay: Frederick and Fanny Hatton. Photography: Joseph August.

Cast: Charles Jones, Marian

Nixon, Ben Hendricks, Trilby Clark, Charles Coleman, Jack Herrick, Jacqueline Gadsden, Lydia Yeamans Titus, Monte Collins, Harry Lonsdale.

Big Dan O'Hara (Jones), opens up a camp for boxers after his wife leaves him while he's away at war. He takes in a beautiful woman (Nixon), and the way is cleared for their romance when Dan's wife dies.

192 The Big Fight

1930, Sono Art-World Wide Pictures, 59 minutes. Director: Walter Lang. Supervision: James Cruze. Adaptation: Walter Woods. Photography: Jackson Rose.

Cast: Ralph Ince, Lola Lane, Guinn Williams, Stepin Fetchit, Wheeler Oakman, James Eagle, Robert E. O'Connor, Edna Bennett, Tony Stabeneau, Larry McGrath.

It's another gangsters and prizefighters film with a helpless woman in the background.

A manicurist's brother will be framed for murder because of a large debt he owes to a gangster unless she agrees to give her boxer-boyfriend (Williams) some drugged water during the big fight.

She doesn't, but the boxer's manager (Oakman) does. However, the boxer's water boy (Fetchit) innocently substitutes good water for the bad, allowing the hero to win the fight, while the cops take care of the baddies.

193 Big Pal

1925, Royal Pictures, 4,543 feet. Director: John G. Adolfi. Story: Jules Furthman.

Cast: William Russell, Julanne Johnston, Mary Carr, Mickey Bennett, Hayden Stevenson, William Bailey.

Heavyweight boxer Russell saves a judge's daughter from a runaway horse and romance begins.

Once again, the old kidnapping storyline is used. This time it's the boxer's young nephew, who is threatened with harm unless Russell throws the big fight in the fifth round. As usual with the kidnapping plot, the nephew escapes in time and appears at ringside with the judge's daughter to inspire Russell to victory.

194 The Big Punch

1948, Warner Brothers, 80 minutes. Director: Sherry Shourds. Producer: Saul Elkins. Screenplay: Bernard Girard. Story: George Brown. Photography: Carl Guthrie. Editor: Frank Magee.

Cast: Gordon MacRae, Wayne Morris, Lois Maxwell, Mary Stuart, Anthony Warde, Jimmy Ames, Marc Logan, Eddie Dunn.

Give **The Big Punch** credit for trying something a little different, even though the results don't lift it much above the usual "B" film.

MacRae and Morris portray boxers taking totally different paths: Morris gives up the ring to become a minister, while MacRae gets mixed up with the ever-present crooked boxing ring.

MacRae refuses to take a dive and when the gang kills a cop who's on to the scheme, he's framed for the murder and takes refuge with Morris.

195 The Bigger They Are

1931, Vitaphone, 18 minutes.

Primo Carnera and Little Billy the midget are tramps at the start of this short; but as you might expect, Carnera becomes a boxer and Billy his manager.

196 Bill Manages a Prizefighter

1915, Komic Films, 865 feet.

Cast: Fay Tincher, Tammany Young, Tod Browning, Eddie Dillon.

The fight manager of the title diverts the attention of the champ with a beautiful girl so that his boxer can win.

197 Billion Dollar Scandal

1933, Paramount Pictures,

Guinn Williams, center, as "The Tiger," listens to Stepin Fetchit while hugging Lola Lane in the James Cruze production of The Big Fight. (The Museum of Modern Art/Film Stills Archive.)

76 minutes. Director: Harry Joe Brown. Producer: Charles E. Rogers. Story: Gene Towne, Graham Baker. Photography: Charles Stumac.

Cast: Robert Armstrong, Constance Cummings, Olga Baclanova, Frank Morgan, James Gleason, Irving Pichel, Warren Hymer, Sidney Toler, Frank Albertson, Berton Churchill.

A boxing manager who's also an expert masseur (Armstrong) is released from jail and manages to hook on as a private gym instructor of a wealthy oilman.

Because of his job, he gets to hear a lot of tips, and he makes a lot of money until he's fed a phony tip for fooling around with his boss's daughter.

198 Billy's Book on Boxing

1911, British, B&C Films, 400 feet. Director: H.O. Martinek.

A man boxes everyone in sight until he, too, is finally floored in this comedy short.

199 Black and White

1910, British, Barker Films, 473 feet.

The Jack Johnson-Jim Jeffries fight inspired more films than any other single sporting event in history. This burlesque of the fight by Will Barker was the first of four made in 1910 in England alone.

The others were **Great Fight at All-Sereno, The Great Black vs. White Prize Fight,** and **The Man to Beat Jack Johnson.**

As some of the titles indicated, it was the race factor which most fascinated the filmmakers and the audiences. Many other films on the fight would periodically crop up in the United States, Britain and France.

200 Black Thunderbolt

1922, A.A. Millman, 7 reels.

Speaking of the great boxer, Jack Johnson, this film was filmed in Spain while Johnson was in exile there. Unfortunately, prints of this film appear to have been lost and information about it is scanty at best.

201 Blarney

1926, Metro Goldwyn Mayer, 6,055 feet. Director: Marcel DeSano. Photography: Ben Reynolds. Editor: Lloyd Nosler.

Cast: Renee Andoree, Ralph Graves, Paulett Duval, Malcolm White, Margaret Seddon.

An Irish girl who has made some money in the United States pays the transatlantic fare for a boxer from her home town. Complications ensue when he falls for another girl, but he's eventually brought back to form.

202 Blue Blazers

1922, Western Pictures, 5 reels. Directors: Robert Kelly, Charles W. Mack.

Cast: Lester Cuneo, Francillia Billington, Fannie Midgley, Bert Sprotte, Roy Watson, Phil Gastrock.

Tired of the phony life, a boxing champ goes West only to be robbed by thugs. He winds up on a ranch run by a beautiful girl and her mom who are having trouble meeting their mortgage payments.

Naturally, there's a villain to defeat—he's got his covetous eyes on the property, which contains oil; and he's prepared to marry the girl to get it.

203 Blue Eagle

1926, Fox Film Corp., 6,200 feet. Director: John Ford. Screenplay: L.G. Rigby. Photography: George Schneiderman.

Cast: George O'Brien, Janet Gaynor, William Russell, Robert Edeson, David Butler, Phil Ford, Ralph Sipperly, Margaret Livingston, Jerry Madden, Harry Tenbrook.

When the two heroes aren't busy fighting each other, there are Germans to battle during World War I.

Leaders of rival neighborhood gangs, not only do they love the same girl, but they find themselves as stokers on the same battleship during the war. Finally, they're allowed to battle it out in the ring on the battleship, but an impolite German submarine interrupts the fight by torpedoing the ship.

After the war, they continue battling each other until they find a common enemy in some drug smugglers. Defeating the baddies together, they decide to stage a fight between themselves at the end just to see who will win.

204 Blue Smoke

1935, British, Fox, 74 minutes. Director: Ralph Ince. Producer: John Barrow. Screenplay: Fenn Sherie, Ingran D'Abbes. Photography: Alex Bryce.

Cast: Tamara Desni, Ralph Ince, Bruce Seton, Ian Colin, Eric Hales, Hal Walters, Beryl DeQuerton, Wilson Coleman, Jock McKay.

A love triangle concerning a girl, a gypsy boxer and his rival.

205 Body and Soul

1947, United Artists, 104 minutes. Director: Robert Rossen. Producer: Bob Roberts. Screenplay: Abraham Polonsky. Photography: James Wong Howe. Editors: Francis Lyon, Robert Parrish.

Cast: John Garfield, Lilli Palmer, Hazel Brooks, Anne Revere, William Conrad, Joseph Pevney, Canada Lee, Lloyd Goff, Joe Devlin, John Indrisano (referee), Art Smith.

By the mid 1940's, after nearly countless mediocre productions, boxing movies were in the doldrums. **Body and Soul** singlehandedly revived the genre.

Winning an Academy Award for best editing, John Garfield was nominated for best actor for his portrayal of Charley Davis, a Jewish boy from the slums who rose to be champ, but found the going tough once he got there.

Inspired by a New York State

inquiry into fight fixing, **Body and Soul** mixed outstanding acting and haunting camerawork with Abraham Polonsky's memorable dialogue (Polonsky would later become a victim of blacklisting during the McCarthy era).

Former welterweight contender Canada Lee is especially poignant as a boxer with a blood clot on the brain, while William Conrad as Quinn, the manager, and Joseph Pevney, as the mobster whose most famous line is "everybody dies" are equally memorable.

Charley's rise and fall is depicted in flashback form as he's waiting for a fixed fight to begin.

As he rises to the top, his shopkeeper parents declare, "All over Europe they're killing people like us, but over here, Charley's a champeen."

Once he's champion, however, Charley finds himself getting deeper and deeper into debt to gangster Roberts (Pevney) to support his lifestyle.

Even the boxing cliché of virtuous girl vs. vamp seems fresh here. Virtuous Lilli Palmer, who sees through the gangster far earlier than Charley does, tells her boyfriend: "I can't marry you—that would just mean marrying him." Hazel Brooks is on tap as the vamp.

After having lost his best friend Ben (Canada Lee), his girl and his family's respect, Charley finds himself doublecrossed in the ring in what was supposed to be a draw and fights to win in boxing scenes that were extremely graphic for their time.

206 Body and Soul

1981, Cannon Group, 115 minutes, Color. Director: George Bowers. Producers: Menahem Golan, Yoram Globus. Screenplay: Leon Isaac Kennedy. Photography: James Forrest. Editors: Sam Pollard, Skip Schoolnik.

Cast: Leon Isaac Kennedy, Jayne Kennedy, Peter Lawford, Perry Lang, Nikki Swassy, Mike Grazzo, Kim Hamilton, Muhammad Ali.

Resemblances between this and 1947's **Body and Soul** are so thin, it would be almost sacrilege to call it a remake.

This version was made to cash in on Kennedy's success as a boxer in **Penitentiary.** He portrays an aspiring black medical student who becomes a pro boxer to earn some money.

A beautiful television commentator (Jayne Kennedy) falls for him, while gangster Lawford nearly succeeds in corrupting him.

Ali has a brief role as himself.

207 The Body Punch

1929, Universal Pictures, 4,786 feet. Director: Leigh Jason. Screenplay: Harry O. Hoyt. Adaptation: Clarence J. Marks. Photography: Joseph Brotherton. Editor: Frank Atkinson.

Cast: Jack Daugherty, Virginia Browne Faire, George Kotsonaros, Wilbur Mack, Monte Montague, Arthur Millett.

A boxer (Daugherty) and a wrestler (Kotsonaros) who are constantly at each other's throats stage a benefit match against each other. The boxer is framed with a stolen bracelet by a rival for a girl's love, but the real thief turns out to be the wrestler.

208 Bomber (aka **Capitaine Malabar, Dit 'La Bombe'**)

1982, Italian, Color. Director: Michele Lupo, Screenplay: Marcello Fondato, Francesco Scardamaglia. Photography: Georgia Di Battista.

Cast: Bud Spencer, Jerry Cala, Mike Miller, Valeria Cavalli.

Bearded behemoth Spencer, who's enormously popular in Europe and who's best known for his roles in spaghetti westerns, portrays a boxing champion turned boat skipper who's offered a new job by a trainer.

209 Born to Fight

1938, Conn, 64 minutes. Director: Charles Hutchinson. Producer: Maurice A. Conn. Adaptation: Sascha Baranley from a story by Peter B. Kyne. Photography: Arthur Reed.

Cast: Frankie Darro, Kane Richmond, Jack LaRue, Frances Grant, Sheila Manora, Harry Harvey, Monty Collins.

Fight manager Richmond goes into hiding after he unintentionally injures a gangster. He meets fighter Darro and trains him to become a winner.

210 The Bowery

1933, United Artists, 92 minutes. Director: Raoul Walsh. Adaptation: Howard Estabrook, James Gleason. Photography: Barney McGill.

Cast: Wallace Beery, Jackie Cooper, George Raft, Fay Wray, Bert Kelton, George Walsh, Oscar Apfel, Herman Bing, Tammany Young, John Kelly.

This isn't really a boxing film, but maybe, again, it is.

Beery and young Cooper, who scored in **The Champ,** are reunited in a typically robust Raoul Walsh film about life on the Bowery in days gone by.

The emphasis is on the rivalry between Brooklyn Bridge jumper Steve Brodie (Raft) and Chuck Connors (Beery) over practically everything from women to fighting ability. Brodie wins the girl, but Connors beats him in a climactic fight on a river barge.

211 Bowery Blitzkrieg

1941, Monogram, 62 minutes. Director: Wallace Fox. Producer: Sam Katzman. Screenplay: Sam Robins. Editor: Robert Golden.

Cast: Leo Gorcey, Bobby Jordan, Huntz Hall, Warren Hull, Charlotte Henry, Keye Luke, Bobby Stone, Donald Haines, Martha Wentworth, David Gorcey, Ernest Morrison.

The Dead End Kids have become the East Side Kids, led by Leo Gorcey, who in this episode is a boxer who takes quick cash for fixed fights until he's reformed during the Golden Gloves tournament and becomes amateur champ. That, despite the fact that hoods try to frame him and he gives some blood to help save a pal.

212 The Boxer (aka **The Boxer and the Death**)

1963, Czechoslovakia Film, 120 minutes. Director: Peter Solan. Screenplay: Josef Hen, Solan, Tibor Virchta. Photography: Tibor Brath.

Cast: Stefan Kujetic, Manfred Krug, Valentina Thielova, Josef Kondrat, Edwin Marian, Gerhard Rachold, Jindrich Bobek, Jan Jovacik, Magda Godoleova.

Nazi concentration camp commandant Krug is really a boxer at heart, and he yearns for an adequate sparring partner.

He picks out an inmate (Kujetic) and allows him to fatten up for a bout which he insists will be fair. The inmate, who has been overcome by smoke from the gas chambers, is torn between boxing to win—and facing possible death if he does despite the commandant's vows—and losing intentionally.

213 The Boxer

1977, Japanese, Toei Films, 95 minutes, Color. Director: Shuji Terayama. Screenplay: Shiro Ishimori, Rio Kishida, Terayama. Photography: Tatsuo Susuki.

Cast: Bunta Sugawara, Kentaro Shimizu.

A rising boxer suddenly quits in the middle of a bout he's winning and leaves his family.

His eyesight slowly failing him, he lives only with his dog until a young boxer persuades him to be his manager. A stormy relationship between the two follows.

214 Boxing Fever

1909, British, Cricks and Martin, 600 feet.

Director A.E. Coleby stars as a man who fights with everyone he meets until he's finally dealt a knockout blow--by his wife.

215 Boxing for Points

1897, Edison.

Possibly the first American boxing film, this depicts some military students boxing. The camera, operated by one of Thomas A. Edison's employees, was so large and hard to handle, it was difficult to move.

216 Boxing Gloves

1929, Metro Goldwyn Mayer, 2 reels. Director: Anthony Mack. Producer: Hal Roach. Photography: Art Lloyd, F.E. Hershey. Screenplay: Roach, Robert F. McGowan. Editor: Richard Currier.

Joe and Chubby of Our Gang fight over Jean in a boxing arena run by Manny and Farina. They end up knocking each other out after each was told the other would take a fall.

217 Boxing Kangaroo

1896, British, 40 feet. Director: Burt Acres.

A man boxes a kangaroo in this, the earliest known boxing movie.

218 Boxing Match or Glove Contest

1896, British, 40 feet. Director: Burt Acres.

From the director of **Boxing Kangaroo** comes this epic, the first known film involving a boxing match between two humans: Sgts. Barrett and Pope.

219 Branded Man

1928, Rayart Pictures, 6,089 feet. Director: Scott Pembroke. Scenario: Tod Robbins, Arthur Hoerl. Photography: Hap Depew. Editor: Charles A. Post.

Cast: Charles Delaney, June Marlowe, Gordon Griffith, George Riley, Andy Clyde, Erin LaBissoniere, Lucy Beaumont.

A wealthy tenement owner leaves his unfaithful wife for Mexico, where he becomes a top boxer. He meets an old girlfriend and romance blazes anew. When his unfaithful wife is killed by a lover, the way is clear for the wealthy boxer to marry his love.

220 Breakdown

1952, Realart, 76 minutes.

Director-Producer: Edmond Angelo. Screenplay: Robert Abel. Photography: Paul Ivano. Editor: Robert M. Leeds.

Cast: William Bishop, Wally Cassell, Ann Richards, Anne Gwynne, Sheldon Leonard, Richard Benedict, John Vosper.

Ward boss Leonard frames Bishop for manslaughter during a political campaign. When he's freed from prison, Bishop becomes a top boxer under the tutelage of his new manager, Cassell, a physically handicapped man who lives a new life through the boxer.

221 Broadway Billy

1926, Rayart Pictures, 5,954 feet. Director: Harry J. Brown. Scenario: Henry R. Simon.

Cast: Billy Sullivan, Virginia Brown Faire, Jack Herrick, Hazel Howell.

Billy Brookes (Sullivan) must box to pay the bills of his wife who spends it faster than he can make it.

222 Broken Blossoms (aka **Yellow Man and the Girl**)

1919, United Artists, 6,013 feet. Director-Producer-Screenplay: D.W. Griffith. Original story: Thomas Burke. Photography: G.W. "Billy" Bitzer, Hendrik Sartov. Editor: James Smith.

Cast: Lillian Gish, Richard Barthelmess, Donald Crisp, Arthur Howard, George Beranger, Norman "Kid McCoy" Selly.

Photoplay Magazine called **Broken Blossoms** "the first genuine tragedy of the movies" and contrasted its limited sets to the huge ones Griffith used for **Intolerance.**

Coming as it did from the director of **Birth of a Nation** with its controversial treatment of blacks, **Broken Blossoms'** tale of love between an unhappy white girl and a "Yellow Man" was quite risky for 1919.

Gish portrays the physically and mentally abused daughter of boxer Battling Burrows, described in the film as "an abysmal brute from the jungles of East London." She's such an unhappy child that to smile she must put her fingers on her mouth and lift it up.

After a particularly severe beating, she stumbles into the curio shop of the Yellow Man, a disillusioned Chinese who came to England full of hope for mankind.

He shows Gish the first kindness she's known in her life; but when Burrows discovers she's staying with him, he wrecks the apartment, drags her back and beats her to death. The Yellow Man then kills Burrows, carries Gish's body back to his room and kills himself.

223 Broken Blossoms

1936, British, Twickenham Films, 87 minutes. Director: Hans Brahm. Producer: Julius Hagen. Adaptation: Emlyn Williams. Photography: Curt Courant.

Cast: Emlyn Williams, Dolly Haas, Arthur Margetson, C.V. France, Basil Radford, Edith Sharp, Ernest Jay, Gibb McLaughlin.

The fact that not many people today know that there was ever a remake of **Broken Blossoms,** with Williams as the Yellow Man, should tell you something about its quality, despite the fact that D.W. Griffith helped out during the production. Williams simply could never get the accent down right, and the film simply could never match up to the original.

224 Broken Bottles

1920, British, Gaumont-Around the Town, 2,000 feet. Director-Writer: Leslie Henson.

Cast: Leslie Henson, Nora Howard, Stanley Brightman, Peggy Carlisle.

In an obvious twist on **Broken Blossoms,** the boxer gets beaten up by his drunken daughter and is killed by his opponent in the ring.

225 The Burning Trail

1925, Universal Pictures, 4,783 feet. Director: Arthur Rosson. Adaptation: Isadore Bernstein. Photography: Gilbert Warrenton.

Cast: William Desmond, Albert J. Smith, Mary McIvor, Harry Tenbrook, James Corey, Jack Dougherty, Edmund Cobb.

When a boxer accidentally kills his opponent, he quits the ring and, taking Horace Greeley's advice, heads west, where he gets a job as a ranch cook.

He eventually becomes a hero by saving a sheepman from some rough hombres and the man's daughter from a fire.

226 Cain and Mabel

1936, Warner Brothers, 89 minutes. Director: Lloyd Bacon. Story: H.C. Witwer. Adaptation: Laird Doyle. Photography: George Barnes. Editor: William Holmes.

Cast: Clark Gable, Marion Davies, Allen Jenkins, Roscoe Karns, Walter Catlett, David Carlysle, Hobart Cavanaugh.

Gable is a rising boxer whose face remains untouched throughout, and Davies is an ex-waitress on the way up as a musical star. She gets her big break when the lead in the show walks out.

Gable's fight manager, Davies' producer and a press agent concoct a torrid romance between the two to gain headlines, and naturally by the time the last reel unspools, it's become a real one.

A remake of 1924's **The Great White Way.**

227 Call of the Road

1920, I.B. Davidson, 6,000 feet. Director-Writer: A.E. Coleby.

Cast: Victor McLaglen, Phyllis Shannaw, Warwick Ward, Philip Williams, A.E. Coleby, Adeline Hayden Coffin, Ernest A. Douglas, H. Nicholls-Bates, Olive Bell.

A nobleman is disowned because of his gambling, but he becomes a boxer and later saves his kin from a thief.

228 Campus Champs

1931, Pathe, 14 minutes. Director: Fred Guiol. Producer: Fred Laily. Screenplay: Harry Fraser. Editor: Fred Maguire.

Cast: Nat Carr.

A small-town tailor bets his entire bankroll on the local champ at a college fight with a masked boxer. The masked man, however, turns out to be the tailor's son who's attending a college in a neighboring town.

The tailor then switches his cheering to his son, despite his huge bet.

229 The Canvas Kisser

1925, Paul Gerson Pictures, 5 reels. Director: Duke Worne. Story: Grover Jones. Photography: Alfred Gosden.

Cast: Richard Holt, Ruth Dwyer, Garry O'Dell, Cecil Edwards.

As the title suggests, the hero is a boxer who makes a lot of money by betting on his opponents and then taking falls in the ring until he's reformed by the love of a beautiful woman.

230 Catch As Catch Can

1931, Metro Goldwyn Mayer, 2 reels. Director: Marshall Neilan.

Cast: Guinn "Big Boy" Williams, Zasu Pitts, Thelma Todd, Billy Gilbert.

A boxer gives Zasu a new hat and tells her he'll do well if she wears it to his bout; but, during the fight, the hat keeps on getting bounced from one place to another.

231 Celebrity

1928, Pathe Exchange, 6,145 feet. Director: Tay Garnett. Producer: Ralph Block. Screenplay: Garnett, George Dromgold, based on a play by William Keefe. Photography: Peverell Marley. Editor: Doane Harrison.

Cast: Robert Armstrong, Clyde Cook, Lina Basquette, Dot Farley, Jack Perry, Otto Lederer, David Tearle.

To build up fighter Kid Reagan (Armstrong) for a title bout, his manager, Circus (Cook), hires a journalist to write poems under the boxer's name and two female vaudeville performers to play his mother and girlfriend.

Once he's gotten enough publicity, Kid Reagan is able to get the title bout only to find that the girl (Lina Basquette) has walked out. He wins the bout and gets together to live happily ever after with the girl.

232 The Champ

1931, Metro Goldwyn Mayer, 85 minutes. Director: King Vidor. Scenario and Dialogue: Leonard Praskins. Original Story: Frances Marion. Photography: Gordon Avil.

Cast: Wallace Beery, Jackie Cooper, Roscoe Ates, Irene Rich, Edward Brophy, Hale Hamilton, Jesse Scott, Marcia Mae Jones, Lee Phelps, Frank Hagney.

If imitation is the highest form of flattery, as the saying goes, then **The Champ** is no doubt the most flattered sports film ever. Not only did it spawn two direct remakes—**The Clown,** a 1953 non-sports film, and 1979's **The Champ**—but literally dozens of movies in which a broken down has-been is redeemed by the love of a child.

The Champ still holds up today despite its unabashed tear-jerking and few will dispute it deserved its nomination as best picture of the year. Frances Marion's story did win the Oscar as did Beery, sharing the best actor award with Fredrick March.

Beery is a hopelessly boozing ex-boxing champ who's reduced to cleaning stables at a racetrack. When he's not drinking, he's gambling away whatever money he has, much to the chagrin of his son Dink (Cooper).

When the ex-champ's wife visits the track, wanting to give the kid a better environment, the boxer makes a comeback.

Reviewers even in 1931 called the climax a bit sentimental, but the Beery-Cooper combo proved magic at the box office.

Racing scenes were filmed at the Caliente Race Track.

233 The Champ

1979, Metro Goldwyn Mayer, 121 minutes, Color. Director: Franco Zeffirelli. Producer: Dyson Lovell. Screenplay: Walter Newman, based on a story by Frances Marion. Photography: Fred J. Koenekamp. Editor: Michael J. Sheridan.

Cast: Jon Voight, Ricky Schroeder, Faye Dunaway, Jack Warden, Arthur Hill, Strother Martin, Joan Blondell, Mary Jo Catlett, Elisha Cook, Jeff Blum, Shirlee King.

All the basic elements of the 1931 original were present, but the magic that made the oldie click wasn't there, and all that remained was the over-sentimentality.

Schroeder as the little boy, T.J., was an adequate fill-in for Jackie Cooper and Faye Dunaway was fitting for the rich mother, but who nowadays could replace Wallace Beery?

Voight was a fatal choice in this case. Whereas Beery was the prototype ugly hero and convincing as a drunken bum, Voight was too much the pretty boy type for audiences to really believe he was a boxer.

Moreover, as talented as Voight may be, Beery had a genius for being both comic and poignant at the same time, something few actors could match.

234 Champ for a Day

1953, Republic Films, 90 minutes. Director-Producer: William A. Seiter. Screenplay: Irving Shulman, based on the story, "The Disappearance of Dolan," by William Fay. Photography: John L. Russell, Jr. Editor: Fred Allen.

Cast: Alex Nicol, Audrey Totter, Charles Winniger, Hope Emerson, Joseph Wiseman, Barry Kelley, Henry Morgan, Horace McMahon, Jesse White, Grant Withers.

What's happened to boxer Nicol's manager? He's disappeared without a trace, and it's up to the fighter to find out. It turns out he was murdered by fight-fixing racketeers.

Set in a Midwest city, Nicol wins a fight; but his next one is fixed so he'll win that too. Nicol throws the racketeers a curve by angering his opponent so badly that Our Hero loses on his own.

Meanwhile, Nicol manages to prove who killed his manager.

235 The Champeen

1923, Pathe, 2 reels. Director: Robert F. McGowan. Producer-Screenplay: Hal Roach. Photography: Len Powers.

It's Knockout Jimmy, the Irish Giant, vs. Terribul Jackie, the Bone Crusher, over the love of Mary in this early Our Gang short. Mary winds up spurning them both for a milquetoast.

236 The Champion

1915, Essanay Films, 1,816 feet. Director-Screenplay: Charles Chaplin. Photography: Rollie Totheroh.

Cast: Charles Chaplin, Edna Purviance, Leo White, G.M. Anderson, Bud Jamison, Ben Turpin, Lloyd Bacon.

Lovable Charlie somehow becomes a sparring partner for Spike Dugan, who's in training to fight the champ. Putting a horseshoe in his glove, Charlie winds up knocking out the challenger and facing the champ himself. He wins with the help of his dog.

237 Champion

1949, United Artists, 99 minutes. Director: Mark Robson. Producer: Stanley Kramer. Screenplay: Carl Foreman. Story: Ring Lardner. Photography: Frank Planer. Editor: Harry Gerstad.

Cast: Kirk Douglas, Marilyn Maxwell, Arthur Kennedy, Paul Stewart, Ruth Roman, Lola Albright, Luis Van Rooten, John Day, Harry Shannon.

Hard-hitting exposés of the boxing world were "in" after 1947's **Body and Soul** revived the genre. Whereas in **Body and Soul** it was the outside corrupting forces which brought down the boxer, in **Champion** it's the corrupting forces from within which spell doom for fighter Midge Kelly, whose portrayal by Kirk Douglas won an Academy Award nomination.

Lardner's original story had Kelly as a heel from the start; but to gain audience sympathy, he was portrayed as a nice guy at the film's opening.

As Kelly ascends to the middleweight title, his rottenness takes over as he dumps manager Stewart, abandons his wife for vamp Maxwell and punches out crippled brother Kennedy.

The brutal title fight at the end of the film is one of the best ever put on celluloid. Film editor Harry Gerstad won the Academy Award for his efforts.

238 The Champ's a Chump

1936, Columbia Pictures, 18 minutes.

Cast: Guinn "Big Boy" Williams, Louis Prima and his swing band.

Williams goes to college in an effort to lure the school's champ boxer into going pro.

239 Charlie Chan at Ringside

When Warner Oland, who portrayed Charlie Chan, died during this 1938 production, 20th Century-Fox had so much footage shot, it decided to turn it over to the studio's other great Asian detective—and so the film **Mr. Moto's Gamble** was born (see listing under that title).

240 Childish Things

1969, Filmword, 93 minutes, Color. Director-Photography: John Derek. Writer-Producer: Don Murray. Editor: Maurice Wright.

Cast: Don Murray, Linda Evans, David Brian, Angelique Pettyjohn, Don Joslyn, Gypsy Boots, Erik Holland, George Atkinson.

The only claim to fame for **Childish Things** is that star Murray wrote and produced it, and actor Derek directed and filmed it.

The plot, such as it is, has boxer Derek arriving at Brian's farm for boozers and proceeds to woo his benefactor's young daughter.

241 The Circus Cyclone

1925, Universal Pictures, 4,397 feet. Director-Story: Albert Rogell. Photography: Pliny Horne.

Cast: Art Acord, Moe McCrea, Ben Corbett, Nancy Deaver, Cesare Gravina, Albert J. Smith, Hilliard Karr, George Austin, Gertrude Howard, Jim Corey.

When cowboy Jack Manning (Acord) stops circus owner Steve Brant (Smith) from beating a horse after he's rejected by the lovely Doraldina (Deaver), the two men agree to a boxing match with the winner getting the horse. Manning wins the bout, but true to his character, Brant refuses to take defeat lying down and frames the girl's father for bank robbery.

It's up to the good guys to find the real robbers in time to save the father from being lynched.

242 City for Conquest

1940, Warner Brothers, 105 minutes. Director-Producer: Anatole Litvak. Screenplay: John Wexley, from a novel by Aben Kandel. Associate Producer: William Cagney. Photography: Sol Polito. Editor: William Holmes.

Cast: James Cagney, Ann Sheridan, Anthony Quinn, Arthur Kennedy, Frank Craven, Donald Crisp, Elia Kazan, Frank McHugh, George Tobias, Jerome Cowan, Lee Patrick.

There's a lot of **Golden Boy**, the 1939 boxing hit, in **City for Conquest** in its mixture of pugilism and the arts; but top-notch performances make it a strangely neglected film.

Cagney is an aspiring welterweight who'd rather drive a truck, but who boxes to raise money for tuition for brother Kennedy's music career. He's simply unbeatable in the ring until an opponent puts resin on his gloves, blinding Cagney on contact.

Cagney goes through a tormenting period of self-pity and antagonizes those closest to him in the process, while they achieve the success that will now never be his.

His sweetheart (Sheridan) becomes a top dancing partner to rival Anthony Quinn, while his brother winds up conducting at Carnegie Hall while Cagney opens up a newsstand at Times Square.

If the plot sounds like a soap opera, it sure is; but in the hands of Cagney and the others, it's quality soap.

243 City Lights

1931, United Artists, 81 minutes. Director-Screenplay: Charles Chaplin. Photography: Rollie Totheroh, Gordon Pollock.

Cast: Charles Chaplin, Virginia Cherrill, Florence Lee, Harry Myers, Allan Garcia, Hank Mann.

Chaplin, once again portraying the Tramp, falls in love with a blind flower girl. In an effort to raise money to prevent her eviction, he actually gets a job--as a manure shoveler--but is fired for being late.

Desperate for cash, he's talked into a boxing match by a pug who promises to take it easy on him and split the winnings if Charlie will agree to lie down. The boxer runs out of the gym at the last minute, however, when he learns the police are about to grab him.

That leaves Charlie to fight a mean brute, who insists that "winner take all" and who casually flattens a just-victorious fighter in the locker room and a boisterous fan while on his way into the ring.

Charlie's hilarious strategy is to keep dancing behind the referee while striking his foe with hidden blows. His strategy gets everyone so confused at one point he has the brute and the referee throwing punches at each other while Charlie watches. Later, the two boxers knock each other to the canvas. The brute stands as the referee begins the count on Charlie. As Charlie rises, the brute falls down, and the ref begins the count on him. The brute rises and Charlie falls down again, etc.

244 City of Bad Men

1953, 20th Century Fox, 82 minutes, Color. Director: Harmon Jones. Producer: Leonard Goldstein. Screenplay: George W. George, George F. Slavin. Photography: Charles G. Clarke.

Cast: Dale Robertson, Jeanne Crain, Richard Boone, Lloyd Bridges, Carole Matthews, Carl Betz, Whitfield Connor, Hugh Sanders.

Set in Carson City, Nevada in 1897, Robertson and his pals, fresh from an unsuccessful role in the Mexican Revolution, enroll as deputies with the intent of stealing the proceeds from the Jim Corbett-Doug Fitzsimmons fight. It's up to sweetie Crain to change Robertson and set him against his crooked pals.

245 Clancy's Kosher Wedding

1927, Film Booking Offices of America, 5,700 feet. Director: Arvid E. Gillstrom. Screenplay: J.G. Hawks. Adaptation: Curtis Benton. Story: Al Boasberg. Photography: Charles Boyle.

Cast: George Sidney, Will Armstrong, Ann Brody, Mary Gordon, Sharon Lynn, Ed Brady, Rex Lease.

The Cohens, owners of a clothing store, are upset that daughter Leah (Sharon Lynn) loves Tom Clancy (Rex Lease), whose father owns an adjacent store.

Tom agrees to fight the Cohens' choice for their daughter, a boxer named Izzy Murphy (Ed Brady) with the winner getting the girl. The respective fathers, in the meantime, wager everything they have on the fight. Clancy wins and the Cohens are forced onto the street, but the Clancys take them in as partners as Leah and Tom marry.

Once again, the women are portrayed in this comedy as little more than objects to be fought over, although there's a slight difference here.

Usually, the woman is portrayed as going only with the winner. In **Clancy's Kosher Wedding**, Leah actually tries to dissuade Tom from winning, knowing that it will ruin her own father.

246 Come and Get It

1929, FBO Pictures, 5,164 feet. Director: Wallace Fox. Scenario: Frank Howard Clark. Photography: Virgil Miller. Editor: Della King.

Cast: Bob Steele, Jimmy Quinn, Betty Welsh, William Welsh, Harry O'Connor, Marin Sais, James B. Leong.

Navy boxing champ Breezy Smith (Steele) is attacked by Regan and Singapore Joe. The villains follow him home where Regan winds up killing a neighbor and pinning the murder on Breezy's dad.

Singapore Joe offers to spill the beans on his ex-pal for $1,000, and Breezy enters a boxing match to win the money to clear his dad.

247 Comic Boxing Match

1899, British, Warwick Trading Co., 150 feet.

It's a tall man vs. a short man.

248 Confessions of Tom Harris

1972, 98 minutes, Color. Directors: John Derek, David Nelson. Producer-Screenplay: Derek.

Cast: Don Murray, Linda Evans, David Brian, Gary Clarke, Logan Ramsey.

Derek and Murray, who teamed on the always-to-be-forgotten **Childish Things**, are reunited in the making of **Confessions of Tom Harris**, another boxing film which almost no one has ever seen.

Here, Murray plays a totally rotten boxer.

249 Conflict (aka **The Abysmal Brute**)

1936, Universal, 60-63 minutes. Director: David Howard. Screenplay: Charles A. Logue, Walter Weems, based on a story by Jack London. Photography: A.J. Stout.

Cast: John Wayne, Jean Rogers, Tommy Bupp, Eddie Borden, Ward Bond, Frank Sheridan, Bryant Washburn, Frank Hagney, Margaret Mann, Lloyd Ingraham.

Wayne and Bond run a crooked fight racket as they travel about in 1890's lumber camps. Shades of **The Champ**, Wayne turns over a new leaf with the influence of an orphan boy and a lady reporter who's posing as a social worker.

250 The Contender

1944, Producers Releasing Corp., 63 minutes. Director: Sam

Newfield. Producer: Bert Sternbach. Photography: Robert Cline. Screenplay: George Sayer, Jay Doten, Raymond Schrock.

Cast: Buster Crabbe, Arline Judge, Julie Gibson, Donald Mayo, Glenn Strange, Milton Kibbee, Roland Drew, Sam Flink, Duke York, George Turner.

Borrowing a bit from **City for Conquest,** truck driver Crabbe becomes a boxer to pay the tuition at his son's military school.

As Crabbe rises up the ladder, of course he falls under the influence of a vamp as he leaves the influence of virtuous sports writer, Arline Judge.

Just as he's about to hit rock bottom because of all the night life, he realizes the error of his ways. To boot, his son would rather be a journalist.

251 Corinthian Jack

1921, British, Master Films, 5,000 feet. Director-Screenplay: Walter Courtenay Rowden. Story: Charles E. Pearce.

Cast: Victor McLaglen, Kathleen Vaughan, Warrick Ward, Dorothy Fane, Malcolm Tod, Conway Dixon, William Lenders, Roy Raymond.

A beautiful girl is saved from the evil clutches of a nobleman by a boxer. The film was re-released in a drastically cut version in 1926 as **Fighting Jack.**

252 The Count of Ten

1928, Universal Pictures, 5,557 feet. Director: James Flood. Presented by: Carl Laemmle. Screenplay: Harry O. Hoyt, Albert DeMond. Photography: Virgil Miller, Ben Kline. Editor: George McClure.

Cast: Charles Ray, James Gleason, Jobyna Ralston, Edythe Chapman, Arthur Lake, Charles Sellon, George Magrill.

It's the manager to the rescue of his beleaguered fighter in this adaptation of a **Red Book** magazine story by Gerald Beaumont.

And who better to play the manager than James Gleason who made a career out of such roles? His fighter is Johnny McKinney (Ray), whose father-in-law and troublesome brother-in-law move right in when he marries Betty (Ralston), a pretty counter girl.

The in-laws prove such a financial strain that poor Johnny has to keep on fighting and fighting until he breaks his hand. It's up to Gleason to kick the in-laws out and let the two young lovers live happily ever after.

253 The Coward (aka **They Called Him Coward)**

1915, British, Hepworth, 1,525 feet. Director: Frank Wilson. Story: Stewart Rome.

Cast: Stewart Rome, Chrissie White, Lionelle Howard, Nichol Simpson.

A boxer has a lot on his mind during the big bout: his baby is undergoing a serious eye operation.

254 The Cowboy and the Prizefighter

1950, Eagle Lion, 60 minutes, Color. Director: Lewis D. Collins. Screenplay: Jerry Thomas, based on the "Red Ryder" comic strip by Fred Harman. Photography: Gilbert Warrenton.

Cast: Jim Bannon (Red Ryder), Little Brown Jug (Little Beaver), Emmett Lynn, Don Haggerty, Karen Randle, John Hart, Marshall Reed, Forrest Taylor, Lou Nova.

Western hero Red Ryder is saved by a man who's out to get a traveling fight promoter who he believes is responsible for his father's death. It's up to Red Ryder and his little sidekick, Little Beaver, to straighten things out.

255 The Crowd Roars

1938, Metro Goldwyn Mayer, 87 minutes. Director: Richard Thorpe. Producer: Sam Zimbalist. Photography: John Seitz. Screenplay: Thomas Lennon, George Bruce, George Oppenheimer.

Cast: Robert Taylor, Lionel Stander, Maureen O'Sullivan, Frank Morgan, Edward Arnold, Jane Wyman, Charles D. Brown, William Gargan, Nat Pendleton, Donald Barry, J. Farrell MacDonald.

Young star Taylor, who was a box office sensation in **A Yank at Oxford**, this time is Tommy "Killer" McCoy, the son of a drunken ex-vaudevillian (Morgan).

McCoy, whose last opponent died in the ring, is now under contract to big-time gambler, Jim Cain (Arnold). The boxer falls in love with Cain's daughter, Sheila, who thinks her pop is a stockbroker. Naturally, dad disapproves.

The good, old reliable kidnapping subplot is pulled out of the script storage once again as Sheila and McCoy's father are held hostage by the evil gambler, Pug Welsh, who orders McCoy to take a dive in the eighth round.

You guessed it--they escape (don't they always?). Pop McCoy uses an old vaudeville juggling act to distract and then bop the guards; and Sheila rushes to Madison Square Garden. Our Hero is taking a terrible beating; but as soon as he sees Sheila alive and well, his opponent starts seeing stars.

The storyline of **The Crowd Roars** is older than the hills; but with an expert cast--especially with the latest heart throb Taylor--audiences didn't seem to mind. It was remade in 1947 as **Killer McCoy** with Mickey Rooney.

256 The Croxley Master

1921, British, Screen Plays, 3,900 feet. Director: Percy Nash. Screenplay: Harry Engholm, based on a novel by Sir Arthur Conan Doyle.

Cast: Dick Webb, Dora Lennox, Jack Stanley, Joan Ritz, Cecil Morton York, Louis Rihil, Mabel Penn, J.T. MacMillan, Ernest Wallace, George Turner.

A Welsh doctor's aide who needs money to begin his own practice turns to boxing to raise the dough.

257 The Dangerous Coward

1924, Monogram Pictures, 4,830 feet. Director: Albert Rogell. Producer: Harry J. Brown. Story: Marion Jackson. Photography: Ross Fisher.

Cast: Fred Thomson, Al Kaufman, Jim Corey, Hazel Keener, Frank Hagney, Andrew Arbuckle, David Kirby.

For some strange reason, it seems that all disgruntled boxers headed west, at least according to the number of 1920's films on the subject.

The Dangerous Coward is distinguished mainly by the names of its main characters: The Lightning Kid, Our Hero, who believes that he has permanently injured his opponent, the Weazel, and Battling Benson, the foe he takes on at the film's climax.

258 Dangerous Kiss

1961, Japanese, Toho Films. Director: Yuzo Kawashima.

Cast: Akira Takarada, Michiyo Aratama, Reiko Dan, Mitsuko Kusabue, Akemi Kita, Ichiro Nakatani, Seizaburo Kawazu, Haruko Togo, Takao Zushi.

We admit we haven't seen this one; it appears to focus on a boxer's relationship with 4 women.

259 Daring Years

1923, Equity, 6,782 feet. Director: Kenneth Webb. Producer-Story: Dan Carson Goodman.

Cast: Mildred Harrist, Clara Bow, Charles Emmett Mack, Joe King, Mary Carr, Tyrone Power, Skeets Gallagher.

The eternal triangle casts its evil spell once again as a dancer becomes involved with a boxer (King) and another man (Mack). When the jealous boxer is accidentally shot, the girl must save her beloved.

260 Day of the Fight

1951, RKO Radio Pictures, 16 minutes. Director-Photography-Editor-Sound: Stanley Kubrick.

Narrator: Douglas Edwards.

Kubrick's very first film focuses on the preparations for a big bout by middleweight boxer Walter Cartier.

261 De Woild's Champeen

1931, Tiffany, 18 minutes. Director: Frank Strayer. Story and Dialogue: Scott Darling.

Cast: Paul Hurst.

A boxing champ is accidentally knocked out by this comedy short's hero at a society affair.

262 The Defeated Victor

1959, Italian, Serena Film, 95 minutes. Director: Paolo Heusch. Screenplay: Fausto Tozzi. Photography: Robert Gerardi.

Cast: Maurizio Arena, Giovanna Ralli.

The fall of a veteran fighter parallels the rise of a young one in this story as seen through the eyes of the boxers' women. The veteran's wife, who has lived through the good years with her man, must adjust her lifestyle as he begins his slide.

263 Dempsey Returns

1932, Independent, 18 minutes.

The story of boxing great, Jack Dempsey, is narrated by Curtis Benton. Dempsey's career from his win over Jess Willard to his loss to Gene Tunney is highlighted.

264 Double or Nothing

1936, Vitaphone, 20 minutes. Director: Joseph Henabery. Story: Cyrus Wood, George Bennett.

Cast: Phil Harris, Leah Ray.

When a fighter walks out of training camp, Harris is persuaded to impersonate him and finds himself being kidnapped.

265 Dress Parade

1927, Pathe Exchange-DeMille Pictures, 6,599 feet. Director: Donald Crisp. Screenplay: Douglas Z. Doty. Photography: Peverell Marley. Editor: Barbara Hunter.

Cast: William Boyd, Bessie Love, Hugh Allan, Walter Tennyson, Maurice Ryan, Louis Natheaux, Clarence Geldert.

Film vaults are loaded with stories about military academies in which the hero arrives with a superior attitude until he learns the hard way otherwise.

Boyd portrays a boxing champion who attends West Point and vies for the hand of the commander's daughter.

266 The Duke Comes Back

1937, Republic, 62 minutes. Director: Irving Pichel. Story: Lucien Cary. Photography: Harry Neumann.

Cast: Allan James, Heather Angel, Genevieve Tobin, Frederick Burton, Joseph Crehan, Ben Weldon, John Russell.

The boxing hero saves his society gal's dad from financial ruin. Winning the world's championship wasn't good enough for dear old dad, who threatens to disinherit his daughter for stooping to marry anyone as low as a boxer.

When the hero, who had retired from the ring, starts boxing again to get his father-in-law out of a $200G hole, dad eventually relents.

267 The Duke of Chicago

1949, Republic, 59 minutes. Director: George Blair. Producer: Stephen Aver. Screenplay: Albert DeMond, based on a novel by Lucien Cary. Photography: John Mac Burnie. Editor: Cliff Bell.

Cast: Tom Brown, Audrey Long, Grant Withers, Paul Harvey, Skeets Gallagher, Lois Hall, Matt McHugh, Joseph Crehan.

Attention all publishers! If your business is in financial trouble, why not enter boxing to raise the money? Actually, hero Tom Brown had been a middleweight champion before turning to publishing.

He rejects an offer for a fixed fight and wins the money he needs despite a broken hand.

268 The Duke Steps Out

1929, Metro Goldwyn Mayer, 6,201-6,236 feet. Director: James Cruze. Adaptation-Continuity: Raymond Schrock, Dale Van Every. Story: Lucien Cary. Photography: Ira Morgan. Editor: George Hively.

Cast: William Haines, Joan Crawford, Karl Dane, Jack Roper, Delmar Daves, Luke Cosgrave, Herbert Prior.

A millionaire's son (Haines) strikes out on his own and decides to go to college when he falls in love with a beautiful college gal (Crawford).

The problem is, he's also a prizefighter; and in this light comedy, that causes some romatic complications until the two get together happily at the end.

269 Dumbells in Ermine

1930, Warner Brothers, 6,300 feet. Director: John G. Adolfi. Screenplay: Harvey Thew. Photography: Dev Jennings.

Cast: Robert Armstrong, Barbara Kent, Beryl Mercer, James Gleason, Claude Gillingwater, Julia Swayne Gordon, Arthur Hoyt, Mary Foy, Charlotte Merriam.

A Virginia socialite is torn between her love for a boxer (Armstrong) and the evangelist (Hoyt) her mother wants her to marry. Good old Grandma (Mercer) pushes for the boxer and eventually Mom is won over.

James Gleason, who as usual plays a wisecracking fight manager, is credited with writing the dialogue for this adaptation of the play, "Weak Sisters," by Lynn Starling.

270 Dynamite Dan

1924, Aywon Film Corp., 4,850 feet. Director-Scenario: Bruce Mitchell. Photography: Bert Longenecker.

Cast: Kenneth McDonald, Frank Rise, Boris Karloff, Eddie Harris, Diana Alden, Harry Woods, Jack Richardson.

The hero of the title (McDonald) becomes a boxer after knocking out the champ who was harassing his girlfriend.

Dan wins his first 21 fights by first-round knockouts before getting the chance to meet the heavyweight champ in a real bout.

271 East Side, West Side

1927, Fox Film Corp., 8,154 feet. Director-Adaptation: Allan Dwan. Photography: George Webber.

Cast: George O'Brien, Virginia Valli, J. Farrell MacDonald, Dore Davidson, Sonia Nodalsky, Edward Garvey, Holmes Herbert.

A boxer whose mom and stepfather were killed in an accident sets out to find his real dad. He finds a benefactor in Gilbert Van Horn (Herbert), a wealthy man who, of course, is his father.

The fighter (O'Brien) gives up the ring to become an engineer, perhaps to better figure out all the complicated plot turns in this glossy soap opera.

272 Edith and Marcel

1982, French, Color. Director: Claude Lelouch. Screenplay: Lelouch. Photography: Jean Boffety.

Cast: Evelyne Bouix, Marcel Cerdan, Jr., Jacques Villeret, Francis Huster, Jean-Claude Brialy, Jean Bouise, Charles Gerard, Charlotte de Turckheim.

The director of **A Man and a Woman** this time focuses on the romance between the great French singer, Edith Piaf, and a boxer.

273 The Egg-Crate Wallop

1919, Paramount, 5 reels. Director: Jerome Story. Story: Julian Josephson.

Cast: Charles Ray, Colleen Moore, Jack Connelly, Fred Moore, Otto Hoffman, J.P. Lockner, George Williams.

When the express office is robbed, the hero (Ray), who's the manager, is suspected. He becomes a professional boxer after fleeing the scene and is sent into a bout as a substitute.

And who is the foe? The real thief, who had made an unsuccessful play for the hero's girlfriend, the daughter of the express company's general manager. After taking a terrible whupping the first few rounds, the hero finds the strength to defeat the villain and clear his name.

274 Every Which Way but Loose

1978, Warner Brothers, 119 minutes, Color. Director: James Fargo. Producer: Robert Daley. Screenplay: Jeremy Joe Kroneberg.

Cast: Clint Eastwood, Sondra Locke, Geoffrey Lewis, Beverly D'Angelo, Ruth Gordon, Walter Barnes, George Chandler, Roy Jenson, James MacEachin.

Philo Beddoe (Eastwood), a truck driver who enjoys country music and earning extra cash in bare knuckles fights, traipses around the countryside with his two sidekicks--Clyde the orangutan, whom he won in a fight, and a human (Lewis). Feisty old mom (Gordon) is around to get the laughs left over by the orangutan.

In between fights, Beddoe manages to stay one step ahead of an ornery motorcycle gang and a Los Angeles cop who are after his scalp and one step behind the object of his affections, a country western singer (Locke).

A big box office hit, **Every Which Way but Loose** inspired a sequel, **Any Which Way You Can**, but its main claim to fame on the sports film roster is that the brawny victorious Beddoe is rejected at the end by Locke in favor of a non-athletic type, a rarity indeed in sports films.

275 Ex-Champ

1939, Universal, 64-72 minutes. Director: Phil Rosen. Producer: Burt Kelly. Screenplay: Alex Gottlieb, Edmund L. Hartmann. Story: Gordon Kahn. Photography: Elwood Bredell. Editor: Bernard Burton.

Cast: Victor McLaglen, Tom Brown, Nan Grey, Constance Moore, William Frawley, Donald Briggs, Samuel S. Hinds, Marc Lawrence, Kid Chissel, Thurston Hall, Charles Halton.

A former boxing champ (McLaglen) who's now a doorman lives in the past and drinks heavily, mainly because his son is an ungrateful snotnose.

It seems the lad's education took nearly every penny of dad's boxing money, and now the boy is pretending to be an orphan while wooing a banker's daughter.

When the son faces jail over some stock misappropriations, it's up to the rising welterweight being trained by dad to come through and earn enough money to make up the deficit.

276 Excuse My Glove

1936, British, Alexander, 75 minutes. Director: Redd Davis. Producers: Howard Alexander, Joe Rock. Screenplay: Val Valentine, Katherine Strueby. Photography: Jack Willson.

Cast: Len Harvey, Archie Pitt, Betty Ann Davies, Olive Blakeny, Wally Patch, Ronald Shiner, Arthur Finn, Vera Bogetti, Bobbie Comber, Billy Wells.

A conniving manager can't stop our hero, a glass collector, from becoming a boxing champ. The hero is portrayed by real-life boxer Harvey, who plays a shy man who becomes a fighter after winning a bout at a fair.

277 Fat City

1972, Columbia, 96 minutes, Color. Director: John Huston. Producer: Ray Stark. Screenplay: Leonard Gardner. Photography: Conrad Hall. Editor: Margaret Booth.

Cast: Stacy Keach, Jeff Bridges, Susan Tyrell, Candy Clark,

Nicholas Colasanto, Art Aragon, Curtis Cokes, Sixto Rodriguez, Billy Walker, Wayne Mahan.

Director Huston has a soft spot in his heart for life's misfits, and he certainly has two to work with in **Fat City.**

Veteran fighter Tully (Keach) is a skid row bum, the result of too many women and too much liquor. Working out for a comeback try, he befriends the young Ernie (Bridges) and encourages him to become a pro.

The two men's stories are juxtaposed as they train together by hiring themselves out as migrant farm workers, with Tully starting to see a new woman and Bridges' relationship with his wife changing because of his boxing.

Atmosphere, rather than action, is the key as the viewer comes to the realization that these are both two of life's losers, and that Ernie could well become the Tully of tomorrow.

Huston originally sought Marlon Brando for Keach's role. Tyrell won a nomination for best supporting actress.

278 The Fear Fighter

1925, Rayart Pictures, 4,800 feet. Director: Albert Rogell. Story: Grover Jones. Photography: Ross Fisher.

Cast: Billy Sullivan, Ruth Dwyer, J.P. McGowan, Spike Robinson, Jack Herrick, Gunboat Smith, Phil Salvadore.

We've heard of fathers opposing their daughter's marriage before, but **The Fear Fighter** offers a comic switch. The hero, Billy Griffin (Sullivan), must box his prospective father-in-law before he can get permission to marry.

He's beaten so badly he gets amnesia and eventually lands in jail. There, his cellmate teaches him to box; and Griffin becomes a top lightweight contender on his release.

In the championship fight, a blow restores his memory, but woe! Now Griffin can't remember how to fight since he didn't know how before he got amnesia.

Being beaten badly, his girlfriend has some harsh words for him that rally him to victory on his own.

279 The Fifty-Shilling Boxer

1937, British, George Smith, 74 minutes. Director: MacLean Rogers. Producer: George Smith. Story: Guy Fletcher. Photography: Geoffrey Faithfull.

Cast: Bruce Seton, Nancy O'Neil, Moore Marriott, Eve Gray, Charles Oliver, Aubrey Malla Lieu.

How many circus clowns have become pro boxers? The hero (Seton) of this one is a total flop as an actor when he's hired to portray a pug but his prowess with his fists impresses a fight promoter in the audience.

280 The Fight

1971, Cinerama Releasing Corp., 26 minutes, Color. Director-Producer: William Greaves.

There have been newsreel films on major boxing matches since nearly the beginning of film history, and we are not attempting to cover them all here.

However, as this one is about **The Fight** between Muhammad Ali and Joe Frazier, and as many filmgoers felt they had been cheated and misled after viewing this 26-minute short, we are including it here.

A total of 12 cameras were used to photograph the action, and there's nothing wrong with that. The problem is that many customers felt the publicity for the film indicated they would see the entire fight, when in reality only six rounds are shown.

A feature length documentary on the Ali-Frazier fight was released in 1974 under the title **The Fighters** (see separate listing).

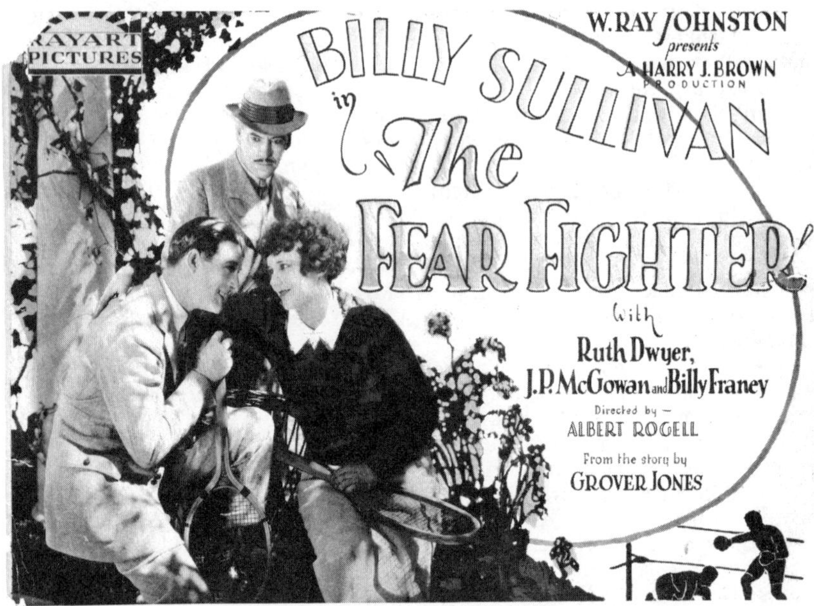

The great John L. Sullivan's nephew starred in this silent–era boxing movie.

281 Fight for Love (aka **The Other Fellow**)

1908, Edison Co., 475 feet. No credits available.

A fight between sailors over some girls is broken up by officers who allow them to have a real boxing match. A **Variety** review of the film stated "There is a man behind the sheet (screen) who interjects appropriate remarks at interesting points."

282 The Fight Never Ends

1947, Alexander Productions. Producer: William Alexander.

Cast: Joe Louis, Ruby Dee, Mills Brothers, William Greaves, Emmett "Babe" Wallace, Harrell Tillman, Elwood Smith, Gwendolyn Tynes.

Boxing great Joe Louis plays himself as he strives to cut down juvenile delinquency in what press material for the film describes as "a story as powerful as the Brown Bomber himself."

283 The Fighter

1952, United Artists, 78 minutes. Director: Herbert Kline. Producer: Alex Gottlieb. Screenplay: Kline, Aben Kandel, based on "The Mexican" by Jack London. Photography: James Wong Howe. Editor: Edward Mann.

Cast: Richard Conte, Vanessa Brown, Lee J. Cobb, Frank Silvera, Roberta Haynes, Hugh Sanders, Claire Carleton, Martin Garralaga, Argentina Brunetti, Rudolfo Hoyos, Jr.

A quite respectable action film in its own right, **The Fighter** has the distinction of being the only American sports movie to be remade as a Russian propaganda film; and it's pretty easy to see why.

The background of the Mexican Revolution provides a natural setting to illustrate workers shedding the yoke of imperialism.

In this version, however, Conte portrays Filipe Rivera, a Mexican who crosses into El Paso, Texas and joins a group plotting the overthrow of Diaz. Rivera's family had been killed by Diaz's soldiers.

To raise money for the cause, Rivera faces a top contender in a winner-take-all boxing match.

The Russians remade the film in 1957 under the original title of the Jack London film, **The Mexican.** The American version came on the heels of the success of MGM's **Right Cross** in 1950, another boxing film with a Mexican as the hero.

284 The Fighters

1974, Walter Reade Organization, 114 minutes, Color. Producer-Director-Editor: William Greaves.

The 1971 Ali-Frazier fight is the focus of this full-length documentary, which includes much footage of the 15-rounder won by Ali as well as a lot of scenes of backstage activity.

285 Fighter's Paradise

1924, Phil Goldstone Productions, 4,800 feet. Director: Alvin J. Neitz. Scenario: J.F. Natteford.

Cast: Rex Baker, Andrew Waldron, Dick Sutherland, Jack Curtis, Harry Burns, Kenneth Benedict, Margaret Landis.

Here's another 1920s boxing western in which a timid counterman is forced into a fight and becomes a top boxer after a blow to the head.

286 Fighting Billy

1915, British, Cricks, 521 feet. Director-Scenario: W.P. Kellino.

A short gag film in which a ruffian is defeated by a goat which has boxing gloves on its horns.

287 Fighting Champ

1933, Monogram, 57 minutes. Director: J.P. McCarthy. Story: Wellyn Totman. Photography: Archie Stout.

Cast: Bob Steele, Arletta Duncan, Duncan King, Kit Guard, George Chesebro, Frank Ball, Lafe McKee.

The setting may be out West, but the old fight-fixing racket is still the same in this Grade B shoot-em-up.

288 The Fighting Deacon (aka **The Life of Tiger Flowers**)

1926, Theatrical Owners Booking Association, 5 reels. Writer-Producer: Walk Miller.

The story of middleweight boxer Theodore "Tiger" Flowers, who defeated Harry Greb for the title, is presented from his time in the Army during World War I and his tutelage by Walk Miller.

289 The Fighting Fool

1929, British, BSFP, 10 minutes. Director: Jack Harrison. Screenplay: Chick Farr.

Cast: Chick Farr, Herbert Cyril, Harry Terry.

A boxer is defeated by a "dandy" despite the fact the latter never lands a punch.

290 Fighting Fools

1949, Monogram, 89 minutes. Director: Reginald LeBorg. Producer: Jan Grippo. Screenplay: Edmond Seward, Gerald Schnitzer, Bert Lawrence. Photography: William Sickner. Editor: William Austin.

Cast: Leo Gorcey, Huntz Hall, Gabriel Dell, Frankie Darro, Billy Benedict, David Gorcey, Bernard Gorcey, Benny Bartlett, Lyle Talbot, Eddie Gribbon.

The East Side Kids tackle a crooked boxing racket run by baddie Talbot after one of their friends is killed in a rigged fight.

291 Fighting Gentleman

1932, Freuler, 69 minutes. Director: Fred Newmayer. Story: Edward Sinclair. Photography: Edward Kull. Editor: Fred Bain.

Cast: William Collier, Jr., Josephine Dunn, Natalie Moorhead,

Crauford Kent, Lee Moran, Pat O'Malley, James J. Jeffries.

When Grade B boxing films (and many Grade A ones while we're at it) aren't focusing on fixed fights, they're about a boxer torn between the virtuous girl back home and the wicked gold digger.

The mechanic-boxer hero of the title neglects the wife at home for a vamp only to lose a big fight. Once he learns the error of his ways, it's back to the training room for another try.

292 The Fighting Heart

1925, Fox Film Corp., 6,978 feet. Director: John Ford. Scenario: Lillie Hayward, based on "Once to Every Man" by Larry Evans. Photography: Joe August.

Cast: George O'Brien, Victor McLaglen, Billie Dove, J. Farrell MacDonald, Diana Miller, Francis Ford, Edward Piel, James Marcus, Bert Woodruff.

It's one of the axioms of the auteur theory of the cinema that directors keep on making the same film over and over.

Although plot-wise, **The Fighting Heart** bears no resemblance to director Ford's 1952 classic **The Quiet Man,** its climactic street battle could be called a distant cousin.

Whereas **The Quiet Man** was light and enjoyable film fare, with its most memorable sequence a long fight spilling through a town and into the countryside, **The Fighting Heart** is comparably heavy going.

The constant in both climactic fight sequences is that the heavy is Victor McLaglen, himself a former boxer who once fought Jack Johnson.

McLaglen portrays Soapy Williams, evil heavyweight champion-bootlegger whose liquor caused a death.

The family of the hero, Denny Bolton (O'Brien), was noted for heavy drinking and he, too, is suspected of it and is scorned by his girlfriend. Bolton becomes a boxer with the sole intent of beating Williams in the ring.

Because he's good enough to pose a threat to Williams, his girlfriend vamp (Miller) makes a play for him to get him to break training.

An out-of-shape Bolton loses the match in the ring, but later wins the street fight with Williams.

293 Fighting Mad (aka **Joe Palooka in Fighting Mad**)

1948, Monogram, 74 minutes. Director: Reginald LeBorg. Producer: Hal E. Chester. Screenplay: Ralph S. Lewis, Bernard D. Shamberg. Story: Ralph S. Lewis, Bernard D. Shamberg. Photography: William Sickner. Editor: Roy Livingston.

Cast: Joe Kirkwood, Leon Errol, Elyse Knox, John Hubbard, John Indrisano, Patricia Dane, Charles Cane, Wally Vernon, Frank Hyers, Jack Shea, Jack Roper, Eddie Gribbon.

Many consider this the best of the Joe Palooka series. The comic strip hero is blinded during a bout and undergoes an operation. His sight is restored, but he's ordered to lay off fighting for a year or he may go permanently blind.

Meanwhile, Palooka's manager Knobby Walsh (Errol) has taken in a new fighter but gets involved with some gamblers, and it's up to Joe to risk blindness (shades of **Rocky II**!) to come to the aid of his pal.

294 Fighting Mad

1957, British, Border Films, 53 minutes. Director: Denis Kavanagh. Producer: Edwin J. Fancey. Screenplay: Jennifer Wyatt. Photography: Hal Morey.

Cast: Joe Robinson, Adrienne Scott, Beckett Bould, Jack Taylor.

A boxer helps his uncle fend off crooks who are trying to muscle in on an oil claim. Here's still another tale of a fighter who swears off the game after killing an opponent in the ring.

295 The Fighting Marine

1926, Pathe, 10 Chapters. Director: Spencer G. Bennet. Screenplay: Frank Leon Smith.

Cast: Gene Tunney.

Chapter One: The Successful Candidate; Chapter Two: The Second Attack; Chapter Three: In the Enemy's Trap; Chapter Four: The Desperate Foe; Chapter Five: Entombed. Chapter Six: The Falling Tower; Chapter Seven: Waylaid; Chapter Eight: Challenged; Chapter Nine: The Signal Shot; Chapter Ten: Fired and Hired.

Boxing champ Tunney got plenty of opportunity to display his fistic prowess in this chapter play, for which he was paid a $24,000 salary plus 25 percent of the gross receipts.

296 Fighting Youth

1925, Columbia Pictures, 5 reels. Director: Reeves Eason. Adaptation: Dorothy Howell. Story: Paul Archer. Photography: George Meehan.

Cast: William Fairbanks, Pauline Garon, Jack Britton, George Periolat, William Norton Bailey, Pat Harmon, Frank Hagney, Tom Carr.

Two of boxing movies' time honored clichés are rolled up into one here—the kidnapping of the hero and his escape just in time for the big fight and the ringside plea to the beaten boxer from his sweetheart which gives him the strength to win.

The plot involves a young socialite (Fairbanks) who gets into so many fights outside the ring that he's asked to fight a charity match with Murdering Mooney (Hagney), who beat up his sweetheart's brother.

297 The Filthy Five (aka **The Dirty Five**)

1968, Extraordinary Films, 96 minutes. Director-Photography: Andy Milligan. Producer: William Mishkin. Screenplay: Gerald Jacuzzo.

Cast: Matt Garth, Anne Linden, Jackie Colton, Nick Orzel, Maha, Gerald Jacuzzo, Mark Jenkins, Maggie Rogers, Mary Carter, Larry Ree, Maggie Dominic.

Lovers of sleaze films may find enough in this cheapie to keep them happy. A boxer gives up his ring career for a role in a television series, but his involvement with a drug addict co-star makes the hero's prostitute girl friend jealous. It's about as high class as it sounds.

298 Fisticuffs

1929, Educational, 2 reels. Director: Henry W. George.

Cast: Lupino Lane, Wallace Lupino, Harry Dunkinson, Ruth Eddings.

Set in the 1800's, Lane is a bumbling blacksmith's apprentice who loves his boss's daughter. The blacksmith trains another helper to box the Belfast Biffer and bets all he has on the bout.

The Biffer, however, is a no-good villain and has his opponent kidnapped, leaving it up to Our Hero to take his place in the ring and win the bout and the girl.

299 The Flanagan Boy (aka **Bad Blonde**)

1953, British, Hammer Films, 81 minutes. Director: Reginald Le Borg. Producer: Anthony Hinds. Screenplay: Richard Landau, Guy Elmes. Story: Max Catto. Photography: Walter Harvey.

Cast: Frederick Valk, Barbara Peyton, John Slater, Sidney James, Toby Wright, Marie Burke, George Woodbridge.

A boxer is persuaded to try to kill his promoter by the latter's wife.

300 Flesh and the Fury

1952, Universal-International, 82 minutes. Director: Joseph

Pevney. Producer: Leonard Goldstein. Screenplay: Bernard Gordon. Story: William Alland. Photography: Irving Glassberg. Editor: Virgil Vogel.

Cast: Tony Curtis, Jan Sterling, Mona Freeman, Wallace Ford, Connie Gilchrist, Katherine Locke, Joe Gray, Ron Hargrave, Harry Guardino, Harry Shannon, Harry Raven.

The underdog is established here in the person of a deaf mute prizefighter (Curtis) who undergoes an operation to restore his hearing.

Enter the ever-present two women of the boxing movies: The Vamp—in the person of Jan Sterling—and The Innocent—in the form of writer Mona Freeman.

Of course, there are complications during the title fight when Curtis again loses his hearing.

301 Fling in the Ring

1955, Columbia, 2 reels. Director: Jules White.

Cast: The Three Stooges, Richard Wessel, Claire Carlton, Frank Sully.

A remake of the Stooges' earlier short, **Fright Night**, finds the comedians facing a lot of hot water if their boxer wins.

302 Float Like a Butterfly, Sting Like a Bee

1969, Grove Press, 94 minutes. Director-Producer-Photography-Editor: William Klein.

Cast: Muhammad Ali, Joe Louis, Jersey Joe Walcott, Kingfish Levinsky, Evil Eye Finkel, Malcolm X.

Yet another feature documentary on the life of Muhammad Ali takes its title from the champ's description of his boxing style after his first knockout of Sonny Liston.

303 Flying Fists Series

In the early to mid 1920's, light heavyweight champ Benny Leonard appeared in this series of 2-reel boxing shorts which were highlighted by the appearance of a "black shadow" which appeared when things appeared worst for the hero.

Titles in the series include **Breaking In, Hitting Hard, Soft Muscles** and the most famous of the series, **Jazz Bout.**

Jazz Bout, produced in 1924 by Henry Ginsberg and Jacob Wilk and written by Sam Hellman, finds the boxing hero giving up the ring at his girlfriend's urging.

He becomes the saxophonist in a jazz band but agrees to fight again when he's accused of being afraid. When he's being badly beaten in the ring, his band appears and inspires him to fight harder.

304 Flying Fists

1938, Victory, 63 minutes. Director: Bob Hill. Screenplay: Basil Dickey. Story: Rock Hawkey. Photography: Bill Hyer.

Cast: Herman Brix, Jeanne Martel, Fuzzy Knight, J. Farrell MacDonald, Guinn Williams, Dickie Jones, Charles Williams.

A champ who retired at the urging of his girl returns to the ring when her father finds himself in need of money.

305 Footlight Serenade

1942, 20th Century-Fox, 81 minutes. Director: Gregory Ratoff. Producer: William Le Baron. Screenplay: Robert Ellis, Helen Logan, Lynn Starling. Story: Fidel La Barbra, Kenneth Earl. Photography: Lee Garmes.

Cast: Victor Mature, John Payne, Betty Grable, Jane Wyman, James Gleason, Phil Silvers, Cobrina Wright, Jr.

Broadway actor Payne, who's secretly married to chorus girl Grable, must sweat out most of this musical while Mature, a boxing champ who has a role in the play, makes a pass at her.

Payne gets his chance to wallop the champ during a scene in the play in which he's supposed to spar with Mature.

"I won, don't worry," Benny Leonard tells his mom from ringside during the first episode in the Flying Fists series. (The Museum of Modern Art/Film Stills Archive.)

306 For My Lady's Happiness

1926, British, Frederick White Co., 2,201 feet. Director: Harry Parkinson. Screenplay: Andrew Soutar.

Cast: Phil Scott.

A boxer's victory saves a fair lady from an unhappy marriage.

307 For the Love of Pete

1936, Vitaphone, 16 minutes. Director: Lloyd French. Story: Jack Henley, Burnet Hershey.

Cast: Robert Norton, Shemp Howard.

Comic strip boxer Joe Palooka was first portrayed on the screen by Stu Erwin in 1934's **Palooka.** In the late 1940's, Monogram produced a series of Joe Palooka features starring Joe Kirkwood as the champ.

In the 1930's, however, Norton starred as Palooka in Vitaphone shorts. In **For the Love of Pete,** he's first a baggage room worker, then an employee of a clothing store when the town's boxing hopeful against the champ is put out of commission and Joe must take his place.

308 The Fortunate Fool

1933, British, Associated British, 73 minutes. Director: Norman Walker. Producer: Jack Eppel. Story: Dion Titheradge. Photography: Alan Lawson.

Cast: Hugh Wakefield, Joan Wyndham, Jack Raine, Elizabeth Jenns, Arthur Chesney, Sara Allgood, Bobbie Comber, Mary Mayfren.

An ex-boxer and a poor girl are helped by a rich writer.

309 Fortune's Child

1919, Vitagraph, 5 reels. Director: Joseph Gleason. Screenplay: Lawrence McCloskey.

Cast: Kempton Greene, Gladys Leslie.

A beautiful girl's pure love for a boxer causes his regeneration.

310 The Fourth Musketeer

1923, R-C Pictures, 5,800 feet. Director: William K. Howard.

Producer: J.G. Caldwell. Photography: William O'Connell.

Cast: Johnny Walker, Eileen Percy, Philo McCullough, Kate Lester, Eddie Gribbon, William Scott, George Stone.

Brian O'Brien (Walker) quits the ring to open up a garage only to find his wife fooling around with another man. He gets the chance to win her back when he foils a jewelry theft.

311 Fright Night

1947, Columbia Pictures, 2 reels. Director: Edward Bernds.

Cast: The Three Stooges, Cy Schindell, Dick Wessel, Harold Brauer, Claire Carleton.

Shemp Howard's first film with the comedy team finds the Stooges as fight managers who learn that they'll be killed if their boxer wins. This was remade in 1955 as **Fling in the Ring.**

312 Game Chicken

1926, British, Frederick White Co., 2,150 feet. Director: Harry B. Parkinson. Screenplay: Andrew Souter.

Cast: Billy Wells.

Boxer Hen Pearce's victory over Joe Berks helps get a lady out of debt.

313 The Gay Corinthian

1924, British, Butcher, 5,300 feet. Director: Arthur Rooke. Screenplay: Eliot Stannard, based on a novel by Ben Bolt.

Cast: Victor McLaglen, Betty Faire, Cameron Carr, Humberton Wright, George Turner, Donald McCardle.

Romance is afoot in this period piece involving a boxer, some gypsies and a girl who's the subject of a bet. It was re-released in a cut version in 1926 as **The Three Wagers.**

314 Gentleman Jim

1942, Warner Brothers, 104 minutes. Director: Raoul Walsh. Producer: Robert Buckner. Screenplay: Vincent Lawrence, Horace McCoy. Photography: Sid Hickox. Editor: Jack Killifer.

Cast: Errol Flynn, Alexis Smith, Jack Carson, Alan Hale, John Loder, William Frawley, Minor Watson, Madeleine Le Beau, Rhys Williams, Arthur Shields, Dorothy Vaughan, Ward Bond.

If you don't mind Hollywood taking liberty with some facts, **Gentleman Jim** is certainly the most thoroughly enjoyable boxing biography ever put on screen.

James J. Corbett, as portrayed by Flynn, is everything but a gentleman as he spends much of the film getting into trouble with his mouth.

Covering his days from the time he was a bank clerk in San Francisco to his championship bout with the great John L. Sullivan, Corbett, according to the film, gets his first big break when he helps a judge out of a jam at an illegal bare knuckle fight.

He eventually works himself into the exclusive Olympic Club where he bests an imported boxing teacher and later a pro. All this while wooing the daughter of a millionaire. The climactic bout in 1892 with John L. is a real dandy.

315 Gentleman Joe Palooka

1946, Monogram, 65 minutes. Director-Screenplay: Cyril Endfield. Producer: Hal E. Chester. Photography: William Sickner. Editor: Ralph Dixon.

Cast: Joe Kirkwood, Jr., Leon Errol, Guy Kibbee, Elyse Knox, Lionel Stander, Stanley Prader, H.B. Warner, Tommy Harmon, Fred Steele.

The famous comic strip boxing hero wins the title early in this one. He's duped by crooked politician Kibbee into fronting for the transfer of some federal land which is actually a coverup for an oil land grab.

When Joe finds out he's been used, he quits the ring in disillusionment until he helps expose the crooks.

Real-life middleweight champ Fred Steele is featured in a cameo role congratulating Joe on winning a fight.

316 The Girl from Monterey

1943, Producers Releasing Corp., 60 minutes. Director: Wallace Fox. Producer: Jack Schwarz. Screenplay: Arthur Hoerl. Story: George Green, Robert Gordon. Photography: Marcel Le Picard. Editor: Robert Grandali.

Cast: Amida, Edgar Kennedy, Veda Ann Borg, Jack La Rue, Terry Frost, Anthony Caruso, Charles Williams, Bryant Washburn, Guy Zanett, Wheeler Oakman.

Don't let the title fool you; **The Girl from Monterey** is a boxing musical set in New York.

Amida manages boxer Caruso, who happens to be her brother. Problem is, she's in love with Frost, another boxer, and doesn't want them to fight but the boxing commission forces them to.

Frost's manager, in the meantime, sets vamp Van Borg on Caruso to keep him out of shape.

317 Glory Alley

1952, Metro Goldwyn Mayer, 73 minutes. Director: Raoul Walsh. Producer: Nicholas Nayfask. Screenplay: Art Cohn. Photography: William Daniels. Editor: Gene Ruggiero.

Cast: Ralph Meeker, Leslie Caron, Kurt Kaszner, Gilbert Roland, John McIntyre, Louis Armstrong, Jack Teagarden, John Indrisano.

Boxer Meeker, who has an old head injury, flees the ring before a middleweight title bout and is branded a coward by the denizens of New Orleans' Glory Alley.

He wins the medal for valor in Korea and pays for an operation to restore the sight to Caron's blind dad, but must still prove he's no coward in the boxing ring.

318 The Glove Slingers

1939, Columbia, 2 reels. Director: Jules White.

Cast: Noah Beery, Jr., Shemp Howard, Paul Hurst, Dorothy Vaughn.

With a little plagiarism of 1934's **Palooka,** this two-reel short inaugurated a series of **Glove Slingers** shorts.

Like the hero in **Palooka,** Beery plays a young man whose father was a boxer and whose mother is set against him following those footsteps into the ring.

Other titles in the series include **Mitt Me Tonight, Glove Affair, Socks Appeal** and **Fresh As a Freshman,** with the casts in a constant state of flux. David Durand, Bill Henry and Dick Hogan were others who portrayed the lead.

319 Glove Taps

1937, Metro Goldwyn Mayer, 1 reel. Director: Gordon Douglas. Producer: Hal Roach. Photography: Art Lloyd. Editor: William Ziegler.

When Alfalfa of Our Gang is challenged to a fight by tough kid Butch, Porky and Buckwheat come to his aid with a loaded glove.

320 The Goat Getter

1925, Rayart Pictures, 5,040 feet. Director: Albert Rogell. Screenplay: Grover Jones. Photography: Lee Garmes.

Cast: Billy Sullivan, Johnny Sinclair, Kathleen Myers, Virginia Vance, Eddie Diggins, William Buckley, Joe Moore.

Sullivan is knocked out by the lightweight champ but follows him around from town to town, trying to get his goat and goad him into a rematch.

He finally gets his chance in Hollywood where the champ is making a movie.

321 Golden Boy

1939, Columbia Pictures, 98 minutes. Director: Rouben

Mamoulian. Producer: William Perlberg. Screenplay: Lewis Meltzer, Daniel Taradash, Sarah Y. Mason, based on the play by Clifford Odets. Photography: Nick Musuraca, Karl Freund. Editor: Otto Meyer.

Cast: William Holden, Barbara Stanwyck, Adolph Menjou, Lee J. Cobb, Sam Levene, Ed Brophy, Beatrice Blinn, Don Beddoe, Joseph Calleia.

The film that propelled Holden to stardom finds him shunning a promising career as a violinist for a career in the ring.

He falls in love with the girlfriend (Stanwyck) of manager Menjou. She at first urges him to keep on fighting; but when she falls in love with him, urges him to quit the dirty racket.

When racketeer Calleia buys his contract and Stanwyck marries Menjou, things get really rough for Holden, who winds up killing an opponent in the ring.

Whereas the original play by Odets ended in suicide, there's a happy ending in the film version.

322 Golden Gloves

1940, Paramount, 66 minutes. Director: Edward Dmytryk. Screenplay: Maxwell Shane, Lewis R. Foster. Photography: Henry Sharp. Editor: Doane Harrison.

Cast: Richard Denning, Jean Cagney, J. Carrol Naish, Robert Paige, William Frawley, Edward S. Brophy, Robert Ryan, George Ernest, David Durand, Sidney Miller, Alec Craig.

Tired of seeing gangsters dominate the boxing game, sportswriter Paige organizes a "clean" boxing tournament.

Villain Naish, however, doesn't take the competition lying down and hires a pro boxer to enter the amateur tournament and ruin it.

It's up to heroine Jean Cagney (Jimmy Cagney's kid sister) to spur Our Hero to victory with the usual between rounds plea.

323 Golden Gloves Story

1950, Eagle Lion, 76 minutes. Director: Felix Feist. Producer: Carl Kreuger. Screenplay: Feist, Joe Ansen. Story: D.D. Beauchamp, William F. Sellers. Photography: John L. Russell, Jr. Editor: William F. Claxton.

Cast: James Dunn, Dewey Martin, Gregg Sherwood, Kevin O'Morrison, Kay Westfall, John "Red" Kullers and Tony Zale, Arch Ward, Johnny Behr, and Issy Kline as themselves.

It's nice boy (O'Morrison) vs. nasty boy (Martin) in the amateur tournament. They're both in love with a referee's daughter and in a break of tradition with the usual portrayal of women in sports films, she chooses nasty boy after he's beaten by O'Morrison but undergoes a personality change.

Clips from real Golden Gloves tournament bouts are featured.

324 The Great Black vs. White Prize Fight

1910, British, Gaumont, 395 feet.

One of innumerable reenactments and burlesques inspired by the Jack Johnson-Jack Jeffries championship bout.

325 The Great Fight at All-Sereno

1910, British, Kineto, 350 feet. Director: Theo Bouwmeester.

Another film inspired by the Johnson-Jeffries match.

326 The Great Fight for the Championship in Our Court

1911, British, Urban Trading Co., 355 feet.

A burlesque of the Jack Johnson-Wells fight.

327 The Great John L.

1945, United Artists, 96 minutes. Director: Frank Tuttle. Producers: Frank R. Mastroly, James Edward Grant. Screenplay: Grant. Fight Sequences: John Indrisano. Photography: James Van Trees. Editor: Theodore Bellinger.

Cast: Greg McClure, Linda Darnell, Barbara Britton, Leo Sullivan, Otto Kruger, Wallace Ford, George Matthews, Robert Barrat, J.M. Kerrigan, Richard Martin.

McClure, who had been a Warner Brothers extra, got his big shot at stardom (and blew it) in this screen biography of John L. Sullivan.

Starting out as a boastful strong boy in Boston, he rises to boxing champ in the 1880's and later becomes a drunk after being dethroned, before lifting himself up again and becoming a proponent of clean living.

328 Great Scout and Cathouse Thursday

1976, American-International, 102 minutes, Color. Director: Don Taylor. Producers: Jules Buck, David Korda. Screenplay: Richard Shapiro. Photography: Alex Phillips, Jr. Editor: Sheldon Kahn.

Cast: Lee Marvin, Oliver Reed, Robert Culp, Elizabeth Ashley, Strother Martin, Sylvia Miles, Kay Lenz, Howard Platt.

Marvin and Reed seek revenge on their former partner Culp in the Old West. They plot to steal the proceeds from a boxing match.

329 The Great White Hope

1970, 20th Century Fox, 103 minutes, Color. Director: Martin Ritt. Producer: Lawrence Turnman. Screenplay: Howard Sackler. Photography: Burnett Guffey. Editor: William Reynolds.

Cast: James Earl Jones, Jane Alexander, Lou Gilbert, Joel Fluellen, Chester Morris, Robert Webber, Marlene Warfield, R.G. Armstrong, Hal Holbrook, Beah Richards, Moses Gunn, Lloyd Gough, Scatman Crothers.

Based on the successful Broadway play, **The Great White Hope** is a thinly disguised dramatization of the life of Jack Johnson, the first black heavyweight champ, although the main character's name here is Jack Jefferson.

After winning the crown in 1910, he runs afoul of bigots by taking a white mistress and is sentenced to three years in prison in Illinois.

Jefferson (Jones) escapes to Canada while disguised as a member of a black baseball team and winds up in Europe. In Paris, he finds no one has nerve enough to face him after he gives a foe a savage beating, and he's reduced to humiliating cabaret roles in Germany.

After his mistress drowns herself, he's offered a reduction in his prison sentence if he'll take a dive during a title bout with a white challenger in Havana.

We won't give away the ending here, but we will say it differs from the facts of Johnson's life.

330 The Great White Way

1924, Goldwyn-Cosmopolitan Distributing Co., 9,800-10,000 feet. Director: E. Mason Hopper. Scenario: L. Dayle. Adaptation: Luther Reed. Story: H.C. Witwer. Photography: Harold Wenstrom. Editor: Walter Futter.

Cast: Oscar Shaw, Anita Stewart, Tom Lewis, T. Roy Barnes, Dore Davidson, Ned Wayburn, Harry Watson, G.L. "Tex" Rickard, Pete Hartley, J.W. McGurk, Earle Sande, Kid Broad, Johnny Gallagher.

A number of well-known sports, theater, and newspaper people appear as themselves in this comedy which was remade in 1936 as **Cain and Mabel** with Clark Gable and Marion Davies.

They're played here by Shaw and Stewart as a boxer and a chorus dancer respectively who are victimized by a press agent (Barnes) who invents a romance between the two. Naturally, they eventually do fall in love.

Some of the more well-known personalities appearing as themselves are Witwer, Damon

Runyon, George McManus (of "Bringing Up Father" fame) and Winsor McKay.

331 The Greatest

1977, Columbia Pictures, 101-114 minutes, Color. Director: Tom Gries. Producer: John Marshall. Screenplay: Ring Lardner, Jr., based on "The Greatest: My Own Story" by Muhammad Ali, Herbert Muhammad, Richard Durham. Photography: Harry Stradling, Jr. Editor: Byron Brandt.

Cast: Muhammad Ali, Ernest Borgnine, Lloyd Haynes, John Marley, Robert Duvall, David Huddleston, Ben Johnson, James Earl Jones, Dina Merrill, Paul Winfield, Arthur Adams, Skip Homeier, Phillip MacAllister, Roger Mosley.

The life of Muhammad Ali (nee Cassius Clay, Jr.) has been the subject of so many screen documentaries, it's only natural that there would be a dramatized account starring Ali himself.

With actual footage from Ali's fights, the film traces his career from his formal training under Dundee to his refusal to be inducted in the Army and his bout with George Foreman.

332 Hammer

1972, United Artists, 92 minutes, Color. Director: Bruce Clark. Producer: Al Adamson. Screenplay: Charles Johnson. Photography: Bob Steadman.

Cast: Fred Williamson, Bernie Hamilton, Vonetta McGee, William Smith, Charles Lampkin, Elizabeth Harding, Mel Stewart.

Black boxer Williamson works his way up from the docks to a title contender through Big Sid (Lampkin) a local crime czar. He's ultimately told he must throw a fight or a mob hit man (Smith) will kill his girl.

333 The Happy Warrior

1917, Harma, 3,468 feet. Director: F. Martin Thornton. Story: A.S.M. Hutchinson.

Cast: James Knight, Evelyn Boucher, Joan Legge, Minna Grey, Harry Lorraine, Sydney Lewis Ransome, H. Agar Lyons, Leslie Howard, Roy Byford, Jeff Barlow.

A circus boxer has grown up unaware that he's the rightful heir to a title. When he learns of his heritage, he is torn between accepting it or letting his friend become the new lord.

334 The Happy Warrior

1925, Vitagraph, 7,865 feet. Director: J. Stuart Blackton. Scenario: Marian Constance. Story: A.S.M. Hutchinson. Photography: Paul Allen.

Cast: Malcolm McGregor, Alice Calhoun, Mary Alden, Anders Randolf, Olive Borden, Gardner James, Otto Matieson, Wilfred North, Eulalie Jensen, Andree Tourneur.

A remake of the 1917 film about a boxer who is unaware that he's the rightful Lord Bordon.

335 Hard Times (aka **The Streetfighter**)

1975, Columbia, 92 minutes. Director: Walter Hill. Producer: Lawrence Gordon. Screenplay: Hill, Bryan Gindorff, Bruce Henstell. Photography: Philip Lathrop. Editor: Roger Spottiswoode.

Cast: Charles Bronson, James Coburn, Jill Ireland, Strother Martin, Maggie Blyde, Michael McGuire, Robert Tessier, Nick Dimitri.

Set in 1930's New Orleans, hobo Bronson ties in with gambler Coburn to make a lot of money off Bronson's fists in illegal bare knuckles fights.

The combination of Bronson's drawing power at the box office (particularly in Europe) and Hill's intense visual style made this a big hit, and its hard-hitting fights perhaps inspired the bare fist battles in Clint Eastwood's **Every Which Way but Loose** and **Any Which Way You Can.**

336 The Harder They Fall

1956, Columbia, 109 minutes. Director: Mark Robson. Producer: Philip Yordan. Screenplay: Yordan, based on the novel by Budd Schulberg. Photography: Burnett Guffey. Editor: Jerome Thomas.

Cast: Humphrey Bogart, Rod Steiger, Jan Sterling, Mike Lane, Max Baer, Jersey Joe Walcott, Edward Andrews, Harold J. Stone, Carlos Montalban, Nehemiah Persoff, Felice Orlandi, Herbie Faye, Joe Greb, Abel Fernandez.

Along with **Body and Soul** and **Champion, The Harder They Fall** forms part of the big three exposés of the savage world of boxing with **Requiem for a Heavyweight** running a close fourth. Loosely based on the career of Primo Carnera, **The Harder They Fall** is noteworthy for its extremely brutal boxing scenes.

A huge South American boxer named Toro Moreno (Lane) is brought to the United States by heartless manager Steiger and is built up into a contender and gate attraction through a series of fixed fights.

Sports columnist Eddie Wallis (Bogart), who needs the money, helps with the buildup even though he knows Moreno isn't really that good.

Baer portrays Buddy Brannen, a boxer eager to beat Moreno, while Jersey Joe Walcott portrays a sympathetic trainer.

337 He Couldn't Take It

1934, Monogram, 65 minutes. Director: William Nigh. Screenplay: Dore Schary.

Cast: Ray Walker, Virginia Cherrill, George E. Stone, Stanley Fields, Dorothy Granger, Jane Darwell, Paul Porcasi.

A good-for-nothing tries out boxing, bus driving and other occupations before he finally accomplishes something by helping to expose a mob attorney.

338 He Would Be an Athlete

1907, French, Urban Eclipse, 491 feet.

The hero of the title tries out boxing, rugby and steeplechasing only to wind up heavily bandaged in bed.

339 The Heart of a Man

1959, British, Everest, 92 minutes. Director: Herbert Wilcox. Screenplay: Jack Trevor. Story: Pamela Bower.

Cast: Frankie Vaughan, Anne Heywood, Tony Britton, Anthony Newley, George Rose, Hogan "Kid" Bussey.

A former seaman tries a number of jobs to earn needed money, including trying his hand as a boxer.

340 Heart Punch

1915, Universal. Director-Screenplay: Stuart Paton.

Cast: Jess Willard, Katherine Lee, Marie Wierman, Bobby Vernon, Bert Roach, Howard Crampton, Allan Holubar.

With heavyweight Jess Willard slated for a big title bout with Jack Johnson, Universal executives believed he would prove a natural drawing card at the box office.

So for the fee of $1,000, they paid him to star in **Heart Punch** in which he portrays a boxer whose wife wants him to quit. It's up to their daughter to bring the two together again.

Willard's real-life handlers, Tom Jones and Jack Curley, were also given roles. Production was hampered by the insistence of Willard's managers that their boxer put in only an 8 a.m. to 5 p.m. day.

341 Heart Punch

1932, Mayfair, 62 minutes. Director: Breezy Eason. Producer: Fanchon Royer. Story: Frank Howard Clark. Photography: George Meehan. Editor: Jeanne Spencer.

Cast: Lloyd Hughes, Wheeler Oakman, Marion Schilling, George

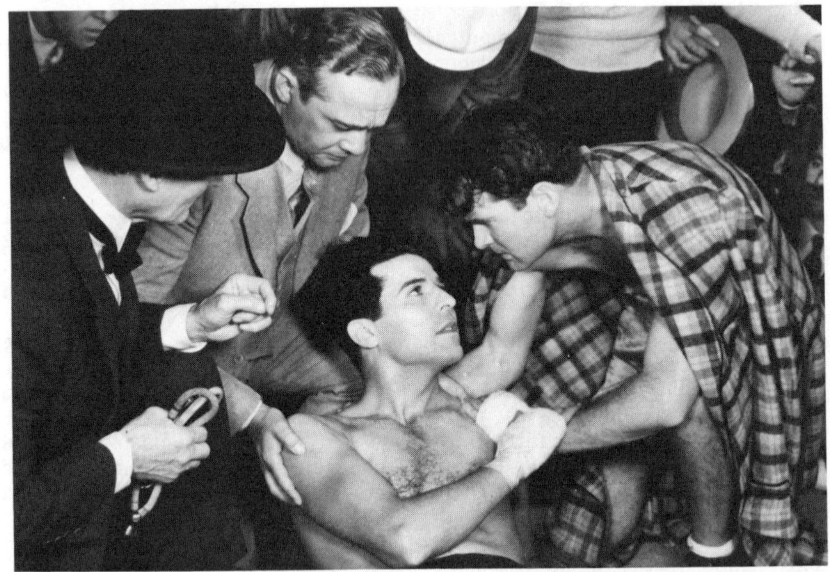

A dramatic moment from the 1932 Mayfair production of Heart Punch. (The Museum of Modern Art/Film Stills Archive.)

Lewis, Mae Busch, Walter Miller, Gordon De Main, James Leong.

A boxer who killed his foe in the ring with a punch to the heart finds himself falling in love with the dead man's sister.

342 Her Father Said No

1927, R-C Pictures, 6,308 feet. Director: Jack McKeown. Story: H.C. Witwer. Photography: Lyman Broening.

Cast: Danny O'Shea, Mary Brian, Al Cooke, Kit Guard, John Steppling, Frankie Darro, Gene Stone, Betty Caldwell.

A boxer who opens a resort for fat millionaires provides the laughs in this sports comedy. Boxer O'Shea is cheated out of a victory by a referee and is spurned by his sweetheart's father.

The boxer then gives up his career to elope with his girlfriend and open up the spa, which is attended by her father, who brings along his own choice for a son-in-law, not knowing that his daughter has already married.

343 Here Comes Mr. Jordan

1941, Columbia, 93 minutes. Director: Alexander Hall. Producer: Everett Riskin. Screenplay: Seton I. Miller, Sidney Buchman, based on a play by Harry Segall. Photography: Joseph Walker. Editor: Viola Lawrence.

Cast: Robert Montgomery, Claude Rains, Evelyn Keyes, Edward Everett Horton, Rita Johnson, James Gleason, John Emery, Donald MacBride, Don Costello, Benny Rubin, Lloyd Bridges, Tom Hanlon, John Kerns.

An all-time comedy-fantasy classic, **Here Comes Mr. Jordan** was nominated for the Academy Award for best picture while Montgomery's portrayal of boxer Joe Pendleton got him a nomination for best actor. It did win the Oscar for best screenplay.

Pendleton, who enjoys flying airplanes and playing the saxophone when he isn't fighting, finds himself in heaven after his plane crashes; but it seems there's a big mistake. Messenger 7013 (Horton) has inadvertently claimed Pendleton's body 50 years before schedule; and it's up to Mr. Jordan (Rains), 7013's boss, to make amends.

The problem is, Pendleton's manager, Max Corkle (Gleason, who else?), has already had the body cremated; and the boxer refuses an offer to be reborn.

After a long search for a body in good physical condition to place Pendleton's soul in, he winds up in the body of Bruce Farnsworth, a crooked millionaire who had just been drowned by his wife and his private secretary.

He falls in love with Bette Logan (Keyes), whose father has landed in trouble with the law because of Farnsworth's crooked scheming. He gets her dad out of trouble and asks her if she will always be able to recognize him by looking in his eyes.

He also, with great difficulty and with the aid of a saxophone, convinces Corkle who he really is so he can get into shape for a title fight.

But Farnsworth's body is murdered again by his wife and secretary; and this time Pendleton lands in the body of Murdoch, his rival, who is boxing the champ because Our Hero is now dead. During the bout, Murdoch is shot by gangsters and falls to the canvas, only to get up with Pendleton's soul to win the fight.

He must then convince Betty of his identity and does so by looking into her eyes. Mr. Jordan erases his memory of what has happened, but the two still feel they've met.

A non-sports sequel, **Down to Earth,** was made in 1947 with Rita Hayworth in the starring role. Rains repeated his role as Mr. Jordan, and Gleason portrayed a theatrical manager.

A 1978 remake, **Heaven Can Wait,** changed the milieu from the boxing ring to the football field and starred Warren Beatty and Julie Christie.

344 High and Handsome

1925, R-C Pictures, 5,669 feet. Director: Harry Garson. Scenario: Rex Taylor. Story: Gerald Beaumont. Photography: Ernest Hallor.

Cast: Maurice B. Flynn, Ethel Shannon, Tom Kennedy, Ralph McCullough, Jean Perry, Marjorie Bonner, John Gough.

Cop Joe Hanrahan (Flynn) is suspended from the force for a public fight with his rival for a girl. A shady fight promoter, who had earlier been warned by Hanrahan about the bad conditions at his arena, sees the opportunity to promote a boxing match between the two rivals.

During the fight, the stands collapse; and we don't really have to tell you who wins the bout and the girl, do we?

345 High Hats and Low Brows

1932, RKO-Pathe, 18 minutes. Director: Harry Sweet. Screenplay: Ralph Ceder. Story: Arthur "Bugs" Baer. Editor: Fred Maguire.

Cast: Harry Gribbon, James Gleason, Mae Busch, Gertrude Astor.

Based on one of Baer's Ruff-town Stories, this one has a boxer attending a society affair being KO'd by the butler.

346 His Last Fight

1914, Vitagraph, 731 feet. Director-Screenplay: Ralph Ince.

Cast: Ralph Ince, Anita Stewart, Gladden James.

A former boxing champion who has taken a job as first mate on an ocean liner gives his life defending a young couple on their honeymoon.

347 His Rise to Fame

1927, Excellent Pictures, 5,790 feet. Director: Bernard

McEveety. Story: Victoria Moore. Photography: Marcel Le Picard.

Cast: George Walsh, Peggy Shaw, Bradley Barker, Mildred Reardon, Martha Petelle, William Nally, Ivan Linow.

Lazy Jerry Drake (Walsh), who has never done anything worthwhile in his life, decides to become a boxer after a shady boxing promoter (Barker) has one of his fighters beat him up over the dancer they both desire (Shaw).

He becomes a title contender, rescues his girl from the villains and goes on to the title fight.

348 Hogan's Alley

1925, Warner Brothers, 6,875 feet. Director: Roy Del Ruth. Adaptation: Darryl Francis Zanuck. Story: Gregory Rogers. Photography: Charles Van Enger. Editor: Clarence Kolster.

Cast: Monte Blue, Patsy Ruth Miller, Willard Louis, Ben Turpin, Louise Fazenda, Charles Conklin, Max Davidson, Herbert Spencer, Frank Hagney, Nigel Barrie, Frank Bond.

Lefty O'Brien (Blue) defeats Battling Savage (Hagney) for the boxing title, but can't win over the father of his sweetheart, Patsy Ryan (Miller), who lives in an Eastside neighborhood of New York known as Hogan's Alley.

We won't go into all the melodramatic plot twists and turns except to say that the climax involves Our Hero attempting to rescue his beloved from a runaway train by using an airplane.

349 Hold Everything

1930, Warner Brothers, 7,513 feet. Director: Roy Del Ruth. Screenplay: Robert Lord. Story: Buddy De Sylva, John McGowan, Ray Henderson, Lew Brown. Photography: Dev Jennings. Editor: William Holmes.

Cast: Joe E. Brown, Georges Carpentier, Winnie Lightner, Sally O'Neil, Edmund Breese, Bert Roach, Jack Curtis, Jimmy Quinn, Dorothy Revier, Tony Stabeneau.

Brown plays Ging Schiner, a boxer scheduled to appear in a preliminary to the heavyweight bout featuring Georges La Verne (Carpentier), in this early musical comedy.

The manager of Bob Morgan (Stabeneau), La Verne's opponent, hires a hood to put La Verne out of the way when his offer to fix the fight is refused; but Schiner saves the day and with some romantic complications out of the way, it's on to the two big fights.

350 The Hollywood Stadium Mystery

1938, Republic, 66 minutes. Director: David Howard. Producer: Armand Schaefer. Story: Stuart Palmer. Photography: Ernest Miller. Editor: Edward Mann.

Cast: Neil Hamilton, Evelyn Venable, Jimmy Wallington, Barbara Pepper, Lucien Littlefield, Lynn Roberts, Reed Hadley, Smiley Burnette.

The murder of sporting world figures was a popular Grade B film topic in the 1930's. Already, there had been films in which baseball players, football players, softball players and jockeys had been murdered in front of the fans, so why not boxing? Here the fighter is killed just as he's about to enter the ring with the champ. We won't tell whodunnit.

The murder of a soccer star would be next in England's **The Arsenal Stadium Mystery** in 1939.

351 Hooks and Jabs

1933, Educational Films, 2 reels. Director: Arvid E. Gillstrom.

Cast: Harry Langdon, Nell O'Day, William Irving, Frank Moran, Vernon Dent.

Comedian Langdon is mistakenly taken for a boxer in this short.

352 Hot News

1953, Allied Artists, 61 minutes. Director: Edward Bernds. Producer: Ben Schwalb. Screenplay: Charles R. Marion, Elwood Ullman. Photography: Carl Guthrie. Editor: Bruce B. Pierce.

Cast: Stanley Clements, Gloria Henry, Ted de Corsia, Veda Ann Borg, Scotty Beckett, Paul Bryar, Myron Healy, Hal Baylor.

When Healy is killed during a fight, boxer-turned-sports columnist Clements wages a crusade to break up de Corsia's gambling ring.

Henry portrays his editor and girlfriend.

353 House of Temperly

1914, British, London Film Co., 4,500 feet. Director: Howard Shaw. Story: Arthur Conan Doyle.

Cast: Charles Maude, Ben Webster, Lillian Logan, Charles Buck, Edward O'Neil, Wyndham Guise, Cecil Morton York.

The House of Temperly faces ruin unless Sir Charles' fighter can win a $100,000 match, but the villainous Sir John has the boxer kidnapped.

Sir Charles's brother must step into the ring himself and try to save the day.

354 How Winky Fought for a Bride

1914, British, Bamforth, 990 feet. Director: Cecil Birch.

One of the "Winky" short comedy film series starring Reggie Switz. Here, he gets a boxer to fight his rival for a girl.

355 The Idol of Millions

1936, Noel, 22 minutes. Compiled by: Leon Britton.

Narrator: Thornton Fisher.

A documentary about boxing great Jack Dempsey, ending with the opening of his New York restaurant.

356 Impersonation of Britt-Nelson Fight

1905, Lubin, 177 feet.

In the early days of filmmaking, it was quite common to hire lookalikes for recreations of big fights and to film the action in such a way as if it looked like the real thing. Here, the Battling Nelson-Jimmy Britt fight is restaged.

357 In the Blood

1923, British, Butcher, 6,100 feet. Director: Walter West. Scenario: J. Bertram Brown. Story: Andrew Soutar.

Cast: Victor McLaglen, Lillian Douglas, Cecil Morton York, Kenneth McLaglen, Clifford McLaglen, John Glidsen.

Framed by his stepmother for a theft, a man must enter the boxing ring when his father's fighter is drugged by the villains in this period piece.

358 In This Corner

1948, Eagle Lion, 62 minutes. Director: Charles F. Riesner. Producer: David L. Stephenson. Screenplay: Burk Symond, Fred Niblo, Jr. Photography: Guy Roe. Editor: Norman Colbert.

Cast: Scott Brady, Anabel Shaw, Jimmy Millican, Mary Meade, Charles D. Brown, Johnny Indrisano, Robert Bice, John Doucette.

Navy vet Brady, who once accidentally killed a pal with a punch, becomes a boxer.

When he refuses to go for a fixed fight, his manager (Millican) makes it appear as if Brady has killed his sparring partner with a punch. That reawakens Brady's mental block and hampers his fighting while his girlfriend seeks out the supposedly dead sparring partner.

359 Invitation to Happiness

1939, Paramount, 97 minutes. Director-Producer: Wesley Ruggles. Screenplay: Claude Binyon. Story: Mark Jerome. Photography: Leo Tover. Editor: Alma Macrorie.

Cast: Fred MacMurray, Irene Dunne, Charlie Ruggles, Billy Cook, William Collier, Sr., Marion Martin, Oscar O'Shea, Eddie Hogan.

Here's a nice little boxing film that's a little different. The beginning is pretty routine—socialite Dunne falls for the egotistical boxer her father has just purchased the contract of.

They marry, and while his son is being born, he's busy fighting in Boston. Ten years later, he's still boxing and has a shot at the title; but when he comes home for a visit he finds he's a total stranger to his son because he's been away most of the time.

MacMurray, who portrays the boxer, must decide what's most important for him—his career or his family's love.

360 The Irish in Us

1935, Warner Brothers, 84 minutes. Director: Lloyd Bacon. Story: Frank Orsatti. Screenplay: Earl Baldwin. Photography: George Barnes.

Cast: James Cagney, Pat O'Brien, Olivia DeHavilland, Frank McHugh, Allen Jenkins, Mary Gordon, J. Farrell MacDonald, Thomas Jackson, Harvey Perry.

A change of pace comedy for Cagney in which he portrays a fight manager who has two brothers—a cop (O'Brien) and a fireman (McHugh).

Cagney takes on a fighter with the monicker Carbarn Hammerschlog (Jenkins), but he goes on a drunken binge with McHugh before the big bout and Cagney must take his place in the ring.

361 The Iron Man

1931, Universal, 72 minutes. Director: Tod Browning. Producer: Carl Laemmle, Jr. Screenplay: Francis E. Faragoh, based on a novel by W.R. Burnett.

Cast: Lew Ayres, Robert Armstrong, Jean Harlow, John Miljan, Eddie Dillon, Mike Donlin, Ned Sparks, Sam Blum, Morris Cohan.

A boxer's worst enemy is his cheating wife in this hit boxing film which was remade in 1937 as **Some Blondes Are Dangerous** and as **Iron Man** again in 1951.

Ayres plays a lightweight champ who does fine in the ring as long as he stays away from his unfaithful wife (Harlow), who manages to split up the boxer and his manager (Armstrong). The climactic fight pits Ayres against his old manager's new boxer.

Villainous John Miljan socks Harlow in the jaw, a shocking scene to 1931 audiences.

362 The Iron Man

1951, Universal-International, 82 minutes. Director: Joseph Pevney. Producer: Aaron Rosenberg. Screenplay: George Zuckerman, Borden Chase. Story: W.R. Burnett. Photography: Carl Guthrie. Editor: Russell Schoengarth.

Cast: Jeff Chandler, Evelyn Keyes, Stephen McNally, Joyce Holden, Rock Hudson, Jim Backus, Jim Arness, Steve Martin, Doris Cole, Mushy Callahan.

Coal miner Coke Mason (Chandler) becomes a boxer so he can earn enough money to open up a radio shop in this much-changed remake of the 1931 **Iron Man** and 1937's **Some Blondes Are Dangerous.**

His savagery in the ring earns him the disdain of fight fans; and when his manager tries to fix a fight, he drops him.

Meanwhile, vamp Holden is out to steal his heart from Evelyn Keyes, as Mason must learn to control his killer style in the ring.

363 Is Zat So?

1927, Fox Film Corp., 6,950 feet. Director: Alfred E. Green. Scenario: Philip Klein. Photography: George Schneidermann.

Cast: George O'Brien, Edmund

Lowe, Douglas Fairbanks, Jr., Kathryn Perry, Cyril Chadwick, Doris Lloyd, Jack Herrick, Philippe De Lacy, Richard Maitland.

Based on a comedy by James Gleason and Richard Taber, it concerns the friendship and romantic affairs of fight manager Hap Hurley (Lowe), boxer Chick Cowan (O'Brien) and millionaire Blackburn (Fairbanks). It was remade in 1935 as **Two Fisted.**

364 Jack Johnson

1970, Big Fights, Inc., 90 minutes. Director: William Cayton. Producer: Jim Jacobs. Script: Al Bodian. Photography: Larry Garinger. Editor: John Dandre.

Narration: Kevin Kennedy. Jack Johnson's Voice: Brock Peters.

A far-ranging documentary on the life of the first black heavyweight champ contains much rare footage including his big fight with James Jeffries in 1910, his loss in Havana to Jess Willard in 1915, his race with Barney Olfield, his marriages to white women, his career in Hollywood and his exile in Europe.

There's also footage with actor Victor McLaglen, who once fought Johnson.

365 Jealousy

1934, Columbia, 66 minutes. Director: Roy William Neill. Screenplay: J.M. March, Kubec Glasman. Story: Argyle Campbell. Photography: John Stumar.

Cast: George Murphy, Nancy Carroll, Donald Cook, Raymond Walburn, Arthur Hohl, Inez Courtney.

The trick ending of **Jealousy** has divided critics and viewers alike in their opinion of whether it ruined the film. Although it's rarely screened today, prints are available from several sources, so we won't give away that ending.

A jealous boxer knocks out his girl's boss. She marries the fighter only on the condition that he'll never get that jealous again; but when the couple experience financial difficulties, she goes to work for her old boss again.

It's all perfectly innocent, but the boxer finds the pair in a hotel room and kills the employer. Just as the jury is about to bring in a verdict of "not guilty," the boxer confesses.

As he's walking to the last mile...

366 Joe Louis Story

1953, United Artists, 88 minutes. Director: Robert Gordon. Producer: Sterling Silliphant. Screenplay: Robert Sylvester. Photography: Joseph Brun. Editor: David Kummins.

Cast: Coley Wallace, Paul Stewart, Hilda Simms, James Edward, John Marley, Ossie Davis, Dotts Johnson, Evelyn Ellis, Carl Rocky Latimer, John Marriott, P. Jay Sidney, Buddy Thorpe, Ruby Goldstein.

Ask ten people who portrayed Joe Louis in his screen biography, and we'll bet you at least six of them will say the boxing great portrayed himself. We tried it. That's how convincing Coley Wallace was in the lead.

Mixing in some actual fight footage, it's done in flashback style, with sportswriter Stewart serving as narrator, the usual style for a 1950s sports biography.

The boxing highlights of the film are his two bouts with Max Schmelling—the first one which he lost and the rematch he won. The last bout dramatized is his 1951 defeat at the hands of Rocky Marciano.

367 Joe Palooka, Champ

1946, Monogram, 72 minutes. Director: Reginald LeBorg. Producer: Hal E. Chester. Screenplay: George Moskov, Albert de Pina. Story: Chester, based on the comic strip by Ham Fisher. Photography: Ken Kline.

Cast: Joe Kirkwood, Jr., Leon Errol, Elyse Knox, Eduardo

Ciannelli, Joe Sawyer, Elisha Cook, Jr., Saul McDaniel, Robert Kent, Sarah Padden, Michael Mark, Lou Nova, Jimmy McLarnin.

Cameos: Joe Louis, Manuel Ortiz, Ceferino Garcia, Henry Armstrong.

The first depiction of the comic strip boxer on screen was 1934's **Palooka** with Stu Erwin and Jimmy Durante. Also in the 1930's, there was a series of Joe Palooka shorts.

Joe Palooka, Champ began a popular Monogram series which ran until 1951. As this is the opening episode, Palooka (Kirkwood) is discovered by manager Knobby Walsh (Errol) and built up into a title contender despite the efforts of gangsters led by Ciannelli.

368 Joe Palooka in Humphrey Takes a Chance

1950, Monogram, 62 minutes. Director: Jean Yarbrough. Producer: Hal E. Chester. Screenplay: Henry Blankfort. Photography: William Sickner. Editor: Edward J. Kay.

Cast: Joe Kirkwood, Leon Errol, Gil Lamb, Tom Neal, Lois Collier, Jack Kirkwood, Andrew Tombes, Robert Coogan, Tim Ryan, Mary Happy, Chester Conklin, Heinie Conklin.

Palooka's pal Humphrey is involved with a crooked fight promoter (Neal) and his crooked politician pals in this series entry which is highlighted by a pie-throwing fight near the end.

369 Joe Palooka in the Big Fight

1949, Monogram, 66 minutes. Director: Cyril Endfield. Producer: Hal E. Chester. Screenplay: Stanley Prager. Photography: Mack Stengler. Editor: Fred Maguire.

Cast: Joe Kirkwood, Leon Errol, Lina Romay, David Bruce, Lyle Talbot, Eddie Gribbon, George O'Hanlon, Virginia Welles, Greg McClure, Taylor Holmes, Frank Fenton, Jack Roper.

Palooka is set up as a drunk on the eve of a big fight by a crooked gang led by sports columnist Bruce. Later, he's framed for the murder of a girl who wanted to spill the beans on the racket to Joe, and he's got to track down the real culprits himself.

370 Joe Palooka in the Counterpunch

1949, Monogram, 65 minutes. Director: Reginald LeBorg. Producer: Hal E. Chester. Screenplay: Henry Blankfort, Cyril Endfield. Photography: Otho Lovering.

Cast: Joe Kirkwood, Leon Errol, Elyse Knox, Sheila Ryan, Eddie Gribbon, Douglas Fowley, Douglas Dumbrille, Joe Herrera, John Indrisano, Marcel Journet, Walter Sande.

Palooka helps a federal agent crack a counterfeiting ring while aboard a ship heading for South America.

He later has to fight the Latin American champion with a hand he injured fighting the gang.

371 Joe Palooka in the Squared Circle

1950, Monogram, 63 minutes. Director: Reginald LeBorg. Producer: Hal E. Chester. Screenplay: Jan Jeffrey. Story: B.F. Melzer. Photography: Mike Picard.

Cast: Joe Kirkwood, James Gleason, Lois Hall, Edgar Barrier, Myrna Dell, Robert Coogan, Dan Seymour, Charles Halton, Frank Jenks, Greg McClure, Eddie Gribbon, Jack Roper.

Palooka witnesses a mob killing and, taking his story to the newspapers, declares war against crime with the gangsters out for his scalp.

In the title bout, Joe must fight off the effects of being drugged as well as elude the punches of his opponent.

372 Joe Palooka in the Triple Cross

1951, Monogram, 60 minutes. Director: Reginald LeBorg. Producer: Hal E. Chester. Screenplay: Jan Jeffrey. Story: Harold Bancroft. Photography: William Sickner.

Cast: Joe Kirkwood, James Gleason, Cathy Downs, John Emery, Steve Brodie, Don Harvey, Rufe Davis, Jimmy Wallington, Mary Young, Eddie Gribbon, Sid Tomack.

The series finale has Knobby Walsh (by now played by James Gleason) and Joe's wife (Downs) kidnapped by crooks who want Palooka to take a dive. One of the male villains disguises himself as Joe's aunt.

In the boxing finale, Joe is knocked out of the ring, but manages to punch out one of the heavies and climb back into the ring before the count of ten.

373 Joe Palooka in Winner Take All

1948, Monogram, 64 minutes. Director: Reginald LeBorg. Producer: Hal E. Chester. Screenplay: Stanley Rubin. Fights staged by: John Indrisano. Photography: William Sickner. Editor: Otho Lovering.

Cast: Joe Kirkwood, Elyse Knox, Stanley Clements, William Frawley, John Shelton, MaryBeth Hughes, Sheldon Leonard, Frank Jenks, Lyle Talbot, Jack Roper, Eddie Gribbon, Big Ben Moroz, Hal Fieberling.

Palooka battles 7-footer Moroz and later Fieberling for the championship. In between, he must foil a kidnapping plot by gamblers who want him to throw a match.

374 Joe Palooka Meets Humphrey

1950, Monogram, 65 minutes. Director: Jean Yarbrough. Producer: Hal E. Chester. Screenplay: Henry Blankfort. Photography: William Sickner. Editor: Otho Lovering.

Cast: Joe Kirkwood, Leon Errol, Robert Coogan, Jerome Cowan, Joe Besser, Don McGuire, Pamela Blake, Donald McBride, Eddie Gribbon, Clem Bevans, Frank Sully.

Palooka faces simple-minded Humphrey in a charity bout while on his honeymoon and the two become good friends.

375 Keep Fit

1937, British, Associated British, 82 minutes. Director-Screenplay: Antony Kimmins, Austin Melford. Producer: Basil Dean. Photography: John W. Boyle.

Cast: George Formby, Kay Walsh, Gus McNaughton, Edmund Breon, George Benson, Evelyn Roberts, Denier Warren, Hal Walters, Leo Franklyn.

Bumbling comic Formby this time is a department store barber who must watch a muscleman in a number of competitions for the love of a manicurist.

Good triumphs over brawn in the boxing match finale.

376 Keep Punching

1939. Director: John Clein.

Cast: Henry Armstrong, Canada Lee, Dooley Wilson, Alvin Childress, Francina Everett.

A black boxer is wooed away by a temptress, but the good woman in his life wins him back in time for him to be in shape for the big bout.

377 Kelly the Second

1936, Metro Goldwyn Mayer, 70-85 minutes. Director: Gus Meins. Producer: Hal Roach. Story: Jeff Moffitt, William Terhune. Adaptation: Jack Jeune, Gordon Douglas. Photography: Art Lloyd.

Cast: Patsy Kelly, Guinn "Big Boy" Williams, Pert Kelton, Charley Chase, Edward Brophy, Harold Huber, Max Rosenbloom, Billy Gilbert.

A trucker who excels at street fights becomes a pro boxer under the tutelage of a woman (Kelly) in this rarely-screened-today MGM comedy.

Williams, as the boxer, must deal with his huge appetite as well as his ring foe Rosenbloom.

378 Kent the Fighting Man

1916, British, Gaumont, 5,500 feet. Director: A.E. Coleby. Scenario: Rowland Talbot. Story: George Edgar.

Cast: Billy Wells, Hetty Payne, A.E. Coleby, Arthur Rooke, Charles Vane, Sidney Bland, Frank Dane, Nelson Phillips, Harry Lofting, Fred Drummond, Tom Coventry.

Bombardier Billy Wells is cast as a disowned gambler who becomes a top boxer.

379 The Kid Comes Back

1938, Warner Brothers, 61 minutes. Director: B. Reeves Eason. Producer: Bryan Foy. Screenplay: George Bricker. Story: E.J. Flanagan. Photography: Arthur Edeson.

Cast: Wayne Morris, Barton MacLane, Dickie Jones, June Travis, Max Rosenbloom, Joseph Crehan, Frank Otto.

Morris, who was a big hit as the boxer in 1937's **Kid Galahad,** is cast this time as a young street fighter who's taken under the wing by vet boxer MacLane.

MacLane loses his chance at a title fight when the champ retires, but soon finds himself lined up against his protege for the championship.

By now, however, Morris is in love with MacLane's daughter and is quite fond of the old man, so he refuses to fight him and has to be goaded into the match.

Who will win?

380 Kid Dynamite (aka **Queen of Broadway)**

1943, Monogram, 73 minutes. Director: Wallace Fox. Producers: Sam Katzman, Jack Dietz. Screenplay: Gerald Schnitzer. Story: Paul Ernst. Photography: Mack Stengler. Editor: Carl Pierson.

Cast: Leo Gorcey, Huntz Hall, Bobby Jordan, Gabriel Dell, Pamela Blake, Sammy Morrison, Benny Bartlett, Dave Durand.

The East Side Kids are in action again, with Gorcey slated to battle the champ of the West Side before being kidnapped. Jordan must step in to take his place in the ring.

381 The Kid from Brooklyn

1946, RKO Radio Pictures, 114 minutes. Color. Director: Norman Z. McLeod. Producer: Samuel Goldwyn. Screenplay: Don Hartman and Melville Shaverson, based on the 1936 screenplay **The Milky Way** by Grover Jones, Frank Butler and Richard Connell and the play by Lynn Root and Harry Clork. Photography: Gregg Toland. Editor: Daniel Mandell.

Cast: Danny Kaye, Virginia Mayo, Vera-Ellen, Steve Cochran, Eve Arden, Walter Abel, Lionel Stander, Fay Bainter, Clarence Kolb, Victor Cutler, Charles Cane, Jerome Cowan, Don Wilson, Johnny Downs, Knox Manning, Kay Thompson.

A remake of the 1936 Harold Lloyd comedy **The Milky Way** proved to be a hit for Danny Kaye as shy milkman Burleigh Sullivan, who accidentally knocks out the middleweight champ.

Manager Walter Abel, through a series of setups, makes Kaye believe he's a real fighter until he faces the championship fight.

As he did in innumerable fighting films, ex-boxer John Indrisano served as boxing instructor and technical adviser on **The Kid from Brooklyn.**

382 The Kid from Kokomo (aka **Orphan of the Ring)**

1939, Warner Brothers, 92 minutes. Director: Lewis Seiler. Screenplay: Jerry Wald, Richard Macaulay. Story: Dalton Trumbo. Photography: Sid Hickox.

Cast: Wayne Morris, May Robson, Pat O'Brien, Joan Blondell, Jane Wyman, Stanley Fields, Sidney Toler, Max Rosenbloom, Ed Brophy, Winifred Harris.

Boxer Morris would rather be back on the farm than in the ring, so manager O'Brien hires an old alcoholic-kleptomaniac (Robson) to pose as the fighter's long-lost mom to get him back to boxing.

This was Morris' third portrayal of a boxer—the previous two coming in 1937's **Kid Galahad** and 1938's **The Kid Comes Back** and his least successful.

383 Kid Galahad (aka **The Battling Bellhop)**

1937, Warner Brothers, 100 minutes. Director: Michael Curtiz. Producer: Hal Wallis. Screenplay: Seton I. Miller. Story: Francis Wallace. Photography: Gaetabo Gaudio.

Cast: Edward G. Robinson, Bette Davis, Wayne Morris, Humphrey Bogart, Harry Carey, Joseph Crehan, Jane Bryan.

A farm boy who's a hotel bellhop is persuaded by promoter Robinson and mistress Bette Davis to become a boxer when they see how good he is with his fists.

The naive lad runs afoul of gangster Bogart and complications ensue when he falls for Robinson's gal. A popular film, it was remade in 1962 with Elvis Presley and in 1941 as a carnival movie, **The Wagons Roll at Night.**

384 Kid Galahad

1962, United Artists, 95 minutes, Color. Director: Phil Karlson. Producer: David Weisbart. Screenplay: William Fay. Photography: Burnett Guffey. Editor: Stuart Gilmore.

Cast: Elvis Presley, Gig Young, Lola Albright, Joan Blackman, Charles Bronson, Ned Glass, Robert Emhardt, David Lewis, Liam Redmond, Michael Dante, Judson Pratt.

After being discharged from the Army, Walter Gulick (Presley) becomes a sparring partner at a Catskills training camp in this very loose remake of the 1937 Warner Brothers version.

Young, in the Edward G. Robinson role, feels Gulick is good pro material and the youth earns the label Galahad after he saves Albright from some hoods.

After giving up boxing, Gulick comes back to face a good veteran fighter after he learns that Young has been threatened by the hoods.

385 Kid Glove Kisses

1932, Universal, 2 reels. Director: Harry J. Edwards. Story: Francis J. Martin.

Cast: Slim Summerville, Eddie Gribbon, Edward Le Saint.

A bugler courts an Army officer's daughter in this two-reel short, which has a boxing finale.

386 Kid Hayseed

1928, Educational, 2 reels. Director: Charles Lamont.

Cast: Big Boy, Lila Leslie, Lorraine Rivero, Jackie Levine, Jack Miller.

Big Boy, the tiny tot star with the big derby, is tricked by the neighborhood bully, Kid Bolony, into meeting him inside the boxing ring.

387 Kid Monk Baroni

1952, Realart, 79 minutes. Director: Harold Schuster. Screenplay: Aben Kandel. Photography: Charles Van Enger. Editor: Jason Bernie.

Cast: Leonard Nimoy, Richard Rober, Bruce Cabot, Mona Knox, Jack Larson, Budd Jaxon, Archer McDonald, Kathleen Freeman.

Long before television's Mister Spock was featured on **Star Trek,** Nimoy portrayed Paul Baroni, whose face was so disfigured (although he didn't have pointed ears) that he was called Monk.

A concerned priest (Rober) teaches Baroni how to box and gets him involved in some of the church's social programs.

Turning pro under the tutelage of Cabot, he undergoes plastic surgery and turns his back on the priest, falling in love with gold-digger Knox, who spurns him after taking his money. As if that wasn't bad enough, Baroni has become a defensive fighter, not wanting to get his new face messed up.

Baroni eventually gives up boxing to head the church's athletic programs.

388 Kid Nightingale

1939, Warner Brothers, 56 minutes. Director: George Amy. Screenplay: Charles Belden, Raymond Schrock. Story: Lee Katz. Photography: Arthur Edeson. Editor: Frederick Richards.

Cast: John Payne, Jane Wyman, Walter Catlett, Harry Burns, Ed Brophy, Charles Brown, John Ridgely.

In **Golden Boy**, it was a violinist turned boxer. Here, Payne portrays an opera-singing waiter who enters the ring and is built up into a contender through a series of fixed bouts.

The promoter's gimmick is to have a band play at each of Payne's knockouts and to have him sing.

Wyman comes to the rescue by discovering the fights were crooked and getting him into real shape for the big fight.

389 Killer McCoy

1947, Metro Goldwyn Mayer, 103 minutes. Director: Roy Rowland. Producer: Sam Zimbalist. Screenplay: Frederick Hazlitt Brennan, Thomas Lennon, George Bruce, George Oppenheimer. Photography: Joseph Ruttenberg. Editor: Ralph E. Winters.

Cast: Mickey Rooney, Bob Steele, James Dunn, Sam Levene, Douglas Croft, David Clarke, Brian Donlevy, Ann Blyth, Tom Tully, Mickey Knox, James Bell, Gloria Holden.

A remake of 1938's **The Crowd Roars** with Robert Taylor, the boxer's class shrunk from a heavyweight to a lightweight for star Rooney.

Rooney earns the name "killer" by accidentally causing the death of a ring opponent and ties in with gambler Donlevy, in the role played by Edward Arnold in the original.

Dunn portrays Rooney's drunken vaudevillian pop, while Blyth is the gambler's daughter the boxer falls in love with.

390 The Killers

1946, Universal-International, 103 minutes. Director: Robert Siodmak. Producer: Mark Hellinger. Screenplay: Anthony Veiller, based on a story by Ernest Hemingway. Photography: Woody Bredell. Editor: Arthur Hilton.

Cast: Burt Lancaster, Ava Gardner, Edmond O'Brien, Albert Dekker, Sam Levene, Vince Barnett, Virginia Christine, Charles McGraw, William Conrad, Jack Lambert.

In a small, isolated town, a gas station attendant just calmly lies in bed as two hired gunmen murder him, even though he knew they were coming.

Why? A determined cop vows to find out why as the story is unraveled through flashbacks.

The gas station attendant, it turns out, was a former boxer who "could really take it." In one particularly effective scene, as the boxer (Lancaster) is being revived after a knockout, his manager is talking, in his presence, about replacing him.

The boxer, lured into a gang of crooks by femme fatale Gardner, participates in a payroll robbery and is doublecrossed.

The Killers was remade in 1964, but the boxing hero was changed into an auto racer.

391 Killer's Kiss

1955, United Artists, 67 minutes. Director-Screenplay-Photography-Editor: Stanley Kubrick. Producers: Kubrick, Morris Bousel.

Cast: Frank Silvera, Jamie Smith, Irene Kane, Jerry Jarret, Mike Dana, Felice Orlandi, Ralph Roberts, Phil Stevenson, Julius Adelman, David Vaughan.

Light years away from his **2001, A Space Odyssey** and other big budget hits, Kubrick did just about everything in this Manhattan-based drama filmed on a shoestring.

The plot isn't much: A second-rate boxer (Smith) protects the dancer who lives across from him from the desires of crime boss Silvera. The film is more atmosphere than anything else.

392 King for a Night

1933, Universal, 70-78 minutes. Director: Kurt Neumann. Screenplay: William Anthony McGuire, Jack O'Donnell, Scott Pembroke.

Cast: Chester Morris, Helen Twelvetrees, Alice White, John Miljan, Grant Mitchell, George E. Stone, George Meeker, Frank Albertson, Warren Hymer, Wade Boteler, Max Rosenbloom.

The sister of middleweight Bud "Kid" Gloves (Morris) kills the promoter (Miljan) who made a fool of her, but the boxer takes the blame.

Will he go to the chair? The ending may surprise you.

393 Kings of the Ring

1944, Irwin A. Lesser-Martin J. Lewis, 95 minutes. Photography: Jack Rieger.

Narrator: Nat Fleischer.

The editor of **Ring Magazine** narrates this compilation of some of boxing's greatest fights.

Among the boxers featured are Joe Louis, Billy Conn, Max Baer, Jack Johnson, Tommy Burns, Bill Squires, Lou Nova, Jack Dempsey, Georges Carpentier, Primo Carnera and Gene Tunney.

394 The Knockout (aka **Counted Out, The Pugilist**)

1914, Keystone, 2 reels. Director-Producer: Mack Sennett.

Cast: Fatty Arbuckle, Charlie Chaplin, Edgar Kennedy, Minta Durfee, Mack Swain, Al St. John, Slim Summerville, Charlie Chase, Mack Sennett, the Keystone Cops.

With a cast like this, does the plot really matter? It's all slapstick of the highest order with the referee taking more punches than the boxers, and Fatty starting a wild chase by shooting off a gun at the end of the bout.

395 The Knockout

1923, British, Napoleon, 6,000 feet. Director: Alexander Butler. Story: Walter Summers.

Cast: Rex Davis, Lillian Hall, Josephine Earle, Tom Reynolds, Julian Royce, Mickey Brantford.

A boxer is knocked out and hallucinates that his wife is killed and that he's kidnapped, among other things.

396 The Knockout

1925, First National Pictures, 7,450 feet. Director: Lambert Hillyer. Scenario: Joseph Poland, Earle Snell, based on "The Come-Back" by Morris De Camp Crawford. Photography: Roy Carpenter. Editor: Arthur Tavares.

Cast: Milton Sills, Lorna Duveen, John Philip Kolb, Edward Lawrence, Harry Jed Prouty, Claude King.

An arm injury forces the world's light heavyweight champ, Sandy Donlin (Sills) to find a new line of work, so he becomes foreman of a lumber camp.

Falling in love with the daughter (Duveen) of his boss's rival and seeing that his boss will stop at nothing to put the man out of business, Donlin re-enters the ring, risking serious injury, to get enough money to bail his prospective father-in-law out of financial trouble.

397 The Knockout

1932, Metro Goldwyn Mayer, 2 reels. Director: Anthony Mack. Producer: Hal Roach.

Cast: Mickey Daniels, Grady Sutton, Eddie Morgan, Gordon Douglas, Mary Kornman, Jacqueline Wells.

Daniels accidentally KO's

champ Douglas after he annoys his girl friend and takes his place in the ring in this comedy short.

398 Knock-Out

1936, German, Bavaria-Film AB, 86 minutes. Director: Karl Lamac.

Cast: Max Schmeling, Anny Ondra, Hans Schonrath, Samson Koerner, Hans Richter, Meyer Falkow.

A Nazi-made musical comedy boxing film starring heavyweight Schmeling and his wife, Ondra.

399 Knockout

1941, Warner Brothers, 71 minutes. Director: William Clemens. Producer: Edmund Grainger. Screenplay: M. Coates Webster. Story: Michael Fessier. Photography: Ted McCord. Editor: Doug Gould.

Cast: Arthur Kennedy, Olympe Bradna, Virginia Field, Anthony Quinn, Cliff Edwards, Richard Ainley, Tom Garland, Cornel Wilde, Vera Lewis.

Fight manager Quinn won't let his newlywed boxer (Kennedy) quit the ring. His efforts to find new jobs blocked, Kennedy must fight to earn some more money because a baby is on the way.

But Kennedy's troubles are just beginning. A beautiful heiress vamps him and his mouthpiece is drugged during the big fight.

400 Knockout

1965, Turn of the Century Fights, Inc., 42-50 minutes. Director-Producer: William Cayton.

Narrator: Kevin Kennedy.

A compilation film of 19 top fights that was combined in 1969 with **Knockout #2** to make one feature film.

Among the boxers featured are Jack Dempsey, Gene Tunney, Sugar Ray Robinson, Ingemar Johansson, Jess Willard, Joe Louis, Percy Bassett, Max Baer, Archie Moore, Cassius Clay (Muhammad Ali), Jack Johnson, and Rocky Marciano.

401 Knockout

1977, Turn of the Century Fights, Inc., 104 minutes. Director: Jim Jacobs. Producer: William Cayton. Editor: Steve Lott.

Narrator: Kevin Kennedy.

An updated version of **Knockout** and **Knockout #2**, the film includes the Ali-Frazier fight in Manila, the Foreman-Frazier and Foreman-Norton fights.

402 Knockout Blow

1912, British, Kineto, 575 feet. Director: F. Martin Thornton.

The British Film Institute describes this as "a famous hard-fought encounter in the boxing ring."

403 The Knockout Kid

1925, Rayart Pictures, 4,901 feet. Director: Albert Rogell. Scenario: Forrest Sheldon.

Cast: Jack Perrin, Molly Malone, Eva Thatcher, Bud Osborne, Martin Turner, Ed Burns, Jack Richardson.

Haven't we described this one before? Maybe it just sounds like so many other 1920's boxing films although this one's a comedy.

The son of a millionaire is disowned for boxing and heads west, where he becomes involved with romance and cattle rustlers.

404 Knockout Kisses

1933, Sennett, 18 minutes. Director George Marshall.

The gag here is that the hero must face a pair of twins in the ring. Each round they change places unknown to him so that he's got to face a rested boxer each time.

The hero's manager is a woman, à la **Be Yourself**.

405 Knockout #2

1966, Turn of the Century Fights, Inc., 50 minutes. Director-Producer: William Cayton.

Narrator: Kevin Kennedy.

Twenty-five more title bouts which were combined with the

first **Knockout** movie to form one 110-minute feature in 1969.

Among the boxers featured are James J. Jeffries, Jake La-Motta, Rocky Graziano, Dick Turpin, Sonny Liston, Primo Carnera, Jack Sharkey, Jack Johnson and many more.

406 Knockout Reilly

1927, Paramount Pictures, 7,080 feet. Director: Malcolm St. Clair. Screenplay: Pierre Collings, Kenneth Raisbeck. Story: Albert Payson Terhune. Photography: Edward Cronjager.

Cast: Richard Dix, Harry Gribbon, Mary Brian, Jack Renault, Osgood Perkins, Lucia Backus Seger, Larry McGrath, Myrtland La Varre.

A steel mill hand knocks out a masher, who turns out to be Killa Agerra (Renault).

The girl's brother (Gribbon) happens to be an ex-boxer himself, and he takes the steel worker (Dix) in hand and starts training him.

Our Hero is framed for a shooting and is sent to prison, where he keeps in shape on the rockpile.

407 Lady and Gent

1932, Paramount, 84 minutes. Director: Stephen Roberts. Story: Grover Jones, William Slavens. Photography: Harry Fischbeck.

Cast: George Bancroft, Wynne Gibson, Charles Starrett, James Gleason, John Wayne, Morgan Wallace, James Crane.

A prizefighter and a nightclub owner sacrifice their all for the sake of an orphan boy who grows up to be a football star.

When the youth (Starrett) decides to foresake football for boxing, it's up to daddy (Bancroft) to teach the boy a lesson.

It was remade in 1939 as **Unmarried.**

408 Lady on the Tracks

1968, Czech, Royal Films International, 83 minutes, Color. Director: Ladislave Rychman. Screenplay: Vratislav Blazek. Photography: Josef Hanus.

Cast: Jirina Bohdalova, Radoslave Brzbohaty, Frantisek Peterka, Libuse Geprtova, Stanislav Fiser.

A trolley conductress in Prague falls for a boxer when she catches hubby with another woman. The unfaithful husband decides he wants his wife back and takes boxing lessons.

The finale is a boxing match between the husband and his wife's lover in front of an arena filled with trolley conductresses all hoping the husband will be thrashed. He is, but he wins back his wife's love.

409 L'Air De Paris

1954, French, Corona, 100 minutes. Director: Marcel Carne. Screenplay: Jacques Siguid, Carne. Photography: Roger Hubert. Editor: Henri Rust.

Cast: Jean Gabin, Arletty, Roland Lesaffre, Mario Daems, Folco Lulli, Jean Paredes, Simone Paris.

A little-known film from the director of such earlier French classics as **The Children of Paradise** and **Port of Shadows.** Gabin is an over-the-hill boxer now running a gym who likes what he sees in a young railroad worker and starts training him to be champion.

Gabin's wife dislikes the youth (Lesaffre), who's involved with a woman who later dumps him.

410 The Last Challenge

1916, British, London, 3,200 feet. Director: Harold Shaw. Story: Bannister Merwin.

Cast: Chesterfield "Billie" Goode, Jem Smith, G.T. Dunning, Toff Wall, Sam Howard, Eugene Corri.

An ex-champ, now an innkeeper, re-enters the ring to battle the rival of his daughter's beloved.

411 The Last Fight

1982, Best Film and Video, 86 minutes, Color. Director-Screenplay: Fred Williamson. Producer: Jerry Masucci. Photography: James Lemmo. Editor: Daniel Lowenthal.

Cast: Fred Williamson, Joe Spinell, Ruben Blades, Darlanne Fluegel, Willie Colon, Salvador Sanchez, Don King, José "Chegui" Torres.

Salsa star Blades plays a singer who runs up a huge gambling debt and is forced to become a boxer to pay it off. What's worse, he develops a blood clot on the brain and still keeps on fighting.

The film was dedicated to the memory of Sanchez, who plays a boxer in the film. Sanchez, a featherweight, was killed in a car crash before the film's release.

412 The Last Man on Earth

1924, Fox Film Corp., 6,637. Director: J.P. Blystone. Scenario: Donald W. Lee. Photography: Allan Davey.

Cast: Buck Black, Jean Johnson, Earle Foxe, Grace Cunard, Gladys Tennyson, Derelys Perdue, Maryon Aye, Clarissa Selwynne.

Here's a boxing comedy that's truly unique.

In futuristic 1954, a mysterious disease kills every male over the age of 14. Every male, except, that is, a hermit who went off by himself after his beloved rejected him.

His identity discovered, he's sold for $10 million to the government and brought to the U.S. Senate chambers, where the female senators from California and Virginia battle it out in a boxing ring for the right to own him.

But whether either will wind up with him is questionable as his original sweetheart hears about the fight and attends it.

413 Last of the Mohee-Cans

1926, 1,677 feet.

A boxer tells his own twisted version of **Last of the Mohicans** at a party given by the rival for a girl. The host challenges him to fight any boxer chosen by the host.

It's rough going in the ring until each time the boxer is knocked down, his manager gets him back up with a pin prick.

414 The Last Round

1914, British, The Barker, 2,650 feet. Director: Bert Haldane. Story: Rowland Talbot.

Cast: Thomas H. MacDonald, Blanche Forsythe, Fred Paul, J. Hastings Batson.

The daughter of a colonel who's in the clutches of a loan shark agrees to marry him to prevent him from foreclosing on her father.

To the rescue comes a young officer who loves the girl and who finds a top boxer he can wager on. The loan shark puts the boxer out of commission, leaving it up to the officer to enter the ring himself and fight for his girl.

415 Laughing Irish Eyes

1936, Republic, 70 minutes. Director: Joseph Santley. Story: Sidney Sutherland, Wallace Sullivan. Photography: Milton Krasner, Reggie Lanning. Editor: Joseph H. Lewis.

Cast: Phil Regan, Walter C. Kelly, Evalyn Knapp, Ray Walker, Mary Gordon, Warren Hymer, Betty Compson, Herman Bing, Clarence Muse, Russell Hicks.

The head of the Irish-American Athletic Association (Kelly) returns to Ireland to lure the best Irish fighter he can find back to the states. He brings his beautiful daughter with him as bait.

Their catch is a Cork blacksmith who manages to sing four songs while fighting his way to the top.

416 Leather Gloves

1948, Columbia, 75 minutes. Director-Producers: Richard Quine, William Asher. Screenplay: Brown

Holmes, Based on a **Saturday Evening Post** story by Richard English. Photography: Henry Freulich. Editor: Viola Lawrence.

Cast: Cameron Mitchell, Virginia Grey, Jane Nigh, Sam Levene, Henry O'Neill, Blake Edwards, Bob Castro, Sally Corner, Stanley Andrews, Eddie Acuff.

An off-beat boxing film with a touch of **The Best Years of Our Lives** features Mitchell as a war veteran who was a top boxer before World War II, but who now just drifts from place to place.

Needing some money, he talks himself into a boxing match in a small, isolated town and then agrees to take a dive for a fee.

However, he gets to like the young man he's going to face in the ring even though he's his rival for the local girl he meets. If the young man wins, his triumph over a name boxer will carry him to the big time, and as Mitchell knows all too well, eventual heartbreak as the kid isn't that good.

If the kid loses, he'll stay back home with the girl.

Will Mitchell take the easy way out and take a dive? Or will he face the wrath of gamblers and beat the kid? That's the dilemma he grapples with until the final round.

417 The Leather Pushers

From 1922 to 1924 and again in 1930 and 1931, Universal produced a series of two-reelers based on stories by H.C. Witwer which appeared in **Collier's.**

Starring Reginald Denny, the man who appeared in more boxing movies than anyone else, they concerned a college youth out to find his own way in the world by becoming a prizefighter. Billy Sullivan, a nephew of the Great John L., replaced Denny in some of the episodes.

In the 1922-24 series, episodes seven to 12 have the title **The New Leather Pushers.**

1922-24 series. Director: Harry A. Pollard. Scenario: Pollard, Harvey Thew.

1. **Let's Go;** 2. **Round Two;** 3. **Payment Through the Nose;** 4. **A Fool and His Money;** 5. **The Taming of the Shrewd;** 6. **Whipsawed;** 7. **Young King Cole;** 8. **He Raised Kane;** 9. **Chickasha Bone Crusher;** 10. **When Kane Met Abel;** 11. **Strike Father, Strike Son;** 12. **Joan of Newark;** 13. **The Wandering Two** (the only three-reeler in the series); 14. **The Widower's Mite;** 15. **Don Coyote;** 16. **Something for Nothing;** 17. **Columbia the Gem and the Ocean;** 18. **Barnaby's Grudge;** 19. **That Kid from Madrid;** 20. **He Loops to Conquer;** 21. **Girls Will Be Girls;** 22. **A Tough Tenderfoot;** 23. **Swing Bad the Sailor;** 24. **Big Boy Blue.**

1930-31 Series. Director: Albert Kelley. Screenplay: Douglas Doty, Ralph Ceder, Harry Fraser.

1. **Kid Roberts;** 2. **Hammer and Tongs;** 3. **The Knockout;** 4. **The Come-Back;** 5. **The Mardi Gras;** 6. **All for a Lady!** 7. **Framed!** 8. **The Lady Killer;** 9. **Kane Meets Abel;** 10. **The Champion.**

418 The Leather Pushers

1940, Universal, 64 minutes. Director: John Rawlins. Screenplay: Larry Rhine, Ben Chapman, Maxwell Shane. Photography: Stanley Certes. Editor: Arthur Hilton.

Cast: Richard Arlen, Andy Devine, Astrid Allwyn, Douglas Fowley, Charles D. Brown, Shemp Howard, Horace McMahon, Charles Lane, Wade Boteler, George Reed, Eddie Gribbon.

The Arlen-Devine team provided a number of good grade B action films.

Here, Arlen is the trainer for wrestler Devine when promoter Fowley decides Arlen would make a good boxer. Giving him a big buildup through phony fights, his efforts are belittled by a woman sportswriter who winds up winning his contract in a raffle.

The new team winds up having the last laugh as Arlen rises to the top.

419 The Leather Saint

1956, Paramount, 86 minutes. Director: Alvin Ganzer. Producer: Norman Retchin. Screenplay: Ganzer, Retchin. Photography: Haskell B. Boggs. Editor: Floyd Knudtson.

Cast: John Derek, Paul Douglas, Jody Lawrence, Cesar Romero, Ernest Truex, Richard Shannon, Rick Vera, Edith Evanson, Lou Nova, Baynes Barron, Bill Baldwin, Courtland Shepard.

Father Gil Allen (Derek) is an Episcopalian minister totally devoted to caring for young polio victims. When money is desperately needed for better facilities, he decides that the only way he can raise the necessary funds is to enter the boxing ring.

His manager (Douglas) and a shady promoter (Romero) find his behavior a bit strange for a boxer but never suspect he's a clergyman. When it's revealed, the predictable results ensue.

420 The Legendary Champions

1968, Turn of the Century Fights, 77 minutes. Director-Writer: Harry Chapin. Producer: William Cayton. Editors: Bernie Gagliano, Max Coggiola.

Narrator: Norman Rose.

The crew responsible for the **Knockout** compilation films is back but with something slightly different.

This time, they concentrate on the boxing era from 1882 to 1929 and focus as much on their out-of-the-ring careers as they do on their boxing matches.

It's the film's theme that the boxers were as much a part of the show business world as of the sports world as it covers the vaudeville careers of Sullivan, Corbett and others.

421 Let's Do It Again

1975, Warner Brothers, 112 minutes, Color. Director: Sidney Poitier. Producer: Melville Tucker. Screenplay: Richard Wesly. Story: Timothy March. Photography: Donald M. Morgan.

Cast: Bill Cosby, Sidney Poitier, J.J. Walker, John Amos, Calvin Lockhart, Ossie Davis, Paul Harris, Denise Nichols, George Foreman, Lee Chamberlin, Mel Stewart, Julius Harris.

The sequel to **Uptown Saturday Night** finds Cosby and Poitier in New Orleans as members of the Sons and Daughters of Shaka Lodge.

Poitier, who has a strange hypnotic power, uses it on a skinny boxer to turn him into a title contender to help raise money for the organization and bewilder gangsters Amos and Lockhart.

422 Lieutenant Daring Defeats the Middleweight Champion

1912, British, B&C, 1,190 feet. Director: Charles Raymond. Scenario: Harold Brett.

Cast: Percy Moran, Ivy Martinek, Charles Calvert, Edward Durrant, J.W. Bremmer, Harold Brett, Frank Bradley.

Our Hero escapes from those always-present kidnappers in time to win the bout and the colonel's beautiful daughter.

423 Life of Jimmy Dolan

1933, Warner Brothers, 71 minutes. Director: Archie Mayo. Adaptation: David Boehm and Erwin Gelsey from the play, **The Sucker**, by Bertram Milhauser and Beulah Marie Dix. Photography: Arthur Edeson.

Cast: Douglas Fairbanks, Jr., Loretta Young, Aline McMahon, Guy Kibbee, Lyle Talbot, Fin Dorsay, Shirley Grey, George Meeker, John Wayne.

A fighter who has just won the championship is involved in the accidental death of a reporter. When his manager is killed in a flaming car crash after the killing, everyone thinks it's the boxer (Fairbanks) who's dead except for detective Kibbee.

The fighter takes refuge at a health farm; and at the risk of exposing his identity, he accepts a $500-a-round bout to help pay off the farm's mortgage.

Wayne has a small role as a prizefighter.

The film was remade in 1939 as **They Made Me a Criminal** with John Garfield.

424 Little Miss Smiles

1922, Fox Film Corp., 4,884 feet. Director: Jack Ford. Scenario: Jack Strumwasser, Dorothy Yost, from "Little Aliens" by Myra Kelly. Photography: David Abel.

Cast: Shirley Mason, Gaston Glass, Arthur Rankin, George Williams, Sidney D'Albrook, Richard Lapan.

When the mother of a poor New York tenement family starts going blind, their son strives to become a prizefighter over his parents' objections. His sister loves a doctor; but when a gambler turns his attentions to her, the brother shoots him.

Be assured all turns out well, however.

425 Little Orphan Annie

1938, Paramount, 57 minutes. Director: Ben Holmes. Producer: John Speaks. Screenplay: Bud Wilson Schulberg, Samuel Ornitz, based on the comic strip by Harold Gray. Photography: Frank Redman. Editor: Robert Bischoff.

Cast: Ann Gillis, Robert Kent, June Travis, J. Farrell MacDonald, J.M. Kerrigan, Sarah Padden, James Burke.

Loan sharks have free rein in Annie's tenement neighborhood so the little girl of comic strip fame persuades the residents to pool their expenses and back a boxer for a share of his purse.

The loan sharks kidnap the fighter before the big bout (what else is new?), but a horde of neighborhood women rescue him and get him to the arena on time (have you ever seen them get to the arena too late?).

426 The Lollipop Cover

1965, Continental, 82-85 minutes. Director-Producer: Everett Chambers. Screenplay: Chambers, Don Gordon, based on an idea by Nancy Valentine. Photography: Michael Murphy. Editor: James D. Mitchell.

Cast: Don Gordon, Carol Seflinger, George Sawaya, Annette Valentine, David White, John Marley, Bert Remsen, Midge Ware, Cliff Carnell, Carolyn Hughes, Lee Philips.

A 9-year old girl who's been abandoned by her drunken dad still believes in the basic goodness of people, and when things get too depressing she starts looking at the world through brightly-colored lollipop covers.

Into her life comes a cynical boxer who has hitchhiked to the city for the money his sister supposedly has been holding for him.

427 The Loser Wins

1915, British, Burlingham Standard, 993 feet. Director: Ernest G. Batley.

The girl weds the loser for once after he and a rival box for a Red Cross fund.

428 Love and Fighting

1947, Finnish, Fenno Filmi, 90 minutes. Director: Yigo Norta. Producer: Bio Kuva. Screenplay: Tex Westerberg.

Cast: Sirkka Sipila, Kullervo Kalske, Assi Raine, Irja Ranniko, Hannes Hayrinen, Joel Asikainven.

We must confess that all we can find out about this Finnish entry is that it's described as a "boxing comedy romance."

429 Luck

1923, Mastodon Films, 6,442 feet. Scenario: Doty Hobart. Story:

Jackson Gregory. Photography: Charles E. Gilson, Neil Sullivan.

Cast: Johnny Hines, Robert Edeson, Edmund Breese, Violet Mersereau, Matthew Betts, Harry Fraser, Polly Moran, Charles Murray, Flora Finch.

Robert Carter (Hines) makes a bet for $100,000 that he can start without a cent and make $10,000 in a year. He wins a prize-fight and uses the proceeds to start building a new town.

When he rescues a judge's daughter from a cave-in, the new town's success is assured, and Carter wins the bet.

430 Mabel's Married Life

1914, Keystone, 891 feet. Directors: Charles Chaplin, Mabel Normand.

Cast: Charles Chaplin, Mabel Normand, Mack Swain, Charles Murray, Hank Mann, Harry McCoy, Alice Davenport.

Mabel buys Charlie a boxing dummy after he failed to protect her from a wolf.

Arriving home drunk, Charlie mistakes the dummy for a real person and picks a fight with it. In the Chaplin style, Charlie loses to the dummy.

431 Madison Square Garden

1932, Paramount, 70 minutes. Director: Harry Joe Brown. Producer: Charles L. Rogers. Story: Thomas Burtis. Photography: Henry Sharp.

Cast: Jack Oakie, Marian Nixon, Thomas Meighan, William Boyd, ZaSu Pitts, Lew Cody, William Collier, Sr., Robert Elliott, Warren Hymer.

The routine fight-fixing story doesn't really matter; what distinguishes **Madison Square Garden** from all the rest is the free-for-all climax in which real-life sports celebrities, including Jack Johnson and many others, do battle with the baddies.

Collier portrays the manager of Oakie, his usual wisecracking self as a boxer, and of Hymer, a wrestler. When he's offered the job as a matchmaker at the Garden, he turns it down rather than give up his two proteges. The two then walk out on him so he can take the job.

Boyd and Cody are the new heavies, who resort to using loaded gloves; and when their scheme is discovered, that's when the real fun begins.

The sports celebrities, who portray Madison Square Garden employees in the film, help track down, and then beat up the villains.

432 The Main Event

1927, Pathe Exchange, 6,472 feet. Director: William K. Howard. Adaptation-Continuity: Rochus Gliese. Story: Paul Allison. Photography: Lucien Andriot. Editor: Claude Berkeley.

Cast: Vera Reynolds, Rudolph Schildkraut, Charles Delaney, Ernie Adams, Julia Faye, Robert Armstrong.

Boxer Johnnie Regan (Delaney) falls for night club dancer Glory Frayne (Reynolds), the girl friend of Regan's ring foe, Red Lucas (Armstrong).

The faithful Glory plots to keep Regan out of training, thus assuring a victory for her boyfriend; but she soon discovers that she really loves Regan.

433 The Main Event

1938, Columbia, 55 minutes. Director: Danny Dare. Producer: Ralph Cohn. Story: Harold Shumate. Adaptation: Lee Loeb. Photography: Allen G. Siegler. Editor: Al Clark.

Cast: Robert Paige, Jacqueline Wells, Arthur Loft, John Gallaudet, John Tyrrell, Thurston Hall.

Paige is a detective on the trail of a boxer, who's the willing victim of a kidnapping plot in this bottom-of-the-bill programmer.

434 The Main Event

1979, Warner Brothers, 112 minutes, Color. Director: Howard Zieff. Producers: Barbra Streisand, Jon Peters. Screenplay: Gail Parent, Andrew Smith. Photography: Mario Tosi. Editor: Edward Warschilka.

Cast: Barbra Streisand, Ryan O'Neal, Paul Sand, Whitman Mayo, Patti D'Arbanville, Chu Chu Malave, Richard Lawson, James Gregory, Badja Medu Djora.

Cosmetics queen Streisand's empire is falling apart on her: Her accountant has run off with most of her money, and her main asset is now a third-rate boxer named Kid Natural (O'Neal).

O'Neal doesn't even really want to fight anymore. He'd rather run a driving school, which is in the shape of a boxing glove.

However, as Streisand is desperate (she originally acquired his contract as a tax loss), she talks him into it and she becomes his manager.

435 Man from Down Under

1943, Metro Goldwyn Mayer, 102 minutes. Director: Robert Z. Leonard. Screenplay: Well Root, Thomas Seller. Story: Bogart Rogers, Mark Kelly. Photography: Sidney Wagner. Editor: George White.

Cast: Charles Laughton, Donna Reed, Horace McNally, Richard Carlson, Binnie Barnes, Clyde Cook, Arthur Shields, Christopher Severn, Hobart Cavanaugh, Andre Charlot.

There's a little bit of just about everything here. Australian Army Sgt. Laughton takes two orphan Belgian kids home with him at the end of World War I, leaving entertainer Barnes on the dock.

Putting the girl in private school, he raises the boy (Carlson) to be the lightweight Australian boxing champ, while a shoulder injury keeps the lad out of the Army.

Laughton buys a hotel with the boxing winnings, but Barnes shows up and in revenge takes it away from him via gambling.

Then World War II breaks out, the boy and girl fall in love, but are they related? As we said, a little bit of everything here.

436 The Man I Love

1929, Paramount Famous Lasky Corp., 6,669 feet. Director: William Wellman. Screenplay: Herman J. Mankiewicz. Photography: Henry Gerrard. Editor: Allyson Shaffer.

Cast: Richard Arlen, Pat O'Malley, Mary Brian, Charles Sullivan, Harry Green, Jack Oakie, Leslie Fenton, Sailor Vincent, Robert Perry.

A Los Angeles boxer named Dum-Dum Brooks marries Celia Fields (Brian) and heads for New York, where he signs with promoter McCarthy (O'Malley).

The boxer (Arlen) is an instant success and is slated to fight for the championship but gets involved with another woman and his wife leaves him.

Dum-Dum has trouble in the championship bout until his wife appears to urge him on and...you know the rest.

437 The Man to Beat Jack Johnson

1910, British, Tyler, 280 feet.

Cast: Willie Saunders.

Another film inspired by the Johnson-Jeffries fight.

438 Mandingo

1975, Paramount, 126 minutes, Color. Director: Richard Fleischer. Producer: Dino De Laurentiis. Screenplay: Norman Wexler, based on the novel by Kyle Onstott and a play by Jack Kirkland. Photography: Richard H. Kline. Editor: Frank Bracht.

Cast: James Mason, Susan George, Percy King, Ken Norton, Rachel Ward, Branda Sykes, Lillian Hayman, Roy Poole.

In the Old South, King, son of slave-breeder Mason, makes

a lot of money gambling on black boxer Norton. When he beds Sykes, George goes to bed with Norton in retaliation.

With the emphasis on sex and violent action, audiences, of course, loved it; and a sequel, **Drum**, was the result.

439 Mannequin

1933, British, Real Art, 54 minutes. Director: George A. Cooper. Producer: Julius Hagen. Story: Charles Bennett.

Cast: Harold French, Diana Beaumont, Whitmore Humphries, Richard Cooper, Ben Welden, Faith Bennett, Vera Bogetti, Anna Lee.

The same old story about a boxer who leaves his sweetheart for a society dame but learns better.

440 Matilda

1978, American International, 105 minutes, Color. Director: Daniel Mann. Producer: Albert Ruddy. Screenplay: Ruddy, Timothy Galfas, based on the book by Paul Gallico. Photography: Jack Woolf, Editor: Allan A. Jacobs.

Cast: Elliott Gould, Robert Mitchum, Harry Guardino, Clive Revill, Karen Carlson, Roy Clark, Lionel Stander, Art Metrano, Larry Pennell.

Did they really make a feature film about a boxing kangaroo, which is portrayed by a man inside a suit? Yes they did, although this nonsense isn't quite as bad as it sounds.

Gould is the down-and-out talent agent who strikes it rich on the kangaroo's boxing ability, while Carlson is the animal lover out to see that Matilda isn't exploited.

441 Meet the Champ

1933, Paramount, 2 reels. Director: Del Lord. Story and Adaptation: Luther Reed, Ralph Ceder, Scott C. Cleethorpe. Editor: Maurice Wright.

Cast: Walter Catlett, Eugene Palette.

A cow milking contest is held inside a boxing ring with all the attendant atmosphere of a boxing bout.

442 Melody of My Heart

1936, British, Butchers, 82 minutes. Director: Wilfred Noy. Producers: Brandon Fleming, George Barclay. Screenplay: Fleming.

Cast: Lorraine la Fosse, Derek Oldham, Bruce Seton, Hughes Macklin, Dorothy Vernon, MacArthur Gordon, Colin Cunningham, Bombardier Billy Wells.

The opera **Carmen** is the basis for this minor musical of a cigarette factory worker who rejects her lover in favor of a boxer.

443 The Mexican

1957, Russian, Artkino, 82 minutes, Color. Director: V. Kaplunovsky. Screenplay: E. Braginsky. Story: Jack London. Photography: S. Polyanov.

Cast: O. Strizhenov, B. Andreyev, D. Sagal, N. Rumyanseva, V. Dorofeyav, T. Samoilova.

The Mexican Revolution is an ideal subject for a Russian movie. What's surprising is that **The Mexican,** based on a story by Jack London, is actually a remake of a 1952 film, **The Fighter,** which was made in the United States.

Some Mexican revolutionaries plotting the overthrow of the government are based in Los Angeles. Needing money for the cause, the hero agrees to a 17-round winner-take-all boxing match.

444 Mike Wins the Championship

1914, British, 595 feet. Director: Dave Aylott.

Mike wins his boxing match, but loses one to his wife.

445 The Milky Way

1936, Paramount, 80 minutes. Director: Leo McCarey. Producer: E. Lloyd Sheldon. Screenplay: Grover Jones, Frank Butler, Richard Connell. Photography: Al Gilks. Editor: LeRoy Stone.

Cast: Harold Lloyd, Adolphe Menjou, Verree Teasdale, Helen Mack, William Gargan, Dorothy Wilson, Lionel Stander, Charles Lane.

This comedy about a shy milkman who becomes a boxing champ was remade ten years later as **The Kid from Brooklyn** with Danny Kaye.

The Milky Way represented a comeback for silent comedian Lloyd as his first soundie hit. He plays the milkman whose only real talent is knowing how to duck.

When middleweight champ Gargan is knocked out by Stander, Lloyd gets the credit and gets the nickname "The Killer."

In the title bout with the champ, Lloyd's only real chance for success lies in putting him to sleep.

446 Monkey on My Back

1957, United Artists, 93 minutes. Director: Andre de Toth. Producer: Edward Small. Screenplay: Crane Wilbur, Anthony Veiller, Paul Dudley. Photography: Maury Girtsman. Editor: Grant Whytock.

Cast: Cameron Mitchell, Dianne Foster, Paul Richards, Jack Albertson, Kathy Garver, Lisa Golm, Barry Kelley, Dayton Lommis, Brad Harris.

The mid-1950's brought a number of hard-hitting dramas on drug addiction to the screen. The three most notable were **Man with the Golden Arm, A Hatful of Rain** and **Monkey on My Back.**

Monkey on My Back is the story of welterweight and lightweight boxing champ Barney Ross, a hero at Guadalcanal during World War II. He becomes a drug addict when he contracts malaria after being wounded and develops a need for morphine.

The film pulls no punches in depicting Ross' struggle to go "cold turkey" and his six months in a hospital trying to get rid of that monkey on his back.

447 Mountains of Manhattan

1927, Lumas Film Corp., 5,785 feet. Director: James P. Hogan. Scenario: Alyce Garrick. Story: Herbert C. Clark. Photography: Ray June. Editor: Edith Wakeling.

Cast: Dorothy Devore, Charles Delaney, Kate Price, George Chesebro, Bobby Gordon, James P. Hogan, Clarence Wilson, Robert Homans.

A boxing champ quits to study engineering, but lands a construction job on a skyscraper to earn some money. He runs afoul of a villainous foreman, and the climax has the two battling on the girders high above Manhattan.

448 Movie Movie

1978, Warner Brothers, 105 minutes, Color and Black and White. Director-Producer: Stanley Donen. Screenplay: Larry Gelbart, Sheldon Keller. Photography: Charles Rosher, Jr., Bruce Surtees. Editor: George Hively.

Cast: George C. Scott, Harry Hamlin, Art Carney, Trish Van Devere, Eli Wallach, Ann Reinking, Red Buttons, Jocelyn Brando, Michael Kidd.

A "double feature" plus coming attractions, all affectionately spoofing 1930's movies.

The first "feature," in black and white, is **Dynamite Hands,** in which Hamlin is the law student hopeful who needs $250,000 for his sister's eye operation.

He becomes a boxer under Scott's tutelage and wins his first 29 fights—28 by knockout—and comes home with a grand total of $300.

The filmmakers have studied

their genre well and every spoofing plot turn rings true to the 1930's films. Naturally, there's a shady gambler (Wallach) who sets the ever-present vamp on him.

Hamlin, who had earlier told his fiancée "don't you know the minute I met you I lost all interest in women" leaves her for the vamp and is later ordered by Wallach to take a dive in the championship bout.

With his parents betting their store on him, Hamlin is getting beaten badly in the ring until guess what? His sister appears, and makes the token ringside plea to Hamlin.

Scott is murdered by Wallach after the fight, but Hamlin becomes a lawyer fast enough to prosecute him himself.

The coming attractions are for an aviation film while the "second feature," in color, is **Baxter's Beauties**, a takeoff on Busby Berkeley backstage musicals.

Scott, who had a long melodramatic death scene in **Dynamite Hands**, gets another one in the second half.

449 Mr. Hex

1946, Monogram, 63 minutes. Director: William Beaudine. Producer: Jan Grippo. Screenplay: Cyril Endfield. Photography: James Brown. Editor: Seth Larsen.

Cast: Leo Gorcey, Huntz Hall, Bobby Jordan, Gabriel Dell, Bill Benedict, David Gorcey, Bernard Gorcey, Eddie Gribbon, Gale Robbins, Sammy Cohen, John Indrisano.

The East Side Kids (Bowery Boys) want to help a singer raise money for his sick mother, so Gorcey hypnotizes Hall into believing he's a top boxer.

Gangsters, in the meantime, try to steal Gorcey's coin which he uses to hypnotize Hall and hire an evil eye (Cohen) to rattle the boxer in the ring.

450 Mr. Moto's Gamble

1938, 20th Century Fox, 60-71 minutes. Director: James Tinling. Producer: John Stone. Screenplay: Charles Belden, Jerry Cady, based on a character created by John P. Marquand. Photography: Lucien Andriot.

Cast: Peter Lorre, Keye Luke, Dick Baldwin, Lynn Bari, Douglas Fowley, Harold Huber, Jane Regan, Max Rosenbloom, Pierre Watkin, Ward Bond, Lon Chaney, Jr.

This mystery started out as **Charlie Chan at Ringside**, but when Warner Oland died during production, the film was turned over to the Japanese detective, Mr. Moto (Lorre).

Moto runs a detective school in this one, and Luke and pupil Rosenbloom try to find out who poisoned a boxer.

451 Navy Bound

1951, Monogram, 60 minutes. Director: Paul Landres. Producer: Wilbur F. Broidy. Screenplay: Sam Rocca, based on a **Collier's** magazine story by Talbert Josselyn. Photography: Harry Neumann. Editor: Otho Levering.

Cast: Tom Neal, Wendy Waldron, Regis Toomey, John Abbott, Murray Alper, Paul Bryar, Harvey Parry.

A Navy boxing champion leaves the service to help his family's tuna fishing business, but when the family experiences financial difficulties, he takes on a professional challenger in the ring.

452 The Navy Way

1944, Paramount, 74 minutes. Director: William Berke. Screenplay: Maxwell Shane. Photography: Fred Jackman, Jr., Editor: Howard Smith.

Cast: Robert Lowery, Jean Parker, Bill Henry, Roscoe Karns, Sharon Douglas, Robert Armstrong, Richard Powers, Larry Nunn.

Set at the Great Lakes Naval

Training Station, this potboiler service drama finds boxer Lowery a reluctant inductee because it deprives him of a shot at the title. Rest assured that by the final reel, he's a true red, white and blue Navy man.

453 New Champion

1925, Columbia Pictures, 4,470 feet. Director: Reeves Eason. Story: Dorothy Howell. Photography: George Meehan.

Cast: William Fairbanks, Edith Roberts, Frank Hagney, Al Kaufman, Lotus Thompson, Lloyd Whitlock, Bert Apling.

A blacksmith's assistant (Fairbanks) takes the place of Knockout Riley (Hagney) when the latter injures his hand. Fighting under Riley's name, the blacksmith's aide overcomes a poor start to win the championship and a girl's hand.

454 News Hounds

1947, Monogram, 68 minutes. Director: William Beaudine. Producer: Jan Grippo. Screenplay: Edmond Seward, Tim Ryan. Photography: Marcel Le Picard. Editor: William Austin.

Cast: Leo Gorcey, Huntz Hall, Bobby Jordan, Gabriel Dell, Billy Benedict, Bernard Gorcey, David Gorcey.

Another East Side Kids-Bowery Boys comedy finds Leo Gorcey's paper being sued over a story about a fight-fixing racket, but some missing photos hold the key.

455 The Night Bird

1928, Universal Pictures, 6,702 feet. Director: Fred Newmeyer. Scenario: Earle Snell. Story: Frederick Hatton, Fanny Hatton. Photography: Arthur Todd. Editor: Maurice Pivar.

Cast: Reginald Denny, Betsy Lee, Sam Hardy, Harvey Clark, Corliss Palmer, Jocelyn Lee, Alphonse Martel, George Bookasta.

Universal's favorite boxer, Denny, portrays a light heavyweight named Kid Davis in this romantic comedy. Afraid of girls, he meets a young woman who has fled home so she won't have to marry a man she doesn't love.

Davis and the girl (Lee) fall in love, but the match is split up by the boxer's manager (Hardy). In the title bout, Our Hero is losing badly because of a broken heart.

In a slight switch from the usual cliche, this time it's a male plea at ringside—that of the girl's brother—which stirs Our Hero to victory.

456 The Night I Fought Jack Johnson

1913, Vitagraph, 196 feet.

Two men—one in blackface and the other in a business suit—box each other before ending up dancing.

457 Night Parade (aka **Sporting Life**)

1929, RKO Productions, 6,503-6,665 feet. Director: Malcolm St. Clair. Producer: William Le Baron. Scenario: James Gruen, George O'Hara. Story: George Abbott, Edward Paramore, Hyatt Daab. Photography: William Marshall. Editor: Jack Kitchen.

Cast: Hugh Trevor, Lloyd Ingraham, Dorothy Gulliver, Aileen Pringle, Robert Ellis, Lee Shumway, James Dugan.

A middleweight champ who expects to lose his next fight anyway agrees to take a dive at the urging of a mobster and a vamp, who has gotten him out of shape.

A friendly sportswriter gets wind of the plot and tells the lad's dad; and, yes, there's a ringside plea in the climactic bout.

458 No Way Back

1949, British, Eros, 72 minutes. Director: Stefan Osiecki. Producer: Derrick de Marney. Screenplay: Osiecki, de Marney, based on a story by Thomas Burke. Photography: Robert Navarro.

Cast: Terence de Marney, Eleanor Summerfield, Jack Raine, John Salew, Shirley Quentin, Denys Val Norton, Gerald C. Lawson, Tommy McGovern.

A boxer known as "The Croucher" is forced to give up the ring when his sight is damaged during a fight, and he joins up with a gangster.

459 Nobby Wins the Cup

1914, British, Ecko, 505 feet. Director: W.P. Kellino.

Short comedy in which the hero trains to be a boxer.

460 The Noble Art

1920, British, Martin's Photoplays, 2,000 feet. Director-Scenario: Fred Goodwins.

Cast: Fred Goodwins.

A weakling takes up boxing for the sake of a girl and winds up the winner of both her love and the bout.

461 The Notorious Elinor Lee

1940, Micheaux Film Corp. Director: Oscar Micheaux. Producers: Micheaux, Hubert Julian.

Cast: Edna Mae Harris, Robert Earl Jones, Gladys Williams, Carmen Newsome, Vera Burelle, Laura Bowman, Juano Hernandez, Amanda Randolph.

There's nothing really new here, except that it's an all-black cast. Vamp Harris tries to get rising fighter Jones to throw a fight.

462 Off Limits

1953, Paramount, 87 minutes. Director: George Marshall. Producer: Harry Tugend. Screenplay: Hal Kanter, Jack Sher. Photography: J. Peverell Marley. Editor: Arthur Schmidt.

Cast: Bob Hope, Mickey Rooney, Marilyn Maxwell, Stanley Clements, Eddie Mayshoft, Jack Dempsey, Marvin Miller, John Ridgely, Norman Leavitt, Art Aragon.

When lightweight champ Bullets Bradley (Clements) is drafted, his shady backers force manager Wally Hogan (Hope) to enlist to make sure he stays in shape while in the Army.

When ladies man Hogan passes the physical while Bradley flunks, the manager realizes it was part of a scheme to get him out of the way, and he vows to find another fighter.

Along comes meek little Tuttle (Rooney) who keeps on bugging Hope to train him. At first he's just strung along, but he's eventually trained to meet the champ.

The funniest scene has Bradley and his opponent slugging it out inside the ring while two of Hogan's many girlfriends stage a boxing match with each other outside the ring.

Dempsey portrays a referee who has difficulty remembering how to count up to ten.

463 Oh, Baby!

1927, Universal Pictures, 7,152 feet. Director-Story: Harley Knoles. Scenario: Arthur Hoerl. Photography: Marcel Le Picard, Stuart Kelson.

Cast: Little Billy, David Butler, Madge Kennedy, Creighton Hale, Ethel Shannon, Flora Finch.

The midget manager of a heavyweight contender is talked into posing as a friend's non-existent daughter for the benefit of the man's aunt.

The night of the big fight, the manager just barely manages to get out of the house and to the arena, dressed in women's clothes and wig, in time to help out his fighter.

Numerous celebrities appear during the boxing scenes at Madison Square Garden, including Damon Runyon and Bugs Baer.

464 On the Run

1958, British, United Artists, 70 minutes. Director: Ernest Morris. Screenplay: Brian Clemens, Eldon Howard.

Cast: Neil McCallum, Susan Beaumont, William Hartnell, Gordon Tanner, Philip Savile, Gilbert Winfield.

A boxer who refused to take a dive flees for his life and takes refuge in a garage.

465 On Your Toes

1927, Universal Pictures, 5,918 feet. Director: Fred Newmeyer. Scenario: Earle Snell, Gladys Lehman. Photography: Ross Fisher.

Cast: Reginald Denny, Barbara Worth, Hayden Stevenson, Frank Hagney, Gertrude Howard, George West.

If this is a 1920's Universal boxing film, then it must be starring Reginald Denny.

This time he's the son of former champion Kid Roberts and is more interested in teaching dance than boxing. However, he's shamed into fighting by the lovely daughter of fight manager Jack Sullivan.

After initial failure in the boxing ring, he becomes good enough to face Punch Mello (Hagney) for the title.

466 One Hour to Live

1939, Universal, 61 minutes. Director: Harold Schuster. Screenplay: Roy Chanslor. Photography: George Robinson.

Cast: Charles Bickford, John Litel, Doris Nolen, Samuel S. Hinds, Paul Guilfoyle, Jack Carr, Robert Emmett Keane, Emory Parnell, John Gallaudet, Olin Howland.

It's police detective Bickford vs. murderous fight manager Litel, who has married the cop's sweetheart.

467 One Punch O'Day

1926, Rayart Pictures, 5,064 feet. Director: Harry J. Brown. Scenario: Henry R. Symonds.

Cast: Billy Sullivan, Charlotte Merriam, Jack Herrick, William Malan, Eddie Diggins.

An ace boxer falls in love with a girl whose father is in a lot of trouble. People have invested their life savings in an oil well, and he's about to lose the land to a villain.

The boxer helps out his prospective father-in-law by raising money through a bout.

468 One-Round Hogan

1927, Warner Brothers, 6,357 feet. Director: Howard Bretherton. Screenplay: Charles R. Condon. Photography: Norman Brodin.

Cast: Monte Blue, Leila Hyams, James J. Jeffries, Frank Hagney, Tom Gallery, Texas Kid, Abdul the Turk.

Blue portrays the son of a famous boxer, is a light heavyweight champ himself. During a bout with his best friend—Blue's sweetheart's brother—the friend is knocked out. His friend is later killed by his manager, who blames it on Blue.

The climax is a boxing match between Blue and the manager.

469 One Round Jones

1946, Sepia Arts.

Cast: Eddie Green, Lorenzo Tucker.

Little-known comedy about the antics of a black boxer.

470 One Round O'Brien

1912, AB. Director: Mack Sennett.

Cast: Fred Mace, William J. Butler, Clarence Parr, Frank Evans.

A reasonably popular series of films featuring Mace as a boxer began with this episode. Subsequent episodes were **One Round O'Brien Comes Back** (1913), **One Round O'Brien Comes East** (1913), **One Round O'Brien's Flirtation** (1913) and **One Round O'Brien in the Ring Again** (1914).

471 Over the Wall

1938, Warner Brothers, 72 minutes. Director: Frank Mac-

Donald. Screenplay: Crane Wilbur, George Bricker. Story: Warden Lewis E. Lawes. Photography: James Van Trees. Editor: Frank Magee.

Cast: Dick Foran, June Travis, John Litel, Dick Purcell, Veda Ann Borg, George E. Stone, Ward Bond, John Hamilton, Jonathan Hale, Tommy Bupp.

A year before the release of **Kid Nightingale** comes this story, written by a prison warden, about a singing boxer.

The fighter (Foran) is framed for murder by racketeer Purcell and has a rotten attitude until he's straightened out by the prison chaplain (Litel) and becomes the lead singer in the prison choir.

472 Palooka

1934, United Artists, 80-86 minutes. Director: Benjamin Stoloff. Story: Gertrude Purcell, Jack Jevne and Arthur Kober, based on the comic strip by Ham Fisher. Photography: Arthur Edeson. Editor: Grant Whytock.

Cast: Stuart Erwin, Jimmy Durante, Robert Armstrong, Lupe Velez, Marjorie Rambeau, Mary Carlisle, William Cagney, Thelma Todd, Franklyn Ardell, Tom Dugan, Guinn Williams.

The first screen appearance of comic strip hero Joe Palooka, played by Stuart Erwin, is more Jimmy Durante's show as fight manager Knobby Walsh.

Palooka is a country bumpkin who rescues Walsh from a beating following an automobile accident. Impressed with the youth's fistic skills, he lures him to the big city to be a boxer.

When Momma Palooka finds out, she's furious because the last thing she wanted her son to be was a boxer. It seems Dear Old Dad was quite a fighter in his day before walking out on Momma.

Palooka has some early success, thanks to his foe (Hagney) being drunk, until golddigger Velez sinks her hooks into him. It's up to Momma to get rid of Velez, while Dad (Armstrong) arrives on the scene in time to give his son some pointers.

473 Pardon Our Nerve

1939, 20th Century-Fox, 65-67 minutes. Director: H. Bruce Humberstone. Producer: Sol M. Wurtzel. Screenplay: Robert Ellis, Helen Logan. Story: Hilda Stone, Betty Reinhardt. Photography: Charles Clarke.

Cast: Lynn Bari, June Gale, Guinn Williams, Michael Whalen, Edward Brophy, Ward Bond, John Miljan, Tom Kennedy.

Two quick-thinking city girls talk a Minnesota waiter (Williams) into posing as a boxer at a society party. When he accidentally knocks out the champ, he's convinced to enter the boxing ring.

The girls talk a bill collector into financing him, and their quick wits earn him some early success until some of their tricks are discovered.

474 The Patent Leather Kid

1927, First National Pictures, 11,955 feet. Director-Producer: Alfred Santell. Scenario: Winifred Dunn. Adaptation: Adela Rogers St. Johns. Story: Rupert Hughes. Photography: Arthur Edeson, Ralph Hammeras, Alvin Knechtel.

Cast: Richard Barthelmess, Molly O'Day, Lawford Davidson, Matthew Betz, Arthur Stone, Raymond Turner, Hank Mann, Walter James, Lucien Prival, Nigel De Brulier.

The Patent Leather Kid (Barthelmess), a tough New York City boxer, could care less about patriotism during World War I. When his girl friend goes overseas to entertain the troops, he feels only anger.

However, when the boxer and his trainer are drafted and the latter is killed in battle, the Patent Leather Kid becomes a hero; and even though he's partially paralyzed, he's now a real patriot.

475 Penitentiary

1980, Jerry Gross Organization, 98 minutes, Color. Director-Producer-Writer: Jamaa Fanaka. Photography: Marty Ollstein. Editor: Betsy Blanket.

Cast: Leon Isaac Kennedy, Thommy Pollard, Hazel Spear, Floyd Chatman, Badja Djoia, Wilbur "Hi Fi" White.

A big hit with urban audiences, it inspired a sequel, **Penitentiary II.**

Kennedy is framed for murder and must use his fists to fight off the sexual advances of other inmates. His skill lands him on the prison boxing team, where victories earn visitation rights by females and the possibility of early parole.

476 Penitentiary II

1982, United Artists/MGM, 103-109 minutes. Color. Director-Producer-Writer: James Fanaka. Photography: Steve Posey. Editor: James E. Nownes.

Cast: Leon Isaac Kennedy, Glynn Turman, Ernie Hudson, Mr. T, Beggy Blow, Sephton Moody, Donovan Womack, Malik Carter, Stan Kamber, Cephus Jaxon.

Many people think Mr. T had his film debut in **Rocky III** as the notorious Clubber Lang. Uh, uh, it was here. That's about the only thing that distinguishes this sequel to **Penitentiary,** for which they pulled out a script that was old in 1930 and dressed it up with lots of sex, violence and foul language.

Too Sweet (Kennedy), the boxing champ of the original, really doesn't want to fight anymore, but Half-Dead, aided by Do Dirty and Simp (are you following this?), kill the hero's girl after raping her to make him fight. They're out for revenge against him for what he did in the first film.

As if that's not enough, the villains apparently saw a lot of old boxing films on TV, because they pull the old kidnapping trick, threatening to kill Too Sweet's sister unless he takes a dive against the champ.

The title bout is being held at the prison and Too Sweet is really taking a whupping because he loves his sister. But he, too, must have seen a lot of old boxing movies because as soon as he learns that his brother-in-law has freed her, he gains strength and floors the champ.

477 The Personality Kid

1934, Warner Brothers, 70 minutes. Director: Alan Crosland. Adaptation: F. Hugh Herbert, Erwin Gelsey. Story: Gene Towne, C. Graham Baker.

Cast: Pat O'Brien, Glenda Farrell, Claire Dodd, Henry O'Neill, Robert Gleckler, Thomas Jackson, Arthur Vinton, Clarence Muse, Clay Clement, George Cooper.

O'Brien is a wise guy boxer who likes to laugh and dance. He betrays his wife for a wealthy illustrator, but there's a catch: His wife has been getting all his contracts for him and has been matching him with nobodies.

478 Pimple Beats Jack Johnson

1914, British, Folly Films, 790 feet. Director-Scenario: Fred and Joe Evans.

Cast: Fred Evans.

The British comic dreams he beats the great black boxer.

479 Pimple's Sporting Chance

1913, British, Folly Films, 495 feet. Director-Scenario: Fred and Joe Evans.

Cast: Fred Evans.

Pimple wins a boxing match to help save a widow from eviction.

480 A Pitboy's Romance

1917, British, I.B. Davidson-Tiger, 4,000 feet.

Director-Scenario: A.E. Coleby.

Cast: Arthur Rooke, Jimmy Wild, Tommy Noble, A.E. Coleby, J. Hastings Batson.

A boxer gets revenge on the man who jilted his former sweetheart.

481 The Pittsburgh Kid

1941, Republic, 76 minutes. Director: Jack Townley. Producer: Armand Schaeffer. Screenplay: Earl Felton, Houston Branch, based on the story "Kid Tinsel" by Octavus Roy Cohen. Photography: Reggie Lanning. Editor: Ernest Nims.

Cast: Billy Conn, Jean Parker, Dick Purcell, Alan Baxter, Veda Ann Borg, Jonathan Hale, Ernest Whitman, John Kelly, Etta McDaniel, Dick Elliott.

If you want to know why Billy Conn never made it big in the movies, all you have to do is watch him play himself in this film made right after his bout with Joe Louis.

Conn's manager dies at the opening of the film, and Hale wants to take over so he sics his vamp daughter on him.

The scheme fails and Conn winds up fighting the title bout against Hale's fighter (Jack Roper) in this easily-forgotten saga.

482 Pocket Boxers

1903, British, R.W. Paul, 8 minutes. Director: W.R. Booth.

Two men take out tiny boxers from their pockets and make a bet on the fight.

483 Pride of the Bowery (aka **Here We Go Again**)

1940, Monogram, 63 minutes. Director: Joseph H. Lewis. Producer: Sam Katzman. Screenplay: George Plympton. Adaptation: William Lively. Story: Steven Clemson. Photography: Robert Kline. Editor: Robert Golden.

Cast: Leo Gorcey, Bobby Jordan, Kenneth Howell, Mary Ainslee, Bobby Stone, Donald Haines, David Gorcey, Sunshine Sammy Morrison, Kenneth Harlan, Nick Stuart, Lloyd Ingraham.

The East Side Kids' Muggs (Leo Gorcey) is a Golden Gloves boxer who yearns to train in the wild open spaces. His pals trick him into joining the Civilian Conservation Corps, where he's slow catching on to the rules.

When he refuses to shake hands after a bout with a fellow camper, the others give him the silent treatment.

To help out a pal who's stolen some money and needs to return it, Muggs turns pro and gets beaten badly, although he earns the money. When he returns the money to the captain's drawer, however, he's accused of stealing it. The real culprit finally confesses, however; but in a unique final twist which sets this apart from other boxing movies, Muggs is winning his final bout handily when the ringside plea from a beautiful girl friend causes him to be distracted and knocked out.

484 The Pride of the Fancy

1920, British, G.B. Samuelson, 6,000 feet. Director: Albert Ward. Story: George Edgar.

Cast: Rex Davis, Daisy Burrell, Tom Reynolds, Fred Morgan, Dorothy Fane, Wyndham Guise, Pope Stamper.

A boxer wins the bout and the girl despite the efforts of the villain, so what else is new?

485 Prince of Broadway

1926, Chadwick. Director: John Gorman. Adaptation: Frederic Chapin.

Cast: George Walsh, Alyce Mills, Freeman Wood, Robert Roper, Tommy Ryan, Charles McHugh, G. Howe Black, Frankie Genaro, Billy Papke, Leach Cross, Gene Delmont.

The "Prince of Broadway" loses his heavyweight title because of too much wine and women, and to boot, he loses his contract.

It's a childhood sweetheart who gives him the inspiration to get back on the winning track.

486 The Prize Fighter

1967, Polish. Director: Julian Dziedzina. Screenplay: B. Tomaszewski, J. Suszko. Photography: M. Sprudin.

Cast: Daniel Olbrychski.

Olbrychski portrays a man who's straightened out by becoming a boxer.

487 The Prize Fighter

1979, New World Pictures, 99 minutes. Color. Director: Michael Preece. Producer: Lang Elliott. Screenplay: Tim Conway, John Myers. Photography: Jacques Haitkin. Editor: Fabien Tordjmann.

Cast: Tim Conway, Don Knotts, David Wayne, Robin Clark, Cisse Cameron, Mary Ellen O'Neill, Michael La Guardia.

With Conway and Knotts in the cast, you know you ain't getting Shakespeare. They're penniless in the 1930's and get involved in a fixed fight scheme with mobster Clark hoping to take away Wayne's gym, with the latter placing his bets on fighter Conway.

488 The Prizefighter and the Lady

1933, Metro Goldwyn Mayer, 90 minutes. Director: W.S. Van Dyke. Story: Frances Marion. Adaptation: John Lee Mahin, Jr., John Meehan. Photography: Lester White.

Cast: Max Baer, Myrna Loy, Primo Carnera, Jess Willard, Jim Jeffries, Jack Dempsey, Walter Huston, Otto Kruger, Vince Barnett, Robert McWade, Muriel Evans, Jean Howard.

Ex-boxer Baer not only fights, but sings and dances in this adaptation of a story by the author of **The Champ,** which is noteworthy for the number of big name boxers who appear.

Primo Carnera, who portrays Baer's opponent in the final bout, refused to be knocked out, so the original ending of the film had to be changed. The film studio paid Carnera an extra $10,000 to be added to his $35,000 fee so that the boxer would accept a draw!

During the final battle in the film, Baer is beaten to a pulp by Carnera for the first ten rounds until his estranged wife (Loy) and his ex-manager (Huston) show that they're still with him.

489 Punch Drunks

1934, Columbia, 18 minutes. Director: Lou Breslow.

Cast: The Three Stooges, Dorothy Granger, Arthur Housman, William Irving, Jack "Tiny" Lipson, Billy Fletcher.

Every time Curly hears "Pop Goes the Weasel," he turns into a fighting demon. When the violinist playing it at ringside breaks his fiddle, Curly starts getting beaten to a pulp until the song is played on a phonograph.

490 Put Up Your Hands

1919, American Film Co., 5 reels. Director: Edward Sloman. Screenplay: L.V. Jefferson.

Cast: Marjarita Fisher, George Periolat, Emory Johnson, Hayward Mack, William Mong, Kate Price, Bull Montana.

Men prove no match in the boxing ring for the female hero of this western comedy.

491 The Quiet Man

1952, Republic, 129 minutes, Color. Director: John Ford. Producer: Merian C. Cooper. Screenplay: Frank S. Nugent. Story: Maurice Walsh. Photography: Winton C. Hoch, Archie Stout. Editor: Jack Murray.

Cast: John Wayne, Maureen O'Hara, Victor McLaglen, Barry Fitzgerald, Ward Bond, Mildred Natwick, Arthur Shields, Francis Ford, Jack Roper, Al Murphy, Eileen Crowe, Sean McClory, Charles Fitzsimmons.

Wayne portrays Sean Thornton, who returns to his native Ireland after killing a man in the ring.

He buys a cottage in Innisfree where he was born, but that angers McLaglen, because the cottage Wayne buys divides his land from that of a wealthy widow, and McLaglen wanted it for himself.

Wayne, in the meantime, falls for O'Hara, McLaglen's sister, and guess who must give permission for her to marry him?

The big brawl between Wayne and McLaglen at the end is one of the great sequences of director Ford's career as it endlessly spills throughout the town and into the countryside.

But it's not the plot of **The Quiet Man** which earned it the nomination for best picture and the Academy Award for best director and best color cinematography. It's the lighthearted script acted by an expert cast, the magnificent Irish countryside and the touch of a master director which provide the best feel for life in Ireland yet presented on screen.

492 Raging Bull

1980, United Artists, 128 minutes. Director: Martin Scorcese. Producers: Irwin Winkler, Robert Chartoff. Screenplay: Paul Schrader and Mardik Martin, based on a book by Jake LaMotta with Joseph Carter and Peter Savage. Photography: Michael Chapman. Editor: Thelma Schoonmaker.

Cast: Robert DeNiro, Cathy Moriarty, Joe Pesci, Frank Vincent, Nicholas Colasanto, Theresa Saldana, Frank Adonos, Mario Gallo, Frank Topham, Lois Anne Flax, Eddie Mustafa Muhammad.

DeNiro won the Academy Award for his portrayal of Bronx-born middleweight champ Jake LaMotta, and there are very few around who would dispute that he earned it.

Not many actors would willingly put on 50 pounds for the sake of a film, as DeNiro did to portray the boxer in later years. No pun intended, **Raging Bull** pulls no punches as it follows the moody fighter's career starting in 1941 with extremely brutal, slow-motion fight scenes and tumultuous and seemingly nearly-as-violent home life sequences.

Just about everything is covered, including his being barred for throwing a fight, his career as a night club entertainer and his jailing on a morals charge.

493 Rainbow Ranch

1933, Monogram, 54 minutes. Director: Harry Frazer. Producer: Paul Malvern. Story: Frazer, Harry O. Jones. Photography: Archie Stout.

Cast: Rex Bell, Cecelia Parker, Robert Kortman, Henry Hall, Gordon de Maine, Phil Dunham.

A navy boxing champ (Bell) heads out West to avenge himself on the villain who killed his uncle, stole his land and took his girl, but finds himself framed.

494 Red Hot Hoofs

1926, R-C Pictures, 4,681 feet. Director: Robert DeLacey. Adaptation: F.A.E. Pine. Story: George Washington Yates, Jr. Photography: John Leezer.

Cast: Tom Tyler, Frankie Darro, Dorothy Dunbar, Stanley Taylor, Harry O'Connor, Al Kaufman, Barney Furey.

Ranch foreman Tom Buckley (Tyler) must fight the villainous Battling Jack Riley (Kaufman) to bail out the brother of the girl he loves, in another 1920s boxing western. It seems the lad stole some funds from the bank where he works.

After the inevitable kidnapping plot by Riley, who of course also loves the girl (Dunbar), the outcome is predictable.

495 The Referee

1922, Selznick Pictures-Select Pictures, 4,665 feet. Director: Ralph Ince. Scenario: Lewis Allen Browne. Story: Gerald Beaumont. Photography: William Wagner.

Cast: Conway Tearle, Anders

Randolf, Gladys Hulette, Gus Platz, Frank Ryan, Joe Humphries, Patsy Haley.

Middleweight champion McArdle (Tearle) is injured in an accident, ending his boxing career. After becoming known for his honesty as the owner of a pool hall, he's offered a job as a referee.

Meanwhile, his sweetheart's father doesn't want her having anything to do with anyone connected with the fight game.

During the big bout, McArdle discovers that it's fixed and ends the fight, thus changing his future father-in-law's mind about him.

496 Requiem for a Heavyweight

1962, Columbia, 85-87 minutes. Director: Ralph Nelson. Producer: David Susskind. Screenplay: Rod Serling. Photography: Arthur J. Ornitz. Editor: Carl Lerner.

Cast: Anthony Quinn, Jackie Gleason, Mickey Rooney, Julie Harris, Stan Adams, Herbie Faye, Jack Dempsey, Steve Belloise, Lou Gilbert, Arthur Mercante.

Here's a trivia question: In what film did Muhammad Ali make his debut? That's right, Ali (here Cassius Clay) portrays the young boxer who knocks out Mountain Rivera (Quinn) at the beginning of this great boxing film.

Quitting the ring after 17 years of being punched around, Rivera gets a job as athletic director at a summer camp through the efforts of social worker Harris.

His unscrupulous manager (Gleason), who's in heavily to gamblers, ruins it all for him by getting him soused.

Despite all the wrongs heaped upon him by Gleason, when Quinn realizes that his manager's life may actually be in danger, he agrees to humiliate himself by going into the wrestling ring in full Indian costume and doing a war dance during the match.

497 Ribbons and Boxing Gloves

1914, Biograph, 543 feet.

A ribbon salesman who's losing his girl to a top boxer takes lessons and manages to floor the champ.

498 Right Cross

1950, Metro Goldwyn Mayer, 89 minutes. Director: John Sturges. Producer: Armand Deutsch. Screenplay: Charles Schnee. Photography: Norbert Bodine. Editor: David Rackin.

Cast: June Allyson, Dick Powell, Ricardo Montalban, Lionel Barrymore, Tom Powers, Marilyn Monroe (unbilled), Teresa Celli, Barry Kelley, John Gallaudet, Ken Tobey.

Right Cross can be considered a landmark sports film in terms of its treatment of minorities and women in sports.

Montalban is a Mexican-American boxer with what could be described as a persecution complex. He loves Allyson, the daughter of manager Barrymore, but is in constant fear that he'll lose her to sportswriter Powell the instant he stops winning.

When Barrymore's health won't let him manage Montalban anymore, Allyson takes over.

Right Cross is the first sports film to bring to the fore in a major production the particular sensitivities of minority athletes. It's no coincidence that within two years there would be two other major productions about Mexican boxers—**The Ring** and **The Fighter.**

The romance with Allyson is precedent-setting as well, although it would be some time before a black-white love affair would be portrayed on screen.

Right Cross is also significant for its serious handling, unlike the ilk of **Be Yourself,** or even **Take Me Out to the Ball Game,** of a woman involved in the world of sports. And Montalban's fear that he'll lose her once he starts losing is true to the fickle presentation of women in sports films that's occurred time and time again since the silent era. **Right Cross** is one of the exceptions to that.

499 The Right That Failed

1922, Metro Goldwyn Mayer, 5 reels. Director: Bayard Veiller. Adaptation: Lenore Coffee. Photography: Arthur Martinelli.

Cast: Bert Lytell, Virginia Valli, DeWitt Jennings, Philo McCullough, Otis Harland, Max Davidson.

A boxer breaks his wrist while winning the lightweight title and falls in love with a high society gal at a vacation resort. At first, he keeps his profession a secret from her; but eventually he's accepted for what he is.

500 Right to the Heart

1941, 20th Century-Fox, 72 minutes. Director: Eugene Forde. Producer: Sol M. Wurtzel. Screenplay: Walter Bullock. Story: Harold McGrath. Photography: Virgil Miller. Editor: Louis Loeffler.

Cast: Joseph Allen, Jr., Brenda Joyce, Cobina Wright, Jr., Stanley Clements, Don DeFore, Hugh Beaumont, Charles D. Brown, Frank Orth, Phil Tead, William Haade.

Flattened by a boxer in a nightclub fight and disowned by his rich aunt for his constant irresponsible behavior, Allen decides to attend a fighter's camp to get into shape for a return fight against the pug.

He falls in love with the daughter of the camp trainer.

501 The Ring

1927, British, Wardour, 8,007-8,454 feet. Director-Screenplay: Alfred Hitchcock. Producer: John Maxwell. Photography: John J. Cox.

Cast: Carl Brisson, Lilian Hall-Davis, Ian Hunter, Billy Wells, Forrester Harvey, Harry Terry, Gordon Harker, Eugene Corri.

Considered minor Hitchcock, **The Ring** marked The Master's first hookup with cameraman Cox, who would shoot all of his subsequent features until 1933.

The Ring can be cited as a prime example of the presentation of women as fickle.

A carnival boxer who is engaged to a ticketseller is beaten by an Australian champ, who also makes love to the woman.

The carnival boxer eventually does marry the woman, only to have her leave him for the champ. The two men finally meet again in the ring with the cuckolded hubby flooring the champ and winning back his fickle wife.

502 The Ring

1952, United Artists, 79 minutes. Director: Kurt Neumann. Screenplay: Irving Shulman. Photography: Russell Harlan. Editor: Bruce B. Pierce.

Cast: Gerald Mohr, Lalo Rios, Rita Moreno, Robert Arthur, Robert Osterloh, Martin Garralaga, Jack Elam, Peter Brocco, Julia Montova.

Prejudice against Mexican-Americans is what drives a young boxer (Rios) to try for the top to try to make the "Anglos" respect him.

Winning his first eight bouts under the tutelage of manager Mohr despite the objections of his loved ones to his chosen profession, the youth seeks bouts he's not ready for and is badly beaten.

When a waitress refuses to serve him, he realizes that the respect he's earned in the boxing ring is only superficial, and he also eventually learns of other ways he can help his people.

503 Ring and the Belle

1941, Columbia, 2 reels. Director: Del Lord.

Cast: Andy Clyde, Vivien Oakland, Jack Roper, Dudley Dickerson, Vernon Dent.

Comedian Clyde has a problem

as a fight manager when his boxer skips town.

504 Ringside

1949, Lippert Pictures, 63 minutes. Director: Frank McDonald. Producer: Ron Ormond. Screenplay: Daniel Ullman. Photography: Ernest Miller. Editor: Hugh Winn.

Cast: Red Barry, Sheila Ryan, Margia Dean, Joseph Crehan, John Cason, Tom Brown, Tony Canzoneri, Joey Adams, Lyle Talbot, Frankie Van.

Here's a low budget film that comes close to being a total ripoff of Cagney's **City for Conquest.**

Barry portrays a concert pianist whose boxer brother (Brown) is blinded during a championship bout. That much is nearly identical with **City for Conquest.** But this one focuses on the pianist rather than the blinded brother as Barry gives up his musical career and trains to be a boxer so he can avenge himself upon the champ.

There are complications along the way as Barry falls in love with his brother's girl friend, but as brother Brown is starting to fool around with his nurse, all works out okay.

505 Ringside Maisie

1941, Metro Goldwyn Mayer, 95 minutes. Director: Edwin Marin. Producer: J. Walter Rubin. Screenplay: Mary McCall, Jr. Editor: Frederick Y. Smith.

Cast: Ann Sothern, George Murphy, Robert Sterling, Virginia O'Brien, Natalie Thompson, Max Rosenbloom, Rags Ragland, Jonathan Hall, John Indrisano, Eddie Simms.

The fifth in the Maisie comedy series finds the Brooklyn gal involved with a boxer (Sterling) and his greedy manager (Murphy).

506 Ripped Off (aka **The Boxer**)

1971, Italian, 83 minutes, Color. Director: Franco Prosperi.

Cast: Robert Blake, Ernest Borgnine, Gabriele Ferzetti, Catherine Spaak, Thomas Milian.

To borrow from the title, this is a modern-day ripoff of **The Life of Jimmy Dolan** and **They Made Me a Criminal** in which boxer Blake is framed for the murder of his manager, and he's tracked by detective Borgnine.

Although it's an Italian production, **Ripped Off** was filmed in Chicago.

507 Rocco and His Brothers

1961, French-Italian, Astor Pictures, 120-180 minutes. Director: Luchino Visconti. Screenplay: Visconti, Suso Cecchi D'Amico, Pasquale Festa Campanile, Enrico Medioli. Photography: Giuseppe Rotunno. Editor: Mario Serandrei.

Cast: Alain Delon, Annie Girardot, Claudia Cardinale, Renato Salvatori, Katina Paxinou, Roger Hanin, Paolo Stoppa, Suzy Delair, Spiros Focas, Max Cartier, Rocco Vidolazzi.

The corrupting influences of life in the big city form the focus of Visconti's mammoth melodrama, which exists in several versions of varying lengths.

A recently-widowed woman travels with her sons from the south of Italy to live in Milan. The family finds life in the big city tough; and one of the brothers, Simone (Salvatori) enjoys some success as a boxer and takes a prostitute as his lover. She leaves him, however, when he gets too possessive.

Another brother, Rocco (Delon) falls for her, incurring the wrath of jealous Simone, who has turned to a life of crime. Rocco also becomes a professional boxer and signs a long-term contract to repay the homosexual boxing patron his brother has robbed. The plot twists include murder and betrayal.

508 Rocky

1976, United Artists, 119-121 minutes. Color. Director: John

G. Avildsen. Producer: Irwin Winkler. Screenplay: Sylvester Stallone. Photography: James Crabe. Editor: Richard Halsey.

Cast: Sylvester Stallone, Talia Shire, Burt Young, Carl Weathers, Burgess Meredith, Thayer David, Joe Spinell, Bill Baldwin, Joe Frazier, Al Salvani, Frank Stallone.

Rocky, the ultimate underdog, won the Academy Award for best picture, best director and best editing, spawned two sequels and inspired a whole spate of imitations.

Stallone plays Rocky Balboa, "The Italian Stallion," a stumblebum Philadelphia club fighter who's a total failure at whatever he does.

Suddenly, out of nowhere, heavyweight champ Apollo Creed (Weathers), as part of his own personal celebration of the American bicentennial, gives him a shot at the title as part of a publicity gimmick.

While Creed takes the match lightly, Rocky sees it as the only chance he'll ever have and trains hard to the strains of Bill Conti's now famous "Rocky" theme, as he punches meat, jogs and runs up and down the steps of the city's landmarks. No more collecting for loan shark Spinell for him.

Rocky has found new meaning to his life in the person of shy, homely Adrian (Shire) while the boxer's love makes her come out of her shell.

The finale boxing match is a blockbuster, with Rocky clearly outclassed and the eventual loser; but he gains the respect of the entire world by his refusal to give up and the way which he fights.

According to some sources, the real-life inspiration for **Rocky** was New Jersey heavyweight Chuck Wepner, whose nickname was "the Bayonne Bleeder" and who had a title shot against Muhammad Ali.

509 Rocky II

1979, United Artists, 119 minutes, Color. Director-Screenplay: Sylvester Stallone. Producers: Irwin Winkler, Robert Chartoff. Photography: Bill Butler. Editor: Danford B. Greene. Boxing Technical Advisor: Al Salvani.

Cast: Sylvester Stallone, Talia Shire, Burgess Meredith, Burt Young, Carl Weathers, Tony Burton, Joe Spinell, Leonard Gaines, Sylvia Meals, Frank McRae, Bill Baldwin.

In case you missed it the first time around, the first ten minutes of the sequel reprise the blockbuster boxing match of the original.

After the bout, Rocky is told he can never fight again or he'll risk permanent injury to the eye that was so badly battered and cut during the match.

Meanwhile, his efforts to get a permanent job outside the ring meet with failure.

His opponent in the match, Apollo Creed, is being inundated with mail claiming that he can't beat Rocky again, so he tries goading Rocky into a bout, calling him the Italian Chicken as poor Rocky ponders whether to risk eye injury. Of course, the audience knew he would accept or there wouldn't have been a sequel, would there?

The match itself tries to outdo the original, with both fighters taking more punches than any sane referee would allow, thanks to a little dramatic license, and at one point knock each other to the floor.

510 Rocky III

1982, United Artists/MGM, 99 minutes, Color. Director-Screenplay: Sylvester Stallone. Producers: Irwin Winkler, Robert Chartoff. Photography: Bill Butler. Editors: Don Zimmerman, Mark Warner.

Cast: Sylvester Stallone, Carl Weathers, Talia Shire, Burt

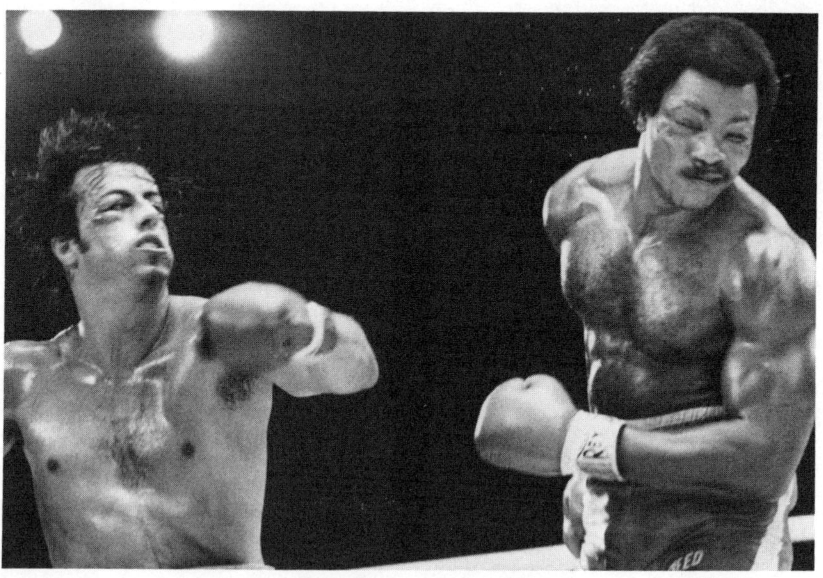

Rocky Balboa (Sylvester Stallone), left, and Apollo Creed (Carl Weathers) slug it out in the championship bout rematch in Rocky II. (From the United Artists release Rocky II, © 1979 United Artists Corporation.)

Young, Burgess Meredith, Mr. T, Ian Fried, Al Silvani, Wally Taylor, Tony Burton, Hulk Hogan.

Now that Rocky is heavyweight champ, how do you keep sympathy for him as the underdog? The answer: Introduce rooting, tooting, muscle-bound meanness personified in the person of challenger Clubber Lang (Mr. T).

Rocky is now peaceably married with a son and ignores manager Mickey's (Meredith's) advice to retire.

Beaten and humiliated in the ring by Lang, Rocky finds a new friend in his former opponent, Apollo Creed, who helps him train for the rematch.

One of **Rocky III**'s highlights is charity boxing-wrestling match between Rocky and Thunderlips (Hulk Hogan).

511 Rodney Stone

1920, British, Screen Plays, 6,341 feet. Director-Producer: Percy Nash. Screenplay: W. Courtenay Rowden, based on a novel by Sir Arthur Conan Doyle. Photography: S.L. Eaton.

Cast: Lionel D'Aragon, Cecil Morton York, Ethel Newman, Frank Tennant, Frank Adair, Fred Morgan, Douglas Payne, Ernest Wallace.

In 1796, the "son" of a blacksmith becomes a fighter. In actuality, he's the son of a peer with a dreaded family secret in this period piece which is also highlighted by a coach race.

512 Rough House Rosie

1927, Paramount, 5,952 feet. Director: Frank Strayer. Screenplay: Louise Long, Ethel Doherty, from a **Saturday Evening Post** story by Nunnally Johnson. Photography: James Murray, Hal Rosson.

Cast: Clara Bow, Reed Howes, Arthur Housman, Doris Hill, Douglas Gilmore, John Miljan.

On the night of the big fight, a nightclub girl leaves her wealthy lover and goes to the ring to root for her former boyfriend, whom she had previously jilted.

513 The Roughneck

1924, Fox Film Corp., 7,619 feet. Director: Jack Conway. Scenario: Charles Kenyon. Story: Robert William Service. Photography: George Schneiderman.

Cast: George O'Brien, Billie Dove, Harry T. Morey, Harvey Clark, Charles Sellon, Cleo Madison, Buddy Smith.

A young boxer flees to the South Seas, fearing he has killed an opponent in the ring. He jumps ship and beats a shark to the nearest island where who should he find? Dear Old Mom, who thought he had been killed years before.

But he finds things aren't all that peaceful on the island. He must fight the evil seaman Mad McCara (Morey) who lured his mother to the island and who is now making improper advances to a young woman (Dove).

514 Run for the Wind

1966, British, 95 minutes. Director: Lindsay Shonteff. Screenplay: Jeremy Craig Dryden.

Cast: Francesca Annis, Sean Caffrey, Shawn Phillips, Mark York, Jack Smethurst, George Pastell, Sheena Campbell.

A woman who jilted her boxer boyfriend for a singer finds the fighter doesn't want her back.

515 Scrap Iron

1921, Associated First National Productions, 6,747 feet. Director: Charles Ray. Adaptation: Finis Fox. Photography: George Ricard.

Cast: Charles Ray, Lydia Scott, Vera Steadman, Tom Wilson, Tom O'Brien, Stanton Heck, Charles Wheelock.

Our Hero gets into all kinds of trouble when his dear invalid mother convinces him to give up boxing. Branded a coward by his mill co-workers, his girl leaves him and he's fired when he gets back to work late from lunch.

You just know he's going to get back into that ring and redeem himself.

516 Sea Legs

1930, Paramount, 5,673 feet. Director: Victor Heerman. Scenario: Marion Dix. Story: George Marion. Photography: Allen Siegler. Editor: Doris Drought.

Cast: Jack Oakie, Lillian Roth, Harry Green, Eugene Pallette, Jean Del Val, Albert Conti, Andre Cheron.

Navy lightweight champ Searchlight Doyle (Oakie) is forced to impersonate a wealthy good-for-nothing who must serve in the navy of Sainte Cassette to receive an inheritance in this lightweight musical comedy.

517 Second Chance

1953, RKO Radio Pictures, 81 minutes. Color. Director: Rudolph Mate. Producer: Sam Wiesenthal. Screenplay: Oscar Millard, Sydney Boehm. Photography: William Snyder. Editor: Robert Ford.

Cast: Robert Mitchum, Jack Palance, Linda Darnell, Sandro Ciglio, Rodolfo Hoyos, Jr., Reginald Sheffield, Margaret Brewster, Roy Roberts, Salvador Baguez.

Hailed as RKO's first film in 3-D and stereophonic sound, the boxing scenes take a back seat to the exciting climax which finds good guy Mitchum battling hit man Palance in a cable car stranded thousands of feet over the ground.

Mitchum is an American boxer who's fighting nobodies throughout South America until he gets his head screwed on right again following the death of a ring opponent.

He becomes the protector of a gangster's girl (Darnell), who's fleeing from Palance who is out to: (A) Kill her so she can't testify before a Senate committee; or (B) Run away with her himself.

When the three of them and a number of other persons are

trapped in a cable car, which is about to plunge down the mountainside, Mitchum finds he has to finally use his full punching power to get the better of Palance.

518 Secrets of a Nurse

1938, Universal, 75 minutes. Director: Arthur Lubin. Screenplay: Tom Lennon, Lester Cole. Story: Quentin Reynolds.

Cast: Helen Mack, Dick Foran, Edmund Lowe, Clarence Muse.

Nurse Mack becomes involved with a boxer (Foran) who is falsely accused of murder.

519 Sergeant Joe Louis on Tour

1943, Toddy Films.

A short documentary made during World War II which features the great black boxer's tours for the Army.

520 The Set-Up

1949, RKO Radio Pictures, 72 minutes. Director: Robert Wise. Producer: Richard Goldstone. Screenplay: Art Cohn, from the poem by Joseph Moncure March. Photography: Milton Krasner. Fights staged by: John Indrisano.

Cast: Robert Ryan, Audrey Totter, George Tobias, Alan Baxter, Wallace Ford, Percy Helton, Hal Fieberling, Darryl Hickman, Kenny O'Morrison, James Edwards.

The only boxing feature to be inspired by a poem, all the action in this very much underrated and neglected work takes place in one night and on one block of a small city.

Ryan is Stroker Thompson, an over-the-hill fighter who is perenially just one more bout away from making the big time.

When a customer at the seedy arena sees the poster for the fight outside, he says incredulously, "Is he still fighting? I remember him when I was a kid."

Thompson is such a sure bet to lose that his crooked manager (Tobias) doesn't even bother telling him he's supposed to take a dive.

Meanwhile, faithful (for a change!) wife Totter just wants him to quit while he still has his full senses.

Much of the action is centered around the locker room where all the boxers on the night's card swap stories. There are the usual assortment of characters including the punch-drunk oldtimer who represents Thompson's future and the naive beginner (Hickman) who symbolizes his past.

When Thompson somehow manages enough strength to win his bout, he becomes the target of racketeers who are upset at being doublecrossed, even though the boxer knew nothing about the set-up.

521 The Shakedown

1929, Universal Pictures, 6,613-6,753 feet. Director: William Wyler. Scenario: Charles A. Logue, Clarence J. Marks. Photography: Charles Stumar, Jerome Ash. Editor: Lloyd Nosler.

Cast: James Murray, Barbara Kent, George Kotsonaros, Wheeler Oakman, Harry Gribbon.

Murray plays a professional "fall guy" who travels around from city to city making himself known as a good fighter, but who later takes dives for a fee.

Arriving in Boonton, he falls in love and becomes father to an orphan boy and decides to change his life. He must overcome public hostility once his past is made public, to defeat the local boxing hero Battling Roff (Kotsonaros).

522 The Shock Punch

1925, Paramount Pictures, 6,151 feet. Director: Paul Sloane. Screenplay: Luther Reed. Story: John Monk Saunders. Photography: William Miller.

Cast: Richard Dix, Frances Howard, Percy Moore, Theodore Babcock, Gunboat Smith, Walter Long.

Ironworker Randall Savage

(Dix) is also a top boxer and the rival of Bull Malarkey (Long) for the daughter of an architect. He must battle not only ring opponents, but the efforts of Malarkey to stall construction and ruin the girl's dad.

523 Side Streets

1933, British, MGM, 47 minutes. Director: Ivar Campbell. Producer: Norman Loudon. Screenplay: Philip Godfrey.

Cast: Arnold Riches, Jane Wood, Diana Beaumont, Paul Neville, Harry Terry, Dora Levis, Gunnar Moir.

An unemployed man enters a boxing match to earn some money, while at the same time trying to save his fiancée's mom from the clutches of a blackmailing ex-husband.

524 The Sidewalks of New York

1923, Lester Park, 5,500 feet. Director: Lester Park. Scenario: Willard King Bradley.

Cast: Hanna Lee, Bernard Siegel, Templar Saxe.

This little-known film, regardless of its quality, must be considered a sports movie landmark for its theme of women's rights and its acknowledgment of women as athletes.

A woman refuses to marry her father's favorite and is kicked out of the house. She goes on to win the ladies world championship boxing match and save her dad from being evicted.

525 The Singing Boxer

1933, Paramount, 2 reels. Director: Leslie Pearce. Producer: Mack Sennett. Screenplay: W.C. Fields.

Cast: Donald Novis.

Six years before **Kid Nightingale** came this comedy short, which is just what it sounds like.

526 The Snob Buster

1925, Rayart Pictures, 4,970 feet. Director: Albert Rogell. Scenario: Forrest Sheldon. Photography: Ross Fisher.

Cast: Reed Howes, Wilfred Lucas, David Kirby, Gloria Grey, George French, Ray Johnston, Max Asher.

The son of a millionaire returns home from World War I such a changed man that his father commits him to an insane asylum, for his new democratic views.

He escapes and goes to stay with his war buddy, an ex-boxer, and falls in love with his friend's sister.

Running afoul of another boxer, the two agree to a public bout, but the millionaire has his son put away in the asylum again (this may sound like a comedy, but it isn't). Guess what, he escapes again, but is being beaten badly in the ring until, you guessed it, the girl's ringside plea.

The cops raid the place before the bout is finished, but the two fighters resume the match on their own after getting away.

527 So This Is Love

1928, Columbia, 5,611 feet. Director: Frank Capra. Producer: Harry Cohn. Story: Norman Springer. Photography: Ray June. Editor: Arthur Roberts.

Cast: Shirley Mason, William Collier, Jr., Johnnie Walker, Ernie Adams, Carl Gerard, William H. Strauss.

A dress designer loves a counter girl, but she only has eyes for a boxer and even has the poor schnook design clothes for her that will attract the boxer's attention.

However, the girl sours on the boxer when he starts bullying the designer, who to get the girl's love, starts training to be a boxer himself.

Prior to the big bout between the two rivals, the counter girl, to help the designer, starts feeding the champ just about everything in the deli so he'll be overfed for the fight.

528 The Social Lion

1930, Paramount, 5,403 feet. Director: A. Edward Sutherland. Story: Octavus Roy Cohen.

Cast: Jack Oakie, Mary Brian, Olive Borden, William Bechtel, Richard Cummings.

Boxing and polo mix in this early sound comedy. Oakie is boxer Marco Perkins, who after being badly defeated in the ring, becomes a member of an exclusive polo club—at first for laughs—until it's learned he's an excellent polo player.

The boxer ignores a hat-check girl who loves him for a snobbing society gal until he learns better. After telling his society "friends" off, he returns to boxing to try to win the championship.

529 Society Girl

1932, Fox Film Corp., 72 minutes. Director: Sidney Lanfield. Photography: George Barnes. Adaptation: Charles Braban.

Cast: James Dunn, Peggy Shannon, Spencer Tracy, Walter Byron, Bert Hanlon, Marjorie Gatson, Eula Guy Todd.

You can tell how old this one is by the place Tracy, who portrays a fight manager, has in the billing. A society girl strings along a boxer (Dunn), at first for laughs. It becomes no laughing matter for Dunn, however, when he breaks training for her and winds up being KO'd.

530 Soigne Ton Gauche

1936, French, Cady-Films. Director: Rene Clement. Producer: Fred Orain. Screenplay: Jacques Tati.

Jacques Tati, often described as the French Charlie Chaplin and who would go on to fame for his Mr. Hulot character in the 1950's and 60's, stars in this early short as a valet who's quite skilled at boxing.

531 Un Soir De Rafle (Night Raid)

1931, French, Osso Films. Director: Carmine Galloni. Screenplay: Henri Decoin.

Cast: Albert Prejean, Annabella, Lucien Baroux, Edith Mara, Constant Remy.

This just goes to prove the French can make cliche-ridden boxing films like everyone else.

Prejean is a singing seaman who loses his passion for the ocean after he rescues a cabaret singer from the police. After he beats an ex-champ in a carnival boxing match, he decides to begin a pro ring career and before long is French boxing champ.

Along comes the inevitable Vamp to steal Our Hero from his beloved cabaret singer, sap him of his strength and lead to his defeat because of lack of training in the European championship bout. A sadder, but wiser, Prejean then returns to the singer.

532 Some Blondes Are Dangerous

1937, Universal, 65-68 minutes. Director: Milton Carruth. Producer: E.M. Asher. Screenplay: Lester Cole. Photography: George Robinson. Editor: Frank Gross.

Cast: William Gargan, Noah Beery, Jr., Dorothy Kent, Nan Grey, Roland Drew, Polly Rowles, John Butler, Lew Kelly, Eddie Roberts, Ed Stanley, Joe Smallwood, Walter Friedman.

A remake of 1931's **The Iron Man** features Beery as the champ who marries gold-digger Kent, with Grey as the nice girl he left behind and Gargan as his manager.

He eventually splits up with his manager and finds out about his wife's infidelity. He later faces his old manager's new protege in the big fight.

It was remade again in 1951 as **The Iron Man.**

533 Some White Hope

1915, Vitagraph, 858 feet.

Cast: Donald McBride.

One of dozens of films inspired by Jack Johnson's career, this is a burlesque of his fight with Jess Willard. A braggart dreams he replaces Willard in the ring and knocks out an unidentified black champ in the first round.

He's awakened when his wife throws a jug of water over him.

534 Somebody Up There Likes Me

1956, Metro Goldwyn Mayer, 112 minutes. Director: Robert Wise. Producer: Charles Schnee. Screenplay: Ernest Lehman, based on the autobiography of Rocky Graziano with Rowland Barber. Photography: Joseph Ruttenberg. Editor: Albert Akst.

Cast: Paul Newman, Pier Angeli, Everett Sloane, Eileen Heckart, Harold J. Stone, Sal Mineo, Joseph Buloff, Sammy White, Arch Johnson, Steve McQueen, Dean Jones, Courtland Shepard, Harry Wisman, Terry Rangno.

The screen role of Rocky Graziano was originally intended for that rebel without a cause himself, James Dean. When the movie idol was killed in a car crash, it proved the big break for Paul Newman's movie career.

The film's foreword carries this quote from boxer Graziano: "This is the way I remember it...definitely."

It traces the boxer's life from age 8, when his drunken father, a disillusioned fighter himself, uses the boy as a punching bag to amuse his alcoholic friends.

Graziano as a youth gets into deeper and deeper trouble with the law, going from one institution to another and later being dishonorably discharged from the army.

It's through his love for boxing and for a beautiful Jewish girl (Angeli) that Graziano begins to make something worthwhile of his life until a new roadblock crosses his path.

A gangster pal (Loggia) tries to convince him to throw a fight, and when he refuses he gets into trouble anyway for not reporting it.

Then he must still fight for the championship.

The film won Oscars for best black and white cinematography and for best black and white art direction. Set mostly in New York City.

535 A Son of David

1920, British, Broadwest, 4,700 feet. Director: Hay Plumb. Scenario: Benedict James. Story: Charles Barnett.

Cast: Poppy Wyndham, Ronald Colman, Arthur Walcott, Joseph Pacey, Constance Backner, Robert Vallis, Vesta Sylva.

An orphan boy is adopted by a rabbi and when he grows up boxes the man he believes killed his real dad.

536 Speakeasy

1929, Fox Film Corp., 5,775 feet. Director: Benjamin Stoloff. Scenario: Frederick H. Brennan, Edwin Burke. Editor: J. Edwin Robbins.

Cast: Lola Lane, Stuart Erwin, Paul Page, Warren Hymer, Helen Ware, Erville Alderson, James Guilfoyle, Joseph Cawthorn, Marjorie Beebe, Sailor Vincent.

Middleweight fighter Paul Martin (Page), having just lost the title bout, refuses to grant an interview to a woman reporter (Lane), who makes up a story that he's going to make another try for the championship.

Naturally, the two eventually fall in love; and the reporter proves that the boxer's manager (Hymer) is a two-timing crook. Martin must enter the ring alone during his rematch for the crown.

537 The Spirit of Youth

1929, Tiffany-Stahl, 6,216 feet. Director: Walter Lang. Story:

Eve Unsell, Elmer Harris. Photography: John Boyle. Editor: Desmond O'Brien.

Cast: Larry Kent, Dorothy Sebastian, Betty Francisco, Maurice Murphy, Anita Fremault, Donald Hall, Charles Sullivan, Sidney D'Albrook, Douglas Gilmore.

A navy boxing champ in love with a librarian meets a rich girl who turns his head. The rich girl convinces the champ to appear in a benefit bout, but he's blinded by resin on his foe's glove.

The librarian proves her true love and sticks by her man, while the rich heiress falls by the wayside.

The fighter being blinded by resin on his opponent's gloves predates Cagney's blinding by the same method in **City for Conquest.**

538 Spirit of Youth

1938, Grand National, 65-70 minutes. Director: Harry Fraser. Producer: Lew Golder. Screenplay: Arthur Hoerle.

Cast: Joe Louis, Clarence Muse, Mantan Moreland, Edna Mae Harris, Cleo Desmond, Mae Turner, Clarence Brooks, Anthony Scott, Janette O'Dell.

It was because Joe Louis acted (although some harsh critics said they wouldn't exactly call it that) in films, that many persons to this day believe Louis played himself in his screen biography.

There's absolutely nothing in **Spirit of Youth** to distinguish it from hundreds of other boxing movies except for the great boxer's appearance and, with the exception of white ring opponents, an all-black cast.

The boxing great portrays Joe Thomas, a rising ring star who's devoted to his mother until he falls into the clutches of a nightclub performer (Harris).

Out of shape from too much wine and women, he's knocked out in his next fight but is determined to make a comeback.

Harris, in the meantime, realizes she's no good for him and summons the pure girl from back home.

In his rematch, Thomas is being beaten to a pulp until guess who arrives; and with the 4,567th ringside plea in movie history (or so it seems) he gets up off the mat and wins.

539 Splinter's in the Navy

1931, British, Twickenham, 76 minutes. Director: William Forde. Producer: Julius Hagen. Screenplay: R.P. Weston, Bert Lee, Jack Marks.

Cast: Sydney Howard, Frederick Bentley, Helena Pickard, Paddy Browne, Lew Lake, Hal Jones, Reg Stone.

A sailor must beat the navy boxing champ (how come it's never the army?) to win his girl.

540 Square Joe

1921, ESL Colored Featured Productions.

Cast: Joe Jeanette, John Lester Johnson, Bob Slater, Marian Moore.

Very little is known about this apparently long-lost feature except that Jeanette and Johnson portray a pair of black boxers.

541 The Square Jungle

1955, Universal-International, 86 minutes. Director: Jerry Hopper. Producer: Albert Zugsmith. Screenplay: George Zuckerman. Photography: George Robinson. Editor: Paul Weatherwax.

Cast: Tony Curtis, Pat Crowley, Ernest Borgnine, Paul Kelly, Jim Backus, Leigh Snowden, John Day, Joe Vitale, John Marley, David Janssen, Kay Stewart, Frank Marlowe, Joe Louis as himself.

Curtis portrays Eddie Quaid, a grocery clerk with a drunken father (Backus). Quaid becomes middleweight champion after a brutal fight with the reigning title holder (Day) but loses it in a rematch when the ref (Marley) is quick to stop the fight.

In an indictment of the brutality of the sport, the ref, criticized for stopping the second fight, allows the third title match between the two to go too far, with Curtis seriously injuring his opponent.

542 The Square Ring

1955, Republic, 83 minutes. Directors: Michael Ralph, Basil Dearden. Producer: Michael Baker. Screenplay: Robert Westerby. Photography: Otto Heller. Editor: Peter Bezencenet.

Cast: Jack Warner, Robert Beatty, Bill Owen, Maxwell Reed, Bill Travers, George Rose, Alfie Bass, Ronald Lewis, Sidney James, Joan Collins, Kay Kendall.

Released in 1953 in Great Britain, but in the United States two years later, **The Square Ring** takes a cue from **The Set-up** in that most of the action is confined to the dressing room of a boxing arena and the assortment of fighters within it.

It focuses on five fighters: A novice facing his first fight (à la **The Setup**), a punch drunk, a braggart, an ex-champ who hopes to regain his wife by winning back his crown and a boxer who's been told by his manager to take a dive.

543 The Sting II

1982, Universal, 102 minutes, Color. Director: Jeremy Paul Kagan. Producer: Jennings Lang. Screenplay: David S. Ward. Photography: Bill Butler. Editor: David Garfield.

Cast: Mac Davis, Jackie Gleason, Teri Garr, Oliver Reed, Karl Malden, Ben Rifkin, Jose Perez, Val Avery, Michael D. Aldredge, John Hancock, Larry Hankin, Bert Remsen.

In this sequel to **The Sting,** Lonigan (Reed) seeks revenge on the merry band of con men who took him for a fortune several years earlier.

He murders a lifelong friend of head con man Gleason and blames it on oafish hood Malden. Gleason seeks his own revenge on Malden by setting up a phony boxing scheme in which pal Davis poses as a top boxer.

The sting is to get Malden to invest a fortune on the phony boxer, who, of course, will then take a dive; but Davis must fight to win when Reed's manipulations cause a change of plans.

544 The Street of Sin

1928, Paramount Famous Lasky Corp., 6,218 feet. Director: Mauritz Stiller.

Scenario: Chandler Sprague. Story: Josef Von Sternberg, Benjamin Glazer.

Cast: Emil Jannings, Fay Wray, Olga Baclanova, George Kotsonaros, John Gough, Johnnie Morris, John Burdette.

Retired boxer Basher Bill (Jannings) takes refuge in a Salvation Army shelter, pretending to go straight while in reality he's a notorious criminal.

He's reformed by Elizabeth (Wray), the pure girl who runs the shelter and eventually sacrifices his own life to protect her from his gang.

545 Sunday Punch

1942, Metro Goldwyn Mayer, 76 minutes. Director: David Miller. Producer: Irving Starr. Screenplay: Fay and Michael Kanin. Photography: Paul Vogel. Editor: Albert Akst.

Cast: William Lundigan, Jean Rogers, Guy Kibbee, Dan Dailey, Jr., J. Carrol Naish, Connie Gilchrist, Sam Levene, Leo Gorcey, Rags Ragland, Douglass Newland, Anthony Caruso.

In a slightly offbeat plot that may have been the inspiration for 1948's **Leather Gloves,** a Swedish boxer named Olfa Jensen (Dailey) who's in love with the same girl as his ring opponent (Lundigan) faces a dilemma.

He knocks out Lundigan, who returns to his medical studies,

and in a break of tradition with the usual portrayal of women in sports films, gets the girl even though he lost.

546 The Super Fight

1970 Woroner Productions-Computer Sports, Inc., 70 minutes. Director-Producer: Murry Woroner. Photography: Howard Winner, Willard Jones. Editors: Oscar Barber, William Hallahan, Ralston Prince.

Cast: Rocky Marciano, Muhammad Ali, Chris Dundee, Angelo Dundee, Mel Ziegler, Ferde Pacheco, Joe Louis, Jersey Joe Walcott, Jim Braddock, Max Schmeling, Jack Kearns, Jr., Nat Fleischer.

A documentary about the great fight between Rocky Marciano and Muhammad Ali in which Ali was KO'd in the 12th round. Huh? The two never fought, you say?

They did in this film, which features a simulated bout between the two with the results determined by a computer. There are even scenes at the "training camps" of the two fighters and off-screen interviews with some great boxers of the past.

547 The Swell-Head

1927, Columbia Pictures, 5,484 feet. Director: Ralph Graves. Producer: Harry Cohn. Screenplay: Robert Lord. Photography: Conrad Wells.

Cast: Ralph Graves, Johnnie Walker, Eugenia Gilbert, Mildred Harris, Mary Carr, Tom Dugan.

Lefty Malone (Graves), who is a partner in a moving business and has a sick mother, gets into an altercation with boxer Spug Murphy and does so well he accepts an offer to fight professionally.

His early successes in the ring go to his head, and he's shocked back to his senses by Murphy, who beats him. However, Malone's mother gets well, and he learns the meaning of true love with his girl friend.

548 The Swellhead

1930, Tiffany Productions, 7,040 feet. Director: James Flood. Scenario: Richard Cahoon, Adele Buffington. Story: A.P. Younger. Photography: Jackson Rose, Art Reeves. Editor: Richard Cahoon.

Cast: James Gleason, Johnny Walker, Marion Shilling, Natalie Kingston, Paul Hurst, Freeman Wood.

A young woman (Shilling) is the only one in the world to believe in the abilities of Cyclone Hickey (Walker), a braggart and a troublemaker with little proven ability.

The girl convinces Johnny Trump (played by James Gleason, who else?) to manage him. After a stormy relationship with the boxer, Trump helps turn him around and justify the girl's faith in him.

549 Swing Fever

1943, Metro Goldwyn Mayer, 80 minutes. Director: Tim Whelan. Producer: Irving Starr. Screenplay: Nat Perrin, Warren Wilson. Photography: Charles Rosher. Editor: Ferris Webster.

Cast: Kay Kyser, Max Rosenbloom, Marilyn Maxwell, Nat Pendleton, Curt Bois, William Gargan, Lena Horne.

Rube Kyser has special hypnotic powers in this musical comedy. He's tricked into using them by a girl who wants her boy friend manager's boxer to win the championship.

550 A Swingin' Affair (aka **Rebel in the Ring**)

1963, Bengal International, 76-85 minutes. Director-Associate Producer: Jay O. Lawrence. Producer: Gunther Collins. Screenplay: Bill George, Michael Connors, Tony Rock. Photography-Editor: Murray DeAtley.

Cast: Arlene Judge, Bill Wellman, Jr., Baynes Barron, Susan Sturidge, Sandra Gale Bettin, John Indrisano, Johnny Reno, Teri Garr, Ernie de la Fuente, Dick Dale and His Del-Tones.

Here's an ultra cheapjack production which does have a slightly offbeat plot, but is so badly done it has to rank among the worst boxing films of all time.

The twist is that Johnny Kwalski would rather study to run a steamship company than box, while his mom wants him to follow in dad's footsteps and become a big-time pro fighter.

While Johnny keeps his boxing career secret from the college fraternity he's pledging for, in fear that the snobs won't want a "commoner," the boxing public can't understand why "Kid Gallant" can only box occasionally, not knowing the youth is a college student.

After listening to some of the worst rock and roll music ever recorded on film and some lackluster boxing scenes, all turns out well, despite Kid Gallant losing the big fight.

The boxing scenes are so bad the arena is kept dark to try to hide the fact there are only about two rows of unexcited spectators. It's also the only film in memory in which the fight announcer has to struggle to read the play-by-play onscreen with his lines written on a piece of paper clearly in front of him.

"This . . . is . . . one . . . of . . . the . . . most . . . exciting . . . bouts . . . in . . . the . . . history . . . of this arena," the announcer monosyllabilizes in a monotone during the climactic bout.

551 Tennessee Champ

1954, Metro Goldwyn Mayer, 72 minutes, Color. Director: Fred M. Wilcox. Producer: Sol Baer Fielding. Screenplay: Art Cohn, based on "Lord in His Corner" by Eustace Cockrell. Photography: George Folsey. Editor: Ben Lewis.

Cast: Dewey Martin, Keenan Wynn, Shelley Winters, Earl Holliman, Charles Buchinsky (Bronson), Yvette Dugay, Dave O'Brien, Frank Richards, Jack Kruschen.

Religious prizefighter Martin finally gets through to con artist Wynn by the finale of this boxing comedy. Wynn pulls Martin out of the river and becomes his manager.

Martin keeps on winning because he has the "Lord in his corner," until Wynn tries a crooked deal. By the time of the finale bout against a boxer portrayed by Charles Buchinsky (who would later change his name to Charles Bronson), Wynn has seen the light.

552 There Ain't No Justice

1939, British, Ealing-Capad, 83 minutes. Director: Pen Tennyson. Producer: Sergei Nolbandov. Story: James Curtis. Adaptation: Sergei Nolbandov. Screenplay: James Curtis, Tennyson, Nolbandov. Photography: Mutz Greenbaum.

Cast: Jimmy Hanley, Edward Rigby, Mary Clare, Edward Chapman, Phyllis Stanley, Jill Furse, Nan Hopkins, Michael Wilding, Richard Norris.

Bribed to lose the bout, a mechanic turned boxer decides to win instead.

553 There's Life in the Old Dog Yet

1908, British, London Cinematograph Co., 280 feet. Director: S. Wormald.

Cast: Jem Mace.

A veteran boxer makes a comeback.

554 They Made Me a Criminal

1939, Warner Brothers, 92 minutes. Director: Busby Berkeley. Producer: Hal Wallis. Screenplay: Sig Herzig. Photography: James Wong Howe. Editor: Jack Killifer.

Cast: John Garfield, Gloria Dickson, Claude Rains, Ann Sheridan, May Robson, John Ridgely, Barbara Pepper, Ward Bond, Leo Gorcey, Billy Halop, Bobby Jordan, Huntz Hall.

A remake of **The Life of Jimmy Dolan** finds Garfield as the new middleweight champ after decking his opponent. Having a unique boxing style, he attributes his success in a victory speech to staying away from booze and women and dedicates his win to his dear old mom.

At a private victory party, Garfield is stewed to the gills and is fooling around with a woman when he confides to a guest that his dear old mom is long dead and that his speech was just hogwash.

The guest turns out to be a newspaper reporter, who despite pleas by Garfield and his manager, insists upon doing a story. Garfield takes a swing at him and passes out. The manager hits the reporter over the head with a bottle, and seeing that he's dead flees the scene.

Garfield awakens to find that he's supposedly been killed in a car crash (which the manager was in), and that he's been accused of murdering the reporter.

He flees to an Arizona ranch where he befriends a group of city boys (the Dead End Kids) and falls in love with the sister of one of them.

The girl's love softens Garfield's cynical view of life, and he agrees to fight in an exhibition bout to raise funds for the ranch.

Garfield's unique style puts cop Rains on his trail. Rains' police career was earlier marred by his sending the wrong man to the electric chair. Will he turn Garfield in?

555 They Never Come Back

1932, Weiss Brothers, 64 minutes. Director: Fred Newmeyer. Story: Arthur Hoerl. Photography: James Diamond.

Cast: Regis Toomey, Dorothy Sebastian, Gertrude Astor, Earle Foxe, Greta Granstedt, Eddie Woods, George Byron, James J. Jeffries, Little Billy.

A boxer not only breaks his arm, but finds himself framed by a jealous rival for a girl's love.

556 The Third String

1914, British, London, 1,990 feet. Director: George Loane Tucker. Screenplay: W.W. Jacobs.

Cast: Frank Stanmore, Jane Gail, George Bellamy, Judd Green, Charles Rock, Charles Vernon.

A comedy in which a man, to impress a barmaid, impersonates a boxer and finds himself in the boxing ring with the champ.

557 The Third String

1932, British, Welsh-Pearson, 65 minutes. Director-Producer: George Pearson. Screenplay: George Pearson, James Reardon, A.R. Rawlinson. Story: W.W. Jacobs.

Cast: Sandy Powell, Kay Hammond, Mark Daly, Alf Goddard, Charles Paton, Sydney Fairbrother, Pollie Emery.

A remake of the 1914 comedy in which a sailor poses as an Australian boxing champ to impress a barmaid and then must fight the girl's ex-boy friend.

The girl runs off with another man after all the shenanigans.

558 The Tiger

1978, Yugoslavian, Yugoslavia Film, 90 minutes, Color. Director: Milan Jelic. Screenplay: Gordon Milic. Photography: Piedrag Popovic. Editor: Lana Vukobratovic.

Cast: Ljubisa Samardzic, Slavko Simac, Vera Cukie, Bata Zivojnovic, Pavic Vujicic.

A veteran boxer who's never been much good, but who has always been honest and helped others, has a constantly nagging wife. After one last fight, his wife leaves him; eventually, he unwillingly begins a life of crime.

He winds up in jail and forms a prison boxing team.

559 The Tip-Off

1931, RKO Radio Pictures, 70 minutes. Director: Albert Rogell. Story: George Kibbe Turner. Adaptation: Earl Baldwin. Photography: Edward Snyder. Editor: Charles Craft.

Cast: Eddie Quillan, Robert Armstrong, Ginger Rogers, Jean Peers, Ralf Harolde, Charles Sellon, Mike Donlin.

An employee in a radio repair shop becomes a boxer and runs afoul of mobsters when he falls for a gangster's girl (Rogers).

Armstrong portrays a fighter who befriends the hero (Quillan) in this comedy.

560 Title Shot

1982, Cinepax, 96 minutes, Color. Director: Karen Bromley. Producer: Rob Iveson. Screenplay: John Saxton. Story: Richard Gabourie. Photography: Henry Fiks. Editor: Ronald Sanders.

Cast: Tony Curtis, Richard Gabourie, Susan Hogan, Allan Royal, Robert Delbert, Natsuko Ohama, Jack Duffy, Sean McCann, Taborah Johnson.

The publicity for this limited-release film says it best. Showing a picture of Curtis, it states "This man owns the champ...and the champ is worth more dead than alive," showing a man aiming a gun.

561 Toboggan

1934, French, Gaumont Franco-Film Aubert, 90 minutes. Director-Screenplay: Henri Decoin.

Cast: Georges Carpentier, Arlette Marchal, John Anderson, Francois Descamps, Raymond Corby.

Actual footage of French boxing great Carpentier is included in this feature about an aging fighter (Carpentier) who attempts a comeback against Anderson.

Just to prove that the French aren't any better in their portrayals of women on screen, Carpentier is pushed into his comeback by a woman who leaves him after he's defeated.

562 A Touch of Leather (aka **Death Blow**)

1968, British, Olympic International, 65 minutes. Director: Olaf Ericson.

Cast: Terry Brogan, Joyce Lee.

A promoter drops his boxer like a hot potato when he's no longer needed.

563 Tough Enough

1983, 20th Century-Fox, 107 minutes, Color. Director: Richard O. Fleischer. Producer: William S. Gilmore. Screenplay: John Leone. Photography: James A. Contner. Editor: Dann Cahn.

Cast: Dennis Quaid, Warren Oates, Carlene Watkins, Stan Shaw, Pam Grier, Bruce McGill.

A country western singer (Quaid) who wants more money to support his wife and child enters a tough man elimination boxing tournament sponsored by an unscrupulous promoter (Oates).

As he slugs his way to the national finals through a series of elimination bouts, he realizes, in between singing engagements, that Oates is just out to exploit him and that the bouts are just another form of show business.

564 Transatlantic Trouble (aka **Take It from Me**)

1937, British, Warner Brothers, 78 minutes. Director: William Beaudine. Producer: Irving Asher. Story: John Meehan, Jr., J.O.C. Orton. Photography: Basil Emmott.

Cast: Max Miller, Betty Lynne, Buddy Baer, Clem Lawrence, Zillah Bateman, James Stephenson, Joan Miller.

A fight manager pursues his boxer, who has just eloped and is honeymooning aboard an ocean liner, and is mistaken for a millionaire.

565 Treat 'Em Rough

1942, Universal, 59-61 minutes. Director: Ray Taylor. Producer: Marshall Grant. Screenplay: Roy Chanslor, Bob Williams. Photography: George Robinson.

Cast: Eddie Albert, Peggy Moran, William Frawley, Lloyd Corrigan, Truman Bradley, Mantan

Moreland, Joe Crehan, Ed Pawley, Dewey Robinson, Monte Blue.

An ex-middleweight champ who boxed against his dad's wishes helps clear his father of graft charges when a million barrel shortage is discovered.

566 Twinkletoes

1926, First National Pictures, 7,833 feet. Director: Charles Brabin. Scenario: Winifred Dunn, based on "Twinkletoes, a Tale of Chinatown" by Thomas Burke. Photography: James Van Trees.

Cast: Colleen Moore, Kenneth Harlan, Tully Marshall, Gladys Brockwell, Warner Oland, Lucien Littlefield, John Philip Kolb, Julanne Johnston, William McDonald.

A dancing girl (Moore) falls in love with a married boxer (Harlan) in a London slum district. The boxer's jealous wife, in revenge, turns the girl's burglar dad in to the police.

When the wife is killed in an accident, it frees the boxer and the girl to live happily ever after—following an unsuccessful suicide try by the girl.

567 Two Fisted

1935, Paramount, 60 minutes. Director: James Cruze. Screenplay: Sam Hellman, Francis Martin, Eddie Moran, from the play "Is Zat So?" by James Gleason and Richard Taber. Photography: Harry Fischbeck.

Cast: Lee Tracy, Roscoe Karns, Grace Bradley, Kent Taylor, Gail Patrick, Gordon Westcott, G.P. Huntley, Jr., Billy Lee, John Indrisano.

A remake of **Is Zat So?** finds fight manager Tracy and boxer Karns in tight financial straits. They sign on as protectors of a socialite and baby boy, and the finale is a bout in the drawing room between Karns and another fighter.

568 Two-Fisted Gentlemen

1936, Columbia, 68 minutes. Director: Gordon Wiles. Producer: Ben Pivar. Story: Tom Van Dycke. Photography: John Stumar. Editor: James Sweeney.

Cast: James Dunn, June Clayworth, George McKay, Thurston Hall, Gene Morgan, Paul Guilfoyle, Harry Tyler.

The only thing that distinguishes this from the hundreds of other boxing films in this chapter is that the boxer's manager is a woman.

569 Two Mad Boxers

1910, French, Pathe Freres, 312 feet.

During a boxing match, two fans start a bout of their own and nothing stops them. They KO a cop and wind up on a raft where they both eventually fall into the water.

570 United States Smith

1928, Lumas Film Corp., 7,022 feet. Director: Joseph Henabery. Producer: Harold Shumate. Scenario: Curtis Benton. Photography: Ray June.

Cast: Eddie Gribbon, Lila Lee, Mickey Bennett, Kenneth Harlan, Earle Marsh.

Ace marine boxer Gribbon comes home to the U.S.A. for a boxing title match and befriends a Russian orphan.

He's all set to throw the fight to get money for the boy's education, when a plea from the lad convinces him to fight to win.

571 Unmarried

1939, Paramount, 64 minutes. Director: Kurt Neumann. Screenplay: Lillie Howard, Brian Marlow. Story: Grover Jones, William S. McNutt. Photography: Harry Fischbeck. Editor: Stuart Gilmore.

Cast: Helen Twelvetrees, Buck Jones, Donald O'Connor, John Hartley, Robert Armstrong, Sidney Blackmer, Larry Crabbe,

Edward Pawley, William Haade, Jack Roper.

Cowboy star Buck Jones stars in this remake of 1932's **Lady and Gent** as an unsuccessful boxer.

He loves Twelvetrees, a night-club owner during Prohibition days, after she loses the club. They sacrifice all to raise the son of Jones' manager, who was killed in a holdup; but the boy, who becomes a football star, would rather be a boxer, and it's up to stepdad to straighten him out.

572 Uppercut O'Brien

1929, Educational Films, 2 reels. Director: Earle Rodney. Producer: Mack Sennett.

Cast: Andy Clyde, Harry Gribbon, Marjorie Beebe, Bert Swor, James Leong.

Clyde is boxer Gribbon's manager in this early talkie short.

573 Uppercuts

1928, Educational, 2 reels. Director: Walter Graham. Producer: Al Christie.

Cast: Jack Duffy, Stella Adams, Bill Irving, Violet Bird, Bill Blaisdell, Kid Wagner.

His films are rarely screened nowadays, but Jack Duffy in his day was well-known as a character named Grandpa, who had a set of whiskers that would make Gabby Hayes blush.

Here, he's the president of the Anti-Prizefighting League who gets mixed up in, that's right, a prizefight.

574 Valley of the Moon

1914, Bosworth, 6 reels.

Cast: Jack Conway, Myrtle Stedman, Ernest Garcia, Rhea Haines.

Based on a story by Jack London, this finds boxer Billy Roberts marrying and promising his wife he'll never fight again.

He becomes a teamster but finds himself in desperate financial straits because of a strike so he accepts a 20-round fight at $1 a round without telling his wife. He tells her, when asked about his bruises, that he was beaten by scabs.

575 The Victor

1923, Universal Pictures, 4,880 feet. Director: Edward Laemmle. Scenario: E. Richard Schayer, based on the **Redbook** magazine story "Two Bells for Pegasus" by Gerald Beaumont. Photography: Clyde De Vinna.

Cast: Herbert Rawlinson, Dorothy Manners, Frank Currier, Eddie Gribbon, Otis Harlan, Esther Ralston, Tom McGuire.

The eldest son of a financially ailing British nobleman comes to the United States to marry the daughter of a chewing gum magnate, but he can't go through with it.

He meets an actress who helps him out; and, after he knocks out a well-known fighter in a restaurant argument, becomes such a good prizefighter that he earns enough money to save his father's estate and marry the girl.

576 Vincent, Francois, Paul and the Others

1974, French, Gaumont, 118 minutes, Color.

Director: Claude Sautet. Screenplay: Jean-Loup Debadie, Claude Neron, Sautet. Photography: Jean Boffety. Editor: Jacqueline Thiedot.

Cast: Yves Montand, Michel Piccoli, Serge Reggiani, Gerard Depardieu, Stephane Audrane.

A character study basically concerned with three middle-aged men finds Vincent losing his business, wife and mistress; physician Francois losing his wife and Paul taking a new lover.

They befriend a young boxer (Depardieu) and help him win. The boxer then quits the ring to get a job in a factory.

577 Walkover

1969, Polish, New Yorker Films, 77 minutes. Director-Screenplay: Jerzy Skolimowski. Photography: Antoni Nurzynski. Editor: Barbara Krzyczmonik.

Cast: Aleksandra Zawieruszanka, Jerzy Skolimowski, Krzysztof Chamiec, Franciszek Pieczka, Andrzej Herder, Elzbieta Czyzewska.

The 1969 date is the time of American release although **Walkover** was produced in 1965 by Film Polski.

Director Skolimowski, Poland's best-known director after Wajda and Polanski, plays the lead who interrupts a trip when he sees a girl he knew in college.

He was expelled from the school, and his only income now is from boxing. She gets him a job at a factory, and he's persuaded to be in a boxing tournament.

After winning his first fight, he's declared the winner in a "walkover" because his foe fails to show. The opponent, however, later demands and gets another chance when he claims he was bribed not to show up.

578 Walloping Kid

1926, Aywon Film Corp., 4,900 feet. Director-Screenplay: Robert J. Horner. Photography: Bert Baldridge.

Cast: Kit Carson, Jack Richardson, Dorothy Ward, Frank Whitson, Al Kaufman, Jack Herrick, Pauline Curley.

The Walloping Kid (Carson) must give up boxing to head West and run his father's ranch but finds that it's being plagued by a gang of rustlers.

579 The Way of the World

1920, British, I.B. Davidson, 5,000 feet. Director-Scenario: A.E. Coleby.

Cast: A.E. Coleby, Gordon Coghill, Charles Vane, Babs Ronald, Cherry Hardy, Olive Bell, H. Nicholls-Bates.

A man adopts a poor child and winds up beating her father in the boxing ring.

580 We're All Gamblers

1927, Paramount Famous Lasky Corp., 5,935 feet. Director: James Cruze. Screenplay: Hope Loring. Story: Sidney Howard. Photography: Bert Glennon.

Cast: Thomas Meighan, Marietta Millner, Cullen Landis, Philo McCullough, Gertrude Claire, Gunboat Smith.

A heavyweight boxer reared as an adopted child from New York's lower east side conceals his love over many years for a society woman because of the class differences between the two. She also loves him, but because of her upbringing fails to tell him until the final reel.

581 When Giants Fought

1926, British, Frederick White Co., 2,085 feet. Director: Harry B. Parkinson. Screenplay: Andrew Soutar.

Cast: Joe Beckett, Frank Craig, Wyndham Guise, James Knight, George Wynn, Alex Hunter.

A drama set against the background of the fight between Tom Cribb and black boxer Thomas Molyneux.

582 When's Your Birthday

1937, RKO Radio Pictures, 77 minutes. Director: Harry Beaumont. Producer: Davis Loew. Screenplay: Harry Clark. Cartoon segment: Leon Schlesinger. Photography: George Robinson. Editor: Jack Ogilvie.

Cast: Joe E. Brown, Marian Marsh, Fred Keating, Edgar Kennedy, Suzanne Kaaren, Margaret Hamilton, Minor Watson, Frank Jenks.

If you don't mind the pun, this comedy rides on the heels of the 1936 success **Three Men on a Horse** (see Horses and Other Animals chapter).

Astrologer Brown is hired

by gambler Watson to predict the winners of boxing matches and horse races, but he can only do it when the stars are right.

He also goes on to become a top welterweight, but again can only fight well when the moon is in its ascendancy.

583 Whiplash

1948, Warner Brothers, 91 minutes. Director: Lew Seiler. Producer: William Jacobs. Screenplay: Maurice Geraghty, Harriet Frank, Jr. Story: Kenneth Earl. Adaptation: Gordon Kahn. Photography: Peverell Marley. Editor: Frank Magee.

Cast: Dane Clark, Alexis Smith, Zachary Scott, Eve Arden, Jeffrey Lynn, S.Z. Sakall, Alan Hale, Douglas Kennedy.

As boxer Clark sits groggy with a concussion during a bout at Madison Square Garden, he reminisces about how he got into this mess.

An artist, he has a brief affair with Smith and she runs out on him. Tracking her down, he finds her singing in her husband's nightclub.

The husband (Scott), an ex-boxer, was crippled in a car accident and becomes Clark's manager, reliving his career through the younger man. He, of course, finds out about his wife's extra-marital affair; but despite his efforts, Clark wins the fight (and Smith).

584 The White Hope

1915, British, Hepworth, 3,650 feet. Director: Frank Wilson. Scenario: Victor Montefiore. Story: W.H. Trowbridge.

Cast: Stewart Rome, Violet Hopson, Lionelle Howard, John MacAndrews, Frank Wilson, George Gunther.

A period piece involving a heavyweight boxer, romance and nobility.

585 The White Hope

1922, British, Walter West, 6,300 feet. Director: Frank Wilson. Story: W.H. Trowbridge.

A longer version of the 1915 film.

586 The White Hope on Championship

1914, British, Heron, 710 feet.

A tall boxer and a short boxer slug it out.

587 The White Masks

1921, Merit Film Corp., 5 reels. Director: George Holt. Scenario: Marian Hatch. Story: Ett Corr. Photography: Reginald Lyons.

Cast: Franklyn Farnum, Al Hart, Virginia Lee, Shorty Hamilton.

Jack Bray (Farnum) incurs the wrath of the leader of a masked vigilante group when he falls in love with a saloon pianist (Swenson).

Despite the gang's efforts, Bray's fighter, Battling Rush (Hamilton), wins the bout; and Bray wins his battle with the gang's leader, saloon owner Jim Dougherty (Hart) for the girl.

588 Willie vs. Bombardier Wells

1913, French, Eclair, 940 feet. Director: Victorin Jasset.

Cast: Bombardier Billy Wells, Willy Sanders.

Wells battles, if you can call it that, tiny Willie, who has to be lifted on his second's shoulders to reach Wells.

589 The Windjammer

1926, Rayart Pictures, 5,016 feet. Director: Harry J. Brown. Scenario: Grover Jones.

Cast: Billy Sullivan.

A sissy manages to defeat a boxing champ and, of course, win the fickle love of the girl.

590 The Winner

1915, British, Cricks, 1,114 feet. Director: Charles Calvert. Story: Reuben Gillmer.

Cast: J. Palmer.

Here's a real switch: The girl marries the boxer who loses the fight over her.

591 The Winner

1947, Russian, Artkino, 89 minutes. Director: Andrei Frolow. Screenplay: Sergei Vladimirsk, V. Yurenev. Photography: V. Petrov.

Cast: Vladimir Volodin, Anastasia Zuyeva, Ilya Perevertsev, Irina Cheredniachenko, Vassily Gribnov.

A Siberian athlete who's in love with a swimmer decides to try for the Russian boxing title. After riding two weeks on a train to get there, he loses, but decides to try again.

592 The Winner

1965, French, Robert Kingsley & Noelle Gillmor, 82 minutes. Director-Writer: Francois Reichenback. Producer: Pierre Braunberger. Photography: Reichenback, Jean Marc Ripert.

Cast: Abdoulaye Faye, Marcel Bruchard, Miloc Pladner, Luce Vidi.

A semi-documentary about the life of Faye, a Senegalese boxer who's visiting Paris for the first time and is in training for a fight.

593 Winner Take All

1924, Fox Film Corp., 5,949 feet. Director: W.S. Van Dyke. Scenario: Ewart Adamson. Story: Larry Evans. Photography: Joseph Brotherton, E.D. Van Dyke.

Cast: Buck Jones, Peggy Shaw, Edward Hearn, Tom O'Brien, Lilyan Tashman, William Norton Bailey, Ben Deeley.

Perry Blair (Jones) is fired from his job for fighting but is signed by promoter Dunham (Deeley) as a pro boxer.

He quits the ring when he's told to fight in a fixed match but is convinced to fight one more time on a winner-take-all basis.

594 Winner Take All

1932, Warner Brothers, 66 minutes. Director: Roy Del Ruth. Story: Gerald Beaumont. Photography: Robert Kurrie.

Cast: James Cagney, Marian Nixon, Guy Kibbee, Clarence Muse, Virginia Bruce, Dickie Moore, Allen Lane.

Cagney gained fame in 1931's **Public Enemy** for rubbing a grapefruit in a woman's face. Here, he goes one better, dousing one with seltzer and kicking another in the rear.

He's a boxer who undergoes plastic surgery when his nose is broken; and then, fearful that his face will be messed up again, develops a new defensive style. When his nose is broken again, a society girl he fell for walks out on him, and he realizes it's the pure, simple girl he loves.

595 Winner Take All

1939, 20th Century-Fox, 61-62 minutes. Director: Otto Brower. Screenplay: Francess Hoffman, Albert Ray. Story: Jerry Cady.

Cast: Tony Martin, Gloria Stuart, Henry Armetta, Slim Summerville, Kane Richmond, Robert Allen, Inez Falange.

Cowboy-turned-waiter-turned boxer Martin scores a lucky win in a charity bout and gets conceited after gamblers rig a number of fights for him to win.

Reporter Stuart must teach him a lesson, and he starts training to win for real.

596 The Winning Wallop

1926, Lumas Film Corp., 5,000 feet. Director: Charles Hutchinson. Photography: James Brown.

Cast: William Fairbanks, Shirley Palmer, Frank Hagney, Charles K. French, Melvin McDowell, Crauford Kent, Jimmy Aubrey.

The son of a wealthy man wins the amateur boxing title

at college and winds up taking a job at a ladies gymnasium in this comedy based on a story by L.V. Jefferson.

Lazy by nature, he's forced by events into appearing in a championship bout.

597 Woman Wise

1937, 20th Century-Fox, 62 minutes. Director: Allen Dwan. Producer: Sol M. Wurtzel. Screenplay: Ben Markson. Photography: Robert Planck.

Cast: Rochelle Hudson, Michael Whalen, Thomas Beck, Alan Dinehart, Douglas Fowley, George Hassell, Astrid Allwyn, Chick Chandler, Pat Flaherty.

A sports editor helps to bust open a phony fight racket.

598 Wonder Man

1920, Robertson-Cole Co., 7 reels. Director: John G. Adelphi. Scenario: Joseph W. Farnham. Story: Daniel Carson Goodman. Photography: G. Benoit.

Cast: Georges Carpentier, Faire Binney, Florence Hulings, Downing Clarke, Cecil Owen, Robert Barrat, William Halligan, John Burkell, Francois Deschamps, Jack Blumenfeld.

French boxing champ Carpentier portrays a French Secret Service agent assigned to track down the villains responsible for stealing valuable contracts between the United States and France.

Some American friends get him into an exclusive country club where it's suspected the culprits hang out. He winds up entering an amateur boxing tournament at the club and is being beaten up by the cad until his girlfriend urges he win and guess what happens?

Carpentier's real-life manager—Deschamps—and his sparring partner—Blumenfeld—have roles in the film.

599 World in My Corner

1956, Universal-International, 82 minutes. Director: Jesse Hibbs. Producer: Aaron Rosenberg. Screenplay: Jack Sher. Story: Sher, Joseph Stone. Photography: Maury Gertsman. Editor: Milton Carruth.

Cast: Audie Murphy, Barbara Rush, Jeff Morrow, John McIntire, Tommy Hall, Howard St. John, Chico Vejar.

A boy from the slums rises to a welterweight contender only to find he can't get a shot at champ Vejar, who is controlled by promoter St. John.

The boxer (Murphy) wants to marry Rush, the daughter of his domineering benefactor, but needs money for that, so he agrees to a fixed fight with Vejar. During the bout, he changes his mind and wins, but the injuries he suffers during the fight end his ring career.

600 The World's Champion

1922, Paramount Pictures, 5,030 feet. Director: Philip Rosen. Adaptation: J.E. Nash, Albert Shelby Le Vino, based on the play "The Champion, a Comedy in Three Acts" by Thomas Louden and A.E. Thomas. Photography: Charles Edgar Schoenbaum.

Cast: Wallace Reid, Lois Wilson, Lionel Belmore, Henry Miller, Jr., Helen Dunbar, Leslie Casey, Stanley J. Sandford, W.J. Ferguson, Guy Oliver.

When a prosperous man's son (Reid) dares to approach a noblewoman (Wilson), he is beaten by Lord Brockington (Sandford) and disowned by his father.

He goes to America where he becomes a boxing champ and returns home to find the noblewoman, in need of money, serving as his father's secretary.

Beating Lord Brockington in a fight and giving up boxing to become an attorney, he is re-accepted by his father and also, of course, gets the girl.

Football

The combination of the wide open spaces of the football field, the grueling physical contact of the sport and the clock ticking away to the final seconds have proven a lure few movie studios can resist.

Between 1920 and 1940, college football films were grinded out by the dozen. Just those with the word college in the title alone include **The College Boob, The College Coach, College Days, The College Hero, College Humor, College Love, The College Lovers, Collegiate,** etc. etc.

Most of these were as indistinguishable as the titles. **Strongheart,** made in 1914 and remade in 1925 as **Braveheart,** is the first major football classic, dealing with an Indian brave at Columbia University who sacrifices himself for the good of his team.

Nearly everyone has heard of **Knute Rockne, All American,** but few today have seen **The Spirit of Notre Dame,** in which J. Farrell MacDonald's portrayal of the Notre Dame coach was so impressive he was forever typecast in similar roles.

Touchdown (1931) was a breakthrough picture as far as football is concerned because the coach ultimately places the well-being of his players ahead of winning the game, which he doesn't. It sparked many imitations. By the time **Knute Rockne** came out in 1940, however, the college football film was a tired genre with grid films having trickled down to an occasional slapstick comedy such as **Life Begins in College.**

Knute Rockne breathed new life into football films, inspiring such biographical films as **The Iron Major, Spirit of Stanford** and **Spirit of West Point.** After a handful of gridiron films in the early 1950s such as **The All American, Saturday's Hero** and **Crazylegs, All American,** football all but disappeared from American screens until the mid-to-late 1960s, with **The Fortune Cookie, John Goldfarb, Please Come Home** and **Paper Lion.**

The new permissiveness of the screen allowed filmmakers to stress the violence of pro football in **The Longest Yard** and **North Dallas Forty** as the gridiron made a screen comeback, but nothing like its heyday in the 20s.

In **Full Moon High** (1981), a football star becomes a werewolf and must wait 20 years to play in the big game and lead his team to victory.

As for cliches, we count 70 last-minute touchdowns. It wouldn't make an interesting film, we guess, if the winning touchdown was scored in the first half and the heroes win 27-0.

We also count 29 films in which the hero is suspended, kidnapped or quits and returns to the team in time to lead it to victory.

601 Against All Odds

1984, Columbia Pictures, 125 minutes, Color. Director: Taylor Hackford. Producers: Hackford, William S. Gilmore. Screenplay: Eric Hughes. Photography: Donald Thorin. Editor: Fredric and William Steinkamp.

Cast: Jeff Bridges, Rachel Ward, James Woods, Alex Karras,

Richard Widmark, Jane Greer, Dorian Harewood, Swoosie Kurtz, Saul Rubinek, Pat Corley, Bill McKinney, Allen Williams.

An updating of Jacques Tourneur's 1947 film noir, **Out of the Past** finds Jeff Bridges as Terry Brogan, a veteran professional football player who is suddenly cut by the Los Angeles Outlaws despite his insistence he's fully recovered from some injuries.

He's hired by a sleazy acquaintance (Woods) to track down an heiress who has run off to the Yucatan. The trail leads to romance (with Rachel Ward) and the killing in self-defense of Brogan's football pal, trainer Hank Sully (Karras), who has been forced by financial necessities to become a hit man.

More of an action and romance film than a sports film (there are training camp scenes but no game action scenes), it's nevertheless of interest in the sports genre for its treatment of how athletes are treated once their playing days are over.

When he's released, Brophy's agent will no longer have anything to do with him. Other ex-athletes, in need of funds, join Woods' gambling syndicate.

602 The All-American

1932, Universal, 73 minutes. Director: Russell Mack. Adaptation: Frank Wood, Ferdinand Reyney. Story: Richard Schayer, Dale Van Every.

Cast: Richard Arlen, John Darrow, Andy Devine, Gloria Stuart, James Gleason, Preston Foster, Merna Kennedy, Harold Waldridge, Earl McCarthy, Ethel Clayton.

Featuring a number of the day's top football coaches, including Pop Warner, and about two dozen real-life top college players, **The All-American**'s story line also cuts a bit above the average.

The action begins during All-American Arlen's last grid game. Afterwards, rather than continuing in school to get his degree, he quits for some fast money selling some bonds.

He soon finds that life off the gridiron is no bed of roses and starts gambling his money away and hanging out with cheap women.

When kid brother Darrow becomes a college football hero as well and gets a swelled head, Arlen gets the chance to help show him the light by embarrassing him in a charity game between past and present All-Americans.

603 The All American

1953, Universal, 83 minutes. Director: Jesse Hibbs. Producer: Aaron Rosenberg. Screenplay: D.D. Beauchamp. Adaptation: Robert Yale Libett. Story: Leonard Freeman. Photography: Maury Gertsman. Editor: Edward Curtiss.

Cast: Tony Curtis, Lori Nelson, Richard Long, Mamie Van Doren, Gregg Palmer, Paul Cavanagh, Herman Hickman, Morgan Jones, Stuart Whitman, Frank Gifford, Tom Harmon.

The credits read more like an All-American scorecard than as a movie. Besides the presence of Gifford and Harmon in the cast, the director, Jesse Hibbs, was an All American in 1933 at USC and the screenwriter, D.D. Beauchamp, took the honors in 1927. In addition, cast member Herman Hickman once coached the Yale grid squad.

Curtis plays Nick Bonelli, an All-American quarterback with a swelled head who's brought down several notches when his parents, en route to see him play, are killed in a bus crash.

He quits school and football but later enrolls at a snooty college, which, of course, also has a grid team. He gets into a lot of trouble at the new school; but when it's the day of the big game, he's reinstated and, of course, leads the team to victory.

604 All-American Kickback

1931, Educational Films, 2 reels. Director: Del Lord. Producer: Mack Sennett.

Cast: Andy Clyde, Harry Gribbon, Marjorie Beebe.

Gribbon's a football player in this comedy short.

605 All the Right Moves

1983, 20th Century-Fox, 91 minutes. Color. Director: Michael Chapman. Producer: Stephen Deutsch. Screenplay: Michael Kane. Photography: Jan De Bont. Editor: David Garfield.

Cast: Tom Cruise, Craig T. Nelson, Lea Thompson, Charles Cioffi, Gary Graham, Paul Carafotes, Christopher Penn, Sandy Faison, Donald A. Yannessa, James A. Baffico.

In its own way, **All the Right Moves** can be considered a "prequel" to 1953's **Saturday's Hero.** Stef Djordjevic (Cruise), the young high school football hero of **All the Right Moves**, comes from the same mold as Steve Novak of **Saturday's Hero.**

Both the college grid star of **Saturday's Hero** and his younger counterpart in the later film are using sports as their springboards out of the dingy steel towns which have seemingly held their families hostage forever.

Whereas **Saturday's Hero** focuses on the grid star's disillusionment with the high pressure sports of the outside world, **All the Right Moves** details Stef's uphill struggle to leave the fictional town of Ampipe, Pa. (in reality Johnstown, Pa.).

Standing directly in Stef's way is Coach Nickerson (Nelson) who wants to leave Ampipe as badly as the youth and who needs a big win over the school's arch rival to land a big-time college coaching job.

Stef, meanwhile, is being heavily recruited but wants a school where he can also get a top education.

The football scenes are memorable. On the day of the big game against the wealthy suburban school, there's a downpour, and the players on the field are half buried in the mud.

Stef does well, and Ampipe has the lead in the final minute when Coach Nickerson makes a fatal mistake. Instead of having his team simply fall on the ball, he has them trying to run it out near their own end zone. The ball is fumbled on the wet turf, and the rivals fall on it to win the game.

In the locker room, Nickerson blames Stef's friend for the loss; and when Our Hero stands up for his pal, he's suspended.

And when some angry townspeople vandalize the coach's house later, Stef is innocently present and is kicked off the team.

Suddenly, no college will take Stef and he appears doomed to work in the same steel mill as the rest of his family. The coach holds the only key out.

His girl friend Lisa (Thompson) also offers an interesting counterpoint. A good student herself, she wonders about the fairness of a system which provides full scholarships for athletes while ignoring those who can make other contributions to society.

The rival school's coach is played by Don Yannessa, a long-time football coach in Aliquippa, Pa., who served as technical adviser and trained the actors (many of them school football players themselves) for the grid scenes.

606 Ashamed of Parents

1921, Warner Brothers, 6 reels. Director: Horace G. Plympton. Photography: Jack Brown.

Cast: Charles Eldridge, Jack L. Bohn, Edith Stockton, Walter McEvan, W.J. Goss.

A self-sacrificing shoemaker (Eldridge) manages to raise enough money to send his son (Bohn) to college.

The lad becomes a big grid star and becomes engaged to an upper-class girl (Stockton); but as the title indicates, he's ashamed of his father's humble background and tells him not to come to the wedding. All works out for the best, however, when the girl meets the selfless father and gets to like him.

607 The Band Plays On

1934, Metro Goldwyn Mayer, 87 minutes. Director: Russell Mack. Adaptation: Bernard Schubert, Ralph Spence, Harvey Gates. Photography: Leonard Smith. Editor: William Levanway.

Cast: Robert Young, Stuart Erwin, Leo Carrillo, Betty Furness, Ted Healy, Preston Foster, Russell Hardie, William Tannen.

Young, Erwin, Hardie and Tannen are juvenile delinquents who are caught stealing a car. They're sent to a special program run by grid coach Foster, who spots their natural talent and gradually molds them into a top college backfield.

Three of them later walk out on him but change their minds and come back in time for the big game. In a break of tradition with the majority of football films, the youths, after being kept on the bench by the coach, get into the game late; but their team doesn't win.

The result is one of the few ties in grid movie history.

608 The Big Game

1936, RKO Radio Pictures, 73 minutes. Director: George Nicholls, Jr. Producer: Pandro S. Berman. Story: Francis Wallace. Adaptation: Irwin Shaw. Photography: Harrry Wild.

Cast: Philip Huston, James Gleason, June Travis, Bruce Cabot, Andy Devine, C. Henry Gordon, Guinn Williams, John Arledge, Frank M. Thomas, Billy Gilbert.

Author Irwin Shaw's first effort for the big screen is an expose of the evils of college recruiting and the then-growing influence of gamblers on the college football scene.

Featuring a number of top college grid stars in the cast, it includes a free-for-all on the playing field, which was supposedly inspired by a real-life battle during a NYU-Fordham game. Oh, yes, there's a kidnapping.

609 Black Sunday

1977, Paramount, 143 minutes, Color. Director: John Frankenheimer. Producer: Robert Evans. Screenplay: Ernest Lehman, Kenneth Ross, Ivan Moffat, based on a novel by Thomas Harris. Photography: John A. Alonzo. Editor: Tom Rolf.

Cast: Robert Shaw, Bruce Dern, Marthe Keller, Fritz Weaver, Steven Keats, Bekim Fehmiu, Michael V. Gazzo, William Daniels, Walter Gotell, Victor Campos, Walter Brooks and Pat Summerall, Joe Robbie, Robert Wussler, and Tom Brookshier as themselves.

Keller, a Black September terrorist, and Dern, an ex-Vietnam POW, plot to commandeer a blimp, fly over the Orange Bowl during the Super Bowl and unleash pellets that will kill thousands of people in an effort to end U.S. aid to Israel.

Israeli agent Shaw smokes out the plot and engages in a race against time to save the lives of thousands of innocent people.

610 The Blindness of Love

1916, Metro, 5 reels. Screenplay: B.A. Rolfe.

Cast: Julius Steger.

The son of a piano factory owner is a big football hero but is expelled from school for some shenanigans during a victory celebration.

The son can do no wrong in his father's eyes until dad takes him into the family business, and the son proceeds to ruin it.

The old man is reduced to being a piano tuner but has a tearful reconciliation with his boy at the end.

611 Bonzo Goes to College

1952, Universal-International, 78-80 minutes. Director: Frederick de Cordova. Producer: Ted Richmond. Screenplay: Leo Lieberman, Jack Henley, based on characters created by Raphael David Blau and Ted Berkman. Photography: Carl Guthrie. Editor: Ted Kent.

Cast: Maureen O'Sullivan, Edmund Gwenn, Charles Drake, Gigi Perreau, Gene Lockhart, Irene Ryan, Guy Williams, John Miljan, David Janssen, Jerry Paris, Frank Nelson.

A sequel to the popular **Bedtime for Bonzo**, this comedy does not star Ronald Reagan, as did the original.

That amazing chimp Bonzo leaves the circus and befriends the daughter of a college football coach. Passing the college entrance exams, he becomes the team's star quarterback.

In a spoof of football film cliches, Bonzo is kidnapped by gangsters to keep him out of the big game; but naturally he escapes and gets to the game to lead the team to victory as the seconds tick down.

612 A Boy Named Charlie Brown

1969, National General, 85 minutes, Color. Director: Bill Melendez. Producer: Lee Mendelson. Screenplay: Charles M. Schulz based on his comic strip. Editors: Robert T. Gillis, Charles McCann, Steve Melendez.

In this feature-length Peanuts cartoon, Charlie Brown's football team loses its 99th game in a row, sending him straight to Lucy's psychiatry box.

He later wins his school's spelling bee, but loses in the national finals on the word "beagle," despite the presence of Snoopy, the world's most famous beagle.

613 Braveheart

1925, Producers Distributing Corp., 7,256 feet. Director: Alan Hale. Presented by: Cecil B. DeMille. Adaptation: Mary O'Hara. Story: William Churchill DeMille. Photography: Faxon M. Dean.

Cast: Rod LaRocque, Lillian Rich, Robert Edeson, Arthur Housman, Tyrone Power, Jean Acker, Frank Hagney.

The title is slightly changed; but **Braveheart** is a remake of 1914's **Strongheart**, the first great football film.

When his tribe's fishing rights are threatened by a canning corporation, a young Indian (LaRocque) is sent to college to get a law degree so he can protect them.

He becomes an All-American grid star but is expelled when he takes the blame for a friend for selling the team's signals to an opponent. He still manages to win the court battle for his tribe's fishing rights.

614 Brotherly Love

1928, Metro Goldwyn Mayer, 6,053 feet. Director: Charles F. Reisner. Scenario: Earl Baldwin, Lew Lipton. Story: Patterson Margoni. Photography: Henry Sharp. Editor: George Hively.

Cast: Karl Dane, George K. Arthur, Richard Carlyle, Jean Arthur, Edward Connelly.

A prison comedy which no doubt influenced the baseball comedy **Up the River** (1930) concerns the relationship between a prison guard (Dane) and a small barber (George Arthur) who both love the warden's daughter.

The guard, who's responsible for the barber being in prison in the first place, puts him on the prison football team, fully expecting him to be beaten to a pulp.

The barber proves to be a star, however, and the guard, who gets into some trouble, is sent to another prison. Released from jail, the barber still wants to play in the big grid game against the guard's new team.

615 Brown of Harvard

1917, William N. Selig, 6 reels. Director: Harry Beaumont.

Cast: Tom Moore, Hazel Daly, Sidney Ainsworth, Warner Richmond, Walter McGrail, Nancy Winston, Alice Gordon, Kempton Greene, Frank Joyner, Robert Ellis.

Based on a play by Rida Johnson Young and Gilbert P. Coleman, this is an early version of the rah-rah film remade by MGM in 1926.

It concerns a swell-headed youth who enrolls at Harvard, is disgraced during a crew race but becomes a big football hero.

616 Brown of Harvard

1926, Metro Goldwyn Mayer, 7,941 feet. Director: Jack Conway. Screenplay: A.P. Younger, based on a play by Rida Johnson Young and Gilbert P. Coleman. Photography: Ira H. Morgan. Editor: Frank Davis.

Cast: Jack Pickford, Mary Brian, Francis X. Bushman, Jr., Mary Alden, David Torrence, Edward Connelly, Guinn Williams, Ernest Gillen, William Haines.

Tom Brown (Haines), the ladies man at Harvard, opposes the quiet McAndrews (Bushman) for the affections of a teacher's daughter (Brian).

During a big crew meet against Yale, Brown replaces his rival as stroker but causes his team to lose when he collapses.

Disgraced, he goes out for the football team and is eventually declared a hero when he gives his rival the chance to score during the big game.

617 The Cheerleader

1928, Lumas Film Corp., 5,772 feet. Director: Alvin J. Neitz. Adaptation: Jack Casey. Story: Lee Authmar. Photography: Edward Gheller. Editor: Edith Wakeling.

Cast: Ralph Graves, Ralph Emerson, Harold Goodwin, Gertrude Olmstead, Shirley Palmer, Donald Stuart, Duke Martin, Lillian Langdon, Bobby Nelson, Ruth Cherrington.

Two college chums get into a whole lot of hot water and one is forced, on the day of the big game, to act only as a cheerleader; but rest assured that by the end of the final reel both will be in there to lead their team to glory.

618 The Cheer Leader

1930, Vitaphone, 9 minutes.

Cast: Tom Douglas.

An ailing college student is forced to cheer his team to victory from the window of his dormitory.

619 The Cheerleaders

1973, Conemation, 84 minutes, Color. Director: Paul Glickler. Producers: Glickler, Richard Lerner. Screenplay: Glickler, Tad Richards, Ace Baandige. Photography: Lerner. Editor: Glickler.

Cast: Stephanie Fondue, Denise Dillaway, Jovita Bush, Debbie Lowe, Sandy Evans, Kim Stanton, Richard Meatwhistle, John Jacobs, Patrick Wright, Jay Lindner.

In this softcore "X" film, the cheerleaders come up with a novel way to help their team win: They tire the opposing team out by sacrificing themselves sexually before the big game.

Even that's not quite enough. The cheerleaders' only virgin must make the biggest sacrifice of all during half time to ensure the team's victory.

620 The Cheerleaders' Wild Weekend

1979, Dimension, Color. Director: Jeff Werner. Producer: Chuck Russell. Screenplay: D.W. Gilbert, Jason Williams. Photography: Paul Ryan.

Cast: Kristine De Bell, Jason Williams, Janet Blythe, Hana

Byrbo, Tracy King, Anthony Lewis, Lachelle Price, Janie Squire, Ann Wharton, Robert Huston.

They're back again.

621 Choices

1981, Oaktree Productions, 90 minutes, Color. Director: Silvio Narizzano. Producers: Alicia Rivera Alon, Rami Alon. Screenplay: Rami Alon. Photography: Hanania Baer.

Cast: Paul Carafotes, Victor French, Lelia Goldoni, Val Avery, Dennis Patrick, Demi Moore, Billy Moses.

Ever since **Bang the Drum Slowly,** films about persons who overcame great personal handicaps or illness to become athletic stars have been in vogue (although, of course, there had been films in the past on the subject such as **The Stratton Story**).

In the little-seen **Choices,** a partially-deaf high school football player is told by a physician that he can't play.

At first, the youth is depressed but then starts fighting back. He learns how to understand signals despite his handicap and eventually appeals for the permission to play.

622 Classmates

1908, AM&B, 310 feet. Director: Wallace McCutcheon.

One of the earliest fiction football films finds a celebration going on after a college grid team victory. A woman knocks a masher down the stairs, and he gets into a fight with another man.

623 The College Boob

1926, Harry Garson Productions, 5,340 feet. Director: Harry Garson. Adaptation: Gerald C. Duffy. Story: Jack Casey. Photography: James Brown.

Cast: Lefty Flynn, Jean Arthur, Jimmy Anderson, Bob Bradbury, Jr., Cecil Ogden, Dorothea Wolbert, William Malan, Raymond Turner.

A rube promises his family he won't engage in sports at college, only to become the school boob through the efforts of a jealous bully.

After beating up some of his tormentors, he's persuaded to go out for the football team and helps the team win, but then lives up to his promise to his family until his girl friend convinces them otherwise.

624 College Coach

1933, Warner Brothers, 75 minutes. Director: William A. Wellman. Screenplay: Niven Busch, Manuel Seff. Photography: Arthur Todd.

Cast: Dick Powell, Ann Dvorak, Pat O'Brien, Arthur Byron, Lyle Talbot, Hugh Herbert, Guinn Williams, Donald Meek, Harry Beresford.

In a break of tradition, the coach of the title (O'Brien) is actually given a romantic interest to show that he's only a tough guy on the outside.

Powell, who gets to sing, is a chemistry major who scores three touchdowns in the last 10 minutes of the big game to lead his team to victory.

625 College Days

1926, Tiffany Productions, 7,300 feet. Director-Scenario-Supervision: A.P. Younger. Photography: Milton Moore, Mack Stengler. Editor: James C. McKay.

Cast: Marceline Day, Charles Delaney, Pat Harmon, James Harrison, Duane Thompson, Brooks Benedict, Kathleen Key, Edna Murphy, Robert Homans, Gibson Gowl.

Through a series of romantic misunderstandings, a University of California grid player is expelled, but later reinstated.

When the big game comes, however, he's suspended again for helping out his girl friend and breaking training rules. But if he didn't get into the big game in the fourth quarter and do you

The action is fast and furious on the gridiron in the 1926 film College Days. (The Museum of Modern Art/Film Stills Archive.)

know what, this wouldn't be a Hollywood movie, would it?

626 The College Hero

1927, Columbia Pictures, 5,628 feet. Director: Walter Lang. Screenplay: Dorothy Howell. Photography: Joseph Walker. Editor: Arthur Roberts.

Cast: Bobby Agnew, Pauline Gaton, Ben Turpin, Rex Lease, Charles Paddock, Joan Standing, Churchill Ross.

A college freshman (Agnew) and his roommate (Lease) become best friends on and off the football field, although Lease secretly loves Agnew's girl (Gaton).

During football practice, Lease intentionally trips Agnew, injuring him seriously. The remorseful Lease starts drinking, and after his pal helps win the game, the two are reconciled.

627 College Hounds

1930, Metro Goldwyn Mayer, 22 minutes. Directors: Jules White, Zion Myers.

An all-dog cast is featured in this short comedy in which, yes, there's a plot to kidnap the team's star player. The dogs play a game attended by hundreds of canines in the stands.

628 College Humor

1933, Paramount, 68 minutes. Director: Wesley Ruggles. Story: Dean Fales. Adaptation: Claude Binyon, Frank Butler, Photography: Leo Tover.

Cast: Bing Crosby, Jack Oakie, Richard Arlen, Mary Carlisle, Mary Kornman, George Burns, Gracie Allen, Joseph Sauers, Lona Andre.

If Bing is the star, you know that music is just as prominent as the plot.

He plays a college professor who becomes a radio star and steals the heart of a grid star's girl. Her brother (Oakie), a really fresh freshman, becomes the team's new star and scores two touchdowns in the final quarter.

629 College Love

1929, Universal, 6,145-6,864 feet. Director: Nat Ross. Producer: Carl Laemmle, Jr. Scenario: John B. Clymer, Pierre Couderc. Story: Leonard Fields. Photography: George Robinson. Editor: Ted Kent.

Cast: George Lewis, Eddie Phillips, Dorothy Gulliver, Churchill Ross, Hayden Stevenson, Sumner Getchell.

A romantic comedy with the usual two football players in love with the same girl. Flash Thomas (Phillips) and Bob Wilson (Lewis) both love Dorothy (Gulliver).

Wilson covers for his pal and rival, who's attending a party against training rules, but is eventually found out and gets into trouble.

Benched, he, of course, gets in the game and the two friends play together to help the team to victory while Wilson gets the girl.

630 College Lovers

1930, First National Pictures, 5,633 feet. Director: John G. Adolfi. Scenario: Douglas Doty. Story: Earl Baldwin. Photography: Frank Kesson. Editor: Frederick Y. Smith.

Cast: Jack Whiting, Marion Nixon, Wade Boteler, Guinn Williams, Frank McHugh, Russell Hopton, Richard Tucker, Charles Judels, Phyllis Crane.

Would'ja believe another comedy about football players in love with the same gal? This has an added twist, however, in that it's three in love with Madge (Nixon).

Eddie (Hopton) and Tiny (Williams) both love her, although she's secretly engaged to Frank (Whiting). Eddie and Tiny battle over her during halftime and they're benched; but the romantic complications are sorted out before the game's end, and they play together to help the team win.

631 The College Orphan

1915, Universal, 6 reels.

Cast: Carter De Haven, Louise Morrison, Gloria Fonda, Val Paul, William Canfield, Flora Parker De Haven, Lule Warrenton, Doc Crane.

Set against a football background, a wild teenager must redeem himself when another student causes him to be expelled and disinherited.

632 College Rhythm

1934, Paramount, 75 minutes. Director: Norman Taurog. Adaptation: Walter DeLeon, John McDermott, Francis Martin. Story: George Manon, Jr. Photography: Leo Tover, Ted Tetzlaff.

Cast: Joe Penner, Lanny Ross, Jack Oakie, Helen Mack, Lyda Roberti, Mary Brien, George Barbiler, Franklin Pangborn, Mary Wallace, Dean Jagger, Joseph Sauers.

Oakie plays his usual conceited football star but this musical comedy offers a slightly different plot: The team is fighting to save an old department store.

633 The College Widow

1927, Warner Brothers Pictures, 6,616 feet. Director: Archie L. Mayo. Adaptation: Paul Schofield, Peter Milner, based on "The College Widow, a Pictorial Comedy in Four Acts" by George Ade. Editor: Clarence Kolster.

Cast: Dolores Costello, William Collier, Jr., Charles Hill Mailes, Guinn "Big Boy" Williams, Douglas Gerrard, Anders Randolf, Robert Ryan, Sumner Getchell.

The lovely daughter (Costello) of an Atwater College professor uses her natural charms to lure top football players to the school after the college president (Mailes) faces firing over the team's poor showing.

Loosely remade in 1930 as **Maybe It's Love.**

634 The Collegians

Between 1926 and 1929, Universal produced a long series of two-reel shorts about life at fictional Calford College. As the titles indicate, the series' main focus was on sports of all kinds; but for some reason, the series is remembered in some quarters as being mainly football.

George Lewis, Hayden Stevenson and Churchill Ross were among the series' regular stars. Carl Laemmle, Jr. was the producer and wrote the stories; and the directors included Harry Edwards, Robert Hill, Wesley Ruggles, Nat Ross, Harry Fraser and Ben Holmes.

Here, in the order of their release, are the series titles:

1. **Benson at Calford**; 2. **Fighting to Win**; 3. **The Last Lap**; 4. **Around the Bases**; 5. **Fighting Spirit**; 6. **The Relay**; 7. **Flashing Oars**; 8. **Breaking Records**; 9. **Crimson Colors**; 10. **Winning Five**; 11. **The Dazzling Coeds**; 12. **A Fighting Finish**; 13. **Samson at Calford**; 14. **The Winning Punch**; 15. **Running Wild**; 16. **Splashing Through**; 17. **Sliding Home**; 18. **The Junior Year**; 19. **Calford vs. Redskins**; 20. **Kicking Through**; 21. **Calford in the Movies**; 22. **Paddling Co-Eds**; 23. **Fighting for Victory**; 24. **Dear Old Calford**; 25. **Calford on Horseback**; 26. **The Bookworm Hero**; 27. **Speeding Youth**; 28. **The Winning Point**; 29. **Farewell**; 30. **King of the Campus**; 31. **The Rivals**; 32. **On Guard**; 33. **Junior Luck**; 34. **The Cross Country Run**; 35. **The Varsity Drag**; 36. **Flying High**; 37. **On the Side Lines**; 38. **Use Your Feet**; 39. **Splash Mates**; 40. **Graduation Daze**.

635 Collegiate

1926, R-C Pictures, 4,718 feet. Director: Del Andrews. Adaptation: James Gruen. Story: Jean Dupont. Photography: Jules Cronjager.

Cast: Donald Keith, Alberta Vaughn, John Steppling, Alys Murrell, Frankie Adams, William Austin, Charles Cruz.

The daughter of a millionaire works her way through college rather than marry the snob her father has selected and falls in love with a football star.

The player is suspended wrongly for allegedly cheating on a test. The girl also gets into trouble and is locked in her dorm, but she escapes in time for her boy friend to get in the game.

636 Come On, Leathernecks

1938, Republic, 65 minutes. Director: James Cruze. Producer: Herman Schlom. Screenplay: Sidney Salkow, Dorell and Stuart McGowan. Photography: Ernest Miller. Editor: Edward Mann.

Cast: Richard Cromwell, Marsha Hunt, Leon Ames, Edward Brophy, Bruce McFarlane, Robert Warwick, Howard Hickman, Walter Miller.

An Annapolis quarterback is torn between service to his country and accepting an enticing offer from the pros. The film's title should tell you what the unsurprising final choice is.

The quarterback (Cromwell) becomes involved in an arms smuggling plot in the Philippines, where he's followed by a persistent recruiter (Brophy).

637 Convict's Code

1939, Monogram, 53 minutes. Director: Lambert Hillyer. Producer: E.B. Derr. Screenplay: John W. Krafft. Photography: Arthur Martinelli. Editor: Russell Schoengarth.

Cast: Robert Kent, Anne Nagel, Sidney Blackmer, Victor Kilian, Norman Willis, Maude Eburne, Ben Alexander, Pat Flaherty.

Those ever-present gamblers want a grid star out of the way for a big game so they frame him on a bank robbery charge, and he serves three years in prison.

He gets a job as chauffeur to the head gambler, whose sister falls in love with him.

638 The Cowboy Quarterback

1939, Warner Brothers, 54 minutes. Director: Noel Smith. Producer: Bryan Foy. Screenplay: Fred Niblo, Jr., based on a play by Ring Lardner and George M. Cohan. Photography: Ted McCord. Editor: Doug Gould.

Cast: Bert Wheeler, Marie Wilson, Gloria Dickson, DeWolf Hopper, William Demarest, Eddie Foy, Jr., William Gould, Charles Wilson, Eddie Acuff, Clem Bevans.

A low-budget remake of **Fast Company** and **Elmer the Great,** the only difference being that football has replaced baseball as the hero's occupation.

A country rube (Wheeler) is discovered tossing potato sacks in a grocery story owned by Wilson and is signed by Demarest to play for the Packers.

Despite the usual interference from the usual racketeers, he's able to win the game almost single-handedly in the final seconds.

639 Crazylegs, All American

1953, Republic, 87 minutes. Director: Francis D. Lyon. Producer-Screenplay: Hall Bartlett. Photography: Virgil E. Miller. Editor: Cotton Warburton.

Cast: Elroy "Crazylegs" Hirsch, Lloyd Nolan, Joan Vors, James Millican, Bob Waterfield, Bob Kelley, James Brown, Win Hirsch, John Brown, Norman Field, Louise Lorimer and the Los Angeles Rams.

The filmmakers had a problem: Who do you get to portray a then-aging Crazylegs Hirsch as a high school teenager? The answer: Aging Crazylegs Hirsch himself, beanie and all, looking nearly as old as his parents in the film. Somehow he got away with it.

Narrated by Nolan, who portrays his former football coach, the film incorporates a lot of newsreel footage of the grid great in action.

It dramatizes his rise to stardom at the University of Wisconsin, where he earns letters in football, basketball, baseball and track, and later at Michigan.

Joining the Chicago Rockets after a stint in the Marines, he's seriously injured and his career is jeopardized; but Crazylegs refuses to give up. He joins the Los Angeles Rams and after switching to end from the backfield, makes a comeback.

640 The Draw-Back

1928, Educational, 2 reels. Director: Norman Taurog.

Cast: Johnny Arthur, Kathryn McGuire, Wallace Lupino, Al Thompson.

As the title indicates, the hero of this short comedy is more of a liability than an asset on the field; but the farm boy who was the butt of the college's practical jokes winds up as the big game's unlikely hero and wins the girl.

641 The Drop Kick

1927, First National, 6,900 feet. Director: Millard Webb. Adaptation: Winifred Dunn. Story: Katherine Brush. Photography: Arthur Edeson, Alvin Knechtel.

Cast: Richard Barthelmess, Barbara Kent, Eugene Strong, Brooks Benedict, Dorothy Revier, James Bradbury, Jr., Alberta Vaughn, Hedda Hopper, George Pearce.

Boy, you think you have troubles? Pity poor football star Jock Hamill (Barthelmess). He's accused of murdering his coach, who actually committed suicide because he couldn't afford his unfaithful wife's expenses.

And who does the wife (Revier) want as her new boy friend? That's right, Our Hero. Hamill's Dear Mother rides to the rescue, wringing the real story out of the unfaithful wife to clear her son.

Elroy "Crazylegs" Hirsch portrayed himself in the film Crazylegs, All American. (Courtesy Elroy Hirsch.)

Meanwhile, lest we forget this is a football film, Hamill is singlehandedly messing up the big game because of everything on his mind. It all boils down to the drop kick of the title. Will he make it? Have you ever known a hero in a 1920's football film not to make it?

642 Easy Living

1949, RKO Radio Pictures, 77 minutes. Director: Jacques Tourneur. Producer: Robert Sparks. Screenplay: Charles Schnee. Story: Irwin Shaw. Photography: Harry J. Wild. Editor: Frederic Knudtson.

Cast: Victor Mature, Lucille Ball, Lizabeth Scott, Sonny Tufts, Lloyd Nolan, Paul Stewart, Jack Paar, Gordon Jones, Don Beddoe, James Backus and the Los Angeles Rams.

The fickle woman rears her ugly head in another sports film. This time it's Scott who begins to stray when husband Mature's pro grid skills begin to decline.

He's got some heart trouble, but he keeps on playing lest he lose his wife for good. As usual, there's a nice girl (Ball) who loves Mature and counterbalances Scott who does stay with him at the end.

643 Eyes Right!

1926, Goodwill Pictures, 4,500 feet. Director: Louis Chaudet. Adaptation: Leslie Curtis. Story: Ernest Grayman. Photography: Allen Davey.

Cast: Francis X. Bushman, Jr., Robert Hale, Larry Kent, Flobelle Fairbanks, Dora Dean, Frederick Vroom.

A poor lad (Bushman) who can't afford the tuition at the San Diego Army and Navy Academy pays his way through by washing dishes in the school kitchen.

He works his way up to a cadet and becomes a star player on the girdiron but falls for the commandant's niece (Fairbanks).

That incurs the jealousy of an upperclassman, who frames him and gets him suspended from the big game. Naturally, he's cleared in the nick of time and brings his team from far behind to win.

644 The Fable of the Higher Education

1914, Essanay.

Cast: Wallace Beery, Leo White, R. Belder.

Do people attend college to get an education? Of course not, they go to play football. That's the theme of this early satire.

645 A Fan's Notes

1972, Canadian, Warner Brothers, 90 minutes. Director: Eric Till. Screenplay: William Kinsolving. Story: Frederick E. Exley. Photography: Harry Makin.

Cast: Jerry Orbach, Patricia Collins, Burgess Meredith, Rosemary Murphy, Conrad Bain, Julia Robinson.

The son of a football star gets to accept the fact that he'll never follow in his father's footsteps.

646 Father Was a Fullback

1949, 20th Century-Fox, 84 minutes. Director: John M. Stahl. Producer: Fred Kohlmar. Screenplay: Aleen Leslie, Casey Robinson, Mary Loos, Richard Sale, from a play by Clifford Goldsmith. Photography: Lloyd Ahern. Editor: J. Watson Webb, Jr.

Cast: Fred MacMurray, Maureen O'Hara, Betty Lynn, Rudy Vallee, Thelma Ritter, Natalie Wood, Jim Backus, Richard Tyler, Buddy Martin, Mickey McCardle.

Grid coach MacMurray has enough problems while suffering through a losing season in this pleasant family film, but one of his daughters writes an article about her supposed sex life that almost gets him fired.

Wife O'Hara helps hubby fight off the alumni, led by Vallee, who are out for his scalp. Meanwhile, the coach gets some tips from grid star Tyler that help the team out; and he solves his problems with daughters Wood and Lynn.

647 Fighting Youth

1935, Universal, 80 minutes. Director: Hamilton MacFadden. Producer: Fred S. Meyer. Screenplay: Henry Johnson, Florabel Muir, MacFadden. Photography: Eddie Snyder.

Cast: Charles Farrell, June Martel, Andy Devine, J. Farrell MacDonald, Ann Sheridan, Eddie Nugent, Herman Bing, Phyllis Fraser, Charles Wilson.

Radicals try to take over a college campus through subversion, and what better way than to try to influence the top football star?

The star is swept off his feet by a radical woman, and his performance on the field promptly suffers. With the aid of a G-man who's working to expose the radicals, the star is soon set right; and with three minutes left to go in the important game, guess who scores two touchdowns?

648 Finney

1969, Gold Coast, 72 minutes, B&W and Color. Director-Producer-Editor-Screenplay: Bill Hare. Photography: Jack Richards.

Cast: Robert Kilcullen, Bill Levinson, Joan Sundstrom, Anthony Mockus, Dick Stanwood, Ricky Hill, Dwight Lawrence, Jerry Kaufherr.

A veteran Chicago Bears tackle turns down a job as defensive coach after being told he's cut after 13 years in the pros.

He tries his hand at painting football scenes, but no one wants to buy them so he eventually becomes a bartender.

Football sequences in **Finney** are in color. The rest of the film is black and white.

649 Flight

1929, Columbia, 9,005-10,670 feet. Director: Frank Capra. Producer: Harry Cohn. Scenario: Howard J. Green. Story: Ralph Graves. Photography: Joseph Walker, Joe Novak: Editors: Ben Pivar, Maurice Wright, Gene Milford.

Cast: Ralph Graves, Jack Holt, Alan Roscoe, Harold Goodwin, Jimmy De La Cruze, Lila Lee.

Lefty Phelps (Graves) makes a crucial misplay in a big football game and joins the Marines where he befriends Panama Williams (Holt). The two, of course, love the same girl (Lee) and become involved in a revolution in Nicaragua.

650 Football Now and Then

1953, RKO Radio Pictures, 1 reel, Color. Director: Jack Kinney. Story: Lance Nolley. Animation: John Sibley, George Nicholas, Fred Moore.

A Walt Disney cartoon in which a boy and his grandfather watch a football game between Bygone University and Present State on television and discuss the differences between old-time football and modern grid action.

651 Football Romeo

1938, Metro Goldwyn Mayer, 1 reel. Director: George Sidney. Producer: Jack Chertok. Screenplay: Hal Law, Robert A. McGowan, Jack White.

Alfalfa's the reluctant hero in a game against Butch's Assassins in this Our Gang comedy short. He's blackmailed into playing by Carla, who threatened to reveal the contents of a note he wrote.

652 Football Royal

1955, Warner Brothers, 10 minutes, Color. Director-Photography: Andre de la Varre. Screenplay: Charles Tedford. Editor: Rex Steele.

This one's a little different than the ordinary sports short documentary, so we're including it here. It details a strange form of football played in Florence, Italy. Two teams of 27 players in medieval costume play a mixture of American style football, rugby, soccer and basketball.

653 A Football Warrior

1908, The Edison Co., Director: F.S. Armitage.

An early football movie filmed in New Jersey for Thomas A. Edison's company.

654 Force of Impulse

1961, Sutton Pictures, 84 minutes. Director: Saul Swimmer. Producer: Peter Gayle. Screenplay: Francis Swann. Story: Swimmer, Tony Anthony. Photography: Clifford Poland. Editor: Gene Milford.

Cast: Robert Alda, J. Carroll Naish, Tony Anthony, Jeff Donnell, Jody McCrea, Bruce Talbot, Lionel Hampton, Christina Crawford, Kathy Barr, Teri Hope.

A delivery boy who's also the star for his high school football team must overcome the objections of his sweetheart's wealthy parents.

655 The Fortune Cookie

1966, United Artists, 125 minutes. Director-Producer: Billy Wilder. Screenplay: Wilder, I.A.L. Diamond. Editor: Daniel Mandell.

Cast: Jack Lemmon, Walter Matthau, Ron Rich, Cliff Osmond, Lurene Tuttle, Harry Holcombe, Harry Davis, Archie Moore, Keith Jackson, Herbie Faye, Billy Beck.

CBS cameraman Harry Hinkle (Lemmon) is rammed into on the sidelines by Boom Boom Jackson (Rich) during a Minnesota Vikings-Cleveland Browns game.

Willie Gingrich, a lawyer who's so shady he thinks nothing of taking money out of poor boxes and who's Hinkle's brother-in-law, convinces the cameraman to sue everyone in sight.

Gingrich (Matthau) gets Hinkle to fake the symptons of a severe back injury as private eyes and doctors try to prove the masquerade. Hinkle, in the meantime, gets pangs of conscience when the grid star, upset at having crippled someone, becomes his nurse.

This was one of the best Lemmon-Matthau comedies.

656 The Forward Pass

1929, First National, 4,920-7,246 feet. Director: Eddie Cline. Scenario: Howard Emmett Rogers. Story: Harvey Gates. Photography: Arthur Todd. Editor: Ralph Holt.

Cast: Douglas Fairbanks, Jr., Loretta Young, Guinn Williams, Marion Byron, Bert Rome, Lane Chandler, Phyllis Crane, Allan Lane, Floyd Shackleford and the USC football team.

The star quarterback (Fairbanks) for Sanford College calls it quits after taking a lot of punishment from the opposition one game.

Called a coward by a teammate (Lane) and tricked into playing by a girl, he does play, but poorly. The two players fight with each other in the locker room and become friends, joining to lead the team to victory.

657 Francis Goes to West Point

1952, Universal-International, 83 minutes. Director: Arthur Lubin. Producer: Leonard Goldstein. Screenplay: Oscar Brodney. Photography: Carl Guthrie. Editor: Milton Carruth.

Cast: Donald O'Connor, Lori Nelson, Alice Kelley, Palmer Lee, William Reynolds, Les Tremayne, Otto Hulbett, David Janssen, James Best.

Francis the Talking Mule is back in action helping out pal O'Connor again. O'Connor is appointed to West Point after he saves a nuclear plant from sabotage.

With the mule helping him out with advice, O'Connor joins the football team but is expelled just before the big game with Navy. Following every football film cliche, he's allowed back in time to help steer the team.

658 The Freshman

1925, Pathe Exchange, 75 minutes. Directors: Sam Taylor, Fred Newmeyer. Screenplay: Taylor, John Grey, Ted Wilde, Tim Whelan.

Cast: Harold Lloyd, Jobyna Ralston, Brooks Benedict, James Anderson, Hazel Keener, Joseph Harrington, Pat Harmon, Charles Stevenson, Grady Sutton, Oscar Smith.

Undoubtedly one of the greatest sports comedies of all time and one of the few Lloyd features still generally accessible to the public features the great silent-era clown as Harold Lamb, a freshman at Tate University.

Football sequences for **The Freshman** were shot between quarters of the East-West game at the Berkeley Bowl. A major portion of those sequences were used with soundtrack added as the opening sequence for 1947's **The Sin of Harold Diddlebock,** a kind of "semi" sequel to **The Freshman.**

Lamb's only impressions of college life come from a football movie; and when he arrives at Tate, described by the titles as "a large football stadium with a college attached," he's ridiculed by some upperclassmen for the greeting. ("I'm just a regular fellow. Step right up and call me Speedy.") and little jig Lamb lifts from that movie.

Among his chief tormentors is Chet Trask (Anderson), the school's football star.

He's made the laughing stock (unknown to him) of the entire campus when he's tricked into giving a welcoming speech in front of the entire student body and a very nervous kitten creates havoc.

While trying out for the football team, he ruins the team's tackling dummy. The coach (Harmon), described as a man "so tough he shaves with a blowtorch," makes Lamb serve as the new tackling dummy for the whole team and keeps him on the squad strictly for laughs.

Hoping to become a big man on campus, Lamb sponsors a party that backfires when his suit, made by an ailing tailor who didn't have time to complete it, keeps on falling to pieces.

Lamb gets his chance on the football field in the big game when the coach has no one else to put in. He ruins his big chance to be a hero when he stops short of the goal line after mistaking the factory whistle for the game whistle, but finally lands on the goal line—his face full of chalk—to win the game and become the campus hero.

Story-wise, **The Freshman** is alarmingly similar to the twice-made baseball comedy, **The Pinch Hitter,** but Lloyd's greatness as a comedian makes the former film a classic while **The Pinch Hitter** has fallen by the wayside.

659 The Galloping Ghost

1931, Mascot, 12 chapters. Director: Reeves Eason. Supervising Editor: Wyndham Gittens. Story: Helmer Bergman, Ford Beebe, Gittens. Photography: Benjamin Kline, Ernest Miller, Tom Galligan. Editors: Ray Snyder, Gilmore Walker.

Cast: Harold "Red" Grange, Dorothy Gulliver, Tom Dugan, Gwen Lee, Francis X. Bushman, Jr., Theodore Lorch, Walter Miller, Edward Hearn, Ernie Adams, Tom London, Stepin Fetchit.

Chapter One: The Idol of Clay; Chapter Two: The Port of Peril; Chapter Three: The Master Mind; Chapter Four: The House of Secrets; Chapter Five: The Man Without a Face; Chapter Six: The Torn $500 Bill; Chapter Seven: When the Lights Went Out; Chapter Eight: The Third Degree; Chapter Nine: The Sign in the Sky; Chapter Ten: The Vulture's Lair; Chapter Eleven: The Radio Patrol; Chapter Twelve: The Ghost Comes Back.

Legendary football hero Grange, who had earlier starred in two silent sports films (**One Minute to Play, A Racing Romeo**) got his chance to display his vocal cords as well as his gridiron ability in this serial in which those ever-present evil gamblers attempt to fix football games.

Grange finds himself being framed for throwing games and must survive an extraordinary number of perils before clearing his name by the final episode.

660 The Girl Said No

1930, Metro Goldwyn Mayer, 5,772-8,382 feet. Director: Sam Wood. Adaptation: Sarah Y. Mason. Story: A.P. Younger. Photography: Ira Morgan. Editors: Frank Sullivan, Truman K. Wood, George Boemler.

Cast: William Haines, Leila Hyams, Polly Moran, Marie Dressler, Francis X. Bushman, Jr., William Janney.

There's no Mrs. Robinson from **The Graduate** here, but the college football hero, fresh out of college, grabs his girl friend from the altar to prevent her marriage to another man in this early talkie comedy.

661 The Gladiator

1938, Columbia, 70 minutes. Director: Edward Sedgwick. Producer: David L. Loew. Screenplay: Charlie Melson, Arthur Sheekman, based on a novel by Philip Wylie. Photography: George Schneiderman.

Cast: Joe E. Brown, Man Mountain Dean, June Travis, Dickie Moore, Lucien Littlefield, Robert Kent, Eddie Kane.

The usual Brown comedy hi-jinks about as he wins money at a movie promotion and uses it to enroll at college where he wrestles Man Mountain Dean and becomes a big football hero.

662 Good News

1930, Metro Goldwyn Mayer, 8,100 feet. Director: Nick Grinde. Screenplay: Frances Marion, based on a play by Laurence Schwab, Lew Brown, Frank Mandel and B.G. DeSylva. Photography: Percy Hilburn. Editor: William LeVanway.

Cast: Mary Lawlor, Stanley Smith, Bessie Love, Cliff Edwards, Gus Shy, Lola Lane, Delmar Daves, Thomas Jackson, Billy Taft, Frank McGlynn, Dorothy McNulty.

Tait College's chances of winning the big game are jeopardized when the team's star (Smith) is suspended for poor grades because of a romance. He's reinstated in time in this musical comedy, remade 17 years later.

663 Good News

1947, Metro Goldwyn Mayer, 95 minutes, Color. Director: Charles Walters. Producer: Arthur Freed. Screenplay: Betty Comden, Adolph Green, based on the play by Laurence Schwab, Lew Brown, Frank Mandel and B.G. DeSylva. Photography: Charles Schoenbaum. Editor: Albert Akst.

Cast: Peter Lawford, June Allyson, Patricia Marshall, Joan McCracken, Ray McDonald, Mel Torme, Robert Strickland, Donald McBride, Tom Dugan, Clinton Sundberg, Jane Green.

Lawford, captain of Tait College's football team, falls for a finishing school gal who won't give him the time of day until she learns he's heir to a pickle empire.

The girl tries to impress everyone with her French but mouths expressions like "quel fromage" (what cheese) when she means to say "quel domage" (what a pity).

He jilts the librarian (Allyson) who teaches him French so he can impress the gold digger, but she later agrees to be his tutor so he can pass a makeup test and play in the big game.

664 The Great Alone

1922, American Releasing Corp., 5,912 feet. Directors: Jacques Jaccard, James Colwell. Story: Jaccard. Photography: Frank B. Good.

Cast: Monroe Salisbury, Laura Anson, Walter Law, Richard Cummings, Maria Law, George Waggoner.

A half-breed Indian from the Yukon (Salisbury) is a football star on the field but ignored by everyone off the field at Stanford University except innocent Mary (Maria Law).

He quits school and returns home only to find he must save Mary during a blizzard.

665 The Gridiron Flash (aka **The Luck of the Game**)

1935, RKO Radio Pictures, 62 minutes. Director-Screenplay: Glen Tryon. Story: Nicholas Barrows, Earle Snell. Photography: John W. Boyle.

Cast: Eddie Quillan, Betty Furness, Grant Mitchell, Edgar Kennedy, Grady Sutton, Joseph Sauers, Margaret Dumont.

A college coach likes what he sees of convicted bank robber Quillan during a game with a prison team and promises to get him pardoned if he'll play for the school.

Naturally, he accepts and even begins a romance with the coach's niece.

Some of his old ways are still with him; and he starts to leave with some stolen jewels, but finds that college has changed him and he returns in time to help his team win.

666 Gus

1976, Buena Vista, 96 minutes, Color. Director: Vincent McEveety. Producer: Ron Miller. Photography: Frank Phillips. Editor: Robert Stafford.

Cast: Edward Asner, Don Knotts, Gary Grimes, Tim Conway, Liberty Williams, Dick Van Patten, Ronnie Schell, Bob Crane, Tom Bosley, Harold Gould, Dick Butkus, Dick Enberg, Johnny Unitas.

With Don Knotts as the coach and Conway the villain, you know this isn't going to be **Knute Rockne, All American.**

Asner, owner of the Atoms, the worst team in the history of football, is desperate. So desperate, he reaches into Yugoslavia to sign up a youthful athlete (Grimes) and his pet mule Gus who can kick 100-yard field goals.

After some legal difficulties, the mule is allowed to play and leads the team into the playoffs.

Meanwhile, Asner's assistant (Williams) falls for Grimes, and she dumps boy friend Butkus, who later turns up on another team and guns for Grimes' scalp.

As in most Disney sports comedies, there's the usual kidnapping (or is it mulenapping) plot by the villains and the usual escape in time.

667 The Guy Who Came Back

1951, 20th Century-Fox, 91 minutes. Director: Joseph Newman. Producer: Julian Bloustein. Screenplay: Allan Scott. Photography: Joseph La Shelle. Editor: William B. Murphy.

Cast: Paul Douglas, Joan Bennett, Linda Darnell, Don DeFore, Billy Gray, Zero Mostel, Walter Burke, Henry Kulky, Dick Ryan, Robert B. Williams.

Harry Joplin (Douglas) is an aging, overweight pro football player who refuses a coaching job in hopes of still making a comeback.

Leaving Bennett for a model (Darnell), he earns some money as a wrestler. Meanwhile, the outbreak of a war causes a player shortage, and he gets his shot at a comeback only to realize that he really is through.

The model also sends him back to his wife.

The film's most poignant scene is when Joplin, giving a

speech, realizes that what was funny to other people when he was a star isn't the same coming from a has-been.

668 The Halfback

1917, Conquest Pics, 3 reels. Director: Ben Tourbett. Story: Ralph Henry Barbour.

Cast: Yale Boss, Ogden Childs, Scott Fletcher, T. McNamara, Harry Warington, Frank Gargan.

A kid from the other side of the tracks makes good on the gridiron despite the efforts of his rival, a rich kid.

669 Harmon of Michigan

1941, Columbia, 65 minutes. Director: Charles Barton. Producer: Wallace MacDonald. Screenplay: Howard J. Green. Story: Richard Goldstone, Stanley Rauh, Fredric Frank. Photography: John Stumar. Editor: Arthur Seid.

Cast: Tom Harmon, Forest Evashevski, Anita Louise, Oscar O'Shea, Warren Ashe, Stanley Brown, Ken Christy, Tim Ryan, William Hall, Larry Parks, Lloyd Bridges, Chester Conklin.

Harmon, a 1940 All-American, stars as himself. After graduation from college, he's got a swelled head and quits an assistant coaching job.

He lands a new post under wise old Pop Branch (O'Shea) but quits that one as well to coach another school where he wins on an illegal play before changing his attitude and winding up with Branch again.

Forest Evashevski, Harmon's teammate at Michigan, also appears as himself.

670 Harold Teen

1928, First National, 7,541 feet. Director: Mervyn LeRoy. Producer: Allan Dwan. Screenplay: Tom J. Geraghty, based on the comic strip. Photography: Ernest Haller. Editor: LeRoy Stone.

Cast: Arthur Lake, Mary Brian, Lucien Littlefield, Jack Duffy, Jack Egan, Alice White, Hedda Hopper, Ben Hall, William Blakefield, Ed Brady, Fred Kelsey.

Lake, who would go on to become the screen's Dagwood in the Blondie series, plays another comic strip character here.

Harold moves to the city from the country where he becomes one of the most popular students at his high school as a football star, fraternity member and director of the school play in this easy-to-take comedy.

671 Heaven Can Wait

1978, Paramount, 100 minutes, Color. Directors-Producers: Warren Beatty, Buck Henry. Screenplay: Beatty, Robert C. Jones, Don Zimmerman. Photography: William A. Fraker; Editors: Robert C. Jones, Don Zimmerman.

Cast: Warren Beatty, Julie Christie, James Mason, Jack Warden, Charles Grodin, Dyan Cannon, Buck Henry, Vincent Gardenia, Dolph Sweet, R.G. Armstrong.

A remake of the 1941 boxing comedy **Here Comes Mr. Jordan.** Instead of the hero (Beatty) being a boxer, he's an aging football player who's called up to heaven by mistake before his time is up and put in the body of an industrialist.

Mason has the Claude Rains role as the angel who corrects the error, while Warden, as the football coach, is in the role made famous by James Gleason.

The industrialist's wife (Cannon) and her boy friend (Grodin) plot to murder the industrialist a second time. In the meantime, the hero finds true love with Christie as he tries to prove to her and Warden his true identity.

672 Hero for a Day

1939, Universal, 65 minutes. Director: Harold Young. Producer: Ken Goldsmith. Screenplay: Harold Buchman. Story: Matt Taylor. Photography: John Boyle.

Cast: Charley Grapewin, Anita Louise, Dick Foran, Burton Churchill, Emma Dunn, David Holt, Richard Lane.

A bottom-of-the-bill programmer that's undeservedly been relegated to the bottom of the sports film pileup, **Hero for a Day** is a modest little attempt to show what happens to grid stars when their days of glory are gone.

Grapewin is a night watchman who had been an All-American grid star 35 years earlier and who becomes the special invited guest when his old school plays in a big game. When his old school wins in an exciting finish, he collapses.

Stock footage is used for the grid scenes and one shot shows the players with their numbers on backwards, indicating the scene was reversed.

673 High School Hero

1946, Monogram, 69 minutes. Director: Arthur Dreifuss. Producer: Sam Katzman. Screenplay: Dreifuss, Hal Collins. Photography: Ira Morgan. Editor: Ace Herman.

Cast: Freddie Stewart, June Preiser, Noel Neill, Ann Rooney, Jackie Moran, Frankie Darro, Warren Mills, Milt Kibbee, Pierre Watkin, Douglas Fowley.

Little is new plotwise in this low budget musical comedy as the boys from Whitney High School, whose football team reminds no one of Notre Dame, try to figure out how to win while also getting ready for a talent show.

674 Hold 'Em Jail

1932, RKO Radio Pictures, 63 minutes. Director: Norman Taurog. Screenplay: S.J. Perelman, Walter DeLeon, Mark Sandrich. Photography: Len Smith. Editor: Artie Roberts.

Cast: Bert Wheeler, Robert Woolsey, Edna May Oliver, Roscoe Ates, Edgar Kennedy, Betty Grable, Paul Hurst.

The comedy team of Wheeler and Woolsey is framed and sent to Bidemore Prison where coach Hurst is trying to build a winning football team out of a real bunch of losers.

The team is so bad their archrivals may play their next game against some reform school boys instead of Bidemore.

With the help of some chloroform they use to put the opposing team to sleep, Wheeler and Woolsey turn things around.

Hold 'Em Jail was one of a number of films inspired by the success of **Up the River,** a comedy about a prison baseball team.

675 Hold 'Em Navy!

1937, Paramount, 82 minutes. Director: Kurt Neumann. Screenplay: Erwin Gelsey, Lloyd Corrigan. Story: Albert S. LeVino. Photography: Henry Sharp.

Cast: Lew Ayres, Mary Carlisle, John Howard, Benny Baker, Tully Marshall, Elizabeth Patterson, Archie Twitchell, Lambert Rogers, Lee Bennett, Alston Cockrell, Frank Nelson.

The tradition and goals of the U.S. Naval Academy are at the core of this routine story about a freshman (Ayres) and an upperclassman (Howard) who are at odds over the love of a girl.

When it comes down to the nitty-gritty, however, they unite to lead their team to a win over Army in the closing seconds of the game.

676 Hold 'Em Yale

1928, Pathe Exchange, 7,056 feet. Director: Edward H. Griffith. Scenario: George Dromgold, Sanford Hewitt, from a play by Owen Davis. Adaptation: Dromgold. Photography: Arthur Miller. Editor: Harold McLernon.

Cast: Rod LaRocque, Jeanette Loff, Hugh Allan, Joseph Cawthorn, Tom Kennedy, Jerry Mandy.

Lightweight comedy with LaRocque portraying an Argentinian who woos a professor's daughter and is the big hero in a football game against Princeton.

677 Hold 'Em Yale

1935, Paramount, 61 minutes. Director: Sidney Lanfield. Producer: Charles Rogers. Story: Damon Runyon. Adaptation: Paul Gerard Smith, Eddie Welch. Photography: Milton Krasner.

Cast: Cesar Romero, Larry "Buster" Crabbe, Patricia Ellis, William Frawley, Andy Devine, George Barbier, Warren Hymer, Grant Withers, George E. Stone.

Four ticket scalpers (Frawley, Devine, Hymer and Stone) wind up with a disinherited heiress on their hands when she's dumped by a playboy.

She falls in love with a Yale benchwarmer and the four, after much difficulty, get the coach to put him in the game against Harvard, which he does help to win.

678 Hold That Co-Ed (aka **Hold That Girl**)

1938, 20th Century-Fox, 80 minutes. Director: George Marshall. Producer: Darryl F. Zanuck. Screenplay: Karl Tunberg, Don Ettlinger, Jack Yellen. Photography: Robert Planck.

Cast: John Barrymore, George Murphy, Marjorie Weaver, Joan Davis, Jack Haley, George Barbier, Ruth Terry, Donald Meek, Glenn Morris, Johnny Downs, Paul Hurst, Guinn Williams.

In a spoof on Louisiana politician Huey Long, Barrymore portrays a gubernatorial candidate who schemes to attract votes by building up the football team of a needy university.

His main opponent, in the meantime, is doing the same thing at another school.

Barrymore's team includes some strange recruits, including some wrestlers and Joan Davis, a drop kick specialist who encounters a lot of difficulty carrying the ball against the wind.

679 Hold That Line

1952, Monogram, 67 minutes. Director: William Beaudine. Producer: Jerry Thomas. Screenplay: Charles Marion, Tim Ryan. Photography: Marcel Le Picard.

Cast: Leo Gorcey, Huntz Hall, John Bromfield, Veda Ann Borg, Mona Knox, Gloria Winters, Taylor Holmes, Bernard Gorcey, Gil Stratton, Jr., David Condon, Pierre Watkin.

Two of the Bowery Boys (Leo Gorcey, Huntz Hall) attend an Ivy League college as part of a bet by alumni that even the coarsest of youths can be transformed by an education.

They join the football team and go head on against those ever-present gamblers.

680 Horse Feathers

1932, Paramount, 70 minutes. Director: Norman McLeod. Story: Bert Kalmar, Harry Rubry, S.J. Perelman. Photography: Ray June.

Cast: Marx Brothers, Thelma Todd, David Landau, Florine McKinney, James Pierce, Nat Pendleton, Reginald Barlow.

Groucho is Prof. Quincy Adams Wagstaff, the new president of Huxley College, who is determined to improve the school's football team by hook or by crook, and mostly by crook.

As Groucho is told the college has had a new president every year since 1888, he replies "and that's the year we won our last football game."

He heads to a local speakeasy upon hearing that two top professional football players hang out there; and after a sequence in which he tricks Chico into giving the secret password "swordfish" to enter the place mistakes him and Harpo for the two pros.

Handing them a contract, Chico complains that the paper

is blank, to which Groucho responds "that's all right. We'll fill in something later." When he realizes there's no official seal on the document, Groucho complains it isn't legal, but Harpo produces a real, live seal.

Needless to say, there's chaos on and off the gridiron, with Groucho not below plotting to kidnap members of the opposing team (a switch on the usual cliche in which the good guys get kidnapped) and Todd sent to woo Groucho and steal Huxley's signs. The finale game is a literal circus with banana peels on the field and elastic attached to the ball.

681 How to Watch Football

1938, Metro Goldwyn Mayer, 1 reel. Director: Roy Rowland.

Cast: Robert Benchley, Joyce Compton, John Butler, Eddie Acuff, Diane Cook.

One of Benchley's one-reel comedy shorts in which he "explains" just what the title says.

682 Howard Jones

In 1931, Educational Films came out with a series of films narrated by USC coach Howard Jones on how to play football. Typical titles were **Spring Training** and **Penalties** and each ran about 10 minutes.

683 The Huddle

1932, Metro Goldwyn Mayer, 103 minutes. Director: Sam Wood. Photography: Harold Wenstrom. Editor: Hugh Wynn.

Cast: Ramon Novarro, Madge Evans, Una Merkel, Ralph Graves, John Arledge, Frank Albertson, Kane Richmond.

Based on a novel by Francis Wallace, the locale has been changed from Notre Dame to Yale as it follows steel worker Novarro (who also sings Italian ballads) through his entire four years at the university.

Novarro thinks he's a hot shot because he's a top football star, but learns humility after losing out in some school elections and failing to win a girl. In the finale game against Harvard, he plays with appendicitis.

684 The Iron Major

1943, RKO Radio Pictures, 90 minutes. Director: Ray Enright. Producer: Robert Fellows. Screenplay: Aben Kandel, Warren Duff. Photography: Robert de Grasse. Editor: Robert Wise.

Cast: Pat O'Brien, Ruth Warrick, Robert Ryan, Leon Ames.

A tribute to grid coach Frank Cavanaugh, who wouldn't quit despite extreme adversity, **The Iron Major** covers four decades of his life.

Returning home from World War I wounded and partially blind, he becomes football coach at Boston College, later switching to Fordham.

Despite a doctor's warning that he can only have a few more years of active life, he just keeps on coaching, eventually going blind in 1932.

685 John Goldfarb, Please Come Home!

1965, 20th Century-Fox, 96 minutes, Color. Director: J. Lee Thompson. Producer: Steve Parker. Screenplay: William Peter Blatty. Editor: William B. Murphy.

Cast: Shirley MacLaine, Peter Ustinov, Richard Crenna, Jim Backus, Scott Brady, Fred Clark, Wilfrid Hyde-White, Harry Morgan, Richard Deacon, Jerome Cowan, Telly Savalas.

From the same man who wrote **The Exorcist** comes a madcap comedy about the Jewish coach of an Arab football team. Crenna is "Wrong Way" Goldfarb, so named because of his exploits on the gridiron. As a spy plane pilot, he does it again, crashing in Fawzia instead of Russia.

He's forced by the infantile king (Ustinov) to coach the kingdom's inept football squad, or he'll be turned over to Russia. It seems the king's son was cut by Notre Dame, and he wants his team to beat them.

Meanwhile, Goldfarb tries to help photographer (MacLaine) who has managed to get herself trapped in the king's harem.

Comes the big game in the desert and Notre Dame refuses to lose as ordered by the State Department, so MacLaine saves the day by taking the ball and the gentlemanly Notre Dame squad won't tackle her.

686 The Kick-Off

1926, Excellent Pictures, 6,000 feet. Director: Wesley Ruggles. Story: H.H. Van Loan (or Ruggles, sources disagree). Photography: Frank Zukor.

Cast: George Walsh, Leila Hyams, Earle Larrimore, Bee Amann, W.L. Thorne, Joseph Burke, Jane Jennings.

The new boy, Tom Stephens (Walsh), at Farnsworth College, makes good as quarterback despite dirty tricks and being framed by his rival for a girl's hand. Yes, Our Hero is late for the game; and yes, he wins the game for Farnsworth.

687 The Kickoff

1931, Metro Goldwyn Mayer, 2 reels. Director: George Stevens. Producer: Hal Roach.

Cast: Mickey Daniels, Grady Sutton, David Rollins, Mary Kornman, Betty Bolen, Harry Bernard, Leo Willis, Charlie Hall.

In case you thought the plots of football comedy shorts were any different, this entry in the Boy Friends series finds the good guys' coach and star being kept out of the game by those inevitable racketeers, but the good guys winning just the same.

688 King of the Gamblers

1948, Republic, 60 minutes. Director: George Blair. Producer: Stephen Aver. Screenplay: Albert De Mond, Bradbury Foote. Photography: John MacBurnie. Editor: Robert Leeds.

Cast: William Wright, Thurston Hall, Janet Martin, Stephanie Bachelor, George Meeker, Jonathan Hale, Wally Vernon, William Henry, James Cardwell.

When a football player threatens to reveal a game-fixing scheme in which a sports editor is involved, he's murdered and another player is framed for the crime; and it's up to District Attorney Wright to straighten out the mess.

689 The Kinky Coaches and the Pom Pom Pussycats (aka **Crunch**)

1981, Canadian Summer Vista Pictures, 90 minutes, Color. Director: Mark Warren. Producer: Jim Hanley. Screenplay: Douglas Ditonot, Richard Saver, Bruce Calman.

Cast: John Vernon, Robert Forster, Norman Fell.

Players chase girls, girls chase players, etc. Vernon and Forster are high school coaches and Fell a sportscaster in a limp comedy originally filmed in 1979.

690 Knute Rockne

At the beginning of the 1930s, Pathe and Universal released a series of shorts, directed by Albert Kelley and about 10 minutes each, starring legendary college coach Knute Rockne, who gave pointers on how to play the game.

Titles in the series include **Backfield Play, Carry On, Famous Plays, Offensive System, Shifts, The Last Yard, Touchdown** and **Two Minutes to Go.**

691 Knute Rockne, All American

1940, Warner Brothers, 97 minutes. Director: Lloyd Bacon. Producer: Hal Wallis. Screenplay: Robert Buckner, based on the private papers of Mrs. Knute Rockne. Photography: Tony Gaudio. Editor: Ralph Dawson.

Boy, couldn't any team today use a running back like the one in 1926's The Kick Off, starring George Walsh. (The Museum of Modern Art/Film Stills Archive.)

Cast: Pat O'Brien, Gale Page, Ronald Reagan, Donald Crisp, Albert Basserman, John Qualen, Dorothy Tree, John Litel, Henry O'Neill, Owen David, Jr., Johnny Sheffield, Nick Lukats, Kane Richmond, William Marshall, William Byrne and Howard Jones, Glenn "Pop" Warner, Alonzo Stagg, Wiliam Spaulding as themselves.

WARNING: It's our understanding that many prints of this all-time football classic which are being shown on TV and videotape lack the film's most famous line: "Let's go out and win this one for the Gipper."

Retitled **A Modern Hero** in Great Britain, this is the most famous football film of all time and served as a springboard for Reagan, who portrays grid star George Gipp, to get a wider variety of roles.

O'Brien's portrayal of the famed Notre Dame coach stands out as a highlight of his long career, and the studio never had any doubts about selecting him for the role.

Reagan was selected over about ten other actors, and only after he convinced them that he was a football player at college.

The film covers Rockne's entire life, opening with his emigration to the United States from Norway and ending with a eulogy by Crisp after the coach is killed in a plane crash.

It shows him earning tuition to attend Notre Dame by working in a Chicago post office and later marrying Bonnie Skiles (Page), upon whose memoirs much of the film is based.

As coach, it depicts him developing his team's famous passing attack and stresses his relationship with his players, particularly Gipp and the Four Horsemen.

Above all, it's emphasized that Rockne was a molder of men, determined to win—but fairly—and a gentleman as well, who wasn't slowed down even by a serious illness.

When Gipp, dying of pneumonia

tells his coach, "Some day when things are tough, maybe you can ask the boys to go in there and win just once for the Gipper." Rockne remembers that toward the end of the movie when his team is being beaten by Army. That's when he rallies them with his "Gipper" speech. Let's just hope the print you watch has it.

692 The Lady Objects

1938, Columbia, 66 minutes. Director: Eric C. Kenton. Producer: William Perlberg. Screenplay: Gladys Lehman, Charles Kenyon. Photography: Allen G. Siegler. Editor: Al Clark.

Cast: Lanny Ross, Gloria Stuart, Joan Marsh, Roy Benson, Pierre Watkin, Robert Paige, Arthur Loft.

A college halfback marries a criminal lawyer after graduation. They separate, and he becomes a nightclub singer and gets involved in a murder.

693 The Last Game

1978, EO Corp., 105 minutes, Color. Director-Editor: Martin Beck. Producer: Earl Owensby. Screenplay: Tom McIntyre. Photography: Darrell Cathcart.

Cast: Howard Segal, Terry Alden, Jerry Rushing, Toby Wallace, Mike Allen, Bob Supan, Joan Hotchkis, Julian Morton, Max Ivey, Ed Grady.

Poor Cory Gantt goes non-stop from 4 a.m. each day working two jobs, going to classes at a small North Carolina college and vying for the starting quarterback job.

The sole support of his blind father, his life is complicated by a wealthy and obnoxious alumnus who wants his own son to be the starting quarterback. The alumnus threatens to have the coach fired unless Cory is benched and also offers, as an added incentive, a $100,000 gift to the school.

Cory's dad, who attends the games, is heartbroken at his son's benching. The youth, in the meantime, loses his fickle girl friend to the new quarterback and gets into trouble in school when he falls asleep in class from working the two jobs.

Needless to say, as the film's title gives away all, Cory gets his chance in the big—and last—game of the season and even gets to spurn his fickle girl friend, who returns to him after he becomes the hero.

694 The Laugh-Back

1930, Universal, 20 minutes. Director: Stephen Roberts. Story: Nick Barrows, Sidney Levee.

Cast: Monte Collins, Jack White.

Coach White is driven crazy by the antics of bungler Collins on the gridiron.

695 Life Begins in College

1937, 20th Century-Fox, 80-90 minutes. Director: William A. Seiter. Producer: Harold Wilson. Screenplay: Karl Tunberg, Don Ettlinger, from stories by Darrell Ware. Photography: Robert Planck.

Cast: Ritz Brothers, Joan Davis, Tony Martin, Gloria Stuart, Fred Stone, Nat Pendleton, Dick Baldwin, Joan Marsh, Jed Prouty, Lon Chaney, Jr., Elisha Cook, Jr., Frank Sully.

Those loony Ritz Brothers bide their time on the bench until the last two minutes of the game until Coach Stone has no one else to put in.

Pendleton portrays a wealthy Indian football player who helps save the coach's job.

696 Live Wires

1921, Fox Film Corp., 4,290 feet. Director: Edward Sedgwick. Scenario: Jack Strumwasser. Story: Sedgwick, Charles E. Cooke.

Cast: Johnnie Walker, Edna Murphy, Lefty James, Frank Clark, Wilbur Higby, Hayward Mack, Alberta Lee.

A football star (Walker) is called away from training for a big game when his father dies, and learns there's no money left for his education.

Some crooks trick his mother into signing away their property, and then try to get him to throw the game. Needless to say, the baddies are overcome; and Our Hero helps win the game, but it's the manner he gets there that's interesting. He's lifted from a moving train by an airplane to take him there.

697 The Long Gray Line

1955, Columbia, 138 minutes, Color. Director: John Ford. Producer: Robert Arthur. Screenplay: Edward Hope, based on "Bringing Up the Brass" by Marty Maher and Nardi Reeder Champion. Photography: Charles Lawton, Jr.

Cast: Tyrone Power, Maureen O'Hara, Robert Francis, Donald Crisp, Ward Bond, Betsy Palmer, Phil Carey, Peter Graves, Harry Carey, Jr., Milburn Stone, James Sears, Norm Van Brocklin.

Based on Marty Maher's autobiography, it covers his 50-year involvement with sports and the cadets at West Point, from his start as an athletic trainer and swimming instructor.

698 The Longest Yard

1974, Paramount, 121 minutes, Color. Director: Robert Aldrich. Producer: Albert S. Ruddy. Screenplay: Tracy Kennan Wynn. Story: Ruddy. Photography: Joseph Bivoc. Editor: Michael Luciano.

Cast: Burt Reynolds, Eddie Albert, Ed Lauter, Michael Conrad, Jim Hampton, Harry Caesar, John Steadman, Charles Tymer, Richard Kiel, Mike Henry, Ray Nitschke, Joe Kapp, Bernadette Peters, Ernie Wheelwright, Bob Tessier.

A total of 47 minutes of **The Longest Yard** is devoted to bone-crunching grid action; and if that isn't the record, we're sure it comes close.

Itself another descendant of **Up the River** and a direct influence on **Victory**, the World War II-era soccer film with Sylvester Stallone, it's a comedy-drama with the focus on a game between a prison's prisoners and the guards, with each side of course out for the other's throats.

In prison on a stolen car rap, Reynolds is blackmailed by warden Albert into arranging the game and is then told to make sure the prisoners lose. You don't think he listens, do you? Reynolds, who had been kicked out of pro football for point shaving, assembles a crew called "The Mean Machine," eager to play the prison's brutal guards.

After being threatened with new charges that'll keep him in prison for a long time, Reynolds agrees to the warden's call to throw the game if it's agreed that the guards will let up on the prison team once they're 21 points ahead.

It soon becomes obvious to Reynolds' teammates that he's throwing the game; and when he fakes an injury and leaves the game, no one will sit near him. However, when the guards continue to physically punish the prisoners' team even after they're 21 points ahead, Reynolds re-enters to lead them to a last-minute victory.

699 Makers of Men

1931, Columbia, 67 minutes. Director: Edward Sedgwick. Story: Howard J. Green, Sedgwick. Photography: L.W. McConnell.

Cast: Jack Holt, Richard Cromwell, John Marsh, Robert Alden, John Wayne, Walter Catlett, Natalie Moorhead, Richard Tucker, Ethel Waters.

Cromwell walks out on the team after a couple of losses and a conflict with the coach in this generally undistinguished grid programmer. How come the winning touchdown in the big game is never in the third quarter?

700 Making the Varsity

1928, Excellent Pictures, 6,400 feet. Director: Cliff Wheeler. Story: Elsie Werner, Bennett Southard. Photography: Edward Kull. Editor: Les Anthony.

Cast: Rex Lease, Arthur Rankin, Gladys Hulette, Edith Yorke, Florence Dudley, Carl Miller, James Latta.

The football action in this forgotten film is one of the few from the 1920's to offer anything really different.

A football star knocks out his own brother during the first quarter of the big game when he discovers that he's going to throw the game. Their team goes on to victory and the wayward brother, who had led a loose and fast life and amassed gambling debts, reforms.

701 M*A*S*H

1969, 20th Century-Fox, 116 minutes, Color. Director: Robert Altman. Producer: Ingo Preminger. Screenplay: Ring Lardner, Jr. Story: Richard Hooker. Photography: Harold Stine. Editor: Danford B. Greene.

Cast: Elliott Gould, Donald Sutherland, Tom Skerritt, Sally Kellerman, Robert Duvall, Jo Ann Pflug, Rene Auberjonois, Roger Bowen, Gary Burghoff, Michael Murphy, Bud Cort, Fran Tarkenton, Ben Davidson, Buck Buchanan, Howard Williams, Jack Concannon, John Myers, Tom Woodeschick.

There have been entire books written about M*A*S*H and especially about the popular TV series it inspired, so we'll concentrate mainly on the memorable football sequence.

U.S. Army surgeons Hawkeye Pierce (Sutherland), Trapper John McIntyre (Gould) and Duke Forrest (Skerritt) lead a totally undisciplined madcap existence that directly contrasts to the horrors of war they witness in their Korean War operating room.

Their constant stunts bring them into conflict with by-the-book Maj. Frank Burns (Duvall) and Major O'Houlihan (Kellerman), who's in charge of the nurses and earns the nickname Hot Lips.

After a series of adventures, Hawkeye boasts to a general investigating O'Houlihan's complaints that the M*A*S*H unit has a good football team and is challenged to a game with $5,000 at stake.

During a no-holds-barred game in which marijuana is passed around freely, the unit wins the game and the bet through the help of a pro player and some underhanded antics.

702 The Mating

1915, Mutual, 5 reels. Scenario: C. Gardner Sullivan.

Cast: Bessie Barriscale, Lewis J. Cody, Enid Markey, Walter Whitman, Margaret Thompson, Ida Lewis.

A girl pretends a football hero is her sweetheart to make her boy friend jealous.

703 Maybe It's Love

1930, Warner Brothers, 6,568 feet. Director: William Wellman. Screenplay: Joseph Jackson. Story: Mark Canfield. Photography: Robert Kurrie. Editor: Edward McDermott.

Cast: Joan Bennett, Joe E. Brown, James Hall, Laura Lee, Anders Randolf, Sumner Getchell, George Irving, Howard Jones, Russell Saunders, Stuart Erwin and members of the All-American football team.

A soundie remake of the 1927 Warner's film **The College Widow** finds the president of Upton College (Irving) facing firing unless the football team beats Parsons for the first time in 12 years. The president's daughter (Bennett), to save her father, uses her beauty

A tense moment on the gridiron from Making the Varsity. (The Museum of Modern Art/Film Stills Archive.)

and charm to recruit some top players for the team.

When her scheme is discovered, the team pretends to be drunk before the big game but they relent and win.

704 Monkey's Uncle

1965, Buena Vista, 87 minutes, Color. Director: Robert Stevenson. Screenplay: Tom and Helen August. Photography: Edward Colman. Editor: Cotton Warburton.

Cast: Tom Kirk, Annette Funicello, Leon Ames, Frank Faylen, Arthur O'Connell, Leon Tyler, Norman Grabowski, Alan Hewitt, Connie Gilchrist, Cheryl Miller.

A sequel to the Disney studios' **The Misadventures of Merlin Jones** finds the scientific genius (Kirk) up to more loony experiments.

He discovers that sleep learning works and uses it on a couple of stupid football players to prove his point. Meanwhile, the college is offered $1 million if it will drop its football program and $10 million if it gets a man to fly.

705 Mr. Doodle Kicks Off

1938, RKO Radio Pictures, 77 minutes. Director: Leslie Goodwins. Producer: Robert Sisk. Screenplay: Bert Granet. Story: Mark Kelly. Photography: Russell Metty.

Cast: Joe Penner, William B. Davidson, June Travis, Richard Lane, Frank M. Thomas, Ben Alexander, Billy Gilbert, Jack Carson, Alan Bruce, George Irving, Pierre Watkin.

The father of a musically-inclined weakling (Penner) who hates sports of any kind promises his old college a huge endowment if it turns his son into an athlete.

Everyone nearly goes crazy trying, especially the football team, which physically throws him across the goal line for a score.

However, it's discovered that Penner goes wild every time he hears "Pop Goes the Weasel," so the school band plays it in time for him to kick the winning field goal.

This sounds suspiciously similar to the 1934 Three Stooges comedy short, **Punch Drunks,** in which Curly becomes an unbeatable boxer every time he hears "Pop Goes the Weasel."

706 The Naggers Go Rooting

1931, Vitaphone, 9 minutes. Director: Alfred Goulding.

Cast: Mr. and Mrs. Jack Norworth.

The family battles through a traffic jam in the parking lot. Then Mrs. Norworth nags her husband all game long and the two fight with other fans.

707 Navy Blue and Gold

1937, Metro Goldwyn Mayer, 93 minutes. Director: Sam Wood. Producer: Sam Zimbalist. Screenplay: George Bruce. Photography: John Seitz. Editor: Robert J. Kern.

Cast: Robert Young, Tom Brown, James Stewart, Paul Kelly, Lionel Barrymore, Billie Burke, Florence Rice, Frank Albertson, Samuel S. Hinds, Minor Watson.

"It is not the victory which is important, it is how the game is played," Barrymore tells the Navy football team.

Cadet Stewart doesn't exactly fit the mold Barrymore had in mind. He enrolls under an assumed name because of his father's earlier disgrace and puts himself above the institution.

He finally fits into the Navy way of thinking and manages to clear his dad's name to boot.

Of course, when it's discovered who he really is, there's a big to-do, but you just know he's going to be allowed to play the big game vs. Army.

708 The New Halfback

1929, Educational Films, 2 reels. Director: Mack Sennett.

Cast: Andy Clyde, Harry Gribbon, Marjorie Beebe, Bert Swor, Wade Botelier, Patsy O'Leary.

Gribbon is the grid player and veteran comedian Clyde the college dean in this short.

709 North Dallas Forty

1979, Paramount, 119 minutes, Color. Director: Ted Kotcheff. Producer: Frank Yablans. Screenplay: Kotcheff, Yablans, Peter Gent. Photography: Paul Lohmann. Editor: Jay Kamen.

Cast: Nick Nolte, Mac Davis, Charles Durning, Dayle Hadden, Bo Swenson, Steve Forrest, G.D. Spradlin, Dabney Coleman, Savannah Smith, John Bottoms, Marshall Colt, John Matuszak.

So scathing and realistic was this serio-comic exposé of the underside of pro football that the NFL refused to cooperate.

Nolte is Phillip Elliott, a veteran wide receiver for the North Dallas Bulls. When we first see him wake up in the morning, we notice there's hardly an inch of his body that's unscarred; and to get ready for a game he's got to pump himself up with drugs and tape himself up like a mummy.

Davis is his quarterback friend, Spradlin reprises his coach's role of **One on One** and Durning is the assistant who's never without his bottle of Maalox which he drinks straight from the bottle.

After all his years of service, Elliott finds himself accused of having an immature attitude.

The football action scenes are probably the most brutal and gut-crunching ever filmed.

710 Number One

1969, United Artists, 105 minutes, Color. Director: Tom Gries. Producer: Walter Seltzer. Screenplay: David Moessinger. Photography: Michel Hugo. Editor: Richard Brockway.

Cast: Charlton Heston, Jessica Walter, Bruce Dern, John Randolph, Diana Muldaur, G.D. Spradlin, Richard Elkins, Mike Henry, Al

Hirt, Ernie Barnes and the New Orleans Saints.

Ron "Cat" Catlan (Heston), the Saints' 40-year-old quarterback, is under a lot of pressure to retire. His marriage is on the rocks; and he's turned down a number of business offers even though he's coming off a serious knee injury, and a rookie quarterback (Elkins) is impressing team officials.

He keeps on playing with the aid of a knee brace and some drugs and proves to everyone his competitiveness by masterminding a skillful touchdown drive, but is ultimately pummeled by the defense and winds up on the ground motionless by the end of the game.

711 One Minute to Play

1926, R-C Pictures, 7,732 feet. Director: Sam Wood. Story: Byron Morgan. Photography: Charles Clarke.

Cast: Red Grange, Mary McAllister, Charles Ogle, George Wilson, Ben Hendricks, Jr., Lee Shumway, Al Cooke, Kit Guard, Lincoln Stedman, Jay Hunt, Edythe Chapman.

This is the football film it seems nearly everyone has heard about, because it stars grid great Grange as Red Wade, but few have seen because it's rarely screened nowadays.

Wade plays football against his father's wishes and naturally becomes his college's star. When Pop finds out, he threatens to withdraw an endowment to the school if he continues to play.

Now think a minute. Would Hollywood hire Red Grange to star in a film if he didn't get into the big game at the end? So, naturally, dad is eventually won over.

712 $1,000 a Touchdown

1939, Paramount, 71 minutes. Director: James Hogan. Producer: William C. Thomas. Screenplay: Delmar Daves. Photography: William Mellor. Editor: Chandler House.

Cast: Joe E. Brown, Martha Raye, Eric Blore, Susan Hayward, John Hartley, Syd Saylor, Joyce Mathews, George McKay, Matt McHugh, Tom Dugan.

Brown helps Raye, who has inherited a university, turn the school into a dramatic college and build up the football team so the school can gain publicity and, ultimately, some more cash.

A game against a pro team is arranged, and Raye promises the pro team $1,000 for every touchdown.

713 One Yard to Go

1931, Educational Films, 2 reels. Director: William Beaudine. Story: John A. Waldron, Earl Rodney, Walter Weems, Jack Jevne.

Comedy short with Marjorie Beebe engaged to a fortune hunter but actually in love with a halfback.

714 Out of It

1969, United Artists, 97 minutes. Director-Screenplay: Paul Williams. Producer: Edward Pressman. Photography: John G. Avildsen. Editor: Ed Orshan.

Cast: Jon Voight, Barry Gordon, Lada Edmund, Jr., Gretchen Corbett, Peter Grad, Martin Gray, Oliver Bery.

Voight is the high school grid star and bully at a Long Island school. When Gordon starts dating his girl friend, Voight injures him during practice and then burns the youth's jacket.

Gordon gets revenge by proving that bullies are cowards by scaring him with a cigarette lighter shaped like a gun.

715 Over the Goal

1937, Warner Brothers, 63 minutes. Director: Noel Smith. Producer: Bryan Foy. Screenplay: William Jacobs, Anthony Coldeway. Photography: Warren Lynch. Editor: Frank Dewar.

Cast: William Hopper, June

A scene from the 1926 film One Minute to Play, which featured the Galloping Ghost himself, Red Grange. (The Museum of Modern Art/Film Stills Archive.)

Travis, Mabel Todd, Willard Parker, Gordon Oliver, William Harrigan, Johnny Davis, Raymond Hatton, Eddie Anderson, Hattie McDaniel and the USC football team.

What a predicament for Our Hero! He's promised his girl friend he'll never play football again because another knee injury could cripple him for life.

Yet the university will get a huge endowment if the team beats Squeedunk U. On the other hand, Our Hero's family will lose a lot of money if his team wins. Sound complicated?

Our Hero is framed and put in jail but still manages to get to the game in time.

716 Paper Lion

1968, United Artists, 105 minutes, Color. Director: Alex March. Producer: Stuart Miller. Screenplay: Lawrence Roman, based on a novel by George Plimpton. Photography: Morris Harzband, Peter Garbarini. Editors: Sidney Katz, John Carter, Louis San Andes.

Cast: Alan Alda, Lauren Hutton, David Doyle, Ann Turkel, Sugar Ray Robinson, Frank Gifford, Vince Lombardi, Alex Karras and members of the Detroit Lions.

Author George Plimpton (Alda) gets a brainstorm: Wouldn't it make a terrific story if he were able to train with a pro football team, get into a real game and then write about his experiences?

After all, he'd already pitched against a baseball all-star team (and got rocked) and boxed three rounds with Sugar Ray Robinson (and been decked).

Vince Lombardi and other coaches turn down his idea, telling him he's liable to be hurt in the violent world of pro football. But the Detroit Lions decide to give it a try.

At first, his identity is a secret. He tells his teammates he's been playing in Canada, but when they see his total lack of ability, they get suspicious. When his identity is discovered, there's a lot of resentment from players who don't want to risk injury and put their careers on the line for a publicity stunt.

He becomes the target of practical jokes, and they even dupe him into believing he's leading a touchdown drive during a practice game. But he gradually earns their respect by sticking out a tough training schedule and manages to get into a pre-season game against the St. Louis Cardinals, nearly blowing the game.

717 Pardon My Stripes

1942, Republic, 64 minutes. Director: John H. Aver. Producer: Albert J. Cohen. Screenplay: Lawrence Kimble, Stuart Palmer. Photography: John Alton.

Cast: Bill Henry, Tom Kennedy, Edgar Kennedy, Sheila Ryan, Harold Huber, Paul Hurst, Cliff Nazarro.

Here's another prison sports comedy directly inspired by the success of 1930's **Up the River.**

Grid star Henry runs the wrong way for a touchdown during a game, but he gets a job from a gangster who won a bundle because of his blunder.

The player is told to bring some cash from Los Angeles to Chicago, but the money falls out of the airplane and right into the courtyard of the state prison.

Knowing he's doomed unless he retrieves the cash, he manages to get into the prison where he plays in a frantic prison football game while trying to find the money.

718 Peggy

1950, Universal-International, 77 minutes, Color. Director: Frederick De Cordova. Producer: Ray Dietrich. Screenplay: George F. Slavin, George W. George. Editor: Ralph Dawson.

Cast: Diana Lynn, Charles Coburn, Rock Hudson, Charlotte Greenwood, Barbara Lawrence, Charles Drake, Connie Gilchrist, James Best, Jack Kelly, Jerome Cowan, Griff Barnett.

The slight plot is really only a pretext for the pageantry of the Rose Bowl Parade in this comedy programmer.

Two sisters are competing with each other to be queen of the Tournament of Roses, even though one is secretly married to Hudson, a football star for Ohio State. Adding to the problem is the fact that daddy Coburn can't stand Hudson.

Footage from the Rose Bowl game between Ohio State and California is shown.

719 Pigskin

1928, Educational, 2 reels. Director: Norman Taurog. Producer: Jack White.

Cast: Lige Conley, Otto Frees, Mary O'Brien, Peg O'Neill, Jack Lloyd, Sunshine Hart.

Diminutive Roscoe Redknapp (Conley), a benchwarmer for his college team, get his chance to play when everyone else is injured in this two-reel comedy.

His rival for the love of a professor's daughter is the biggest player on the opposing team and sees it as his chance to pulverize the smaller Redknapp.

Through a series of events, the scheme backfires, and Redknapp winds up the hero and gets the girl.

720 Pigskin Palooka

1937, Metro Goldwyn Mayer, 1 reel. Director: Gordon Douglas. Producer: Hal Roach, Photography: Art Lloyd. Editor: William Ziegler.

Our Gang's Alfalfa brags to Darla that he's a big football hero at military school even though he's never played a minute.

When he gets back home, he's forced to play for Spanky's All-Stars and somehow winds up the game's hero.

721 Pigskin Parade

1936, 20th Century-Fox, 90-93 minutes. Director: David Butler. Screenplay: Harry Tugend,

Jack Yellen, William Conselman. Story: Arthur Sheekman, Nat Perrin, Mark Kelly. Photography: Arthur Miller.

Cast: Judy Garland, Stuart Erwin, Betty Grable, Patsy Kelly, Johnny Downes, Jack Haley, Arline Judge, Dixie Dunbar, Tony Martin, Elisha Cook, Jr., Eddie Nugent, Charles Wilson, Alan Ladd, Si Jenks.

Noteworthy as Judy Garland's feature debut, 11 songs are featured in this comedy about a second-rate school which manages to conquer the mighty Yale football team.

Erwin plays the hick quarterback who kicks better barefooted—this is years before this style came into vogue in the NFL—while Haley is a coach from Flushing.

Some of the promo material we have from this film spells Garland's first name as "Juddy."

722 The Plastic Age

1925, B.P. Schulberg Productions, 6,488 feet. Director: Wesley Ruggles. Adaptation: Eve Unsell, Frederica Sagor. Story: Percy Marks. Photography: Gilbert Warrenton, Allen Siegler.

Cast: Donald Keith, Clara Bow, Henry B. Walthall, Gilbert Roland, Mary Alden, J. Gordon Edwards, Jr., Felix Valle, David Butler.

A track star (Carver) falls in love in college, and his career goes steadily downhill until his sweetheart (Bow) sees what she's doing to him and dumps him.

He then becomes a football star, winning the big game, and the two lovers are reunited.

723 The Pom Pom Girls

1976, Crown International, 90 minutes. Color. Director-Producer-Screenplay: Joseph Ruben. Photography: Stephen M. Katz. Editor: George Bowers.

Cast: Robert Carradine, Jennifer Ashley, Lisa Reeves, Michael Mullins, Bill Adler, James Gammon.

The intense rivalry between two California high schools and between Carradine and Adler in particular takes a back seat, as you might expect, to the amours of the girls in the title.

724 Pop Warner

Similar to the Howard Jones and Knute Rockne series, Universal produced a number of these shorts in the early 1930's starring another one of the giants of grid coaching. Directed by Albert Kelley, titles include **Developing a Football Team, Football 40 Years Ago, Trick Plays** and, believe it or not, **Soccer.**

725 Pretty Maids All in a Row

1971, Metro Goldwyn Mayer, 92 minutes, Color. Director: Roger Vadim. Producer-Screenplay: Gene Roddenberry, based on a novel by Francis Fellini.

Cast: Rock Hudson, John David Carson, Angie Dickinson, Keenan Wynn, Telly Savalas, Roddy McDowell, William Campbell, Joy Bang.

Not really a sports film, but it deserves passing mention with Hudson as a coach who kills girls after making love to them to keep them from talking.

726 The Quarterback

1926, Paramount, 7,114 feet. Director: Fred Newmeyer. Adaptation: Ray Harris. Story: William Slavens McNutt, William O. McGeehan. Photography: Edward Cronjager.

Cast: Richard Dix, Esther Ralston, Harry Beresford, David Butler, Robert Craig, Mona Palma.

Jack Stone (Dix) is the son of the quarterback for the 1899 team of Colton College, who, when he married, pledged to remain a student at the school until Colton defeated State University on the gridiron.

In 1926, he and his son are now schoolmates because Colton still hasn't been able to beat State.

Jack and his pal Lumpy Goggins (Butler) hone up their football passing and receiving by delivering milk.

With the big game against State approaching, Jack finds himself suspended but is reinstated in time to help Colton win.

727 The Quarterback

1940, Paramount, 71 minutes. Director: H. Bruce Humberstone. Producer: Anthony Veiller. Screenplay: Robert Pirosh. Photography: Leo Tovar. Editor: Alma Macrorie.

Cast: Wayne Morris, Virginia Dale, Lillian Cornell, Edgar Kennedy, Alan Mowbray, Jerome Cowan, Rod Cameron, William Frawley, Walter Catlett, Frank Burke.

Although they're both comedies from the same studio, this is not a remake of 1926's **The Quarterback.**

Morris plays twins—one a football hero and the other a bookworm—who both court lovely Miss Dale. The studious one gets an athletic scholarship based on his brother's feats.

Naturally, there are gamblers around; and the football-playing brother manages to get to the game in the nick of time to bail out his relieved twin and harried coach Frawley.

728 Rackety Rax

1932, Fox Film Corp., 65 minutes. Director: Alfred Werker. Story: Joel Sayre. Adaptation: Ben Markson, Lou Breslow.

Cast: Victor McLaglen, Nell O'Day, Arthur Pierson, Alan Dinehart, Allen Jenkins, Vincent Barnett, Esther Howard, Stanley Fields.

The head of a sports racketeering empire (McLaglen) wants to have his own football team. He fails in his attempts to buy Navy and West Point so settles on Canarsie College where he puts together an entire team of gangsters.

The climax pits Canarsie's gangster team with another team of racketeers put together by a bootlegger.

729 Reckless

1984, United Artists/MGM, 90 minutes, Color. Director: James Foley. Producer: Edgar J. Sherick, Scott Rudin. Screenplay: Chris Columbus. Photography: Michael Ballhaus. Editor: Albert Magnoli.

Cast: Aidan Quinn, Daryl Hannah, Kenneth McMillan, Adam Baldwin, Cliff de Young, Lois Smith, Dan Hedaya, Billy Jacoby, Toni Kalem.

Reckless can serve as a companion piece to 1983's **All the Right Moves** as both are about youths whose main desire is to leave the dreary steel town their families have called home for years.

Whereas in **All the Right Moves,** the young hero used football to get out, young Aidan Quinn takes a totally opposite approach in **Reckless.**

A totally anti-social lad, he's unpopular with most of the other students because of his wild and unpredictable behavior and winds up being kicked off the football team. He runs afoul of the snobbish and bullyish quarterback (Baldwin), whose father is a big shot at the steel mill, by wooing his girl (Hannah).

Quinn is fond of racing his motorcycle right up to the edge of a cliff to see how far he can go without falling off. When his father is killed in an industrial accident, he burns down the house.

After some steamy sex scenes in the school pool and boiler room where Quinn sets up house after hours, he races his cycle into the school and asks Hannah to come away with him. Will she go?

730 Red Clay

1925, Universal, 4,626 feet. Director: Ernst Laemmle. Scenario: Charles Logue, Frank L. Inghram.

Story: Sarah Saddoris. Photography: Ben Kline.

Cast: William Desmond, Marceline Day, Noble Johnson, Lola Todd, Albert J. Smith, Byron Douglas, Billy Sullivan, Felix Whitefeather, Ynez Seabury.

An Indian chief is drafted during World War I and saves the life of the son of a congressman while fighting in France. When the war ends, the chief enrolls at college where he becomes a football star and starts dating the sister of the man he saved.

Red Clay is more interesting as an early statement against prejudice than as a sports film.

731 Return to Campus

1975, Cinepix, 100 minutes, Color. Director-Producer-Screenplay: Harold Cornsweet. Photography: Steve Shuttack, Pierre Janet.

Cast: Earl Keyes, Ray Troha, Al Raymond, Robert Gutin, Paul Jacobs, Arnold Palmer, Helen Killinger, Norma Joseph, Jesse White, Connie O'Connell, Tom Harmon.

Written and directed by a former Ohio State football star, **Return to Campus** deals with a man (Keyes) who was drafted during World War II after three years as star kicker for the team.

He's now well-to-do and retired and is asked by a high school coach (Raymond) to help teach kicking to his players. That inspires him to think about returning to college to finish his fourth year. He invents a device that he fits in his shoe that lets him kick tremendous field goals, and he helps Ohio State win.

732 Rise and Shine

1941, 20th Century-Fox, 92 minutes. Director: Allan Dwan. Producer: Mark Hellinger. Screenplay: Herman Mankiewicz, based on "My Life and Hard Times" by James Thurber. Photography: Edward Cronjager. Editor: Allen McNeil.

Cast: Jack Oakie, George Murphy, Linda Darnell, Walter Brennan, Milton Berle, Sheldon Leonard, Donald Meek, Paul Harvey, Ruth Donnelly, Raymond Walburn.

Lunatic characters inspired by James Thurber set this musical comedy above some of the rest.

Berle is a gambler who bets on Oakie's team and sends ex-player Murphy, now an entertainer, in to protect him but then decides to switch his bets for the last game.

The plot has little that's new—Oakie is kidnapped, but gets to the game in time for a wacky final two minutes—but it's the strange characters which make it entertaining.

733 Rosalie

1937, Metro Goldwyn Mayer, 123 minutes. Director: W.S. Van Dyke. Producer: William A. McGuire. Screenplay: McGuire, based on a play by McGuire and Guy Bolton. Photography: Oliver T. Marsh. Editor: Blanche Sewell.

Cast: Nelson Eddy, Eleanor Powell, Frank Morgan, Edna May Oliver, Ray Bolger, Ilona Massey, Billy Gilbert, Reginald Owen, Tom Rutherford, George Zucco.

One of MGM's biggest-budget musicals features Eddy as a singing West Point football star who also has his own airplane.

He's in love with Powell, a Balkan princess; and together they help the royal family escape to the United States during a Communist revolution.

734 Rose Bowl

1936, Paramount, 72 minutes. Director: Charles Barton. Story: Francis Wallace. Adaptation: Marguerite Roberts. Photography: Henry Sharp.

Cast: Tom Brown, Larry "Buster" Crabbe, Eleanor Whitney, William Frawley, Benny Baker, Nydia Westman.

Brown and Baker head for college, where they have trouble

getting girls because Crabbe is hoarding them all. Basically, a totally routine college grid film.

735 Rose Bowl Story

1952, Monogram, 73 minutes, Color. Director: William Beaudine. Producer: Richard Herrmance. Screenplay: Charles R. Marion. Photography: Harry Neumann. Editor: Walter Hanneman.

Cast: Marshall Thompson, Vera Miles, Richard Rober, Natalie Wood, Keith Larsen, Tom Harmon, Ann Doran, James Dobson, Jim Backus, Clarence Kolb.

A selfish football star thinks only of going to the pros until he's set on the right track and lets his blocker go in for the big touchdown.

À la **Peggy**, there's a lot of footage of the pageantry of the Tournament of Roses and stock footage of the Rose Bowl action cut in.

736 Salute

1929, Fox Film Corp., 7,610 feet. Director: John Ford. Screenplay: James K. McGuinness. Story: Tristram Tupper, John Stone. Photography: Joseph August. Editor: Alex Troffey.

Cast: George O'Brien, Helen Chandler, Frank Albertson, David Butler, John Wayne, Ward Bond, Stepin Fetchit, Lumsden Hare, Joyce Compton, Clifford Dempsey, William Janney.

Filmed in Annapolis, the traditions of the Naval Academy get a going over as a young midshipman finds the going too tough and quits.

Spurred on by his girl friend, however, he returns and scores a big touchdown in the game against Army.

It's a bit ironic that the Naval Academy, which once rejected director Ford because of poor eyesight, offered its full cooperation in this story about inter-service rivalry.

737 Satan's Cheerleaders

1977, World Amusement, 92 minutes, Color. Director: Greydon Clark. Producer: Alvin L. Fast. Screenplay: Clark, Fast.

Cast: John Ireland, Yvonne De Carlo, Jack Kruschen, John Carradine, Jacquelin Cole, Kerry Sherman, Alissa Powell, Sherry Marks, Hillary Horan.

En route to a game, a group of cheerleaders is trapped in a town run by the sheriff (Ireland) who heads a Devil-worshipping cult.

One of the girls discovers she possesses special powers. When the girls finally do arrive at the game, you know the opposing team doesn't stand a chance.

738 Saturday's Hero (aka **Idols in the Dust**)

1951, Columbia, 111 minutes. Director: David Miller. Producer: Buddy Adler. Screenplay: Millard Lampell, Sidney Buchman, based on the novel "The Hero" by Lampell. Photography: Lee Garmes. Editor: William Lyon.

Cast: John Derek, Donna Reed, Sidney Blackmer, Alexander Knox, Elliot Lewis, Otto Hulet, Howard St. John, Wilbur Robertson, Alvin Baldock.

A high school football star in a New Jersey mill town seeks to rise above the factory status of his Polish immigrant family.

Counterpointing the status of Steve Novak (Derek) as a hero is his brother, a veteran of World War II, who still can't find a job.

Disregarding the advice of a newsman who has served as his mentor, Novak selects a school known for its academic standards and turns down offers from the traditional football powers.

He's taken under the wing of T.C. McCabe (Blackmer), a wealthy alumnus who wants to build his alma mater into a football power and who provides football recruits with phony jobs and expense accounts.

With Novak's help, the school becomes a football powerhouse, and the newsman sells himself out to McCabe, becoming a publicity agent whose sole purpose is to build Novak into an All-American candidate.

All of a sudden, coaches from all over the country are swarming over the campus offering the top players money to defect to their schools; and McCabe must top their offers.

Novak begins to realize he's simply being used when he seriously injures his shoulder when an opposing player admits he was paid to put him out of the game.

Against the wishes of the coach (Hulet), Novak is ordered to play the next game even though he's risking a crippling blow to his injured shoulder.

When he's hurt again, Novak returns home to the mill town to start afresh. His ignored father dead and his brother still resentful, he plans to work days while continuing his education at night.

He does wind up ahead of the game, however, as his sweetheart (Reed), the niece of McCabe, decides to escape the clutches of her domineering uncle to join him.

Saturday's Hero is a searing indictment of the college recruiting system and makes an interesting companion piece—along with **Reckless**—for **All the Right Moves**, which is about a high school football star eager to leave his steel mill home town.

739 Saturday's Heroes

1937, RKO Radio Pictures, 58 minutes. Director: Edward Killy. Producer: Robert Sisk. Screenplay: Paul Yawitz, Charles Kaufman, David Silverstein. Story: George Templeton. Photography: Nicholas Musuraaca. Editor: Frederic Knudtson.

Cast: Van Heflin, Marian Marsh, Frank Jenks, Al St. John, Richard Lane, Dick Hogan, Alan Bruce, Minor Watson, Willie Best, Walter Miller, Crawford Weaver, George Irving.

Grid star Heflin comes into contact with hypocrisy among the faculty and professionalism in the college football ranks in this forerunner to **Saturday's Hero**, which also has some comic moments.

740 Saturday's Millions

1933, Universal, 75 minutes. Director: Edward Sedgwick. Story: Lucian Cary. Adaptation: Dale Van Every. Photography: Charles Stumar.

Cast: Robert Young, Lelia Hyams, Johnny Mack Brown, Andy Devine, Grant Mitchell, Mary Carlisle, Joe Sauers, Mary Doran, Paul Porcasi, Richard Tucker.

A cocky grid star romances a railroad president's daughter while working his way through college by doing laundry routes.

With a cast that includes several All-Americans, the cocky star learns the value of team play; and in the big game refuses to let the coach sub for him even though he has a broken hand.

He fumbles the ball on the goal line with the game on the line, but his new attitude wins him the girl. **Saturday's Millions** was one of a number of films inspired by 1931's **Touchdown** in which the hero doesn't win the big game.

741 Semi-Tough

1977, United Artists, 108 minutes, Color. Director: Michael Ritchie. Producer: David Merrick. Screenplay: Walter Bernstein. Photography: Charles Rosher, Jr. Editor: Richard A. Harris.

Cast: Burt Reynolds, Kris Kristofferson, Jill Clayburgh, Robert Preston, Bert Convy, Roger Mosley, Lotte Lenya, Richard Maser, Carl Weathers, Brian Dennehy, Joe Kapp, Mary Jo Catlett, Ron Silver.

Clayburgh, the daughter

of eccentric team owner Preston, rooms with both Reynolds and Kristofferson.

When she decides to marry Kris, Burt does everything he can to thwart the wedding. Oh, yes, they do manage to get in some football in between the shenanigans.

742 70,000 Witnesses

1932, Paramount, 69 minutes. Director: Ralph Murphy. Story: Cortland Fitzsimmons. Photography: Henry Sharpe.

Cast: Phillips Holmes, Dorothy Jordan, Charlie Ruggles, Johnny Mack Brown, J. Farrell MacDonald, Lew Cody, David Landau, Kenneth Thompson, Guinn "Big Boy" Williams.

When a football player (Brown) is murdered, suspicion falls on another player, Holmes, whose brother is a professional gambler. We promise not to reveal whodunnit.

MacDonald, as usual, is the coach.

This was the daddy of a whole spate of 1930's films in which sports stars were murdered, including **Death on the Diamond, Girls Can Play, The Arsenal Stadium Mystery** and others.

743 The Sin of Harold Diddlebock

1947, United Artists, 90 minutes. Director-Producer-Screenplay: Preston Sturges. Photography: Robert Pittack. Editor: Tom Neff.

Cast: Harold Lloyd, Frances Ramsden, Jimmy Conlin, Raymond Walburn, Franklin Pangborn, Margaret Hamilton, Arline Judge, Al Bridge, Edgar Kennedy, Frank Moran.

The football climax of the 1925 comedy classic **The Freshman** is the starting point of **The Sin of Harold Diddlebock.**

With footage from **The Freshman** cut in, Diddlebock (Lloyd) is offered a job in an advertising agency for winning the big game. He accepts only to be stuck in a clerical job over the next 22 years. Meeting a track tout, he gets drunk and wins several hundred thousand dollars at the track.

Using the money to buy a circus and a hansom cab, he wakes up broke and with a hangover and winds up selling the circus.

In the film's most memorable comedy sequence, he's hanging above the ground from a leash. If he falls, he's dead; but at the other side of the leash is a lion!

744 Smith of Minnesota

1942, Columbia, 66 minutes. Director: Lew Landers. Producer: Jack Fier. Screenplay: Robert D. Andrews. Photography: Philip Tannura. Editor: Mel Thorsen.

Cast: Bruce Smith, Arline Judge, Warren Ashe, Don Beddoe, Kay Harris, Robert Stevens, Roberta Smith, Rosemary DeCamp, Maurice Murphy, Dick Hogan, Douglas Leavitt.

Following the pattern of **Harmon of Michigan** and **The Spirit of Stanford,** Columbia featured Bruce Smith, All-American halfback from the University of Minnesota, in the supposedly true story of his own life.

The ads blazed: "Watch a typical kid learn the kind of real-life heroism the Axis is learning to fear. It's a real-life heart-filled drama of today. Have a seat on the 50-yard line for the thrill-packed drama of a great All-American."

The story line has a film studio sending writer Ashe to the University of Minnesota to live with Smith and come up with a different kind of screenplay about the captain of the undefeated 1941 team. The writer finds the quiet Smith almost boring at first until he learns of his background and of the forces which drive him to great gridiron exploits.

A highlight of the film is a recreation of a 1910 game between Minnesota and Michigan in which Smith's father played—and lost.

As this is a wartime gridiron film, **Smith of Minnesota** ends with the star's enlistment in the Navy.

745 The Snob

1921, Realart Pictures, 4,015 feet. Director: Sam Wood. Scenario: Alice Eyton. Story: William J. Neidig. Photography: Alfred Gilks.

Cast: William E. Lawrence, Wanda Hawley, Edwin Stevens, Sylvia Ashton, Walter Hiers, Julia Faye, Richard Wayne.

The daughter of an oil millionaire meets a football star (Lawrence) but snubs him when she finds out he's working as a waiter to pay his way through college.

After a change of heart, she takes a job as a waitress to prove that she's a changed woman and to win his heart.

746 So This Is College

1929, Metro Goldwyn Mayer, 6,104-9,143 feet. Director: Sam Wood. Screenplay: Al Boasberg, Delmar Daves. Photography: Leonard Smith. Editor: Frank Sullivan.

Cast: Elliott Nugent, Robert Montgomery, Cliff Edwards, Sally Starr, Polly Moran, Phyllis Crane, Oscar Rudolph, Dorothy Dehn, Max Davidson, Ann Brody.

Two lifelong pals (Nugent, Montgomery) are at odds over a woman (Starr) at the University of Southern California where they're also members of the grid team.

When they find out about her schemes, they both dump her in time for their game against Stanford.

747 Son of Flubber

1963, Buena Vista, 100 minutes. Director: Robert Stevenson. Producers: Bill Walsh, Ron Miller. Screenplay: Walsh, Don Dagradi, based on a story by Samuel W. Taylor and on books by Danny Dunn. Photography: Edward Colman. Editor: Cotton Warburton.

Cast: Fred MacMurray, Nancy Olson, Keenan Wynn, Tommy Kirk, Ed Wynn, Leon Ames, Ken Murray, William Demarest, Charlie Ruggles, Paul Lynde, Bob Sweeney, Stuart Erwin.

A sequel to **The Absent Minded Professor**, MacMurray uses flying rubber (flubber) gas on the football team this time instead of the basketball team at sorry Medfield College.

He has a new invention—an artificial rain cloud which can break glass.

When the flubber gas is used to inflate a football player, he's tossed by the team downfield like a pigskin. The football winds up going to outer space when kicked.

748 The Sophomore

1929, Pathe Exchange, 5,799-6,526 feet. Director: Leo McCarey. Adaptation: Joseph Franklin Poland. Story: Corey Ford, T. H. Wenning. Photography: John J. Mescall. Editor: Doane Harrison.

Cast: Eddie Quillan, Sally O'Neil, Stanley Smith, Jeanette Loff, Russell Gleason, Sarah Padden, Brooks Benedict, Spec O'Donnell, Walter O'Keefe.

A football star runs off the field in the middle of the game when he discovers that it's his girl friend who's been paying his way through college after he lost all his money in a craps game.

That's a change of pace from the usual college football comedy.

749 Spirit of Notre Dame

1931, Universal, 78 minutes. Director: Russell Mack. Producer: Carl Laemmle, Jr. Story: E.R. Schayer, Dale Van Every. Photography: George Robinson.

Cast: Lew Ayres, William Bakewell, J. Farrell MacDonald, Andy Devine, Harry Barris, Sally Blane, Nat Pendleton, Moon Mullins and as The Four Horsemen—Don

Miller, Elmer Layden, Jim Crowley, Harry Stuhldreher.

After playing coaching legend Knute Rockne here, J. Farrell MacDonald was forever typecast as a firm but understanding coach or trainer. His performance is less famous than Pat O'Brien in **Knute Rockne, All American**, but no less inspired.

A tribute to the Notre Dame coach, **Spirit of Notre Dame** includes newsreel footage of game action.

Ayres portrays a conceited high school star who expects to set the world on fire at Notre Dame, only to find out he's expected to block for Blakewell, who gets a swelled head himself.

The two eventually learn the Notre Dame way of doing things and make up with each other for the good of the team.

750 Spirit of Stanford

1942, Columbia, 74 minutes. Director: Charles Barton. Producer: Sam White. Screenplay: Howard J. Green, William Brent, Nick Lucatz. Photography: Franz F. Blaner, John Stumar. Editor: James Sweeney.

Cast: Frankie Albert, Marguerite Chapman, Matt Willis, Ernie Nevers, Lloyd Bridges, Forrest Tucker, Shirley Patterson, Kay Harris, Robert Stevens.

Stanford's All-American quarterback Frankie Albert plays himself in this supposedly autobiographical tale of a grid star who turns pro just before a big college game, but who returns when his roommate gets sick. Naturally, he wins the game.

Football star Ernie Nevers also appears as himself.

751 Spirit of West Point

1947, Film Classics, 75 minutes. Director: Ralph Murphy. Producers: John W. Rogers, Harry Joe Brown. Screenplay: Tom Reed. Photography: Lester White. Editor: Harvey Manger.

Cast: Doc Blanchard, Glenn Davis, Alan Hale, Jr., Robert Shayne, Anne Nagel, George O'Hanlon, Michael Browne, Bill Stern, Harry Wismer, Tom Harmon, Rudy Wissler.

Made while they were on a 60-day furlough after their graduation from West Point, Army's two great grid stars portray themselves as they're tempted with offers to turn pro.

One of their teammates, Mileaway McCarty (Browne) accepts an offer.

Except for footage of the two greats, this is a generally routine grid potboiler.

752 The Split

1968, Metro Goldwyn Mayer, 90 minutes. Color. Director: Gordon Flemyng. Producer: Irwin Winkler, Robert Chartoff. Screenplay: Robert Sabaroff, based on the novel "The Seventh" by Richard Stark. Photography: Burnett Guffey. Editor: Rita Roland.

Cast: Jim Brown, Diahann Carroll, Julie Harris, Ernest Borgnine, Gene Hackman, Jack Klugman, Warren Oates, James Whitmore, Donald Sutherland.

This is kind of an updated version of Stanley Kubrick's 1956 **The Killing**, with the locale changed from a racetrack to the Los Angeles Coliseum.

A gang of crooks steals over $500,000 during a championship football game, but have a falling out after the robbery and start killing each other off.

753 Sport Parade

1932, RKO Radio Pictures, 63 minutes. Director: Dudley Murphy. Adaptation: Corey Ford, Francis Cockrell. Story: Jerry Horwin. Additional Dialogue: Robert Benchley. Photography: J. Roy Hunt.

Cast: Joel McCrea, William Gargan, Walter Catlett, Richard "Skeets" Gallagher, Marian Marsh, Robert Benchley, Clarence H. Wilson, Ivan Linow.

McCrea and Gargan, both star football players in college, head in different directions after graduation.

Gargan becomes a reporter while McCrea, whose head has outgrown his hat, finds himself turning down an offer to throw a professional game but becoming a pro wrestler by the end of the film.

Naturally, they both love the same girl.

Benchley nearly steals the show as a radio announcer.

754 Start Cheering

1938, Columbia, 78 minutes. Director: Albert Rogell. Story: Corey Ford. Screenplay: Eugene Solow, Richard E. Wormser, Philip Rapp. Photography: Joseph Walker. Editor: Gene Havlick.

Cast: Charles Starrett, Jimmy Durante, Walter Connolly, The Three Stooges, Broderick Crawford, Professor Quiz, Raymond Walburn, Joan Perry.

Movie star Starrett antagonizes an entire football team, led by Crawford, when he enrolls at college and has all the girls swooning over him.

Instead of a frantic finish on a football field to climax the film, there's a race to make a radio broadcast.

755 Strongheart

1914, Klaw and Erlanger, 1,144 feet. Director: James Kirkwood. Supervisor: D.W. Griffith.

Cast: Lionel Barrymore, Henry B. Walthall, Alan Hale, Antonio Moreno, Blanche Sweet.

The first truly major football film is set at New York's Columbia University, where an Indian (Walthall) enrolls so he can learn how to improve life back on the reservation for his people.

When the team's football star (Barrymore) sells plays to the opposition, Walthall takes the blame so the star can play and the team win.

The Indian, however, becomes disillusioned and heads back home, only to find his tribe won't accept his white girlfriend and the white man won't accept him.

Strongheart was remade in the 1920's as **Braveheart.**

756 Sunny Skies

1930, Tiffany Productions, 6,994 feet. Director: Norman Taurog. Scenario: Earl Snell. Story: A.P. Younger. Photography: Arthur Reeves. Editor: Clarence Kolster.

Cast: Benny Rubin, Marceline Day, Rex Lease, Marjorie Kane, Greta Granstedt, Wesley Barry, Robert Randall.

The hero of this musical comedy saves his roomie's life with a blood transfusion while under suspension, but naturally he's returned to the team and despite giving blood has enough strength to lead good old Standtech to victory.

757 Sweetie

1929, Paramount Famous Lasky Corp., 6,303-8,969 feet. Director: Frank Tuttle. Screenplay: George Marion, Jr., Lloyd Corrigan. Photography: Alfred Gilks. Editor: Verna Willis.

Cast: Stuart Erwin, Nancy Carroll, Wallace MacDonald, Helen Kane, Stanley Smith, Jack Oakie, William Austin, Charles Sellon, Aileen Manning.

In between ten songs, there is a plot about a chorus girl who inherits a college and who orders that athletes whose grades don't meet standards won't be able to play.

One of the team's stars (Smith), who earlier had spurned her, fails; but he and the team's other hero (Oakie) naturally get to play and help the school win.

758 Swing That Cheer

1933, Universal, 63-70 minutes. Director: Harold Schuster. Producer: Max H. Golden. Screenplay: Charles Grayson, Lee Loeb. Story: Thomas

Ahearn, F. Maury Schuster. Photography: Elwood Bredell.

Cast: Tom Brown, Robert Wilcox, Andy Devine, Constance Moore, Ernest Truex, Doodles Weaver, Margaret Early, Raymond Parker, Samuel S. Hinds, David Oliver.

A football star who thinks he's the greatest is taught a lesson by his pal, his blocker, when the latter fakes an injury to show him what life would be like without a good blocker.

Needless to say, the star learns his lesson; and the two pals start working together for the good of the team.

759 The Swinging Cheerleaders

1974, Centaur Releasing Corp., 94 minutes, Color. Director: Jack Hill. Producer: John Prizer. Screenplay: Jane Witherspoon, Betty Conklin. Photography: Alfred Taylor. Editor: Mort Tubor.

Cast: Jo Johnston, Rainbeaux Smith, Colleen Camp, Ron Hajek, Rosanne Katon, Jason Sommers, Ian Sander, George Wallace.

Softcore sex is the main attraction as a journalism student becomes a cheerleader to write an exposé on the exploitation of women.

She manages to thwart a plot by the football coach to throw a big game.

760 That's My Boy

1932, Columbia, 71 minutes. Director: Roy William Neill. Adaptation: Norman Krasna, based on a novel by Francis Wallace. Photography: Joseph August. Editor: Jack Dennis.

Cast: Richard Cromwell, Dorothy Jordan, Mae Marsh, Arthur Stope, Douglas Dumbrille, Lucien Littlefield and the USC football team.

The obviously small Cromwell is described in the film as a "tricky runner" to alibi his casting in this tale of a grid star working his way through school.

He gets knee-deep in a stock scheme and has to make good his investors' losses.

761 That's My Boy

1951, Paramount, 98 minutes. Director: Hal Walker. Producer: Hal Wallis. Screenplay: Cy Howard. Photography: Lee Garmes. Editor: Warren Low.

Cast: Dean Martin, Jerry Lewis, Ruth Hussey, Eddie Mayehoff, Marion Marshall, Polly Bergen, Hugh Sanders, John McIntire, Tom Harmon.

From the 1920's through the 1950's, it seemed that every major comedian had to make at least one sports film. The team of Martin and Lewis made three—this one, **The Caddy** and **Money from Home**, a horse racing comedy—unless you want to include **Sailor Beware** because of its boxing sequence.

Lewis plays, as usual, the weakling bungler who becomes the hero in spite of himself.

He is totally dominated by his father (Mayehoff), a wealthy alumnus who forces the coach (Sanders) to keep him on the football team despite his total ineptitude. The father hires a grid star (Martin) to keep an eye on him and make him an athlete.

762 Three Little Pigskins

1934, Columbia, 2 reels. Director: Raymond McCarey.

Cast: The Three Stooges, Lucille Ball, Gertie Green, Phyllis Crane, Walter Long, Joseph Young, Milton Douglas, Harry Bowen, Lynton Brent, Bud Jamison, Charles Dorety.

Chaos reigns when those lovable (or hatable depending upon your view) Stooges are mistaken for grid stars.

763 Time Out for Lessons

1939, Metro Goldwyn Mayer, 1 reel. Directors: Edward Cahn, Bud Murray. Producer: Jack Chertok. Screenplay: Hal Law,

Robert A. McGowan. Photography: Robert Planck. Editor: Ralph E. Goldstein.

There's more lecturing than romping in this change of pace Our Gang short.

Alfalfa's father, upset about his son's grades, tells him he won't be able to play football in college unless he takes "time out for lessons." He tells him he can play as long as he studies diligently.

764 The Time, The Place, and the Girl

1929, Warner Brothers, 5,200-6,339 feet. Director: Howard Bretherton. Screenplay: Robert Lord, based on a play by Frank R. Adams, Joseph E. Howard and Will Hough. Photography: John Stumar. Editor: Jack Killifer.

Cast: Grant Withers, Betty Compson, Gertrude Olmstead, Gerald King, Bert Roach, James Kirkwood, Vivian Oakland, John Davidson.

Not to be confused with the 1946 musical of the same name, this one concerns a beautiful tutor (Olmstead) who falls in love with a conceited football star, who falls for a socialite, who gets him involved in a phony stock scheme, etc. etc.

765 Touchdown

1931, Paramount, 79 minutes. Director: Norman McLeod. Adaptation: Grover Jones, William S. McNutt, from the novel "Stadium" by Francis Wallace.

Cast: Richard Arlen, J. Farrell MacDonald, Peggy Shannon, Jack Oakie, Regis Toomey, George Barbier, George Irving, Charles D. Brown, Herman Brix, Jim Thorpe, Howard Jones, Charles Starrett.

One of the forgotten landmarks in sports film history features Arlen as a win-at-all-costs football coach.

Touchdown was different than other sports films inasmuch as it featured an unglamorous view of the game, had an unsavory lead character and the team lost the big game at the finale.

J. Farrell MacDonald, just removed from his role as Knute Rockne in **Spirit of Notre Dame,** is featured as another fatherly coach here, in contrast to Arlen's character.

A former All-American, Arlen refuses to tolerate defeat and sends in an injured player. The result is the team wins the game, but the player lands in the hospital while Arlen begins to alienate his friends.

In the finale, the same situation comes up again. Arlen, however, resists temptation and keeps a young player (Starrett) who has a concussion on the bench while his team goes down to defeat. The coach, however, earns the respect of those around him.

Following **Touchdown,** there were a number of football films in which the hero wins by losing the big game.

766 Touchdown, Army

1938, Paramount, 69 minutes. Director: Kurt Neumann. Screenplay: Lloyd Corrigan, Erwin Gelsey. Photography: Victor Milner. Editor: Arthur Schmidt.

Cast: John Howard, Robert Cummings, Mary Carlisle, Owen Davis, Jr., William Frawley, Benny Baker, Minor Watson, Raymond Hatton.

Nearly every cliche in the book is thrown in here with one minor twist.

Cummings is the usual West Point cadet who has no respect for the rules and traditions of the Academy; and if you've been reading this chapter up until now, you know that on the day of the big game, he's in trouble.

You also know that he's allowed out just in time to play; and, of course, you're aware that he and his rival for the lovely lady's hand play together for the good of the team to win.

The one twist is that Cummings'

rival (Howard), runs the wrong way until Cummings alerts him with a rebel yell.

767 Triple Pass

1928, Biltmore Pictures, 4,800 feet.

Cast: William Barrymore.

Alas, **Triple Pass** appears to be one of those films for which no prints exist today. All that we know about it is that it does somehow involve football.

768 Triple Threat

1948, Columbia, 71 minutes. Director: Jean Yarbrough. Producer: Sam Katzman. Screenplay: Joseph Carole, Don Martin. Photography: Vincent Farrar. Editor: Jerome Thoms.

Cast: Richard Crane, Gloria Henry, Mary Stuart, John Litel, Pat Phelan, Joseph Crehan, Harry Wismer, Bob Kelley, Tom Harmon.

If ever there was a run-of-the-mill football film, this is it. Crane plays a conceited college star who has to adjust to the pros and to a romance that affects his play on the field.

The story focuses on two Rose Bowl heroes—the selfish Don Whitney of Western U. who wins the game by disobeying the coach's orders; and the noble Joe Nolan of State U., who'd rather go to medical school than play football.

After the pair wind up on the Los Angeles Rams as rookie roommates, Whitney learns the hard way about becoming a team player.

The only thing noteworthy about it is the number of pro stars who appear. They include Bob Waterfield, Sammy Baugh, Paul Christman, Johnny Clement, Bill Dudley, Sid Luckman, Charles Trippi, Steve Van Buren, Indian Jack Jacobs, Paul Governali and Boley Dancewicz.

769 Trouble Along the Way

1953, Warner Brothers, 109 minutes. Director: Michael Curtiz. Producer: Melville Shavelson. Screenplay: Shavelson, Jack Rose. Story: Douglas Morrow, Robert Hardy Andrews. Photography: Archie Stout. Editor: Owen Marks.

Cast: John Wayne, Charles Coburn, Donna Reed, Marie Windsor, Sherry Jackson, Douglas Spencer, Leif Erickson, Dabbs Greer, Tom Tully, Chuck Connors, Bill Radovich.

Wayne here is a pool shark and a bookmaker, but he also happens to be a darn good football coach. Even though his antics have gotten him fired from other schools, he's hired by the rector of St. Anthony's College (Coburn), whose school badly needs a money-making team. Wayne goes about his task by stacking up the team with ringers.

The coach, in the meantime, gets involved with probation officer Reed in a custody battle for his daughter (Jackson).

770 Two Minute Warning

1976, Universal, 115 minutes, Color. Director: Larry Peerce. Producer: Edward S. Feldman. Screenplay: Edward Hume, based on a novel by George LaFountaine. Photography: Gerald Hirschfeld. Editor: Eve Newman, Walter Hannemann.

Cast: Charlton Heston, John Cassavetes, Martin Balsam, Marilyn Hassett, David Janssen, Jack Klugman, Gena Rowlands, Walter Pidgeon, Brock Peters, Joe Kapp.

(NOTE: A longer version with subplot added exists on television prints.)

Cassavetes and Heston are cops out to stop a sniper who causes mayhem during a football game. The film's chief attraction, pushed heavily in its trailers, was the mob panic scene as the frantic crowd tries to get out of the stadium.

Howard Cosell, Dick Enberg, Frank Gifford and Merv Griffin have minor roles.

771 Two Minutes to Go

1921, Associated First National Pictures, 5,920 feet. Director: Charles Ray. Story: Richard Andres. Photography: George Rizard.

Cast: Charles Ray, Mary Anderson, Lionel Belmore, Lincoln Stedman, Truman Van Dyke, Gus Leonard, Tom Wilson, Bert Woodruff, Francois Dumas, Phillip Dunham.

Chester Burnett (Ray) quits the football team when his father gets into financial trouble. He gets a job as a milkman, and ashamed to tell his girl friend (Anderson), he keeps it a secret.

When the Big Game comes up, Chester returns to the team but plays uninspired ball until he learns that his dad is out of trouble and his girl friend is backing him all the way.

772 Two Minutes to Play

1937, Victory, 69 minutes. Director: Bob Hill. Producer: Sam Katzman. Story: William Buchanan. Photography: Bill Hyer. Editor: Charles Henkel.

Cast: Herman Brix, Eddie Nugent, Jeanne Martel, Betty Compson, Grady Sutton, Duncan Renaldo, David Sharpe, Sammy Cohen, Forrest Taylor.

The eternal triangle rears its all-too-familiar head as two students are bitter rivals for the hand of a coed. As they're both football stars, that leads to trouble on and off the field.

The twist is that the two lads' dads were also bitter rivals.

The two players settle their differences and stage the winning touchdown drive in the time span mentioned in the title.

773 Up the River

1938, 20th Century-Fox, 75 minutes. Director: Alfred Werker. Producer: Sol M. Wurtzel. Screenplay: Lou Breslow, John Patrick. Story: Maurine Watkins. Photography: Peverell Marley. Editor: Nick DeMaggio.

Cast: Preston Foster, Tony Martin, Phyllis Brooks, Slim Summerville, Arthur Treacher, Sidney Toler, Alan Dinehart, Bill Robinson, Edward Gargan.

1930's **Up the River** proved so successful, it spurred many imitations and this remake with the sport changed from baseball to football (See Baseball chapter).

Foster and Treacher are stars for their prison football squad. When they learn the mother of their pal Martin has been swindled by Toler, they disguise themselves as women and escape.

They're expert con men themselves, so after beating the crooks they return to prison in time for the big game and find the warden is more interested in winning it than punishing them for escaping.

774 Varsity Show

1930, Vitaphone, 11 minutes.

A college football team appears in drag for the big varsity show.

775 We Went to College

1936, Metro Goldwyn Mayer, 64 minutes. Director: Joseph Santley. Producer: Harry Rapf. Screenplay: Richard Marbaum, Maurice Rapf. Photography: Lester White.

Cast: Charles Butterworth, Walter Abel, Hugh Herbert, Una Merkel, Edith Atwater, Walter Catlett, Charles Trowbridge, Tom Ricketts.

The big football game is the focal point of three days of wild happenings at a homecoming for grad Butterworth, who runs onto the field to tackle an opposing player and prevent his scoring a touchdown.

776 West Point

1927, Metro Goldwyn Mayer, 8,090-8,134 feet. Director: Edward Sedgwick. Story: Raymond L. Schrock. Photography: Ira Morgan. Editor: Frank Sullivan.

Cast: William Haines, Joan Crawford, William Bakewell,

Neil Neely, Ralph Emerson, Leon Kellar, Raymond G. Moses.

Here's the antithesis of 1929's **Salute** which glorified the Naval Academy and its football team.

In **West Point**, a conceited grid star (Haines) has trouble adjusting to the Academy's way of doing things and quits when the going gets rough.

Persuaded to return, he becomes the hero in the big game against Navy and has the proper team spirit.

777 West Point Widow

1941, Paramount, 63 minutes. Director: Robert Siodmak. Producer: Sol C. Siegel. Screenplay: F. Hugh Herbert, Hans Kialy. Story: Anne Wormser. Photography: Theodor Sparkuhl. Editor: Archie Marshek.

Cast: Anne Shirley, Richard Carlson, Richard Denning, Frances Gifford, Maude Eburne, Janet Beecher.

Nurse Shirley marries Army grid star Denning and has a baby by him, but the boy's family has the marriage annulled so the lad can finish his education.

In the meantime, intern Carlson falls for her.

778 While Thousands Cheer (aka **Gridiron Graft, Crooked Money**)

1940, Million Dollar Productions.

Cast: Kenny Washington, Gladys Snyder, Joni Le Gon, Florence O'Brien, Ida Belle, Mantan Moreland, Reginald Fenderson, Lawrence Criner.

A football tale involving an attempt to bribe players.

779 White Flannels

1927, Warner Brothers, 6,820 feet. Director: Lloyd Bacon. Scenario: C. Graham Baker, based on a story by Lucian Cary in the **Saturday Evening Post.** Photography: Ed du Par.

Cast: Jason Robards, Louise Dressler, Virginia Brown Faire, Warner Richmond, George Nichols, Brooks Benedict, Rose Blossom, Rosemary Cooper.

The wife of a coal miner scrimps and saves for enough money to send her son (Robards) to college, where he becomes a big football star and falls in with the well-to-do crowd.

Anxious to watch her son play, she gets a job as a waitress in a town cafe; but when her identity is revealed during a big victory celebration at the site, the lad's phony friends desert him and he returns to his roots.

He saves a lifelong friend from a mine accident and weds his childhood sweetheart.

780 Win That Girl

1928, Fox Film Corp., 5,337 feet. Director: David Butler. Scenario: John Stone, based on a story by James Hopper in the **Saturday Evening Post.** Photography: Glen MacWilliams. Editor: Irene Morra.

Cast: David Rollins, Sue Carol, Tom Elliott, Roscoe Karns, Olin Francis, Mack Fluker, Sidney Bracey, Janet MacLeod, Maxine Shelly, Betty Recklaw.

The title says almost all as the women are once again portrayed as loving only the winners.

Pity poor Johnny Norton III (Rollins). His father and grandfather were both on teams which were defeated by a rival school led by members of the Brawn clan.

He's long been their great bright hope to finally beat the Brawns, but he just doesn't seem to have it on the gridiron. Comes the big game, however, he gets his break when other players are injured and proves his worth to "win that girl."

781 Yale vs. Harvard

1927, Metro Goldwyn Mayer, 2 reels. Director: Robert F. McGowan. Producer: Hal Roach. Photography: Art Lloyd. Editor: Richard Currier.

Our Gang's football team takes on a rival.

782 Yes Sir, That's My Baby

1949, Universal-International, 82 minutes, Color. Director: George Sherman. Producer: Leonard Goldstein. Screenplay: Oscar Brodney. Photography: Irving Glassberg. Editor: Ted J. Kent.

Cast: Donald O'Connor, Charles Coburn, Gloria DeHaven, Joshua Shelley, Barbara Brown, Jim Davis, James Brown, Michael Dugan, Hal Fieberling, Patricia Alphin.

A very slight, but easy-to-take musical comedy about ex-GIs who enroll at college and come into conflict with the wives when they want to play football.

783 Yesterday's Heroes

1940, 20th Century-Fox, 66 minutes. Director: Herbert I. Leeds. Producer: Sol M. Wurtzel. Screenplay: Irving Cummings, Jr., William Conselman, Jr. Story: William Brent. Photography: Charles Clarke.

Cast: Robert Sterling, Jean Rogers, Ted North, Katharine Aldridge, Russell Gleason, Richard Lane, Edmund MacDonald, George Irving, Pierre Watkin, Harry Hayden.

Success on the gridiron interferes with a young medical student's studies. Meanwhile, he ignores true love Rogers for widow Aldridge until the final reel.

784 The Young Animals

1968, American-International, 93-99 minutes, Color. Director-Producer: Maurice Dexter. Screenplay: James G. White. Photography: Ken Peach. Editor: Sid Levin.

Cast: Tom Nardini, Patty McCormack, David Macklin, Joanna Frank, Zooey Hall, Russ Bender, Arthur Peterson, Keith Taylor, The American Revolution.

As the title indicates, violence and exploitation are more the rule here than plot or sincerity.

Set at an Arizona high school, it's about the tensions between Mexican-American students and their bigoted math teacher/football coach who they want fired.

Violence, rape and other such situations abound.

Golf

Except for a series of British films in the 1920s based on stories by P.G. Wodehouse and a brief flurry of activity in the early 1950s with **Follow the Sun, Pat and Mike** and **The Caddy**, golfing features have been few and far between with the majority being comedies.

Of the numerous films with golfing sequences, perhaps the most unique is in **Bruce Lee, We Miss You** (1981) in which the kung fu hero tracks down the man allegedly responsible for the death of film star Lee.

Meeting on the golf course, the villain shoots a number of golf balls rapid-fire at the hero who catches them in mid-air. The two then clash in kung fu combat, using golf clubs as weapons as they chase each other around the golf course.

In **How to Commit Marriage**, Bob Hope plays golf with a chimpanzee.

785 Affinities

1922, W.W. Hodkinson Corp., 5,484 feet. Director: Ward Lascelle. Scenario: H. Landers Jackson. Story: Mary Roberts Rinehart. Photography: Joe Scholz, Abe Scholtz.

Cast: John Bowers, Colleen Moore, Joe Bonner, Grace Gordon, Pietro Sosso.

An avid golfer (Bowers) neglects his wife who starts seeing another man (Bonner). Bowers, in turn, starts seeing Bonner's wife until the comic affairs are all straightened out.

786 All Teed Up

1930, Metro Goldwyn Mayer, 2 reels. Director: Edgar Kennedy. Producer: Hal Roach.

Cast: Charlie Chase, Thelma Todd, Tenen Holtz, Edgar Kennedy, Dell Henderson, Carl Stockdale, Nelson McDowell, Harry Bowen.

Chase causes country club chaos when he plays golf.

787 Always a Gentleman

1929, Educational, 2 reels. Director: Norman Taurog.

Cast: Lloyd Hamilton, Edna Gregory, Al Thompson, Jack Miller.

Hamilton is invited to be part of a foursome. While his behavior is strange—he mistakes an umbrella for a club and keeps on hitting the same person with his shots—his companions seem even stranger.

When he's invited to their home later, he finds out why. They're inmates from an asylum.

788 Banning

1967, Universal, 102-110 minutes, Color. Director: Ron Winston. Producer: Dick Berg. Screenplay: James Lee. Photography: Loyal Griggs. Editor: Terry Williams.

Cast: Robert Wagner, Anjanette Comer, Jill St. John, Guy Stockwell, James Farentino, Susan Clark, Howard St. John, Sean Garrison, Mike Kellin, Gene Hackman.

Wagner, a golf pro at an exclusive country club, is under a lot of pressure during a big tournament. Not only is Farentino gunning for his job, but Stockwell, his old nemesis, is on the scene causing him some romantic problems. It seems Stockwell is the one who ruined Wagner's golfing career with charges of dishonesty.

789 Bobby Jones

In the very early 1930's, Vitaphone released a number of shorts featuring golfing great Bobby Jones. They were distinguished from the host of other instructional series, such as those featuring Howard Jones, Knute Rockne, Babe Ruth, Johnny Farrell et al. by the large number of well-known movie stars who appeared in them.

Directed by George Marshall, they ranged in length from 8 to 14 minutes.

We have listed the first 11 shorts in the first series and the first three in the second series. The stars who appear in each are listed after the title.

First Series

1. **How I Play Golf—The Putt-R** (sic), Richard Barthelmess, Joe E. Brown, Frank Craven. 2. **Chip Shots,** Charles Winniger, John Halliday, William Davidson, Robert Elliott. 3. **The Niblick.** 4. **The Master Niblick,** Leon Errol. 5. **The Medium Irons,** Junior Coughlan. 6. **The Big Irons.** 7. **The Spoon,** Walter Huston, Zelma O'Neal, John Halliday. 8. **The Brassie.** 9. **The Driver.** 10. **Trouble Shots,** Edward G. Robinson, Douglas Fairbanks, Jr. 11. **How I Play Golf,** James Cagney, Joe E. Brown, Louise Fazenda, Evalyn Knapp.

Second Series

1. **How to Break 90: The Grip,** Joe E. Brown. 2. **Position and Backswing,** Guy Kibbee. 3. **Hip Action,** W.C. Fields, Warner Oland.

790 Bombs and Boobs

1926, Short Films Syndicate, 482 feet. Animation: Bud Fisher.

Those cartoon characters, Mutt and Jeff, travel to Russia only to be chased by the Russian golf champ, Poison Ivan, who throws bombs at them.

791 The Caddy

1953, Paramount, 95 minutes. Director: Norman Taurog. Producer: Paul Jones. Screenplay: Edmund Hartmann, Danny Arnold. Photography: Daniel L. Fapp. Editor: Warren Low.

Cast: Dean Martin, Jerry Lewis, Donna Reed, Barbara Bates, Joseph Calleia, Fred Clark, Clinton Sundberg, Howard Smith, Marshall Thompson, Housely Stevenson, Jr. and Tom Harmon, Ben Hogan, Byron Nelson, Julius Boros, Lighthorse Harry Cooper as themselves.

Lewis is an ace golfer, but like Katharine Hepburn in **Pat and Mike,** he's got a slight problem. Whereas Hepburn froze whenever her boyfriend was watching, Lewis does her one better. He becomes a clown whenever ANYONE is watching, it seems.

Instead, under his tutelage, pal Martin is built up into a top contender; but the ungrateful playboy identifies Lewis as only being his caddy and shunts him to the background.

The climactic golf match is pure mayhem with Martin and Lewis never finishing the round while disrupting the games of many of the top pros.

The song "That's Amore" is featured.

792 Caddyshack

1980, Warner Brothers, 90-107 minutes, Color. Director: Harold Ramis. Producer: Douglas Kenney. Screenplay: Kenney, Ramis, Brian Doyle-Murray. Photography: Stevan Larner. Editor: William Carruth.

Cast: Chevy Chase, Bill Murray, Rodney Dangerfield, Ted Knight, Michael O'Keefe, Sarah Holcomb, Scott Colomby, Cindy Morgan, Brian Doyle-Murray, Albert Salmi.

"It's the slobs vs. the snobs" blared the radio and television ads for this no-holds-barred comedy, as the caddies and friends take on the stuffy members of an exclusive country club.

Chase is the club's golf pro who takes caddy O'Keefe under his wing. Murray is a crazy greenskeeper who's determined to get rid of a pesky gopher even if it means dynamiting the golf course. Dangerfield is an uncouth slob who recently came into a lot of money while Knight is the leader of the snobs, a rich judge.

Caddyshack's funniest sequence is when a discarded Clark bar is thrown into the swimming pool. As the theme from **Jaws** is played, the candy bar floats closer and closer to the swimmers until it's spotted. As someone shouts "doody, doody," there's a frantic race to get out of the pool, which is later drained.

793 Change of Heart

1938, 20th Century-Fox, 59 minutes. Director: James Tinling. Producer: Sol M. Wurtzel. Screenplay: Frances Hyland, Albert Ray. Photography: Daniel B. Clark.

Cast: Gloria Stuart, Michael Whalen, Lyle Talbot, Detmar Watson, Jane Darwell.

Until **Pat and Mike,** nearly every film which depicted women as athletes was a bottom-of-the-bill programmer, like this one.

Stuart plays a top golfer whose husband isn't interested in the game until his wife starts pairing with a male golfer. He then begins honing up on golf.

794 Chester Forgets Himself

1924, British, Stoll, 2,179 feet. Producer: Andrew P. Wilson Editor: Challis N. Sanderson.

Cast: Ena Evans, Nelson Ramsey, Jameson Thomas, Harry Beasley, H. Clavering Craig, Nell Emerald.

To impress a girl, Chester puts on intellectual airs on the golf course, but it isn't until he starts cursing after being hit by a ball that she takes any interest in him.

795 Dangerous Golfers

1905, British, Clarendon, 350 feet. Director: Percy Snow.

Everything that's in the way of the golfers in the title is destroyed when they swing their clubs.

796 Dead of Night

1946, British, Ealing, 102 minutes. Directors: Alberto Cavalcanti, Charles Crichton, Basil Dearden, Robert Hamer. Screenplay: John V. Baines, Angus MacPhail with additional dialogue by T.E.B. Clarke. Stories: H.G. Wells, Angus Mac Phail, E.F. Benson, John V. Baines. Photography: Douglas Slocombe, Stan Pavey. Editor: Charles Hasse.

Cast: Mervyn Johns, Michael Redgrave, Renee Gadd, Roland Culver, Mary Merrall, Frederick Valk, Barbara Leake, Sally Ann Howes, Basil Radford, Michael Allan.

Each of the guests at a country weekend tells of his or her experiences with the supernatural.

In the only lighthearted segment, two avid golfers are in love with the same girl and decide to play a match to determine who gets the right to woo her. When one of the men wins by cheating, his friend immediately drowns himself in the nearest water trap as the winner marries the girl.

The dead golfer, however, returns to haunt his ex-pal by playing nasty tricks on the links; but after he decides to lift the curse, he can't remember how.

In another segment, a race car driver who's recuperating from a bad crash has a premonition of a deadly accident.

797 Divot Diggers

1936, Metro Goldwyn Mayer, 2 reels. Director: Robert F. McGowan. Producer: Hal Roach. Photography: Francis Corby. Editor: Louis McManus.

When the caddies walk out during a pay dispute, members of Our Gang take their places and run amok on the course.

798 Don't Hook Now

1943, United Artists, 2 reels.

Cast: Bing Crosby, Bob Hope, Ben Hogan, Sam Snead, Byron Nelson, Jimmy Demaret, Ralph Guldahl, Jimmy Hines.

Musical comedy mixes with actual footage from the Bing Crosby Golf Tournament in this two-reeler, which features Bing crooning "What More Do You Want—Vaudeville" on the links.

799 The Fable of the Kid Who Shifted His Ideals to Golf and Finally Became a Baseball Fan and Took The Only Known Cure

1916, Essanay, 1 reel. Director: Richard Foster Baker.

At least the kid didn't have to try and fit the title of this short onto a movie theater marquee.

800 Follow the Sun

1951, 20th Century Fox, 93-96 minutes. Director: Sidney Lanfield. Producer: Samuel G. Engel. Screenplay: Frederick Hazlitt Brennan. Photography: Leo Tover. Editor: Barbar McLeam.

Cast: Glenn Ford, Anne Baxter, Dennis O'Keefe, June Havoc, Larry Keating, Roland Winters, Nana Bryant, Sam Snead, James Demaret, Cary Middlecoff, Harold Blake, Ann Burr.

The real-life story of Ben Hogan, **Follow the Sun** was the first American-made feature golf film since the 1930's; and it's no mere coincidence that it was followed a year later by **Pat and Mike** and in 1953 by **The Caddy.** Both of the latter films followed the example of **Follow the Sun** which included many of the game's top golfers in the cast to lend an air of authenticity.

The story is quite straightforward, but the production values and acting are quite good. Hogan (Ford) weds his childhood sweetheart from Texas (Baxter), and she sticks by him through his early struggle to make money on the golf circuit.

Just as he nears the top, he's seriously injured in an automobile accident, and she still sticks by him.

Hogan, who early in his career shunned contact with the public, is inspired to make a comeback through the support of his fans.

801 Follow Thru

1930, Paramount-Publix Corp., 8,386 feet. Black and white with color segments. Director-Screenplay: Laurence Schwab, Lloyd Corrigan. Producers: Schwab, Frank Mandel. Photography: Henry Gerrard, Charles Boyle. Editor: Alyson Shaffer.

Cast: Charles Rogers, Nancy Carroll, Zelma O'Neal, Jack Haley, Eugene Pallette, Thelma Todd, Claude King, Albert Gran, Don Tomkins, Kathryn Givney.

Based on a play by Lew Brown, B.G. De Sylva, Ray Henderson and Laurence Schwab, this early musical comedy is about a woman golfer who loses a championship match but falls in love with a handsome golf instructor while doing so.

802 A Foozle at the Tee Party

1915, Roach Studios.

Cast: Harold Lloyd.

Comedian Lloyd, in his role as Lonesome Luke, winds up knocking out a golfer.

803 Foozle Takes Up Golf

1911, British, Hepworth, 450 feet. Director: Frank Wilson.

Short comedy about the woes of a golfer.

804 Gall and Golf

1917, Vitagraph. Director: Lawrence Semon. Producer: Graham Baker.

Cast: Lawrence Semon, Florence Curtis.

Semon and Curtis, a couple of pickpockets, meet at the Blue Blood Country Club and decide to form a partnership on the golf course. They succeed until they're finally spotted and have to make a run for it.

805 Golf Chump

1932, RKO Radio Pictures, 2 reels. Director: Harry Sweet.

Cast: Edgar Kennedy, Florence Lake, Dot Farley, William Eugene, Eddie Boland.

Kennedy, in his role as Mr. Average Man, creates comic havoc on a golf course.

806 The Golf Game and the Bonnet

1913, Vitagraph, 689 feet. Director: George D. Baker. Screenplay: Gregory Ker.

Cast: John Bunny, Flora Finch, Wallie Van, Richard Leslie, Roma Raymond, Jack Harvey, Arthur Cozine, Claire McCormick.

Bunny goes out golfing with the boys instead of going home to help his wife clean. When he's hit in the eye with a ball, he buys a hat for his wife to try to made amends.

Arriving home, he spots his wife beating a carpet and, going behind it, pretends that she caused his black eye. She winds up apologizing to him.

807 The Golf Specialist

1930, RKO Radio Pictures, 2 reels. Director: Monte Brice.

Cast: W.C. Fields.

Fields recreates his vaudeville routine of a golfer who's hampered by a whole string of events.

808 Golf Widows

1928, Columbia, 5,592 feet. Director: Erle C. Kenton. Scenario: W. Scott Darling. Photography: Arthur Todd.

Cast: Harrison Ford, Vera Reynolds, Sally Rand, Kathleen Key, Will Stanton, John Patrick.

Comic complications abound as two wives (Key, Rand) fume over being neglected by their golfing husbands.

To teach their husbands a lesson they go to the horse races in Mexico with two men who are in on the scheme. The husbands grab the bait, but the jealous fiancée of one of the two men gets in on the act as well.

809 The Golfers

1929, Educational, 21 minutes. Director: Mack Sennett.

Cast: Andy Clyde, Harry Gribbon, Thelma Hill, Patsy O'Leary, Bert Swor, Charlie Guest.

Hill is taking golf lessons from real-life pro Charlie Guest. Her dad in this comedy short wants her to wed Mr. Palooka (Gribbon), a millionaire who boasts that he once struck oil on the golf course.

Clyde portrays his rival for the girl's hand.

810 Golfing (aka **Comic Golf**)

1913, British, Hewitt Films, 900 feet. Director: G. Fletcher Hewitt.

Cast: Harry Lauder, Neil Kenyon.

Some more comic antics on the golf course featuring stars from the stage.

811 Golfing Extraordinary, Five Gentlemen

1896, British, 40 feet. Director: Birt Acres.

British film pioneer Acres holds the distinction of having made the very first sports film comedy. One member of a golfing fivesome swings and misses and then falls down. That's the whole film.

812 Green Grass Widows

1928, Tiffany-Stahl, 5,334 feet. Director: Alfred Raboch. Story: Viola Brothers Shore. Photography: Jackson Rose. Editor: Robert J. Kern.

Cast: John Harron, Walter Hagen, Gertrude Olmstead, Hedda Hopper, Lincoln Stedman, Ray Hallor.

Golf pro Walter Hagen appears as himself, and naturally he's painted in a good light. When a college youth enters a tournament

British golfing great Walter Hagen autographs some balls for his admirers in Green Grass Widows. (The Museum of Modern Art/Film Stills Archive.)

to raise enough money to complete his education, Hagen throws the match on the last hole to allow the lad to win.

The youth (Harron), however, realizes what the pro has done; and he and his newlywed wife vow to name their first child after Hagen.

813 Humours of Amateur Golf

1906, British, Urban Trading Co., 400 feet.

A very fat golfer has a very small caddy.

814 Johnny Farrell

In 1931, Pathe released a series of shorts ranging in length from 8 to 11 minutes featuring open champ Farrell giving instructions. Titles include **Golf, Duffer Swings** and **Under Par.**

815 Kid Boots

1926, Paramount, 5,650-8,565 feet. Director: Frank Tuttle. Screenplay: Tom Gibson, based on the play by Anthony McGuire, Otto Harbach and J.P. McCarthy. Photography: Victor Milner.

Cast: Eddie Cantor, Clara Bow, Billie Dove, Lawrence Gray, Natalie Kingston, Malcolm Waite, William Worthington.

An athlete (Gray) who is trying to obtain a divorce from a chorus girl (Kingston) inherits $3 million so naturally she contests it.

Using an alias, he becomes a professional golfer and Kid Boots (Cantor), a former tailor's aide he has befriended, his top caddy. With the help of a swimming teacher (Bow), there's a happy ending.

816 The Long Hole

1924, British, Stoll, 2,278 feet. Producer: Andrew P. Wilson. Editor: Challis N. Sanderson.

Cast: Roger Keyes, Charles

Courtneidge, Daphne Williams, Harry Beasley.

In this adaptation of a P.G. Wodehouse story, two men engage in a match of cross-country golf for the right to court a girl they've both fallen in love with.

At the end, the suitors learn that she's already engaged.

817 Love in the Rough

1930, Metro Goldwyn Mayer, 85 minutes. Director: Charles F. Reisner. Adaptation: Sarah Y. Mason from the play by Vincent Lawrence.

Cast: Robert Montgomery, Dorothy Jordan, Benny Rubin, J.C. Nugent, Dorothy McNulty, Tyrrell Davis, Harry Burns, Allan Lane, Roscoe Ates, Catherine Moylan, Edwards Davis.

A remake of the 1927 comedy **Spring Fever** concerns a conceited golfer (Montgomery) at an exclusive country club who changes his ways for the love of a beautiful girl (Jordan), but must still win the crucial final match.

818 Match Play

1930, Educational, 2 reels. Director: Mack Sennett.

Cast: Walter Hagen, Leo Diegel, Andy Clyde, Marjorie Beebe, Bud Jamison.

Real-life pros Hagen and Diegel must put up with the comic antics of Clyde and Beebe on the course.

819 McNab's Visit to London

1905, British, Alpha Trading Co., Director: Arthur Cooper.

Cast: Arthur Cooper, Ruby Vivian.

A Scottish golfer visits London and all but wrecks his host's home.

820 Now You See Him, Now You Don't

1972, Buena Vista, 88 minutes, Color. Director: Robert Butler. Producer: Ron Miller. Screenplay: Joseph L. McEveety. Story: Robert L. King.

Cast: Kurt Russell, Joe Flynn, Cesar Romero, Jim Backus, Michael McGreevey, Joyce Menges.

The usual 1970's Disney potboiler about a college youth (Russell) who discovers how to make himself invisible deserves passing mention for its golf course sequences.

The youth helps college president Flynn win one match, but Flynn loses without his help in another.

821 Once You Kiss a Stranger

1969, Warner Brothers, 106 minutes, Color. Director: Robert Sparr. Producer: Harold A. Goldstein. Screenplay: Frank Tarloff, Norman Katkov. Photography: Jacques Marquette. Editor: Marjorie Fowler.

Cast: Paul Burke, Carol Lynley, Martha Hyer, Peter Lind Hayes, Philip Carey, Stephen McNally, Whit Bissell, Elaine Devry, Kathryn Givney, Jim Raymond, George Fenneman.

This is a remake of 1951's **Strangers on a Train**, but any other comparison between this and the Hitchcock classic are purely coincidental.

A deranged woman (Lynley) who is about to be committed seduces a professional golfer (Burke) who is facing a sudden death playoff against another golfer (Carey). Unaware that he's being photographed and taped, Burke jokingly agrees to Lynley's suggestion that she kill his opponent and he kill her psychiatrist.

When she goes through with her suggestion by running over the rival golfer with a cart and clubbing him with one of Burke's irons, she demands that he keep his end of the bargain.

Hitchcock's original concerned a tennis pro with Robert Walker as the deranged schemer and the villain's homosexuality implied. By changing sexes in this remake, the filmmakers emphasized some more sordid aspects.

Comedian Andy Clyde, left, Leo Diegel and Marjorie Beebe marvel at golf pro Walter Hagen's mammoth drive in the Educational short Match Play. (The Museum of Modern Art/Film Stills Archive.)

822 Ordeal by Golf

1924, British, Stoll, 1,894 feet. Producer: Andrew P. Wilson. Editor: Challis N. Sanderson.

Cast: Harry Beasley, Edwin Underhill, Jack Powell, Jean Jay, E. Ashley Marvin, Moore Marriott, Ewan Allan.

Two employees in line for promotion must play a round of golf with their boss, in another adaptation of a P.G. Wodehouse story.

823 Part Time Wife

1930, Fox Film Corp., 6,500 feet. Director: Leo McCarey. Screenplay: McCarey, Raymond L. Schrock, Howard Green. Photography: George Schneiderman. Editor: Jack Murray.

Cast: Edmund Lowe, Leila Hyams, Tom Clifford, Walter McGrail, Louis Payne, Sam Lefkin, George Corcoran.

Lowe plays a man who's too wrapped up in his business affairs to pay any attention to his wife (Hyams) who loves to play golf. When she takes McGrail as her golfing partner, hubby and wife separate.

In an attempt to win his wife back, Lowe takes up golf and with the help of caddy Clifford, gets her back. Fox remade the film in 1938 as **Change of Heart.**

824 Pat and Mike

1952, Metro Goldwyn Mayer, 94 minutes. Director: George Cukor. Producer: Lawrence Weingarten. Screenplay: Ruth Gordon, Garson Kanin. Photography: William Daniels. Editor: George Boemler.

Cast: Katharine Hepburn, Spencer Tracy, Aldo Ray, William Ching, Sammy White, Jim Backus, Charles Buchinski (Bronson), Loring Smith, George Mathews, Phyllis Povah, Chuck Connors, Carl Switzer, Mae Clark and Tom Harmon, Gussie Moran, Babe Zaharias, Don Budge, Alice Marble, Frank Parker, Betty Hicks, Beverly Hanson, Helen Dettweiler as themselves.

A landmark in women's sports

films is also grand entertainment thanks to the Tracy-Hepburn team, a biting script by the Gordon-Kanin husband and wife team and expert handling by veteran director Cukor, whose specialty was handling so-called "women's" pictures.

Hepburn is Pat Pemberton, a college teacher who joins her boy friend on the links with a snooty couple who may give the school a huge endowment, depending upon the outcome of the golf match.

After completely bungling the match and tired of the non-stop yapping of the snooty woman, she grabs a club and reels off a succession of six perfect drives off the tee.

It seems that whenever her boy friend is watching, poor Pat simply freezes up. To prove to her fiancé (Ching) that she really is good, Backus talks her into entering a major golf tournament.

She beats all comers; but on the 18th hole against golfing great Babe Zaharias, she blows a putt because Ching has decided to come and watch her.

Despite Ching's objections, she signs a contract with unscrupulous manager Mike Conovan (Tracy), who also manages a dumb punch-drunk fighter, Davie Hucko (Ray), the victim of knockouts in his last four fights, and a losing horse.

Also excelling in other sports, Pat embarks on a cross-country pro tennis tour and in the finals is beating pro Gussie Moran until the boy friend shows up again.

Suddenly, the net grows to 10 feet high; and she can't shoot over it. Her opponent's racket grows to huge proportions while hers shrinks to the size of a ping pong paddle. And the next thing she knows, she's being revived in the locker room.

In the meantime, of course, Pemberton and Conovan begin to fall in love, with him seeing her face superimposed on his horse.

Conovan decides to go legit and turns down an ultimatum from three gangsters that she throw the big golf tournament. After she beats up the gangsters who are attacking Conovan, the two eventually realize they love each other; and not even the boy friend's evil eye stare can stop her from winning the tourney.

Until **Pat and Mike**, when women were shown as athletes—that's when they were shown at all—it was usually to either portray them as laughing stocks daring to try to equal the ability of men.

While the form of **Pat and Mike** may be comedy, there's no mistaking the prowess of the women athletes in the film as Zaharias makes one incredible shot after another on the links and Moran matches it on the tennis court.

As we mentioned in the opening chapter, practically every great sports movie focuses on the conflict within rather than a conflict imposed from without.

We don't laugh at Hepburn because there's no question in the film that she's a spectacular athlete. Rather, we laugh because we can sympathize with the inner conflict of the two leads—with she trying to shake off the traditional female shackles which her boy friend wants to place on her and with Conovan trying to understand that a woman is physically superior to him.

825 The Ramblin' Galoot

1926, Associated Exhibitors, 4,438 feet. Director: Fred Bain. Story: Bair Cross. Photography: Ray Ries.

Cast: Buddy Roosevelt, Violet LaPlante, Frederick Lee.

Say, guess what we have here? Nothing else but a golf western as a cowboy teaches a banker and his daughter how to play golf on their ranch.

In the meantime, good old villainy is afoot as a gang of counterfeiters tries to frame him; and when all else fails, they resort to the good old kidnapping scheme.

826 Rhubarb

1970, British, Avalon, 37 minutes. Director-Screenplay: Eric Sykes.

Cast: Harry Secombe, Eric Sykes, Jimmy Edwards, Johnny Speight, Kenneth Connor, Graham Stark.

A cop and a vicar engage in a slapstick golf match.

827 Rodney Fails to Qualify

1924, British, Stoll, 2,062 feet. Producer: Andrew P. Wilson. Editor: Challis N. Sanderson.

Cast: Lionelle Howard, Phyllis Lytton, Dallas Cairns, Victor Robson, Harry Beasley, Sheila Astley, E. Spalding, H. Clavering Craig.

A golfer and a poet are rivals for the love of a girl in another adaptation of a P.G. Wodehouse story.

828 Scroggins Plays Golf

1911, British, Cricks and Martin, 410 feet. Director: A.E. Coleby.

When a golfer loses his ball, he uses eggs and fruit instead.

829 Spring Fever

1927, Metro Goldwyn Mayer, 6,705 feet. Director: Edward Sedgwick. Screenplay: Albert Lewin, Frank Davis, based on a play by Vincent Lawrence. Photography: Ira Morgan. Editor: Frank Sullivan.

Cast: William Haines, Joan Crawford, George K. Arthur, George Fawcett, Eileen Percy, Edward Earle, Lee Moran, Bert Woodruff.

A conceited shipping clerk (Haines) is an expert golfer and manages to join an exclusive country club, where he ruffles some feathers by his failure to observe the etiquette of the game.

He labels his favorite golf club "sweetheart" and presents it to his girl friend (Crawford) after he falls in love. It's her love which changes him; and in the climactic tournament, she comes out of the crowd to give him "sweetheart," which he uses to win.

Remade in 1930 as **Love in the Rough.**

830 The Suffragette's Downfall or Who Said 'Rats'?

1911, British, Acme, 515 feet. Director: Fred Rains.

A henpecked husband, played by director Rains, sets loose some rats on his golfing wife in a short that's not exactly a landmark in the portrayal of women in sports.

831 Three Little Beers

1935, Columbia, 14 minutes. Director: Del Lord.

Cast: The Three Stooges, Bud Jamison.

The Stooges, while making a beer delivery, manage to foul up a golf tournament.

832 Tom Thumbs Down

1931, Vitaphone, 8 minutes.

Cast: Bobby Jarvis, Harry McNaughton.

It's comedy time in the only miniature golf non-documentary we know of. McNaughton's tutelage makes Jarvis the champ of the miniature circuit.

833 West of Broadway

1926, Producers Distributing Corp., 5,186 feet. Director: Robert Thornby. Adaptation: Harold Shumate, based on a story by Wallace Smith, "New York West," in **Blue Book Magazine.** Photography: Georges Benoit.

Cast: Arnold Gray, Priscilla Dean, Walter Long, George Hall, William Austin, Majel Coleman.

A woman-hating Wyoming rancher converts part of his ranch into—guess what, a golf course and hires a pro named Freddy—who turns out to be a girl.

They become involved in a cattle rustling scheme, and the villains resort to the old kidnapping trick again; but as usual, there's a happy ending.

Horses and Other Animals

In a way, the motion picture as we know it today began with a horse race. Although there had been a number of devices producing an effect similar to motion, it wasn't until 1877 that, for all intents and purposes, a continuous picture was produced.

That was the year Eadweard Muybridge and John D. Isaacs set up a number of cameras side by side at the edge of a racetrack. Each had a snapshot shutter that was kept open by a thin silk thread spread across the track and attached to a wall on the opposite end. When Leland Stanford's racehorse crossed each thread, the cameras snapped in rapid succession, producing, in effect, a continuous picture.

The British film pioneer, Burt Acres, also made horse racing one of his early subjects with the filming of the 1895 Derby.

As filmmaking progressed, it wasn't long before it was realized that horseracing provided a relatively easy-to-film milieu that provided instant excitement with last minute wins by the nose. And if the budget didn't allow for staging a race, it was easy enough just to use stock footage with a couple of close-ups of the actors spliced in to give the illusion the sequence was filmed fresh.

Racing films by the dozens were made in England during the 1910's and 1920's, with a good many of them directed by Walter West and starring Violet Hopson, often dealing with the nobility.

By the early 1920's, just as many were being made in the United States, and the cliches which developed in those early films remained in the genre throughout the years.

It seems there was always a mortgage at stake on the big race, with a villain always casting his evil eye on the property (or the nobleman's title as the case may be). The villain would stop at nothing to stop the hero or heroine's horse from even getting the chance to win.

When attempts to dope the horse failed, the villain would set the barn on fire. If that failed, too, he could resort to the usual kidnapping trick; but, darn it, the hero always seems to escape in time from those.

And there were other ways. Jockeys could be bribed; and if they turned down the offer, they could be framed, according to racing movies. The jockeys could also be injured or bumped off, but that usually meant the hero or heroine would ride the horse him- or herself. Drat, foiled again!

Sometimes the jockey was his own villain, fighting his greedy instincts and getting a second chance to prove to the world and himself that he's not such a bad fellow after all.

As far as women go, horse racing movies were unique inasmuch as they were equal opportunity employers. Where women, at least until the 1960's, were generally unacceptable as athletes in movies at least in the filmmakers' minds, they were perfectly convincing as jockeys and the annals of horse-racing movie history are filled with stories about women who take the reins in the big race and ride to victory.

The most famous equestrian film of them all, for example, **National Velvet,** features Elizabeth Taylor as a girl who disguises herself as a jockey and wins, only to be disqualified when it's discovered she's a girl.

With the box office success of **The Champ** (1931), a boxing movie, and **Little Miss Marker** (1934), stories about bums who were transformed by children became commonplace, nowhere more evident than in horse racing films.

Just to name a few, there were **Fast Companions, Little Miss Thoroughbred, King of the Turf, Salty O'Rourke, Race Track, Stablemates** and, of course, two remakes of **Little Miss Marker.**

When filmmakers had a horse-racing plot and wanted to try something a little different, they switched the milieu to the dog track.

Polo films, in the meantime, seem to be mainly old football scripts that have been dusted off and transferred from the gridiron.

We are not including rodeo films because we feel they belong in the western film genre. We also are not including fox hunting for the same reasons we are omitting bullfighting and hunting movies—we feel they, too, belong in other genres.

With horse racing films in particular, you run into the problem of crossing genres, particularly with the western movies. If we listed every western that had a horse race in it, there would probably be enough in this chapter alone for an entire book; therefore, we've been selective to include only those we believe play an integral part of the plot. The others we will leave to the many fine western reference works on the market.

Among the dozens of films which aren't included in the main listings but which deserve footnotes in the history of horse racing movies are: **The Double Event, Easy Money** (1934), **The Fabulous Suzanne,** in which a waitress wins by sticking a lucky pin into a racing form, **Five to One, Gypsy Colt,** in which a girl's pet horse is sold to a racing stable but escapes across the desert, **His First Command,** the phony track schemes of **The Sting** and **I'd Give My Life, It Happened Tomorrow, Jake the Plumber, The Kibitzer, Looking for the Derby Result, Lucky Carson, Madame Louise, The Man in the Saddle** (1928), **My American Wife, Rollin' Home** (1946), **The Payoff, Reckless Living** (1931), **The Ridin' Streak, The Right to Live, Sandy** (1917), **The Saturday Night Kid, Smith's Wives, A Sporting Double, Three Pals, Tip on a Dead Jockey,** and **Wolf Law.**

In polo, we have listed **Social Lion** under boxing because we feel it more appropriately belongs there, while **On Top of the World** (1936) and **Times Square Lady** (1935) are of peripheral interest to dog racing fans.

Racing and Equestrian

834 All In

1936, British, Gainsborough, 71 minutes. Director: Marcel Varnel. Producer: Michael Balcon. Screenplay: Leslie Arliss, Val Guest, based on a play "Tattenham Corner" by Gibb McLaughlin, Glennis Lorimer.

Cast: Ralph Lynne, Gina Malo, Jack Barry, Claude Dampier.

Complications arise when the nephew of an antigambling crusader winds up the owner of a racing stable.

835 All for Peggy

1915, Universal, 1 reel. Producer: Joseph De Grasse.

Cast: Lon Chaney, Pauline Bush.

Chancy, the Man of 1,000 Faces, this time is a horse trainer whose daughter (Bush) disguises herself as a boy and rides the horse to victory.

836 April Love

1957, 20th Century-Fox, 99 minutes, Color. Director: Henry Levin. Producer: David Weisbart. Screenplay: Winston Miller, based on a novel by Agnew Chamberlain.

Photography: Wilfred Cline.

Cast: Pat Boone, Shirley Jones, Dolores Michaels, Arthur O'Connell, Matt Crowley, Jeanette Nolan, Brad Jackson.

A remake of 1944's **Home in Indiana** finds singer Pat Boone as a city youth with a criminal record who finds a new lease on life in Kentucky and becomes a winning trotting driver.

837 The Arizona Sweepstakes

1926, Universal, 5,418 feet. Director: Clifford S. Smith. Scenario: Isadore Bernstein. Photography: Harry Neumann.

Cast: Hoot Gibson, Helen Lynch, Philo McCullough, Emmett King, Turner Savage, George Ovey, Tod Brown.

A cowboy (Gibson) who's suspected of a murder in San Francisco returns to his native Arizona and enters a big horse race to bail his sweetheart's father out of financial difficulty.

838 At the Races

1934, Vitaphone, 10 minutes. Director: Joseph Henabery. Screenplay: Jack Henley.

Cast: Edgar Bergen.

Bergen's dummy, Charlie McCarthy, is a jockey with all the "inside" dope on the races.

839 Atta Boy's Last Race

1916, Triangle, 5 reels. Director: George Siegmann. Screenplay: Tod Browning.

Cast: Dorothy Gish, Keith Armour, Carl Stockdale, Adele Clifton, Loyola O'Connor, Fred H. Turner.

There's not much new in this tale of a ranch mortgage hanging in the balance of the big horse race.

840 The Attempted Nobbling of the Derby Favourite

1905, British, Cricks and Sharp, 540 feet. Director: Tom Green.

A scheme to dope the favored winner in the race is thwarted.

841 Aunt Clara

1954, British, British Lion, 84 minutes. Director: Anthony Kimmins. Producers: Colin Lesslie, Anthony Kimmins. Screenplay: Kenneth Horne, Roy Miller, based on a novel by Noel Streatfeild.

Cast: A.E. Matthews, Margaret Rutherford, Ronald Shiner, Fay Compton, Nigel Stock, Jill Bennett, Raymond Huntley, Eddie Byrne, Sidney James.

A sweet religious old lady (Rutherford) inherits a whorehouse, a number of greyhounds and a racecourse racket, among other things. She turns the shady rackets into fund-raising operations for her charities in this gentle comedy.

842 Beautiful Kitty

1923, British, Butcher, 4,480 feet. Director-Producer: Walter West. Scenario: J. Bertram Brown.

Cast: James Knight, Violet Hopson, Robert Vallis, Arthur Walcott, Pollie Emery, Fred Percy.

A man spends his track winnings to invest in a racehorse.

843 The Belles of St. Trinian's

1954, British, British Lion, 91 minutes. Director: Frank Launder. Producers: Launder, Sidney Giliat. Screenplay: Launder, Giliat, Val Valentine, inspired by the cartoons by Ronald Searle. Editor: Thelma Connell.

Cast: Alastair Sim, Joyce Grenfell, George Cole, Hermione Bradley, Betty Ann Davies, Renee Houston, Beryl Reid, Joan Sims, Irene Handle, Mary Merrall.

The first in a comedy series about the little "monsters" in girl form who inhabit St. Trinian's school finds the sweet young things thwarting a plot to steal the favorite in the big race.

It seems the headmistress (Sims in drag) has bet all available cash through her bookie brother (also Sims) in an attempt to get the school out of debt.

844 Big Boy

1930, Warner Brothers, 6,275 feet. Director: Alan Crosland. Screenplay: William K. Wells, Perry Vekroff, Rex Taylor, based on a play by Harold Atteridge. Photography: Hal Mohr. Editor: Ralph Dawson.

Cast: Al Jolson, Claudia Dell, Louise Closser Hale, Noah Beery, Lloyd Hughes, Eddie Phillips, Lew Harvey, Tom Wilson, Franklin Batie, John Harron, Carl White.

With Jolson around, you know this is a musical. He's a singing jockey, in blackface, who has trained Big Boy for the Kentucky Derby for the owners, who need a victory to get out of financial trouble.

Two of the family members unknowingly fall in with some shady characters who plan to put in their own jockey and throw the big race, but the plan is foiled by Jolson.

845 The Big Race

1934, Showmen's Pictures, 62 minutes. Director: Fred Newmeyer. Story: Hugh Cummings. Photography: George Meehan. Editor: S. Roy Luby.

Cast: Boots Mallory, John Darrow, Paul Hurst, Frankie Darro, Phillips Smalley, Katherine Williams, James Flavin.

When a stable owner's son is suspected of doping horses, not only is he disowned but his girl friend breaks off their engagement.

With barely enough money to buy food for himself, he and a friend somehow manage to train an unknown horse and enter it against his dad's favorite.

846 Bill As a Jockey

1910, Lux, no credits available.

Bill inherits a prize racehorse from his uncle and enters it in a race which he wins. He starts flirting with a female admirer at the track but is later discovered by his wife.

Bill rides away in fright, but his wife manages to track him down and starts beating him. He promises her he'll behave in the future.

847 Bill's Legacy

1931, British, Twickenham, 57 minutes. Director: Harry J. Revier. Producer: Julius Hagen. Screenplay: Leslie Fuller, Syd Courtenay.

Cast: Leslie Fuller, Mary Clare, Angela Joyce, Syd Courtenay, Ethel Leslie, Ivan Crowe.

A working man spends his inheritance on a racehorse.

848 Black Beauty

1921, Vitagraph, 7 reels. Director: David Smith, Scenario: William B. Courtney. Adaptation: Lillian Chester, George Randolph Chester, based on the novel by Anna Sewell. Photography: Reginald Lyons.

Cast: Jean Paige, James Morrison, George Webb, Bobby Mack, John Steppling, Leslie T. Peacock, Adele Farrington, Charles Morrison, Molly McConnell, Colin Kenny.

As anyone who has read Anna Sewell's 1877 novel knows, **Black Beauty** is by no means a horse racing film. It has, however, been a favorite subject for filmmakers over the years and has been shot more than half a dozen times, the first version being in 1906. The plots of these versions range from anything involving a black horse to being reasonably faithful to Sewell's tale, told from the horse's viewpoint, as he's passed from one owner to another, including noblemen, cabbies, junkmen and the like.

In this version, the only one we are giving in any kind of detail, there is a horse racing sequence. Other versions of **Black Beauty** made after this were in 1933, 1946, 1957 and 1971.

Kelly Reno, who has just ridden his horse to victory, is cheered on by, from left, Teri Garr, Mickey Rooney and Clarence Muse in The Black Stallion. (From the United Artists release The Black Stallion, © 1979 United Artists Corporation.)

849 The Black Stallion

1979, United Artists, 118 minutes, Color. Director: Carroll Ballard. Producers: Fred Roos, Tom Sternberg. Screenplay: Melissa Mathison, Jeanne Rosenberg, William D. Wittliff, based on a novel by Walter Farley. Photography: Caleb Deschanel. Editor: Robert Dalva.

Cast: Kelly Reno, Mickey Rooney, Teri Garr, Clarence Muse, Hoyt Axton, Michael Higgins, Ed McNamara, Dogmi Larbi, John Burton, John Buchanan, Kristen Vigard, Fausto Tozzi.

In what is unquestionably the most beautifully photographed horse racing film ever, young Alec (Reno) first meets the Arabian stallion during an ocean voyage with his father in 1949.

When the ship sinks, the horse and the boy wind up together on a desert island, where they become great pals. When they're rescued, the boy and the horse go home to the farm; but the stallion escapes.

He's found by Henry Dailey (Rooney), a retired trainer, who spots the stallion's racing potential and trains him to race against the two top thoroughbreds with Alec on his back.

Cass-ole, an Arabian stud from Houston, was selected to play the stallion after a studio search that spanned five nations.

Sardinia was chosen for the island scenes, and Toronto, Canada subbed for the New York locations. The final race sequence, set in Chicago, was actually filmed at Fort Erie Racetrack on the Ontario border.

850 The Black Stallion Returns

1983, United Artists, 93-103 minutes, Color. Director: Robert Dalva. Producers: Tom Sternberg, Fred Roos, Doug Claybourne. Screenplay: Richard Kletter, Jerome Kass, based on a novel by Walter Farley. Photography: Carlo Di Palma. Editor: David Holden.

Cast: Kelly Reno, Vincent

Spano, Allen Goorwitz, Woody Strode, Ferdinand Mayne, Teri Garr, Dogmi Larbi, Angelo Infanti, Luigi Mezzanotte, Franco Citti, Joe Murphy.

With Walter Farley's novel inspiring 15 sequels, it's not surprising there should be a film sequel to the highly successful **The Black Stallion.**

In **The Black Stallion Returns,** the horse's Arab owners kidnap the champion from the farm of young Alec Ramsay (Reno). Despite his young age, he uses his wits to follow them to the Sahara in an attempt to reclaim the horse.

After an eventful trek through the desert to the kingdom of Abu Ben Ishak (Mayne), he must ride the stallion in a difficult cross-desert race in order to reclaim him. Five dozen of Morocco's top horsemen were recruited by the filmmakers for this race.

851 Blondie's Holiday

1947, Columbia, 61 minutes. Director: Abby Berlin. Producer: Burt Kelly. Screenplay: Constance Lee. Photography: Vincent Farrar. Editor: Jerome Thoms.

Cast: Penny Singleton, Arthur Lake, Larry Simms, Marjorie Kent, Jerome Cowan, Grant Mitchell, Sid Tomack, Eddie Acuff.

The usual shenanigans and mixups abound in this Blondie series entry, but the day is saved because Dagwood rescues a bank president's wife during a raid on a bookie joint.

852 Blue Blood

1951, Monogram, 72 minutes, Color. Director: Lew Landers. Producer: Ben Schwalb. Screenplay: W. Scott Darling. Photography: Gilbert Warrenton. Editor: Ray Livingston.

Cast: Bill Williams, Jane Nigh, Arthur Shields, Audrey Long, Harry Shannon, Lyle Talbot, William J. Tunnen, Harry Cheshire, Milton Kibbee.

A trainer discovers that the reason a horse keeps on losing at the track is its fear of the starter's red flag, so he tries to get the horse to overcome that handicap.

Comes the big race and the baddies have their jockey garbed in red. Oh, yes, there are also two women in love with the same man. Ho hum.

853 Blue Fire Lady

1978, Australian, Australian-International, 95 minutes, Color. Director: Ross Dimsey. Producer: Antony I. Ginnare. Screenplay: Bob Manumli. Photography: Vincent Monton. Editor: Tony Patterson.

Cast: Cathryn Harrison, Mark Holden, Peter Cummings, Marion Edward, Lloyd Cunnington, Anne Sutherland, Gary Waddell, John Wood.

The racehorse hates brutal trainer Cummings and will only let the heroine (Harrison) handle him. She, in the meantime, is in love with rock star Holden.

854 Blue Grass of Kentucky

1950, Monogram, 69 minutes, Color. Director: William Beaudine. Producer: Jeffrey Bernerd. Screenplay: W. Scott Darling. Photography: Gilbert Warrenton. Editor: Otho Lovering.

Cast: Bill Williams, Jane Nigh, Ralph Morgan, Robert Henry, Russell Hicks, Ted Hecht, Dick Foote, Jack Howard, Bill Terrell, Stephen S. Harrison, Pierre Watkin.

Williams refuses Nigh's marriage offers because she's the daughter of a millionaire. What he doesn't know, however, is that the horse he and dad Morgan have entered in the Kentucky Derby was sired by the champ owned by the girl's father.

855 The Bookmaker

1907, British, R.W. Paul, 140 feet. Director: J.H. Martin.

A bookie welshes on the bets after watching the race.

856 Boots Malone

1951, Columbia, 103 minutes. Director: William Dieterle. Producer-Screenplay: Milton Holmes. Photography: Charles Lawton, Jr. Editor: Al Clark.

Cast: William Holden, Johnny Stewart, Stanley Clements, Basil Ruysdael, Carl Redi, Ed Begley, Henry Morgan, Ann Lee, Whit Bissell.

The good-for-nothing jockey agent Boots Malone (Holden) befriends a neglected rich lad (Stewart) who hangs around the track. Strictly for the money, Holden strings him along by teaching him how to be a jockey.

Before long, as you have probably guessed by now, Holden forms a genuine attachment to the 15-year-old and bucks both gangsters and the boy's mother to try to make the kid's riding debut a success.

857 The Boy from Indiana

1950, Ventura-Eagle Lion, 66 minutes. Director: John Rawlins. Screenplay: Otto Englander. Photography: Jack Mackenzie. Editor: Merrill White.

Cast: Lon McAllister, Lois Butler, Billie Burke, George Cleveland, Victor Cox, Jerry Ambler, Allen Church, Jeanne Patterson.

Horse owner Cleveland, in desperate straits, dopes his quarter-miler, which manages to win several races. With wandering youth McAllister as his jockey, the horse wins the big race, with Cleveland's ranch on the line, despite being gored by a bull earlier.

858 Boy Woodburn

1922, British, George Clark Productions, 5,761-7,300 feet. Director-Screenplay: Guy Newall. Story: Alfred Olivant. Photography: H.I. Harris.

Cast: Guy Newall, Ivy Duke, A. Bromley Davenport, Mary Rorke, Cameron Carr, John Alexander, Charles Evemy, Douglas Munro.

A motherless colt is raised by a trainer's daughter to be the Grand National champ.

859 Bred in Old Kentucky

1926, R-C Pictures, 5,285 feet. Director: Eddie Dillon. Story: Louis Weadock, C.D. Lancaster. Photography: Phil Tannura.

Cast: Viola Dana, James Mason, Jerry Miley, Jed Prouty, Roy Laidlaw, Josephine Crowell.

A girl mortgages a Kentucky estate and bets all on her racehorse which is injured during a fixed race and has to be shot.

She falls in love with the wealthy horse owner (Miley) whose jockey ran into her horse; but when she discovers he had nothing to do with the incident she thwarts a scheme to substitute a lookalike during a race in which he has lot at stake.

860 Breezing Home

1937, Universal, 64 minutes. Director: Milton Carruth. Producer: Edmund Grainger. Screenplay: Charles Grayson, based on the story "I Hate Horses" by Finley Peter Dunne, Jr. and Philip Dunne. Photography: Gilbert Warrenton.

Cast: Binnie Barnes, William Gargan, Wendy Barrie, Raymond Walburn, Alma Druger, Alan Baxter, Willie Best, Michael Loring, Elisha Cook, Jr., Granville Bates, John Hamilton.

When a crooked gambler takes a thoroughbred named Galaxy, its trainer (Gargan) comes along. When the horse is injured during a fixed race, he accuses the beautiful lady (isn't there always one?) of the film of being in on it.

Everything is righted when the horse wins the next race, despite another attempt at fixing the outcome.

861 The Bride Wore Boots

1946, Paramount, 85 minutes. Director: Irving Pichel. Producer: Seton I. Miller. Screenplay: Dwight Mitchell Wiley, based on a play by Harry Segall. Photography: Stuart Thompson, Gordon Jennings. Editor: Ellsworth Hoagland.

Cast: Barbara Stanwyck, Robert Cummings, Robert Benchley, Diana Lynn, Patricia Knowles, Peggy Wood, Willie Best, Natalie Wood, Gregory Muradian, Mary Young.

Cummings is an author who hates horses with a passion. He has two problems: His wife (Stanwyck) runs a breeding farm; and one of the horses, Albert, has taken a fancy to him.

Through a series of antics, Cummings winds up riding Albert during the steeplechase finale and tries to stay in the saddle long enough for the horse to win.

862 Broadway Bill

1934, Columbia, 90 minutes. Director: Frank Capra. Scenario: Robert Riskin. Story: Mark Hellinger. Photography: Joseph Walker.

Cast: Warner Baxter, Myrna Loy, Walter Connolly, Helen Vinson, Douglas Dumbrille, Raymond Walburn, Lynne Overman, Clarence Muse, Frankie Darro.

Sure it's sentimental stuff; but in the hands of an expert cast and director Frank Capra, who would later make such films as **It's a Wonderful Life**, **Mr. Smith Goes to Washington** and **Mr. Deeds Goes to Town**, it's grand entertainment. Capra had hoped to get Clark Gable for the lead but couldn't.

Racehorse Broadway Bill's owner (Baxter) is broke and doesn't even have enough money to pay his entry fee. Baxter, who had married into a wealthy family, bolted over the social confinement.

The cards get stacked up even more as Baxter is jailed and his horse attached for an unpaid feed bill. Despite having been ill and his jockey paid off by gamblers, Broadway Bill still manages to win the big race but then drops dead.

Add some romance and you have a film successful enough to be remade in 1950 as **Riding High**.

863 By a Nose (aka **Photo Finish**)

1957, French, Rank, 90-100 minutes. Director: Norbert Carbonneaux. Screenplay: Carbonneaux, Albert Simenon. Photography: Roger Dormoy. Editor: Jacqueline Thiedot.

Cast: Fernand Gravey, Jean Richard, Louis de Funes, Jacques Duby, Darry Cowl, Max Revol, Micheline Dax.

A comedy about a hick who meets two con men at the racetrack.

864 By the Shortest of Heads

1915, British, Barker, 3,500 feet. Director: Bert Haldane. Story: Jack Hulcup.

Cast: George Formby, Jr., Jack Tessier, Moore Marriott, Jack Hulcup, Percy Manton.

The bastard son of nobility is adopted by a horse trainer and winds up winning the big race "by the shortest of heads."

865 The Calendar (aka **Bachelor's Folly**)

1931, British, Gainsborough-British Lion, 80 minutes. Director: T.H. Hunter. Producer: Michael Balcon. Screenplay: Angus MacPhail, Robert Stevenson, based on a play by Edgar Wallace. Photography: Bernard J. Knowles.

Cast: Herbert Marshall, Edna Best, Gordon Harker, Anne Grey, Nigel Bruce, Alfred Drayton, Allan Aynesworth, Leslie Perrins, Melville Cooper.

A down-and-out horse owner is banned from the track after being accused of deliberately losing a race. Instead of the butler being the villain, here the ex-convict helps his employer prove his innocence.

866 The Calendar

1948, British, Gainsborough,

80 minutes. Director: Arnold Crabtree. Producer: Anthony Darborough. Screenplay: Geoffrey Kerr, based on the play by Edgar Wallace. Photography: Reginald Wyer.

Cast: Greta Gynt, John McCallum, Raymond Lovell, Diana Dors, Sonia Holm, Leslie Dwyer, Charles Victor, Barry Jones, Felix Aylmer, Sydney King.

A remake of the 1931 version, here the bankrupt horse owner is proven innocent of any wrongdoing by a girl trainer.

867 Casey's Shadow

1978, Columbia, 110 minutes, Color. Director: Martin Ritt. Producer: Ray Stark. Screenplay: Carol Sobieski. Story: John McPhee. Photography: John A. Alonzo. Editor: Sidney Levin.

Cast: Walter Matthau, Alexis Smith, Robert Webber, Murray Hamilton, Andrew A. Rubin, Stephen Burns, Susan Myers, Michael Hershewe.

The All-American Futurity for quarter horses at Ruidoso, New Mexico, provides the backdrop for a poor Cajun family's battle agains the rich and powerful.

Lloyd Bourdelle (Matthau) is the Louisiana horse trainer with three motherless sons. The oldest (Rubin) serves as his father's assistant, the middle son (Burns) is a jockey and the youngest, Casey (Hershewe) is simply devoted to horses and becomes attached to the colt they raise.

The horse, named Casey's Shadow, soon attracts a lot of attention; but the family turns down offers by wealthy horse owners Smith and Hamilton. It also comes into conflict with brutal trainer Webber.

Despite a serious injury to the horse, it enters the big race against doctor's orders.

868 Chain Lightning

1922, Arrow Film Corp., 4,969 feet. Director-Producer: Ben Wilson. Scenario: J. Grubb Alexander, Agnes Parsons. Photography: Harry Gersted.

Cast: Norval MacGregor, Joseph W. Girard, William Carroll, Jack Dougherty, Ann Little.

A girl (Little) comes home from school only to find her horse, Chain Lightning, has been sold by her father because of financial troubles to another southern colonel. Her father, who's also ill, bets all his money on the horse to win the big race.

Through a chain of events, the girl winds up riding the horse to victory.

869 Champions

1984, Embassy Pictures, 115 minutes, Color. Director: John Irvin. Producer: Peter Shaw. Screenplay: Evan Jones, based on the novel "Champion's Story" by Bob Champion. Photography: Ronnie Taylor.

Cast: John Hurt, Edward Woodward, Jan Francis, Ben Johnson.

Here's the true story of how British jockey Bob Champion (Hurt) won his battle over cancer and then rode a crippled horse everyone had given up on to win the 1981 Grand National.

There's much graphic footage of Champion's treatment for cancer and how he went against medical advice to resume his career as a jockey.

He rescues a horse named Aldaniti from the scrap heap and enters it in England's big horse race.

870 Charlie Chan at the Race Track

1936, 20th Century-Fox, 70 minutes. Director: H. Bruce Humberstone. Adaptation: Robert Ellis, Helen Logan, Edward T. Lowe, based on a character created by Earl Derr Biggers. Photography: Harry Jackson.

Cast: Warner Oland, Keye Luke, Helen Wood, Thomas Beck,

Alan Dinehart, Gavin Muir, Gloria Roy, Jonathan Hale, Frankie Darro, G.P. Huntley, Jr.

A shipboard murder, a camera that shoots darts, a switch of horses and assorted other skullduggery all are solved by the great Chinese detective by the time the final reel unspools.

871 Checkers

1937, 20th Century-Fox, 79 minutes. Director: H. Bruce Humberstone. Producer: John Stone. Screenplay: Lynn Root, Frank Fenton, Robert Chapin, Karen DeWolf. Photography: Daniel B. Clark.

Cast: Jane Withers, Stuart Erwin, Una Merkel, Marvin Stephens, Minor Watson, Francis Ford, June Carlson, Andrew Tombes, John Harrington, Spencer Charters.

If this is a horse racing film, there's a mortgage at stake. This time it's Merkel battling a stonehearted banker as Withers and Erwin nurse a horse back to health.

The jockey must escape from jail in time for the big race.

872 Cheyenne

1929, First National Pictures, 5,944 feet. Director: Albert Rogell. Scenario: Marion Jackson. Story: Bennett Cohen. Photography: Frank Good. Editor: Fred Allen.

Cast: Ken Maynard, Gladys McConnell, James Bradbury, Jr., William Franey, Charles Whittaker.

A rodeo star helps out a girl who's involved with horse racing because her dad is in deep financial trouble in this oater.

873 The Chorus Lady

1924, Producers Distributing Corp., 6,020 feet. Director: Ralph Ince. Adaptation: Bradley King, based on a play by James Grant. Photography: Glen Gano.

Cast: Margaret Livingston, Alan Roscoe, Virginia Lee Corbin, Lillian Elliott, Lloyd Ingraham, Mervyn LeRoy, Philo McCullough, Eve Southern.

A prize horse, blinded in a stable blaze, wins the big race anyway after the horse's owner postponed his impending marriage.

Comic misunderstandings abound when the hero (Roscoe) finds his girl friend (Livingston) with a well-known gambler (McCullough).

874 Colleen

1927, Fox Film Corp., 5,301 feet. Director: Frank O'Connor. Screenplay: Randall H. Faye. Photography: George Schneiderman.

Cast: Charles Morton, Madge Bellamy, Sammy Cohen, Tom Maguire, Sidney Franklin, J. Farrell MacDonald, Marjorie Beebe, Ted McNamara.

A poor Irish lad loves a rich girl in this tale of the Old Sod and horse racing.

875 Come On George

1939, British, ATP, 88 minutes. Director: Anthony Kimmins. Producer: Jack Kitchin (sic). Screenplay: Anthony Kimmins, Leslie Arliss, Val Valentine. Photography: Ronald Neame.

Cast: George Formby, Pat Kirkwood, Joss Ambler, Ronald Shiner, Cyril Raymond, George Hayes, George Carney, Syd Crossely, C. Denier Warren, Gibb McLaughlin.

Madball British comic Formby is an ice cream vendor who through a series of misadventures winds up as a stableboy to a temperamental racehorse which bears a resemblance to him.

After defeating the ever-present racetrack mobsters, he rides the horse in the big race to the predictable result, but not without a few laughs along the way.

876 The County Fair

1932, Monogram, 67 minutes. Director: Louis King. Producer: I.E. Chadwick. Story: Roy Fitzroy.

Cast: Hobart Bosworth, Marion Shilling, Ralph Ince, William Collier,

Jr., Snowflake, Kit Guard, Otto Hoffman, Arthur Millett, Thomas R. Quinn, Edward Kane

The usual nonsense about a horse's owners struggling to raise enough money for the big race and coming up against gangsters before riding to victory.

877 County Fair

1937, Monogram, 71 minutes. Director: Howard Bretherton. Producer: E.B. Derr. Screenplay: John T. Neville. Photography: Arthur Martinelli. Editor: Donald Barralt.

Cast: John Arledge, Mary Lou Lender, J. Farrell MacDonald, Fuzzy Knight, Jimmy Butler, Harry Worth, William Hunter.

A jockey is framed by gangsters when his horse is doped and winds up being suspended. He romances a farmer's daughter and enters her horse, Rainbow, in the big race to--surprise, surprise--help pay off the mortgage on the farm.

878 County Fair

1950, Monogram, 76 minutes, Color. Director: William Beaudine. Producer: Jeffrey Bernard. Screenplay: W. Scott Darling. Photography: Gilbert Warrenton. Editor: Richard Heermance.

Cast: Rory Calhoun, Jane Nigh, Florence Bates, Warren Douglas, Raymond Hatton, Emory Parnell.

Give the filmmakers a "B" for at least trying something a little different as horse owners and track personnel conspire to allow a worn-out harness horse to win one final victory.

879 Crazy Over Horses (aka **Win, Place and Show**)

1951, Monogram, 65 minutes. Director: William Beaudine. Producer: Jerry Thomas. Screenplay: Tim Ryan, Max Adams. Photography: Marcel Le Picard.

Cast: Leo Gorcey, Huntz Hall, Gloria Sanders, William Benedict, Bernard Gorcey, David Gorcey, Bennie Bartlett, Allen Jenkins, Tim Ryan.

The usual Bowery Boys hijinks abound as they're given a racehorse in payment for a bill and come up against some hoodlums.

880 Cruiskeen Lawn

1922, Irish, Irish Photoplays, 4,500 feet. Director-Scenario: John MacDonagh. Producer: Norman Whitten.

Cast: Tom Moran, Kathleen Armstrong, Jimmy O'Day, Fred Jeffs, Chris Sylvester, Fay Sargent.

Despite being doped by a rival, a poor squire's horse manages to win the big race.

881 The Curate at the Races

1909, British, Hepworth, 575 feet. Director: Lewin Fitzhamon.

Cast: Harry Buss.

A drunken curate gets into some trouble with a bookie.

882 Dandy Dick

1935, British, Wardour, 75 minutes. Director: William Beaudine. Producer: Walter C. Mycroft. Screenplay: Frank Miller, William Beaudine, Clifford Grey, Will Hay, based on a play by Sir Arthur Wing Pinero. Photography: Jack Parker.

Cast: Will Hay, Edmond Knight, Nancy Burne, Davy Burnaby, Mignon O'Doherty, Syd Crosseley, Wally Patch.

The village vicar needs funds to repair the church spire and opportunity knocks when his sister, the wife of a jockey, brings home a racehorse. Risking all he has on the horse, he finds himself accused of doping before all the complications are sorted out.

883 David Harum

1934, Fox Film Corp., 82 minutes. Director: James Cruze. Adaptation: Walter Woods, based on a novel by Edward Westcott. Photography: Hal Mohr. Editor: Jack Murray.

Cast: Will Rogers, Marie Dressler, Evelyn Venable, Kent Taylor, Stepin Fetchit, Noah Beery, Roger Imhof, Frank Melton, Charles Middleton.

As with any film starring Will Rogers, it's not so much the plot that counts but the great American humorist-philosopher's personality which makes the film.

He and deacon Middleton cheat each other on horse deals until he winds up with a horse everyone thinks is a loser.

It turns out the horse will respond only to music, so the film's heroine gets the band to play during the trotting race finale and the horse pays off 10-1 on a $4,500 bet.

884 A Day at the Races

1937, Metro Goldwyn Mayer, 109-111 minutes. Director: Sam Wood. Producers: Irving Thalberg, Max Siegel. Screenplay: Robert Pirosh, George Seaton, George Oppenheimer. Photography: Joseph Ruttenberg. Editor: Frank Hall.

Cast: The Marx Brothers, Allan Jones, Maureen O'Sullivan, Margaret Dumont, Douglas Dumbrille, Esther Muir, Sig Rumann, Vivien Fay, Frank Darro, Charles Trowbridge, Carole Landis.

Not that the plot ever really matters in any Marx Brothers comedy, but Groucho is Dr. Hugo Z. Hackenbush, a horse doctor who becomes head of the Standish Sanitarium.

Needless to say, by the time the Marx Brothers have finished wreaking havoc at the racetrack and at the sanitarium, everyone involved is ready to be committed.

The film's most famous sequence is when Groucho, who's trying to place a bet at the track, meets ice cream vendor Chico, who stops him from placing a bet on Sun-Up. Telling him the horse is the worst on the track, he sells him a "horses code" for $1. Actually, the code was free, but there was a $1 printing charge.

When Groucho "can't make heads or tails" out of the code, Chico goes back to his cart and instead of pulling out some "tootsie fruitsie" ice cream, comes up with a master code book, which is free except for a "delivery charge."

When Groucho still can't make sense out of the code, Chico sells him a set of breeder's guides at $1 each or a "bargain" rate of four for $5. While Groucho is going through his ever-growing stack of books, Chico places a bet on Sun-Up.

By the time Chico is finished, Groucho has ten more books. Finally ready to bet, Groucho learns that the race has already been won by Sun-Up at 40-1.

Dumping his books into Chico's ice cream cart as the con man counts his winnings, Groucho starts hawking ice cream the way Chico did.

885 The Day the Bookies Wept

1939, RKO Radio Pictures, 53 minutes. Director: Leslie Goodwins. Producer: Robert Sisk. Screenplay: Bert Granet, George Jeske. Story: Daniel Fuchs. Photography: Jack Mackenzie.

Cast: Joe Penner, Betty Grable, Richard Lane, Tom Kennedy, Thurston Hall, Bernadene Hayes, Carole Hughes, Jack Arnold.

Some taxi drivers pool their money to buy a racehorse named Hiccup, who as you may have guessed is an alcoholic.

On the day of the big race, he wins after drinking a full load of beer.

886 A Dead Certainty

1920, British, Broadwest, 4,494 feet. Producer: Walter West. Screenplay: P.L. Mannock, based on a novel by Nat Gould.

Cast: Gregory Scott, Poppy Wyndham, Cameron Carr, Harry Royston, Mary Masters, Wallace Bosco.

The boy friend of an evil

nobleman's niece comes under a lot of pressure to lose the big horse race.

887 Derby Day

1923, Pathe, 2 reels. Director: Robert F. McGowan. Producer-Screenplay: Hal Roach.

After getting into the racetrack for free, Our Gang is inspired to hold a derby of their own for a $5 purse with a mule, cow, goat and dog as the entrants. It doesn't really matter, however, as the whole things turns into a real circus with Farina winning on his tricycle.

888 Derby Day

1952, British, British Lion, 84 minutes. Director: Herbert Wilcox. Screenplay: John Baines. Photography: Max Greene. Editor: Bill Lewthwaite.

Cast: Anna Neagle, Michael Wilding, Googie Withers, John McCallum, Peter Graves, Suzanne Cloutier, Gordon Harker.

Divided into three main segments, **Derby Day** follows three pairs of people as they spend a day at the track.

The first story involves murder, with the couple being arrested just as they're collecting their winnings; the second involves a servant and a film star; and the third a man and woman who have both lost loved ones.

889 Devil on Horseback

1954, British, British Lion, 88 minutes. Director: Cyril Frankel. Screenplay: Neil Paterson, Montagu Slater, Geoffrey Orme. Photography: Denny Densham. Editor: Sidney Stone.

Cast: Googie Withers, John McCallum, Jeremy Spenser, Meredith Edwards, Liam Redmond, Sam Kydd, Malcolm Knight, Vic Wise.

A conceited young jockey (Spenser) learns the hard way that winning the race isn't everything from former jockey Redmond after the lad causes the death of one of his mounts.

890 Dime with a Halo

1963, Metro Goldwyn Mayer, 94 minutes. Director: Boris Sagal. Producer-Screenplay: Laslo Vadnay, Hans Wilhelm. Photography: Philip H. Lathrop. Editor: Ralph E. Winters.

Cast: Rafael Lopez, Barbara Luna, Roger Mobley, Paul Langton, Robert Carricart, Manuel Padilla, Larry Domasin, Tony Maxwell, Vito Scotti, Jay Adler.

Five young Tijuana boys pool their money every week to bet $2 at the racetrack. Short of cash one week, they steal a dime from a church poorbox.

Their horse wins and they're due over $80,000, but they have difficulty finding the adult who places their bets for them. When he's found, he dies of a heart attack; and the winning ticket flies away into the wind.

The lads return the dime to the poorbox.

891 The Dixie Handicap

1925, Metro Goldwyn Mayer, 6,509 feet. Director: Reginald Barker. Adaptation: Waldemar Young, based on a **Redbook Magazine** story by Gerald Beaumont. Photography: Percy Hilburn. Editor: Daniel J. Gray.

Cast: Frank Keenan, Claire Trevor, Lloyd Hughes, Otto Hoffman, John Sainpolis, Otis Harland, Ruth King, Joseph Morrison, Edward Martindel, William Quirk.

A southern judge's daughter (Trevor) is brought up in luxury, never knowing of her father's desperate financial condition. The judge (Keenan) places all his hopes on a horse named Dixie, but soon is forced to sell it and eventually loses his home and starts drinking heavily.

The judge's friend (Hughes) buys Dixie after it's injured during a race and nurses the colt back to health so he can enter it in the Kentucky Derby. The colt, of course, wins, the judge's estate is restored and the daughter and the judge's friend get married.

892 Don't be a Dummy

1932, British, First National, 54 minutes. Director: Frank Richardson. Producer: Irving Asher. Screenplay: Brock Williams.

Cast: George Harris, William Austin, Garry Marsh, Muriel Angelus, Mike Johnson, Sally Stewart, Katherine Watts, Charles Castella.

A barred racehorse owner and his jockey clear their names when they pose as a ventriloquist and his dummy and overhear the real crooks tell how they framed the pair.

893 Don't Bet on Love

1933, Universal, 62 minutes. Director-Screenplay: Murray Roth.

Cast: Lew Ayres, Ginger Rogers, Charles Grapewin, Shirley Grey, Merna Kennedy, Tom Dugan, Robert E. O'Conner.

A plumber (Ayres) experiences fantastic luck at the track even though his girl friend (Rogers) can't stand gambling. She calls off the wedding after she learns the honeymoon is slated to be in Saratoga. He goes on to pick 26 winners in a row.

894 Down the Stretch

1927, Universal, 6,910 feet. Director: King Baggot. Screenplay: Curtis Benton, based on the story "The Money Rider" by Gerald Beaumont in **Redbook Magazine.** Photography: John Stumar.

Cast: Robert Agnew, Marian Nixon, Virginia True Boardman, Ward Crane, Lincoln Plummer, Jack Daugherty, Ben Hall, Otis Harlan, Edna Gregory.

A youth (Agnew) follows the footsteps of his father as a jockey and enjoys success until he's injured in an accident.

When he returns to work, he's overweight; and his brutal trainer (Plummer) forces him to diet until he's so weak he can hardly stand. After winning the big race, he faints and the trainer is fired, with the lad taking his place.

895 Down the Stretch

1936, Warner Brothers, 58 minutes. Director: Williams Clemens. Screenplay: William Jacobs. Photography: Arthur Todd.

Cast: Mickey Rooney, Patricia Ellis, Dennis Moore, William Best, Gordon Hart, Frank Faylen, Charles Wilson.

Rooney plays the son of a well-known jockey who's the only one able to ride a temperamental horse. When he falls in with bad elements, he winds up being banned at American racetracks, but gets another chance and proves his mettle in the English Derby.

896 Down Under Donovan

1922, British, Stoll, 5,900 feet. Director: Harry Lambert. Scenario: Forbes Dawson, based on a novel by Edgar Wallace.

Cast: Cora Goffin, W.H. Benham, Bertram Parnell, William Lugg, W.H. Willits, Peggy Surtees, Cecil Rutledge.

Despite the shenanigans of a rival, an ex-convict's horse wins that inevitable big race.

897 Dream of the Race-Track Fiend

1905, American Mutoscope and Biograph Co., 8 minutes. Photography: G.W. Bitzer.

A drunk falls asleep and dreams of winning a fortune at the race-track and then entertaining his friends on a yacht. He falls overboard and wakes up in his bathtub.

898 Dry Rot

1955, British, Remus, 87 minutes. Director: Maurice Elvey. Producer: Jack Clayton. Screenplay: John Chapman, based on his play. Photography: Arthur Grant.

Cast: Ronald Shiner, Brian Rix, Peggy Mount, Sidney James, Joan Sims, Heather Sears, Miles Malleson.

Comedy about some bookies who face disaster if the favorite wins, so they try to switch him with a doped ringer.

899 Easy Come, Easy Go

1947, Paramount, 77 minutes. Director: John Farrow. Producer: Kenneth Margowan. Screenplay: Francis Edwards Faragon, John McNulty, Anne Froehlick. Photography: Daniel L. Fapp. Editor: Thomas Scott.

Cast: Barry Fitzgerald, Diana Lynn, Sonny Tufts, Dick Foran, Frank McHugh, Allen Jenkins, John Litel, Arthur Shields, Frank Faylen, James Burke, George Cleveland.

Pleasant enough minor film fare about an elderly Irishman (Fitzgerald) whose only real pleasure in life is betting on the horses, so much so that he has a long line of creditors and gets in the way of his daughter's love life.

900 Educated Evans

1936, British, Warner Brothers, 86 minutes. Director: William Beaudine. Producer: Irving Asher. Screenplay: Frank Launder, Robert Edmunds, based on a novel by Edgar Wallace.

Cast: Max Miller, Nancy O'Neil, Clarice Mayne, Albert Whelan, Hal Walters, Robert English, Percy Walsh, Julien Mitchell, George Merritt.

A track tipster rises to be trainer for a stable owner.

901 The Electric Horseman

1979, Columbia-Universal, 121 minutes, Color. Director: Sydney Pollack. Producer: Ray Stark. Screenplay: Robert Garland. Photography: Owen Rolzman. Editor: Sheldon Kahn.

Cast: Robert Redford, Jane Fonda, Valerie Perrine, Willie Nelson, John Saxon, Nicholas Coster, Allan Arbus, Wilford Brimley, Will Hare, Basil Hoffman, Timothy Scott.

Sonny (Redford) is an alcoholic former rodeo star who has sold his soul to promote a horrible product called Ranch Breakfast. He's not above making himself something akin to a riding neon sign.

When he sees a prize racehorse named Rising Star being humiliated and mistreated as a special attraction in Las Vegas, it's too much for him. He kidnaps the horse and begins a long trek to turn it loose in Utah. He's accompanied by a woman reporter (Fonda).

The Electric Horseman was a rare co-production between two major studios.

902 Esther Waters

1948, British, GFD-Rank, 108 minutes. Directors: Ian Dalrymple, Peter Proud. Screenplay: Michael Gordon, William Rose. Photography: C. Pennington-Richards, H.E. Fowle. Editor: Brereton Porter.

Cast: Dirk Bogarde, Cyril Cusack, Kathleen Ryan, Alexander Parker, Fay Compton, Ivor Bernard, Margaret Diamond, Mary Clare.

Get our your handkerchiefs for Victorian soap opera of the highest order. A pretty young maid falls in love with a groom who loves to gamble, but he (Bogarde) runs away with another woman.

Years of misery follow as she (Ryan) has his child and must board him out. Finding her lover again, she convinces him to marry her for the sake of their son. However, he gambles away all their money on horses and dies, leaving the family again in poverty.

The film's Derby Day sequence is climaxed by the victory of Fred Archer (Parker), the first American to win it.

903 Eyes of Fate

1933, British, Sound City,

67 minutes. Director: Ivar Campbell. Producer: Norman Louden. Story: Holloway Horn.

Cast: Valerie Hobson, Allen Jeayes, Terrence De Marney, Faith Bennett, Nellie Bowman, O.B. Clarence, Tony Halfpenny, Edwin Ellis.

A bookie cleans up at the track by reading the results in tomorrow's newspaper until he reads about his own death.

The much more well-known **It Happened Tomorrow,** made in 1944 with Dick Powell, followed the same basic plotline.

904 Fast Companions

1932, Universal, 71 minutes. Director: Kurt Neumann. Story: Gerald Beaumont. Photography: Arthur Edeson.

Cast: Tom Brown, James Gleason, Maureen O'Sullivan, Andy Devine, Mickey Rooney.

Gleason and jockey Brown are racing con men who have a special kind of racket. They build up a horse by having it win some minor races; and then when the suckers place all their money, they hold the horse back in the big races.

Along comes an orphan (Rooney) into their lives; and as so often happens in racetrack movies, their personalities change and they straighten themselves out.

Universal dusted off the script in 1936, changed the sport from horse racing to boxing, and filmed **Conflict** with John Wayne as the crooked boxer (see Boxing chapter).

905 Fast Company

1953, Metro Goldwyn Mayer, 67 minutes. Director: John Sturges. Producer: Henry Berman. Screenplay: William Roberts. Photography: Harold Lipstein. Editor: Joseph Dervim.

Cast: Polly Bergen, Howard Keel, Nina Foch, Marjorie Main, Robert Burton, Horace McMahon, Sig Arno, Iron Eyes Cody, Joaquin Garay.

Keel, who owns a no-good nag of his own, is also caring for a horse which has been willed to Bergen. He wants the horse for himself, so he makes sure the horse keeps on losing in an attempt to get her to sell him cheaply.

Bergen finds out about the scheme and starts racing the horse herself; but never fear, she and Keel ultimately get together in this track comedy.

906 Father Tom

1921, Playgoers Pictures, 5 reels. Director: John B. O'Brien. Scenario-Editor: Rodney Hickok. Story: Carl Krusada. Photography: Lawrence E. Williams.

Cast: Tom Wise, James Hill, May Kitson, Myra Brooks, James Wallace, Ray Allen, Harry Boler, Alexander Clark.

This could be subtitled **Father Tom Knows Best** as the good reverend (Wise) does it all. However, he irks the mother of Bob Wellington (Clark) when he acts as matchmaker between him and a pretty orphan girl who owns a horse.

Mrs. Wellington (Allen) threatens to refuse to renew the mortgage on the church, so the two young lovers enter the horse in a race to raise enough money for dear Father Tom. Villainy is afoot as the horse is kidnapped, but none other than Father Tom rescues it in time.

907 Father's Derby Trip (aka **Father and the Bookmaker**)

1906, British, Cricks and Sharp, 385 feet. Director: Tom Green.

Father wins, but the bookie welshes on the bet.

908 The Favourite for the Jamaica Cup

1913, British, B&C, 948 feet. Director: Charles Raymond.

Cast: Dorothy Foster, Percy

Moran, John Glover, George Melville, Harry Lorraine.

The villainous gambler will stop at nothing to try to kill the horse in the title, including wrecking the entire train.

909 Fighting Chance

1955, Republic, 70 minutes. Director: William Witney.

Cast: Rod Cameron, Ben Cooper, Julie London, Taylor Holmes, Howard Wendell, Mel Welles, Bob Steele, Paul Birch, Carl Milletaire, Rodolfo Hoyos, Jr., John Damler.

It's the old romantic triangle again with a horse trainer and a jockey both in love with Julie London.

910 Fighting Thoroughbreds

1939, Republic, 65 minutes. Director: Sidney Salkow. Producer: Armand Schaefer. Screenplay: Wellyn Totman. Photography: Jack Marta.

Cast: Ralph Byrd, Mary Carlisle, Robert Allen, Gabby Hayes, Marvin Stephens, Charles Wilson, Kenne Duncan, Victor Kiljan, Eddie Brian.

Horse Romeo romances Horse Juliet. A Kentucky Derby winner woos a female horse owned by a bitter rival and they have a son which grows up to be a Derby winner himself.

911 Flying Fifty (aka **The Flying Fifty-Five**)

1939, British, Admiral, 72 minutes. Director: Reginald Denham. Producer: Victor M. Greene. Screenplay: Victor M. Greene, Vernon Clancy, Kenneth Horne, based on a novel by Edgar Wallace.

Cast: Derrick de Marney, Nancy Burne, Marius Goring, John Warwick, Peter Gawthorne, D.A. Clarke-Smith, Amy Veness, Ronald Shiner, Billy Gray.

The son of a horse owner, posing as a stablehand, is blackmailed to lose the big race.

912 The Flying Fifty-Five

1924, British, Stoll, 4,900 feet. Director-Screenplay: A.E. Coleby.

Cast: Lionelle Howard, Stephanie Stephens, Brian B. Lemon, Lionel D'Aragon, Frank Perfitt, Bert Darley.

An earlier version of the Edgar Wallace story, although with a slightly different title, finds a nobleman posing as a stableboy and riding a horse to victory when the villain injures the real jockey.

913 The Flying Horseman

1926, Fox Film Corp., 4,971 feet. Director: Orville O. Dull. Scenario: Gertrude Orr, based on "Dark Rosaleen" by Max Brand in **Country Gentlemen Magazine.** Photography: Joe August.

Cast: Buck Jones, Gladys McConnell, Bruce Covington, Harvey Clark, Silver Buck, Walter Percival, Hank Mann.

Boy, is Ridley (Percival) ever the villain in this horse racing western. Not only does he hate kids, he frames the hero (Jones) for murder and plots to get a ranch and the owner's daughter by foul means.

Naturally, Our Hero escapes from jail in time for the big race and saves the ranch from ruin. It seems that there's always a mortgage hanging in the balance of a movie horse race.

914 Follow That Horse!

1960, British, Seven Arts, 80 minutes. Director: Alan Bromly. Producer: Thomas Clyde. Screenplay: Alfred Shaughnessy, based on the novel "Photo Finish" by Howard Mason. Photography: Norman Warwick. Editor: Gerald Turney-Smith.

Cast: David Tomlinson, Cecil Parker, Richard Wattis, Mary Peach, Dora Bryan, Raymond Huntley, Sam Kydd, George Pravda, John Welsh, Peter Copley.

A bumbling British civil servant

(Tomlinson) flirts with a racehorse owner's daughter when he should be paying attention to the physicist he's accompanying to a NATO conference.

The scientist is trying to get out of the country with some microfilm; but instead of getting into the getaway van, he gets into a horse van, where a racehorse swallows the microfilm after it falls into the hay.

From there on, it's a frantic scramble between the call of nature, Communist spies and Tomlinson to retrieve the film.

915 For the Love of Mike

1960, 20th Century-Fox, 87 minutes, Color. Director-Producer: George Sherman. Screenplay: D.D. Beauchamp. Photography: Alex Philips. Editor: Frederick Smith.

Cast: Richard Basehart, Arthur Shields, Red Allen, Armando Silvestre, Elsa Cardenas, Michael Steckler, Danny Bravo, Stuart Erwin.

A young Indian boy pulls his quarter horse through all kinds of hardships, including a threat from a mountain lion, to win the race and help pay for the church.

916 A Fortune at Stake

1918, British, Broadwest, 6,500 feet. Director-Producer: Walter West. Story: Nat Gould.

Cast: Violet Hopson, Gerald Ames, Edward O'Neill, James Lindsey, Gwynne Herbert, Windham Guise, Tom Coventry.

The eternal triangle looms with a jockey falling in love with the wife of a nobleman.

917 The Frame-Up

1937, Columbia, 59 minutes. Director: D. Ross Lederman. Story: Richard E. Wormser. Adaptation: Harold Shumate. Photography: Benjamin Kline.

Cast: Paul Kelly, Jacqueline Wells, George McKay, Robert E. O'Connor, Raphael Bennett, Wade Boteler, Edward Earle, C. Montague Shaw, John Tyrrell.

A track detective is an unwilling accessory in a plan to cheat the track but uses his wits to get the crooks. There are two major racing sequences.

It all concerns the switching of a horse named Red Rodger.

918 Francis Goes to the Races

1951, Universal, 88 minutes. Director: Arthur Lubin. Producer: Leonard Goldstein. Screenplay: Oscar Brodney, David Stern. Photography: Irving Glassberg. Editor: Milton Carruth.

Cast: Donald O'Connor, Piper Laurie, Cecil Kellaway, Jesse White, Barry Kelly, Hayden Rorke, Vaughn Taylor, Larry Keating, Peter Brocco, Don Beddoe, George Webster.

Where better to get a horse racing tip than from the horse's mouth? And if your best friend is a talking mule, so much the better.

That's the situation in this first sequel to the original **Francis** as Peter Stirling (O'Connor) goes to work with a horse breeder.

When gangsters take over the ranch, Francis (voice supplied by Chill Wills) talks to his horse friends and gives his pal a list of winners to help raise some money to bail out the place. When Stirling obtains a horse which seems to have a inferiority complex, good reliable Francis turns psychiatrist to straighten her out so she can win the big race.

919 From Hell to Heaven

1933, Paramount, 67 minutes. Director: Eric C. Kenton. Adaptation: Percy Heath, Sidney Buchman, based on a play by Lawrence Hazard. Photography: Henry Sharp.

Cast: Carole Lombard, Jack Oakie, Adrienne Ames, David Manners, Sidney Blackmer, Verna Hillie, James C. Eagles.

Racing characters of all types and descriptions descend

upon a hotel at a racing resort in this **Grand Hotel** imitation.

There's the stable owner down to his last dollars and desperately needing a win, a jockey who's been threatened, a couple trying to win at the track so they can return what the husband embezzled from his job and a number of other characters.

920 The Galloping Major

1951, British, International Film Distributors, 82 minutes. Director: Henry Cornelius. Screenplay: Cornelius, Monja Danischewsky. Photography: Stanley Pavey. Editor: Geoffrey Foot.

Cast: Basil Radford, Jimmy Hanley, Janette Scott, A.E. Matthews, Rene Ray, Hugh Griffith, Joyce Grenfell, Sidney James.

A retired army officer, now an impoverished owner of a pet shop, gets 300 people to pay one pound apiece and purchase a horse to enter the Grand National. After a series of complications, the horse manages to win.

921 The Gambling Sex

1932, Freuler, 60 minutes. Director: Fred Newmeyer. Story: F. McGrew Willis. Photography: Edward Kull. Editor: Fred Bain.

Cast: Grant Withers, Ruth Hall, Baston Williams, John St. Polis, Jean Porter, Jimmy Eagles.

With racing scenes set against the mountains of Miami, Florida (don't blame us—we didn't film this. It's not our fault all the racing scenes have mountains in the background), a rich girl learns the value of money once she starts gambling it away on the horses.

922 A Game of Chance

1932, British, Equity British, 65 minutes. Director: Charles Barnett. Story: John F. Argyle.

Cast: John F. Argyle, Margaret DeLane, Jack Marriott, Eileen Lord, Thomas Moss.

A trainer comes in conflict with a crooked bookie.

923 Garrison's Finish

1923, Allied Producers and Distributors, 7,898 feet. Director: Arthur Rosson. Screenplay: Elmer Harris, based on a novel by William B.M. Ferguson. Photography: Harold Rosson.

Cast: Jack Pickford, Madge Bellamy, Charles A. Stevenson, Tom Guise, Ethel Grey Terry, Lydia Knott, Clarence Burton.

With actual footage from the Kentucky Derby spliced in, this deals with a jockey who's suspended after being framed by the baddie and who gets amnesia during a fight. There's also the usual barn fire.

Our Hero gets a job with a colonel (what else?), saves his life from the same baddie who framed him, rescues a kidnapped horse and enters the Kentucky Derby. Guess where he finishes?

924 Garry Owen

1920, British, Welsh-Pearson, 5,900 feet. Director-Screenplay: George Pearson. Story: H. DeVere Stacpoole.

Cast: Fred Groves, Hugh E. Wright, Moyna McGill, Bertram Burleigh, Arthur Cleave, Alec Thompson.

A widower winds up winning the English Derby and the hand of his daughter's governess.

925 Gentleman at Heart

1941, 20th Century-Fox, 67 minutes. Director: Ray McCarey. Producer: Walter Morosco. Screenplay: Lee Loeb, Harold Buchman. Story: Paul Hervey Fox. Photography: Charles Clarke. Editor: J. Watson Webb.

Cast: Cesar Romero, Carole Landis, Milton Berle, J. Carrol Naish, Jerome Cowan, Elisha Cook, Jr., Kane Richmond, Matt McHugh, Richard Derr, Rose Hobart.

When successful bookie Romero meets the beautiful manager of an art shop (Landis), he's determined to get some culture, so he takes over Berle's art gallery in payment of a racing debt.

To his surprise, he finds that the art world has the same number of shady characters as the track world.

926 Gentleman from Dixie

1941, Monogram, 61 minutes. Director: Al Herman. Producer: Edward Finney. Screenplay: Fred Myton. Photography: Marcel Le Picard. Editor: Fred Bain.

Cast: Jack LaRue, Marian Marsh, Clarence Muse, Mary Ruth, John Holland, Herbert Rawlinson, Joe Hernandez.

A man who was framed gets out of prison and becomes a race-horse trainer, but he still gets the opportunity for revenge on the one who railroaded him and to fall in love.

927 Gentleman from Louisiana

1936, Republic, 67 minutes. Director: Irving Pichel. Producer: Nat Levine. Screenplay: Gordon Rigby, Joseph Fields. Photography: Ernest Miller, Jack Marta.

Cast: Eddie Quillan, Charles Sale, Charlotte Henry, Marjorie Gateson, John Miljan, Pierre Watkin, Snub Pollard, John Kelly.

Set in the days of the Great John L. and Diamond Jim Brady, an apprentice jockey climbs the ladder to success despite the machinations of the villains and an accident during an important race.

928 The Gentleman Rider (aka **Hearts and Saddles)**

1919, British, 5,000 feet. Director-Producer: Walter West.

Cast: Violet Hopson, Stewart Rome, Gregory Scott, Cameron Carr, Violet Elliott.

All the villainy in England can't stop Our Hero from winning the big race on his girl's horse.

929 A Girl in Every Port

1952, RKO Radio Pictures, 86 minutes. Director-Screenplay: Chester Erskine. Producers: Irwin Allen, Irving Cummings, Jr. Story: Frederick Hazlitt Brennan. Photography: Nicholas Musuraca. Editor: Ralph Dawson.

Cast: Groucho Marx, William Bendix, Marie Wilson, Don DeFore, Dee Hartford, Gene Lockhart, George E. Stone, Rodney Wooten, Percy Helton, Hanley Stafford, Teddy Hart.

Marx and Bendix are veteran sailors whose files on their antics take up more space than the documents on World War II. When Bendix comes into an inheritance, he's warned by Groucho that "they sell sailors elephants" (the name of the story on which the movie is based), but the sailor is conned anyway into buying a nag with sore ankles.

At first, Groucho is interested only in helping his pal get his money back; but when they learn the horse has a healthy twin which is owned by screwball carhop Wilson, the comic antics get complicated.

Hiding the twin horses on ship, they become involved with gangsters, saboteurs, an admiral's niece and others, and wind up riding both twins in the same race to the befuddlement of the track announcer.

930 Glory

1956, RKO Radio Pictures, 99 minutes, Color. Director-Producer: David Butler. Screenplay: Peter Milne. Story: Gene Markey. Photography: Wilford M. Cline. Editor: Irene Morra.

Cast: Margaret O'Brien, Walter Brennan, John Lupton, Byron Palmer, Charlotte Greenwood, Lisa Davis, Gus Schilling, Hugh Sanders, Walter Baldwin, Harry Tyler.

Child star Margaret is grown-up here and gets to sing three songs for her orchestra. She and Greenwood operate their Kentucky racing stable on a shoestring budget.

Their prize horse, Glory,

doesn't earn enough money to pay for feed, let alone the fee for the Kentucky Derby, so the pair's friends at the track all pitch in.

931 Going Places

1939, Warner Brothers, 84 minutes. Director: Ray Enright. Producer: Hal B. Wallis. Screenplay: Sig Herzig, Jerry Wald, Maurice Leo. Story: Victor Mapes, William Collier, Jr.

Cast: Dick Powell, Anita Louise, Louis Armstrong, Ronald Reagan, Allen Jenkins.

Powell is a horse-shy sporting goods salesman who through a series of circumstances is mistaken for a well-known rider and winds up winning a big race.

932 Gold Heels

1924, Fox Film Corp., 6,020 feet. Director: William S. Van Dyke. Scenario: John Stone, Frederic Chapin, based on "Checkers: A Hard Luck Story" by Henry Martyn Blossom. Photography: Arthur Todd.

Cast: Robert Agnew, Peggy Shaw, William Norton Bailey, Harry Tracey, James Douglas, Lucien Littlefield, Carl Stockdale, Fred Butler.

Two penniless racetrack characters come to a small town, where one of them (Agnew) gets a job in a store owned by a man who also owns an over-the-hill horse named Gold Heels.

He buys the horse and gets it back into shape. Meanwhile, the store owner's daughter (Shaw) has raised money for some orphans, but it's stolen and Our Hero is jailed; but you don't think he's still in there by the time the race rolls around, do you?

933 Golden Hoofs

1941, 20th Century-Fox, 68 minutes. Director: Lynn Shores. Producers: Walter Morosco, Ralph Dietrich. Screenplay: Ben Grauman Kohn. Story: Roy Chanslor, Thomas Langan. Photography: Lucien Andriot. Editor: James Clark.

Cast: Jane Withers, Charles Rogers, Katherin Aldridge, George Irving, Buddy Pepper, Cliff Clark, Philip Hurlick, Sheila Ryan, Howard Hickman.

Because of financial difficulties, Withers' granddad (Irving) sells his trotting farm to Rogers who wants to convert it to a racehorse farm, but Jane persuades him otherwise.

934 Grand National Night (aka **Wicked Wife)**

1953, British, Renown Pics, 81 minutes. Director: Bob McNaught. Producer: Phil C. Samuel. Photography: Jack Asher. Screenplay: McNaught, from a play by Dorothy and Campbell Christie.

Cast: Nigel Patrick, Moira Lister, Beatrice Campbell, Betty Ann Davies, Michael Hordern, Noel Purcell.

A rather complicated story of a racehorse owner who accidentally kills his spouse and then stuffs the body in someone else's car.

935 The Great Coup

1919, British, Broadwest, 4,400 feet. Director: George Dewhurst. Producer: Walter West. Scenario: J. Bertram Brown, based on a novel by Nat Gould.

Cast: Stewart Rome, Poppy Wyndham, Gregory Scott, Cameron Carr.

When her mother conspires to bribe the jockey, the adopted daughter of a nobleman rides her sweetheart's horse to victory herself.

936 The Great Dan Patch

1949, United Artists, 92 minutes. Director: Joseph Newman. Producer-Screenplay: John Taintor Foote. Photography: Gilbert Warrenton. Editor: Fred W. Berger.

Cast: Dennis O'Keefe, Gail Russell, Ruth Warrick, Charlotte Greenwood, Henry Hull, John

Hoyt, Arthur Hunnicutt, Clarence Muse, Harry Lauter.

The story of the great harness horse from Indiana at the turn of the century is told in low-key style as chemist O'Keefe leads his horse to one victory after another and a host of track records.

It's not one of the great sports films, but its farm-based simplicity still makes for good entertainment.

937 The Great Game (aka **The Straight Game**)

1918, British, I.B. Davidson, 6,000 feet. Director-Screenplay: A.E. Coleby. Story: Andrew Soutar.

Cast: Bombardier Billy Wells, A.E. Coleby, Earnest A. Douglas, Judd Green, H. Nichols Bates, Eve Marchew.

Boxing great Wells stars in another one of the endless British racing films about nobility—this time a squire's son must win a race to gain his inheritance.

938 The Great Mike

1944, Producers Releasing Corp., 72 minutes. Director: Wallace Fox. Photography: Jocky A. Feindel. Screenplay: Raymond Schrock.

Cast: Stuart Erwin, Buzzy Henry, Pierre Watkin, Alfalfa Switzel, Edythe Elliott, Bob Meredith, Lane Chandler, Ed Cassidy, William Halligan, Gwen Kenyon.

The sentiment is poured on as thick as syrup as a young boy is convinced a milk wagon horse can be a racing champion.

The boy and his horse become involved in a rigged race scheme, and the lad's dog sacrifices his life for the horse.

939 The Great Turf Mystery

1924, British, Butcher, 5,250 feet. Director-Producer: Walter West. Story: J. Bertram Brown.

Cast: Violet Hopson, James Knight, Warwick Ward, Marjorie Benson, Arthur Walcott, M. Evans.

The horse of a millionaire's son is doped by the trainer of a lady owner.

940 Green Grass of Wyoming

1948, 20th Century Fox, 89-92 minutes, Color. Director: Louis King. Producer: Robert Bassler. Screenplay: Martin Berkeley, based on a novel by Mary O'Hara. Photography: Charles Clarke. Editor: Nick De Maggio.

Cast: Charles Coburn, Peggy Cummins, Robert Arthur, Lloyd Nolan, Burl Ives, Geraldine Wall, Charles Hart, Will Wright, Herbert Heywood, Richard Garrick.

A kind of sequel to **My Friend Flicka** and **Thunderhead, Son of Flicka** finds a Romeo and Juliet-type romance between the children of two rival trotting families, with Coburn's kin (Cummins) falling for Nolan's son (Arthur).

Arthur buys a mare, but she's lured away by the outlaw stallion Thunderhead. He brings both horses back; but later, when the mare falters down the stretch, it's discovered she's having a foal.

The two rival families eventually settle their differences.

The film is proof you can have a good racing film without villains, burning stables, crooked jockeys, kidnappings or horses that respond to magic passwords.

941 Harnessed Lightning

1947, Universal-International, 17 minutes. Director: Harold James Moore. Producer: Thomas Mead. Screenplay: Frank Kelly. Narrator: Ed Herlihy.

Horse trainer Tom Berry trains his harness horses for the Hambletonian.

942 Harrigan's Kid

1943, Metro Goldwyn Mayer, 80 minutes. Director: Charles Reisner. Producer: Irving Starr. Screenplay: Martin Berkeley, Alan Friedman. Story: Borden Chase. Photography: Walter Lundin. Editor: Ferris Webster.

Cast: Bobby Reddick, William Gargan, Frank Craven, J. Carrol Naish, Russell Hicks, Selmer Jackson, Jay Ward.

A young jockey is encouraged to play it straight by a barred jockey who takes him under his wing.

943 Heart of Virginia

1948, Republic, 60 minutes. Director: R.G. Springsteen. Producer: Sidney Picker. Screenplay: Jerry Sackheim. Photography: John MacBurnie. Editor: Irving M. Schoenberg.

Cast: Janet Martin, Robert Lowery, Frankie Darro, Paul Hurst, Sam McDaniel, Tom Chatterton, Bennie Bartlett, Glen Vernon, Edmund Cobb.

Darro, playing a jockey as usual, loses his confidence when he causes the death of a friend during a race, but a girl's faith in him gets him back on the right track (no pun intended).

944 Her Second Chance

1926, First National Pictures, 6,420 feet. Director: Lambert Hillyer. Story: Mrs. Wilson Woodrow. Photography: John W. Boyle. Editor: George McGuire.

Cast: Anna Q. Nilsson, Huntly Gordon, Dale Fuller, Charlie Murray, Sam De Grasse, William J. Kelly.

A mountain girl changes her identity after getting out of reform school and plots revenge against the judge who sentenced her. She enters her horse in a race the judge's horse is entered in, but has a change of heart when she learns a cad has switched horses on the judge and informs him of the plot.

945 His Last Dollar

1914, Paramount, 4 reels. Story: David Higgins, Baldwin G. Cooke.

Cast: David Higgins, Betty Gray, Hal Clarendon, E.L. Davenport, Wellington Playter, Jack Pickford, Nat Deverich.

Con men swindle a jockey (Higgins) out of his ample winnings; but he gets a new shot at glory when he bets on his friend's horse and the jockey is injured. He not only wins the race, but the girl.

946 His Last Race

1923, Phil Goldstone Productions, 5,800 feet. Director: Reeves Eason, Howard Mitchell. Photography: Jackson Rose.

Cast: Rex Baker, Gladys Brockwell, William Scott, Harry Depp, Noah Beery, Pauline Starke, Robert McKim.

A resort owner's former flame shows up and romance flares anew. She's now a widow with a son in ill health, so he enters a horse-race to raise money to take care of the little tyke and to marry her.

Naturally, there's villainy afoot as there's a plot to take away his land and kidnap his faithful steed.

947 Home in Indiana

1944, 20th Century-Fox, 103-106 minutes, Color. Director: Henry Hathaway. Producer: Andre Daven. Screenplay: Winston Miller. Story: Agney Chamberlain. Photography: Edward Cronjager. Editor: Harmon Jones.

Cast: Walter Brennan, Lon McAllister, Jeanne Crain, Charlotte Greenwood, June Haver, Ward Bond, Charles Dingle, Robert Condon, Charles Saggau, Willie Best, George Reed.

One of the all-time favorite racing movies, it was remade with Pat Boone in 1957 as **April Love.**

Filmed in Indiana, Kentucky and Ohio, it concerns a semi-retired horseman (Brennan), once one of the top men around, who's now down on his luck and down to his last horse.

Nephew McAllister arrives from the big city after his aunt dies and finds he likes horses and country life. It also helps that two women (Crain and Haver) are interested in him.

McAllister borrows money from Crain and raises a filly who becomes champion trotter.

948 Home on the Range

1935, Paramount, 54 minutes. Director: Arthur Jacobson. Producer: Harold Hurley. Photography: William Mellor. Screenplay: Harold Shumate.

Cast: Jackie Coogan, Randolph Scott, Evelyn Brent, Dean Jagger, Addison Richards, Fuzzy Knight, Ann Sheridan.

Based on **Code of the West** by Zane Grey, Scott and Coogan are brothers who own a racehorse stable and who are menaced by the usual perils of racing movies: The mortgage and the villain who wants the ranch and who resorts to all kinds of sneaky tricks.

A forest fire is the sole added attraction prior to the inevitable big race to raise money to pay off the mortgage.

949 The Home Stretch

1921, Paramount, 4,512-4,602 feet. Director: Jack Nelson. Producer: Thomas H. Ince. Scenario: Louis Stevens, based on "When Johnny Comes Marching Home" by Charles B. Davis in **Metropolitan Magazine.** Photography: Bert Cann.

Cast: Douglas MacLean, Beatrice Burnham, Walt Whitman, Mary Jane Irving, Wade Boteler, Jack Singleton, Margaret Livingston, Joe Bennett, George Holmes.

Johnny (MacLean) inherits a racehorse but loses all his money when he rescues a woman in danger on the track, causing his horse to lose the race. The woman's husband hires him to manage a hotel where he falls in love with a girl.

950 The Homestretch

1947, 20th Century-Fox, 99 minutes, Color. Director: H. Bruce Humberstone. Producer: Robert Bassler. Screenplay: Wanda Tuchock. Photography: Arthur Arling.

Cast: Cornel Wilde, Maureen O'Hara, Glenn Langan, Helen Walker, James Gleason, Henry Stephenson, Tommy Cook, Margaret Bannerman, Ethel Griffies.

Here's another prime example of why 20th Century-Fox is the king of horse racing movies as the plot takes a background to the color of eleven top racetracks around the world.

Some of the best racing sequences ever put on film are a major part of the story of a gambler (Wilde) who shares his love of the track with the love of his wife (O'Hara), a sheltered lass from Boston.

She follows him from track to track from the United States to Jamaica to England as she's puzzled by his relationship with Walker, who lends him money.

Divorce is in the winds until Wilde stakes his last dollar on the Kentucky Derby to win enough money to build up his Maryland stables.

951 The Horse in the Grey Flannel Suit

1969, Buena Vista, 113 minutes, Color. Director: Norman Tokar. Producer: Winston Hibler. Screenplay: Louis Pellatur, based on the book "Year of the Horse" by Eric Hatch. Photography: William Snyder. Editor: Robert Stafford.

Cast: Dean Jones, Diane Baker, Lloyd Bochner, Fred Clark, Ellen Janov, Morey Amsterdam, Kurt Russell.

This belongs in the "horsemanship" category rather than racing as Jones is an advertising man under grouchy boss Clark.

He loves the boss's daughter, a riding enthusiast, and comes up with an idea that links the girl's skill as a horsewoman with a sales pitch.

The final 26 minutes of the film are devoted to a Washington,

D.C., horsemanship competition that's rivaled on screen only by **International Velvet.**

952 The Horse with the Flying Tail

1961, Buena Vista, 47 minutes, Color. Director-Producer: Larry Lansburgh. Screenplay: Janet Lansburgh. Photography: Hannes Staudinger, Werner Kurz, Robert Carmet, James Bauden, Sidney Zucker, Larry Lansburgh. Editor: Warren Ames

Narrator: Bill Bryan.

Injun Joe begins his career stealing food from an Indian village but soon becomes a jumper for a former cavalry officer. He moves on to be owned by a fox hunter and later a brutal trainer.

As this is a Disney film, however, he's rescued from the trainer by the coach of the U.S. Equestrian team who renames him Nautical; and he goes on to fame as the horse whose tail flies up in the air whenever he does anything.

953 A Horseman of the Plains

1928, Fox Film Corp., 4,399 feet. Director: Benjamin Stoloff. Scenario: Fred Myton. Story: Harry Sinclair Drago. Photography: Dan Clark.

Cast: Tom Mix, Sally Blance, Heinie Conklin, Charles Byer, Lew Harvey, Grave Marvin, William Ryno.

Sheriff Mix helps out a gal whose ranch is, you guessed it, in mortgage trouble, and, you guessed it again, he's kidnapped by the baddies before the big race, but, of course, he gets there in time to win it.

More a western than a horse racing film.

954 The Horsemen

1951, Russian, Artkino, 100 minutes, Color. Director: Konstantin Yudin. Screenplay: M. Volpin, N. Erdman. Photography: L. Gelein.

Cast: Sergei Yur, T. Gridov, Tamara Chernova, S. Solyus, N. Mordvinov, R. Plyaft, R. Shpigel.

An unusual blend of war and horse racing culminates in a Cossack cavalry charge against the Nazis during World War II.

Opening in 1939, the young farmer hero's steadfast faith in his horse pays off in victory at the racetrack. When war breaks out, the farmer joins the underground; and when he's injured, the horse brings him out safely.

955 Hot Heels (aka **Patents Pending, Painting the Town**)

1928, Universal, 5,864 feet. Director: William James Craft. Screenplay: Harry O. Hoyt (even though the screen credits list Jack Foley and Vin Moore). Photography: Arthur Todd. Editor: Charles Craft.

Cast: Glenn Tryon, Tod Sloan, Patsy Ruth Miller, Greta Yoltz, James Bradbury, Sr., Lloyd Whitlock.

When a theatrical group finds out a message summoning them to an engagement in Cuba was a bad joke, they enter their trick horse in a race to try to regain some of their money.

956 Hot Tip

1935, RKO Radio Pictures, 70 minutes. Director: Ray McCarey. Story: William Slavens McNutt. Photography: Jack Mackenzie.

Cast: James Gleason, ZaSu Pitts, Margaret Callahan, Russell Gleason, Ray Mayer, J.M. Kerrigan, Arthur Stone, Donald Kerr, Kitty McHugh.

Diner owner Gleason's horse handicapping costs his brother the money he was going to use for his marriage, so the restaurateur must hock everything he has to try to win the money back for him.

957 How Jones Saw the Derby

1905, British, Warwick, 1,905 feet. Director: Charles Raymond.

The race is run backwards, at least through the eyes of a drunk.

958 How Pimple Saved the Kissing Cup

1913, British, Folly Films, 595 feet. Director-Screenplay: Fred and Joe Evans.

Cast: Fred and Joe Evans.

A lowly stableboy rescues a nobleman's horse from a villain and rides it to victory in the big race.

959 Hubby Goes to the Races

1912, British, Hepworth, 600 feet. Director: Frank Wilson.

Cast: Harry Buss.

A poor schnook is mistakenly identified as a bookie who welshed on a bet.

960 Hundred to One

1933, British, Twickenham, 45 minutes. Director: Walter West. Producers: Julius Hagen, Harry Cohen. Screenplay: Basil Mason.

Cast: Arthur Sinclair, Dodo Watts, David Nichol, Edmund Hampton, Derek Williams.

A horse purchased by an Irishman never does amount to much, but its foal winds up a Derby winner.

961 The Hundredth Chance

1920, British, Stoll, 6,585 feet. Director: Maurice Elvey. Screenplay: Sinclair Hill, based on a novel by Ethel M. Dell.

Cast: Dennis Neilson-Terry, Mary Glynne, Eille Norwood, Sydney Seaward, Teddy Arundell, Patrick Key.

A woman with a crippled brother weds a horse trainer.

962 The Hurricane Kid

1925, Universal, 5,296 feet. Director: Edward Sedgwick. Scenario: E. Richard Schayer. Adaptation: Raymond L. Schrock. Story: Will Lambert. Photography: Virgil Miller.

Cast: Hoot Gibson, Marion Nixon, William A. Steele, Violet La Plante, Arthur Machley, Harry Todd, Fred Humes.

With a beautiful girl's ranch at stake, the Hurricane Kid (Gibson) wins the big horse race against another ranch.

963 In Old Kentucky

1920, First National, 7 reels. Director: Marshall Neilan. Screenplay: Thomas J. Geraghty, from a play by Charles T. Dazey.

Cast: Anita Stewart, Mahlon Hamilton, Edward Coxen, John Currie, Edward Connolly, Adele Farrington, Marcia Manon, Frank Duffy.

Here's an action-packed melodrama in which the heroine outdoes the hero for a change. A poor mountain lass not only saves the lives of the hero and the horse, but she wins the big horse race for him.

964 In Old Kentucky

1927, Metro Goldwyn Mayer, 6,646 feet. Director: John M. Stahl. Scenario: A.P. Younger. Adaptation: Younger, Lew Lipton, based on a play by Charles T. Dazey. Photography: Maximilian Fabian. Editor: Basil Wrangell, Margaret Booth.

Cast: James Murray, Helene Costello, Stepin Fetchit, Wesley Barry, Dorothy Cumming, Edward Martindel, Harvey Clark, Carolynne Snowden, Nick Cogley.

Here's another version of the same play by Dazey that was filmed in 1920. A World War I veteran returns to his Kentucky horse breeding estate a drunkard and finds the place in dire financial straits.

The family's fortunes take a turn for the better when a racehorse the hero (Murray) had during the war and which used to belong to the estate is repurchased and entered in the Kentucky Derby.

965 In Old Kentucky

1935, Fox Film Corp., 86 minutes. Director: George Marshall.

Producer: Edward Butcher. Screenplay: Sam Hellman, Gladys Lehman from a play by Charles T. Dazey. Photography: L.W. O'Connell.

Cast: Will Rogers, Dorothy Wilson, Bill Robinson, Russell Hardie, Louis Henry, Alan Dinehart, Charles Sellon, Eddie Tamblyn, Fritz Johannet, Bobby Rose.

Released after Rogers' death, this third version of the Dazey play has been altered to fit the humorist's unique personality and is more a comedy than anything else, in contrast to the melodramatics of the two earlier versions.

966 In the Stretch

1914, Ramo, 4 reels. Story: Will A. Davis. Adaptation: Davis, Phil Scorelle.

Cast: Phil Scorelle, Stuart Holmes, Courtney Collins, William S. Rising, Jack Hopkins.

A jockey is tempted to join a race-fixing scheme but decides against it and is sent to prison anyway. When he gets out, he makes the most of his chance to clear his name by winning the big race.

967 International Velvet

1978, United Artists/MGM, 125 minutes, Color. Director-Writer-Screenplay: Bryan Forbes. Photography: Tony Imi. Editor: Timothy Ree.

Cast: Tatum O'Neal, Nanette Newman, Christopher Plummer, Anthony Hopkins, Peter Barkworth, Dinsdale Landen, Sara Bullen, Jeffrey Byron.

It's more than 30 years after the setting of **National Velvet** and the little girl from the classic 1944 film has grown up to be a childless divorcée (Newman) who's having a serious relationship with author Plummer.

Into their lives comes orphan O'Neal from America to stay with her British aunt. She's unable to adjust to her new environment and even runs away from home, but she develops an attachment to a horse and turns out to be just as good in the saddle as Velvet.

After a struggle, she makes the British Olympic equestrian team coached by Hopkins, who drives her harder than she ever imagined.

The final half hour of the film deals with Olympic equestrian events. There's also a subplot with an American Olympian who begins a relationship with the girl.

968 Into the Straight

1950, Australian, Universal-International, 80 minutes. Director-Producer: Tom O. McCreadle. Screenplay: Zelma Roberts.

Cast: Charles Tingwell, Muriel Steinbeck, George Randall, Nonnie Piefer, James Workman, Margot Lee.

The only thing interesting about this Australian quickie is that it proves that they can make totally routine track films Down Under just as poorly as anywhere else.

969 It Ain't Hay

1943, Universal, 80 minutes. Director: Erle C. Kenton. Producer: Alex Gottlieb. Screenplay: Allen Boretz and John Grant, based on "Princess O'Hara" by Damon Runyon. Photography: Charles Van Enger. Editor: Frank Gross.

Cast: Bud Abbott, Lou Costello, Grace McDonald, Cecil Kellaway, Patsy O'Connor, Eugene Pallette, Shemp Howard, Eddie Quillan, Mike Mazurki, Samuel S. Hinds.

Leave it to Lou to get things all screwed up in this slapstick remake of 1935's **Princess O'Hara.** He's a hack driver who's sent to the racetrack to pick up a nag for the taxi but takes a prize racehorse by mistake.

When it comes to the big race, none other than Costello is jockeying it. This is the film in which Abbott and Costello do their fodder and mudder routine.

970 I've Got a Horse

1938, British, British Lion, 77 minutes. Director-Producer: Herbert Smith. Screenplay: Fenn Sherie, Ingran D'Abbes, Sandy Powell. Photography: George Stretton.

Cast: Sandy Powell, Norah Howard, Felix Aylmer, Evelyn Roberts, Wilfrid Hyde White, D.A. Clarke-Smith, Edward Chapman, Frank Atkinson, Kathleen Harrison.

Farce about a gambler who's given a horse in settlement for a bet and who enters it in the big race. Lo and behold, the horse is winning when, at a crucial moment, it begins doing circus tricks because its trainer was originally from the circus.

971 I've Gotta Horse

1965, British, Windmill, 92 minutes. Director: Kenneth Hume. Producers: Larry Parnes, Kenneth Hume. Screenplay: Ronald Wolfe, Ronald Chesney. Story: Parnes, Hume.

Cast: Billy Fury, Michael Medwin, Amanda Barrie, Bill Fraser, John Pertweek, Leslie Dwyer, The Bachelors, The Gamblers.

A rock singer juggles his time between the racetrack, where he has a horse entered in the Derby, and trying to get to the show on time.

972 The Jockey

1910, French, Pathe. No credits available.

When a jockey gets himself drunk, a young stableboy proves himself by winning the race.

973 The Jockey

1914, British, Sunny South, 1,150 feet. Director: F.L. Lyndhurst.

Cast: Will Evans, Arthur Conquest, George Grave.

A jockey leaves the track during the 2:30 race to take care of some business and returns in time to win the 4:30 race.

974 Johnny Get Your Hair Cut

1927, Metro Goldwyn Mayer, 6,781 feet. Director: B. Reeves Eason, Archie Mayo. Scenario: Florence Ryerson. Story: Gerald Beaumont. Photography: Frank Good. Editor: Sam S. Zimbalist.

Cast: Jackie Coogan, Mattie Witting, Maurice Costello, Pat Hartigan, James Corrigan, Bobby Doyle, Knute Erickson.

An orphan boy (Coogan) who loves horses saves the life of an owner's daughter and is allowed to ride in a big race.

975 Judith Buys a Horse

1939, British, Butcher, 17 minutes. Director: Lance Comfort.

Cast: Judy Dick.

A girl's father buys her a horse, which she trains to win the race.

976 Just Crazy About Horses

1978, Fred Baker Films, 105 minutes, Color. Directors: Jim Lovejoy, Joe Wemple, Victor Kanefsky. Producers: Lovejoy, Wemple. Photography: Peter Stein, Cotter Watt, Ted Churchill, Mike Lerme. Editor: Samuel D. Pollard.

Narrator: Tammy Grimes.

If you ever wanted to know about the workings of the high society of the racing world, this feature documentary is for you.

Concentrating on the big money involved in the race circuit from stud farm to the track, the highlight is a detailed mating scene. The mating cost the mare's owner $33,000.

An auction for the high rollers and a fox hunting sequence are also included.

977 Just My Luck

1957, British, Rank, 86 minutes. Director: John Paddy Carstairs. Producer: Hugh Stewart. Screenplay: Alfred Shaughnessy, Peter Blackmore.

Cast: Norman Wisdom, Margaret Rutherford, Joan Sims, Sabrina, Delphi Lawrence, Edward Chapman.

Wisdom is one of Britain's top comics, yet his films are rarely shown in the United States. This one involves a gambler who wins his bet only to have the bookies welsh on him.

978 Kentucky

1938, 20th Century-Fox, 95 minutes, Color. Director: David Butler. Producer: Darryl F. Zanuck. Screenplay: Lamar Trotti, John Taintor Foote. Photography: Ernest Palmer, Ray Rennahan. Editor: Irene Morra.

Cast: Loretta Young, Richard Greene, Walter Brennan, Douglas Dumbrille, Karen Morley, Russell Hicks, Moroni Olsen, Willard Robertson, Eddie Anderson.

One of the best of the Fox studio's many fine racing dramas earned Brennan the Oscar as best supporting actor.

It's a Romeo and Juliet-type story with Young and Greene members of feuding Kentucky families, begun during the Civil War when soldiers led by a member of Greene's family took over the stables of Brennan, Young's uncle.

When Greene trains Young's horse to win the Kentucky Derby, all is forgiven on both sides.

979 The Kentucky Derby

1922, Universal, 5,398 feet. Director: King Baggot. Scenario: George C. Hull, based on a play by Charles T. Dazey. Photography: Victor Milner.

Cast: Reginald Denny, Lillian Rich, Emmet King, Lionel Belmore, Walter McGrail, Gertrude Astor, Bert Woodruff, Anna Hernandez, Pat Harmon, Wilfred Lucas.

When the son of a Kentucky colonel rebuffs a marriage proposal by a couple of fortune hunters, one of them frames the youth (Denny) for the theft of some funds from his father.

Returning home after three years, he discovers who the villain is and exposes a plot against his father's hope for the Derby.

980 Kentucky Handicap

1926, Rayart, 5,420 feet. Director: Harry J. Brown. Scenario: Henry Roberts Symonds.

Cast: Reed Howes, Robert McKim, Alice Calhoun, Lydia Knott, Josef Swickard, James Bradbury, Jr.

Framed by a baddie and barred from the track, the good guy has to put up his horse as security for a loan only to find the villain has obtained the notes.

The good guy has to beat the confession out of the villain and winds up winning the race.

981 Kentucky Pride

1925, Fox Film Corp., 6,597 feet. Director: John Ford. Scenario: Dorothy Yost. Photography: George Schneiderman.

Cast: Henry B. Walthall, J. Farrell MacDonald, Gertrude Astor, Malcolm Waite, Belle Stoddard, Winston Miller, Peaches Jackson.

A Kentucky horse owner (Walthall) loses most of his top horses in a card game and must stake the rest of his fortune on a horse named Virginia's Future. It breaks a leg during the Futurity, and he not only goes broke, but his wife (Astor) deserts him.

The horse's trainer (MacDonald) nurses Virginia's Future, who is later sold and gives birth to a colt named Confederacy, who winds up winning the Futurity and restoring the horseman's fortune.

982 The Killing

1956, United Artists, 84 minutes. Director-Screenplay: Stanley Kubrick. Producer: James B. Harris. Photography: Lucien Ballard. Editor: Betty Steinberg.

Cast: Sterling Hayden, Loleen Gray, Vince Edwards, Jay C. Flippen, Ted De Corsia, Marie Windsor, Elisha Cook, Jr., Joe Sawyer, Tim Carey, Maurice Oboukhoff, Jay Adler.

Based on the novel **Clean**

Break by Lionel White, the focus is on a $2 million racetrack robbery.

Among the shady characters involved are the mastermind (Hayden), an ex-convict; the track cashier (Cook); a crooked cop (De Corsia); a drunk (Flippen); a wrestler (Oboukhoff) and a bartender (Sawyer). Hood Edwards tries to muscle in on the deal.

While the wrestler starts a riot as a diversion inside near the pay window, throwing cops around like dolls, the other part of the scheme is to shoot one of the horses during the race as a further diversion.

As Hayden is about to board an airplane with the stolen loot, his suitcase flies open and the cash is scattered in the wind.

The Split, a drama about thieves who have a falling out after robbing a football stadium during a game, was inspired by **The Killing.**

983 The King of the Turf

1926, Film Booking Offices of America, 6,210 feet. Director: James P. Hogan. Continuity: J. Grubb Alexander. Adaptation: John C. Brownell, Louis Joseph Vance. Photography: Jules Cronjager.

Cast: George Irving, Patsy Ruth Miller, Kenneth Harlan, Al Roscoe, Kathleen Kirkham, Mary Carr, Eddie Phillips, David Torrence, William Franey.

A southern colonel (Irving) is framed by his partner (Torrence) and goes to prison. The partner confesses his crime on his deathbed, but his wife puts it in the safe and the colonel must serve out his sentence.

When he gets out of prison, a horse trainer he met in prison (Harlan) learns about the confession, and the colonel's name is cleared. His horse, in the meantime, wins the big race.

984 King of the Turf

1939, United Artists, 88 minutes. Director: Alfred E. Green. Producer: Edward Small. Story-Adaptation: George Bruce. Photography: Robert Planck. Editor: Grant Whytock.

Cast: Adolphe Menjou, Roger Daniel, Dolores Costello, William Demarest, Walter Abel, Alan Dinehart, Harold Huber, Milburn Stone.

Of all the films about little children redeeming fallen stars that were made after 1931's **The Champ** (see Boxing chapter), this ranks as one of the best.

In typical "fall of the mighty" fashion, Menjou once was a top stable owner who has become an alcoholic. Bumming a ride in a train's horse car, he meets a young runaway (Daniel) who's crazy about horse racing.

The two become pals and manage to buy a racehorse for $2. Under Menjou's training, the horse becomes a winner with the kid as jockey until the lad's mother shows up to take him back home.

In typical 1930's sentimental fashion, the mother turns out to be the woman he deserted years ago, and the lad is his own son. Menjou orders the boy to throw the next race and pretends to be drunk, knowing the kid will return to a better life with his mother.

985 Kissing Cup's Race

1920, British, Hopson Productions, 6,337 feet. Director: Walter West. Screenplay: J. Bertram Brown, Benedict James, based on a poem by Campbell Rae Brown.

Cast: Violet Hopson, Gregory Scott, Clive Brook, Arthur Walcott, Philip Hewland, Joe Plant, Adeline Hayden.

Yet another in the seemingly endless line of racing films about a nobleman thwarting the schemes of villains to win the big race.

986 Kissing Cup's Race

1930, British, Butcher, 75

minutes. Director: Castleton Knight. Screenplay: Knight, Blanche Metcalfe, based on a poem by Campbell Rae Brown.

Cast: Stewart Rome, Madeline Carroll, John Richard Cooper, Chili Bouchier, Moore Marriott.

A remake of the silent in which a poor nobleman keeps young colt Kissing Cup after selling off all his other horses. The colt helps him regain his fortune.

987 Ladies Crave Excitement

1935, Mascot, 69 minutes. Director: Nick Grinde. Screenplay: Wellyn Totman. Story: John Rathmell. Photography: Ernie Miller, William Nobles.

Cast: Norman Foster, Evelyn Knapp, Esther Ralston, Eric Linden, Purnell Pratt, Gilbert Emery.

The rivalry between two newsreel outfits takes a new turn when the ace cameramen for Union Newsreel falls in love with the daughter of the owner of Globe Newsreel.

The cameraman gets into hot water when he films some crooks doping a racehorse owned by the rival and gives the story to the newspapers. The baddies steal the film from him before he can give it to his boss.

988 The Lady Owner

1923, British, Broadwest, 5,129 feet. Director-Producer: Walter West. Screenplay: J. Bertram Brown (some sources list his name as J. Brinton Brown).

Cast: Violet Hopson, Fred Raines, Arthur Walcott, Edwin Ellis, Marjorie Benson.

A nobleman retires and moves to the country under a false name. He meets the female owner of a racing stable and tries to set up a marriage between her and his son.

The son thwarts a plan by the villain, who holds the mortgage on her property, to dope her horse and rides it himself to victory.

989 The Lady's from Kentucky

1939, Paramount, 75 minutes. Director: Alexander Hall. Producer: Jeff Lazarus. Screenplay: Malcolm Stuart Boylan. Story: Rowland Brown. Photography: Theodor Sparkuhl.

Cast: George Raft, Ellen Drew, Hugh Herbert, ZaSu Pitts, Lew Payton, Louise Beavers, Forrester Harvey, Harry Tyler.

Gambler Raft has lost all his money but still has a promising racehorse. He convinces his partner, Drew, to keep on racing the animal, eventually ruining it. Raft then learns his lesson.

990 The Law of the Wild

1934, Mascot, 12 chapters. Directors: Armand Schaefer, Reeves Eason. Supervising Editor: Wyndham Gittens. Story: Ford Beebe, John Rathmell, Al Martin. Screenplay: Sherman Lowe, Eason. Photography: Ernest Miller, William Nobles. Editor: Earl Turner.

Cast: Rex, King of the Wild Horses; Rin Tin Tin, Jr.; Ben Turpin, Bob Custer, Lucile Browne, Richard Cramer, Ernie Adams, Edmund Cobb, Charles Whitaker, Dick Alexander.

Chapter One: The Man Killer; Chapter Two: The Battle of the Strong; Chapter Three: The Cross-eyed Goony; Chapter Four: Avenging Fangs; Chapter Five: A Dead Man's Hand; Chapter Six: Horse Thief Justice; Chapter Seven: The Death Stampede; Chapter Eight: The Canyon of Calamity; Chapter Nine: Robber's Roost; Chapter Ten: King of the Range; Chapter Eleven: Winner Takes All; Chapter Twelve: The Grand Sweepstakes.

Rex, a magnificent wild stallion is captured by the young hero (Custer) and is befriended by smart dog Rinty. However, villains kidnap Rex and turn him into a successful racehorse.

There's a falling out among the thieves, however, and Our Hero finds himself being framed for the murder of one of them. He clears his name with the help of Rinty while Rex is entered in a big race in the final chapter.

991 The Lemon Drop Kid

1934, Paramount, 60 minutes. Director: Marshall Neilan. Producer: William La Baron. Screenplay: Howard Greene, J.P. McEvoy, from a story by Damon Runyon. Photography: Henry Sharp.

Cast: Lee Tracy, Helen Mack, William Frawley, Minna Gombell, Babe LeRoy, Robert McWade, Henry Walthall.

Coming on the heels of the success of **Little Miss Marker** was this sentimental track-based story involving a no-good track tout who reforms for the sake of a kid.

The tout (Tracy) moves to a small town where he finds a new life. He commits a crime to raise money to get a specialist for a kid but is undone by his fondness for lemon drops. Everything turns out well, however.

Bears little resemblance to the 1951 remake.

992 The Lemon Drop Kid

1951, Paramount, 91 minutes. Director: Sidney Lanfield. Producer: Robert L. Welch. Screenplay: Edmund Hartmann, based on a story by Damon Runyon. Photography: Daniel L. Fapp. Editor: Archie Marshek.

Cast: Bob Hope, Marilyn Maxwell, Lloyd Nolan, Jane Darwell, Andra King, Fred Clark, William Frawley, Sid Melton, Tor Johnson, Harry Belaver, Society Kid Hogan.

Partly directed and written, although uncredited, by Frank Tashlin, any resemblance between this and the 1934 version is strictly coincidental, but still entertaining in its own right.

Hope is his usual wise-cracking self as the Kid, a totally rotten to the core, lying, cheating and lovable track tout. He picks the wrong victim, the moll of a ganster, and the horse finishes in slow motion.

As part of his scheme to raise money to repay the gangster, he turns a gambling den into a refuge for homeless old ladies, but his motive is pure greed. He gradually undergoes a change of personality as the old ladies and the Kid win out over the mobsters.

993 Lily of Killarney (aka **Bride of the Lake**)

1933, British, Associated Producers and Distributors, 86 minutes. Director: Maurice Elvey. Producer: Julius Hagen. Screenplay: H. Fowler Mear, based on a play by Dion Bouricault and an operetta by Charles Benedict. Photography: Sydney Blythe.

Cast: John Garrick, Gina Malo, Dennis Hoey, Leslie Perrins, Stanley Holloway, Sara Allgood, Dorothy Boyd, D.J. Williams, Hughes Macklin, Pamela May.

All the routine stops are pulled in this tale of an impoverished Irishman who must both win the big horse race to keep his land from being foreclosed upon and rescue his kidnapped sweetheart from the villain. Need we say how it turns out?

The music is really the main interest.

994 The Little Adventuress

1938, Columbia, 60 minutes. Director: D. Ross Lederman. Screenplay: Michael L. Simmons. Photography: Henry Freulich. Editor: Al Clark.

Cast: Edith Fellows, Richard Fiske, Jacqueline Wells, Cliff Edwards, Kenneth Harlan, Virginia Howell, Harry C. Bradley, Charles Waldron.

Her parents dead, a young girl brings her horse with her when she goes to live with relatives and trains it for the races.

Rescued from a barn fire, the horse is ill, but naturally gets well enough in time for the big race. Finding out that gamblers have bribed the jockey, the girl rides the horse herself to victory.

995 Little Johnny Jones

1923, Warner Brothers, 6,800-7,165 feet. Directors: Arthur Rosson, Johnny Hines. Adaptation: Raymond L. Schrock, based on a play by George M. Cohan. Photography: Charles E. Gilson. Editor: Clarence Kolster.

Cast: Johnny Hines, Wyndham Standing, Margaret Seddon, Herbert Prior, Molly Malone, Mervyn LeRoy, George Webb, Pauline French.

A comedy in which an American jockey fights all kinds of dastardly deeds en route to the English Derby. The jockey (Hines) is framed, his girl friend (Malone) is the victim of the good old reliable kidnapping trick, and there's all sorts of other villainy, but Our Hero Johnny comes out on top at the end.

996 Little Johnny Jones

1929, First National, 5,020-6,621 feet. Director: Mervyn LeRoy. Screenplay: Adelaide Heilbron, Eddie Buzzell, based on a play by George M. Cohan. Photography: Faxon Dean. Editor: Frank Ware.

Cast: Eddie Buzzell, Alice Day, Edna Murphy, Robert Edeson, Wheeler Oakman, Raymond Turner, Donald Reed.

LeRoy, who played a jockey in the 1923 version, directed this remake which has lots of music and is far different.

After racing a horse to victory, Johnny (Buzzell) leaves his hometown sweetheart (Day) to race in New York where he falls for the obligatory vamp in the form of a show girl (Murphy) who unsuccessfully tries to get him to throw a race.

When he loses anyway, he's falsely accused of throwing it, but gets another chance to race in England and a new shot at regaining his girl friend's love.

997 Little Miss Marker

1934, Paramount, 78-80 minutes. Director: Alexander Hall. Producer: B.P. Schulberg. Screenplay: Walter R. Lipman, Sam Hellman, Gladys Lehman, based on a story by Damon Runyon. Photography: Alfred Glicks.

Cast: Shirley Temple, Adolphe Menjou, Dorothy Dell, John Kelly, Charles Kelly, Lynne Overman, Frank McGlynn, Sr., Jack Sheehan, Gary Owen, Willie Best (billed as Sleep 'n' Eat), James Burke.

One of Temple's greatest successes spawned three remakes—as **Sorrowful Jones** in 1949, the non-sports **40 Pounds of Trouble** in 1963 and **Little Miss Marker** in 1980. It also inspired countless more films about little tykes reforming shady adult characters which had themselves been spawned by the success of 1931's **The Champ.**

She's the daughter of a desperate bettor who leaves her with crooked bookie Menjou as a "marker" on his bet, not knowing that the race has been fixed.

When her father dies, it's up to grumpy Menjou and the rest of Runyon's colorful track characters to take care of her. She turns them into such goody-goody characters that even the gangster boss is persuaded to save her life with a blood transfusion.

998 Little Miss Marker

1980, Universal, 112 minutes, Color. Director-Screenplay: Walter Bernstein. Producer: Jennings Lang. Photography: Phillip Lathrop. Editor: Eve Newman.

Cast: Walter Matthau, Julie Andrews, Tony Curtis, Sara Stinson, Bob Newhart, Lee Grant, Brian Dennehy, Kenneth McMillan, Andrew Rubin, Joshua Shelley.

This remake of the Damon Runyon story finds Matthau perfectly cast as grumpy bookie Sorrowful Jones and Andrews as his girl friend. Its shortcoming is that Sara Stinson as the 6-year-old "marker" on a bet is no substitute for Shirley Temple.

The highlight of this version is a fixed horse race in which the winning horse runs so slow, all the other jockeys have to frantically struggle to hold back their mounts.

Needless to say, the girl reforms Jones.

999 Little Miss Thoroughbred

1938, Warner Brothers, 64 minutes. Director: John Farrow. Associate Producer: Bryan Foy. Screenplay: George Bricker, Albert DeMond. Photography: William O'Connell. Editor: Everett Dodd.

Cast: Janet Chapman, John Litel, Ann Sheridan, Frank McHugh, Eric Stanley, Robert Hemans, Cy Kendall.

Chapman is the 6-year-old orphan of the title in this **Little Miss Marker** clone.

She picks gambler Litel to be her father and changes his luck for the better. He marries Sheridan so that things look right, but you just know everything's going to come out smelling like roses by the final reel.

1000 The Littlest Outlaw

1955, Buena Vista, 75 minutes, Color. Director: Roberto Gavaldon. Producer: Larry Lamsburgh. Screenplay: Bill Walsh, based on a story by Lamsburgh. Photography: Alex Phillips. Editor: Carlos Savage.

Cast: Pedro Armendariz, Joseph Calleia, Rodolfo Acosta, Andres Velasquez, Pepe Ortiz, Laila Maley, Gilberto Gonzalez, Jose Jorvay.

In an unusual move, the Disney studio shot English and Spanish-language versions of this Mexico-based family film simultaneously.

A young boy (Velasquez) has a brutal stepfather who trains a horse to jump higher by placing spindles atop the barrier. During the big competition, the prize horse embarrasses a general (Armendariz) by refusing to jump, because he remembers the pain, and later throws the general's daughter.

When the general orders the animal shot, the lad runs away with him and becomes a fugitive. The horse gets away from the boy and is made the lure in a bull ring, but the kid jumps in and rides it out with a huge jump.

1001 Loco Luck

1927, Universal, 4,827 feet. Director: Cliff Smith. Scenario: Doris Malloy. Adaptation: Isadore Bernstein. Story: Alvin J. Neitz. Photography: Eddie Linden.

Cast: Art Acord, Fay Wray, Aggie Herring, William A. Steele, George F. Marion, Al Jennings.

The horse is the hero in this racing western. A rancher (Acord) faces the usual foreclosure on his property by the villain (Jennings) who wants it because there's oil on it.

Acord enters a horse race to pay off the mortgage, but the unoriginal villain kidnaps him and locks him in a cabin. Acord's trusty steed, however, tracks down his master and frees him, then wins the big race.

1002 Long Odds

1922, British, Stoll, 5,430 feet. Director-Screenplay: A.E. Coleby.

Cast: A.E. Coleby, H. Nicholes-Bates, Frank Wilson, Madge Royce, Harry Marsh.

When a substitute jockey is injured, an ill rider takes his place and wins.

1003 The Long Shot

1939, Grand National, 69 minutes. Director: Charles Lamont. Producer: Franklyn Warner. Adaptation: George Adamson. Story: Harry Beresford, George Callahan. Photography: Arthur Martinelli. Editor: Bernard Loftus.

Cast: Gordon Jones, Marsha Hunt, C. Henry Gordon, George

Meeker, Harry Davenport, George E. Stone, Tom Kennedy, Jason Robards.

The old one about a horse which has been a consistent loser is dusted off again. This time, it's discovered the horse simply can't race in the rail position; so when that's rectified, it wins the Santa Anita.

Oh, yes, there is more of a plot than that, involving a scheme by stable owner Gordon to ruin his rival Davenport in order to get the pretty girl to marry him.

Davenport fakes his own death and leaves the horse which proves to be a winner to Jones and the girl.

1004 Luck of the Irish

1937, British, Paramount, 79-81 minutes. Director-Screenplay: Donovan Pedelty. Producers: Pedelty, Richard Hayward. Story: Victor Haddick. Photography: Jack Wilson.

Cast: Richard Hayward, Kay Walsh, Niall McGinnis, J.R. Mageean, R.H. MacCandless, Charles Fagan, Harold Griffen, Charlotte Tedlie.

Featuring members of the Belfast Repertory Co. and lots of Irish music, this was released in the British Isles in 1935.

With a nobleman's ancestral castle facing ruin, a servant (Hayward) tries to help out his employer by selling phony pottery. The squire has bet all he has on his horse to win the big race.

The horse loses, but a rich American comes to the rescue.

1005 Luck of the Turf

1936, British, Radio, 64 minutes. Director-Producer: Randall Faye. Screenplay: John Hunter. Photography: Geoffrey Faithfull.

Cast: Jack Melford, Moira Lynd, Wally Patch, Moore Marriott, Sybil Grove, Tom Helmore, Peggy Novak.

A schnook has the knack for picking winners at the racetrack for his friends, but never bets himself until he tries to get enough money to marry his sweetheart.

Naturally, he loses, but then stakes all he's got left on a real long shot.

1006 Lucky Blaze

1933, British, Ace, 48 minutes. Director-Screenplay: Widgey R. Newman.

Cast: William Freshman, Vera Sherbourne, Moore Marriott, Freddie Fox, J. Collins.

A jockey is helped out by the squire's daughter in the big race.

1007 Lucky Larkin

1930, Universal, 5,779-5,875 feet. Director: Harry J. Brown. Screenplay: Marion Jackson. Photography: Ted McCord. Editor: Fred Allen.

Cast: Ken Maynard, Nora Lane, James Farley, Harry Todd, Paul Hurst, Charles Clary, Blue Washington.

Lucky Larkin, played by cowboy star Ken Maynard, comes to the rescue of a rancher being victimized by a racing rival jealous of the quality of his horses. Despite the barn fire cliche in which several horses are injured and other dirty tricks, Larkin wins the county race for the good guy.

1008 Lure of the Track

1925, Lee-Bradford Corp., 4,800 feet. Producer: Charles Makranzy.

Cast: Sheldon Lewis, Maclyn Arbuckle, Dot Farley.

The usual stuff about a jockey thwarting the plots of villains to win the big race and save a girl and her father from ruin.

1009 Ma and Pa Kettle at the Fair

1952, Universal-International, 78 minutes. Director: Charles Barton. Producer: Leonard Goldstein. Screenplay: Richard Morris, John Grant. Story: Martin Ragaway,

Leonard Stern, Jack Henley. Photography: Maury Gertsman. Editor: Ted J. Kent.

Cast: Marjorie Main, Percy Kilbride, James Best, Lori Nelson, Ester Dale, Emory Parnell, Oliver Blake, Rex Lease.

Trying to raise money for his daughter's college education, Pa buys a worn-out trotter, which he enters in the race at the fair, but loses. It's Ma to the rescue with winnings for her bread and jam, in this unpretentious entry in the comedy series.

1010 The Man Who Could Not Lose

1914, Famous Players, 5 reels. Story: Richard Harding Davis.

Based on a novel by Richard Harding Davis, it has a broke writer who sees a horse in a dream and becomes a big bettor after he wagers on it at the track and wins.

1011 The March Hare

1956, British, British Lion, 85 minutes, Color. Director: George More O'Ferrall. Producers: Bertram Ostrer, Albert Fennell. Screenplay: Gordon Wellesley, Allan MacKinnon, Paul Vincent Carroll, based on a novel by T.H. Bird. Photography: Jack Hillyard. Editor: Gordon Pilkington.

Cast: Peggy Cummins, Terence Morgan, Martita Hunt, Wilfrid Hyde White, Cyril Cusack, Derrick De Marney, Charles Hawtrey, Maureen Delaney, Ivan Samson.

A leisurely paced Irish fantasy about a nobleman who loses his home and stables by gambling, but stays on when the new owner's daughter thinks he's the groom.

They fall in love and raise a colt to be a Derby contender, with old trainer Cusack around to lend a helping hand. **The Quiet Man** it's not, but for those who love lots of Irish color, this is the next best thing.

1012 Maryland

1940, 20th Century-Fox, 92 minutes, Color. Director: Henry King. Producer: Gene Markey. Screenplay: Ethel Hill, Jack Andrews.

Cast: Walter Brennan, Fay Bainter, Brenda Joyce, John Payne, Charles Ruggles, Hattie McDaniel, Marjorie Weaver, Sidney Blackmer, Ben Carter, Ernest Whitman, Paul Harvey.

After his Oscar-winning performance in **Kentucky** in 1938, 20th Century Fox gave Walter Brennan a role in another racing film and simply gave it the name of another state. The result was another winner for the king of racing film studios.

Payne is forbidden to ride horses by mom Bainter, who's still scarred by the memory of her husband being killed in a hunting accident.

But when he falls in love with the daughter (Joyce) of his dad's old trainer (Brennan), he goes against his mother's wishes and rides in the Maryland steeplechase.

1013 McHale's Navy

1964, Universal, 93 minutes, Color. Director-Producer: Edward J. Montagne. Screenplay: Frank Gill, Jr., G. Carleton Brown. Photography: William Margulies. Editor: Sam E. Waxman.

Cast: Ernest Borgnine, Joe Flynn, Tim Conway, Bob Hastings, Gary Vinson, John Wright, Carl Ballantine, Bill Sands, Yoshio Yoda, Edson Stroll, Jean Willes, George Kennedy.

Anyone who's seen the successful television comedy series on which this is based knows what to expect. PT boat skipper McHale (Borgnine) and his bunch of misfits, based on a Pacific island during World War II, botch a scheme to make money on delayed race results and wind up in debt to the marines.

When bungling Ensign Parker

(Conway) causes their boat to ram a warehouse, they're even more in debt; and crochety Captain Binghamton (Flynn) just can't wait to find something to send them to the brig for.

Salvation comes when they rescue a famous racehorse from a torpedoed ship, glue on some fur so it won't be recognized and enter it in a race. Slapstick galore.

There was a second film based on the series, **McHale's Navy Joins the Air Force.**

1014 A Member of Tattersall's

1919, British, G.B. Samuelson, 6,000 feet. Director-Screenplay: Albert Ward. Story: H.V. Browning.

Cast: Isobel Elsom, Malcolm Cherry, Campbell Cullan, Tom Reynolds, James Lindsey.

A villainous nobleman makes life miserable for a horse racing captain who's in love with a bookie's daughter.

1015 Men of Chance

1931, RKO Radio Pictures, 65 minutes. Director: George Archainbaud. Story: Louis Weltzenkom. Photography: Nick Musucaro.

Cast: Ricardo Cortez, Mary Astor, John Halliday, Ralph Ince, Kitty Kelly.

Cortez is the victim of a scheme by two rival gamblers who get him to marry a girl (Astor) so they can find out his plans and then fix the races.

The girl upsets the scheme when she finds she really loves him and helps him get his money back.

1016 Michael Shayne, Private Detective

1940, 20th Century-Fox, 77 minutes. Director: Eugene Forde. Producer; Sol M. Wurtzel. Screenplay: Stanley Rauh, Manning O'Connor, based on a novel by Brett Halliday. Photography: George Schneidermann. Editor: Al De Gaetano.

Cast: Lloyd Nolan, Marjorie Weaver, Joan Valerie, Walter Abel, Elizabeth Patterson, Donald McBride, Douglas Dumbrille, Clarence Kolb, George Meeker.

The famous detective becomes involved with gamblers, society women and a racetrack scheme.

1017 Mickey

1918, Mabel Normand Feature Film Co., 7 reels. Director: F. Richard Jones. Producer: Mack Sennett. Story: J.G. Hawks. Photography: Hans F. Koenekamp.

Cast: Mabel Normand, Louis Cody, Tom Kennedy, Laura La Varnie, Wheeler Oakman, Minta Durfee, George Nichols, William Colvin.

In 1916, Mack Sennett formed the Normand film company in an effort to please his top star. This was her initial effort, and although it was shelved for two years, it finally opened to favorable critical reviews.

She plays a tomboy who's been raised by her miner dad and an Indian woman and who's sent to live with her nasty aunt so she can get a so-called proper education.

She aids a wealthy man who's attracted to her by masquerading as a jockey and winning the big race, but suffers an injury as she does so. Fear not, there's a happy ending.

1018 The Million Dollar Handicap

1925, Producers Distributing Corp., 6,117 feet. Director: Scott Sidney. Adaptation: F. McGrew Willis, based on "Thoroughbreds" by William Alexander Fraser. Photography: J. Devereaux Jennings, Dewey Wrigley.

Cast: Ralph Lewis, Vera Reynolds, Edmund Burns, Clarence Burton, Tom Wilson, Danny Hoy, Rosa Gore, Walter Emerson, Lon Poff.

Do you have your scorecard ready to follow the melodramatic plot developments? A southern horseman (Lewis) buys a horse named Dixie based on its showing in a race, only to find that it had been doped.

He's paralyzed in a fall from a horse, and to help pay the bills, his son (Emerson) embezzles money from a bank. However, the boy friend (Burns) of the paralyzed man's daughter (Reynolds) proves his love by taking the blame and is fired from the bank.

The girl disguises herself as a male jockey and rides Dixie to win in the big race, which causes her father to undergo a miraculous recovery and lead to a happy ending for all.

1019 Missouri Traveler

1958, Buena Vista, 104 minutes, Color. Director: Jerry Hopper. Producer: Patrick Ford. Screenplay: Norman Shannon Hall, based on a novel by John Burness. Photography: Winston C. Hoch. Editor: Tom McAdoo.

Cast: Brandon de Wilde, Lee Marvin, Gary Merrill, Paul Ford, Mary Hosford, Ken Curtis, Cal Tinney, Frank Cody.

At the turn of the century, a young orphan (de Wilde) runs away to a small town where he's befriended by a newspaper editor (Merrill) and bullied by a farmer (Marvin).

During a July 4th celebration, most of the town roots for de Wilde to beat Marvin in a horse trotting race.

1020 Money from Home

1953, Paramount, 100 minutes, Color, 3-D. Director: George Marshall. Producer: Hal D. Wallis. Screenplay: Hal Kanter, based on a story by Damon Runyon. Photography: Daniel L. Fapp.

Cast: Dean Martin, Jerry Lewis, Marjie Millar, Pat Crowley, Richard Haydn, Robert Strauss, Gerald Mohr, Sheldon Leonard, Jack Kruschen, Society Kid Hogan, Mara Corday.

Good-for-nothing Honey Talk Nelson (Martin), so named because he can sweet talk almost anybody into anything, is forced by mobster Jumbo Schneider (Leonard) to fix a Maryland race after the gangster buys up all his IOUs.

Taking his dimwitted vegetarian veterinarian cousin (Lewis) with him, they're picked up en route by the drunken British jockey of the horse they're supposed to dope up.

Lewis poses as the jockey and winds up riding the horse (well, sort of) in the steeplechase, as Martin falls in love with the lady owner.

Certainly not one of the Martin-Lewis team's better comedies, its only real distinction was that it was in 3-D.

1021 Mr. Celebrity

1942, Producers Releasing Corp., 68 minutes. Director-Screenplay: William Beaudine. Producer: Martin Mooney. Photography: Arthur Martinelli. Editor: Robert Crandall.

Cast: Buzzy Henry, James Seay, Doris Day, William Halligan, Jim Jeffries, Francis X. Bushman, Gavin Gordon, Larry Grey, John E. Ince, Clara Kimball Young, Johnny Berker.

At Celebrity Farm, a haven for ex-show business personalities, a veterinarian (Seay) and his nephew (Henry) nurse a horse called Mr. Celebrity back to health for a run at the championship. The vet, meanwhile, wages a custody fight for the kid against rich grandparents.

1022 Muggs Rides Again

1945, Monogram, 63 minutes. Director: Wallace Fox. Producers: Sam Katzman, Jack Dietz. Screenplay: Harvey Gates. Photography: Ira Morgan. Editor: William Austin.

Cast: Leo Gorcey, Huntz Hall, Billy Benedict, Pierre Watkin, Mendie Koenig, Bud Gorman, John H. Allen, Johnny Duncan, Bernard Thomas.

The East Side Kids, employed at a racetrack, get into hot water when Muggs (Gorcey) is framed and barred as a jockey.

Taking with them a horse given as loan security, they get into even more trouble by keeping it in their clubhouse; but when its owner returns, Muggs is hired for the big race.

They thwart the inevitable doping scheme by the racketeers and Muggs clears his name.

1023 My Brother Talks to Horses

1946, Metro Goldwyn Mayer, 92 minutes. Director: Fred Zinnemann. Producer: Samuel Marx. Screenplay: Morton Thompson, from his book **Joe the Wounded Tennis Player.** Photography: Harold Rosson. Editor: George White.

Cast: Butch Jenkins, Peter Lawford, Charles Ruggles, Edward Arnold, Beverly Tyler, Spring Byington, O.Z. Whitehead, Paul Langton.

In the same vein as **Three Men on a Horse,** Jenkins is a young kid who gets tips straight from the horse's mouth and who becomes the target of gamblers, particularly Ruggles.

Lawford is his older brother and Arnold a rich horse owner. The finale of this light fantasy is the running of the Preakness in Baltimore.

1024 My Old Kentucky Home

1922, American Releasing Corp., 7,382 feet. Director-Producer Ray C. Smallwood. Story: Anthony Paul Kelly. Photography: Michael Joyce, Ollie Leach.

Cast: Monte Blue, Julia Swayne Gordon, Frank Currier, Sigrid Holmquist, Arthur Carew, Lucy Fox, Matthew Betz, Billy Quirk, Pat Harrigan, Tom Blake.

Released from prison after being framed (of course), a Kentucky man returns home to his mother (Gordon). The man never told his mom he was in prison and never wants her to know. His rival, however, conveniently named Con (Carew) so audiences will know he's the villain, constantly threatens to expose his past and eventually does, to no avail.

Blue and his pals realize his mother's horse is incapable of winning the Derby, so they substitute a ringer which wins.

1025 National Velvet

1944, Metro Goldwyn Mayer, 125 minutes, Color. Director: Clarence Brown. Producer: Pandro S. Berman. Screenplay: Theodore Reeves, Helen Deutsch, based on a novel by Enid Bagnold. Photography: Leonard Smith. Editor: Robert Kern.

Cast: Elizabeth Taylor, Mickey Rooney, Donald Crisp, Anne Revere, Angela Lansbury, Juanita Quigley, Butch Jenkins, Reginald Owen, Arthur Shields, Arthur Treacher, Billy Bevan.

There's an interesting story behind the making of this most famous of all horse films. Berman tried to buy the rights to Bagnold's novel as a vehicle for Katharine Hepburn when he was at RKO in 1935. Paramount beat him to the punch, however, but had trouble casting it and sold it to Metro in 1937. When Berman came to Metro in 1941, his interest in it was renewed.

In the role that launched her to fame, Taylor is Velvet Brown, an 11-year-old girl who wins a horse no one else can handle, during a raffle. The tickets for the raffle were paid for by Rooney, an ex-jockey responsible for the death of another rider. Rooney intends to steal from Velvet's family until he's softened by her.

Over the objections of her father (Crisp), she tames the horse and enters it in the Grand National Sweepstakes.

Her mother (Revere) explains that once in a lifetime, everyone is entitled to a move of great folly.

When there are no other jockeys, Velvet rides the horse to victory herself but is disqualified when her sex is discovered.

Revere won an Oscar as Best Supporting Acress for her role as the mother while Kern's editing also earned him an Academy Award.

In 1979, a sequel, **International Velvet**, featured an adult Velvet Brown coping with another young girl and a horse.

1026 Neck and Neck

1931, Sono-Art World Wide, 61 minutes. Director: Richard Thorpe. Producer: George W. Weeks. Story: Betty Burbridge. Photography: Jules Cronjager.

Cast: Glenn Tryon, Vera Reynolds, Walter Brennan, Lafe McKee, Stepin Fetchit.

Undistinguished drama about a boaster who wins a steed during a poker game and trains it to win the race.

1027 Never Back Losers

1967, British, Schoenfeld, 61 minutes. Director: Robert Tronson. Producer: Jack Greenwood. Screenplay: Lukas Heller, based on "The Green Ribbon" by Edgar Wallace. Photography: Bert Mason. Editor: Derek Holding.

Cast: Jack Hedley, Jacqueline Ellis, Patrick Magee, Richard Warner, Derek Francis, Austin Trevor, Harry Locke, George Tovery.

Insurance man Hedley investigates when a famous jockey is killed in a car crash after losing a race in which he was the favorite.

When the jockey's replacement has several near accidents, Hedley discovers gamblers to be behind the events.

1028 New Orleans

1929, Tiffany-Stahl, 6,799 feet. Director: Reginald Barker. Screenplay: John Francis Natteford, Frederick and Fanny Hatton. Photography: Harry Jackson.

Cast: Ricardo Cortez, William Collier, Jr., Alma Bennett.

A loose woman (Bennett) marries the assistant manager of a racetrack (Cortez) after leaving a jockey (Collier) at the altar on their wedding day.

The manager embezzles money from the track to bet on the jockey to keep up with his wife's expenses; and when he wins, she fails to return the money to the safe, and hubby goes to jail.

Not exactly a women's picture.

1029 A Nice Little Bank That Should Be Robbed

1958, 20th Century-Fox, 88 minutes. Director: Henry Levin. Producer: Anthony Muto. Screenplay: Sydney Boehm. Photography: Leo Tover.

Cast: Tom Ewell, Mickey Rooney, Mickey Shaughnessy, Dina Merrill, Madge Kennedy, Frances Bavier, Richard Deacon, Stanley Clements, Tom Greenway.

Pleasant little caper comedy in which horse trainer Rooney talks hypochondriac Ewell into a $30,000 bank robbery.

They buy a racehorse, but since they lost most of the rest of the money to bookie Shaughnessy, they have to rob another bank to get money to enter it in a race.

This time they're caught, and the bank winds up with the horse which turns out to be a winner.

1030 No Control

1927, Producers Distributing Corp., 5,573 feet. Director: Scott Sidney, E.J. Babille. Screenplay: Zelda Sears, Tay Garnett, based on "Speed but No Control" by Frank Condon in the **Saturday Evening Post.** Photography: George Benoit.

Cast: Harrison Ford, Tom Wilson, Toby Claude, Jack Duffy, Phyllis Haver, E.J. Ratcliffe, Larry Steers.

When a circus finds itself in deep financial trouble, it enters a dancing horse in a race to win some money. To prod the horse into going faster and winning the race, the hero gets the circus lion to roar loudly and scare it.

1031 Off to the Races

1937, 20th Century-Fox, 58-59 minutes. Director: Frank R. Strayer. Producer: Max Golden. Screenplay: Robert Ellis, Helen Logan, based on characters created by Katherine Kavanaugh. Photography: Barney McGill.

Cast: Slim Summerville, Jed Prouty, Shirley Deane, Spring Byington, Russell Gleason, Kenneth Howell, George Ernest, June Carlson, Florence Roberts, Bill Mahan.

Uncle George (Summerville) needs the Jones family's help to raise money for the entrance fee for his trotter at the fair. Father Jones winds up taking the reins in this lightweight series entry.

1032 Oh, You Tony!

1924, Fox Film Corp., 6,302 feet. Director: J.G. Blystone. Screenplay: Donald W. Lee. Photography: Daniel Clark.

Cast: Tom Mix, Claire Adams, Dick LaReno, Charles K. French, Earle Foxe, Dolores Rousse, Pat Chrisman, Miles McCarthy, Mathilda Brundage.

Cowboy Mix goes to Washington on behalf of fellow ranchers but winds up losing control of his property to some wicked lobbyists.

He wins back his ranch by staking it all on his horse Tony in a big race.

1033 Old Age Handicap

1928, Trinity Pictures, 5,573 feet. Director: Frank S. Mattison. Scenario: Charles A. Taylor. Photography: Jules Cronjager. Editor: Minnie Steppler.

Cast: Alberta Vaughn, Gareth Hughes, Vivian Rich, Olaf Hytten, Mavis Villiers, Bud Shaw, Jimmy Humes, Carolyn Wethall, Robert Rodman, Arthur Hotaling, Hall Cline.

A poor girl and a banker's daughter vie for the love of a boy. The poor girl, a dancer, endangers her own reputation to save the lad's sister from a ticklish situation and rides his family's in a horse race fixed by the banker.

1034 On the Right Track

1981, 20th Century-Fox, 97-98 minutes, Color. Director: Lee Philips. Producer: Ronald Jacobs. Screenplay-Co-Producers: Tina Pine, Avery Buddy, Richard Moses. Photography: Jack Richards. Editor: Bill Butler.

Cast: Gary Coleman, Maureen Stapleton, Norman Fell, Michael Lembeck, Lisa Eilbacher, Bill Russell, Herb Edelman, David Selburg, C. Thomas Cunliffe.

Little Coleman plays Lester, a shoeshine boy who lives inside a locker at a train station because he's afraid of life "up there."

Beloved by everyone in the terminal, he becomes a big celebrity when it's discovered he has the knack of picking horse race winners.

1035 On Velvet

1938, British, Columbia, 70 minutes. Director-Producer: Widgey R. Newman. Screenplay: John Quin.

Cast: Wally Patch, Joe Hayman, Vi Kaley, Mildred Franklin, Jennifer Skinner, Leslie Bradley, Nina Mae McKinney, Julie Suedo.

Two pals form an advertising company after they lose most of their money at the racetrack and nearly lose their wives in this low grade musical comedy.

All turns out well after a number of complications.

1036 The 100 to 1 Shot, or, a Run Of Luck?

1906, Vitagraph, 10 minutes. Credits unknown.

Some of the earliest examples of parallel cutting are evident in this early melodrama about some big winnings on the racetrack saving some elderly people from eviction. After the horse race, there's a frantic car ride to get to the house in time.

1037 Over the Sticks

1929, British, Cinema Exclusives, 3,345 feet. Director: G.B. Samuelson, A.E. Coleby. Producer: Frank Wheatcroft. Story: Samuelson.

Cast: Tom Shelton, Molly Wright, Billy Phelps.

A racehorse owner fakes his own death after being blackmailed and becomes a successful bookie.

1038 Pardon My Gun

1930, Pathe Exchange, 5,654 feet. Director: Robert De Lacy. Producer: E.B. Derr. Screenplay: Hugh Cummings. Story: Betty Scott. Photography: Edward Snyder. Editor: Fred Allen.

Cast: Sally Starr, George Duryea, Mona Ray, Lee Moran, Robert Edeson, Frank MacFarlane, Tom MacFarlane, Harry Woods, Abe Lyman and His Band.

There's lots of western music in this light tale of two men in love with a rancher's daughter highlighted by an annual horse race.

1039 The Phantom Horse

1956, Japanese, Daiei, 90 minutes, Color. Director: Koji Shima. Photography: Michio Takahashi.

The plot sounds familiar, but the beautiful color photography and straightforward simplicity lift this tale of a horse race saving a family's home above the ordinary.

1040 Phantom of the Turf

1928, Rayart Pictures, 5,905 feet. Director-Producer: Duke Worne. Scenario: Arthur Hoerl. Story: Leota Morgan. Photography: Walter Griffin. Editor: Malcolm Sweeney.

Cast: Rex Lease, Helene Costello, Forrest Stanley, Danny Hoy, Clarence H. Wilson.

The son of the owner of a famous racehorse returns home to find his father dead and a villain claiming to be his guardian. The youth (Lease) unravels the mystery of his dad's death and rides the horse to victory despite the attempts by the baddie (Stanley) to substitute a ringer.

1041 Phar Lap

1983, Australian, 20th Century-Fox, 118 minutes, Color. Director: Simon Wincer. Producer: John Sexton. Screenplay: David Williamson. Photography: Russell Boyd. Editor: Tony Paterson.

Cast: Tom Burlinson, Ron Leibman, Martin Vaughan, Judy Morris, Celia De Burgh, Richard Morgan, Robert Grubb, Georgia Carr, James Steele, Vincent Ball, Peter Whitford.

Originally, the American general release was scheduled for October 1984, but when the death of the prize racehorse Swayle recalled the mysterious death of the Australian champion Phar Lap in 1932, the release date was pushed up two months. Coincidence? Maybe.

This "horse biography" follows Phar Lap from his start as a scrawny little thing to his reign as king of the turf in Australia during the Depression years.

A stableboy (Burlinson) believes in Phar Lap when no one else will and the horse runs only with his young friend's encouragement. The boy keeps the horse's relentless debt-ridden trainer from working Phar Lap to death.

Phar Lap becomes a national hero in Australia to the common man and wins 37 races in three years despite efforts by bookies to kill him and by the Victoria Racing Club which imposes weight handicaps on him.

In Mexico, his owner is told "If something's good, that's okay; but if something's too good, it upsets the whole system," and a few days later Phar Lap dies under mysterious circumstances.

1042 Pickin' a Winner

1932, Vitaphone, 17 minutes, Color. Director: Roy Mack. Story: Jack Henley, Glen Lambert.

During a carnival, a couple of con men win the fire chief's clothes and the town's firehorse, which they enter in a race. The horse is far behind until he hears the fire bell and then sprints to win.

1043 Pimple's the Whip

1917, British, Piccadilly, 2,000 feet. Directors-Screenplay: Fred and Joe Evans.

Cast: Fred Evans.

A plot to kill the favorite in a horse race is thwarted.

1044 Pimple's Three O'Clock Race

1915, British, Piccadilly, 525 feet. Directors-Screenplay: Fred and Joe Evans.

Cast: Fred Evans.

Two men pose as a horse owner and a jockey to sneak in to the racetrack.

1045 Playing the Ponies

1937, Columbia, 2 reels. Director: Charles Lamont.

Cast: The Three Stooges, William Irving, Jack "Tiny" Lipson.

A broken-down racehorse is purchased by the Three Stooges.

1046 Pleasure Before Business

1927, Columbia, 5,569 feet. Director: Frank Strayer. Producer: Harry Cohn. Screenplay: William Branch. Photography: J. O. Taylor.

Cast: Pat O'Malley, Virginia Brown Faire, Max Davidson, Rosa Rosanova, Lester Bernard, Tom McGuire, Jack Raymond, Henri Menjou.

A cigar manufacturer (Davidson) who's in ill health wagers a lot of money on a racehorse named Sarah who won't race unless the jockey speaks to her in Yiddish.

1047 Polly of the Circus

1918, Goldwyn Features, 8 reels. Directors: Charles Horan, Edwin L. Hollywood. Screenplay: Adrian Gil Speare, Emmett Campbell Hall, based on a play by Margaret Mayo.

Cast: Mae Marsh, Vernon Steele, Charles Riegel, Wellington Playter, Charles Eldridge, George Trimble, Lucille La Verne, Dick Lee, John Carr, Mildred Call, Stephen Carr.

Sam Goldfish changed his name to Goldwyn and made this his first production for Goldwyn Features.

A pretty circus rider named Polly (Marsh) is injured and taken to the home of minister Steele, despite the objections of a self-righteous deacon (Riegel), who wants her out of town.

When Toby the Clown falls seriously ill, she enters the horse race at the county fair to raise money for him. She wins, but the clown dies anyway; and when the deacon threatens the minister, she leaves town.

It was remade in 1932.

1048 The Pride of Donegal

1929, British, H.B. Parkinson, 6,412 feet. Director: J. Steven Edwards. Story: Norman Lee.

Cast: Rex Sherren, Robina Maugham, Syd Crossley, Graeme Lom.

An injured racehorse is saved from the scrap heap and recovers to win the Grand National.

1049 Pride of Maryland

1951, Republic, 60 minutes. Director: Philip Ford. Producer: William Lackey. Screenplay: John K. Butler. Photography: John MacBurnie. Editor: Harold Minter.

Cast: Stanley Clements, Peggy Stewart, Frankie Darro, Joe Sawyer, Robert Barrat, Harry Shannon, Duncan Richardson, Stanley Logan, Joseph Crehan, Emmett Vogan, Clyde Cook.

A cheapie production featuring process photography and stock racing shots concerns a jockey who gets a second chance after he's barred for betting on himself.

1050 Pride of the Blue Grass

1939, Warner Brothers, 65 minutes. Director: William McGann. Producer: Bryan Foy. Screenplay: Vincent Sherman. Photography: Ted McCord.

Cast: Edith Fellows, James McCallion, Granville Bates, Sam McDaniels, Arthur Loft, DeWolf Hopper, Frankie Burke.

When a horse falters during the stretch in the Derby, it's discovered he's blind. He's retrained and secretly entered in the Grand National and wins to save the old homestead.

1051 Pride of the Blue Grass

1954, Allied Artists, 71 minutes, Color. Director: William Beaudine. Producer: Hayes Goetz. Screenplay: Harold Shumate. Photography: Harry Neumann. Editor: John Fuller.

Cast: Lloyd Bridges, Vera Miles, Margaret Sheridan, Arthur Shields, Michael Chapin, Harry Cheshire, Cecil Weston, Emory Parnell, Joan Shawlee, Ray Walker.

Miles' faith in Gypsy Prince remains steadfast even after the horse breaks its leg. Under the training of Bridges, it eventually wins the big race.

1052 Princess O'Hara

1935, Universal, 74 minutes. Director: David Burton. Adaptation: Doris Mallory, Harry Clork, based on a story by Damon Runyon.

Cast: Jean Parker, Chester Morris, Leon Errol, Vince Barnett, Henry Armetta, Verna Hillie, Ralph Remley, Dorothy Gray, Anne Howard, Jimmy Fay, Clifford Jones.

Typical Runyonesque characters such as Deadpan, Last Card Louis, Fingers and Pocahantas abound in this tale of a cab driver named King O'Hara who's killed during a taxi war between Vic Toledo and a rival firm.

When O'Hara's daughter blames Toledo, he instructs his drivers to take care of her without her knowing. When they steal a racehorse to sub for a sick taxi horse, she nearly lands in jail.

It was remade in 1943 as **It Ain't Hay** with Abbott and Costello.

1053 A Race for Life

1928, Warner Brothers, 4,777 feet. Director: D. Ross Lederman. Screenplay: Charles R. Condon. Photography: Ed Du Par. Editor: Charles Henkel, Jr.

Cast: Rin Tin Tin, Bobby Gordon, Virginia Brown, Carroll Nye, James Mason, Pat Hartigan.

It's the dog hero of all time, Rin Tin Tin, to the rescue of his master (Gordon) when a rival stable owner tries to prevent the boy from riding his boss's star horse in the big race.

1054 Race for Love

1913, British, Martin, 1,050 feet. Director: Lewin Fitzhamen. Screenplay: Frank C. Barnaby.

Cast: Constance Somers-Clarke, Frank Doller.

Despite being shot by a rival, the hero jockey wins the big race and the girl's love.

1055 Race Street

1949, RKO Radio Pictures, 79 minutes. Director: Edwin L. Marin. Producer: Nat Holt. Screenplay: Martin Rackin, suggested by a story by Maurice Davis. Photography: J. Roy Hunt.

Cast: George Raft, William Bendix, Harry Morgan, Marilyn Maxwell, Frank Faylen, Gale Robbins, Cully Richards, Mack Gray, Russell Hicks, Richard Powers, William Forrest.

When a bookie (Morgan) is killed after refusing to pay racketeers protection money, bookie pal Raft seeks vengeance despite the efforts of an honest cop (Bendix) to help him.

1056 Race Track

1933, World Wide, 78 minutes. Director-Producer: James Cruze. Story: J. Walter Rubin, Wells Root. Adaptation: Walter Lang, Douglas Doty.

Cast: Leo Carrillo, Junior Coghlan, Kay Hammond, Lee Moran, Huntley Gordon, Wilfrid Lucas, Joseph Girard.

Made before **Little Miss Marker**, this still owes its roots to 1931's **The Champ,** in its tale of a waif who reforms a racetrack crook (Carrillo).

As in the 1931 classic, the boy's mother tries to reclaim the lad, who becomes a jockey, and Carrillo is torn on how to handle it.

1057 Race Wild

1926, Ellbee Pictures, 5,240 feet. Director: Oscar Apfel. Photography: William Tuers.

Cast: Rex Lease, Eileen Percy, David Torrence, John Miljan.

More dastardly deeds by the villain, who desires the southern colonel's homestead, go to no avail, as usual. The baddie uncouples the railroad car transporting the colonel's prize horse and dopes the jockey, but the good guy's daughter rides the horse herself.

1058 Racing Blood

1926, Lumas Film Corp., 5,500 feet. Director: Frank Richardson. Screenplay: James Bell Smith. Photography: Ray June.

Cast: Robert Agnew, Anne Cornwall, John Elliott, Clarence Geldert, Charles A. Sellon, Robert Hale.

When a lad's father kills himself after losing the estate to the father of the boy's girl friend, the young lovers break up, with the boy (Agnew) becoming a newspaper reporter.

He later buys a horse which turns out to be one which was stolen by his girl friend (Cornwall), but she doesn't tell him about it.

Entering the horse in the big race, the youth is disqualified because of a weight limit, and the girl rides it and is reunited with her boy friend.

1059 Racing Blood

1938, Conn, 61 minutes. Director: Rex Hale. Producer: Maurice A. Conn. Story: Peter B. Kyne. Adaptation: Stephen Norris. Photography: Robert Doran, William Hyer, Jack Greenhalgh. Editor: Martin G. Cohn.

Cast: Frankie Darro, Kane Richmond, Gladys Blake, Arthur Housman, Jimmy Eagles, Matthew Betz, Si Wills, Snowflake, Bob Tansill, Jones Quintette.

As usual, Darro is the jockey, but what he does to win the race has to be some sort of record.

Not only does he raise a crippled colt which everyone else wants to destroy, but he's kidnapped and shot in the chest. He escapes and steals an ambulance, and, making it to the racetrack just in the nick of time, wins the race.

1060 Racing Blood

1954, 20th Century-Fox, 75 minutes, Color. Director-Producer: Wesley Barry. Screenplay: Sam Rocca. Photography: John Martin. Editor: Ace Herman.

Cast: Bill Williams, Jean Parker, Frankie Darro, Jimmy Boyd, George Cleveland, John Eldridge, Sam Flint, Fred Kohler, Jr., George Steele, Bobby Johnson.

Young Boyd sings four songs in between secretly raising a horse with a cloven hoof everyone wanted destroyed and which ultimately beats its twin in a race.

1061 Racing Lady

1937, RKO Radio Pictures, 59 minutes, Director: Wallace Fox. Producer: William Sistrom. Screenplay: Dorothy Yost, Thomas Lennon, Cortland Fitzsimmons, based on stories by Damon Runyon, J. Robert Byron and Norman Houston. Photography: Harry Wild.

Cast: Smith Ballew, Ann Dvorak, Harry Carey, Berton Churchill, Frank M. Thomas, Ray Mayer, Willie Best, Hattie Mc-Daniel, Harry Jans, Harland Tucker.

Ho hum, nothing's really new in the story about a girl who trains a colt and turns it from a loser into a winner and who falls in love with an automobile executive who wants the horse.

1062 Racing Luck

1948, Columbia, 65 minutes. Director: William Berke. Screenplay: Joseph Carole, Al Martin, Harvey Gates. Photography: Ira H. Morgan. Editor: Henry Batista.

Cast: Gloria Henry, Stanley Clements, David Bruce, Paula Raymond, Harry Cheshire, Dooley Wilson, Jack Ingram.

A totally routine horse racing film which concentrates on the racing and has little plot that's worthwhile.

1063 Racing Romance

1926, Rayart Pictures, 5,352 feet. Director-Producer: Harry J. Brown. Screenplay: Henry Roberts Symonds. Photography: William Tuers.

Cast: Reed Howes, Virginia Brown Faire, Harry S. Northrup, Mathilda Brundage, Victor Potel, Ethan Laidlaw.

Every cliche in the book is tossed in, from the burning stable, to the mortgage depending on the big race, the villain framing the hero and the last-minute attempt to get to the track on time.

The main plot concerns a feud between two Kentucky families and a youth from one family who loves the girl of the other.

1064 Racing Romance

1937, British, Radio, 63 minutes. Director: Maclean Rogers. Producer: A. George Smith. Screenplay: John Hunter. Photography: Geoffrey Faithfull.

Cast: Bruce Seton, Elizabeth Kent, Marjorie Taylor, Eliot Makeham, Ian Fleming, Sybil Grove, Robert Hobbs, Charles Sewell, Michael Ripper.

The old quadrangle--man in love with two women and a horse--gets another working in this tale of an engaged garage owner who buys a racehorse, but his fiancée, is jealous of the animal's female trainer.

Needless to say, true love wins out, and horse and trainer live happily ever after.

1065 Racing Sayings Illustrated

1905, British, Graphic, 260 feet. Director: Harold Jeapes.

A short comedy based on racing sayings.

1066 The Racetrack Murders

1964, W. German, Walter Nanley, 84 minutes. Director: F.J. Gottlieb. Photography: Richard Angst. Editor: Walter Wischniewski. Based on a story by Edgar Wallace.

Cast: Hansborg Felmy, Haas Nielsen, Wolfgang Lukschy, Ann Smyrner.

The brother of an executed man takes revenge 15 years later by murdering off, one by one, members of the household of an aristocratic judge, who owns a racing stable.

The murderer tries to pin the deaths on his brother's former partner, a crooked race-fixing gambler who was responsible for the frame-up.

Shades of the silent days: The heroine, the judge's niece, must ride the horse herself in the big race when both the honest jockey and his crooked replacement are put out of action at the last minute.

Until then, the film is mostly talk, talk, talk. At one point, the police inspector, remarking on the fact that the judge was found with a giant pitchfork sticking out his back, makes the startling announcement to the assembled guests at the castle that "the coroner's report has determined it was murder."

1067 Racetrack Winners (Les As du Turf)

1932, French, Paramount, 86 minutes. Director: Serge de Poligny.

Cast: Pauley Drean Josyane, Janett Flo Barancey Bever, Jeanne Fusier-Girl, Henri Jullien.

A pair of track bums invest what little money they have in a racehorse and win enough to marry a couple of dressmakers despite a bookie who tries to welsh.

1068 The Rainbow Jacket

1954, British, Ealing, 100 minutes, Color. Directors-Producers: Michael Relph, Basil Dearden. Screenplay: T.E.B. Clarke. Photography: Otto Hellers. Editor: Jack Harris.

Cast: Robert Morley, Kay Walsh, Edward Underdown, Wilfrid Hyde White, Sidney James, Honor Blackman, Fella Edmonds, Bill Owen, Charles Victor, Ronald Ward.

Owen, a former champion jockey who has been barred from racing, is allowed another chance but sacrifices himself when he learns that his protégé, in need of money, has been bribed to throw the race.

Owen wants to make sure the youth (Edmonds) doesn't follow his footsteps and makes sure the lad wins the race.

1069 The Rainmaker

1926, Paramount, 7 reels. Director: Clarence Badger. Screenplay: Hope Loring, Louis Duryea Lighton, based on "Heavenbent" by Gerald Beaumont in **Redbook Magazine.** Photography: H. Kinley Martin.

Cast: William Collier, Jr., Georgia Hale, Ernest Torrence, Brandon Hurst, Joseph Dowling, Tom Wilson.

A jockey knows when rain is coming because of an old war wound and lets people believe he can call it by praying. He makes a lot of money from promoters and gamblers who want to know what the track conditions will be like.

When he's thrown during a race, he meets a nurse and later finds her in a desert saloon in a town plagued by drought, so he tries out his touch there.

1070 A Rank Outsider

1920, British, Broadwest, 4,236 feet. Director: Richard Garrick. Producer: Walter West. Scenario: Patrick L. Mannock. Story: Nat Gould.

Cast: Gwen Stratford, Cameron Stratford, Lewis Dayton, John Gliddon, Luther Miles, Martita Hunt.

When his sister's racehorse is stolen, her brother, just back from Australia after being framed, tries to track it down.

1071 The Rawhide Kid

1928, Universal, 5,383 feet. Director: Del Andrews. Screenplay: Arthur Statter. Adaptation: Isadore Bernstein. Story: Peter B. Kyne. Photography: Harry Neumann. Editor: Rodney Hickok.

Cast: Hoot Gibson, Georgia Hale, Frank Hagney, William H. Strauss, Harry Todd, Tom Lingham.

Gibson beats Hagney every year in the annual horse race until the latter wins his horse by gambling. When a merchant and his daughter are driven out of town by Hagney's men, Gibson shelters them and earns enough money to buy back his horse.

The villain refuses, however, and Our Hero steals it and wins the race once again.

1072 Reckless Living

1938, Universal, 65-68 minutes. Director: Frank McDonald. Producer: Val Paul. Screenplay:

Charles Grayson, based on the story "Winner's Circle" by Gerald Beaumont. Photography: Elwood Breden.

Cast: Robert Wilcox, Nan Grey, Jimmy Savo, Frank Jenks, William Lundigan, Charles Judels, Harland Briggs, Constance Moore, Harry Davenport, Eddie Anderson.

Minor vehicle with music about a get-rich-quick racetrack scheme.

1073 Reckless Roads

1935, Majestic, 60 minutes. Director: Burt Lynwood. Producer: Larry Darmour. Story: L.E. Heifetz, H.A. Carlisle. Photography: James S. Brown, Jr.

Cast: Judith Allen, Regis Toomey, Lloyd Hughes, Ben Alexander, Louise Carter, Gilbert Emery.

A wild youth ends up winning a horse race.

1074 The Red Stallion

1947, Eagle-Lion, 81 minutes, Color. Director: Lesley Selander. Producer: Bryan Foy. Screenplay: Robert E. Kent, Crane Wilbur. Photography: Virgil Miller. Editor: Fred Allen.

Cast: Robert Paige, Noreen Nash, Ted Donaldson, Jane Darwell, Ray Collins, Guy Kibbee, Willie Best, Pierre Watkin.

A bear's the villain and the beautiful mountain scenery the hero in this pleasant change of pace.

A boy finds a foal and trains it to race, and it rewards his faith by saving his grandmother's ranch from foreclosure. There's nothing new there, but the film's highlight is a fight between the horse and the bear.

1075 The Reivers

1969, National General, 107 minutes, Color. Director: Mark Rydell. Producer: Irving Ravetch. Screenplay: Irving Ruesch, based on a novel by William Faulkner. Photography: Richard Moore. Editor: Thomas Stanford.

Cast: Steve McQueen, Mitch Vogel, Will Geer, Juano Hernandez, Rupert Crosse, Dub Taylor, Ruth White, Sharon Farrell, Burgess Meredith.

In the early part of the twentieth century, the McCaslin family's first car arrives in Mississippi. A hired hand named Boon (McQueen), the car's official driver, persuades young Lucius (Vogel) to lie so that they can drive the car to Memphis.

The car winds up as the stakes in a race between a horse named Lightning and Coppermine. Lightning proves a bust until a sardine sandwich sets him off and after a series of adventures wins back the car.

1076 The Return of October

1948, Columbia, 87 minutes, Color. Director: Joseph H. Lewis. Producer: Rudolph Mate. Screenplay: Melvin Frank, Norman Panama. Story: Connie Lee, Karen DeWolf. Photography: William Snyder. Editor: Gene Havlick.

Cast: Glenn Ford, Terry Moore, Albert Sharpe, James Gleason, Dame May Whittey, Henry O'Neill, Frederick Tozere, Samuel S. Hinds, Lloyd Corrigan.

Uncle Willie (Gleason) dies, but his niece (Moore) remembers his telling her that if he ever came back, it would be as a horse to win the Derby.

When she sees a horse named October, she's reminded of her uncle and winds up being tried for insanity by people who want her estate. Ford, in the meantime, starts to write a book about her.

1077 Ride, Kelly, Ride

1941, 20th Century-Fox, 59 minutes. Director: Norman Foster. Producer: Sol M. Wurtzel. Screenplay: William Conselman, Jr., Irving Cummings, based on a story by Peter H. Kyne. Photography: Virgil Miller. Editor: Louis Loeffler.

Cast: Eugene Pallette, Marvin

Stephens, Rita Quigley, Mary Healy, Richard Lane, Charles D. Brown, Chick Chandler, Dorothy Peterson, Lee Murray, Frankie Burke.

Jockey Stephens, backed by trainer Pallette and his beautiful daughter (Quigley) thwarts some racketeers who try to get him to throw a race.

1078 Riders Up

1924, Universal, 4,904 feet. Director: Irving Cummings. Scenario: Monte Brice, based on a story by Gerald Beaumont. Photography: Ben Reynolds.

Cast: Creighton Hale, George Cooper, Kate Price, Robert Brower, Ethel Shannon, Edith Yorke, Charlotte Stecens, Harry Tracey, Hank Mann.

A long unsuccessful track tout named the Information Kid finally hits the jackpot in Mexico and plans to return to his family in New England.

Taking a blind friend (Brower) to the track one last time, he learns the man has staked his life savings on the race and tells him the horse won, giving him the money he himself planned to use to go home.

1079 Riding High

1950, Paramount, 112 minutes. Director-Producer: Frank Capra. Screenplay: Robert Riskin. Story: Mark Hellinger. Photography: George Barnes, Ernest Laszlo. Editor: William Hornbeck.

Cast: Bing Crosby, Coleen Gray, Charles Bickford, Frances Gifford, Raymond Walburn, William Demarest, Clarence Muse, Margaret Hamilton, Douglas Dumbrille, Ward Bond, Charles Lane, Frankie Darro.

Capra remade his own **Broadway Bill** (1934), added a lot of music plus cameos by Oliver Hardy and Max Baer and came up with nearly an entertaining a film as the sentimental original.

The basic storyline remains the same—the struggle to raise enough money to enter a faithful horse in the big race, and it proved a good vehicle for Crosby.

1080 Riding to Fame

1927, Ellbee Pictures, 5,367 feet. Director-Screenplay: A.B. Barringer. Photography: Kenneth Gordon MacLean, Robert Cline.

Cast: George Fawcett, Rosemary Theby, Gladys McConnell, Arthur Rankin, Henry Sedley, Lafe McKee.

The hero DOESN'T get to the starting gate on time for once, but did you really think that was going to stop him when the fate of a crippled little girl rests on the outcome of the race? No dastardly deeds by the villain can stand in the way.

1081 The Rocking Horse Winner

1949, British, Universal-International, 91 minutes. Director-Screenplay: Anthony Pelissier, based on a story by D.H. Lawrence. Producer: John Mills. Photography: Desmond Dickinson. Editor: John Seabourne.

Cast: Valerie Hobson, John Howard Davies, Ronald Squire, John Mills, Hugh Sinclair, Charles Goldner, Susan Richards, Cyril Smith, Anthony Holles, Melanie McKenzie.

The British censors forced a change in the ending of this story of the world as seen through a child's eyes. The kid (Davies) develops a knack for picking horse race winners while rocking on his toy horse at home.

To the boy, a lack of money means his mother is unhappy; and the more he wins, the more his mother keeps on spending until the lad whips himself into a frenzy on his rocking horse that nearly proves fatal.

1082 Rogues of the Turf

1910, British, Walturdaw, 685 feet. No credits available.

A plot to bribe the jockey

by a bookie and a tout is thwarted by the stableboy.

1083 Rogues of the Turf

1923, British, Butcher, 5,899 feet. Director: Wilifred Noy. Story: John F. Preston.

Cast: Fred Groves, Olive Sloan, James Lindsay, Mavis Clare, Bobbie Andrews, Clarence Blakiston, Dora Lennon, Nell Emerald, James Reardon.

The ex-wife of a horse trainer becomes involved in a plot to kidnap his racehorse.

1084 Run, Appaloosa, Run

1965, Buena Vista, 48 minutes, Color. Director-Producer-Photography-Story: Larry Lansburgh. Screenplay: Janet Lansburgh. Editor: Fred W. Berger.

Cast: Adele Palacios, Wilbur Plaugher, Jerry Gatlin, Walter Cloud, Jack Keran, Ray Patnaude, Pete Logan, Stan Bergstein, Rex Allen.

When a lion kills an Appaloosa on the Nez Percé reservation in Idaho, a young girl gets permission to raise the colt as a cattle horse.

When the tribe needs money, however, it's sold to a brutal rodeo rider and then becomes part of a clown act. As this is a Disney studio film, however, the girl buys back her horse and enters it in a big race.

1085 Run for the Roses (aka Thoroughbred)

1977, Kodiak, 93 minutes, Color. Director: Henry Levin. Producer: Mario Crespo, Jr., Wolf Schmidt. Screenplay: Joseph C. Prieto, Mimi Avins. Story: Crespo. Photography: Paul Dominguez.

Cast: Vera Miles, Stuart Whitman, Sam Groom, Panchito Gomez, Theodore Wilson, Lisa Eilbacher, Henry Brandon, Pat Renella, James Murphy, Joseph Roman.

A wealthy stable owner (Miles), disappointed that a prize mare's colt is born lame, gives him away to the son of a ranch hand but soon regrets her move.

Through the boy's love and through surgery, the colt becomes a contender for the Kentucky Derby. After the race, the boy turns his back on money to retire the horse, rather than risk injury to him.

The highlight is the detailed horse operation scene.

1086 The Sad Horse

1959, 20th Century-Fox, 78 minutes, Color. Director: James B. Clark. Producer: Richard E. Lyons. Screenplay: Charles Hoffman. Story: Zoe Akins. Photography: Karl Struss. Editor: Richard C. Meyer.

Cast: David Ladd, Chill Wills, Rex Reason, Patrice Wymore, Greg Palmer, Leslie Bradley, David DePaul, William Yip, Eve Brent.

Depressed because its dog mascot has disappeared, a champion racehorse is brought to Wills' horse ranch for a rest. Grandson Ladd and his dog are spending the summer at the ranch while his father is getting remarried, and the boy and the dog help heal the horse's spirits.

There's also some action tossed in as the horse kills a snake and helps out when the boy is endangered by a puma.

1087 The Saint Takes Over

1940, RKO Radio Pictures, 68 minutes. Director: Jack Hively. Producer: Howard Benedict. Screenplay: Frank Fenton, Lynn Root, based on characters created by Leslie Charteris. Photography: Frank Redman. Editor: Desmond Marquette.

Cast: George Sanders, Jonathan Hale, Wendy Barrie, Paul Guilfoyle, Morgan Conway, Robert Emmet Keane, Cyrus W. Kendall, Paul Burke, Pierre Watkin, Robert Middlemass.

The suave sleuth Simon

Templar, aka The Saint, helps out Inspector Fernack (Hale), who's framed by some track racketeers.

1088 Salty O'Rourke

1945, Paramount, 100 minutes. Director: Raoul Walsh. Producer: E.D. Leshin. Screenplay: Milton Holmes.

Cast: Alan Ladd, Gail Russell, William Demarest, Bruce Cabot, Spring Byington, Stanley Clements, Marjorie Woodworth.

Heavily in debt to gangsters, Ladd stakes his last hope on avoiding being murdered on one horse that no one but a barred jockey can ride.

Convincing the jockey (Clements) to take the job, Ladd enrolls him under an assumed name at a school for young jockeys, where he mistakes the teacher's kindness for love. She (Russell) in turn loves Ladd, and the jealous jockey nearly throws the all-important race (at least there's no mortgage involved!) but sees the light in time.

1089 Saratoga

1937, Metro Goldwyn Mayer, 90-94 minutes. Director: Jack Conway. Producer: Bernard H. Hyman. Screenplay: Anita Loos, Robert Hopkins. Photography: Ray June.

Cast: Clark Gable, Jean Harlow, Lionel Barrymore, Walter Pidgeon, Una Merkel, Frank Morgan, Cliff Edwards, George Zucco, Jonathan Hale, Hattie McDaniel, Frankie Darro, Si Jenks, Edward "Bud" Flanagan (aka Dennis O'Keefe).

When Jean Harlow died during production in June 1937, Metro hired Mary Dees to double for her and Paula Winslowe to dub her voice.

Gable is bookie Duke Bradley and Harlow the last in the line of a long-time horse breeding family. She's been brought up to avoid the gypsy life of horse breeders—attending northern tracks in summer and southern tracks in winter—but she still wagers on horses and tries to regain the family breeding farm from Gable.

The big race is notable for its use of slow motion.

1090 The Scarlet Lady

1922, British, Violet Hopson Productions, 6,100 feet. Director: Walter West. Producer: Violet Hopson. Screenplay: J. Bertram Brown.

Cast: Violet Hopson, Lewis Willoughby, Cameron Carr, Arthur Walcott, Gertrude Sterroll.

The villainous trustee of a widow attempts to drug some racehorses.

1091 Scattergood Rides High

1942, RKO Radio Pictures. Director: Christy Cabanne. Producer: Jerrold T. Brandt. Screenplay: Michael L. Simmons. Photography: Jack MacKenzie. Editor: John E. Burch.

Cast: Guy Kibbee, Charles Lind, Jed Prouty, Dorothy Moore, Kenneth Howell, Regina Wallace, Frances Carson, Arthur Aylesworth, Paul White, Walter S. Baldwin, Jr.

An entry in the Scattergood Baines (Kibbee) series in which he's able to dole out his wise advice to the orphaned son of an old friend.

The boy wants to be a jockey but is having some trouble with claiming his inheritance of a racing stable.

1092 Sergeant Murphy

1938, Warner Brothers, 57 minutes. Director: B. Reeves Eason. Producer: Bryan Foy. Screenplay: William Jacobs. Story: Sy Bartlett. Photography: Ted McCord. Editor: James Gibbon.

Cast: Ronald Reagan, Donald Crisp, Mary Maguire, Ben Hendricks, William Davidson, Max Hoffman, Jr., David Newell, Emmett Vogan.

James Cagney turned the

lead role down because he felt it was too minor a production; but Reagan, after a number of bit parts, welcomed the role. He plays a soldier who loves Sarge, an army jumping horse which is deemed unfit for the service because it's too sensitive to loud noises.

The horse is mustered out of the army and wins a number of awards and is later smuggled into England where it wins the Grand National. Supposedly based on a true story.

1093 Shadow of the Thin Man

1941, Metro Goldwyn Mayer, 97 minutes. Director: W.S. Van Dyke. Producer: Hunt Stromberg. Screenplay: Harry Kurnitz, Irving Brecher. Photography: William Daniels. Editor: Robert J. Kern.

Cast: William Powell, Myrna Loy, Barry Nelson, Henry O'Neill, Donna Reed, Alan Baxter, Sam Levene, Stella Adler, Louise Beavers, Dickie Hall.

In the fourth episode of the popular detective series featuring the man and wife detective team of Powell and Loy, the pair probe a series of murders related to racetrack gambling.

There's also a scene at a wrestling match.

1094 The Shamrock Handicap

1926, Fox, 5,685 feet. Director: John Ford. Scenario: John Stone. Story: Peter Bernard Kyne. Photography: George Schneiderman.

Cast: Janet Gaynor, Leslie Fenton, J. Farrell MacDonald, Louis Payne, Georgie Harris, Thomas Delmar, Brandon Hurst, Claire McDowell, Willard Louis, Andy Clark.

An impoverished Irish nobleman, who cares about his tenants, sells part of his stable to a wealthy American and then travels across the sea. He enters an American steeplechase in an effort to regain his fortune.

1095 She Went to the Races

1945, Metro Goldwyn Mayer, 85 minutes. Director: Willis Goldbeck. Screenplay: Lawrence Hazard. Story: Alan Friedman, De Vallon Scott. Photography: Charles Salerno. Editor: Adrienne Fazan.

Cast: James Craig, Francis Gilford, Ava Gardner, Edmund Gwenn, Sig Roman, Reginald Owen.

A real example of 1940's screwball comedy in which racing owner Craig becomes the unwitting stakes in a contest between two women.

In the meantime, some wacky professors dope some horses in the name of scientific research.

1096 Silks and Saddles (aka **Thoroughbreds**)

1929, Universal, 5,809 feet. Director: Robert F. Hill. Story Supervision: J.G. Hawks. Adaptation: Edward Clark, James Gruen. Story: Gerald Beaumont. Photography: Joseph Bretherton. Editor: Daniel Mandell.

Cast: Richard Walling, Marion Nixon, Sam De Grasse, Hayden Stevenson, Montagu Love, Mary Nolan, Otis Harlan.

A jockey (Walling) is fired for throwing a race and the no-good woman who had him do it leaves him. He gets a second chance with his employer when his replacement can't handle the prize horse.

1097 Silver Blaze

1912, British, Franco-British/ Eclair, 22 minutes. Director: Georges Treville (although some sources claim the director was Adrien Caillard).

Cast: Georges Treville, Mr. Moyse.

Sherlock Holmes is called in to investigate when the favorite for the Derby disappears, and the stableboy is found drugged and the jockey dead with a crushed skull.

Holmes, who was staying at the home of the owner, Colonel

Ross, discovers the kidnapper has painted the horse and entered it in the Derby under another name.

Of the three versions of **Silver Blaze** brought to the screen, this earliest one is considered the most faithful to Sir Arthur Conan Doyle's original.

1098 Silver Blaze

1923, British, Stoll, 34 minutes. Director: George Ridgwell. Producer: Jeffrey Bernerd. Screenplay: Geoffrey H. Malins, Patrick L. Mannock, based on a story by Sir Arthur Conan Doyle. Photography: Alfred H. Moise. Editor: Challis N. Sanderson.

Cast: Ellie Norwood, Hubert Willis, Knighton Small, Sam Marsh, Norma Whalley, Sam Austin, Bert Barclay, Tom Beaumont.

Another version of Sherlock Holmes tracing the missing racehorse Silver Blaze and solving a murder.

1099 Silver Blaze (aka **Murder at the Baskervilles)**

1937, British, Astor, 71 minutes. Director: Thomas Bentley. Producer: Julius Hagen. Screenplay: Arthur Macrae, H. Fowler Mear, Arthur Wontner, based on stories by Sir Arthur Conan Doyle.

Cast: Arthur Wontner, Ian Fleming, Lyn Harding, Judy Gunn, Lawrence Grossmith, Arthur Macrae, Ronald Shiner.

In this version, Holmes' old nemesis Moriarty and his friend, Sir Henry Baskerville, are added to the tale of the missing Derby favorite.

The groom is found dead with opium poisoning, and the trainer is later found dead on the moors. As in **Charlie Chan at the Race Track,** there's a gun concealed inside a camera during the big race.

1100 Silver Comes Through (aka **Silver Comes Thru, Silver King Comes Thru)**

1927, Film Booking Offices of America, 5,476 feet. Director-Screenplay: Lloyd Ingraham. Story: Frank M. Clifton. Photography: Mack Stengler.

Cast: Fred Thomson, Edna Murphy, William Courtright, Harry Woods, Mathilde Brundage.

A ranch owner (Courtright) who owes a debt to a man (Woods) gives him several horses, but not Silver King, because he sees the man mistreating it.

The hero (Thomson) thwarts a plot by Woods to kidnap the prize horse prior to the big cross-country race.

1101 The Silver Lining

1919, British, I.B. Davidson, 6,458 feet. Director: A.E. Coleby.

Cast: Bombardier Billy Wells, Ella Milne, Richard Buttery, Warwick Ward, Ralph Forster, George Harrington, Doris Paxman, H. Nicholls-Bates, Olive Colin Bell.

The hero, played by boxer Wells, thwarts yet another scheme to dope a racehorse.

1102 Simple Simon at the Races

1909, British, London Cinematograph Co., 435 feet.

A man is chased and stripped after he stands in for a welshing bookie.

1103 Sing You Sinners (aka **The Unholy Beebes)**

1938, Paramount, 88 minutes. Director-Producer: Wesley Ruggles. Screenplay: Claude Binyon. Photography: Karl Struss. Editor: Alma Ruth Macrorie.

Cast: Bing Crosby, Fred MacMurray, Donald O'Connor, Elizabeth Patterson, Ellen Drew, John Gallaudet, William Haade, Paul White, Irving Bacon, Tom Durgan, Herbert Corthell.

Crosby is the good-for-nothing of the Beebe family, the bane of brother MacMurray's existence and the idol of the baby of the family, O'Connor. MacMurray must keep on putting off his marriage because Crosby won't help out the family by getting a job.

What little money the family gets comes from their singing at nightclubs.

Crosby, who has a penchant for trading, runs off huge winnings at the racetrack by trading tickets with a poor sucker and moves out to California to open a swap shop. When the family joins him, however, they find he's traded the store for a horse.

O'Connor, who becomes the jockey, is threatened by gangsters to lose the race, but Crosby finds out about it in time.

1104 So You Want to Play the Horses

1946, Warner Brothers, 10 minutes. Director: Richard L. Bare.

Cast: Joe McDoakes, Jane Harker, Richard Erdman, Leo White, Clifton Young, Fred Kelsey, Art Gilmore.

An Academy Award nomination went to this short about a racing enthusiast who goes "cold turkey" at his wife's urging but has his racing forms hidden all over the place and continues to bet.

1105 Son of Kissing Cup

1922, British, Butcher, 5,600 feet. Director-Producer: Walter West. Screenplay: J. Bertram Brown. Story: Campbell Rae.

Cast: Violet Hopson, Stewart Rome, Cameron Carr, Arthur Walcott, Lewis Gilbert, Adeline Hayden Coffin, Judd Green, Bob Vallis.

In this follow-up to **Kissing Cup's Race**, a bookmaker bribes an ailing racehorse owner.

1106 Song of Kentucky

1929, Fox, 7,125 feet. Director: Lewis Seiler. Screenplay: Frederick Hazlitt Brennan. Photography: Charles G. Clarke. Editor: Carl Carruth.

Cast: Joseph Wagstaff, Lois Moran, Dorothy Burgess, Douglas Gilmore, Herman Bing, Hedda Hopper, Bert Woodruff.

A Kentucky girl tells a fortune hunter she'll marry him if her horse loses the Kentucky Derby. It does, but she winds up with her true sweetheart anyway.

1107 Sorrowful Jones

1949, Paramount, 88 minutes. Director: Sidney Lanfield. Producer: Robert L. Welch. Screenplay: Melville Shavelson, Edmund Hartmann, Jack Rose, based on a story by Damon Runyon. Photography: Daniel F. Fapp. Editor: Arthur Schmidt.

Cast: Mary Jane Saunders, Bob Hope, Lucille Ball, William Demarest, Bruce Cabot, Thomas Gomez, Tom Pedi, Paul Lees, Houseley Stevenson, Claire Carleton, Harry Tyler.

Hope is more restrained than usual in this remake of **Little Miss Marker.** Saunders is the little girl left as a marker for a bet with bookie Jones (Hope). When the father is rubbed out by mobster Cabot, Hope becomes her surrogate father. Described as a "man who fell in love with money at the age of six and has been going steady ever since," he reforms by stealing a racehorse and bringing it to the girl's hospital bedside.

Ball is the mobster's girl who falls for Hope.

1108 The Speed Demon

1925, Bud Barsky Productions, 5,500 feet. Director: Robert N. Bradbury. Screenplay: Samuel M. Pyke. Editor: Della M. King.

Cast: Kenneth McDonald, Peggy Montgomery, B. Wayne Lamont, Art Manning, Clark Comstock, Jack Pierce, Frank Rice, Barney Oldfield.

A Yank (McDonald) prevents a Kentucky colonel from being suckered by a sharpie into giving up his prize filly.

1109 Speed to Burn

1938, Fox, 60 minutes. Director: Otto Brower. Producer: Jerry

Hoffman. Screenplay: Robert Ellis, Helen Logan, based on a story by Edwin Dial Torgerson. Photography: Edward Snyder.

Cast: Michael Whalen, Lynn Bari, Marvin Stephens, Henry Armetta, Chick Chandler, Sidney Blackmer, Johnny Pirrone, Charles D. Brown, Inez Palange.

When a racehorse belonging to some cops is kidnapped along with the jockey, a kid who helped raise it and a cop (Whalen), must get it back in time for the big race.

1110 The Sport of Kings

1921, British, Granger's Exclusives, 5,100 feet. Director-Screenplay: Arthur Rooke.

Cast: Victor McLaglen, Phyllis Shannon, Douglas Munro, Cyril Percival.

Horse racing and boxing mix once again in a tale of a rich girl who works in the slums.

1111 The Sport of Kings

1931, British, Ideal, 90-98 minutes. Director: Victor Saville. Producer: Michael Balcon. Screenplay: Angus MacPhail, based on a play by Ian Hay. Photography: Alex Bryce.

Cast: Hugh Wakefield, Gordon Harker, Dorothy Boyd, Barbara Gott, Lesloe Henson.

Minor comedy in which a man who hates gambling is talked into wagering on the horses.

1112 The Sport of Kings

1947, Columbia, 67 minutes. Director: Robert Gordon. Producer: William Bloom. Screenplay: Edward Huebsch. Story: Gordon Grand. Photography: Henry Freulich. Editor: Aaron Stell.

Cast: Paul Campbell, Mark Dennis, Gloria Henry, Harry Davenport, Harry Cheshire, Clinton Rosemond, Louis Mason.

Two Yanks (Campbell, Dennis) take over a plantation owned by Davenport after their father wins it by gambling, but find they're not exactly welcome in the South.

They soften the old colonel's stand against them when they enter his horse in a big race.

1113 Sporting Blood

1916, Fox, 5 reels. Director-Screenplay: Bertram Bracken. Photography: R.B. Schellinger.

Cast: Dorothy Bernard, Glen White, DeWitt C. Jennings, George Morgan, Madeleine Le Nard, Claire Whitney.

Life among the upper crust of the racing world is examined in this real old-style melodrama.

1114 Sporting Blood

1931, Metro Goldwyn Mayer, 80 minutes. Director: Charles Brabin. Story: Frederick Hazlitt Brennan. Photography: Harold Rosson.

Cast: Clark Gable, Ernest Torrence, Madge Evans, Lew Cody, Marie Prescott, Harry Holman, Hallam Cooley, J. Farrell MacDonald, John Larkin, Eugene Jackson.

Despite the presence of Gable in the cast, Variety's reviewer lamented "the failure of Metro to put any real names into the picture."

Based on Brennan's story, "Horseflesh," it follows the basic pattern of Anna Sewell's **Black Beauty** transposed to the racetrack as it follows a racehorse from one owner to another.

After its birth, it's sold to a millionaire who, after racing it for awhile, sells it to a man who gives it to his wife as a gift.

The horse falls into the hands of a gambler who nearly ruins the animal. When the gambler is shot, his girl friend takes over and restores it to health; and, learning of a plot to throw the race, cuts the reins so the jockey can't hold it back.

1115 Sporting Blood

1940, Metro Goldwyn Mayer. Director: S. Sylvan Simon. Producer:

Theodore Von Eltz and Dorothy Phillips share the tension of the big race in Tiffany Productions' The Sporting Chance (1925). (The Museum of Modern Art/Film Stills Archive.)

Albert Levoy. Screenplay: Albert Mannheimer, Dorothy Yost, Lawrence Hazard. Story: Grace Norton.

Cast: Maureen O'Sullivan, Lewis Stone, Robert Young, William Gargan, Lynne Carver, Clarence Muse, Lloyd Corrigan, Russell Hicks, George R. Reed.

Stable owner Stone carries on a feud with horse lover Young, who marries one of his daughters.

1116 The Sporting Chance

1925, Truart, 6,696 feet. Director: Oscar Apfel. Adaptation: John P. Bernard. Story: Jack Boyle.

Cast: Theodore von Eltz, Dorothy Phillips, Lou Tellegen, Sheldon Lewis, Andrew Clark, George Fawcett.

A girl breaks off her engagement to the hero and becomes engaged with the villain in order to save her dad from going to jail. The hero also owes the villain money and his horse is taken prior to the big race.

Our Hero, however, steals it and wins the race, earning enough money to pay back the villain and save the girl's father from prison.

1117 The Sporting Chance

1931, Peerless, 63 minutes. Director-Producer: Albert Herman. Story: King Baggott.

Cast: Buster Collier, Claudia Dell, James Hall, Eugene Jackson, Mahlot Hamilton, Hedwig Reicher.

Low budget production which offers nothing that hasn't been seen three dozen times before.

1118 The Sporting Duchess

1915, Lubin, 5 reels. Director: Barry O'Neill.

Cast: Rose Coghlan, George Soulle Spencer, Ferdinand Tidmash, Ethel Clayton, Rosetta Brice.

A jockey walks out on the Duchess of the title, but after seeing what cads her rivals are, returns in time for the big race.

1119 Sporting Life

1918, Paramount, 7 reels.

Director-Producer: Maurice Tourneur. Scenario: Winthrop Kelley, based on a play by Cecil Raleigh and Seymour Hicks.

Cast: Ralph Hicks, Warner Richmond, Charles Eldridge, Charles Craig, Henry West, Constance Binney, Fair Binney, Willette Kershaw.

One film reviewer described how the customers "literally started forward from their seats" during the big Derby racing finale of this old-time melodrama, which mixes boxing and horse racing.

The good Lord Woodstock is desperate for cash and is staking all on a Derby win. His sister loves a prizefighter.

The baddies are thwarted in a plot to dope the boxer and next set the Lord and the fighter against each other, and they wind up meeting in the ring.

In the meantime, the Lord's horse, Lady Love, is kidnapped, but you can guess what happens.

1120 Sporting Life

1925, Universal, 7 reels. Director: Maurice Tourneur. Screenplay: Curtis Benton, based on a play by Cecil Raleigh and Seymour Hicks. Photography: Arthur Todd.

Cast: Bert Lytell, Marian Nixon, Paulette Duval, Cyril Chadwick, Charles Delaney, Ted "Kid" Lewis, Frank Finch Smiles, Kathleen Clifford, George Siegmann.

A remake of the 1918 version with the same director, also mixing boxing with kidnapping and horse racing.

1121 Sporting Love

1937, British, Hammer Productions, 68-70 minutes. Director: J. Elder Wills. Screenplay: Fenn Sherie, Ingram D'Abbes, based on a play by Stanley Lupino. Photography: Eric Cross.

Cast: Stanley Lupino, Laddie Cliff, Henry Carlisle, Eda Peel, Bobby Comber, Clarissa Selwyne.

Lots of music spices up the tale of a couple of broke racehorse owners who come up with wives to try to please a wealthy relative.

1122 The Sporting Lover

1926, First National, 6,642 feet. Director: Alan Hale. Adaptation: Carey Wilson, based on a play by Seymour Hicks and Ian Hay. Photography: Faxon Dean, Robert Newhard. Editor: Edward M. Roskam.

Cast: Conway Tearle, Barbara Bedford, Ward Crane, Charles McHugh, John Fox, Jr., Bodil Rosing, George Ovey.

The fickle woman in sports films rears her ugly head once again as a soldier who has gambled away his prize racehorses falls in love with his nurse, who just happens to be the sister of one of the men who now owns the horses.

After the war, she's about to marry the other owner of the horses when they strike a bargain: The wedding arrangements depend on the outcome of the race. If one horse wins, she marries the hero; and if another does, she marries the villain.

When the wrong horse for Our Hero wins, it's discovered the baddie switched them and all is righted.

1123 A Sportsman's Wife

1921, British, Broadwest, 7,025 feet. Director: Walter West. Story: J. Bertram Brown.

Cast: Violet Hopson, Gregory Scott, Clive Brook, Mercy Hatton, Arthur Walcott, Adeline Hayden Coffin.

A jockey becomes involved in a fixed horse race.

1124 Spring Handicap

1937, British, Associated British, 68 minutes. Director: Herbert Brenon. Producer: Walter C. Mycroft. Screenplay: Elizabeth Meehan, William Freshman, based on a play by Ernest E. Bryan.

Cast: Will Fyffe, Maire O'Neill, Billy Milton, Aileen Marson, Frank Pettingell, David Burns, Hugh Miller.

A man wastes most of his legacy on losing ventures in the realm of horse racing, including owning, betting, bookmaking and tipping.

His wife's the heroine in this comedy.

1125 Stable Companions

1922, British, British Super, 5,960 feet. Director: Albert Ward. Producer: G.B. Samuelson. Story: Walter Summers.

Cast: Clive Brook, Lillian Hall Davis, Robert English, Fred Mason, Arthur Posey, Thomas Walters, James Wigham, Chick Wongo.

One nephew of a wealthy man gets the stables and another gets the money after the man decides to test them by faking his own death.

1126 Stablemates

1938, Metro Goldwyn Mayer, 89 minutes. Director: Sam Wood. Producer: Harry Rapf. Adaptation: Leonard Praskins, Richard Maibaum. Story: Reginald Owen, William Thiele. Photography: John Seitz. Editor: W. Donn Hayes.

Cast: Wallace Beery, Mickey Rooney, Margaret Hamilton, Minor Watson, Marjorie Gateson, Arthur Hohl, Oscar O'Shea.

Another attempt to resurrect the success of **The Champ** doesn't come close but isn't too bad thanks to the lead stars.

Beery is his usual drunken self, this time an ex-veterinarian wanted by the law, while Rooney is an orphan who hangs around the track because he loves horses.

The kid inspires Beery to stay sober enough so that he can perform an intricate operation on a racehorse. Hamilton, in the meantime, is eyeing Beery to be her sixth husband and hires him as a handyman so he can earn enough money for the race entry fee.

Beery intends to use the track winnings to finance Rooney's education.

1127 Steeplechase

1910, French, Gaumont, 229 feet. Credits unknown.

A jockey takes a shortcut through a number of public places until he gets back on the track and wins the race.

1128 The Steeple-Chase

1981, Czech, International Film Exchange, 90 minutes, Color. Director: Jaroslav Soukup. Screenplay: Soukup, Miroslav Vaic. Photography: Richard Valenta. Editor: Jiri Brozek.

Cast: Ladislav Mrkvicka, Pavel Zednicek, Gabriela Csvaldova, Milan Klasek, Josef Vetrovec, Jiri Tomek, Miroslav Masopust, Ivo Niederle, Dana Syslova, Ferdinand Kruta.

When a jockey and a prize horse are injured during a race, the animal's owners hire a discredited rider as trainer for the biggest race of the season—the Pardubice Steeple-Chase.

The two jockeys are pals but enter a beautiful girl to form the eternal triangle, and they split up. The horse's owners, however, sell the animal just before the big race and neither gets to ride in the steeple-chase.

1129 The Stirrup Cup Sensation

1924, British, Butcher, 5,300 feet. Director: Walter West. Screenplay: J. Bertram Brown. Story: Campbell Rae Brown.

Cast: Violet Hopson, Stewart Rome, Cameron Carr, Judd Green, Fred Hearne, Gertrude Sterroll, Bobb Vallis.

A man who has been ruined by a lady horse owner gets his revenge on her.

1130 The Stolen Favourite

1909, British, Clarendon. Director: Percy Stow.

The race is on in the 1981 Czechoslovakian film, The Steeple-Chase. (Courtesy The International Film Exchange.)

A horse is kidnapped, but a heroic stableboy sets it free and gets it to the track on time.

1131 The Stolen Favourite

1926, British, 2,000 feet.

Cast: Steve Donoghue, Lillian Pritchard, Robert English, Bellenden Powell, Chick Farr.

Another version of the story of a kidnapped horse.

1132 The Story of Seabiscuit

1949, Warner Brothers, 92 minutes. Color with black and white newsreel footage. Director: David Butler. Producer: William Jacobs. Screenplay: John Taintor Foote. Photography: Wilfrid M. Cline. Editor: Irene Morra.

Cast: Shirley Temple, Barry Fitzgerald, Lon McAllister, Rosemary DeCamp, Pierre Watkin, William Forrest, Sugarfoot Anderson, William J. Cartledge.

The supposedly true story of how the Howard racing family of California (Watkin, DeCamp, Temple) keeps faith in a puny horse named Seabiscuit and trains it to become one of the greatest champions of all time.

One of the film's highlights is a $150,000 race at Pimlico which also features the horse War Admiral.

1133 Straight, Place and Show

1938, 20th Century-Fox, 66 minutes. Director: David Butler.

Producer: Darryl F. Zanuck. Screenplay: M.M. Musselman, Allen Rivkin, from a play by Damon Runyon. Photography: Ernest Palmer. Editor: Irene Morra.

Cast: The Ritz Brothers, Richard Arlen, Ethel Merman, Phyllis Brooks, George Barbier, Sidney Blackmer, Will Stanton, Ivan Iebedeff, Gregory Gaye, Rafael Storm.

The Ritz Brothers try to do to horse racing what the Marx Brothers did in **Day at the Races.** They enter a wrestling match to raise enough money for the race entry fee and impersonate some Russians where they learn of a scheme by some Russian jockeys to fix the race.

In the final race, three riders wind up on one horse.

1134 The Suburban

1915, The Imp, 4 reels. Producer: George Lessey. Scenario: James Dayton. Story: C.T. Dazy.

Cast: King Baggot, William Bailey, Bradley Shaw, Helen Malone.

Baggot is disowned for marrying in secret and winds up being shanghaied to the South Pacific. He manages to return in time for the Suburban and finds his father's jockey has been kidnapped.

1135 Sucker List

1941, Metro Goldwyn Mayer, 2 reels. Director: Roy Rowland. Screenplay: Douglas Foster. Story: Samuel L. Chain, Alan Friedman. Editor: Albert Akst.

Cast: Lynne Carver, John Archer, Noel Madison, George Cleveland, Norman Willis.

Racetrack touts are exposed in this entry in the Crime Does Not Pay series of shorts.

1136 The Sunset Derby

1927, First National, 6 reels. Director: Albert Rogell. Producer: Charles Rogers. Scenario: Curtis Benton, based on a story by William Dudley Pelley in **American Magazine.** Photography: Ross Fisher.

Cast: William Collier, Jr., Mary Astor, Ralph Lewis, David Kirby, Lionel Belmore, Burt Ross, Henry Barrows, Bobby Doyle, Michael Visaroff.

When a jockey is injured in a race, the owners must sell the horse to pay for the hospital expenses. When the jockey recovers, he finds the new owner mistreating the animal and forces him to sell the horse back to the old owners, who enter it in another race.

1137 Sweepstakes

1931, RKO Radio Pictures, 75 minutes. Director: Albert Rogell. Producer: Charles Rogers. Story: Lew Lipton.

Cast: Eddie Quillan, James Gleason, Marion Nixon, Lew Cody, Paul Hurst, King Baggot, Fred Burton, Billy Sullivan, Lillian Leighton, Mike Donlin.

Jockey Quillan becomes a singing waiter in Mexico after he's barred from the track after throwing a race because of sentimental reasons but gets another chance.

In this one, the secret word which makes the horse go faster is "whoop-de-doo."

1138 Sweepstakes Winner

1939, Warner Brothers, 59 minutes. Director: William McGann. Producer: Bryan Foy. Screenplay: John Kraft, Albert De Mond. Photography: Arthur Edeson. Editor: Frank Magee.

Cast: Marie Wilson, Allen Jenkins, Charles Foy, Johnnie Davis, Jerry Colonna, Vera Lewis, Granville Bates, Eddie Kane.

Waitress Wilson winds up with an old horse which after some comic situations regains its form.

1139 Take a Chance

1937, British, Grosvenor, 73 minutes. Director: Sinclair Hill. Producer: Harcourt Templeman. Screenplay: D.B. Wyndham-

Lewis, G.J. Moresby-White, based on a play by Walter Hackett. Photography: John W. Boyle.

Cast: Claude Hulbert, Binnie Hale, Henry Kendall, Gwen Farrar, Enid Stamp-Taylor, Jack Barty, Harry Tate, Guy Middleton, Kynaston Reeves.

A track tipster finds out the wife of a horse owner is leaking information.

1140 Take Me to Paris

1950, British, AB-Pathe, 72 minutes. Director: Jack Raymond. Producer: Henry Halstead. Screenplay: Max Cotto. Photography: James Wilson.

Cast: Albert Modley, Roberta Ruby, Bruce Seton, Richard Molinas, George Bishop, Leonard Sharp, Jim Gerald.

When a horse which has been used to smuggle counterfeit money across the border goes lame, a loser named "Dunderhead" takes his place during the big race, and, surprisingly, wins, helping to foil the villains.

1141/1142 The Tattooed Police Horse

1964, Buena Vista, 48 minutes, Color. Director-Producer-Story: Larry Lansburgh. Screenplay: Janet Lansburgh. Photography: Edward P. Hughes. Editor: Herman Freedman.

Cast: Sandy Sanders, Charles Seel, George Swinebroad, William Hilliard, Shirley Skiles, Keith Andes.

Trotting horse Jolly Roger is banned from racing as a menace to other horses because of his habit of breaking stride in the stretch.

He's sold to the Boston Mounted Police where a friendly cop (Sanders) cures him, and he's involved in a rescue of a driver who had an accident during a race. The original trainer sees the story and buys him back, giving him another shot at racing.

The title comes from a tattoo on the horse's lip.

1143 Thank Evans

1938, British, Warner Brothers, 78 minutes. Director: Roy William Neill. Producer: Irving Asher. Screenplay: Austin Melford, John Dighton, John Meehan, Jr., based on a story by Edgar Wallace. Photography: Basil Emmott.

Cast: Max Miller, Hal Walters, Polly Ward, Albert Whelan, John Carol, Robert Rendel, Glen Alyn, Freddie Watts, Harvey Braban, Aubrey Mallalieu.

Track tipster Educated Evans returns for more comic hi-jinks when he takes a country vacation during a losing streak.

He outwits a crooked trainer by talking the horse's owner into letting another jockey ride the animal.

1144 That Gang of Mine

1940, Monogram, 61 minutes. Director: Joseph H. Lewis. Producer: Sam Katzman. Story: Alan Whitman. Adaptation: William Lively. Photography: Robert Cline, Harvey Gould. Editor: Carl Pierson.

Cast: Leo Gorcey, Bobby Jordan, Clarence Muse, Dave O'Brien, Donald Haines, David Gorcey, Sunshine Sammy Morrison.

The East Side Kids (ne Dead End Kids) turn to the racetrack as Muggs (Leo Gorcey) has trouble becoming a successful jockey.

He keeps on losing his nerve at critical moments. He finally winds up winning the big race on a horse belonging to a penniless man who raised him from colthood.

1145 That's My Man

1947, Republic, 104 minutes. Director-Producer: Frank Borzage. Screenplay: Steve Fisher, Bradley King. Photography: Tony Gaudio. Editor: Richard L. Van Enger.

Cast: Don Ameche, Catherine McLeod, Roscoe Karns, John Ridgely, Kitty Irish, Joe Frisco, Gregory Marshall, Frankie Darro, Dorothy Adams.

While gambler Ameche turns a colt into a big winner, he's neglecting his wife. On the night their baby is born, he's out playing cards, and later he doesn't even show up at a Christmas party.

It's only a matter of time before things start going wrong as hubby and wife separate and, Ameche's gambling luck goes sour.

With his child gravely ill, the winning horse is taken out of retirement in an effort to raise some needed cash.

1146 They Met in Argentina

1941, RKO Radio Pictures, 76 minutes. Director: Leslie Goodwins, Jack Hively. Producer: Lou Brock. Screenplay: Jerry Cady. Story: Brock, Harold Daniels.

Cast: Maureen O'Hara, James Ellison, Robert Middlemass, Albert Vila, Buddy Ebsen, Robert Barrat, Diosa Costello.

Not even a Rodgers and Hart musical score could prevent RKO from losing a whopping $270,000 on this bomb about an oil tycoon who sends Ellison to Argentina with orders to buy a well-known racehorse at any cost.

Ellison falls in love with O'Hara, the horse owner's daughter.

1147 They're Off

1917, Triangle-Kay-Bee. Director: Roy Neil.

Cast: Enid Bennett.

A successful Wall Street businessman becomes a horse owner with his daughter as jockey. She turns her father's champion horse over to a rancher her father ruined so he can get his ranch back.

1148 They're Off

1919, Goldwyn, 2 reels.

Cast: Smiling Bill Parsons.

A man wins big at the racetrack and turns out to be a judge. He winds up sentencing two men who tried a con game on him.

1149 They're Off

1922, Anchor Film Distributors, 4,331 feet. Director-Screenplay: Francis Ford. Photography: O.G. Hill.

Cast: Peggy O'Day, Phil Ford, Francis Ford, Martin Turner, Frederick Moore.

A mountain girl and a southern colonel's wife meet and discover they are twins separated at birth and decide to change places à la **Prince and the Pauper.** The colonel's wife wants to pursue a career in the theater, and the mountain girl enjoys the good life.

The colonel's villainous half-brother discovers the switch and tries blackmail. When he disables the colonel's jockey on the day of the big race, the mountain girl rides the colonel's horse herself.

1150 They're Off

1933, British, Gaumont, 18 minutes. Director: John Rawlins. Producer: Clayton Hutton.

Cast: Flanagan and Allen.

The misadventures of two bookies.

1151 The Thoroughbred

1916, Triangle, 5 reels. Director: Reginald Barker. Supervision: Thomas H. Ince. Screenplay: C. Gardner Sullivan.

Cast: Frank Keenan, Margaret Thompson, George Fisher, J.J. Dowling, Walter Perry.

A minister's anti-gambling sermons lead to the state banning racing and causing all kinds of problems for a southern colonel in need of money.

He must go to another state in order to race his horse.

1152 The Thoroughbred

1925, Truart, 5,481 feet. Director: Oscar Apfel. Scenario:

L. Renick Brown. Photography: Roland Price.

Cast: Maclyn Arbuckle, Theodore von Eltz, Gladys Hulette, Hallam Cooley, Virginia Brown, Carter De Haven, Thomas Jefferson, Robert Brower.

Poor Robert (von Eltz) has all kinds of problems breaking into high society as he's framed on a bad check charge and purchases a real loser of a horse.

1153 The Thoroughbred

1928, British, Gaumont, 5,608 feet. Director-Producer-Screenplay: Sidney Morgan.

Cast: Ian Hunter, Louise Prussing, H. Agar Lyons, Richard Barclay.

A gambling woman attempts to force a jockey to throw the Derby.

1154 The Thoroughbred

1930, Tiffany Productions, 5,425 feet. Director: Richard Thorpe. Screenplay: John Francis Natteford. Photography: Max Dupont. Editor: Clarence Kolster.

Cast: Wesley Barry, Nancy Dover, Pauline Gaton, Larry Steers, Robert Homans, Walter Perry, Onest Conley.

A jockey is wooed by rival racehorse owners, and, after he wins a number of races for one of them, a vamp for a gambler tries to get him to throw a race.

1155 Thoroughbred

1931, British, Equity British, 64 minutes. Director: Charles Barnett. Producer-Screenplay: John F. Argyle.

Cast: James Benton, Margaret Delane, John F. Argyle, Jack Marriott, Thomas Moss.

An amnesiac horse trainer regains his memory during a racing accident in time to find out he's a wealthy man and save his sweetheart from marrying someone else.

1156 Thoroughbred

1936, Australian, British Empire Films, 78 minutes. Director: Ken G. Hall. Screenplay: Edmond Seward. Photography: George Heath.

Cast: Helen Twelvetrees, Frank Leighton, John Longden, Nellie Barnes.

The favorite for the Melbourne Cup becomes the target for crooks who want it out of the way.

1157 Thoroughbreds

1945, Republic, 56 minutes. Director: George Blair. Producer: Lester Shayne. Photography: William Bradford.

Cast: Tom Neal, Adele Mara, Roger Pryor, Paul Harvey, Gene Garrick, Doodles Weaver, Sam Bernard, Eddie Hall, Charles Sullivan, Tom London, Alan Edwards.

When a cavalry sergeant is discharged at the same time the army is disposing of some horses, he becomes the trainer for a high society girl who buys his mount and turns it into a racehorse.

When the regular jockey can't race, the soldier rides his old horse himself.

1158 Thoroughbreds Don't Cry

1937, Metro Goldwyn Mayer, 80 minutes. Director: Alfred E. Green. Producer: Harry Rapf. Screenplay: Lawrence Hazard. Story: J. Walter Ruben, Eleanor Griffin. Photography: Leonard Smith. Editor: Elmo Vernon.

Cast: Judy Garland, Mickey Rooney, Ronald Sinclair, Sophie Tucker, C. Aubrey Smith, Helen Troy, Frankie Darro, Elisha Cook, Jr., Henry Kolker, Forrester Harvey.

In the first Garland-Rooney teamup pic and the first to give Judy star billing, she plays the niece of Tucker, who runs a boarding school for jockeys.

Teenager Sinclair is brought to the United States by grandfather Smith. When jockey Rooney is barred from the track, the lad takes the reins himself in the big race.

1159 Three Men on a Horse

1936, Warner Brothers, 85 minutes. Director-Producer: Mervyn LeRoy. Adaptation: Laird Doyle, based on a play by John Cecil Holm and George Abbott. Photography: Sol Polito. Editor: Ralph Dawson.

Cast: Frank McHugh, Joan Blondell, Guy Kibbee, Sam Levene, Carol Hughes, Allen Jenkins, Teddy Hart, Edgar Kennedy, Paul Harvey, Eddie Anderson.

All kinds of complications arise when a timid verse writer for greeting cards affectionately known as "Oiwin" (McHugh) has a knack for picking racehorse winners.

Although considered one of the top comedies of its day, it's rarely screened nowadays.

1160 Thunderclap

1921, Fox, 6,745 feet. Director: Richard Stanton. Screenplay: Paul H. Sloane. Photography: George W. Lane.

Cast: Mary Carr, J. Barney Sherry, Paul Willis, Violet Mersereau, Carol Chase, John Daly Murphy, Walter McEwen, Maude Hill, Thomas McCann.

A young man (Willis) who is training his horse Thunderclap for a big race falls in love with the daughter of an evil gambling house proprietor who has taken the girl from a convent. The villain (Sherry) has already caused the girl's mother to be paralytic.

When the villain is caught cheating and owes $40,000, he plots against the hero's horse in the race, but everything is foiled.

1161 Thunderhead, Son of Flicka

1945, 20th Century-Fox, 78 minutes, Color. Director: Louis King. Producer: Robert Bassler. Screenplay: Dwight Cummings, Dorothy Yost, based on a novel by Mary O'Hara. Photography: Charles Clarke.

Cast: Roddy McDowell, Preston Foster, Rita Johnson, James Bell, Diana Hale, Carleton Young, Ralph Sanford, Alan Bridge.

In this sequel to **My Friend Flicka** and predecessor to **Green Grass of Wyoming,** a young lad (McDowell) raises a beautiful white colt to be a top racer, but a tendon injury ends the horse's career.

The horse saves the boy's life and the rancher's herd from a wild albino stallion in a thrilling battle between the two steeds.

1162 Thundering Hoofs

1922, Anchor Film Distributors, 4,514 feet. Director: Francis Ford. Photography: O.G. Hill.

Cast: Francis Ford, Peggy O'Day, Phil Ford, Florence Murth, Harry Kelly.

A gal who's been away at school returns to her Kentucky home to find a plot against a Derby horse, so she rides it herself.

1163 Too Many Winners

1947, Producers Releasing Corp., 60 minutes. Director: William Beaudine. Producer-Screenplay: John Sutherland. Photography: Jack Greenbaigh. Editor: Harry Reynolds.

Cast: Hugh Beaumont, Trudy Marshall, Ralph Dunn, Claire Carleton, Charles Mitchell, John Hamilton.

Famed sleuth Michael Shayne (Beaumont) gets involved with murder and counterfeit pari-mutuel tickets at a racetrack.

1164 Top of the Form

1953, British, GFD, 75 minutes. Director: John Paddy Carstairs. Producer: Paul Soskin. Screenplay: Carstairs, Patrick Kirwane, Ted Willis. Story: Val Guest, Marriott Edgars, Anthony Kimmins, Leslie Arliss.

Cast: Ronald Shiner, Harry Fowler, Alfie Bass, Jacqueline

Pierreux, Anthony Newley, Mary Jerrold, Richard Wattis, Roland Curram, Howard Marion-Crawford.

A bookie who is impersonating a teacher helps his pupils thwart a gang of thieves in this lightweight nonsense.

1165 Torchy Gets Her Man

1938, Warner Brothers, 62 minutes. Director: William Beaudine. Producer: Bryan Foy. Screenplay: Albert De Mond. Photography: Arthur Todd, Warren Lynch. Editor: Harold McLernon.

Cast: Glenda Farrell, Barton MacLane, Tom Kenney, Willard Robertson, George Guhl, John Ridgely, Tommy Jackson.

Top reporter Torchy Blaine (Farrell) helps put an end to a counterfeiting gang which unloads the cash through a racetrack's payoff windows.

1166 The Trainer's Daughter, or, a Race for Love

1907, Edison Co., 10 minutes. Director: Edwin S. Porter.

In this melodrama by film pioneer Porter, the bad guy attempts to fix a race so he can marry the daughter of a horse trainer.

1167 Trouble or Nothing

1946, RKO Radio Pictures, 2 reels. Director: Hal Yates.

Cast: Edgar Kennedy, Florence Lake, Dot Farley, Jack Rice, Dick Elliott, Harry Woods, Harry Harvey, Joe Devlin.

Mr. Average Man (Kennedy) gets mixed up in betting on racehorses in this comedy short.

1168 A Turf Conspiracy

1918, British, Broadwest, 5,600 feet. Director: Frank Wilson. Producer: Walter West. Scenario: Bannister Merwin. Story: Nat Gould.

Cast: Violet Hopson, Gerald Ames, Joan Legge, Cameron Carr, Arthur Walcott, Tom Coventry.

A woman is hired by a group of gamblers to make sure a stable remains under their control.

1169 Two Dollar Bettor (aka **Beginner's Luck)**

1951, Realart, 72 minutes. Director-Producer: Edward L. Cahn. Screenplay: Howard Emmett Rogers. Photography: Charles Van Enger. Editor: Sherman Rose.

Cast: John Litel, Marie Windsor, Steve Brodie, Barbara Logan, Robert Sherwood, Barbara Bester, Walter Kingsford.

The evils of gambling are exposed as a widower starts out placing a simple bet on a racehorse and gets so addicted he embezzles from his bank.

He's killed during a desperate attempt to recoup his losses.

1170 Two in a Crowd

1936, Universal, 80 minutes. Director: Alfred E. Green. Producer: Charles Rogers. Story: Louis R. Foster. Photography: Joseph Valentine.

Cast: Joan Bennett, Joel McCrea, Elisha Cook, Jr., Alison Skipworth, Reginald Denny, Henry Armetta, Andy Clyde, Nat Pendleton, Donald Meek, Milburn Stone.

A top cast highlights this comedy about a broke racehorse owner who finds half of a $1,000 bill from a bank robbery. Unfortunately (or fortunately), a girl finds the other half.

The two get together and get the man's racehorse out of hock. The horse, however, just isn't the same until it sees the cart it dragged while in hock and realizes how well off it is and starts to really run.

1171 Two in Revolt

1936, RKO Radio Pictures, 65 minutes. Director: Glenn Tryon. Producer: Robert Sisk. Story: Earl Johnson, Thomas Storey. Adaptation: Frank Howard Clark, Ferdinand Reyher, Jerry Hutchinson. Photography: Jack Mackenzie. Editor: Fred Knudtson.

Cast: John Arledge, Louise Latimer, Moroni Olsen, Emmet Vogan, Murray Alper.

Minor stuff about the friendship between a racehorse and a police dog and the romance between an owner's daughter and a trainer.

1172 Two Thoroughbreds

1939, RKO Radio Pictures, 62 minutes. Director: Jack Hively. Producer: Cliff Reid. Screenplay: Joseph A. Fields, Jerry Cady.

Cast: Jimmy Lydon, Joan Brodel.

When a boy loves his horse, all obstacles are overcome in the movie.

1173 Two to One on Pimple

1913, British, Folly Films, 370 feet. Directors-Screenplay: Fred and Joe Evans.

Cast: Fred and Joe Evans.

A self-described "horse race burlesque" with the early British comedy team.

1174 Under My Skin

1950, 20th Century-Fox, 86 minutes. Director: Jean Negulesco. Producer: Casey Robinson. Screenplay: Robinson, based on a story by Ernest Hemingway. Photography: Joseph La Shelle. Editor: Dorothy Spencer.

Cast: John Garfield, Micheline Presle, Luther Adler, Orley Lindgren, Noel Drayton, A.A. Merola, Ott George, Paul Bryar, Ann Codee, Steve Geray, Joseph Warfield.

Another sports film modeled after **The Champ** finds Garfield as a crooked jockey in Europe who reforms for the sake of his son and his singer girl friend.

Gambler Adler, however, who has already been doublecrossed by Garfield, insists that he throw the next race to make up for the money he's owed.

Garfield decides to play the race straight and wins the race to gain the respect of his son but loses his own life in the process.

1175 Under the Pampas Moon

1935, 20th Century-Fox, 78 minutes. Director: James Tinling. Producer: B.G. De Sylva. Screenplay: Ernest Pascal, Bradley King. Photography: Chester Lyons.

Cast: Warner Baxter, Ketti Galligan, Velozo Yolanda, John Miljan, J. Carrol Naish, Soledad Jimenez, Jack LaRue, George Irving.

When some entertainers crash-land in South America, gaucho Baxter takes the passengers to his ranch, where they watch him win a horse race despite some shenanigans by his opponent.

When the gaucho refuses to sell his horse to a singer's manager, the opponent is induced to steal it for him. Baxter follows the group to regain his horse.

1176 Unwelcome Stranger

1935, Columbia, 65 minutes. Director: Phil Rosen. Story: William Jacobs. Adaptation: Crane Wilbur. Photography: John Stumar. Editor: Arthur Hilton.

Cast: Jack Holt, Mona Barrie, Jackie Searl, Ralph Morgan, Bradley Page, Frankie Darro, Sam McDaniel, Frank Orth.

A horsebreeder who grew up an orphan believes having any orphans around him is a jinx. He even gets rid of any orphan horses around the track.

When a kid brings a horse to the track, the horseman decides to keep them both around for awhile, but his fortunes take a downturn. When it's discovered the lad is an orphan, the breeder blames him for his troubles.

The youth learns of a plan to fix the big race and decides to ride himself to prove he's no jinx.

1177 Up for the Derby

1933, British, Gaumont-British, 70 minutes. Director: MacLean Rogers. Producer: Herbert Wilcox. Screenplay: R.P. Weston, Bert Lee, Jack Marks.

Cast: Sydney Howard, Mark Daly, Dorothy Bartlam, Frank Harvey, Tom Helmore, Frederick Lloyd, Franklyn Bellamy.

A man who picks horses to bet on by shutting his eyes and sticking pins into his racing form buys a horse which has been ruined by a crooked trainer and builds it back up to be a Derby contender.

1178 The Upland Rider

1928, First National, 5,731 feet. Director: Albert Rogell. Story: Marion Jackson. Photography: Ted McCord. Editor: Fred Allen.

Cast: Ken Maynard, Marian Douglas, Lafe McKee, Sidney Jarvis, Robert Walker, Bobby Dunn, David Kirby.

Maynard rides his palomino bronco for his employer in a race against a villainous horse breeder with the winner getting a major government contract.

1179 Wall of Noise

1963, Warner Brothers, 112 minutes. Director: Richard Wilson. Producer-Screenplay: Joseph Landon, based on a novel by Daniel M. Stein. Photography: Lucien Ballard. Editor: William Ziegler.

Cast: Ty Hardin, Suzanne Pleshette, Dorothy Provine, Ralph Meeker, Simon Oakland, Jimmy Murphy, Murray Matheson, Robert F. Simon, George Petrie, Jim Murray.

Set at the Hollywood Park Racetrack, Hardin portrays a horse owner who falls into the clutches of a stable owner's wife after he breaks up with his girl friend.

The stable owner (Meeker) fires him when he finds out what his wife (Pleshette) is doing, but Hardin scrapes together enough money to buy a horse he believes will be a big winner.

For a change, the horse loses the big race, but Hardin and his girl friend (Provine) are reconciled.

1180 Warned Off

1928, British, B&D, 6,510 feet. Director: Walter West. Producer: Herbert Wilcox. Scenario: Reginald Fogwell, Story: Robert Sevier.

Cast: Tony Wylde, Chili Bouchier, Bert Tracy, Walter Tennyson, Queenie Thomas, Evan Thomas.

A horse owner, expelled from racing, gets a second chance and clears his name in the Grand National.

1181 Weavers of Fortune (aka **Racing Luck**)

1922, British, L.B. Davidson, 5,500 feet. Director: Arthur Rooke. Story: Kinchen Wood.

Cast: Henry Vibart, Derek Glynne, Myrtle Vibart.

A student who's been expelled buys a horse and rides it himself in the Grand National.

1182 Welshed—A Derby Day Incident

1903, British, Gaumont, 195 feet. Director: Alf Collins.

Cast: Alf Collins, A.C. Bromhead.

A bookie who welshes winds up being chased by a mob.

1183 What Price Loving Cup?

1923, British, Walter West Productions, 5,100 feet. Director-Producer: Walter West. Scenario: J. Bertram Brown. Story: Campbell Rae Brown.

Cast: Violet Hopson, James Knight, James Lindsay, Marjorie Berson, Cecil Morton York, Oliver Marks.

A female jockey is the target of a kidnapping plot.

1184 When Dreams Come True

1929, Rayart Pictures, 6,082-6,242 feet. Director: Duke Worne. Scenario: Arthur Hoerl, based on a story by Victor Rousseau. Photography: Hap Depew.

Cast: Rex Lease, Helene Costello, Claire McDowell, Danny Hoy, Ernest Hilliard, Buddy Brown, Emmett King.

Suspicion falls on a blacksmith (Lease) when a wealthy man who refused him permission to marry his daughter is found murdered.

Naturally, he escapes and learns the real villain is the dead man's horse breeding partner, who is now plotting to fix a horse race. The hero must see that his girl's horse wins and get a confession out of the bad guys.

1185 When Romance Rides

1922, Goldwyn Pictures, 5,003 feet. Directors: Eliot Howe, Charles O. Rush, Jean Hersholt. Producer-Adaptation: Benjamin B. Hampton. Photography: Gus Peterson, William Edmonds.

Cast: Claire Adams, Carl Gantvoort, Jean Hersholt, Harry Van Meter, Charles Arling, Tod Sloan, Frank Hayes, Babe London, Mary Jane Irving.

Adams and Gantvoort tame a wild horse in this adaptation of Zane Grey's **Wildfire.**

When her own horse is stolen and her family's entry in the big race is drugged by a rival, the wild horse is entered. The girl discovers the stolen horse has been entered by the villain who loses the race and is eventually exposed.

1186 When Winter Went

1925, Independent Pictures, 5 reels. Director: Reginald Morris.

Cast: Raymond Griffith, Charlotte Merriam.

A freezing man tries to keep warm by reading a book about a southern gentleman whose estate depends on the outcome of a big race. The racing tale unfolds as the man reads.

1187 The Whip

1917, Paragon Co., Director: Maurice Tourneur. Photography: Jan Van der Broeck.

Cast: Irving Cummings, Warren Cook, Paul McAllister, Alfred Hemming, Dion Titherade, Alma Hanlon, June Elvidge, Jean Dumar.

A race between a car and a train outshines the big horse race in this tale of a girl who discovers a plot by a crooked bookie and rides the horse herself after thwarting all the efforts of the villain.

1188 The Whip

1928, First National, 6,056-6,058 feet. Director: Charles J. Brabin. Continuity: Bernard McConville, J.L. Campbell, based on a play by Cecil Raleigh and Henry Hamilton. Photography: James Van Trees. Editor: George McGuire.

Cast: Ralph Forbes, Dorothy Mackaill, Anna Q. Nilsson, Lowell Sherman, Albert Gran, Mare MacDermott, Lou Payne, Arthur Clayton.

A nobleman (Forbes) loses his memory in an automobile crash and falls in love with the daughter (Mackaill) of the nobleman who takes him into his home.

Enter the villainess (Nilsson), a fortune hunter whom Forbes rejected when he found out what she wanted. She conspires with a villain (Sherman) to fake a marriage certificate so she can gain a title from Forbes.

Sherman, meanwhile, attempts to kill the heroine's horse because he's bet heavily on another one; but his efforts are thwarted by the hero, who naturally regains his memory and gets rid of the fortune hunter.

1189 The White Star

1915, British, Holmfirth, 4,893 feet. Director: Bertram Phillips.

Cast: Queenie Thomas, Norman Howard, Rowland Moore, Billy Asher, Arthur Walcott, Alf Foy, Syd Baker.

A ringer is substituted for a girl's racehorse.

1190 Who's Got the Action?

1962, Paramount, 93 minutes, Color. Director: Daniel Mann. Producer-Screenplay: Jack Rose. Photography: Joseph Ruttenberg. Editor: Howard Smith.

Cast: Dean Martin, Lana Turner, Eddie Albert, Nita Talbot, Margo, Walter Matthau, Paul Ford, Lewis Charles, John McGiver, John Indrisano, Jack Albertson, Alexander Rose.

When Martin continually loses money on the horses, Turner tries to keep it all in the family by becoming his bookie with lawyer pal Albert as the intermediary. Suddenly, however, Martin begins to win, and all his pals start betting through the new bookie on the block.

Forced to sell her possessions to pay off the winnings, her comic complications mount when gangster Matthau steps in.

1191 Why Nick Winter Went to the Race

1910, French, Pathe, 555 feet.

Cast: Leon Durac.

A detective hired by two husbands follows their wives to the racetrack, but the women get wise to the tail.

1192 Wild Beauty

1927, Universal, 5,192 feet. Director: Henry MacRae. Scenario: Edward Meagher. Story: Sylvia Bernstein Seid. Photography: John Stumar.

Cast: June Marlowe, Hugh Allan, Scott Seaton, Hayes Robinson, William Bailey, Jack Pratt, J. Gordon Russell.

A World War I veteran brings an army horse home with him and falls in love with the daughter of the owner of a racing stable, who, naturally, is dependent on the big race to save his ranch.

When the owner's horse is injured by a rival's animal, the veteran rides the army horse in its place.

1193 Wildfire

1925, Vitagraph Co. of America, 6,550 feet. Director: T. Hayes Hunter. Photography: J. Roy Hunt.

Cast: Aileen Pringle, Edna Murphy, Holmes Herbert, Edmund Breese, Antrim Short, Arthur Bryson, Tom Blake, Lawford Davidson, Robert Billoupe, Edna Morton.

A woman keeps her ownership of a horse racing stable secret so she won't jeopardize her sister's marriage to a man whose father detests the sport. That works against her, however, as the woman's old boy friend returns after a long absence and plots revenge against the man who holds the mortgage on the stables and whose name the stables bear, not knowing his lover really owns them.

That's just the start of the complicated turn of events, including the usual barn fire, crooked jockeys and last-minute victory by the heroine's horse, Wildfire.

1194 Win, Place or Steal (aka **Three for the Money**)

1975, Cinema National, 81 minutes, Color. Director: Richard Bailey. Producer: Thomas D. Cooney. Screenplay: Anthony Monaco, Bailey.

Cast: Dean Stockwell, Russ Tamblyn, Alex Karras, McLean Stevenson, Alan Oppenheimer, Kristina Holland, Harry Dean Stanton, Liv Von Linden, Scatman Crothers.

A comedy which never went into general release features Stockwell, Karras and Tamblyn as bungling gamblers who steal a roll of tickets and a pari-mutuel machine from a racetrack so they can forge winning tickets, but, of course, things don't go as planned.

According to the film, this is supposedly based on a true story.

1195 Wine, Women and Horses

1937, Warner Brothers, 64

minutes. Director: Louis King. Producer: Bryan Foy. Screenplay: Roy Chanslor, based on a novel by W.R. Burnett. Photography: James Van Trees. Editor: Jack Saper.

Cast: Barton MacLane, Ann Sheridan, Dick Purcell, Peggy Bates, Stuart Holmes, Walter Cassell, James Robbins.

A remake of 1934's **Dark Hazard**, it switches the locale from the dog track to the horse race track, but the basic story remains the same.

MacLane is a compulsive gambler who marries Bates, only to see her leave him. He later marries Sheridan.

1196 Wings of the Morning

1937, British, 20th Century-Fox, 85-88 minutes, Color. Director: Harold Schuster. Screenplay: Tom Geraghty, John Meehan, Brinsley MacNamara, based on "Tale of a Gypsy Horse" by Donn Byrne. Photography: Ray Hennahan.

Cast: Henry Fonda, Annabella, Leslie Banks, Stewart Rome, Harry Tate, Irene Vanbrugh.

The happiness of the young lovers Fonda and Annabella depends upon the outcome of a horse race in this, the first color British feature film.

A gypsy who was once married to a nobleman, but who returned to her own people after being shunned by society, sees her granddaughter fall in love with Fonda in Spain.

1197 The Winner's Circle

1948, 20th Century-Fox, 75 minutes. Director: Felix Feist. Producer: Richard Polimer. Screenplay: Howard J. Green. Photography: Elmer Dyer.

Cast: Johnny Longden, Morgan Farley, Bob Howard, William Gould, John Bernardino, Frank Day, Russ Conway.

Jockey Johnny Longden plays himself in this biography of a racehorse from his birth in Kentucky to triumph at Santa Anita.

1198 Winning the Futurity

1915, Walter Miller Feature Film Co., 4 reels.

Cast: Walter Miller.

Miller, a real-life jockey, plays himself in an old-time melodrama in which the villain, after attempting to drug him and his horse, has him kidnapped (what else?).

Our Hero beats up his captor, jumps through a burning doorway into a stream and swims to safety, of course, managing to get to the racetrack in the nick of time. The title tells the outcome in case you had any doubt.

1199 Winning the Futurity

1926, Chadwick Pictures, 5,500 feet. Director: Scott Dunlap. Adaptation: Finis Fox. Story: Hunt Stromberg.

Cast: Cullen Landis, Clara Horton, Henry Kolker, Otis Harlan, Pat Harmon.

A poor lad rescues a colt from being shot and raises it to be a contender in the Kentucky Futurity. In the meantime, his sweetheart's father gambles away his estate and then dies, but retains a document which states that the estate will go to his daughter if she can raise $100,000 in a year and a half.

Despite the efforts of the scoundrel who won the estate, the poor boy's horse enters the race; and if you haven't guessed the outcome by now, you've probably never seen a movie in your life.

1200 Women First

1924, Columbia, 4,875 feet. Director: B. Reeves Eason. Story: Wilfred Lucas. Photography: Allen Thompson.

Cast: William Fairbanks, Eva Novak, Lydia Knott, Bob Rhodes, Lloyd Whitlock, Andy Waldron, Dan Crimmins, Max Ascher, William Dyer, Merta Sterling.

An ex-jockey becomes a horse trainer on an estate run by a Kentucky colonel's daughter, while the girl's brother becomes their favorite horse's jockey.

A rival stable owner, meanwhile, who is deeply in debt, resorts to the old schemes of drugging the hero and the girl's brother and setting fire to the stables when his bribe offer is refused.

With the hero injured, it's the girl who rides in the big race.

1201 Won by a Head

1920, British, Sterling, 4,198 feet. Director: Percy Nash. Story: John Gabriel.

Cast: Rex Davis, Frank Tennant, Vera Cornish, Wallace Bosco, Douglas Payne, J. Edwards Barber.

A boxer who's accused of murder breaks out of jail to prove his innocence and also wins the big race.

1202 The Yellow Back

1926, Universal, 4,766 feet. Director-Screenplay: Del Andrews. Photography: Al Jones.

Cast: Fred Humes, Lotus Thompson, Claude Payton, Buck Connors, Willie Fung.

A ranch hand who is terrified of horses rides for love when he learns that his girl friend's ranch will be lost unless the family wins a horse race.

1203 You Can't Buy Luck

1937, RKO Radio Pictures, 61 minutes. Director: Lew Landers. Screenplay: Martin Mooney, Arthur T. Horman. Photography: J. Roy Hunt.

Cast: Onslow Stevens, Helen Mack, Vinton Haworth, Maxine Jenning, Paul Guilfoyle, Frank M. Thomas, Willie Best, Dudley Clements, Hedda Hopper.

A racehorse owner believes in "luck insurance" and buys gifts for beautiful women before the races.

When a former sweetheart is murdered, he's convicted and escapes in an attempt to prove his innocence.

Polo and Similar

1204 The Adventures of Rex and Rinty

1935, Mascot, 12 chapters. Directors: Ford Beebe, Reeves Eason. Supervisor: Barney Sarecky. Screenplay: Sarecky, John Rathmell. Story: Eason, Maurice Geraghty, Ray Trampe. Photography: William Nobles. Editor: Dick Fantl.

Cast: Rex, King of the Wild Horses; Rin Tin Tin, Jr.; Kane Richmond, Norma Taylor, Mischa Auer, Smiley Burnette, Harry Woods, Pedro Regas, Hooper Archlet, Wheeler Oakman.

Chapter titles: Chapter One: The God Horse of Sujan; Chapter Two: Sport of Kings; Chapter Three: Fangs of Flame; Chapter Four: Homeward Bound; Chapter Five: Babes in the Woods; Chapter Six: Dead Man's Tale; Chapter Seven: End of the Road; Chapter Eight: A Dog's Devotion; Chapter Nine: The Stranger's Recall; Chapter Ten: The Siren of Death; Chapter Eleven: New Gods for Old; Chapter Twelve: Primitive Justice.

Rex, the Wonder Horse, is worshipped as a god by the natives of Sujan but is captured by the villainous Woods and sold to a greedy rancher in the U.S.

The horse resists all efforts to be turned into a polo horse or racer and escapes, where it teams up with Rin Tin Tin, Jr. The horse and dog become friends and avoid recapture by the villains. A well-known polo player (Richmond) helps return the horse to the island where it faces new perils because the natives have been turned against him.

1205 The Arizona Wildcat

1927, Fox, 4,665 feet. Director: R. William Neill. Scenario: John Stone. Story: Adela Rogers St. Johns. Photography: Dan Clark.

Cast: Tom Mix, Dorothy Sebastian, Ben Bard, Cissy Fitzgerald, Marcella Daly, Doris Dawson.

A cowboy (Mix) meets up with his childhood sweetheart (Sebastian), who is now a member of high society and the target of a couple of crooks.

The villains extend their dirty tricks to the polo field where their team is beating the team of the girl's brother, but Mix manages to get on the field in time and change the course of the game.

1206 The Devil's Pass

1959, French, 20th Century-Fox, 80 minutes, Color. Director: Jacques Dupont. Producer: G. Beauregarde. Screenplay-Commentary: Joseph Kessel. Photography: Raoul Coutard. Editor: Marcelle Lionet.

Narrator: Jean Negron.

Semi-documentary about a horse sport played in Afghanistan where the riders battle each other in a ring.

It follows a youth who trails his brother to an annual meet and discovers his brother's horse has a defective saddle strap.

1207 Don't Tell Everything

1921, Paramount, 4,939 feet. Director: Sam Wood. Scenario: Albert Shelby Le Vino. Story: Lorna Moon. Photography: Al Gilks.

Cast: Wallace Reid, Gloria Swanson, Elliott Dexter, Baby Gloria Wood, Dorothy Cumming.

All kinds of romantic complications ensue when two polo players (Reid, Dexter) both love the same woman (Swanson) and are both injured in the same game.

1208 The Horsemen

1971, Columbia, 100 minutes, Color. Director: John Frankenheimer. Producer: Edward Lewis. Screenplay: Dalton Trumbo, based on the novel by Joseph Kersel. Photography: Claude Renoir. Editor: Harold Kress.

Cast: Omar Sharif, Leigh Taylor-Young, Jack Palance, Peter Jeffrey, Mohammed Shamsi, George Morcell.

It's polo Afghan style with the headless carcass of a calf used instead of a ball.

Sharif is the son of a clan leader and has the reputation as being the best in the game, but after he's seriously injured, must struggle to regain his form.

The exoticness of the locale and the sport make up for the lack of originality of the plot, which when you boil it down, is little different than dozens of football and baseball films of past years transferred to a new location.

1209 The Kid from Texas

1939, Metro Goldwyn Mayer, 70 minutes. Director: S. Sylvan Simon. Producer: Edgar Selwyn. Screenplay: Florence Ryerson, Edgar Allan Woolf, Albert Mannheimer. Photography: Sidney Wagner.

Cast: Dennis O'Keefe, Florence Rice, Anthony Allan, Jessie Ralph, Buddy Ebsen, Virginia Dale, Robert Wilcox, Jack Carson.

A cowboy wants to become a polo star so he stows away on a shipment of horses bound for the high society crowd on Long Island where he meets a beautiful woman.

He flops and leaves the team but hones his skills with a wild west show. The final game matches the snooty team he first played for against his new team composed of cowboys and Indians.

1210 King of the Herd

1927, Aywon Film Corp., 5,600 feet. Director: Frank S. Mattison. Photography: Jack Fuqua.

Cast: Raymond McKee, Nola Luxford, Bud Osborne, Arthur Hotaling, Laura Miskin, Fred Shanley, Evelyn Francisco.

The leader of a herd of wild horses causes a stampede when

it frees a number of horses on a ranch to get at the polo pony it has selected as its mate.

A cowboy (McKee) rescues the rancher's daughter (Luxford) from the stampede and captures the wild horse, training it to enter the polo matches at Santa Barbara against a rival.

1211 Little Giant

1933, Warner Brothers, 70 minutes. Director: Roy Del Ruth. Story: Robert Lord. Photography: Sid Hickox. Editor: Robert Haas.

Cast: Edward G. Robinson, Mary Astor, Helen Vinson, Kenneth Thomson, Shirley Grey, Russell Hopton, Berton Churchill, Donald Dillaway, Louise Mackintosh, Helen Mann.

Polo becomes a symbol of the unattainable in a pleasant tale of a notorious gangster (Robinson, of course!) who tires of his life and decides to go straight and break into society.

He moves into the mansion of a pretty young woman who has fallen on hard financial times but falls into the clutches of a snooty fortune-hunting family.

The society villains decide to take him for a complete sucker, taking his cash and laughing at him behind his back at his pathetic attempts to act like he was born into high society.

His attempts at playing polo are the most comical of all; but when he finds out what's going on, he brings his old gang back together again to teach the snobs a lesson they'll never forget.

The finale has the triumphant gangsters getting together on the polo field for a wacky match among themselves.

1212 Lucky Larrigan

1933, Monogram, 56 minutes. Director: J.P. McCarthy. Producer: Tem Carr. Story: Wellyn Totman. Photography: Archie Stout.

Cast: Rex Bell, Helen Foster, Stanley Blystone, Julian Rivero, Wilfrid Lucas, G.D. Wood, George Chesbro.

A polo star follows his girl friend out West where he meets all kinds of trouble on the ranch of her dad, his father's business partner.

1213 Mickey's Polo Team

1936, United Artists-Disney, 10 minutes, Color.

As we said in the introduction, we are not including every sports cartoon but just key selected ones. This is considered one of the top Mickey Mouse cartoons and features caricatures of Laurel and Hardy, Harpo Marx, Charlie Chaplin, Jack Holt and a host of other "guests."

1214 Native Pony

1954, Argentinian, Adoca, 100 minutes. Director: Ralph Peppier. Screenplay: Hugo Mc-Dougall. Photography: Humberto Peruzzi. Editor: Gerardo Rinaldi.

Cast: Enrique Muino, Alberto Bello, Mario Passano, Roberto Fugazot, Margarita Corona, Lia Casanova.

The development of polo as a national sport in Argentina is traced through the story of a man who loves horses and believes that native Argentinian ponies are better suited for polo than foreign ones.

1215 Neptune's Daughter

1949, Metro Goldwyn Mayer, 92 minutes, Color. Director: Edward Buzzell. Producer: Jack Cumming. Screenplay: Dorothy Kingsley. Photography: Frank Loesser. Editor: Irvine Warburton.

Cast: Esther Williams, Ricardo Montalban, Red Skelton, Betty Garrett, Keenan Wynn, Ted de Corsia, Mike Mazurki.

Like nearly all Esther Williams films, the slim and lightweight plot has music, comedy and above all the star in a bathing suit. Little else matters except the latter.

Here, she's a model for a

swimsuit manufacturer who falls for polo star Montalban. Skelton, as a masseur for a polo club, provides most of the comedy as he tries to play the game.

1216 The Polo Champion

1915, British, Pathe, 2,550 feet. Director: M. Hugon.

Cast: James Carew.

Fickle Flora of the sports films turns up again as an heiress promises to marry the winner of a polo match. Another example of women in sports films admiring only the brawn.

1217 Polo Joe

1936, Warner Brothers, 65 minutes. Director: William McGann. Story-Adaptation: Peter Milne, Hugh Cummings. Photography: L. William O'Connell. Editor: Clarence Kolster.

Cast: Joe E. Brown, Carol Hughes, Richard "Skeets" Gallagher, George E. Stone, Joseph King, Fay Holden, Gordon Elliott.

The king of 1930's sports comedies, Joe E. Brown, is back as a wealthy man who goes all out to impress a girl by pretending he's a polo star. The only problem is he's allergic to horses.

He puts on an inner tube to protect himself, but that only results in his bouncing in the saddle more than riding in it.

1218 A Polo Pony

1941, RKO Radio Pictures, 2 reels. Director: Harry D'Arcy.

Cast: Leon Errol, Bob Graves, James C. Morton, Keith Hitchcock, Warren Jackson, Bud Jamison, Jack Rice, Charlie Hall.

Rubber-legged comedian Errol impersonates an Australian polo star.

1219 The Smart Set

1928, Metro Goldwyn Mayer, 6,476 feet. Director: Jack Conway. Scenario: Byron Morgan, Ann Price. Photography: Oliver Marsh. Editor: Sam S. Zimbalist.

Cast: William Haines, Jack Holt, Alice Day, Hobart Bosworth, Coy Watson, Jr., Constance Howard, Paul Nicholson.

Two polo stars (Haines, Holt) are rivals for the hand of a girl (Day). Haines is booted from the team for failing to have the proper team spirit, and he's also disowned by his father (Nicholson).

In a big match against the British, Nelson is injured and has to leave the game; and Haines is given another chance to redeem himself.

Sounds like a lot of 1920's football films, doesn't it?

1220 Stormy the Thoroughbred

1954, Buena Vista, 45 minutes, Color. Director-Producer: Larry Lansburgh. Screenplay: Bill Walsh. Story: Jack Holt, Carolyn Coggins. Photography: Lansburgh, Floyd Crosby, Hal Ramser. Editor: John Link.

Cast: M.R. Valdez, Robert Skene, George Swinebroad, Alden Roark, Cecil Smith, James Stimmle, George Fanneman.

A Kentucky colt is born long after the normal foaling season, making him kind of an "ugly duckling." Smaller than the other horses, he develops an inferiority complex on the horse farm until he's sold to a ranch which turns him into a polo pony.

In true Disney tradition, Stormy proves to be a champion.

1221 This Sporting Age

1932, Columbia, 71 minutes. Directors: Andrew W. Bennison, A.F. Erickson. Story: J.K. McGuinness. Photography: Teddy Tetzlaff.

Cast: Jack Holt, Evalyn Knapp, Hardie Albright, J. Farrell MacDonald, Walter Byron, Ruth Weston, Shirley Palmer, Hal Price.

A champion army polo player (Holt) gets the chance to get even with the cad (Byron) who compromised his girl friend as a polo match is turned into a private vendetta.

1222 White Pants Willie

1927, First National, 6,350 feet. Director: Charles Hines. Adaptation: Howard J. Green, based on a story by Elmer Holmes Davis. Photography: James Diamond.

Cast: Johnny Hines, Leila Hyams, Henry Barrows, Ruth Dwyer, Walter Long, Margaret Seddon, George Kuwa.

Comedy about a bullied garage mechanic who's mocked for always wearing white pants and who invents some kind of magnetic bumper.

He repairs the car of an automobile manufacturer, putting on the new bumper.

When he's mistaken for a polo star, he gets into the match and becomes a hero and gets financial backing for his invention.

1223/1224 Wild Brian Kent

1936, 20th Century-Fox, 57 minutes. Director: Howard Bretherton. Producer: Sol Lesser. Screenplay: Earle Snell, Don Swift, based on a novel by Harold Bell Wright. Photography: Harry Newman.

Cast: Ralph Bellamy, Mae Clarke, Helen Lowell, Stanley Andrews, Lew Kelly, Eddie Chandler, Richard Alexander, Jack Duffy.

Down-and-out polo player Bellamy winds up on a financially troubled farm owned by a nice old lady and her niece, after talking his way into a free meal at a cafe. He helps them get away from the grasp of a slicker.

Using his equestrian skills, he wins enough money in a horse race to buy them a thresher and uses his polo skills to put out a fire set by the villain who has his eyes on the farm.

Dogs, Goats and Donkeys

1225 Dark Hazard

1934, Warner Brothers, 60-72 minutes. Director: Al Green. Screenplay: Ralph Block, Brown Holmes, based on a novel by W.R. Burnett. Photography: Sol Polito.

Cast: Edward G. Robinson, Genevieve Tobin, Glenda Farrell, Robert Barrat, Gordon Westcott, Robert Cavanaugh, George Meeker, Henry P. Walthall, Sidney Toler, Emma Dunn.

Robinson's a compulsive gambler who habituates the dog racing scene and who is dominated by everyone around him. When his wife (Tobin) leaves him, he takes up with tough Farrell. Remade in 1937 as **Wine, Women and Horses** with the milieu changed to horse racing.

The film is based on a best-seller by W.R. Burnett, who also wrote a book which became one of Robinson's most famous movie roles: **Little Caesar.**

1226 Don't Rush Me!

1935, British, Producers' Distributing Corp., 72 minutes. Director: Norman Lee. Producer: Fred Karno. Screenplay: Con West, Michael Barringer.

Cast: Robb Wilton, Peter Haddon, Muriel Aked, Bobbie Comber, Haver & Lee, Kathleen Kelly, Kenneth Love, Wallace Douglas, Dino Galvani, Hal Walters.

Comedy about two anti-gambling men who become heavily involved in betting on greyhounds.

1227 The Gay Dog

1954, British, Coronet, 87 minutes. Director: Maurice Elvey. Producer: Ernest Gartside. Photography: James Wilson. Screenplay: Peter Rogers, based on a play by Joseph Colton.

Cast: Petula Clark, Wilfred Pickles, Megs Jenkins, John Blythe, Margaret Barton, Russell Enogh, Cyril Raymond.

Raving Beauty, a miner's greyhound, is such a great racer that it can't get decent odds at the track so its owner takes it out of town.

The unscrupulous miner gets greedy when he learns another top dog is in the same race but learns the error of his ways.

1228 Jumping for Joy

1956, British, Rank, 88 minutes. Director: John Petty Carstairs. Producer: Raymond Stross. Screenplay: Jack Davies, Henry E. Blyth.

Cast: Frank Howard, Stanley Holloway, A.E. Mathews, Tony Wright, Susan Beaumont, Alfie Bass, Joan Hickson, Lionel Jeffries, Terence Longdon.

A man who's been fired from his job helps catch a narcotics gang while his greyhound wins at the races.

1229 Kid Stakes

1927, Australian, Ordell-Coyle, 2,000 feet. Producer: Tal Ordell. Screenplay: Ordell, Sid Nicholls.

Cast: "Pop" Ordell, Tal Ordell, Charles Roberts, Ray Salmon, Frank Boyd, Edward Stevens, Billy Ireland, Stanley Funnell.

One of the most famous Australian silent films finds a kid named Fatty and his friends competing against a rival gang in a goat cart race.

1230 Mrs. Brown, You've Got a Lovely Daughter

1968, British, Metro Goldwyn Mayer, 95 minutes, Color. Director: Saul Swimmer. Producer: Allen V. Klein. Screenplay: Thaddeus Vane. Photography: Jack Hildyard. Editor: Tristam Cones.

Cast: Herman's Hermits, Stanley Holloway, Mona Washbourne, Lance Percival, Marjorie Rhodes, Sheila White, Sarah Caldwell, Hugh Futcher, Avis Bunnage.

Peter Noone, lead singer of Herman's Hermits, inherits a greyhound which wins the Manchester heat of the National Greyhound Derby.

His troubles start when he takes the dog to London for the finals. He meets a model and falls in love, but he loses money for the entry fee to a con man and the dog winds up being lost.

The rock group takes on a nightclub gig to get money for the Derby, and the dog is found in time.

1231 One Wild Oat

1951, British, Coronet, 78 minutes. Director: Charles Saunders. Producer: John Croyden. Screenplay: Vernon Sylvaine, Lawrence Huntington.

Cast: Stanley Holloway, Robertson Hare, Sam Costa, Andrew Crawford, Vera Pearce, June Sylvaine, Robert Moreton.

The lady owner of a racing greyhound foils a blackmail plot.

1232 The Outcast

1934, British, Wardour, 74 minutes. Director: Norman Lee. Producer: Walter C. Mycroft. Screenplay: Syd Courtenay, Lola Harvey.

Cast: Leslie Fuller, Mary Glynne, Hal Gordon, Jane Carr, Gladys Sewell, Jimmy Godden, Wallace Geoffry, Pat Aherne.

A greyhound saves the day for a broke bookie by winning despite the efforts of some thugs to stop it.

1233 The Price of Fear

1956, Universal, 79 minutes. Director: Abner Biberman. Producer: Howard Christie. Screenplay: Robert Tallman. Story: Dick Irving Hyland. Photography: Irving Glassberg. Editor: Ray Snyder.

Cast: Merle Oberon, Lex Barker, Charles Drake, Gia Scala, Warren Stevens, Phillip Fine, Mary Field, Tim Sullivan.

A beautiful femme fatale (Oberon) causes all kinds of trouble for dog track owner Barker when he's suspected in the death of his partner.

1234 The Pride of the North

1920, British, I.B. Davidson, 5,165 feet. Director: A.E. Coleby.

Cast: Cecil Humphreys, Nora

Roylance, Richard Buttery, James English, Blanche Kellino, H. Nichols-Bates, Eva Llewellyn.

A greyhound's efforts in the Waterloo Cup race help reconcile a father and son.

1235 The Three Caballeros

1945, RKO Radio Pictures, 70 minutes, Color. Director: Harold Young. Story: Homer Brightman, Ernest Terrazzas, Ted Sears, Bill Peet, Ralph Wright, Elmer Plummer, Roy Williams, William Cottrell, Del Connell, James Bodrero. Editor: John Haliday.

One of several feature length multi-episode animated films produced by the Disney studio during the 1940's features a segment entitled "Little Gauchito" in which a flying donkey wins a race but is disqualified as soon as his wings are discovered.

The other segments--all linked by Donald Duck--are "Strange Birds," about a penguin who can't get used to the cold, and a visit to Mexico by Donald Duck and Joe Carioca the parrot.

Made during World War II, production of **The Three Caballeros** was delayed by the shortage of color film stock.

1236 Track the Man Down

1955, British, Republic, 75 minutes. Director: R.G. Springsteen. Producer: William N. Boyle. Screenplay: Paul Erickson, Kenneth R. Hayles. Photography: Basil Emmott.

Cast: Kent Taylor, Petula Clark, Renee Houston, Walter Rilla, George Rose, Mary Mackenzie, Kenneth Griffith.

A thief who stole the take from a dog track is trailed by a reporter.

1237 The Turners of Prospect Road

1947, British, Grand National, 76 minutes. Director-Producer: Maurice J. Wilson. Screenplay: Patrick Kirwan, Victor Katuna. Photography: Freddie Ford.

Cast: Wilfrid Lawson, Helena Pickard, Maureen Glyne, Amy Veness, Jeanne de Casalis, Peter Bull, Leslie Perrins, Shamus Locke.

A cab driver who finds a greyhound pup helps his daughter raise it into a Derby-class racer. When he refuses to sell the animal to a professional backer, he finds himself framed for drunken driving.

With the help of the driver's friends, the dog gets to run in the big race.

1238 Two on a Doorstep

1936, British, Paramount British, 71 minutes. Director: Lawrence Huntingdon. Producer: Anthony Havelock-Allan. Screenplay: Gerald Elliott, George Barraud.

Cast: Kay Hammond, Harold French, Anthony Hankey, George Mozart, Dorothy Dewhurst, Frank Tickle, Walter Tobias, Ted Sanders.

A big greyhound race is the key to this comedy about a girl who sets up her own bookmaking agency after she keeps on getting calls for a bookie who has the same last name.

1239 Wild Boy

1934, British, Gaumont-British, 73-85 minutes. Director: Albert de Courville. Producer: Michael Balcon. Screenplay: Stafford Dickens.

Cast: Gwyneth Lloyd, Lebnora Corbett, Sonnie Hale, Lyn Harding, Ronald Squire, Flanagano Allen.

Mick the Miller, the real-life greyhound Derby winner, portrays a dog named Wild Boy, one of the litter of a prize-winning greyhound named Wild Man of Borneo.

The owner of Black Prince, realizing that the main threat in the big race is Wild Boy, attempts to kidnap the dog.

Olympics and Track and Field

Films dealing with Olympic sports have appeared in a slow but steady flow ever since the silent days, with the pace picking up every four years as the new Olympics approach.

Olympics star Charles Paddock made several track and field pictures during the 1920's and in one out-races the villain who's riding on a horse. Olympics star Jesse Owens years later would try that stunt in real life.

Leni Riefenstahl's massive Nazi epic **Olympia,** a documentary on the 1936 Olympics in Berlin, remains the standard on which all subsequent documentaries of its kind are judged. With the exception of the 1952 games, there has been at least one general release feature documentary on all summer Olympics games since **Olympia** and on most of the winter games as well.

Not that the 1952 games are unrepresented on film. **The Bob Mathias Story** (1954) contains stock footage of the great Olympian's track feats during those games.

As in other sports, the Olympics have provided the base for a number of screen biographies. Besides Mathias, subjects for screen stories have included Jim Thorpe, Billy Mills, Harold Abrahams and Eric Liddell. It was left to television, however, to tell the story of one of the greatest Olympians of all time, Jesse Owens.

When jogging came into vogue in the 1970's, a spate of track films began appearing on the screen, including **Our Winning Season, Running, Chariots of Fire, Personal Best** and **Running Brave.**

In the 1976 **Second Wind,** a stock-broker foresakes his job and marriage for the thrill of competitive running. In **Peck's Bad Boy Joins the Circus,** that famous imp must run the big race in drag while in **Sam's Song** the hero becomes a star javelin thrower before going on to a film career.

Among the films we consider "on the fringe" which deserve footnotes are **Blue Thunder** (1983) with its super-helicopter designed to combat terrorists in the 1984 Olympics in Los Angeles; **The Gay Braggart** (1965), a Japanese film set during the Tokyo games; **Graduation Day** (1981), a "splatter" movie with a track coach and members of the team becoming involved in murder; **Animalympics,** a satire about just what it sounds like; **Punishment Park** (1971) where conscientious objectors to the Vietnam War are given three days to outrace National Guardsmen who are ordered to shoot to kill; and silent film comedian Harry Langdon's **The Strong Man.** In Walt Disney's **Blackbeard's Ghost,** that infamous pirate helps save his ancestral home and helps an inept track team.

1240 American Odyssey

1980, McKinley Productions/ Media America, 87 minutes, Color. Director-Writer-Editor: Ambrose Salmini. Photography: Salmini, Steve Marts, Peter Salmini, Norv Knight.

Opening with the 1979 New York City Marathon and ending at the Davis campus of the University of California, this documentary focuses on the lives of four runners as they make a cross-country trip across America.

Melody Mayer, an Ohio teacher; Leon Henderson, an Oregon farmer; and Todd Gay, who all begin the trip in New York, are joined in Wyoming by Linda Macias.

1241 Barnyard Olympics

1932, Disney, 7 minutes.

A rhinoceros is Mickey Mouse's chief rival for the laurels.

1242 Billie

1965, United Artists, 83-87 minutes, Color. Director-Producer: Don Weis. Executive Producer: Peter Lawford. Screenplay: Ronald Alexander, based on his play **Time Out for Ginger.** Photography: John L. Russell. Editor: Adrienne Fazan.

Cast: Patty Duke, Jim Backus, Jane Greer, Warren Berlinger, Billy De Wolfe, Charles Lane, Dick Sargent, Susan Seaforth, Ted Bessell, Richard Deacon, Bobby Diamond.

A very minor and low-key comedy that was virtually ignored in its original release, **Billie** was nonetheless a giant step forward in the depiction of women as athletes and the first really significant portrayal since **Pat and Mike.**

Duke is a 16-year-old who causes a major stir by outrunning all the boys on the track team, including her boy friend (Berlinger), who takes a typical chauvinistic attitude.

Her athletic prowess causes problems for dad (Backus), who is running for mayor in a no-holds-barred campaign.

1243 The Bob Mathias Story (aka The Flaming Torch)

1954, Allied Artists, 80 minutes. Director: Francis D. Lyon. Producer: William E. Selwyn. Screenplay: Richard Collier. Photography: Ellsworth Frederics. Editor: Walter Hanaman.

Cast: Bob Mathias, Melba Mathias, Ward Bond, Harry Lauter, Ann Doran, Howard Petrie, Diane Jergens, Paul Bryar.

Using the same formula as they did in the biography **Crazylegs, All American** the previous year, the filmmakers got an aging Mathias to play himself as a teenager in this life story. They even hired his wife to portray herself.

His football career at Stanford, his 1948 decathlon championship in London and his victories in the 1952 Olympics in Helsinki are portrayed mostly through stock footage.

What's lacking is any kind of dramatic tension as Mathias monotones his way from one scene to another without any real crises.

1244 The Campus Flirt

1926, Paramount, 6,702 feet. Director: Clarence Badger. Screenplay: Louise Long, Lloyd Corrigan. Photography: H. Kinley Martin.

Cast: Bebe Daniels, James Hall, El Brendel, Charles Paddock, Joan Standing, Gilbert Roland, Irma Kornelia, Jocelyn Lee.

Filmed at the University of Southern California, the main attraction is track star Charles Paddock appearing as himself.

The plot concerns a snobbish girl (Daniels) who joins her college track team after she's scared by a mouse and shoots past Paddock.

The track coach (Hall) is kidnapped prior to the big meet, and the heroine is also delayed when she tries to rescue him, but everyone gets to the stadium on time in case you were worried.

1245 Chariots of Fire

1981, British, 20th Century-Fox, 123 minutes, Color. Director: Hugh Hudson. Producer: David Puttnam. Screenplay: Colin Welland. Photography: David Watkin. Editor: Terry Rawlings.

Cast: Ben Cross, Ian Charleson, Nigel Havers, Nick Farrell, Daniel Gerroll, Alice Krige, Cheryl Campbell, John Gielgud, Lindsay Anderson, Nigel Davenport, Struan Rodger, Ian Holm, Patrick Magee, Brad Davis, Dennis Christopher.

Featuring a magnificent musical score by Vangelis Papathanassiou, this Oscar winner for best picture was responsible as much as **Rocky** for dispelling the image of the sports film as a money-losing proposition.

Opening in 1919 at Cambridge University where the "flower of a generation" was killed in the Great War, it follows future Olympian Harold M. Abrahams (Cross), who must battle himself and subtle anti-Semitism as he begins his rise to the top when he and a friend become the first collegians in 700 years to complete a college dash against the clock in the courtyard.

Meanwhile, in Scotland, running great Eric Liddell (Charleson) is facing his own inner struggle as he's torn between his love for running and his faith as he contemplates becoming a missionary in China.

Abrahams is pretty sure of himself until he goes to watch Liddell win one day despite falling, and he gets a well-known Arab-Italian track coach to perfect his style.

This further upsets the college brass, not only because of the coach's national origins, but because they feel Abraham's only out for personal glory.

Abrahams and Liddell wind up on the 1924 British Olympic team, but complications set in when Liddell learns the qualifying heat for his event is on Sunday, the Lord's Day.

Just as memorable as the closing track sequences is the locker room scene just prior to the races, as there's complete silence as the Americans (Christopher, Davis) and the Englishmen prepare themselves.

The mark of success of any film is how often it's imitated, and it wasn't long before any running sequence in a film was accompanied by a **Chariots of Fire**-type musical score.

1246 Charlie Chan at the Olympics

1937, 20th Century-Fox, 71 minutes. Director: H. Bruce Humberstone. Producer: John Stone. Screenplay: Robert Ellis, Helen Logan, based on a story by Paul Burger and characters created by Earl Derr Biggers. Photography: Daniel C. Clarke.

Cast: Warner Oland, Keye Luke, Katherine DeMille, Pauline Moore, Allan Lane, C. Henry Gordon, John Eldredge, Layne Tom, Jr., Jonathan Hale, Morgan Walker, Andrew Tombes.

That great Asian detective uses his wits and gets help from the German police as he travels to the Berlin Olympics to solve the mystery of a stolen remote control aircraft device.

Chan's son, Luke, is a member of the United States swimming team in this film, a distinctly rare cinema acknowledgment that Asians, too, are capable of athletic prowess.

1247 Dawn

1979, Australian, Hoyts, 111 minutes, Color. Director: Ken Hannam. Producer-Screenplay: Joy Cavill. Photography: Russell Boyd. Editor: Max Lemon.

Cast: Bronwyn Mackay-Payne, Tom Richards, John Diedrich, Bunney Brooke, Ron Haddrick, Gabrielle Hartley, Carmelina Caterina.

Here's the supposedly true story of Australian swimming champion Dawn Fraser, who won medals in three different Olympics--Melbourne in 1956, Rome in 1960 and Tokyo in 1964--and whose behavior out of the water was almost as active and landed her, if you excuse the pun, in some hot water.

1248 Endgame

1983, Italian, Cinema 80, 96 minutes, Color. Director: Steven Benson. Screenplay: Alex Carver. Photography: Frederico Slonisco. Editor: Tony Larson.

Cast: Al Cliver, Moira Chen, George Eastman, Al Yamanouchi, Jack Davis, Gus Stone, Mario Pedone, Gordon Mitchell, Nat Williams, Christopher Walsh.

It's the year 2025, and the survivors of a nuclear holocaust are ruled by the military group called the Security Service. Soldiers wear SS insignia on their helmets and slaughter innocent mutants on sight (get it?).

The main diversion for the populace is Endgame, in which three hunters have 12 hours to track down and kill their prey—all with extensive live television coverage, including slow motion replay of the "kills."

"Unbeatable" Ron Shannon, one of the game's all-time greats having won the game seven times, wins again and is then recruited by a psychic mutant to lead a telekinetic child to safety outside the city where the peaceful mutants can live in peace.

1249 Feudin', Fussin' and A-Fightin'

1948, Universal-International, 78 minutes. Director: George Sherman. Producer: Leonard Goldstein. Screenplay: D.D. Beauchamp. Photography: Irving Glassberg. Editor: Edward Curtiss.

Cast: Donald O'Connor, Marjorie Main, Percy Kilbride, Penny Edwards, Joe Besser, Harry Shannon, Fred Kohler, Jr., Howland Chamberlain, Edmund Dobb, Joel Franklin, Francis Ford.

A musical comedy featuring the song "Me and My Shadow" has O'Connor as a traveling salesman who's kidnapped by a town when the residents see how fast he can run.

He's then forced to race in the town's annual foot race against another community.

1250 XIVth Olympiad—The Glory of Sport

1948, British, GFD, 130 minutes. Director: Castleton Knight. Photography: Stanley Sayer. Editor: Roy Drew.

Narrators: Bill Stern, Ted Husing, Stewart McPherson.

A total of 16 different versions of this record of the 1948 Olympics were made for the various nations involved.

Besides the action at Wembley Stadium in England, there are scenes in Greece and at the winter games in St. Moritz.

1251 The Games

1970, 20th Century-Fox, 96-97 minutes, Color. Director: Michael Winner. Producers: Winner, Lester Linsk. Screenplay: Erich Segal, based on a novel by Hugh Atkinson. Photography: Robert Paynter. Editor: Bernard Gribble.

Cast: Michael Crawford, Stanley Baker, Ryan O'Neal, Charles Aznavour, Jeremy Kemp, Elaine Taylor, Athol Compton, Fritz Weaver, Kent Smith, Sam Elliott, Leigh Taylor-Young.

As the Rome Olympics approach, four runners from different nations train under widely varying conditions.

There's the aging Czech (Aznavour), who must prove he can still do it; there's the Englishman (Crawford) forced by his domineering coach (Baker) to give up his girl friend; the Yale student (O'Neal) with a heart problem and an aborigine (Compton).

1252 Games of the XXI Olympiad Montreal

1976, Canadian, National Film Board of Canada, 119 minutes, Color. Directors: Jean-Claude Labrecque, Jean Baudin, Marcel Carriere, George Dufaux. Editor: Werner Nord.

Bruce Jenner and gymnast Nadia Comaneci highlight this very straightforward account of the games in Canada.

1253 Get on Your Marks

1973, Greek, Color. Director-Producer-Screenplay-Editor: Theodoros Maranghus. Photography: Nikos Petanidis.

Cast: Vanghelis Kazan, Christis Tolius, Kostas Tsakonas, Vasilis Tsipidis, Fani Toliu, Kostas Alexandrakis.

A provincial tailor hopes to escape his drab life by becoming a track star, but his dreams are dashed in a big city factory.

1254 Girl of My Dreams

1935, Monogram, 65 minutes. Director: Raymond McCarey. Producer: William T. Lackey. Screenplay: George Waggner. Photography: Ira Morgan. Editor: Jack Ogilvie.

Cast: Mary Carlisle, Sterling Holloway, Eddie Nugent, Arthur Lake, Creighton Chaney, Gigi Parrish, Tommy Dugan, Jeanie Roberts, Lee Shumvay.

An intercollegiate track meet forms the background of this musical comedy about a star athlete who pays scant attention to women until the senior class election.

1255 Going Some

1920, Goldwyn, 6 reels. Director: Harry Beaumont. Scenario: Laurence Trimble, based on a story by Rex Beach.

Instead of the old homestead, which has oil on it, dependent upon the outcome of a horse race, this time it's a foot race, but virtually everything else is the same.

When a top runner breaks his toe, the hero must take his place in the big race.

1256 Goldengirl

1979, Avco-Embassy, 104 minutes, Color. Director: Joseph Sargent. Producer: Danny O'Donovan. Screenplay: John Kohn, based on a novel by Peter Lear. Photography: Steven Larner. Editor: George Nicholson.

Cast: Susan Anton, James Coburn, Curt Jurgens, Leslie Caron, Robert Culp, James A. Watson, Jr., Harry Guardino, Ward Costello, Michael Lerner, John Newcombe, Jessica Walter.

Dr. Jurgens raises his adopted daughter to be an Olympics star, making her a virtual human guinea pig as he tries out all kinds of new conditioning methods to make sure she wins three track medals at the 1980 Olympics.

Coburn is the financial genius whose purpose is to be sure everyone makes a fortune off the girl (Anton) who, despite the efforts of everyone to turn her into a robot, is still quite human.

1257 The Grand Olympics

1961, Times Film Corp., 120-142 minutes, Color. Director: Romolo Marcellini. Editor: Marco Sarandici.

The Soviet Union takes away the most medals in the 1960 Olympics in Rome. The film, however, wasn't released in the United States until 1964 and then only in a severely truncated version.

1258 Grenoble (aka **13 Jours en France**)

1969, French, United Productions, 95-115 minutes, Color. Directors: Claude Lelouch, Francois Reichenbach. Producer: Georges Derochles. Photography: Willy Bogner, Jr., Jean Collomb, Guy Gilles, Jean-Paul Janssen, Pierre Willemin. Editor: Claude Barrois.

As originally made by Lelouch, one of France's top commercial film directors, and Reichenbach, this account of the 1968 Winter Olympics ran 115 minutes but was drastically cut for American release.

Highlights include Jean-Claude Killy on skis and Peggy Fleming doing her thing on the ice.

1259 The Hazing

1977, Miraleste Co., 90 minutes, Color. Director: Douglas Curtis. Producers: Curtis, Bruce Shelly. Screenplay: Shelly, David Ketchum.

Cast: Jeff East, Brad David, David Hayward, Charles Martin Smith, Sandra Vacey, Kelly Moran, Jim Boelsen.

East is a naive country boy who goes to college with the hopes of being a big track star. Despite the fact that his older brother caused some problems for the Delts, the top fraternity, with his student activism some years back, East is asked to join the group.

During the initiation ceremonies, he believes that a friend (Smith) is killed and is shocked when the fraternity leader (David) asks him to help cover up the death and to dispose of the body.

1260 Hempa's Bar (aka **Cry of Triumph '57**)

1977, Swedish, Swedish Film Institute, 102 minutes, Color. Director: Lars G. Thelestam. Screenplay: Bosse Andersson. Photography: Joergen Persson. Editor: Sylvia Ingemarsson.

Cast: Krister Hell, Jan Nielsen, Harriet Andersson, Carl-Axel Heiknert.

A paralyzed man has become alienated with his two sons. The younger is a violent delinquent who winds up in a reform school, while the other likes Elvis, but further alienates his dad by losing a big running race.

1261 It Happened in Athens

1962, 20th Century-Fox, 92-100 minutes. Director: Andrew Marton. Producer: James S. Elliott. Screenplay: Laslo Vadnay. Photography: Curtis Courant. Editor: Jodie Copelan.

Cast: Jayne Mansfield, Bob Mathias, Trax Colton, Nico Minardos, Maria Xenia, Lili Valentry, Ivan Triesault, Bill Browne, Brad Harris, Paris Alexander.

During the 1896 revival of the Olympics in Athens, a shepherd (Colton) enters the marathon. Meanwhile, a beautiful actress declares she'll marry the victor, expecting it will be Minardos.

Olympian Mathias has a role as the coach in this minor comedy.

1262 Jim Thorpe—All American (aka **Man of Bronze**)

1951, Warner Brothers, 107 minutes. Director: Michael Curtiz. Producer: Everett Freeman. Screenplay: Freeman, Douglas Morrow. Story: Morrow, Vincent X. Flaherty, based on the biography by Thorpe and Russell G. Birdwell. Editor: Folmar Blangsted.

Cast: Burt Lancaster, Phyllis Thaxter, Charles Bickford, Jack Big Head, Suni Warcloud, Al Mejia, Nestor Paiva.

Lancaster turns in one of his most memorable performances as super athlete Thorpe, from his days on an Indian reservation in Oklahoma to his fall to the depths of poverty.

His rise to the top through amazing Olympic feats suddenly comes crashing down when he's forced to return his medals after it's learned he played pro baseball for next to nothing.

As his athletic prowess fades with age after baseball and football careers, he sinks to the lowest depths of poverty after his son dies, and he's discovered driving a junk truck.

At the end, however, he's finally given the recognition he deserves.

1263 Kings of the Olympics

1948, Westport International, 60 minutes. Editors: Joseph Lerner, Max Rosenbaum.

Narrator: Bill Slater.

A severely edited version of Leni Riefenstahl's **Olympia,** covering the events at the 1936 Olympics in Berlin.

1264 Local Boy Makes Good

1931, Warner Brothers, 69 minutes. Director: Mervyn LeRoy. Story: J.C. and Elliott Nugent. Adaptation: Robert Lord, Raymond Griffith, Ray Enright.

Cast: Joe E. Brown, Dorothy Lee, Ruth Hall, Edward Woods, Edward J. Nugent, John Harrington.

Another 1930's comedy in

which Brown becomes a sports hero despite himself.

Working his way through college in the school bookstore, he meets a beautiful girl from another school and decides to go out for the track team.

When he nearly lances the team captain with a javelin, he runs so fast to get away from him that he makes the team.

1265 Loneliness of the Long Distance Runner (aka **Rebel with a Cause**)

1962, British, Continental, 104 minutes. Director-Producer: Tony Richardson. Screenplay: Alan Sillitoe. Photography: Walter Lassally. Editor: Anthony Gibbs.

Cast: Tom Courtenay, Michael Redgrave, Avis Bunnage, Peter Madden, James Bolam, Julia Foster, Topsy Jane, Dervis Ward, Frank Finlay, Alex McCowen, John Bull, Raymond Dyer.

A teenager from the slums (Courtenay) robs a bakery and winds up in a reform school run by a governor (Redgrave) whose program for rehabilitation is through physical exercise.

The governor spots the youth's running ability and makes him the reformatory's great hope in a big race against a top public school.

Young Colin Smith, the youth, spends a lot of time making lonely practice runs, during which his past life is recalled through flashbacks.

Comes the big race, Smith is clearly the cream of the crop; but just before he crosses the finish line as the winner, he stops short and, in a final gesture of his contempt for society and authority, lets all the other runners pass.

1266 Military Academy

1940, Columbia, 66 minutes. Director: D. Ross Lederman. Screenplay: Karl Brown, David Silverstein. Story: Richard English. Photography: Allen G. Siegler. Editor: Gene Milford.

Cast: Tommy Kelly, Bobby Jordan, David Holt, Jackie Searle, Don Beddoe, Jimmy Butler, Walter Tetley, Earl Foxe, Warren Ashe.

A gangster's son is enrolled at the military school under an assumed name, but the other boys find out and make him an outcast.

The boy (Kelly) proves his mettle by becoming a track and field star, while life at the academy teaches him how to be a good citizen.

1267 Million Dollar Legs

1932, Paramount, 61 minutes. Director: Edward Cline. Story: Joseph L. Mankiewicz. Photography: Arthur Todd.

Cast: W.C. Fields, Jack Oakie, Andy Clyde, Lyda Roberti, Dickie Moore, Susan Fleming, Ben Turpin, Hugh Herbert, George Barbier.

Fields is the crazy president of Klopstokia which is sponsoring an Olympics. He's also the top arm wrestler in a republic where the presidency goes to the strongest.

Oakie's task is to recruit an Olympics team for Klopstokia for the usual Fields madness.

1268 A Million to One

1938, Puritan, 59 minutes. Director: Lynn Shores. Screenplay: John T. Neville. Photography: James Diamond. Editor: Edward Schroeder.

Cast: Herman Brix, Joan Fontaine, Monte Blue, Kenneth Harlan, Reed Howes.

Olympian Brix is cast as, right, an Olympics star who thinks he's the greatest and loses his form because of too much booze. He falls in love with society dame Fontaine.

1269 My Champion

1981, Japanese-U.S., Shochiku, 108 minutes, Color. Director: Gwen Arner. Producer: Yasuhiko Kawano. Screenplay: Richard

Matini. Photography: Kimiaki Kimura.

Cast: Chris Mitchum, Yoko Shimada, Andy Romano, Donald Moffat, Connie Sawyer, Yoko Sugi.

The life of marathon runner Miki Gorman is covered over a 13-year span as she moves from Japan to the United States to live with hubby Mitchum.

Despite the fact she's 40 years old, she wins the women's division of the New York City Marathon and a race in Boston. The film was never generally released in the United States and has appeared mainly on cable television.

1270 My Way (aka **The Winners)**

1974, South African, Joseph Brenner, 92 minutes, Color. Directors-Producers: Emil Nofal, Ray Sergeant. Screenplay: Nofal. Photography: Vincent Cox.

Cast: Joe Stewardson, Madeleine Usher, Tony Jay, Marie Du Toit, Richard Loring, Diane Ridler, John Higgins, Jennifer Meyers, Marcello Fiascanaro.

A man who won the Olympics marathon in 1948 (Stewardson) is now a success in the construction business but drives his kids relentlessly to emulate his success in sports, be it auto racing, swimming, fencing or horsemanship.

Intolerant of failure, he alienates his kids and friends alike until tragedy results.

In the finale, the ex-star enters a marathon to prove he can still push those aging bones, as his family and friends cheer the changed man on.

1271 Nine and Three-Fifths Seconds

1925, A.G. Steen. 5,386 feet. Director: Lloyd B. Carleton. Scenario: Roy Clements. Photography: Edward Jenderson, Gordon Pollock.

Cast: Charles Paddock, Helen Ferguson, George Fawcett, Jack Giddings, Peggy Schaffer, G. Raymond Nye, Otis Harlan.

Olympian Jesse Owens once raced a horse, but that was only for 100 yards.

In this showcase for the talents of Olympics track star Charles Paddock, he outraces a horse to track down the villain who has kidnapped his girl friend. With a scene like that, what can he do for an encore? Set an Olympics sprinting record, or course.

The plot, if anyone really cares after watching Paddock's feats, concerns a college athlete who's disowned by his family and becomes a bum until he's rehabilitated through the love of a rancher's daughter.

1272 Oh, Sport, You Are Brave

1981, Russia, Sovexport, 120 minutes, Color. Directors-Concept: Yuri Ozerov, Boris Rychov. Photography: Nikolai Olonovsky.

For those who missed the 1980 Olympics in Moscow because of the U.S. boycott, here's the official record of the games with politics kept to a minimum.

It includes an animated history of the Olympic games.

1273 Olimpiada 40

1980, Polish, Film Polski, 103 minutes, Color. Director: Andrej Kotkowski. Screenplay: Michal Kamar, Kotkowski. Photography: Witold Adamek.

Cast: Mariusz Benoit, Jerzy Bonisak, Tadeusz Galia, Krystof Jancsar, Rysiard Kotys, Wojiech Psoniak.

One of the ancestors of the soccer film **Victory** has a lieutenant in a German POW camp recognizing a prisoner as a member of the Polish Olympics team he competed against in the 1936 games in Berlin.

The Pole refuses the officer's invitation to train with him; but to keep the prisoners' morale up secretly forms a POW Olympics team which makes its own equipment from makeshift materials on hand.

When the Nazis find out,

the Pole is sent to a concentration camp; but the prisoners defy orders and hold their games anyway.

1274 Olympia

1938, German, Olympia-Film GmbH, 180 minutes. Director: Leni Riefenstahl. Production Leaders: Walter Traut, Walter Grosskopf. Directors of Cameramen: A. Kiekebusch, K. Boenisch, R. Fichtner.

Cameramen: Hans Ertl, Walter Frentz, Guzzi Lantschner, Heinz von Jaworsky, Andor V. Barsy, Wilfried Basse, Josef Dietze, Edmund Epkens, Franz von Friedl, Hans Gottschalk, Richard Groschopp, Willi Hameister, Wolf Hart, Hasso Hartnagel, Prof. Walter Hege, Eberhard van der Heyden, Albert Hockt, Paul Holzki, Werner Hundhausen, Sepp Ketterer, Hugo von Kaweczynski, Herbert Kebelmann, Albert Kling, Ernst Kuntsmann, Leo de Laforgue, A. Lagorio, E. Lambertini, Otto Dantschner, Waldemar Lemke, George Lemki, C. Linke, E. Nitzschemann, Albert Schattmann, Wilhelm Schmidt, Hugo Schulze, L. Schvedler, Alfred Siegert, W. Siehm, Ernst Sorge, H. von Stwolinski, Karl Vass.

Despite the fact it was sponsored as a mammoth Nazi propaganda project, Riefenstahl's chronicle of the 1936 Berlin Olympics remains to this day the ultimate achievement in sports documentaries.

The three-hour film is divided into two equal segments, the first being **Fest der Volker (Festival of the Nations)** and the second **Fest der Schonheit (Festival of Beauty).**

Riefenstahl reportedly wasn't even the first choice for the project, with the initial nod supposedly going to Luis Trenker, who bowed out to make instead **The Emperor of California.** Although Riefenstahl has contended over the years that Nazi Propaganda Minister Goebbels opposed her in the project, the Third Reich nevertheless supplied the funds for it, and there's no documentation to support her assertations.

Already in trouble with the International Olympics Committee over its treatment of Jewish athletes, a special production company was formed to conceal the government's involvement in the film for fear the games would be cancelled if it was believed the movie would be used as propaganda.

Riefenstahl devised a number of techniques that were unique for the time.

For the 100-yard dash, she had the camera mounted on a rail alongside the track to keep up with the runners. For the equestrian events, an automatic camera was placed on the saddle of a horse with a bag of feathers beneath it to reduce the vibrations. For overhead shots, automatic cameras were placed in baskets attached to balloons, and Berliners were told where to return the cameras if they found them on the ground after they landed.

The method for filming the water events was also totally unique. With a special underwater camera, the photographer would be on a high board and as the Olympic diver jumped into the water, so would he.

The airship Hindenburg was also used for overhead shots.

The film's prologue was shot in Greece, featuring nude men and women supposedly symbolizing the origin of the games and ultimately blending into the running of the Olympic torch into the stadium.

The stars of the first part of the film were a Korean marathon runner named Kitei Son, who was entered with the Japanese team, and black American Jesse Owens.

It's particularly interesting that a Nazi film would devote as much footage as it does to Owens' heroics, particularly in light of the fact that Hitler went into a rage when asked to pose with the black star; but for propaganda purposes it was probably a good choice as it gave the illusion the Nazis weren't such racists after all.

The second half features the diving sequence, considered the film's best, and a wide variety of events as well as a lot of footage devoted to the beauty of the human body.

1275 Olympia-Olympia

1972, German, Chronos-Film GMBH, 97 minutes, Color. Director: Jochen Bauer. Screenplay: Jost Von Morr. Editors: D. Gerlach, H. Kruska.

The history of the Olympics from 1896 on is the focus of this documentary made in Germany to tie in with the 1972 games in Munich. It features footage from most of the great achievements of the past.

1276 Olympic Games

1927, Pathe, 2 reels. Director: Anthony Mack. Producer-Screenplay: Hal Roach. Photography: Art Lloyd. Editor: Richard Currier.

Our Gang decides to hold its own backyard Olympics, but the true spirit of brotherhood loses out to slapstick.

1277 Olympic Games in White

1948, Swiss-Swedish, Europa. Director: Torgny Wickman. Photography: Harry Persson, Rene Boeniger, Robert Garbade, Ernst Elsigen, George Alexath, J. Bart, Hans Jaworsky.

The 1948 Winter Olympics in St. Moritz, Switzerland is the subject of this documentary.

1278 Olympic Hero

1928, Zakoro Film Corp., 5 reels. Director: R. William Neill. Scenario-Story: Ronald De Gastro. Photography: Faxon Dean. Editor: Henry Weber.

Cast: Charles Paddock, Julanne Johnston, Donald Stuart, Harvey Clark, Crauford Kent, Jack Selwyn, Bob Maxwell, Aileen Manning, Raoul Paoli.

Re-released by Supreme Pictures under the title **The All American**, footage from the 1924 Olympics is spliced into the tale of a college sprinter (real-life Olympian Paddock) and his rise to the top.

1279 Olympics in Mexico

1970, Mexican, Columbia, 120 minutes, Color. Director-Screenplay: Alberto Isaac. Producer: Federico Amerigo.

All the major events of the 19th Olympic games in Mexico City in 1968 are featured.

1280 Our Winning Season

1978, American-International, 92 minutes, Color. Director: Joseph Ruben. Producer: Joe Roth. Screenplay: Nick Nielphor. Photography: Stephen Katz. Editor: Bill Butler.

Cast: Scott Jacoby, Deborah Benson, Dennis Quaid, Randy Herman, Joe Penny, Jan Smithess, P.J. Soles, Robert Wahler.

Shot in Georgia, Jacoby stars as as high school trackster whose rival on the track and off is Wahler, who leads a gang from another school.

There's a lot of **American Graffiti**-type shenanigans, but in between, Jacoby simply can't beat Wahler until ex-track star Penny, who loves Jacoby's sister, gives him some tips before going to Vietnam to meet his death.

1281 Personal Best

1982, Warner Brothers, 122-124 minutes, Color. Director-Producer-Screenplay: Robert Towne. Photography: Michael Chapman. Editor: Bud Smith.

Cast: Mariel Hemingway, Scott Glenn, Patrice Donnelly, Kenny Moore, Jim Moody, Kari Gosswiller, Jodi Anderson, Martha Watson, Emily Dole.

It's hard to say whether Olympics takes a back seat to the lesbian relationship of track stars Hemingway and Donnelly or vice versa, but it was the sex angle which was stressed rather than sports in the film's promotion.

Glenn is caught in the middle as a strong-willed coach.

1282 Pimple the Sport

1913, British, Folly Films, 580 feet. Directors-Screenplay: Fred and Joe Evans.

Cast: Fred and Joe Evans.

He tries out for the Olympics in this short comedy.

1283 The Poor Nut

1927, First National, 6,897 feet. Director: Richard Wallace. Screenplay: Paul Schofield, based on a story by J.C. and Elliott Nugent. Photography: David Kesson.

Cast: Jack Mulhall, Charlie Murray, Jean Arthur, Jane Winton, Glenn Tryon, Cornelius Keefe, Maurice Ryan, Bruce Gordon, Henry Vibart, William Courtwright.

A top scholar who has an inferiority complex when it comes to sports brags to his girl friend that he's a track star. Going out for the team, he loses to his rival; but another girl gives him the support he needs to try again.

1284 Portrait of a Champion

1979, Hungarian, Hungarofilm, 96 minutes. Director: Forenc Kosa. Photography: Janos Gulyas, Ferenc Kaplar.

Five-time Hungarian pentathlon champion Andras Balczo calls it quits at age 34 as this documentary focuses on his life after his career. Turning down offers to train athletes in other countries, he opts to remain in his native country.

1285 Pumping Iron

1977, Cinema 5, 85 minutes, Color. Directors-Producers: George Butler, Robert Fiore. Photography: Fiore. Editors: Larry Silk, Geof Barty.

Cast: Arnold Schwarzenegger, Lou Ferrigno, Mike Katz, Franco Columbu, Ed Corney, Ken Waller, Serge Nubret, Robin Robinson, Marianne Claire.

An entertaining documentary about the world of body builders which first demonstrated the acting abilities (although some people wouldn't call it that) of Schwarzenegger and Ferrigno.

1286 Raw Courage

1983, New World, 90 minutes, Color. Director: Robert L. Rosen. Producers: Rosen, Ronny Cox. Screenplay: Ronny and Mary Cox. Photography: F. Pershing Flynn. Editor: Steven Polivka.

Cast: Ronny Cox, Tim Maier, Art Hindle, M. Emmet Walsh, William Russ, Lisa Sutton, Hirsha Parady, Noel Conlon, Anthony Palmer, Lois Chiles.

Three buddies set out on a 72-mile endurance run across the New Mexican desert to a small town called Glory, where a hero's welcome awaits them.

Carrying no food and just little bottles of water, the trio has stops planned at a number of water holes and some food buried at the 50-mile mark.

About 20 miles out, however, they run afoul of the Citizens Brigade, a right-wing fanatical group which is on a "survival training" military exercise in the desert. After the Brigade accidentally kills one of the runners, the surviving two must run—and fight—for their lives over the remaining 50 miles.

1287 Red Lips (aka **Cream of the Earth, The Plastic Age**)

1928, Universal, 6,947 feet. Director-Adaptation: Melville Brown. Story: Edward J. Montagne, based on a novel by Percy Marks. Photography: John Stumar. Editor: Ray Curtiss.

Cast: Charles Buddy Rogers, Marion Nixon, Stanley Taylor, Hayden Stevenson, Andy Devine,

Earl McCarthy, Robert Seiter, Hugh Trevor.

When a girl is found in his room, a track star is booted from the team but changes his ways and winds up setting new records.

1288 Rendez-Vous a Melbourne (Melbourne Rendezvous)

1957, French, Gueguen-Gergle-ly-Freemantic, 87-110 minutes, Color. Director: Rene Lucot, assisted by Jean Averty, Serge Griboff, Donald Eckles, Claire Attali. Photography: Jacques Duhamel, Pierre Gueguen, Pierre Leon, Georges Leciere. Editors: Jean Dudrumet, Monique Lacombe.

In an unusual move which upset a number of newsreel and film companies, the Australians sold exclusive rights to coverage of the 1956 Olympics in Melbourne to the French.

In the shorter version for American release, all the water sports were inexplicably edited out.

1289 Return of the Champ

1971, Toho, 99 minutes. Director: Akiyasu Kotani. Producers: Juichi Tanaka, Hikaru Onda. Screenplay: Yasuo Tanami. Photography: Masahu Ueda. Editor: Michiko Ikeda.

Cast: Yuzo Kayama, Kunio Tanaka, Ryoko Sakaguchi, Agnes Lum, Ichiro Arishima, Tatsuji Ebara.

An aide to the president of a South Seas republic and a business executive from Japan both love a television producer (Sakaguchi) who's in New York City to cover the running of the marathon.

An American official promises the island official some help for his country if he beats him in the marathon.

1290 Running

1979, Universal, 101 minutes, Color. Director-Screenplay: Steven Hilliard Stern. Producer: Robert Cooper. Photography: Laszlo George. Editor: Kurt Hirschler.

Cast: Michael Douglas, Susan Anspach, Lawrence Dane, Eugene Levy, Charles Shamata, Lutz Brode, Trudy Young, Murray Westgate, Jennifer McKinney, Jim McKay.

Douglas plays a man who's never finished anything he's started. He dropped out of both med school and law school and never showed up for the Pan American Games he was scheduled to compete in as a runner.

Now he's a shoe salesman who's separated from his wife but still in love with her.

He decides to give sports another try to prove he can do something he starts out to accomplish and overcomes the skepticism of the coach, who remembers him from the Pan Am Games, to make the Olympic team and compete in the marathon.

1291 Running Brave

1983, Buena Vista, 105 minutes, Color. Director: "D.S. Everett" (director Donald Shebib had his name taken off the credits). Producer: Ira Englander. Screenplay: Henry Bean, Shirl Hendryx. Photography: Francois Protat. Editor: Tony Lower, Earl Herdan.

Cast: Robby Benson, Pat Hingle, Claudia Cron, Jeff McCraken, August Schellenberg, Denis Lacroix.

Financed by the Ermineskin Band of Cree Indians, **Running Brave** opened in some parts of the country but not in others and was sold to video markets within six months.

A clone of **Chariots of Fire**, it features Benson, who in earlier films had portrayed a Chicano and an orthodox Jew, as Indian runner Billy Mills who won the gold medal in the 10,000 meter run at the Olympics in Tokyo.

Despite having an impressive high school record, college coach Hingle is reluctant to take him on because he claims Indian runners have a reputation for quitting.

Mills sets out to prove him wrong and achieves an awesome record of victories at college. He falls in love with a white student, but finds her family has trouble accepting him and his people won't accept her.

When the going really gets rough, Mills lives up to Hingle's fears by quitting and returns to the reservation. The death of his brother by suicide, however, renews his ambition, and he joins the Marines where he gets another chance to run and winds up on the Olympics team.

1292 Sapporo Winter Olympics

1972, Japanese, Toho, 100 minutes, Color. Director: Mashiro Shinoda. Screenplay: Nabuo Yamada, Aromu Mushiake, Motoo Ogosawara, Kyoko Kishida. Editor: T. Nagizski.

Shinoda, one of Japan's top contemporary directors, led a team of 52 photographers in this documentary on the winter Olympics at Sapporo.

The highlight is the hockey game between Russia and Czechoslovakia, which had been invaded by the Russians only a few years earlier.

1293 Sport, Sport, Sport

1971, Russian, Mosfilm, 90 minutes, Color. Director: Elem Klimov. Screenplay: H. Klimov. Photography: B. Brozhovsky, O. Zguridi.

Made in 1971 but released internationally just prior to the 1980 Olympics in Moscow, this is a humorous documentary on the history of sports, including track, horse, body building, swimming, training and boxing.

1294 The Sprinter

1984, German, Filmproduktion GmbH, 87 minutes, Color. Director: Christoph Boll.

Cast: Wieland Samolek, Gerhard Olschewski, Renate Muhri.

An effeminate youth is the star of this black comedy in which the hero decides it's time he tried his hand at "normalization." To please his mother, he takes up track in hopes that becoming a sports star will make him less of an embarrassment to his father, a former softball star.

1295 Stadium Nuts

1972, French, CCPC, 80 minutes, Color. Director-Screenplay: Claude Zidi, with the collaboration of Jacques Fansten. Producer: Claude Berri. Photography: Michel Choquet.

Cast: Les Chariots, Martine Kelly, Paul Preboisti, Gerard Croce, Jacques Beller.

Les Chariots, a French rock group, stars in a zany nearly plotless collection of sight gags in which they participate in Olympics-style events such as racing, boxing and pole vaulting.

1296 Star Globe-Trotters

1908, British, Urban Trading Co., 320 feet. Director: W.R. Booth.

Early trick film in which a gymnast who's been hypnotized walks around the world no matter whether it's on ceilings, telegraph wires, etc.

1297 Stay Hungry

1976, United Artists, 102 minutes, Color. Director: Bob Rafelson, Harold Schneider. Producer: Rafelson. Screenplay: Charles Gaines, Rafelson. Photography: Victor Kemper. Editor: John F. Link II.

Cast: Jeff Bridges, Sally Field, Arnold Schwarzenegger, R.G. Armstrong, Robert Englund, Helena Kallianotes, Scatman Crothers, Fannie Flagg, John David Carson.

When Armstrong won't sell his gym, Bridges, who is buying up land all over the place, infiltrates the scene and gets involved with the muscle-builders on the site and falls in love with Field.

Wieland Samolek, right, portrays an effeminate youth who tries to become a track star in the 1984 West German film The Sprinter. (Courtesy Jeffrey L. Wise.)

1298 Strongest Man in the World

1975, Buena Vista, 92 minutes, Color. Director: Vincent McEveety. Producer: Bill Anderson. Screenplay: Joseph L. McEveety, Herman Groves. Photography: Andrew Jackson. Editor: Cotton Warburton.

Cast: Kurt Russell, Joe Flynn, Eve Arden, Cesar Romero, Phil Silvers, Dick Van Patten, Harold Gould, Michael McGreevery, Benson Fong, William Schallert, James Gregory.

Another formula Disney comedy based at Medfield College and a follow-up to **The Computer Wore Tennis Shoes** and **Now You See Him, Now You Don't.**

This time, college prexy Flynn (who died after filming was completed) ties the future of his financially troubled institution to the lab discovery of Russell who has found out how to give people super-human strength.

With a cereal contract on the line, the school holds a weight lifting contest against a rival college.

1299 The Suitors' Competition

1909, Pathe.

A change of pace from the usual sports film of the era inasmuch as the most non-athletic man in the cast winds up getting the girl.

The woman had promised to marry the man who won the most tests of physical strength and ability, including foot races and weight lifting.

However, the non-athlete, who had been made to look ridiculous by the others, stops to rescue a dog trapped by a fire and wins the girl's heart.

1300 Sunny Youth

1935, Russian, Amkino. Director: Paul Koromoitsev.

Cast: A. Shubnaya, M. Savitskaya, A. Lakhtionova, N. Penkovich, V. Gomolyak.

A girl co-worker helps a shipyard employee, who normally hates sports, to become a top swimmer and track star in order to win a girl's favor.

1301 Their Sporting Blood

1918, Nestor, 758 feet. Producer: R.A. Dillon. Screenplay: Harry Wulze.

Cast: Marcia Moore.

Another tale of the fickle woman, this time one involving three suitors who hold a race to decide who will marry her. The winner, however, discovers that she's decided to wed someone else anyway.

1302 Ties for the Olympics

1977, W. German, DFFB, 80 minutes. Director-Editor: Stefan Lukschy. Screenplay: Lukschy, Hartmann Schmige. Photography: Norbert Bunge.

Cast: Machael Beerman, Sylvia Dudek, Erika Fuhrmann, Ullrich Gressiter, Hansi Jochmann, Ute Koska.

When a firm gets a contract to provide the ties for the German Olympic team, the company becomes the target of a probe by a consumer agency.

The company hires a detective to find out who made the complaint in this minor comedy.

1303 Tokyo Olympiad

1965, Japanese, Toho-American-International, 93-132 minutes, Color.

Director: Kon Ichikawa. Producer: Suketaru Taguchi. Photography: Juichi Nagano, Kinji Nakamura, Tadashi Tanaka. English Screenplay: Donald Richie. English Narration: Jack Douglas.

Director Ichikawa's emphasis is on the limits of the human body, and his documentary on the 1964 Tokyo Olympics is considered one of the best sports documentaries ever made.

As with the case of many of these Olympics films, it was cut drastically for its American release.

1304 XXII Olympiad: Moscow 1980

1981, Russian, International Film Exchange, 120 minutes, Color. Director: Yuri Ozerov. Scenario: Ozerov, Boris Rytchikov. Text: Nicholai Dobronravov.

For those who didn't get to see the games, which were boycotted by the United States, this is probably the best opportunity to see what you missed.

1305 2076 Olympiad

1977, Aragon, 90 minutes, Color. Director-Producer-Screenplay: James R. Martin. Photography: Mannuel Whitaker.

Cast: Jerry Zafer, Sandy Martin, Dean Bennett, Joel Camphausen, Joann Secunda, Alan Kirk, Sigrid Heath, Meredith Rile, J.R. Martin.

Uninhibited humor in the mold of **Kentucky Fried Movie** and **The Groove Tube** finds the Olympics of 2076 being televised over Channel DEF, an erotic station. The emphasis of the games has changed to sex.

1306 Village Marathon Race (aka **Our Village Club Holds a Marathon Race**)

1908, British, Warwick Trading Co., 422 feet. Director: Charles Raymond.

Both sexes join in the race sponsored by a village club; but by the time they near the finish line, they have to crawl and wind up falling over the line together.

There's a fight over who won.

1307 Visions of 8

1973, Cinema 5, 105-110 minutes, Color. Directors: Miles Forman, Kon Ichikawa, Claude Lelouch, Juri Ozerov, Arthur Penn, Michael Pfleghar, John Schlesinger, Mai Zetterling. Producer: Stan Margulies. Editors: Robert K. Lamber, Bea Dennis, Geoffrey Rowland.

Eight top-flight international directors focus on different aspects of the 1972 Olympics in Munich. The film includes a lot of footage on the slaughter of Israeli athletes by Arab terrorists.

The directors and their segments are:

Ozerov—"The Beginnings," focusing on the preparations for the games; Zetterling—"The Strongest," about the weight lifters; Penn—"The Highest," about the pole vaulters; Pfleghar—"The Women," which is self-explanatory; Ichikawa—"The 300 Meter Dash"; Lelouch—"The Losers"; Forman—"The Decathlon"; Schlesinger—an homage to a losing marathon runner.

1308 Walk, Don't Run

1966, Columbia, 114 minutes, Color. Director: Charles Walters. Producer: Sol C. Siegel. Screenplay: Sol Saks. Photography: Harry Stradling. Editor: Walter Thompson.

Cast: Cary Grant, Samantha Eggar, Jim Hutton, John Standing, Mikio Takai, Ted Hartley, Ben Astar, George Takei.

The film on which this was based, 1943's **The More the Merrier,** was about the housing shortage in Washington, D.C. during World War II. The locale in this remake is shifted to Tokyo during the Olympics.

Wealthy industrialist Grant arrives in the city; and when he can't find a hotel room anywhere, convinces Eggar to share a room with him.

Along comes Olympic walker Hutton to the games ahead of schedule; and he can't find anywhere either, so it becomes a threesome with Grant gradually becoming the matchmaker for the younger two.

1309 Wee Geordie (aka **Geordie**)

1955, British, British Lion/Times Film Corp., 99 minutes. Director: Frank Launder. Producers: Launder, Sidney Gilliat. Screenplay: Launder and Gilliat, based on a novel by David Walker. Photography: Wilkie Cooper. Editor: Thelma Connell.

Cast: Bill Travers, Alastir Sim, Doris Goddard, Norah Gorsen, Molly Urquhart, Francis de Wolff, Jameson Clarke, Michael Ripper, Raymond Huntley, Jack Radcliffe.

A puny gamekeeper's son in the Scottish Highlands answers an ad for a muscle-building course in this easy-to-take comedy. He becomes an ace hammer thrower and eventually represents Britain in the Olympics in Melbourne, Australia.

1310 White Rock

1977, British, EMI, 76 minutes, Color. Director-Screenplay: Tony Maylam. Producer: Michael Samuelson. Photography: Arthur Wooster. Editor: Gordon Swire.

Narrator: James Coburn.

The 1976 Winter Olympics at Innsbruck, Austria are blended with the music of Rick Wakeman in one of the most unusual Olympics documentaries.

1311 The Wicked Dreams of Paula Schultz

1968, United Artists, 113 minutes, Color. Director: George Marshall. Producer: Edward Small. Screenplay: Burt Styler, Albert E. Lewin, Nat Perrin. Story: Ken Englund. Photography: Jacques Marquette. Editor: Grant Whytock.

Cast: Elke Sommer, Bob Crane, Werner Klemperer, Joey Forman, John Banner, Leon Askin, Maureen Arthur, Robert Carricart, Theo Marruse, Fritz Feld, Larry D. Mann.

Sommer is an East Berlin athlete who models her own uniform when she's unhappy with the prudish Olympic uniform she's supposed to wear. She tires of the East, and after Klemperer makes a play for her, she pole vaults to the West.

The remainder of the comedy concerns the Communists' efforts to get her back.

1312 The World's Greatest Athlete

1973, Buena Vista, 93 minutes,

Color. Director: Robert Scheerer. Producer: Bill Walsh. Screenplay: Gerald Gardner, Dee Caruso. Photography: Frank Phillips. Editor: Cotton Warburton.

Cast: Jan-Michael Vincent, John Amos, Roscoe Lee Browne, Tim Conway, Dayle Haddon, Nancy Walker, Billy DeWolfe, Danny Goldman, Howard Cosell, Frank Gifford, Jim McKay, Bud Palmer, Joe Knapp, Vito Scotti, Philip Ahn.

The usual Disney "underdog" comedy features Vincent as a jungle boy with witchdoctor Browne as his godfather. He's recruited by track coach Amos for an American college.

Conway is the team's assistant coach, so you can imagine how horrible the team is before Vincent turns it around with his jungle heroics.

1313 A Yank at Eton

1942, Metro Goldwyn Mayer, 88 minutes. Director: Norman Taurog. Producer: John Considine, Jr. Screenplay: George Oppenheimer, Lionel Houser, Thomas Phipps.

Photography: Karl Freund, Charles Lawton. Editor: Albert Akst.

Cast: Mickey Rooney, Edmund Gwenn, Ian Hunter, Freddie Bartholomew, Marta Linden, Juanita Quigley, Alan Mowbray, Peter Lawford.

Metro's **Yank at Oxford** with Robert Taylor (see Water chapter) was a huge success, so the studio tried a similar formula film for the younger set.

Rooney is an American who enrolls at the English prep school after his mother remarries. After the usual hard time adjusting to his new surroundings, all turns out well after he wins the traditional school race.

Skates

After being virtually non-existent during the silent era, hockey and ice and roller skating movies burst onto the scene with a bang in the mid-1930's.

The biggest single reason for this sudden burst was a pretty young starlet signed by 20th Century-Fox named Sonja Henie. For several years, all Henie had to do was star in a film and do some ice skating, and the film was a box office hit.

Ice hockey action films and ice show musicals began popping up regularly until the mid-1940's, when they started filtering down to a mere trickle before practically disappearing from the scene until, like football films, the new permissiveness in the cinema allowed for the depiction of violence in hockey and roller derby in films such as **Kansas City Bomber, The Unholy Roller, Slap Shot** and **Rollerball.**

Part of the problem filmmakers have in producing hockey films is the sport usually isn't too popular in the warmer climates, therefore, limiting the box office appeal.

There have been numerous ice show movies made--particularly by Henie--but we feel it would be stretching a point to label most of them as "sports" movies. If there's an Olympics or skating championship connection, we do include these in the main listings.

Among the many we don't, but for the sake of thoroughness list here as footnotes, are **Breaking the Ice, Everything's On Ice, Happy Landing, Hit the Ice, Ice Capades, Ice-Capades** (sic) **Revue, Ice Follies of 1939, Iceland, Murder in the Music Hall, My Lucky Star, One in a Million, Second Fiddle, Silver Skates, Snow White and the Three Stooges, Sun Valley Serenade, Thin Ice** and **Wintertime.** We believe these are more properly classified as musicals.

Other films which deserve mention are Charlie Chaplin's **At the Rink,** the weird characters in hockey uniforms in **Strange Brew** and the hockey sequence in **Hell's Kitchen** in which the headmaster of the reform school uses some ringers. Then there's also **The Million Dollar Hockey Puck.**

We have included the several skateboarding films which cropped up in the late 1970's; but like most fads, they quickly disappeared.

1314 Duke of West Point

1938, United Artists, 107 minutes. Director: Alfred E. Green. Producer: Edward Small. Screenplay: George Bruce. Photography: Robert Planck. Editor: Grant Whytock.

Cast: Louis Hayward, Joan Fontaine, Tom Brown, Richard Carlson, Alan Curtis, Donald Barry, Jonathan Hale, Jed Prouty, Kenneth Harlan, Gaylord Pendleton.

An English rugby star from Cambridge enrolls at West Point, where he becomes involved in the usual troubles adjusting to his new surroundings and, of course, has a rival for the love of a girl.

He joins the academy's hockey team where he proves his mettle.

1315 Face-Off (aka **Winter Comes Early)**

1971, Canadian, Cannon,

101 minutes, Color. Director: George McCowan. Producer: John F. Bassett. Screenplay: George Robertson. Photography: Don Wilder. Editor: Kirk Jones.

Cast: Art Hindle, John Vernon, Derek Sanderson, Trudy Young, Frank Moore, Austin Willis, Sean Sullivan, Steve Perrie.

The Toronto Maple Leafs are in last place and haven't made the playoffs in several years, so the pressure is on coach Vernon.

After much discussion, the team selects young Hindle as the league's top draft choice; but the youth's agent demands a $120,000 bonus, and the team balks. Afraid of the bad publicity and dwindling attendance, the Maple Leafs do sign him.

He falls in love with a peacenik who breaks up with him after watching the violence during the game and the girl becomes a drug addict.

The youth, in the meantime, gets a swelled head from early success until he's suspended for dumping a referee and gets into hot water with his coach.

As one veteran tells him: "You're a slave by choice. We all are. The owner says jump, you jump."

Hockey star Derek Sanderson appears as himself.

1316 The Fireball

1950, 20th Century-Fox, 85 minutes. Director: Tay Garnett. Producer: Bert Friedlob. Screenplay: Garnett, Horace McCoy. Photography: Lester White. Editor: Frank Sullivan.

Cast: Mickey Rooney, Pat O'Brien, Beverly Tyler, James Brown, Marilyn Monroe, Ralph Dumke, Bert Begley, Milburn Stone, Sam Flint, John Hedloe, Glenn Corbett.

Orphan Rooney runs away from priest O'Brien's school and finds he has great ability on roller skates.

He joins the roller derby where he becomes a star and also becomes conceited until he contracts polio. After regaining his health, he's finally learned there's more to life than just looking out for himself and is a changed youth.

1317 Freaky Friday

1976, Buena Vista, 95 minutes, Color. Director: Gary Nelson. Producer: Ron Miller. Screenplay: Mary Rodgers. Photography: Charles F. Wheeler. Editor: Cotton Warburton.

Cast: Jodie Foster, Barbara Harris, John Astin, Patsy Kelly, Dick Van Patten, Vicki Schreck, Sorrell Brooke, Alan Oppenheimer, Ruth Buzzi, Kaye Ballard, Marie Windsor.

Young Foster wishes she could change places with her mom and presto! It happens. Foster's mind is in the body of mom Harris and vice versa to the befuddlement of dad Astin.

While Foster makes a muddle of the housework and learns being an adult isn't that much fun, mom finds it difficult replacing her tomboy daughter on the hockey team.

1318 Freewheelin'

1976, Turtle Releasing Organization, 90 minutes, Color. Director-Producer: Scott Dittrich. Screenplay-Editor: George Van Noy. Photography: Pat Darrin.

Cast: Stacy Peralta, Camille Darrin, Russ Howell, Ken Means, Tom Sims, Mike Weed, Paul Constantineau, Bobby Pierce.

Made during the skateboard craze of the 1970's, **Freewheelin'** follows a boy (Peralta) who practically lives and actually sleeps on his board.

In between romancing Darrin, he quits school and makes plans to go to Australia to become a professional skateboarder.

1319 The Game That Kills

1937, Columbia, 55 minutes.

Director-Producer: Ross Lederman. Screenplay: Grace Neville, Fred Niblo, Jr. Story: J. Benton Cheney. Photography: Benjamin Kline. Editor: James Sweeney.

Cast: Charles Quigley, Rita Hayworth, John Gallaudet, J. Farrell MacDonald, Arthur Loft, John Tyrrell, Paul Fix, Max Hoffman, Jr.

Bottom-of-the-bill programmer in which Quigley becomes a pro hockey player after his brother is killed in a rigged "accident" on the rink.

MacDonald has his usual father image role as the team's trainer, and Hayworth is MacDonald's daughter.

1320 Go for It

1976, World Entertainment, 96 minutes, Color. Director: Paul Rapp. Producers: Rapp, Richard Rosenthal. Executive Producer: Wilt Chamberlain. Screenplay: Neil Rapp. Photography: Rick Robertson, Pat Darren. Editor: John O'Connor.

A documentary which explores the latest youth athletic crazes, particularly skateboarding, surfing, hang gliding and skiing.

1321 Hockey Fever

1983, Norwegian, Norsk Film Als, 103 minutes, Color. Director: Oddvar Bull Tuhus. Screenplay: Tuhus, Bjarne Roennig. Photography: Halvor Naess. Editor: Bjoern Breigutu.

Cast: Rune Dybedahl, Liv Osa, Rolf Soeder, Suerre Anterousdahl, Jorn Donner.

A losing hockey team which is suffering at the box office hires a new coach and manager. The coach has scruples, but the manager will stop at nothing, including dirty tricks, to turn the team around. Meanwhile, a young player is torn between love for his girl and duty to the team.

1322 The Hounds of Notre Dame

1980, Canadian, Fraser, 95 minutes. Color. Director: Zale Dalen. Producer: Fil Fraser. Screenplay: Ken Mitchell. Photography: Ron Orieux. Editor: Tony Cower.

Cast: Thomas Peacocke, Frances Hyland, Barry Morse, David Ferry, Phil Ridley, Lawrence Reese, Lenore Zann.

Graduates of the College of Notre Dame in Saskatchewan provided most of the funding for this tribute to Pere Murray, the school's founder.

Set in 1940, Pere Murray struggles to raise money for the school. Meanwhile, a young lad rises to be leader of the Hounds, the school's championship hockey team.

1323 I See Ice

1938, British, Associated British, 81 minutes. Director: Anthony Kimmins. Producer: Basil Dean. Screenplay: Kimmins, Austin Melford. Photography: Ronald Neame.

Cast: George Formby, Kay Walsh, Cyril Ritchard, Garry Marsh, Betty Stockfeld, Frederick Burtwell, Gordon McLeod, Gavin Gordon, Ernest Sefton.

Bungling photographer's assistant Formby uses a miniature camera he's invented to make amends for his blunders. He photographs a big ice hockey game from which spectators have been barred.

1324 Ice Castles

1979, Columbia, 113-115 minutes, Color. Director: Donald Wrye. Producer: John Kemeny. Screenplay: Wrye, Gary L. Baim. Story: Baim. Photography: Bill Butler. Editor: Michael Kahn.

Cast: Robby Benson, Colleen Dewhurst, Tom Skerritt, Jennifer Warren, David Huffman, Lynn-Holly Johnson.

A small-town girl from Iowa (Johnson) is an up-and-coming contender to join the Olympics team as an ice skater when she's partially blinded.

With the love of her hockey-playing boy friend (Robby Benson) and the support of her father (Skerritt) and home town coach (Dewhurst), she's able to overcome her handicap. Warren portrays the girl's big-time coach.

1325 Idol of the Crowds

1937, Universal, 62-64 minutes. Director: Arthur Lubin. Screenplay: George Waggner, Harold Buckley, based on Waggner's story **Hell on Ice**. Photography: Tem Carr.

Cast: John Wayne, Sheila Bromley, Charles Brokaw, Billy Bussud, Jane Johns, Huntley Gordon, Clem Bevans, Russell Hopton, Hal Neiman, Virginia Brissac, George Lloyd.

Hockey player Johnny Hansen (Wayne) and brother Bussud leave their Maine chicken farm to play on major league rinks and become involved with mobsters.

1326 It's a Pleasure

1945, RKO Radio Pictures, 90 minutes, Color. Director: William Seiter. Producer: David Lewis. Screenplay: Lynn Starling, Elliot Paul.

Cast: Sonja Henie, Michael O'Shea, Bill Johnson, Marie McDonald, Gus Schilling, Iris Adrian, Cheryl Walker, Peggy O'Neill.

Mainly another showcase for the skating talents of Henie, it features the romance between a beautiful skater (guess who) and hockey star O'Shea and the complications which ensue.

1327 Kansas City Bomber

1972, Metro Goldwyn Mayer, 99 minutes, Color. Director: Jerome Freedman. Producer: Marty Elfand. Screenplay: Thomas Rickman, Calvin Clements. Story: Barry Sandler. Photography: Fred Koenekamp. Editor: David Berlatsky.

Cast: Raquel Welch, Patti "Moo-Moo" Cavin, Richard Lane, Kevin McCarthy, Helen Kallianiotes, Norman Alden, Mary Kay Pass, Jeanne Cooper, Martine Bartlett.

Lots of female flesh and blood and guts are on display in this tale of life on the pro roller derby circuit.

Nice girl K.C. Carr (Welch) is a rising star on McCarthy's Portland Loggers, but faces antagonism from fading Jackie Burdette (Kallianiotes) who sees her popularity shifting to the new girl in town.

The plot, however, is secondary to the brutal action of the game and the ample display of women's bodies and is not exactly a "liberation" film for the portrayal of females as athletes.

1328 King of Hockey (aka **King of the Ice Rink**)

1936, Warner Brothers, 57 minutes. Director: Noel Smith. Producer: Bryan Foy. Screenplay: George Bricker. Photography: Lou O'Connell.

Cast: Dick Purcell, Wayne Morris, Anne Nagel, Ann Gilles, Marie Wilson, George E. Stone, Joseph Crehan, Gordon Hart.

Purcell is a hockey star who's a louse but not such a bad guy that he's crooked. He's unjustly accused of being on the take from mobster Stone and is punched in the eye by teammate Morris.

His sweetheart and her sister help raise enough cash for an eye operation, and Purcell risks blindness by disobeying the doctor and playing hockey again.

1329 Lake Placid Serenade

1944, Republic, 85 minutes. Director: Steve Sekely. Screenplay: Dick Irving Hyland, Doris Gilbert. Story: Frederick Kohner.

Cast: Vera Hruba Ralston, Vera Vague, Stephanie Bachelor, Walter Catlett, William Frawley, Audrey Tombes, McGowan & Mack, Robert Livingston, John Litel, Lloyd Corrigan, Eugene Pallette.

A girl (Ralston) wins the Czechoslovakian national skating championship and comes to the

United States to represent her country. When World War II breaks out, she's unable to return but finds romance after a lot of music and a Cinderella twist to the story.

1330 The Long Run

1982, Japanese, Toho, 102 minutes, Color. Director: Ruiko Yoshida. Producer: Kazuo Kuroi. Screenplay: Kunio Aoki, Kikuo Kawasaki. Photography: Motoyoshi Hasegawa.

Cast: Toshiyuki Nagashima, Hiromitsu Suzuki, Kazuko Kato, Tomoko Udagawa.

A Japanese athlete roller skates across America with the backing of an airline, accompanied by a reporter and a camerawoman in this interesting view of Americans as seen through Japanese eyes.

1331 Love Story

1970, Paramount, 100 minutes, Color. Director: Arthur Hiller. Producer: Howard G. Minsky. Screenplay: Erich Segal. Photography: Dick Kratina. Editor: Robert C. Jones.

Cast: Ali MacGraw, Ryan O'Neal, John Marley, Ray Milland, Russell Nype, Katherine Balfour, Robert Modica, Sydney Walker, Walker Daniels, Tommy Lee Jones, Andrew Duncan.

A big box office hit, it concerns the romance between a Radcliffe girl, the daughter of a poor baker, and the hockey-playing son from a wealthy Boston family. The Harvard student weds the Radcliffe girl only to learn she's dying of an incurable disease.

It inspired a sequel, **Oliver's Story.**

1332 Olympic Honeymoon (aka **Honeymoon Merry-Go-Round**)

1936, British, London Screenplays-Fanfare, 63 minutes. Director: Alfred Goulding. Producer: Sidney Morgan. Screenplay: Goulding, Monty Banks, Chetwynd Strode, Joan Morgan, based on the novel by F. Dawson Gratix.

Cast: Monty Banks, Claude Hulbert, Princess Pearl, Sally Gray, Tully Comber, Bob Bowman, the Wembley Lions Ice Hockey Team.

A man on his honeymoon is mistaken for a crack hockey player and helps the British team win a big victory in Switzerland.

1333 Paperback Hero

1973, Canadian, Alliance, 87-93 minutes, Color. Director: Peter Pearson. Producers: James Margellus, John F. Bassett. Screenplay: Les Rose, Barry Pearson. Photography: Don Wilder. Editor: Kirk Jones.

Cast: Keir Dullea, Elizabeth Ashley, John Beck, Dayle Haddon, Franz Russell, George R. Robertson, Margot Lamarre, Ted Fellows, Linda Sorenson, Les Ruby.

This very offbeat hockey film wasn't released until 1975 in the United States, and then only on a very limited basis.

Dullea is a hockey player whose whole life falls apart when his team is folded. His sexual prowess with women fades, and he begins to believe he's in the Old West and has a shootout with police.

1334 People vs. Dr. Kildare

1941, Metro Goldwyn Mayer, 76 minutes. Director: Harold S. Bucquet. Screenplay: William Goldbeck, Harry Ruskin. Story: Max Brand, Lawrence P. Bachmann. Photography: Clyde De Vinna. Editor: Ralph Winters.

Cast: Lew Ayres, Lionel Barrymore, Laraine Day, Bonita Granville, Alma Kruger, Paul Stanton, Red Skelton, Diana Lewis, Walter Kingsford, Eddie Acuff, Tom Conway.

Dr. Kildare and Day save the life of an ice skater (Granville) who's injured in an automobile crash. Despite the fact the operation had to be performed at roadside, Kildare finds himself being sued after her leg is paralyzed.

Everything hinges on the second operation, with good old Dr. Gillespie (Barrymore) on hand to give advice to the young doctor.

1335 Rollerball

1975, United Artists, 129 minutes, Color. Director-Producer: Norman Jewison. Screenplay: William Harrison. Photography: Douglas Slocombe. Editor: Anthony Gibbs.

Cast: James Caan, John Houseman, Maud Adams, John Beck, Moses Gunn, Pamela Hensley, Barbara Trentham, Ralph Richardson, Shane Rimmer, Alfred Thomas, Burnell Tucker, Angus MacInnes.

In the year 2018, there's no more war, poverty or social unrest—and there's also no more democracy. Everything in the world is run by several corporate cartels.

To satisfy the public's natural bloodlust and also to illustrate the triumph of the team over the individual, a sport called rollerball is played.

A combination of roller derby and basketball on motorcycles and stressing violence, Jonathan (Caan) is the best. When he's ordered to retire, however, he asserts his individuality and puts up a fight.

In a bloody championship game with fewer rules imposed on the players, all mayhem breaks loose on the court as the participants are killed or maimed.

1336 Skateboard

1978, Universal, 97 minutes, Color. Director: George Gage. Producers: Harry N. Blum, Richard A. Wolf. Screenplay: Gage, Wolf. Photography: Ross Kelsay. Editor: Robert Angus.

Cast: Leif Garrett, Allen Garfield, Kathleen Lloyd, Richard Van Der Wyk, Tony Alva, Steve Monahan, David Hyde, Ellen Oneal, Anthony Carbone.

A professional skateboard team that closely resembles the Bad News Bears is assembled by Garfield, who needs the money to repay a bookie.

The kids change Garfield's greedy ways, and he refuses to throw the championship meet even though it could cost him his life. When the team's star walks out on him, Garfield pins his hopes on young Brad Harris (Garrett).

1337 Skateboard Madness

1980, American National Enterprises, 88 minutes, Color. Director-Screenplay-Editor: Julian Pena, Jr. Producer: Hal Jepsen. Photography: Jepsen, Craig Nolley, Fred Dogher, Louis Schwartzberg.

Narrator: Phil Hartmann.

Cast: Stacey Peralta, Kent Senatore, Gregg Ayres, Dan "Mini Shred" Smith, Kurt "Mello Cat" Ledterman.

The five-minute cartoons at the beginning and end are more interesting than the film itself.

The nonsensical story about a photographer for Wonder Rolling News who drives four skateboarders around California is merely an excuse for lots of skateboard action documentary-style.

1338 Slap Shot

1977, Universal, 122 minutes, Color. Director: George Roy Hill. Screenplay: Nancy Dowd. Photography: Victor Kemper. Editor: Dede Allen.

Cast: Paul Newman, Michael Ontkean, Lindsay Crouse, Jennifer Warren, Melinda Dillon, Strother Martin, Jerry Houser, Steve Carlson, Jeff Carlson, Dave Hanson, Andrew Duncan.

The Charlestown Chiefs are the world's worst hockey team, and they have trouble drawing flies. To boot, the big factory in town is laying off 10,000 workers, so the team's general manager figures it's time to sell everything, including the team bus.

When player-coach Reggie Dunlop (Newman) sees how the fans enjoy the violence in the sport, he gets an idea how to save the team. He lets loose some absolutely psychotic bespectacled brothers to mash and maul the opposition while the rest of the team, with the exception of idealistic Ned (Ontkean), follows suit.

Suddenly, the Chiefs are the league's hottest draw, and they win as well. The coach, meanwhile, tries to track down the team's elusive owner to convince her to keep the club.

Johnston, Pennsylvania was used for the New England mill town locale of the film.

1339 Top Speed

1982, French, INA, 60 minutes, Color. Director-Screenplay: Robert Kramer. Photography: Richard Copans. Editor: Dominique Forgue.

Cast: Laura Dutilleul, William Chenino, Bernard Ballet, Manuelle Lidsky.

A French girl is good enough on roller skates to enter a contest in the United States, but she and her boy friend struggle to raise the cash for the entry fee.

1340 Tournament Tempo (aka **Gay Blades**)

1946, Republic, 67 minutes. Director-Producer: George Blair. Screenplay: Albert Beich, based on a story by Jack Goodman and Albert Rice. Photography: William Bradford. Editor: Tony Martinelli.

Cast: Allan Lane, Jean Rogers, Edward Ashley, Frank Albertson, Anne Gillis, Robert Armstrong, Jonathan Hale, Paul Harvey.

Comedy mixes with the hockey action—and there's lots of it—as a hockey star is wooed by Hollywood and is torn between two careers.

Rogers is the girl sent by the Hollywood bigwigs to find the right star for their next film.

1341 Trocadero Blue and Yellow

1978, French, Warner Brothers-Columbia, 90 minutes, Color. Director-Screenplay: Michael Schock. Photography: Bernard Lay. Editor: George Klotz.

Cast: Anny Duperey, Lionel Melet, Berangere De Lagatineau, Henri Garcin.

A 10-year-old boy who enters skateboard competitions at the Trocadero near the Eiffel Tower also lives in his own fantasy world.

When he meets a young girl he likes, his photographer mom helps him plot to get her into bed, proving French attitudes toward sex are a bit more liberal than in the U.S.

1342 The Unholy Rollers

1972, American-International, 88 minutes, Color. Director: Vernon Zimmerman. Producers: John Prizer, Jack Bohrer. Screenplay: Howard R. Cohen. Photography: Mike Shea. Editors: George Trirogoff, Yeu-Bun Yee.

Cast: Claudia Jennings, Louis Quinn, Betty Anne Rees, Roberta Collins, Alan Vint, Candice Roman, Jay Varela.

Made to cash in on the success of **Kansas City Bomber**, Jennings is a factory girl who battles with her teammates and opponents when she joins the roller derby.

With foul language and violence galore, there's really not much else worth saying about the story.

1343 White Lightning

1953, Allied Artists, 61 minutes. Director: Edward Bernds. Producer: Ben Schwalb. Screenplay: Charles R. Marion. Photography: Lester White. Editor: Bruce Shoengarth.

Cast: Stanley Clements, Steve Brodie, Gloria Blondell, Lee Van Cleef, Barbara Bestar, Myron Healy, Lyle Talbot, Frank Jenks, Paul Bryar.

Red Devils hockey coach Brodie has his hands full when conceited Clements joins the team, even though he helps them win.

When teammate Healy is suspended for being paid off by gangsters, Clements is the next target for a payoff; but he comes through in the big game.

Soccer, Rugby, Cricket and Hurling

Soccer films have been a staple for audiences outside the United States since the early silent days, particularly in Britain where their plots were similar to American football films. Soccer, in fact, is called football outside the United States.

Despite its immense popularity around the world and growing enthusiasm in this country, soccer films have never been able to catch on here. The only two notable American-made soccer films are **Victory** and **The Boys in Company C; Manny's Orphans,** has been seen by practically nobody except on a cable TV station. A 1983 film, **A Minor Miracle,** finds soccer great Pele helping to coach a team of orphans to victory over a team of older youths. It was never released to theaters.

Cricket, rugby and hurling have had similar fates, particularly because American audiences don't understand the games. When was the last time your television station showed **It's Not Cricket** or **The Final Test**? The reaction of American audiences is similar to that of British audiences insofar as baseball is concerned, one reason why when nearly any American baseball movie is showed there, it's under a different title.

Films on the fringe we feel deserve note include **Kipperbang,** about a young boy who fantasizes about kissing a girl and being a cricket hero; **The Wooden Horse,** with a soccer match as a diversion for a prisoner-of-war escape plan; **The Story of a Woman,** a soap opera with a soccer player as one of the lovers; **Tilly at the Football Match,** a 1914 short; **The Promoter** (aka **The Card**), with Alec Guinness as a social climber who towards the film's end becomes involved with a soccer club; **Paris Is Always Paris,** concerning some Italians in Paris for an international match; **Follow That Camel,** in which the hero joins the Foreign Legion after being accused of cheating at cricket; and **How I Won the War,** in which a troop is assigned to build a cricket field for some VIPs in the middle of the North African desert. When some of them are killed in action, their ghosts return to do the work. In **Raffles,** David Niven plays a cricket star who's also a jewel thief.

1344 Adventures of a Football

1914, British, Urban Trading Co., 250 feet. Director: Stuart Kinder.

A soccer ball has all kinds of adventures, including being chased up a tree.

1345 Allez France! (aka **The Counterfeit Constable**)

1966, French, 87 minutes. Director: Robert Dhery. Producer: Henri Diamant-Berger. Screenplay: Dhery, Pierre Tchernia, Jean Lhote, Colette Brosset. Photography: Jean Tournier, Henri Tiquet. Editor: Albert Jurgenson.

Cast: Robert Dhery, Colette Brosset, Ronald Fraser, Diana Dors, Pierre Olaf, Arthur Mullard, Bernard Cribbins.

Pity poor Henri (Dhery)! The Frenchman, in London for the weekend to attend the championship rugby match between England and France, has a couple of teeth knocked out during the game by an over-enthusiastic fan.

After a long struggle to find a dentist on Sunday, he's told not to open his mouth until the work is finished and becomes involved in a string of comic adventures, including the impersonation of a policeman and the rescue of a film star (Dors).

1346 The Arsenal Stadium Mystery

1939, British, GFD, 84 minutes. Director: Thorold Dickinson. Producers: Josef Somlo, Richard Norton. Screenplay: Dickinson, Donald Bull, based on the novel by Leonard Gribble.

Cast: Leslie Banks, Ian MacLean, Greta Gynt, Esmond Knight, Liane Linden, Brian Worth, Anthony Bushell, Richard Norris, Wyndham Goldie, the Arsenal Football Team.

Continuing the string of 1930's murder mysteries involving sporting events, such as **Death on the Diamond, Mr. Moto's Gamble, 70,000 Witnesses** and **Girls Can Play,** this transfers the murder scene to the soccer field.

A prominent player is murdered during an exhibition match, and all his teammates come under suspicion. Investigating the case is a police inspector who'd rather be producing a talent show in which all the cops wear tutus.

1347 Badger's Green

1934, British, Paramount British, 68 minutes. Director: Adrian Brunel. Screenplay: R.J. Davis, Violet Powell, based on a play by S.D. Sheriff.

Cast: Violet Hopson, Bruce Lister, Frank Moore, David Horne, Sebastian Smith, John Turnbull, Wally Patch, Elsie Irving.

When their cricket green becomes the site of a construction plan, the residents of a small village unite in opposition. The villagers win their battle, and the crucial match against stronger opponents.

1348 Badger's Green

1949, British, GFD, 62 minutes. Director: John Irwin. Producer: John Croydon. Screenplay: William Fairchild. Photography: Walter Harvey.

Cast: Barbara Murray, Brian Nissen, Gary Marsh, Jack McNaughton, Kynaston Reeves, Laurence Naismith.

A remake of the 1934 comedy in which villagers put aside their differences and unite against a businessman who wants to build an amusement park and some bungalows on their cherished cricket green.

1349 Blinker's Spy-Spotter

1971, British, Children's Film Foundation, 58 minutes, Color. Director: Jack Stephens. Producer: Harold Orton. Screenplay: Orton, David Ash. Photography: Mark MacDonald.

Cast: David Spooner, Sally-Ann Marlowe, Brent Oldfield, Edward Kemp, Martin Beaumont.

Our hero Blinker invents a goal repellent which makes him a big soccer star and which naturally attracts all kinds of villains to combat in this lighthearted tale aimed at the younger set.

1350 Boys' Cricket Match and Fight

1900, British, 105 feet. No credits available.

One of the very earliest story films, a fight between two boys' cricket teams results after a batsman is called out.

1351 The Boys in Company C

1977, Columbia, 126 minutes, Color. Director: Sidney J. Furie. Producer: Andre Morgan. Screenplay: Rick Natkin, Furie. Photography: Godfrey Godar. Editors: Michael Berman, Frank Urioste, Alan Pattilo, James Benson.

Cast: Stan Shaw, James Whitmore, Jr., Andrew Stevens, James Canning, Michael Lembeck, Craig Wasson, Scott Hylands, Noble Willingham, Santos Morales.

Young men are caught up in the madness of Vietnam after

undergoing training. En route they're told by an officer that if they want to defeat the enemy, they've got to learn to play his game, and that game is soccer.

Throughout the violence and craziness of the war, they maintain their team, the Muthuhs. Finally, their practice pays off as an exhibition game is arranged in Saigon between them and the Dragons, the top Vietnamese team.

They're told that if they win, they'll get out of combat and go on tour throughout the Pacific. When the game starts, they clearly outclass the competition; but the corrupt and brutal Vietnamese official who runs the other team intervenes with the men's superiors.

The Americans are ordered to lose so as to boost the confidence of the Vietnamese to handle their own affairs. They must then decide whether to go through with it and get out of combat or plan to win and face likely death on the battlefield.

1352 Boys Will Be Boys

1935, British, Gainsborough, 75 minutes. Director: William Beaudine. Producer: Michael Balcon. Screenplay: Will Hay, Robert Edmunds. Photography: Charles Van Enger.

Cast: Will Hay, Gordon Harker, Claude Dampier, Jimmy Hanley, Davy Burnaby, Norma Varden, Charles Farrell, Percy Walsh, Peter Gawthorne.

In a comic device that will be borrowed 14 years later in **It's Not Cricket,** a stolen necklace winds up inside the soccer ball during the big founder's day match at a college headed by Hay.

1353 Cats' Cup Final

1912, British, Empire, 360 feet. Director-Scenario: Arthur Cooper.

A soccer championship is played by teams of toy cats.

1354 The Champions

1983, Hong Kong, Golden Harvest, 100 minutes, Color. Director-Screenplay: Yuen Chun Yeung. Photography: Ma Kwun Wah, Sung Kong Wah. Editor: Cheung Yiu Chung.

Cast: Yuen Biao, Cheung Kok Keung, Dick Wei, Lee Choi Fung, Ko Hung.

An honest-to-goodness kung fu soccer film is played for laughs as the good guy underdogs kick more than just the ball in their game against the baddies.

1355 The Club (aka **Players**)

1980, Australian, Roadshow Distributors, 99 minutes, Color. Director: Bruce Beresford. Producer: Matt Carroll. Screenplay: David Williamson. Photography: Don McAlpine. Editor: William Anderson.

Cast: Jack Thompson, Graham Kennedy, Frank Wilson, Harold Hopkins, John Howard, Alan Cassell, Maggie Doyle.

Thompson is a former soccer star turned coach who becomes involved in the behind-the-scenes power play of a soccer club as there's a move to replace the president.

1356 The Coach

1978, Yugoslavian, Yugo Film, 90 minutes, Color. Director-Screenplay: Purisa Dordevic. Photography: Zika Milic. Editor: Mira Mitic.

Cast: Tansige Uzonovic, Ljuba Tadic, Peter Karsten, Drago Cuma, Dorde Nenadovic, Dijana Sporcic.

A soccer trainer gets the chance to coach a top team and recruits a promising prospect from his home town, who incurs the envy of teammates when he does well.

The coach winds up quitting the team and taking a post with a team from Germany.

1357 Comrade President Centre-Forward

1960, Yugoslavian, UFUS, 92 minutes. Director: Zorz Skrigin. Photography: Velibar Andrejevic.

Cast: Mija Aleksis, Olivera Markowic, Paul Vujosic, Tatjana Beljakova, Peter Kurgic.

A soccer comedy.

1358 Coup de Tete (The Hothead)

1980, French, Quartet, 87 minutes, Color. Director: Jean-Jacques Annaud. Screenplay: Annaud, Francis Veber. Photography: Claude Agostini. Editor: Noelle Boisson.

Cast: Patrick Dewaere, France Dougnac, Jean Bouise, Michel Aumont, Paul Le Person, Robert Dalban, Michel Fortin.

The late Dewaere's outstanding performance highlights this comedy-drama about a social misfit who's a fringe player on his town's soccer team.

When he causes the team's star player to be injured during practice, not only is he cut from the team, he's fired from his factory job.

And when the star player rapes a woman, the team figures Dewaere, because of his physical resemblance, is the perfect patsy to frame for the crime.

The tables begin to turn when the team bus is involved in an accident en route to the biggest game of the year, and Our Hero is sprung from prison. Lo and behold, he's the unlikely hero of the game; and that's when the fun really starts as he takes his revenge on the entire town, which he now has eating out of the palm of his hand.

1359 Cricket Terms Illustrated

1905, British, Crick and Sharp, 230 feet.

Similar to **Racing Sayings Illustrated,** this burlesques terms used in cricket.

1360 Cup Fever

1965, British, Century, 53 minutes. Director-Screenplay: David Bracknell. Producer: Roy Simpson.

Cast: Bernard Crimmins, David Lodge, Dermot Kelly, Norman Rossington, Sonia Graham, Johnny Wade, Denis Gilmore, Susan George, Jim Morgan, Raymond Davis.

The Manchester Football Team and a cop come to the aid of a youth soccer team in its fight against a politician.

1361 The Cup Final Mystery

1914, British, Motography, 2,600 feet. Director: Maurice Elvey.

Cast: Elizabeth Risdon, Fred Groves, Douglas Payne, Joan Morgan, Maurice Elvey.

The good guys' goalie is kidnapped just prior to the Cup Final, but he's rescued by the heroine and, of course, gets there on time for the match.

1362 Cup-Tie Honeymoon

1947, British, Mancunian, 93 minutes. Director-Producer: John E. Blakely. Screenplay: Anthony Toner, Harry Jackson. Photography: Geoffrey Faithfull.

Cast: Sandy Powell, Pat McGrath, Dan Young, Betty Jumel, Violet Farebrother, Frank Groves, Joyanne Bracewell, Vic Arnley, Harold Walden.

A star soccer player is torn between playing for his school team or for his father's team until his girl friend helps him make up his mind.

1363 Doing His Duty

1929, British, BSFP, 13 minutes. Director: Hugh Croise.

Cast: Ernie Lotinger.

A man becomes a cop mainly so he can attend soccer matches.

1364 Fiasco in Milan

1963, French-Italian, Jerand, 104 minutes. Director: Nanni Loy. Producer: Franco Cristaldi.

Photography: Robert Gerardi. Editor: Mario Serandrei.

Cast: Vittorio Gassman, Renato Salvatori, Vicky Ludovisi, Carlo Pisacane, Claudia Cardinale, Nino Manfredi.

A gang of crooks plots the theft of a suitcase filled with money from a soccer pool. They get the suitcase during a soccer match in Milan, but then things start going awry, as the title suggests.

1365 Fight for the Glory

1970, Japanese, Shochiku, 85 minutes, Color. Director: Hirokazu Ichimura. Producer: Kiyoshi Higuchi. Screenplay: Shiro Ishimori. Photography: Masao Kosugi. Editor: Shizu Ozaka.

Cast: Kensaku Morita, Miyoko Akaza, Yuuki Meguro, Chishu Ryu, Shuji Sano, Etsuko Ikuta.

The captain of a university's soccer team runs into all kinds of conflicts on and off the field. A tough disciplinarian with his teammates, he faces antagonism from one student who feels his methods are wrong.

He's also offered a chance to study in Europe, but that would mean breaking his promise to his grandfather to run the family brewery if his team loses the big match.

When the hero is injured, the antagonist is sent into the game and learns the hard way the captain was correct.

1366 Fimpen (aka **The Butt, Stubby**)

1974, Swedish, 90 minutes, Color. Director-Producer-Screenplay-Editor: Bo Widerberg. Photography: John Olsson, Hanno Fuchs, Roland Sterner, Ake Astrand.

Cast: Johan Bergman, Monica Zetterlund, Ernst-Hugo Jaeregard and the Swedish National Soccer Team.

When a 6-year-old boy known as "The Butt" out-dribbles a member of the Swedish National Soccer Team at an impromptu meeting, the lad not only winds up as a member of the team, but becomes a national hero by leading it to victory.

Alas, however, he has trouble signing autographs because he's paid more attention to soccer than to school.

1367 The Final Test

1953, British, GFD, 91 minutes. Director: Anthony Asquith. Producer: R.J. Minney. Screenplay: Terence Ratigan, based on his play. Photography: Bill McLeod.

Cast: Jack Warner, Robert Morley, George Ralph, Adrianne Allen, Brenda Bruce, Ray Jackson, Stanley Mexted, Joan Swimstead, Richard Bebb, Godfrey Evans, Len Hutton.

A number of England's top cricket players are featured in this tale of a great player (Warner) facing his final test match who's upset that his poetry-loving son apparently won't be attending.

The tone for the light story is set when an American senator visiting England sees the newspaper headline: Can England Survive? The visiting official learns the headline refers to the match between England and Australia.

1368 Fish, Football and Girls

1968, Israeli, 90 minutes. Director: Uri Zoher. Producer: A. Deshe. Screenplay: Deshe, Talila Ben-Zackai. Photography: David Gurfinkel. Editor: Anna Goorit.

Cast: Shai K. Opihir, The Hagashah of Israel Trio, Gideon Singer, Gadi Yagil, Bomba Tzur.

Slim comedy featuring a lot of soccer action.

1369 Flight of Death

1914, British, Solograph, 1,250 feet. Screenplay: James Carew, Reginald Owen, Lyston Lyle.

A soccer player turns his heroics from the playing field to the battlefield as he flies into action during World War I.

1370 Footballer's Honour

1914, British, Brittania, 2,600 feet. Director: Lewin Fitzhamon.

Proving that no matter what the sport, film clichés are the same everywhere, a star soccer player escapes from his kidnappers in time to get to the big match.

1371 Goal! (aka **Goal: World Cup 1966)**

1966, British-Liechtenstein, Royal Films International, 107 minutes, Color. Director: Abidine Dino, Ross Devenish. Producer: Octavio Senoret. Photography: Jean-Jacques Flori, David Samuelson, Harry Hart.

Narrator: Nigel Patrick.

World Cup action in England during July 1966 between 16 nations is featured in this documentary, with the highlight being the final between England and West Germany with the host team winning.

1372 The Goalie's Anxiety at the Penalty Kick

1972, West German, Bauer International, 101 minutes, Color. Director: Wim Wenders. Screenplay: Wenders, Peter Handke. Photography: Robbie Muller. Editor: Peter Przygodda.

Cast: Arthur Brauss, Kai Fischer, Erika Pluhar, Libgart Schwarz, Marie Bardiscuhewski, Michael Torst, Edda Kochl, Rudiger Vogler.

A goalie's mind is obviously not on the game as he lets a penalty kick slip into the goal, so he begins a long trek on his own, a familiar theme for director Wenders, whose films usually deal with male wanderlust.

He romances a movie theater cashier and for no apparent reason, strangles her.

The film was released in the United States in 1977.

1373 G'Ole (aka **World Cup Film '82)**

1983, British, Ladbroke, 100 minutes, Color. Director: Tom Clegg. Producers: Drummond Challis, Michael Samuelson. Photography: Harvey Harrison.

Narrator: Sean Connery.

It's more World Cup action, this time at the 1982 games between 24 nations, with Italy coming out victorious.

Musical score was by Rick Wakeman, who also provided the music for **White Rock,** a film about the winter Olympics.

1374 Good and Bad at Games

1983, British, Portman/Quintet Films, 85 minutes, Color. Director: Jack Gold. Producer: Victor Glynn. Screenplay: William Boyd. Photography: Wolfgang Suschitzky. Editors: Laurence Mery-Clark.

Cast: Martyn Stanbridge, Anton Lesser, Laura Davenport, Dominic Jephcott, Frederick Alexander, Graham Seed.

A student from Singapore is accepted by his snooty classmates at school only because he's the top cricket player. Years later, they all face a threat from a student they bullied.

1375 A Good Kick-Off

1910, British, Hepworth, 275 feet. Director: Lewin Fitzhamon.

A rugby game winds up in the river.

1376 The Great Game

1930, British, Gaumont, 79 minutes. Director: Jack Raymond. Producer: L'Estrange Fawcett. Screenplay: W.P. Lipscomb, Ralph Gilbert Bettinson. Story: William Hunter, John Lees. Photography: Basil Emmott.

Cast: John Batten, John Cook, Renee Clama, Randle Ayrton, Neil Kenyon, Kenneth Love, A.G. Poulton, Rex Harrison.

Inept management can't stop a soccer team's march to victory.

A number of top soccer stars appear to add authenticity to the action scenes.

1377 The Great Game

1953, British, Advance, 80 minutes. Director: Maurice Elvey. Producer: David Dent. Screenplay: Wolfgang Wilhelm, based on a play by Basil Thomas. Photography: Phil Grindrod.

Cast: James Hayter, Thora Hird, Goeffrey Toone, Diana Dors, Shand Gibbs, John Laurie and the Brentford Football Club.

A soccer team's manager sets his sights on acquiring a rival club's star player. He stops at nothing to get the player, neglecting his printing business in the process; and once his crooked machinations are found out, he must resign his post and return to his ruined business.

1378 Gregory's Girl

1982, Scottish, Samuel Goldwyn, 91-98 minutes, Color. Director-Screenplay: Bill Forsyth. Producer: Clive Parsons, Davina Belling. Photography: Mohl Coulter. Editor: John Gow.

Cast: Gordon John Sinclair, Dee Hepburn, Chic Murray, Jake D'Arcy, Alex Norton, John Bett, Robert Buchanan, William Greenlees, Graham Thompson, Allison Forster.

The charming simplicity of the tale makes this comedy about a high school soccer goalie who falls in love with the newcomer on his team a surprise international hit. The newcomer happens to be a girl who can play better than many of the guys, in one of the extremely few instances in foreign films where the athletic abilities of women are acknowledged.

1379 Harry the Footballer

1911, British, Hepworth, 531-650 feet. Director: Lewin Fitzhamon.

Cast: Hay Plumb, Gladys Sylvani, Jack Hulcup, Claire Pridelle.

The good guys' star is kidnapped prior to the big game, but he's rescued by the heroine and, of course, gets there on time for the match. Gee, didn't we just say the same thing just a few films ago for **The Cup Final Mystery**?

1380 Head or Tails

1983, Italian, CIDIF, 100 minutes, Color. Director: Nanny Loy. Producers: Luigi and Aurelio De Laurentiis. Screenplay: Loy, Franco Ferrini, Enrico Oldoini, Nino Manfredi, Renato Pozzeto. Photography: Claudio Cirillo. Editor: Franco Fraticelli.

Cast: Nino Manfredi, Renato Pozzetto, Mara Venier, Idi Di Benedetto, Paola Stoppa.

The first segment of this two-part comedy concerns a rural priest who loses his memory during a train trip to the big city and becomes involved in a love affair.

The second half features Manfredi as a blue collar worker whose son, the big star of a youth soccer team, is the apple of his eye until he discovers him making love in the shower to a teammate he calls "moustache."

1381 The Hero (aka **Bloomfield**)

1971, English-Israeli, Avco Embassy, 95-105 minutes, Color. Director: Richard Harris. Producers: John Heyman, Wolf Mankowitz. Screenplay: Mankowitz, Harris. Story: Joseph Gross. Editor: Kevin Connor.

Cast: Richard Harris, Romy Schneider, Kim Burfield, Maurice Kaufman, Yossi Yadin, Shrage Friedman.

Harris' directorial career was grounded practically before it began with the release of this offbeat tale of a young boy in Israel who idolizes an aging soccer star (Harris).

The player, who's being forced into retirement at age 40, grapples with his conscience over a bribe offer to throw his last game.

1382 Hooray Brazil

1982, Brazilian, Embrafilme, 95 minutes, Color. Director-Screenplay: Roberto Farias. Photography: Dib Lufti, Francisco Balbino Nunes. Editor: Roberto and Mauro Farias.

Cast: Reginaldo Farias, Antonio Fagundes, Natalia do Vale, Elizabeth Savalla , Carlos Zara.

An innocent man is tortured by the police in a case of mistaken identity, while outside the streets are jammed with people celebrating Brazil's big soccer game victory over Mexico.

1383 It's Not Cricket

1937, British, First National, 63 minutes, Director: Ralph Ince. Producer: Irving Asher. Screenplay: Henry Kendall. Photography: Basil Emmott.

Cast: Betty Lynne, Claude Hulbert, Sylvia Marriott, Henry Kendall, Clifford Heatherley, Violet Farebrother, Frederick Burtwell.

Because hubby is more passionate about cricket than about her, the heroine (Lynne) pretends to run off with one of his best friends (Hulbert).

1384 It's Not Cricket

1949, British, Gainsborough, 77 minutes. Director: Alfred Roome, Roy Rich. Producer: Betty Box. Story: Bernard McNab, Lyn Lockwood, Gerard Bryant. Photography: Gordon Lang.

Cast: Basil Radford, Naunton Wayne, Susan Shaw, Maurice Denham, Alan Wheatley, Nigel Buchanan, Jane Carr, Leslie Dwyer, Patrick Waddington, Edward Lexy.

Bungling detectives get on the trail of a Nazi who's after a diamond hidden inside a cricket ball.

1385 The Last Game

1964, Russian, Artkino, 88 minutes. Director: Y. Karclov. Screenplay: A. Borschchagovskiy. Photography: Sergey Zaytsev. Editor: K. Aleyeva.

Cast: Y. Volkov, V. Kashpur, Lev Kuravlev, Yuriy Nazarov, V. Nevinnyy, V. Skulme, V. Tomingas.

Set in Kiev during the Nazi occupation in 1942, this was supposedly based on a true incident.

One of the many ancestors of **Victory**, it concerns a soccer match that's arranged between a team of Russian prisoners of war and a crack German squad in what's meant to be a propaganda display of Nazi superiority.

The Soviets are allowed to fatten up and roam around the city at will, but they know if they win, they'll be executed.

When the prisoners see how the whole city is out rooting for them, they plan to win and defeat the Nazis. Unlike the false heroics of **Victory**, the team is then led to the firing squad.

1386 Let's Go, Young Guy!

1967, Japanese, 92 minutes, Color. Director: Katsumi Iwauchi. Screenplay: Yasuo Tanami. Photography: Yuzuru Aizawa.

Cast: Yuzo Kayama, Yuriko Hoshi, Bibani Maeda, Akira Takarada, Chen Man Ling, Hoei Tanaka, To Man Rei.

There are lots of romantic complications as a college soccer player who has a girl friend back home meets a Chinese girl while his team is in Hong Kong for a match.

1387 The Lucky Number

1933, British, Gainsborough, 70-72 minutes. Director: Anthony Asquith. Producer: Michael Balcon. Story: Franz Schulz.

Cast: Clifford Mollison, Gordon Harker, Joan Wyndham, Joe Hayman.

When a professional soccer player is robbed, he leaves a pub owner a lottery ticket as security for his drinks.

The ticket proves to be a big winner; but every time the player attempts to redeem it, something else happens.

1388 Manny's Orphans (aka **Kick**)

1979, Cunningham Films, Color. Director: Sean Cunningham. Producers: Cunningham, Victor Miller. Screenplay: Miller.

Cast: Jim Baker, Malachy McCourt, Xavier Rodrigo, Chet Doherty, Marlon Acuna.

From the man who brought you **Here Come the Tigers** (see Baseball chapter) and **Friday the 13th,** Cunningham here tries another comedy as some streetwise orphans help soccer coach Manny get out of trouble with loan sharks.

Fired from his job at an exclusive school, he takes the coaching position at an orphans' home and leads them to the championship.

Soccer star Werner Roth appears as himself in a sequence at Giants Stadium.

1389 The Match

1981, Hungarian, Hungarofilm, 110 minutes, Color. Director-Screenplay: Ference Kosa. Photography: Sandor Sara.

Cast: Tibor Szilagy, Andras Kozak, Alicija Jachiewics, Gabor Koncz, Ferenc Bessenyei.

A secret policeman who also runs a soccer club murders an umpire he feels blew a big call during a match in the Stalinist era.

When a journalist uncovers evidence against the cop, the newsman is arrested.

1390 My Wife's Enemy

1967, Italian, Magna Pictures, 90 minutes. Director: Gianni Puccini. Screenplay: Bruno Baratti, Renato Castellani, Gianna Puccini, Giuseppe Moccia. Photography: Gianni Di Venanzo.

Cast: Marcello Mastroianni, Giovanni Ralli, Memmo Carotenuto, Luciana Paluzzi, Vittorio De Sica, Andrea Checchi.

Originally made in 1959, this was one of a number of Italian films belatedly released in the U.S. after Mastroianni achieved stardom.

He plays a soccer referee who pays more attention to the playing field than to his merchant wife, and both are having extra-marital affairs.

During a big match, however, the two settle their differences and have a reconciliation.

1391 Old College Badge

1913, British, B&C, 1,256 feet. Director: Charles Raymond.

Cast: Percy Moran, Dorothy Foster, Jack Melville, John B. Glover, J. O'Neil Farrell.

A cricket team comes to the rescue when a Jamaican sugar factory is blown up by a villain, and the hero is imperiled.

1392 The Old Time Soccer

1974, Hungarian. Director: Pal Sandor.

Set against a soccer background, this concerns a doomed Jewish man in 1930's Hungary as fascism rears its ugly head.

1393 Pele

1977, French-Mexican, Televisa, 85 minutes, Color. Director: Francois Reichenbach. Screenplay: Reichenbach, Jacqueline Lefevre. Photography: Reichenbach, Lefevre. Editors: Georges Klotz, Francoise Orsoni.

The Brazilian soccer star Pele is considered by many to be the greatest to have ever played the game; so it's natural, with all the soccer fans around the world, there would be a documentary about him.

1394 Pimple on Football

1914, British, Folly Films, 640 feet. Directors: Fred and Joe Evans.

Cast: Fred and Joe Evans.

Pimple (Fred Evans) brings some laughs as he tries to be a soccer star.

1395 Pimple's Fire Brigade

1912, British, Folly Films, 415 feet. Directors-Screenplay: Fred and Joe Evans.

Cast: Fred and Joe Evans.

When a fire engine arrives at the scene of a fire too late, the firemen decide to play a game of soccer.

1396 Ragged Football

1948, Argentinian, SIFA, 110 minutes. Director: Leopoldo Torres Rios. Screenplay: Ricardo Lorenzo, Jerry Gomez. Photography: Alvaro Barreiro.

Cast: Armando Bo, Santiago Arrieta, Orestes Caviglia, Carmen Valdes, Graciela Lecube, Floren Delbene.

A slum boy's great dream is to be a great soccer star and play in front of thousands of people. Meanwhile, he and his friends have to content themselves with playing on an empty lot using only a ragged ball.

A low budget production, this turned out to be one of Argentina's biggest box office hits of the era.

1397 Rattle of a Simple Man

1964, British, Continental, 96 minutes. Director: Muriel Box. Producer: William Gell. Screenplay: Charles Dyer. Editor: Frederick Wilson.

Cast: Harry H. Corbett, Diane Cilento, Thora Hird, Michael Medwin, Charles Dyer, Hugh Futcher, Brian Wilde, Alexander Davion, David Saire, Barbara Archer.

A soccer buff—who's also nearing 40 and still a virgin—travels to London to see the Cup Final.

He's coerced into betting his motorcycle that he can get a Soho prostitute to come home with him and is surprised when she does, and the two begin a relationship.

1398 Really . . . Incredible

1982, Italian, Titanus, 95 minutes, Color. Director: Carlo Vanzina. Producer: Alessandro Fracassi. Screenplay: Enrico and Carlo Vanzina, Diego Abatantuono. Photography: Alberto Spagnoli. Editor: Raimondo Crociani.

Cast: Diego Abatantuono, Stefania Sandrelli, Massimo Boldi, Teo Teocoli.

Soccer ties three separate short stories together with comic Abatantuono playing a different part in each.

In the first, he's an unemployed man from southern Italy who gets into an altercation with fans of a rival team.

The middle segment has him as a car salesman who leaves his wife and family when he believes he's the winner of a soccer pool.

The final story concerns a truck driver who swaps rigs with another driver so he can attend a big soccer match only to have the truck stolen in Paris.

It was a big box office hit in Italy.

1399 The Rival Captains

1916, British Oak, 970 feet. Director: Ethyle Batley.

Another silent film where the star soccer player is kidnapped by the rival team. This time, it's a dog who rescues him, enabling him to get to the match on time.

1400 Rooney

1958, British, Rank, 88 minutes. Director: George Pollock. Photography: Christopher Challis. Editor: Peter Bozencenet.

Cast: John Gregson, Muriel Pavlow, Barry Fitzgerald, June Thorburn, Noel Purcell, Liam Redmond.

An Irishman is a garbage collector by day and the star of a hurling team on weekends.

A very eligible bachelor, he spends much of the rest of his time warding off the marital advances of his widowed landladies.

He moves to the home of

another widow who has a niece she treats practically like a servant.

1401 Slow Motion

1979, Yugoslavian, Jadram, 90 minutes, Color. Director: Vanca Kiljakovic. Screenplay: Tomislav Sabljak. Photography: Drago Novak.

Cast: Vlatko Dulic, Ivica Vidovic, Mia Oremovic, Kostadinka Velkovska.

An aging soccer star is forced to retire because of a leg injury and becomes a hotel receptionist. He decides to throw a class anniversary party to which no one shows up.

1402 Small Town Story

1953, British, GFD, 69 minutes. Director: Montgomery Tully. Producers: Otto Kreisler, Ken Bennett. Screenplay: George Fisher. Story: Franz Marischka, Maurice Weissberger. Photography: Jo Jago, Peter Hamilton.

Cast: Donald Houston, Susan Shaw, Alan Wheatly, Kent Walton, George Merritt, the Middlesex and Arsenal Cricket Clubs and the Millwall Football Club.

A soccer team will come into a lot of money if it turns itself around and becomes a winner. A star player (Walton) is wooed by his ex-girl friend (Shaw) to join another team, but he finds out, and he helps the good guys.

1403 Spider Football

1977, Hungarian, 87 minutes. Director: Janos Rozsa. Screenplay: Istvan Icardos. Photography: Elemer Ragalyi.

Cast: Jozsef Madaras, Judit Halasz, Adam Rajhona, Hedi Temessy, Robert Koltai, Jozsef Mentes.

An incompetent school principal tries to impress an inspection team by showing them how his classes play "spider football." It's a form of soccer inside the classroom in which the kids slide along the floor on their behinds and kick the ball.

1404 The Stand-Off

1979, Romanian, Romania Film, 96 minutes, Color. Director: Dinu Tanase. Screenplay: Mihai Istratescu. Photography: Vasile Vivi Dragan. Editor: Gheorghe Ilarian.

Cast: Stefan Maitec, Mircea Cretu, Sorina Stanclescu, Dana Siclovan, Gabriela Criper.

Yes, this is a Romanian rugby movie in which the young hero works in a lathe factory but whose real passion is on the rugby field.

He also attends night school. Problems begin when his factory foreman apparently has it in for him and he's injured playing rugby.

1405 This Sporting Life

1963, British, Continental, 129 minutes. Director: Lindsay Anderson. Producer: Karel Reisz. Screenplay: David Storey. Photography: Denys Coop. Editor: Peter Taylor.

Cast: Richard Harris, Rachel Roberts, Alan Badel, William Hartnell, Colin Blakely, Vanda Godsell, Anne Cunningham, Jack Watson, Arthur Lowe, Harry Markham.

"You see something you want, you go out and get it. It's as simple as that." That's the philosophy of rugby player Frank Machin (Harris) who has risen from the mines to be a top star.

He's as totally ruthless off the field as he is on it as he mistreats his girl friend, who eventually dies of a brain hemorrhage.

The film propelled Harris to international stardom and features some really brutal rugby scenes.

1406 Those Glory Glory Days

1983, British, Enigma, 95 minutes, Color. Director: Chris Griffin. Producer: Philip Saville. Screenplay: Julie Welch. Photography: Phil Meheux. Editor: Max Lemon.

Cast: Zoe Nathanson, Julia Goodman, Julia McKenzie, Danny

Blanchflower, Peter Tilbury, Sara Sugarman.

Soccer star Blanchflower appears as himself in this comedy about the only female sports journalist in the stadium press box.

When she's given a ride home by her girlhood idol (Blanchflower), she remembers the days when she and three girl friends were avid fans of the soccer team.

1407 The Tricyclist

1958, French, Pathe, 95 minutes, Color. Director: Jack Pinoteau. Screenplay: Jacques Vilfrid, Jean Aurel, Pinoteau, based on a novel by Rene Fallet. Photography: Pierre Petit. Editor: Georges Arnstam.

Cast: Darry Cowl, Beatrice Altariba, Pierre Mondy, Roger Carol, Jean-Claude Brialy.

A bespectacled buffoon who follows his favorite soccer team on a tricycle wherever they go winds up getting into a game and becoming the unlikely hero.

1408 Trobriand Cricket

1975, New Zealand, University of California, Extension Media Center, 54 minutes. Directors: Jerry W. Leach, Gary Kildea. Produced by the Office of Information, Government of Papua, New Guinea.

Well-received wherever it's been shown, either theatrically or on television, this humorous documentary traces the development of cricket in the Trobriand Islands from its introduction by Methodist ministers to a kind of substitute for tribal warfare.

It shows how the natives change the game for their own purposes, with each side having up to 65 batsmen as neighboring villages play each other.

A narrator tells us "the Trobriand Islands have a population of 15,000 and a unique way of playing cricket."

The special rules allow that the home team always wins the match no matter what. Each "out" is followed by a series of chants by the defensive team.

For those who don't understand cricket, this is as good an introduction as any, as the traditional rules of the game are also explained.

1409 Two Half-Times in Hell

1961, Hungarian, Director: Zoltan Fabri.

To celebrate Hitler's birthday, a Nazi officer stages a soccer match between SS men and concentration camp inmates that's intended as a propaganda show.

As in **The Last Game,** the inmates know they face certain death if they play to win, but they do so anyway.

1410 Up for the Cup

1950, British, Citadel-Byron, 76 minutes. Director: Jack Raymond. Producer: Henry Halstead. Screenplay: Con West, Jack Marks. Photography: Henry Harris.

Cast: Albert Modley, Mai Bacon, Helen Christie, Harold Berens, Wallas Eaton, Jack Melford, Charmian Innes.

An inventor has a series of misadventures on Cup Final day. First, he loses his girl, then his wallet and his ticket to the big Cup Final, but after a series of comic misadventures, all turns out well in the end.

1411 Victory

1981, Paramount, 110 minutes, Color. Director: John Huston. Producer: Freddie Fields. Screenplay: Yabo Yablonsky, Evan Jones. Story: Yablonsky, Djordje Milcevic, Jeff Maguire.

Cast: Sylvester Stallone, Michael Caine, Max Von Sydow, Pele, Carole Laure, Bobbie Moore, Tim Pigott-Smith, Daniel Massey, Anton Diffring, Osvaldo Ardiles, Paul Van Himst, Kazimierz Deyna, Hallvar Thorensen, Mike Summerbee.

A hybrid of at least a half-dozen other films, most notably **The Great Escape,** features Caine

The Trobriand natives reinvent the proper British game of cricket to reflect their own values and traditions in Trobriand Cricket. (Courtesy the University of California Extension Media Center.)

as a British soccer coach now a prisoner of war in a Nazi concentration camp.

Nazi officer Von Sydow recognizes him as a former field opponent and comes up with a propaganda scheme: The Germans were unable to defeat the British soccer team before the war, so he proposes a match between the prisoners of war and a team of the Third Reich's best, to be staged before a large crowd in Paris to prove Nazi superiority.

As in **The Last Game,** the prisoners' team is granted special privileges and is allowed to fatten up.

In the meantime, American POW Stallone, modeled after Steve McQueen's character in **The Great Escape,** keeps on trying to escape and sees the soccer team as the means to do so.

The British leaders of the prisoners oppose the game on the grounds it's pure Nazi propaganda and want Stallone to escape, contact the French underground and arrange an escape plan for the entire team and to be recaptured so he can inform the prisoners of the results.

The big match comes and the prisoners, although still a bit out of shape, put up a good showing although the referees are biased against them.

At half-time, when the underground comes through, the team rejects the chance to escape and stages an incredible comeback at half-time. The team escapes when the crowd, rooting for the prisoners, rushes the field and leads them out.

Unlike **The Last Game** and **Two Half-Times in Hell,** the prisoners in **Victory** had their cake by playing to win and ate it too, by escaping instead of being executed.

Victory also owes a couple of nods to **The Longest Yard, The Wooden Horse** and **Olimpiada 40,** among other prisoner dramas, with perhaps acknowledgment to **The Boxer (The Boxer and Death).**

1412 What Price Victory?
1983, Austrian, Bannert Film, 92 minutes, Color. Director-Editor: Walter Bannert. Screenplay: Bannert, Klaus Kemetmuller. Photography: Hans Polak.

Cast: Heinz Peter Puff, Alexander Bauer, Andras Bauer, Rene Wrba, Nikolas Vogel, Peter Wundsam.

An unscrupulous coach tramples all over his kids, without regards to their feelings, in his passion to win on the soccer field. Even when some of the players are on the verge of physical and emotional breakdown, he gets backing by the principal.

1413 Where's George (aka **The Hope of His Side**)
1935, British, United Artists, 69 minutes. Director: Jack Raymond. Producer: Herbert Wilcox. Screenplay: R.P. Weston, Bert Lee, Jack Marks, John Paddy Carstairs.

Cast: Sydney Howard, Mabel Constonduros, Leslie Sarony, Frank Pettingell, Sam Livesey, Wally Patch.

A blacksmith becomes the unlikely hero of his soccer team.

1414 The Winning Goal
1920, British, G. B. Samuelson, 5,000 feet. Director: G.B. Samuelson. Story: Harold Brighouse.

Cast: Harold Walden, Maudie Dunham, Tom Reynolds, Haidee Wright, Jack Cook.

A number of professional players are featured in the story of a soccer player who's sold to a rival team and who's the big hero of the big match despite having a broken arm.

1415 Yesterday's Hero
1979, British, EMI, 95 minutes, Color. Director: Neil Leifer. Producers: Oscar S. Lerman, Ken Regan. Screenplay: Jackie Collins. Photography: Brian West. Editor: Anthony Gibbs.

Cast: Ian McShane, Suzanne Somers, Adam Faith, Paul Nicholas, Sam Kydd, Glynis Barber, Trevor Thomas.

A former star, now on the skids, is given a chance at a comeback, and he makes the most of it.

Tennis, Handball and Ping Pong

Filmmakers have never been too fond of putting tennis action on screen, perhaps scared off by the physical limitations of the court. Although countless films have had tennis scenes in them, full-length films about tennis have been few and far between.

Pat and Mike (1952), the classic comedy starring Katharine Hepburn and Spencer Tracy, contains some of the best tennis action shots ever put on screen, but we discussed that film at length in the Golf chapter.

Dial M for Murder, Alfred Hitchcock's 1954 film, contains no tennis scenes but features Ray Milland as an aging tennis pro in what we consider a companion piece to Hitchcock's earlier **Strangers on a Train,** discussed later in this chapter. Whereas the protagonist in **Strangers** was a tennis pro in his prime, the villainous Milland in **Dial M** fears his loss of virility and comes up with a murder plot as his answer to his wife's infidelity.

The murder plots in **Strangers** and **Dial M** are strikingly similar. In both, the scheme is to have a total stranger commit the crime so there can be no traceable motive.

Of the many other films which have tennis scenes, the sequence in **Mr. Hulot's Holiday,** in which French comedian Jacques Tati develops a most devastating serve, ranks as the funniest.

1416 Brown's Half Holiday

1906, British, Williamson, 312 feet.

No credits available.

Poor Mr. Brown must help his wife with the cleaning while he'd rather be playing tennis. He gets his wish when he's caught in an explosion from a gas leak and is blown onto a tennis court.

1417 Cardboard Lover

1928, Cosmopolitan, 7,108 feet. Director: Robert Z. Leonard. Scenario: F. Hugh Herbert. Photography: John Arnold. Editor: Basil Wrangell.

Cast: Marion Davies, Andres De Segurola, Jetta Goudal, Nils Asther, Tenen Holtz, Pepe Lederer.

While in Europe with her schoolmates, a young girl, who likes collecting celebrities' autographs, falls in love with the French tennis champ (Asther); her hopes soar when it's discovered his girl friend doesn't love him.

1418 Chance

1980, Polish, Film Polski, 94 minutes, Color. Director-Screenplay: Feliks Falk. Photography: Edward Klosinski.

Cast: Krzysztof Zaleski, Jerzy Stuhr, Elzbieta Kakoszka, Ewa Kolasinska, Slawa Kwasniewska.

A teacher of the arts comes into conflict with a brutal handball coach who dominates the lives of his players on and off the court.

The coach, whose own career was ended by a leg injury, teaches his players to cheat and win at all costs, eventually driving one youth into a suicide attempt.

1419 The Christian Licorice Store

1971, National General, 90 minutes, Color. Director: James Frawley. Producers: Michael S. Laughlin, Floyd Mutrux. Screenplay: Mutrux. Photography: David Butler. Editor: Richard Harris.

Cast: Beau Bridges, Maud Adams, Gilbert Roland, Alan Arbus, Anne Randall, Monte Hellman, Jaclyn Hellman, Dido and Jean Renoir.

A tennis champ falls victim to the Hollywood lure, selling himself into commercialism by doing hair tonic ads and dissipating his body at wild parties.

1420 Fickle Flo's Flirtation

1915, British, Martin. Director: Edwin J. Collins.

Two men are rivals for the love of a girl who's in love with a tennis player.

1421 Hard, Fast and Beautiful

1951, RKO, 74-79 minutes. Director: Ida Lupino. Producer: Collier Young. Screenplay: Martha Wilkerson, based on the novel **Mother of a Champion** by John R. Tunis. Photography: Archie Stout. Editor: William Ziegler.

Cast: Sally Forrest, Claire Trevor, Robert Clarke, Carleton Young, Kenneth Patterson, Joseph Kearns, William Hudson, George Fisher, Arthur Little, Jr., Bert Whitley.

Greedy mom Trevor pushes daughter Forrest to fame on the tennis courts, first at a junior tournament in Philadelphia and later on the professional circuit.

With the help of promoter Young, Trevor lives off her daughter's winnings, pushing her husband (Patterson) to the sidelines and manipulating her daughter's life.

She even attempts to thwart her daughter's romance with Clarke, but the girl eventually realizes she's being used and gives up tennis in favor of true love.

1422 Love, Honor and Behave

1938, Warner Brothers, 68 minutes. Director: Stanley Logan. Screenplay: Clements Ripley, Michel Jacoby, Robert Buckner, Lawrence Kimble. Story: Stephen Vincent Benet. Photography: George Barnes. Editor: Owen Marks.

Cast: Wayne Morris, John Litel, Dick Foran, Mona Barrie, Donald Briggs, Gregory Gaye, Audrey Leonard, Priscilla Lane, Thomas Mitchell, Minor Watson, Dickie Moore.

A Yale tennis player who believes winning is secondary to how you play the game marries a Connecticut girl and comes into conflict with her family.

When she's left alone at night, she begins an affair with a football player until hubby decides to fight back.

1423 Oscar, Champion de Tennis

1932, French. Director-Screenplay: Jacques Tati.

Cast: Jacques Tati.

The great French comedian-director made his film debut with this short in which he first displayed his amazing body dexterity. Tati would later include a tennis scene in his feature **Mr. Hulot's Holiday** (1954) in which he develops a serve so devastating, no one will play with him.

1424 Ping-Pong

1902, British, James Williamson.

Two construction workers take a lunch break, put a board across a tub and hold a ping pong match, using trowels as paddles. They knock their heads together reaching for the ball and wind up fighting.

1425 Players

1979, Paramount, 120 minutes, Color. Director: Anthony Harvey. Producer: Robert Evans. Screenplay: Arnold Schulman. Photography: James Crabe. Editor: Randy Roberts.

Cast: Ali MacGraw, Dean-Paul Martin, Maximilian Schell, Pancho Gonzalez, Steven Guttenberg, Melissa Prophet, Guillermo Vilas, Ian Tirias, John McEnroe, Ille Nastase, Denis Ralston, John Lloyd, Vijay Amritral and other tennis world celebrities.

A young tennis star (Martin), in a Wimbledon match against Guillermo Vilas, remembers his romance with an older woman (MacGraw) who's the kept woman of a tycoon (Schell).

Will she turn her back on Schell's money for the star's sake?

Tennis pro Pancho Gonzalez portrays the young player's trainer.

1426 Racquet

1979, Cal-Am Productions, Color. Director: David Winters. Producers: Winters, Alan Roberts. Screenplay: Steve Michaels, Earle Doud.

Cast: Bert Convy, Lynda Day George, Phil Silvers, Bobby Riggs, Bjorn Borg, Edie Adams, Susan Tyrrell, Dorothy Konrad, Monti Rock III, Tanya Roberts.

A low-budget **Shampoo** ripoff features Convy as a country club tennis pro who eventually finds out to his dismay that there's more to life than just being a stud.

Real-life pro Riggs has a prominent role while Borg appears briefly as himself.

1427 Spring Fever (aka **Sneakers**)

1983, Canadian, Camworld Pics, 100 minutes, Color. Director: Joseph L. Scanlan. Producer: John F. Bassett. Screenplay: Stuart Gillard, Fred Stefan. Photography: Donald Wilder. Editor: Kirk Jones.

Cast: Susan Anton, Frank Converse, Jessica Walter, Stephen Young, Carling Bassett, Shawn Foltz.

Originally made in 1981, but not released generally until two years later, this is another **Bad News Bears** clone transferred to the tennis courts.

It centers on a young girl who makes the Junior National Tournament in Sarasota, Florida, who's ignored by the other girls because her mother (Anton) is a showgirl. The young heroine makes some money on the side by hustling games with adults.

1428 Strangers on a Train

1951, Warner Brothers, 100 minutes. Director: Alfred Hitchcock. Screenplay: Czenzi Ormonde. Adaptation: Whitfield Cook, based on a novel by Patricia Highsmith. Photography: Robert Burke. Editor: William H. Ziegler.

Cast: Farley Granger, Robert Walker, Laura Elliot, Ruth Roman, Leo G. Carroll, Patricia Hitchcock, Marian Lorne, Jonathan Hale.

Hitchcock originally had Raymond Chandler tabbed for the screenplay of this thriller, but the two couldn't see eye-to-eye on the script.

It concerns tennis star Guy Haines (Granger), who's on his way home from a tournament when a stranger named Bruno (Walker) begins a conversation with him.

Before he realizes it, the subject turns to murder, with Bruno suggesting that he will murder a girl for Haines if Haines will commit a murder for him.

Bruno's theory is that because there will be no traceable motives for the crimes, they will be the perfect murders.

Haines believes it was just idle talk until he discovers Bruno was deadly serious and has already achieved his end of the "bargain" and is demanding that Haines fulfill his. To further blackmail the pro, Bruno tells him he's planted a piece of evidence incriminating Haines for the crime.

Strangers on a Train features the most memorable tennis sequence in film annals. During a tennis tournament, there's the usual shot of the spectators' heads turning left and right following the shots. Everyone's head, that is, except Bruno's, whose eyes are fixed on Haines.

The finale, a fight on an out-of-control merry-go-round, is also one of Hitchcock's best.

The film was remade as **Once You Kiss a Stranger** with the locale switched to the golf course and the sexual implications, in **Strangers on a Train** latently homosexual, out in the open as Bruno's character was changed to a woman.

1429 The Sweet Ride

1968, 20th Century-Fox, 109 minutes, Color. Director: Harvey Hart. Producer: Joe Pasternak. Screenplay: Tom Mankiewicz, based on a novel by William Murray. Photography: Robert B. Hauser.

Cast: Tony Franciosa, Michael Sarrazin, Jacqueline Bisset, Bob Denver, Michael Wilding, Michele Carey, Lara Lindsay, Lloyd Gough.

The title refers to the lifestyle of those who live by the beach at Malibu. Franciosa portrays an aging tennis star who becomes involved with actress Bisset and surfer Sarrazin.

The scene turns violent when Bisset is raped and killed by motorcyclists.

1430 What Every Girl Should Know

1927, Warner Brothers, 6,281 feet. Director: Charles F. Reisner. Screenplay: Lois Jackson. Photography: David Abel.

Cast: Ruth Miller, Ian Keith, Carroll Nye, Mickey McBan, Lillian Langdon, Hazel Howell, Carmelita Geraghty.

When an innocent man is sent to prison, his younger sister and brother are sent to an orphanage. It all turns out well, however, as they're adopted by a wealthy man, and the girl becomes a top tennis star.

Water Sports

Because nearly everyone loves the water, films dealing with water sports have appeared in a steady stream (no pun intended) from the silent era to the present. However, the sum total of all these films can be wrapped up with the titles of two movies--**A Yank at Oxford** and **The Endless Summer**--and one key name--Esther Williams.

Otherwise, water films have been generally lackluster and unmemorable with, of course, a few exceptions. Speedboat racing films have been basically auto racing films transposed into the water, while surfing films, with the exception of **Big Wednesday**, have been generally mindless.

A Yank at Oxford, featuring Robert Taylor as a crew team star, was a big box office hit although its plot was strikingly similar to those numerous service academy movies in which the brash and selfish young hero is reformed by the traditions of the grand old institution.

The Endless Summer's box office success spurred numerous other surfing documentaries of a similar vein.

The beautiful Esther Williams was a box office smash herself, and MGM usually spared little expense in staging spectacular water extravaganza numbers wrapped inside mediocre plots because her audiences demanded little else. We've included only two of her films here--**Million Dollar Mermaid**--a biography of Annette Kellerman and a major advance in the portrayal of women athletes on screen, and **Dangerous When Wet**, as we believe most of the rest of her films are basically aquacade-type films and deserve to be classed as musicals.

We have also omitted from the listings most of those mindless teeny bopper beach party-type movies which proliferated the screens in the 1960's. We have included those which dealt with actual surfing competitions.

Among the films we feel are worth at least a mention are **Bernardine**; Buster Keaton's **The Cameraman**, which has a boat racing sequence; the yacht race in Abbott and Costello's **Pardon My Sarong** and the British short **Sports Day.**

1431 All American Sweetheart

1937, Columbia, 62 minutes. Director: Lambert Hillyer. Screenplay: Grace Neville, Fred Niblo, Jr., Michael L. Simmons. Story: Robert E. Kent. Photography: Benjamin Kline. Editor: James Sweeney.

Cast: Patricia Farr, Scott Colton, Gene Morgan, Jimmy Eagles, Arthur Loft, Joe Twerp, Ruth Hilliard, Donald Briggs.

A college crew team's coxswain gambles on a nearby showboat and becomes involved with racketeers who are betting heavily against the school.

Comes the big race and the coxswain has two broken ribs courtesy of the gamblers but goes all out anyway.

1432 The Atlantic Swimmers

1976, West German, 81 minutes, Color. Director-Producer-Screenplay: Herbert Achternbusch. Photography: Joerg Schmidt-Reitwein. Editor: Karin Fischer.

Cast: Heinz Braun, Herbert Achternbusch, Alois Hitzenbichler, Sepp Bierbichier.

Comedy about two friends seeking the prize money for a long-distance swim in the Atlantic Ocean.

1433 Big Time or Bust

1934, Tower, 61 minutes. Director: Sam Newfield. Screenplay: G.W. Sayre. Photography: Harry Forbe.

Cast: Regis Toomey, Gloria Shea, Edwin Maxwell, Walter Byron, Nat Carr, Charles Delaney, Hooper Atchley.

Toomey's a high diver, and Shea's his assistant. Conflict arises when they marry, and Shea becomes a star.

1434 Big Wednesday

1978, Warner Brothers, 126 minutes, Color. Director: John Milius. Producer: Buzz Feitshans. Screenplay: Milius, Dennis Aaberg. Surfing sequences by Greg MacGillivray.

Cast: Jan-Michael Vincent, William Katt, Gary Busey, Patti D'Arbanville, Sam Melville, Lee Purcell, Robert Englund, Barbara Hale.

Macho director Milius turns his attention to Malibu, where he follows the lives of three top surfers from the 1960's on.

1435 Blondie Goes to College

1942, Columbia, 74 minutes. Director: Frank R. Strayer. Producer: Robert Sparks. Screenplay: Lou Breslow. Story: Warren Wilson, Clyde Bruckman, based on the comic strip by Chic Young. Photography: Henry Freulich. Editor: Otto Meyer.

Cast: Penny Singleton, Arthur Lake, Larry Simms, Janet Blair, Jonathan Hale, Danny Mummert, Larry Parks, Adele Mara, Lloyd Bridges, Sidney Melton, Andrew Tombes.

When Dagwood Bumstead catches a football while watching a game, he gets the bug to attend college. Taking leave of his job, he and Blondie drop off Baby Dumpling at military school and enroll at college but keep their marriage a secret. Also being kept secret from Dagwood is the fact Blondie is pregnant again.

When the school jock (Parks) makes a play for Blondie, Dagwood tries his hand at sports. He's a laughing stock at football, but makes the crew team and despite a gallant effort, causes the team to lose.

As if that wasn't enough, he winds up being accused of trying to kidnap his own son; but as usual in this comedy series, all turns out okay.

1436 Blue Murder at St. Trinian's

1958, British, British Lion, 85 minutes. Director: Frank Launder. Producers: Launder, Sidney Gilliat. Screenplay: Launder, Gilliat, Val Valentine. Editor: Geoffrey Foote.

Cast: Terry-Thomas, Alastir Sim, Joyce Grenfell, Sabrina, Lionel Jeffries, Ferdy Mayne, Lloyd Lambie, Lisa Gastoni, Dilys Laye.

Those monstrous little girls from St. Trinian's are back, with police being called out to keep order until a new headmistress for the school arrives.

The girls win a trip to Rome by cheating; and to get out of the country, the jewel thief father (Jeffries) of one of them poses as the headmistress.

He hides the jewels in a ball which winds up being used by the girls in a big international water polo match.

1437 Bull of the Campus

1962, Japanese, Toho, 94 minutes, Color. Director: Toshio Sugie. Screenplay: Ryuzo Kasahara, Yasuo Tanami. Photography: Takeshi Suzuki.

Cast: Yuzo Kayama, Yuriko Hoshi, Reiko Dan, Ken Uehara, Yoko Fujiyama, Akemi Kita, Machiko Naka.

A college swimming star

must conquer love and family problems as well as the opposition, and he becomes a lifeguard at a resort community.

1438 Circus Boy

1947, British, GFD, 50 minutes. Director: Cecil Musk. Producer: Frank Hoare. Screenplay: Musk, Mary Cathcart Borer. Story: Patita Nicholson. Photography: A.T. Dinsdale, C. Marlborough.

Cast: James Kenney, Florence Stephenson, George Stephenson, Denver Hall, Dennis Gilbert, Gwen Bacon.

A young swimmer joins the circus as a clown and overcomes the nervousness which had held him back.

1439 Clambake

1967, United Artists, 100 minutes, Color. Director: Arthur H. Nadel. Producer: Jules Levy, Arthur Gardner, Arnold Lavin. Screenplay: Arthur Browne, Jr. Photography: William Margulies. Editor: Tom Rolf.

Cast: Elvis Presley, Shelley Fabares, Will Hutchins, Bill Bixby, James Gregory, Gary Merrill, Amanda Harley, Suzie Kaye, Jack Good, Angelique Pettyjohn, Olga Kaya.

Wanting to make good on his own, the heir (Presley) to an oil fortune becomes a water ski instructor in Florida. He's also an inventor, creating a hardener he calls "goop."

To impress a girl, he enters the Orange Bowl Power Boat Regatta in a boat designed by Merrill, whose last boat failed to make the grade. Using the "goop," Elvis wins the race.

1440 Dangerous When Wet

1953, Metro Goldwyn Mayer, 95 minutes, Color. Director: Charles Walters. Producer: George Wells. Screenplay: Dorothy Kingsley. Photography: Harold Rosson. Editor: John McSweeney, Jr.

Cast: Esther Williams, Fernando Lamas, Jack Carson, Charlotte Greenwood, Denise Darcel, William Demarest, Donna Corcoran.

Esther swims the English Channel in an attempt to get some money for her family's farm back in Arkansas. She's helped out by champagne salesman Lamas while Carson, a liquid vitamin salesman, becomes involved with the French swimmer.

An underwater Tom and Jerry cartoon is incorporated in this comedy.

1441 The Endless Summer

1966, Cinema V, 91-95 minutes, Color. Director-Producer-Writer-Photography-Editor: Bruce Brown.

Seeking the "perfect wave," this popular documentary follows three surfers, including Brown, on a trip to beaches in Hawaii, Ghana, Malibu, Nigeria, Australia, New Zealand and Tahiti. Its box office success made it the archtype documentary for numerous surfing movies.

1442 The Fantastic Plastic Machine

1969, Crown International, 93 minutes, Color. Director-Producer-Screenplay: Eric and Lowell Blum. Photography: John M. Stephens. Editor: Albert Nalpas.

Cast: Nat Young, Bob McTavish, George Greenough, Skip Frye, Mike Purpus, Margo Godfrey, Joey Hamaski, Steve Bigler, Kenny Morrow, Peter Johnson, Mickey Munoz.

Documentary in which a group of American surfers are defeated in California by Nat Young of Australia, considered by many to be the world's greatest.

They stop off in Fiji and New Zealand en route to Australia in hopes of a rematch and are introduced to a new type of surfboard called the plastic machine.

1443 Fast Life

1932, Metro Goldwyn Mayer, 82 minutes. Director: Harry Pollard.

Adaptation: Byron Morgan, Ralph Spence. Photography: Harold Wenstrom. Editor: Hugh Wynn.

Cast: William Haines, Madge Evans, Conrad Nagel, Arthur Byron, Cliff Edwards, Warburton Gamble, Kenneth Thomson, Albert Gran, Ben Hendricks.

Two navy vets (Haines, Edwards) try to interest a shipbuilder who's in financial trouble in a new speedboat engine they've developed. Naturally, the builder has a beautiful daughter to fall in love with.

Pete Smith does the announcing for the international boat race finale.

1444 Floating College

1928, Tiffany-Stahl, 5,477 feet. Director: George J. Crone. Story-Continuity: Stuart Anthony. Photography: Harry Jackson. Editor: Desmond O'Brien.

Cast: Sally O'Neil, Georgia Hale, William Collier, Harvey Clark, George Harris, E.J. Ratcliffe, Virginia Sale.

A couple of rich sisters are the rivals for the love of a swimming instructor of a floating college.

1445 Follow Me

1969, Cinerama Releasing Corp., 79 minutes, Color. Director-Producer: Gene McCabe. Screenplay: Stanley Ralph Ross. Photography: Mike Margulies, Jim Freeman, Greg MacGillivray. Editors: Fred Brown, Donn Cambern, Gerald Sheppard, William Martin, Almon R. Teeter.

Yet another surfing documentary inspired by the huge success of **The Endless Summer** follows three surfers as they sample the waves in Hawaii, Morocco, Ceylon, India, Hong Kong and Tokyo, where they surf indoors at a pool with artificial waves.

1446 For the Love of Mike

1927, First National, 6,588 feet. Director: Frank Capra. Scenario: J. Clarkson Miller, based on "Hell's Kitchen" by John Moroso. Photography: Ernest Haller.

Cast: Claudette Colbert, Ben Lyon, George Sidney, Ford Sterling, Hugh Cameron, Richard "Skeets" Gallagher, Rudolph Cameron, Mabel Swor.

In New York City's Hell's Kitchen, a German, an Irishman and a Jew raise an abandoned baby boy who grows up and attends Yale.

He becomes an ace on the crew team and falls in love with a delicatessen worker but becomes deeply involved with a gambler who threatens to have him arrested unless he throws the big race.

1447 The Forgotten Island of Santosha

1974, Santosha Productions, 84 minutes, Color. Director-Producer-Writer: Larry Yates. Photography: Spider Wills, Tim Cousins, Greg Weaver, Tom Jewel, Ralph Meyers, Scott Preiss.

Narrator: Rick Ely.

The influence of **The Endless Summer** is still evident here as two surfers seek, instead of the "perfect wave" of the 1966 film, "the most unique wave."

Their travels take them to the South Seas, where they also photograph a number of tribal rituals.

1448 Freshman Love

1936, Warner Brothers, 65 minutes. Director: William McGann. Producer: Bryan Foy. Screenplay: Earl Felton, George Bricker. Story: George Ade. Photography: Sid Hickox.

Cast: Frank McHugh, Patricia Ellis, Warren Hull, Joe Cawthorn, George E. Stone, Mary Treen, Joseph Sawyer, Henry O'Neill.

A musical comedy reworking of the 1927 gridiron film **The College Widow** finds McHugh as the harried coach of a college crew team who must either win or be fired.

The college president's daughter (Ellis) helps him out by using her feminine charms to recruit the best crew available. The team's coxswain turns out to be a band leader who leads the crew in stroking to a jazz rhythm.

1449 A Freshman's Finish

1932, Educational, 19 minutes. Director: William Watson. Producer: Al Christie. Story: Frank Roland Conklin.

Cast: Carlyle Moore, Helen Mann, Sally Sweet, Ronnie Randall.

The college sophomores use dirty tricks in their motor boat race against the freshmen, with the winners getting to attend a dance, in this comedy short.

1450 The Golden Breed

1968, Continental, 88 minutes, Color. Director-Producer-Photography-Editor: Dale Davis.

Another **Endless Summer** clone, with surfers riding the waves in Hawaii, Mexico and California. Among the featured surfers are Butch Van Artsdalen, Mickey Dora, Fred Hemings, Greg Noll, Ricky Grigg, Joey Campbell, Jock Southerland, Nat Young, Steve Doyle and Felipe Pomar.

1451 Ha'Penny Breeze

1950, British, AB-Pathe, 72 minutes. Director: Frank Worth. Producers: Darcy Conyers, Don Sharp. Screenplay: Sharp, Worth. Photography: George Stretton, Gordon Lang.

Cast: Don Sharp, Edwin Richfield, Gwyneth Vaughan, Terry Everett, Eva Rowland, Roger Maxwell, John Powe, Darcy Conyers, Michael Gough.

A war veteran hopes to revive his village, which has fallen on hard times, by making it a center of the yachting industry.

He pins his hopes on a big race. He loses, but his sportsmanship earns him the respect of the winner who hires him to build a new vessel.

1452 The Hermit of Bird Island

1915, Lubin, 3 reels. Story: George W. Terwilliger.

Cast: Mary Keane, Earl Metcalfe.

A girl, engaged to a speedboater who injures his arm, convinces a fisherman to race in his place. When he wins, she turns down his advances, and he becomes a hermit on an island.

Later, guess who is stranded on the same island with him?

1453 Hide-Out

1930, Universal, 5,297 feet. Director: Reginald Barker. Screenplay: Arthur Ripley, Lambert Hillyer. Photography: Gilbert Warrenton. Editor: Harry Marker.

Cast: James Murray, Kathryn Crawford, Carl Stockdale, Lee Moran, Edward Hearn, Robert Elliott, Jackie Hanlon.

A bootlegger becomes the ace of a college boating crew but is tracked down by a cop just prior to the big race.

Testing his declaration that he's reformed, the cop orders the athlete to throw the race. The ex-bootlegger agrees but can't go through with it; and when the cop sees that he's truly reformed, lets him go without arresting him.

1454 Howdy Broadway

1929, Rayart, 6,317 feet.

Cast: Ellalee Ruby, Lucy Ennis, Jack J. Clark, Tommy Christian and His Band.

An early talkie musical comedy featuring Christian as a champion crew team leader who's expelled from school after he's caught during a police raid on a speakeasy.

He finds success as a band leader on Broadway.

1455 I Sailed to Tahiti with an All-Girl Crew

1969, World Entertainment Corp., 95 minutes, Color. Director-Producer: Richard Bare. Screenplay: Bare, Henry Irving. Photography: Leonard Smith, Frederic Gately. Editor: John Schreyer.

Cast: Gardner McKay, Fred Clark, Pat Buttram, Diane McBain, Richard Denning, Edy Williams, Jeanne Ranier.

McKay bets Clark $20,000 he can beat him in a sailboat race to Tahiti while using a crew composed entirely of girls who have never sailed before.

Despite all kinds of dirty tricks by Clark, McKay wins out.

1456 Keep Smiling

1925, Associated Exhibitors, 5,400 feet. Directors: Gilbert W. Pratt, Albert Austin. Story: Herman Raymaker, Clyde Bruckman, Monty Banks. Photography: James Diamond, Lee Garmes, Barney McGill.

Cast: Monty Banks, Robert Edeson, Anne Cornwall, Stanhope Wheatcroft, Glen Cavender, Donald Morelli, Syd Crossley, Ruth Holly, Martha Franklin, Jack Huff.

A youth (Banks) is afraid of the water as a result of a childhood disaster and invents a new kind of life preserver, which he uses to save the life of the daughter of a steamship executive.

He's mistaken for a speedboat racer and winds up on the executive's boat with a man put on the boat by a rival who wants to win the race himself.

Although scared, through a series of mishaps and a lot of luck, the youth manages to win the race and prove the worth of his invention.

1457 Let's Go Collegiate

1941, Monogram, 60 minutes. Director: Jean Yarborough. Producer: Lindsay Parsons. Screenplay: Edmond Kelso. Photography: Jack Ogilvie. Editor: Mack Stengler.

Cast: Frankie Darro, Marcia Mae Jones, Jackie Moran, Keye Luke, Mantan Moreland, Gale Storm, Frank Sully, Frank Faylen.

A truck driver (Sully) is picked up off the street by collegians Darro and Moran and quickly develops into a key member of the crew team after the team's ace is drafted in this minor musical comedy.

1458 The Little Coxswain of the Varsity Eight

1908, Edison, 1 reel. Director: Edwin S. Porter.

An early college crew team film by pioneer Porter.

1459 Mark It Paid

1933, Columbia, 60 minutes. Director: D. Ross Lederman. Screenplay; Charles Condon.

Cast: William Collier, Jr., Jean Marsh.

A speedboat racer is framed after he refuses to throw the race in this low-budget quickie.

1460 Max Becomes a Yachtsman

1913, French, Pathe Freres, 845 feet.

Cast: Max Linder.

The great French silent comedian buys a yacht and enters it in the regatta, but he has to be rescued by a girl after the boat is overturned.

1461 Million Dollar Legs

1939, Paramount, 64 minutes. Director: Nick Grinde. Producer: William C. Thomas. Screenplay: Lewis R. Foster, Richard English. Photography: Harry Fishbeck. Editor: Arthur Schmidt.

Cast: Betty Grable, John Hartley, Donald O'Connor, Jackie Coogan, Dorothea Kent, Joyce Matthews, Peter Hayes, Larry "Buster" Crabbe, Richard Denning, Edward Arnold, Jr.

Not to be confused with the 1932 W.C. Fields film (see Olympics chapter), this features Hartley as the son of a college millionaire benefactor who wants to prove he can make it on his own.

He revives the college's crew team only to find the equipment in terrible condition, so he stakes

Thomas Edison's production company made The Little Coxswain of the Varsity Eight, released in 1908.

some cash on a horse race to raise funds to buy new material.

The team eventually is built up to the point where it defeats the school's traditional rivals.

1462 Million Dollar Mermaid (aka **The One Piece Bathing Suit**)

1952, Metro Goldwyn Mayer, 115 minutes, Color. Director: Mervyn LeRoy. Producer: Arthur Hornblow, Jr. Screenplay: Everett Freeman. Photography: George J. Folsey. Editor: John McSweeney, Jr.

Cast: Esther Williams, Walter Pidgeon, Victor Mature, Jesse White, David Brian, Donna Corcoran, Maria Tallchief, Howard Freeman, Charles Watts, Wilton Graff, Frank Ferguson, James Flavin, James Aubrey, Patrick O'Moore.

Corcoran portrays swimming star Annette Kellerman as a young girl, and Williams as the grown-up swimmer. The real-life Kellerman had starred in a movie entitled **Million Dollar Mermaid** in 1914.

The lavish MGM production features several extravagant water numbers as it traces Kellerman's life from childhood through her days at the New York Hippodrome.

Crippled as a child, she gains strength in her legs through swimming and rises to be a top amateur swimmer. She's spotted by a sports promoter (Mature) while in London after she wins a championship, and she rises to further fame before joining the Hippodrome after a spat with the promoter.

One of the very few biographies of female athletes, it was made the same year as **Pat and Mike.**

1463 Miss Pimple, Suffragette

1913, British, Folly Films, 550 feet. Directors-Screenplay: Fred and Joe Evans.

Cast: Fred and Joe Evans.

Another early Pimple comedy, this time finds him impersonating a suffragette and managing to disrupt a boat race.

1464 Motor Madness

1937, Columbia, 61 minutes. Director: D. Ross Lederman. Screenplay: Fred Niblo, Jr., Grace Neville. Photography: Allen G. Siegler.

Cast: Rosalind Keith, Allen Brook, Marc Lawrence, Richard Terry, J.M. Kerrigan, Arthur Loft, Joseph Sawyer, Ralph Byrd, George Ernest.

A mechanic (Brook) for a small boat manufacturer falls in with racketeers who operate a gambling ship outside the 12-mile limit and who also shield wanted criminals.

He's straightened out by Keith in time for the big international cup race the firm needs to win in order to survive.

1465 Oxford Blues

1984, UA/MGM, 102 minutes, Color. Director-Screenplay: Robert Boris. Producers: Cassian Elwes, Elliott Kastner. Photography: John Stanier. Editor: Patrick Moore.

Cast: Rob Lowe, Ally Sheedy, Amanda Pays, Julian Sands, Julian Firth, Alan Howard, Gail Strickland, Michael Gough, Aubrey Morris, Cary Elwes, Bruce Payne, Anthony Calf.

In 1937, MGM had a big box office hit in **A Yank at Oxford** (see listing this chapter) in which Robert Taylor played a brash American who has to make an adjustment to the traditions of the English university and who becomes a boat crew hero. **Oxford Blues** is an unofficial remake.

Here, Lowe portrays a Las Vegas parking attendant who manages to hustle his way into England's most prestigious educational institution after he falls in love with Lady Victoria (Pays).

His crude manners upset Oxford's traditions of order and propriety, but he manages to land himself a spot on the crew team.

The youth is gradually transformed by Oxford's traditions into someone who understands there's more to life than just looking out for yourself.

The film's finale is a grudge race between Oxford and Harvard along the River Thames.

1466 Pacific High

1980, 90 minutes, Color. Director: Michael Ahnemann. Producer: Roy Edward Disney. Photography: Stephen H. Burum. Editors: Ahnemann, Thomas Stanford.

The only thing really noteworthy about this documentary is that it was produced by Walt Disney's nephew. It concerns an annual sailboat race from Newport Beach, California to Ensenada, Mexico.

1467 Pacific Vibrations

1970, American-International, 92 minutes, Color. Director-Producer - Writer - Photography - Editor: John Severson.

Cast: Jock Southerland, Mike Purpus, Billy Hamilton, Rolf Aurness, David Nuuhiwa, Merv Larson, Spider Wills, Mike Tabeling, Jeff Hakman, Corky Carroll, Rick Griffin.

Another surfing documentary featuring some of the world's best, but this time there is a difference.

The focus is on the ecological problems of California and Hawaii beaches, such as industrialization, shrinking sea life and overcrowding.

1468 The Palm Beach Girl

1926, Paramount, 6,918 feet. Director: Erle Kenton. Scenario: Forrest Halsey. Story: Byron Morgan, based on "Please Help Emily" by Harold Marsh Harwood. Photography: Lee Garmes.

Cast: Bebe Daniels, Lawrence Gray, Josephine Drake, Marguerite Clayton, John G. Patrick, Armand Cortez, Roy Byron, Maude Turner Gordon.

A farm girl goes to live in California with her rich aunts

who try to transform her into a society gal. When she discovers some bootleggers putting some merchandise aboard her millionaire boy friend's speedboat, she winds up having to operate it herself in the big race.

1469 Pride of the Navy

1939, Republic, 65 minutes. Director: Charles Lamont. Screenplay: Ben Markson, Saul Elkins. Photography: Jack Marta.

Cast: James Dunn, Rochelle Hudson, Gordon Oliver, Horace McMahon, Gordon Jones, Charlotte Wynters, Joseph Crehan, Charles Trowbridge.

Dunn, drummed out of the Navy, gets the chance to redeem himself when he becomes a speedboat designer and racer and comes up with a new-style torpedo boat.

1470 Race for Your Life, Charlie Brown

1977, Paramount, 78 minutes, Color. Director: Bill Melendez. Producers: Melendez, Lee Mendelson. Written and created by Charles M. Schulz. Editors: Chuck McCann, Roger Donley.

Voices: Duncan Watson, Greg Felton, Stuart Brotman, Gail Davis, Liam Martin, Kirk Jue, Jordan Warren, Jimmy Ahrens, Melanie Kohn, Tom Muller, Bill Melendez.

The comic strip gang from "Peanuts" goes on summer vacation at Camp Remote and must win a raft race against a bunch of bullies.

True to form, Charlie Brown doesn't win, but neither do the bullies as the little bird Woodstock crosses the finish line first.

1471 Racing Fever

1964, Allied Artists, 90 minutes, Color. Director-Producer-Screenplay: William Grefe. Photography: Julio C. Chavez. Editor: Oscar Barber.

Cast: Joe Morrison, Charles G. Martin, Barbara G. Biggart, Maxine Carroll, Dave Blanchard, Ruth Nadel, John Vella, Ross Stone.

Against the backdrop of Miami's International Gran Prix boat race, a hydroplane racer watches in horror as his dad is killed by a boat driven by a playboy millionaire.

He vows revenge and has a relationship with the man's daughter.

1472 Ride the Wild Surf

1964, Columbia, 101 minutes, Color. Directors: Don Taylor, Art Napoleon. Producers-Screenplay: Art and Jo Napoleon. Photography: Joseph Biroc. Editors: Eda Warren, Howard Smith.

Cast: Fabian, Shelley Fabares, Tab Hunter, Barbara Eden, Peter Brown, Susan Hart, James Mitchum, Anthony Hayes, Roger Davis, Catherine McLeod.

Three surfers (Fabian, Hunter, Brown) arrive in Oahu for a surfing competition and romance. One of them (Brown) makes a dangerous dive in a rocky pool in an effort to make a Hawaiian legend come true and bring big waves.

1473 Roaring Speedboats

1936, Fanchon Royer Productions.

Cast: Arletta Duncan, Duncan Renaldo, William Bakewell.

The hero must overcome dirty tricks by his rival to prove the value of his new supercharger in the big speedboat race.

1474 Rockabilly Baby

1957, 20th Century-Fox, 81 minutes. Director-Producer: William F. Claxton. Screenplay: Will George, William Driskill. Photography: Walter Strenge. Editor: Robert Fritch.

Cast: Gary Vinson, Judy Busch, Virginia Field, Douglas Kennedy, Les Brown, Irene Ryan, Ellen Corby, Lewis Martin, Norman Leavitt, Gene Roth.

The son and daughter of a fan dancer encounter some difficulties in their new school when the word gets out about their mom, but the lad leads the school water polo team to victory, while the girl also achieves some success by joining clubs.

1475 Rolled Stockings

1927, Paramount, 6,249 feet. Director: Richard Rosson. Screenplay: Percy Heath. Photography: Victor Milner. Editor: Julian Johnson.

Cast: James Hall, Louise Brooks, Richard Arlen, Nanny Phillips, El Brendel, David Torrence, Chance Ward.

Upholding his family's tradition, one of two brothers makes his school's crew team, but the other doesn't. They're rivals for the love of the same girl, and the athlete causes his brother to be disgraced but later confesses.

1476 Seaweed Sandwich

1970, Merrill-Hammond Productions, Color. Producer: H. Glenn Merrill. Co-Producer: Steve Hammond. Photography-Editor: Bert Kersey.

The Over-the-Line Championships, two-man volleyball and surfing are among the beachfront activities surveyed in the San Diego area.

1477 Speed Madness

1932, Capitol, 61 minutes. Director: George Crone. Producer: Richard Talmadge.

Cast: Richard Talmadge, Lucien Littlefield, Nancy Drexel, Pat O'Malley, Huntley Gordon, Donald Keith, Charles Sellon.

A rich man's son fires the crooked manager of his dad's boat yard and designs a new kind of boat himself. A big order is dependent upon his winning a race, but those ever-present villainous gamblers make life difficult for him before the final reel.

1478 The Strawberry Statement

1970, Metro Goldwyn Mayer, 103-109 minutes, Color. Director: Stuart Hagmann. Producers: Irwin Winkler, Robert Chartoff. Screenplay: Israel Horovitz, based on a novel by James Simon Kunen. Photography: Ralph Woolsey. Editor: Marjorie Fowler, Fredric Steinkamp, Roger J. Roth.

Cast: Bruce Davison, Kim Darby, Bud Cort, Murray MacLeod, Tom Foral, Danny Goldman, Kristina Holland, Bob Balaban, Israel Horovitz, James Coco, David Dukes.

One of the youth-oriented social protest movies of the Vietnam War era features Davison as a member of the crew team at Western University who attends a demonstration mainly so he can meet girls.

He does meet Darby, a political activist who dislikes sports and who gets Davison increasingly active in the protest movement. Davison recruits the team's coxswain (Cort) and is gradually politicized until the final confrontation between National Guardsmen and the students in which he becomes fully committed.

1479 Student Tour

1934, Metro Goldwyn Mayer, 80 minutes. Director: Charles F. Riesner. Story: George Seaton, Arthur Bloch, Samuel Marx. Photography: Joseph Valentine. Editor: Frank Hull.

Cast: Jimmy Durante, Charles Butterworth, Maxine Doyle, Phil Regan, Douglas Fowley, Florine McKinney, Monte Blue, Nelson Eddy, Herman Brix, Fay McKenzie, Betty Grable.

This musical comedy is dated by the number of big-name stars buried deep in the credits. Durante portrays the trainer for a college crew team on a tour slated to end in a boat race on the Thames against an English team.

Through a series of circumstances, the team's coxswain in the big race is replaced by the heroine (Doyle).

1480 Surfari

1967, Canyon Pictures, 90 minutes, Color. Director-Producer: Milton Blair. Photography-Editor: Don Brown.

Narrator: Don Brown.

Ricky Grigg, the 1967 World Champion Surfer, is the focus of this documentary which includes a short history of surfing.

1481 Surfmovies

1981, Australian, ZDF, 46 minutes, Color. Director-Producer-Screenplay: Albie Thoms. Photography: Oscar Scherl, Keith Lambert. Editor: Lindsay Frazer.

Originally made for Australian television, it traces the history of surfing Down Under since its introduction in World War I by Hawaiian Duke Kahanamoku. It includes clips from surfing movies and interviews with many of the top personalities in the sport.

1482 The Sweetheart of Sigma Chi

1933, Monogram, 73 minutes. Director: Edwin L. Marin. Screenplay: Luther Reed, Albert E. Demond. Story: George Waggner.

Cast: Buster Crabbe, Mary Carlisle, Charles Starrett, Florence Lake, Eddie Tamblyn, Sally Starr, Mary Blackford, Tom Dugan.

The whole plot of this musical revolves around the big crew race with Starrett being unable to participate because of poor grades.

1483 The Sweetheart of Sigma Chi

1946, Monogram, 76 minutes. Director: Jack Bernhard. Producer: Jeffrey Bernard. Screenplay: Frank L. Moss, based on a story by George Waggner. Photography: L.W. O'Connell.

Cast: Phil Regan, Elyse Cox, Alan Hale, Jr., Phil Brito, Ross Hunter, Tom Harmon, Paul Guilfoyle, Anne Gillis, Edward Brophy, Fred Colby, David Holt, Marjorie Hoerner.

A remake of the 1933 musical features Hunter as the college crew team star, Regan as his older brother who runs a night spot near campus and Harmon as the coach.

Crooks Guilfoyle and Brophy attempt to fix the big rowing race.

1484 Swim, Swim, Swim

1927, Paramount, 6,124 feet. Director: Clarence Badger. Screenplay: Lloyd Corrigan. Photography: J. Roy Hunt.

Cast: Bebe Daniels, James Hall, Gertrude Ederle, Josephine Dunn, William Austin, James Mack.

In an unusual sex role reversal, a wallflower (Daniels) trains to be an athlete to win the love of a boy (Hall), the most popular guy on campus.

She becomes the butt of school jokes and unwittingly wins a channel race. When that's found out, the lad rejects her, but she gets a second chance in another swim. Gertrude Ederle appears as herself as the girl's swimming mentor.

1485 Swim Team

1979, Film Tel, 90 minutes, Color. Director-Producer-Screenplay: James Polakof. Photography: Don Cirillo. Editor: Richard Chase.

Cast: Stephen Furst, James Daughton, Richard Young, Jenny Neumann, Elise-Anne, Kim Day, Buster Crabbe, Guy Fitch.

The Whalers, a mixed-age group swimming team composed of rich kids, has lost every meet for the past seven years because, in the words of Furst, "the only thing we were proud of was our partying."

With the arrival of a new coach, the team decides to get serious for a change and try to win, particularly against the rival Sharks, coached by a man the kids call Ouch the Grouch.

Eddie Tamblyn spurs his team on in the 1933 Monogram version of The Sweetheart of Sigma Chi, which was remade in 1946. (The Museum of Modern Art/Film Stills Archive.)

man's front is stripped away more; and by the time he reaches home, he realizes he doesn't really have friends, and he's better able to face reality.

1486 The Swimmer

1968, Columbia, 94 minutes, Color. Director: Frank Perry. Producers: Perry, Roger Lewis. Screenplay: Eleanor Perry, based on a story by John Cheever. Photography: David Quaid. Editor: Sidney Katz.

Cast: Burt Lancaster, Janet Landgard, Janice Rule, Tony Bickley, Marge Champion, Nancy Cushman, John Garfield, Jr., Kim Hunter, Rose Gregorio, Charles Drake, Bernie Hamilton, Joan Rivers, Cornelia Otis Skinner.

A middle-aged Connecticut adman decides to prove he's still got that athletic vitality by swimming across the county pool by pool at the homes of supposed friends until he reaches his own home eight miles away.

At each stop, however, the

1487 Top Speed

1930, First National, 7,200 feet. Director: Mervyn Le Roy. Screenplay: Humphrey Pearson, Henry McCarty, based on a play by Bert Kalmar, Harry Ruby and Guy Bolton. Photography: Sid Hickox. Editor: Harold Young.

Cast: Joe E. Brown, Bernice Claire, Jack Whiting, Laura Lee, Frank McHugh, Rita Flynn, Edwin Maxwell, Edmund Breese, Billy Bletcher, Al Hill, Cyril Ring.

Lots of music is mixed with comedy as two vacationing bond clerks (Whiting, Brown) get mixed up with a speedboat race and with the law.

Whiting substitutes for a fired boat pilot and wins a race he was supposed to throw, while he and Brown get into a lot of hot water over a missing bond certificate.

1488 Up the Creek

1984, Orion, 99 minutes, Color. Director: Robert Butler. Producer: Michael L. Meltzer.

Screenplay: Jim Kouf. Story: Kouf, Jeff Sherman, Douglas Grossman.

Cast: Tim Matheson, Dan Monahan, Stephen Furst, Jeff East, Sandy Helberg, Blaine Novak, James B. Sikking, Jennifer Runyon, John Hillerman.

Animal House-type humor abounds at Lepetomane University, affectionately known as Lobotomy U., as the school enters a rafting competition to put itself on the map.

The members of the team are promised diplomas if they win, and with this crew, that's no easy task. They're led by Bob McGraw (Matheson) who has been expelled from 16 schools.

There are dirty tricks galore among the teams which include a crooked Ivy League team, a girl's team which is more interested in winning boys than winning the race, and a military academy team.

1489 Waves of Change

1970, MacGillivray/Freeman Films, 84-90 minutes, Color. Director - Producer - Writer - Photography: Greg MacGillivray. Editors: MacGillivray, Jim Freeman.

Narrator: MacGillivray.

Still another **Endless Summer** clone featuring surfers Mark Martinson, Nat Young, Corky Carroll, Billy Hamilton and Dave Nuuhiwa and filmed in California, Hawaii, France and Portugal.

1490 Wild, Free and Hungry

1970, Box Office International, 88 minutes, Color. Director: H.P. Edwards. Producer: Gary Graver. Photography: Rahn Vickert.

Cast: Gary Graver, Barbara Caron, Jane Tsentas, John Stone, Monica Gayle, George Todd, Rene Leeland, Butch Griswald, Michael Downing.

Graver races a boat owned by carnival man Stone but loses when the boat is rammed. The owner loses not only his carnival but his wife and money, but by the end of the film he gets the carnival back.

1491 The Winning Boat

1909, Kalem. No credits available.

Two men are the rivals for the love of a girl—again—and enter a boat race. The villainous rival attempts to blow up the hero's boat and then knocks out the good guy, but the girl takes his place at the wheel and wins the race.

1492 The Winning Stroke

1919, Fox, 5 reels. Director: E. Dillon. Scenario: E. Sedgewick, R.L. Schrock.

Cast: George Walsh, Jane McAlpine, John Leslie, William Hayes, Louis Este, William Woodford, Sidnet Marion, Byron Douglas.

When Leslie is hazed, he swears revenge on Walsh, the star rower for the college crew team; and with the help of a crooked gambler crony, gets him suspended from the team.

The hero is reinstated in time for the big race, leads his team to victory, leaps from the boat and swims to shore to beat up his adversary.

1493 A Yank at Oxford

1937, Metro Goldwyn Mayer, 100 minutes. Director: Jack Conway. Producer: Michael Balcon. Screenplay: John Mark Saunders, Leon Gordon, Sidney Gilliatt, Michael Hogan, Malcolm Stuart Boyland, Walter Ferris, George Oppenheimer. Photography: Harold Rosson. Editor: Charles Frend.

Cast: Robert Taylor, Maureen O'Sullivan, Lionel Barrymore, Vivien Leigh, Griffith Jones, Edmund Gwenn, C.F. France, Edward Rigby, Morton Selten, Claude Gillingwater.

Despite the presence of what must be a record number of screenwriters, this was a huge box office success and propelled young star Taylor to instant fame.

It was the inaugural film for Metro's British unit, and Taylor's arrival in London for the shooting caused huge mob scenes.

Metro officials were also reportedly miffed at the casting of then-virtual unknown Leigh in a major role.

The story concerns a brash American track star (Taylor) who's sent off to England with a brass band salute by his home town.

He finds it difficult to adjust to the different way of life at Oxford where he's hazed and made the butt of jokes.

Gradually, he fits in with the way of life and is a changed man. He takes the blame for someone else and is suspended from the team before the big race against Cambridge; but as is usual in this sort of thing, he's reinstated in time.

1494 You Said a Mouthful

1932, Warner Brothers, 70 minutes. Director: Lloyd Bacon. Adaptation: Robert Lord, Bolton Malley. Story: William B. Dover. Photography: Richard Towers.

Cast: Joe E. Brown, Ginger Rogers, Preston Foster, Sheila Terry, Farina, Guinn Williams, Harry Gribbon.

Another 1930's sports comedy featuring Brown as a boob who comes out on top despite himself.

Here he's an office worker who's afraid of water and can't swim, who finds himself being billed as a swimming champ and is entered in a marathon swim from Catalina Island.

He wins the race through sheer luck as he's accidentally hooked by an aquaplane.

Wheels

There's an old saying: The more things change, the more they remain the same. That certainly holds true for auto and motorcycle racing movies. The cars may be more sophisticated and the tracks more elegant, but the same formulas which were successful in the earliest days of filmmaking are still exciting audiences today.

Take the madcap adventures of **Motoring Around the World** (1908), for example, and compare the pitfalls to those in **The Great Race** and even **Safari 3000.** The locales may change, but the basic premise is the same.

All you have to do is look at the number of films which include auto chase sequences to realize that if you give audiences a good one—like **The French Connection, The Seven-Ups** or **Bullitt,** they really won't ask for much more.

Although auto racing films were popular practically from day one, a series of Paramount films starring Wallace Reid which combined comedy with action proved so popular they can be credited with inspiring the spate of racing films which were made during the 1920's.

The plots smacked of horse racing films on wheels. Almost invariably, instead of the beautiful heroine's father being a colonel whose mortgage was staked on the big horse race, he was an auto manufacturer, often with a newfangled invention, whose business depended on the outcome of the race.

Instead of the villainous mortgage holder burning down the barn, there was the rival manufacturer whose henchmen sabotaged the vehicles or ran the good guy's vehicle off the track.

When all else failed, they'd do what the villains in every other sports movie did: Kidnap the hero, who, as elsewhere, somehow always managed to escape and get to the race on time.

The Crowd Roars, a well-made 1932 racing actioner starring James Cagney, pretty much standardized the plots of the early sound era racing films, bringing in the angle of the love triangle. Not that this wasn't present during the silent era, but after the Cagney film, it would become commonplace.

The war years put a temporary end to motor racing films because of the necessity of conserving fuel. The genre made an undistinguished comeback in the early years following the war.

During the 1950's, the teenage hot rod and motorcycling films began appearing, most of them low budget productions; and they began deluging the screen with bigger budgets during the 1960's and with the major studios beginning to produce racing films en masse.

If we tried to list every film which had a drag racing or motorcycle racing sequence, it would make a book in itself. We have particularly omitted many of those low grade motorcycle cult-style films, which invariably have racing, although we have made some exceptions, such as **C.C. and Company,** which stars Joe Namath.

Some of the auto and cycle films we feel deserve mention are **American**

Graffiti and **More American Graffiti,** in which Paul Le Mat's character becomes a racing driver; Pat Boone in **State Fair; Drive a Crooked Road** (1954), in which a mechanic for racing cars joins a bank holdup; **Heartbreaker** (1983); **Way Out, Way In** from Japan; and **The Wild Rebels.**

As for bicycle racing, we have not included Jacques Tati's **Jour de Fete,** but anyone who's seen it remembers the hilarious sequence in which mailman Tati speeds past some bike racers while in the course of his rounds.

Bicycles and Others

1495 A Barrow Race (aka **Wheelbarrow Race**)

1909, French, Gaumont, 321 feet.

Participants in a wheelbarrow race go through many obstacles, including a stream which must be crossed over a narrow plank, and some of them don't make it.

1496 The Bicycle Racer

1983, Colombian, Marco Jara Film Productions, 93 minutes, Color. Director-Screenplay: Lisandro Duque Naranjo.

Three youths train hard with the hopes that one of them will be a champion bicycle racer. When a beautiful girl enters their lives, their training goes downhill, but they recover in time for the race.

1497 BMX Bandits

1983, Australian, 90 minutes, Color. Director: Brian Trenchard-Smith. Producers: Tom Broadbridge, Paul Davies. Screenplay: Patrick Edgeworth. Photography: John Seale. Editor: Alan Lake.

Cast: David Argue, John Ley, Nicole Kidman, Angelo D'Angelo, James Lugton, Brian Marshall.

A group of young BMX bike racers comes across some two-way radios used by some bank robbers to tune in on police frequencies and assist them in their heists.

The kids start selling the radios, while the crooks try to get them back. There's a lot of trick bike riding involved as the baddies chase the kids.

1498 A Boy, a Girl and a Bike

1949, British, GFD-Rank, 91 minutes. Director: Ralph Smart. Producer: Ralph Keene. Screenplay: Ted Willis. Story: Keene, John Sommerfield. Photography: Ray Elton, Frank Bassill. Editor: James Needs.

Cast: John McCallum, Honor Blackman, Patrick Holt, Diana Dors, Maurice Denham, Leslie Dwyer, Anthony Newley.

Set in Yorkshire, a wealthy sports car enthusiast turns his attentions to a pretty young cyclist, creating complications in her relationship with her boy friend, another rider for the biking club.

1499 Breaking Away

1979, 20th Century-Fox, 99 minutes, Color. Director-Producer: Peter Yates. Screenplay: Steve Tesich. Photography: Matthew F. Leonetti. Editor: Cynthia Schneider.

Cast: Dennis Christopher, Dennis Quaid, Daniel Stern, Jackie Earle Haley, Barbara Barrie, Paul Dooley, Robyn Douglas, Hart Bochner, Amy Wright.

An Academy Award winner which inspired a television series is set in Bloomington, Indiana and focuses on the efforts of a youth to win the Little 500 bike race.

It's basically a film about family relationships and class distinctions, as some "townies" who are known as cutters because their parents work in the limestone quarries are looked down upon by the snobbish college kids.

One of the townies, Dave, falls for a college girl and tries to convince her he's an Italian, because he says Italians are the best racers. He goes so far as to call his cat "Fellini" and feed it from a Cinzano dish.

His affection for the Italians dwindles after an Italian racer fouls him.

The thrilling bicycle racing scenes and the warm, basically believable relationships made **Breaking Away** a box office winner.

1500 The Cripple and the Cyclist

1906, French, 354 feet.

A cripple defeats a bicyclist in a race.

1501 The Gang That Couldn't Shoot Straight

1971, MGM, 96 minutes, Color. Director: James Goldstone. Screenplay: Waldo Salt, based on a novel by Jimmy Breslin. Photography: Owen Rolzman. Editor: Edward A. Biery.

Cast: Jerry Orbach, Leigh Taylor-Young, Robert DeNiro, Jo Van Fleet, Lionel Stander, Irving Selbst, Herve Villechaize, Joe Santos.

DeNiro is an Italian bike rider imported to the United States by gangster Kid Sally (Orbach) as part of a scheme to get mob boss Baccala (Stander) in this comedy set in Brooklyn's Red Hook section.

1502 A Push Cart Race

1908, Pathe.

Pushcart vendors stage a race through alleyways and streets and fight each other at the finish line.

1503 The Race in the Head

1974, French, Planfilm, 110 minutes, Color. Director-Writer: Joel Santoni. Photography: Jacques Loisleux.

Belgian bicycle racing star Eddie Merckz is profiled with a lot of footage of his races included.

1504 Remember When (aka **Riding High**)

1937, British, Embassy, 68 minutes. Director: David MacDonald. Producer: George King. Screenplay: H. Fowler Mear. Photography: Hone Glendinning.

Cast: Claude Dampier, John Garrick, Kathleen Gibson, Helen Haye, John Warwick, Billy Merson.

In the 19th century, a small-town blacksmith is helped during a bicycle race by an attorney, who helps him prove the merits of the new design vehicle.

1505 Repairing a Puncture

1897, British, 40 feet. Director: Walter D. Welford.

A pioneer fast motion film in which a cyclist repairs his tire.

1506 Six-Day Bike Rider

1934, Warner Brothers, 73 minutes. Director: Lloyd Bacon. Story: Earl Baldwin. Photography: Warren Lynch.

Cast: Joe E. Brown, Maxine Doyle, Frank McHugh, Gordon Westcott, Arthur Aylesworth, Lottie Williams, William Granger, Dorothy Christy, Harry Seymour.

Comedian Brown tries his hand at yet another sport as he portrays a small town passenger agent who accidentally becomes McHugh's partner in a bike race.

He gets a boost when he goes over a loose track board and starts soaring over the other bikers.

1507 The Six-Day Grind

1936, RKO Radio Pictures, 10 minutes.

Cast: Jane and Goodman Ace.

The radio team Easy Aces diagnoses the six-day bike race in this comedy short.

1508 Skid Kids

1953, British, ABFD, 65 minutes. Director: Don Chaffey. Producer: Gilbert Church. Story:

Jack Howells. Photography: S.D. Onions.

Cast: Barry McGregor, Anthony Lang, Peter Neil, Tom Wells, Angela Monk, A.E. Mathews.

The Burton Road Bullets are evicted from their practice track after they're blamed for a series of bicycle thefts from a nearby factory.

With the big junior track competition coming up, they decide to clear their names and catch the crooks themselves.

Cars and Motorcycles

1509 Across the Continent

1922, Paramount, 5,502 feet. Director: Philip E. Rosen. Screenplay: Byron Morgan. Photography: Charles Edgar Schoenbaum.

Cast: Wallace Reid, Mary MacLaren, Theodore Roberts, Sidney D'Albrook, Lucien Littlefield, Betty Francisco, Walter Long, Jack Herbert, Guy Oliver.

What Reginald Denny was to boxing films in the 1920's, Wallace Reid was for the auto racing film.

Here, he's the son of an automobile manufacturer who disobeys his dad's orders that all employees drive company cars when he buys the product of a competitor at the urging of the man's daughter.

He changes his tune when he discovers the competitor is plotting to sabotage his father's entry in the transcontinental race and drives the car himself.

1510 American Nitro

1979, K.B., 75 minutes, Color. Director-Editor: Bill Kimberlin. Producers: Jim Kimberlin, Tim Geideman.

Drivers Don Prudhomme and Tom McEwen are featured in a documentary on the California funny car racing scene.

1511 Angel on Earth (aka **Mademoiselle Ange**)

1966, French-West German, 84-90 minutes, Color. Director: Geza von Radvanyi. Producer: Artur Braunder. Screenplay: Rene Barjavel. Photography: Roger Hubert. Editor: Rene LeHenaff.

Cast: Romy Schneider, Henri Vidal, Jean Paul Belmondo, Michele Mercier, Margarette Haagen, Erika von Thellmann, Ernst Waldrow, Franz Otto Kruger.

Originally released in 1959, this didn't go into general release until seven years later when both Belmondo and Schneider reached international stardom.

Schneider is race car driver Vidal's guardian angel; and when he's thinking of suicide after a romance turns sour, she helps him win the Grand Prix de Monaco and also acts as matchmaker between him and an airline stewardess (also played by Schneider).

1512 Auto Antics

1939, Metro Goldwyn Mayer, 1 reel. Director: Edward Cahn. Producer: Jack Chertok. Screenplay: Hal Law, Robert A. McGowan. Photography: Harold Marzorati. Editor: Roy Brickner.

Spanky and Alfalfa of Our Gang enter their rocket propulsion car in the kidmobile race; and when Butch tries to sabotage the vehicle, Alfalfa winds up racing it backwards.

1513 Auto Hero

1908. No credits available.

An automobile race is won by a girl.

1514 Barney Oldfield's Race for a Life

1913, Keystone. Director: Mack Sennett. Photography: Lee Bartholomer, Walter Wright.

Cast: Barney Oldfield, Mack Sennett, Mabel Normand, Ford Sterling, Hank Mann, Al St. John.

Yes, the villains really tie the heroine to the railroad tracks in this silent comedy short, and it's up to real-life auto racer Oldfield to come to her rescue.

Villainy's afoot in Barney Oldfield's Race for a Life. (The Museum of Modern Art/Film Stills Archive.)

1515 The Big Wheel

1949, United Artists, 92 minutes. Director: Edward Ludwig. Producers: Harry M. Popkin, Samuel H. Stiefel, Mort Briskin. Screenplay: Robert Smith. Photography: Ernest Laszlo. Editor: Walter Thompson.

Cast: Mickey Rooney, Thomas Mitchell, Michael O'Shea, Mary Hatcher, Spring Byington, Lina Romay, Steve Brodie, Allen Jenkins, Richard Lane.

When the son of a former Indianapolis race driver causes the death of another driver on a western track, no one else will let him drive, so he goes east and hits the dirt tracks.

He finally gets his chance at Indy, and just when it seems he's going to win, his car catches fire and he finishes third. However, he's no longer a brash young man, and he winds up getting the girl.

1516 The Black Rider

1954, British, Butcher, 66 minutes. Director: Wolf Rilla. Producer-Screenplay: A.R. Rawlinson.

Cast: Jimmy Hanley, Rona Anderson, Leslie Dwyer, Lionel Jeffries, Beatrice Varley, Michael Golden, Kenneth Connor.

A reporter becomes involved in a motorcycle race and with a gang of smugglers which is "haunting" a castle.

1517 Blonde Comet

1941, Producers Releasing Corp., 65 minutes. Director: William Beaudine. Producer: George R. Batcheller. Screenplay: Martin Mooney. Story: Philip Juergens, Robin Daniels. Photography: Mervyn Freeman.

Cast: Barney Oldfield, Virginia Vale, Robert Kent, Vince Barrett, William Halligan, Joey Ray, Red Knight, Diana Hughes.

Racing legend Oldfield portrays himself in a fictional piece about an accessories dealer who seeks to make his fortune by installing his own carburetor in the top racing cars.

Meanwhile, the Blonde Comet (Vale) races to help build up her father's tire business and must thwart the tricks of a rival driver.

Newsreel footage of auto races is spliced into this cheapie poverty row production.

1518 Bobby Deerfield

1977, Warner Brothers, 124 minutes, Color. Director-Producer: Sydney Pollack. Screenplay: Alvin Sargent from the novel **Heaven Has No Favourites** by Erich Maria Remarque. Photography: Henri Decae. Additional Racing Photography: Tony Maylam. Editor: Fredric Steinkamp.

Cast: Al Pacino, Marthe Keller, Anny Duperey, Walter McGinn, Norman Nielsen, Stephan Meldegg, Romelo Valli, Jaime Sanchez, Guido Alberti.

A young racing car driver (Pacino) rises to international fame, but his life is empty because he's incapable of real emotions.

That's until he meets the wealthy and mysterious Keller and falls in love with her. She changes his personality; but as this is a **Love Story** clone, she's dying of an incurable disease.

1519 Born Reckless

1937, 20th Century-Fox, 60 minutes. Director: Mal St. Clair. Producer: Sol M. Wurtzel. Screenplay: John Patrick, Robert Ellis, Helen Logan, based on a story by John Andrews. Photography: Daniel B. Clark.

Cast: Rochelle Hudson, Brian Donlevy, Barton MacLane, Robert Kent, Harry Carey, Pauline Moore, Chick Chandler, William Frawley, Francis McDonald, George Wolcott.

An auto racing champion comes to the rescue of a taxi firm being menaced by racketeer MacLane who charges $5 per cab per day for "protection."

1520 Born to Speed

1947, Producers Releasing Corp., 61 minutes. Director: Edward L. Cahn. Producer: Marvin D. Stahl. Screenplay: Crane Wilbur, Scott Darling, Robert B. Churchill. Photography: Jackson Rose. Editor: W. Donn Hayes.

Cast: Johnny Sands, Terry Austin, Don Castle, Frank Orth, Geraldine Wall, Joe Haworth.

To mom's dismay, the son of a driver killed in a track crash joins his dad's mechanic (Orth) and races his father's old midget car.

He also must battle Castle for the affections of Orth's niece, and there's a finale race which features a photo finish.

1521 Buck Privates Come Home

1947, Universal-International, 77-80 minutes. Director: Charles D. Barton. Producer: Robert Arthur. Screenplay: John Grant, Frederic I. Rinaldo, Robert Lees. Story: Richard Macaulay, Bradford Ropes. Photography: Charles Van Enger, David S. Horsley.

Cast: Bud Abbott, Lou Costello, Tom Brown, Joan Fulton, Nat Pendleton, Beverly Simmons, Don Beddoe, Don Porter, Donald McBride, Rex Lease, Myron Healy, Eddie Dunn.

In this sequel to their popular **Buck Privates,** Abbott and Costello smuggle an orphan French girl into the United States at the end of World War II and, through a woman acquaintance who helps them, they meet a man who's developed a new kind of midget racing car.

With the police hot on his tail, Costello leads them on a wild chase on—and mostly off—the track in the vehicle. A short version featuring the chase scene was released as **Midget Car Maniacs.**

1522 Burn 'Em Up Barnes

1921, Mastodon Films, 5,600 feet. Directors: George Andre Beranger, Johnny Hines. Scenario: Raymond L. Schrock. Photography: Ted Beasly, Hal Young, Ned Van Buren.

Cast: Johnny Hines, Edmund Breese, George Fawcett, Betty Carpenter, J. Barney Sherry, Matthew Betts, Richard Thorpe, Julia Swayne Gordon, Dorothy Leeds.

"Burn 'Em Up" Barnes (Hines) seeks to make it on his own when his millionaire automobile manufacturer father believes he's good for nothing except for speeding in cars. He's robbed by a gang of crooks and joins some hoboes in a trip to a small town where he meets a damsel in distress.

1523 Burn 'Em Up Barnes

1934, Mascot, 12 chapters, (also 74 minutes). Directors: Colbert Clark, Armand Schaefer. Supervising Editor: Wyndham Gittens. Screenplay: Al Martin, Armand Schaefer, Barney Sarecky, Sherman Lowe. Story: John Rathmell, Colbert Clark. Photography: Ernest Miller, William Nobles. Editor: Earl Turner.

Cast: Jack Mulhall, Frankie Darro, Lola Lane, Julian Rivero, Edwin Maxwell, Jason Robards, Sr., Francis McDonald, Lloyd Whitlock, Bob Kortman, Tom London, Stanley Blystone.

Chapter titles: Chapter One: King of the Dirt Track; Chapter Two: The News Reel Murder; Chapter Three: The Phantom Witness; Chapter Four: The Celluloid Clue; Chapter Five: The Decoy Driver; Chapter Six: The Crimson Alibi; Chapter Seven: Roaring Rails; Chapter Eight: The Death Crash; Chapter Nine: The Man Higher Up; Chapter Ten: The Missing Link; Chapter Eleven: Surrounded: Chapter Twelve: The Fatal Whisper.

Racing driver "Burn 'Em Up" Barnes (Mulhall) comes to the aid of Marjorie Temple (Lane), who is being menaced by villain Drummond (Robards), who knows her land contains valuable oil deposits and who will stop at nothing to wreck her transportation business and get her to sell him the land at a low price.

Drummond will stop at nothing, including attempts to wreck a school bus full of kids.

1524 Burn 'Em Up O'Connor

1939, Metro Goldwyn Mayer, 70 minutes. Director: Edward Sedgwick. Producer: Harry Rapf. Screenplay: Milton Berlin, Byron Morgan, from "Salute to the Gods" by Sir Malcolm Campbell. Photography: Lester White. Editor: Ben Lewis.

Cast: Dennis O'Keefe, Harry Carey, Cecilia Parker, Nat Pendleton, Alan Curtis, Charley Grapewin, Tom Neal, Si Jenks.

Set at a number of tracks, including the Indianapolis Speedway and Roosevelt Field in New York, O'Keefe plays a brash daredevil race driver who joins with unscrupulous racing car manufacturer Carey, who cares nothing about who gets hurt or killed in his vehicles as long as they win.

Meanwhile, the father of a driver killed in one of Carey's cars is doping the drinks of the racers, and O'Keefe falls in love with Carey's daughter.

1525 Burning Up

1930, Paramount, 4,230-6,000 feet. Director: Phil Rosen. Producer: Joe Rock. Scenario: Frances Guihan. Story: Norman Houston. Photography: Herbert Kirkpatrick.

Cast: Richard Arlen, Mary Brian, Francis McDonald, Sam Hardy, Charles Sellon, Tully Marshall.

Arlen and McDonald portray partners who wind up deadly enemies when the latter goes to work for a crooked auto racing promoter and gets involved in fixed races.

During the finale race, Arlen must thwart McDonald's efforts to drive him off the track.

1526 C.C. and Company

1970, Avco Embassy, 94 minutes, Color. Director: Seymour Robbie. Producers: Allan Carr, Roger Smith. Photography: Charles Wheeler. Editor: Fred Chulak.

Our hero gets the trophy—and the girl—in the silent film version of Burn 'Em Up Barnes. (The Museum of Modern Art/Film Stills Archive.)

Cast: Joe Namath, Ann-Margret, William Smith, Jennifer Billingsley, Don Chastain, Teda Bracci, Tedd King, Mike Battle, Sid Haig, the C.C. Ryders.

C.C. Ryder (Namath) saves a fashion correspondent (Ann-Margret) from being raped by his motorcycle gang; and stealing a cycle to impress her, wins a lot of money in a race.

He comes into conflict with the leader of the gang (Smith) and finally challenges him to a double or nothing race.

Namath's performance in this film was one of the major reasons his acting career never got much above the ground.

1527 California Straight Ahead

1925, Universal, 7,238 feet. Director: Harry Pollard. Scenario: Harry Pollard, Byron Moran. Photography: Gilbert Warrenton.

Cast: Reginald Denny, Gertrude Olmsted, Tom Wilson, Charles Gerrard, Lucille Ward, John Steppling, Fred Esmelton.

When Denny arrives at his own wedding late and slightly drunk, the marriage is called off, and he's disowned by his family.

He gets a second chance when he rescues his fiancée and her folks from some circus animals which have escaped and gets to drive his prospective father-in-law's car in a big race.

1528 Cannonball

1976, New World, 93 minutes, Color. Director: Paul Bartel. Producer: Samuel W. Gelfman. Screenplay: Bartel, Donald C. Simpson. Photography: Tak Fujimoto. Editor: Morton Tuber.

Cast: David Carradine, Bill McKinney, Veronica Hamel, Gerrit Graham, Robert Carradine, Belinda Belaski, Judy Canova, Carl Gottlieb, Archie Hahn, Martin Scorsese.

Drivers vie for $100,000 prize money in an illegal Los Angeles to New York no-holds-barred auto race. The drivers must overcome all kinds of dirty tricks and obstacles with hero

Carradine's main rival being McKinney.

A big-budget, big-name remake, **Cannonball Run,** was released just five years later.

1529 Cannonball Run

1981, 20th Century-Fox, 95 minutes, Color. Director: Hal Needham. Producer: Albert S. Ruddy. Screenplay: Brock Yates. Photography: Michael Butler. Editors: Donn Cambern, William D. Gordean.

Cast: Burt Reynolds, Roger Moore, Farrah Fawcett, Dom DeLuise, Dean Martin, Sammy Davis, Jr., Jack Elam, Adrienne Barbeau, Terry Bradshaw, Jackie Chan, Michael Hui, Bert Convy, Jamie Farr, Peter Fonda, Jimmy "The Greek" Snyder.

Big-name stars abound and plot is kept to a minimum in this remake of **Cannonball** as drivers compete in an illegal cross-country auto race amid car crashes and stunts galore.

Everything is played for laughs, particularly by DeLuise who thinks he's a superhero.

1530 Cannonball Run II

1984, 20th Century-Fox, Color. Director: Hal Needham. Producer: Albert S. Ruddy. Screenplay: Needham, Ruddy, Harvey Miller, based on characters created by Brock Yates. Photography: Nick McLean. Editors: William Gordean, Carl Kress.

Cast: Burt Reynolds, Dom DeLuise, Dean Martin, Sammy Davis, Jr., Jamie Farr, Marilu Henner, Telly Savalas, Shirley MacLaine, Susan Anton, Sid Caesar, Jackie Chan, Tim Conway, Don Knotts, Frank Sinatra, Joe Theismann and many other big-name stars.

Reynolds and DeLuise team up again for another cross-country race with no rules. They drive a "nukemobile" and carry MacLaine and Henner, a couple of show girls, as passengers.

Among their opponents are the son of a sheik who insists on a victory to vindicate the family honor, a limousine driven by an orangutan and a host of wacky characters.

1531 The Checkered Flag

1926, Banner Productions, 6,071 feet. Director: John G. Adolfi. Adaptation: Frederick and Fanny Hatton, based on a novel by John Mersereau.

Cast: Wallace MacDonald, Elaine Hammerstein, Lionel Belmore, Robert Ober, Peggy O'Neil, Lee Shumway, Flora Maynard.

A mechanic (MacDonald) is fired by the villainous general manager (Shumway) of an auto manufacturer for being his rival for the affections of the president's daughter (Hammerstein).

The hero's new design carburetor is stolen by the general manager, but he manages to get it back. The villain, however, prevents the mechanic from getting to the race on time to prove the carburetor's value and the girl must race in his place.

1532 Checkered Flag

1963, Mercury, 83-110 minutes, Color. Director-Screenplay: William Grefe. Producer: Herb Vendig. Photography: J.R. Remy. Editor: Edward B. Mulloy.

Cast: Joe Morrison, Evelyn King, Charles J. Martin, Peggy Vendig.

The alcoholic wife of a race driver plots his death with her lover so she can get his money, but the attempts on his life fail.

Finally, during a car crash, the husband is killed; but the lover loses his legs in the crash while the wife is blinded and disfigured when she tries to save him.

1533 Checkered Flag or Crash

1976, Universal, 92 minutes, Color. Director: Alan Gibson.

Producers: Fred Weintraub, Paul Heller. Screenplay: Michael Allin. Photography: Alan Hume. Editor: Allan Holzman.

Cast: Joe Don Baker, Susan Sarandon, Larry Hagman, Allan Vint, Parnelli Jones, Logan Clark, Dana House.

In a big 1,000-mile backroads race in the Philippines, a fashion photographer (Sarandon) forces Walkaway Madden (Baker) to take her as a passenger. He got his nickname by the number of crashes he's walked away from.

Race promoter Hagman will owe $438,000 if the race is cancelled, so it goes on through landslides, floods and all kinds of detours as Baker and his former partner compete against each other.

1534 Checkpoint

1956, British, Rank, 84 minutes. Director: Ralph Thomas. Producer: Betty E. Box. Screenplay: Robin Estridge. Photography: Ernest Steward. Editor: Frederick Wilson.

Cast: Anthony Steel, Odile Versois, Stanley Baker, James Robertson Justice, Maurice Denham, Michael Medwin, Paul Muller, Anne Heywood.

An auto manufacturer sends Baker to negotiate with a designer. The envoy instead steals the blueprint, kills the watchman and causes an explosion.

He gets out of the country as the co-driver to the hero (Steel) in a big race in Italy.

1535 Corky (aka **Looking Good**)

1972, Metro Goldwyn Mayer, 88 minutes, Color. Director: Leonard Horn. Producer: Bruce Geller. Screenplay: Geller, Eugene Price. Photography: David M. Walsh. Editors: Hugh S. Fowler, Albert P. Wilson.

Cast: Robert Blake, Charlotte Rampling, Patrick O'Neal, Christopher Connelly, Pamela Payton-Wright, Ben Johnson, Laurence Luckinbill, Paul Stevens.

Geller had his name taken off as screenwriter in the final version of this tale of a racing driver (Blake) who's a loser on the track and off. It's set in Texas and Atlanta.

1536 Crack o' Dawn

1925, Rayart, 5,236 feet. Director: Albert Rogell. Scenario: Henry Roberts Symonds, John Wesley Gray. Photography: Lee Garmes.

Cast: Reed Howes, J.P. McGowan, Ruth Dwyer, Henry A. Barrows, Eddie Barry, Tom O'Brien, Ethan Laidlaw.

When partners in an auto manufacturing firm quarrel and split up, their children, who are in love with each other, build their own racing car and enter it, leading to a reconciliation between the two manufacturers.

1537 Crash Drive

1959, British, Danziger, 65 minutes. Director: Max Vernel. Producer: Edward J. Danziger. Screenplay: Brian Clemens, Eldon Howard. Photography: Jimmy Wilson.

Cast: Dermont Walsh, Wendy Williams, Ian Fleming, Anton Rogers, Grace Arnols, Ann Sears, George Roderick.

A paralyzed racing car driver feels sorry for himself until his wife returns to him. He becomes a racing team manager.

1538 The Crowd Roars

1932, Warner Brothers, 84 minutes. Director-Story: Howard Hawks. Photography: Sid Hickox, John Sietmar.

Cast: James Cagney, Joan Blondell, Ann Dvorak, Eric Linden, Guy Kibbee, Frank McHugh, Harry Hartz, Billy Arnold.

Another top-notch role for Cagney finds him as an ace driver whose downfall begins when his kid brother (Linden) joins up with him.

He gets friendly with Dvorak,

causing ill will between the brothers. When Cagney causes driver McHugh's death during a race, it crushes him, and he becomes a tramp.

During the climax at Indianapolis, however, Cagney's brother is injured, and the ex-ace gets behind the wheel once again.

Remade in 1939 as **Indianapolis Speedway.**

1539 The Crowd Roars

1932, French-German.

Cast: Jean Gabin, Helene Perdriere, Francine Mussey, Frank O'Neill.

During the 1930's, it wasn't too unusual for there to be foreign versions of popular American films. This is a European adaptation of the Cagney film, with close-ups of French and German actors being spliced in between long shots from the Warner Brothers production.

1540 The Cyclone Rider

1924, Fox, 6,472 feet. Director-Scenario: Thomas Buckingham. Story: Lincoln J. Carter. Photography: Sidney Wagner.

Cast: Reed Howes, Alma Bennett, William Bailey, Margaret McWade, Frank Beal, Eugene Pallette, Ben Deeley, Evelyn Brent, Charles Conklin, Bud Jamison.

The inventor of a new racing car carburetor will get his prospective father-in-law's approval for marriage if he wins the prize money in a race.

1541 Danger on Wheels

1940, Universal, 61 minutes. Director: Christy Cabanne. Screenplay: Maurice Tombragel, based on the story "Test Drive" by Ben Pivar. Photography: Edward Bredell.

Cast: Richard Arlen, Andy Devine, Peggy Moran, Herbert Corthell, Landers Stevens, Sandra King, Jack Arnold, Harry C. Bradley, John Holmes, Joe King.

Based on the life of thrill show driver Lucky Teeter, and including newsreel clips of him in action, it concerns an experimental motor that's blamed for the death of another driver.

1542 Daredevil

1971, Visualscope, 79 minutes, Color. Director: Robert W. Stringer. Producer: Marvin H. Green. Screenplay: Robert Walsh.

Cast: George Montgomery, Terry Moore, Bill Kelly, Frank Logan.

A race champ causes the death of a fellow driver. The dead man's sister follows him everywhere, causing him bad luck, eventually forcing him to become a drug runner for her undertaker pal.

1543 Daredevil Drivers

1938, Warner Brothers, 60 minutes. Director: B. Reeves Eason. Screenplay: Sherman Lowe. Story: Charles Condon. Photography: Ted McCord. Editor: Harold McLernon.

Cast: Dick Purcell, Gloria Blondell, Gordon Oliver, Charles Foy, Al Hernman, Ferris Taylor, Beverly Roberts.

Racing action mixes with comedy as a track driver is suspended and goes to work for a bus firm.

1544 Daredevils of Earth

1936, British, Hallmark, 57 minutes, Director: Bernard Vorhaus.

Cast: Ida Lupino, Cyril McLaglen, John Loder, Marie Ault, Moore Mariott, George Merritt, Sam Wilkinson.

A champ dirt track cycle racer (McLaglen) gets into a lot of hot water when he causes a rival to crack up on the track.

1545 Dead Man's Curve

1928, FBO Pictures, 5,511 feet. Director: Richard Rosson. Editor-Adaptation: Ewart Adamson. Photography: Phillip Tannura.

Cast: Douglas Fairbanks, Jr., Sally Blane, Charles Byer, Arthur Metcalfe, Kit Guard, James Mason, Byron Douglas.

A racing driver (Fairbanks) blames a faulty engine for his third place finish in a race, but his rival (Byer) for a girl's love blames cowardice. The driver quits and redesigns the engine on his own to prove he was right.

1546 Death Drives Through

1935, British, Clifford Taylor, 63 minutes. Director: Edward L. Cahn. Screenplay: Gordon Wellesley. Story: Katherine Strueby, John Huston.

Cast: Dorothy Bouchier, Robert Douglas, Miles Mander, Percy Walsh, Frank Atkinson, Lillian Gunns.

Another racing romance triangle betweeen the good guy driver and the bad guy driver for the auto firm president's daughter.

1547 Death Is a Number

1951, British, Delman, 50 minutes. Director: Horace Shepherd. Producer: Phyllis Shepherd. Screenplay: Charles H. Shaw. Photography: Phil Grindrod, Harry Long.

Cast: Terence Alexander, Lesley Osmond, Denis Webb, Ingeborg Wells, Peter Gawthorne, Isobel George.

The death of a racing driver ends a curse that lasted 300 years.

1548 Death Race 2000

1975, New World, 78 minutes, Color. Director: Paul Bartel. Producer: Roger Corman. Screenplay: Charles B. Griffith, Robert Thom. Photography: Tak Fujimoto. Editor: Tina Hirsch.

Cast: David Carradine, Simone Griffith, Sylvester Stallone, Louisa Moritz, Mary Woronov.

In the year 2000, the participants gather for the opening of the 20th transcontinental road race. The participants include Frankenstein (Carradine), Machine Gun Joe (Stallone) and such sterling characters as Mathilda the Hun, Nero the Hero and Calamity Jane.

The drivers rack up points by the number of pedestrians they run over. The U.S. President says "I give you what you want" as he starts the race via television.

At one point along the route, the hospital lines up elderly patients in wheelchairs into the cars' path, but Frankenstein goes for the doctors instead.

One by one, however, the drivers are eliminated by an underground group opposing the races, and it soon becomes clear that Frankenstein's new female navigator is in with them.

1549 Deathsport

1978, New World, 83 minutes, Color. Directors: Henry Suso, Allen Arkush. Producer: Roger Corman. Screenplay: Suso, Donald Stewart. Story: Francis Doel. Photography: Gary Graver. Editor: Larry Beck.

Cast: Richard Lynch, David Carradine, Claudia Jennings.

In the distant future, the most popular sport is played in a giant stadium and in an atmosphere reminiscent of the days of the Roman gladiators.

Engaged in a battle to the death are the villainous Statesmen on their Death Machine motorcycles and the virtuous Ranger Guides who live by a special code.

1550 Le Depart

1968, Belgian, Pathe Contemporary, 89 minutes. Director: Jerzy Skolimowski. Producer: Bronka Ricquier. Screenplay: Skolimowski, Andrzej Kostenko. Photography: Willy Kurant. Editor: Bob Wade.

Cast: Jean-Pierre Leaud, Catherine Duport, Paul Roland, Jacqueline Bir, John Dobrynine, Georges Aubrey, Maxane.

A hairdresser's assistant plans to drive a Porsche in a big race, but his employer takes the car out himself for the weekend.

After numerous other developments, the young hero sleeps with a girl and winds up missing the race.

1551 Devil at Your Heels

1982, Canadian, National Film Board of Canada, 102 minutes, Color. Director-Editor: Robert Fortier. Screenplay: David Wildson, Charles Lazer. Photography: Barry Perles.

Daredevil driver Ken Carter, known as the "Mad Canadian," plans for several years to jump across a mile-wide section of the St. Lawrence River in a special rocket-powered vehicle.

The documentary details the financial arrangements and other behind-the-scenes activities and culminates in Carter's unsuccessful jump.

1552 The Devil's Hairpin

1957, Paramount, 83 minutes. Director-Producer: Cornel Wilde. Screenplay: James Edmiston, Wilde. Photography: Daniel L. Fapp. Editor: Floyd Knudtson.

Cast: Cornel Wilde, Jean Wallace, Arthur Franz, Mary Astor, Paul Fix, Larry Pennell, Gerald Milton, Ross Bagdasarian.

A former auto racing champ who caused his younger brother to crash is persuaded to try a comeback.

1553 Did You Hear the One About the Traveling Saleslady?

1968, Universal, 97 minutes, Color. Director: Don Weis. Producer: Si Rose. Screenplay: John Fenton Murray. Story: Jim Fritzell, Everett Greenbaum. Photography: Bud Thackery. Editor: Edward Haire.

Cast: Phyllis Diller, Bob Denver, Joe Flynn, Eileen Wesson, Jeanette Nolan, Paul Reed, Bob Hastings, David Hartman, Eddie Quillan, Eddie Ness.

Set in 1910 Kansas, this remake of 1956's **The First Travelling Saleslady** features Diller as the piano saleslady and Denver as a kooky inventor who destroys her piano.

The finale has Diller racing a wood-burning auto in the county fair to raise mortgage money.

1554 Dirt

1979, American Cinema Releasing, Inc., 95 minutes, Color. Directors: Eric Karson, Cal Naylor. Producers: Allan F. Bodoh, John Patrick Graham. Screenplay: S.S. Schweitzer, Bud Freidgen, Tom Madigan. Photography: R.R. Young. Editor-Associate Producer: Skeeter McKitterick.

Cast: R.R. Young, Parnelli Jones, Rick Mears, Mickey Thompson, Bobby Ferro, Malcolm Smith.

Off-road racing is featured in this documentary as motorcycles, tractors and all kinds of other vehicles race over dirt, swamp, snow and whatever.

1555 Dirty Hero (aka **The Last Hero**)

1983, Japanese, Toei, 102 minutes, Color. Director-Producer: Haruki Kadokawa. Screenplay: Shoichi Maruyama. Photography: Sezo Sengen. Editor: Kioaki Saito.

Cast: Masao Kusakari, Atsuko Asano, Hiroshi Katsuno, Yutaka Hayashi, Eji Okada, Rebecca Holden.

A motorcycle racer is able to maintain a rich lifestyle by living off numerous women, although he's constantly worried about his chances of being killed on the track.

1556 Dirty Mary, Crazy Larry

1974, 20th Century-Fox, 93 minutes, Color. Director: John Hough. Producer: Norman T. Herman. Screenplay: Leigh Chapman, Antonio Santean, based on the novel **The Chase** by Richard Unekis. Photography: Mike Margulies. Editor: Chris Holmes.

Cast: Peter Fonda, Susan George, Adam Roarke, Vic Morrow, Ken Tobey, Roddy McDowell.

A wild and destructive car chase across California ensues when two men steal $150,000 to buy a competition car.

1557 Eat My Dust

1976, New World, 89 minutes,

Color. Director-Screenplay: Charles D. Griffith. Producer: Roger Corman. Photography: Eric Saarinen. Editor: Tina Hirsch.

Cast: Ron Howard, Christopher Norris, Warren Kemmerling, Dave Madden, Robert Broyles, Evelyn Russel.

Tired of changing the toilet paper at the race course, Howard steals a racing car from the track in order to impress a girl and in a cross-country race proves he can outdrive them all.

1558 Evel Knievel

1971, Feature Corp., 90 minutes, Color. Director: Marvin Chomsky. Producers: Joe Solomon, George Hamilton. Screenplay: John Milius, Alan Caillou. Photography: David Walsh. Editor: Jack McSweeney.

Cast: George Hamilton, Sue Lyon, Bert Freed, Rod Cameron, Dub Taylor, Ron Masak, Hal Baylor.

The life of the great daredevil driver is traced from the time he sweet talks his way into a rodeo owned by Taylor to his spectacular motorcycle jumps.

Hamilton portrays him as a man who hates the violence associated with motorcycling.

1559 Excuse My Dust

1920, Paramount, 5 reels. Director: Sam Wood. Adaptation: Will M. Ritchey.

Cast: Wallace Reid, Tully Marshall, Theodore Roberts, Ann Little, Guy Oliver, Otto Brower, James Gordon, Walter Long, Jack Herbert, Fred Huntley.

Another of the Wallace Reid racing series finds him married to the daughter of an auto manufacturer with both wanting him to quit racing.

His father-in-law gets a judge to suspend his driving license for speeding, but Reid races anyway and his wife leaves him.

The finale has he and his father-in-law both getting into racing cars to prevent each other from being hurt by an unscrupulous rival.

1560 Fast and Furious

1927, Universal, 5,684 feet. Director: Melville W. Brown. Adaptation: Raymond Cannon. Story: Reginald Denny. Photography: Arthur Todd.

Cast: Reginald Denny, Barbara Worth, Claude Gillingwater, Armand Kaliz, Lee Moran, Charles K. French, Wilson Benge.

Lighthearted comedy in which Denny, for the love of a girl, impersonates a champion race driver and is forced to compete in a race.

1561 Fast and the Furious

1954, American Releasing Corp., 73 minutes. Directors: Edwards Sampson, John Ireland. Producer: Roger Corman. Screenplay: Jerome Odium, Jean Howell. Story: Corman. Photography: Floyd Crosby. Editor: Edwards Sampson.

Cast: John Ireland, Dorothy Malone, Bruce Carlisle, Marshall Bradford, Jean Howell, Larry Thor, Robin Morse, Bruno De Sota, Iris Adrian.

Framed for murder, Ireland commandeers Malone's car and enters it in a race that will take him across the border into Mexico.

1562 Fast Charlie ... The Moonbeam Rider

1979, Universal, 99 minutes, Color. Director: Steve Carver. Producers: Roger Corman, Saul Krugman. Screenplay: Michael Gleason. Story: Ed Spielman, Howard Friedlander. Photography: William Birch. Editors: Tony Redman, Eric Orner.

Cast: David Carradine, Brenda Vaccaro, L.Q. Jones, R.G. Armstrong, Terry Kiser, Jesse Vint, Noble Willingham, Whit Clay, Ralph James, Bill Hartman, Stephen Ferry.

World War I vet Carradine rounds up his old Army buddies for the first Transcontinental

Motorcycle Race from St. Louis to San Francisco in the 1920's.

When he's doublecrossed by waitress Vaccaro, he's forced to take her and her son on the road with him to get money to enter the race; and then once he's in it, he's got to thwart dirty tricks by his opponents.

1563 Fast Company

1979, Canadian, Danton, 90 minutes, Color. Director: David Cronenberg. Producers: Michael Lebowitz, Peter O'Brien, Courtney Smith. Screenplay: Cronenberg, Smith, Phil Savath. Story: Alan Treen. Photography: Mark Irwin. Editor: Ron Sanders.

Cast: William Smith, John Saxon, Claudia Jennings, Nicholas Campbell, Don Francks, Cedric Smith, Judy Foster, George Buza.

When his oil company sponsor opts for a younger driver, a champion drag racer retaliates by stealing a car.

1564 Fever Heat

1968, Paramount, 109 minutes, Color. Director-Producer: Russel S. Doughten, Jr. Screenplay: Henry Gregor Felson, based on a novel by Angus Vickier. Photography: Gary Young. Editor: Tom Boutross.

Cast: Nick Adams, Jeannine Riley, Norman Alden, Vaughn Taylor, Daxson Thomas, Robert Broyles, Al Ruscio.

Ex-driver Ace Jones (Adams) helps Riley's garage get back on its feet before returning to driving and getting into a rivalry over a girl.

1565 Fireball 500

1966, American-International, 92 minutes, Color. Director: William Asher. Producers: Samuel Z. Arkoff, James H. Nicholson. Screenplay: Asher, Leo Townsend. Photography: Floyd Crosby. Editor: Fred Feitshans.

Cast: Frankie Avalon, Annette Funicello, Fabian, Chill Wills, Harvey Lembeck, Julie Parrish, Douglas Henderson, Baynes Barron, Sandy Reed, Mike Nader, Vin Scully.

After Avalon wins a race against local champion Fabian, Parrish gets him to drive a cross-country night race that's really a front for a South Carolina moonshine operation.

Federal agents blackmail him into helping them break the lid off the operation which is run by Lembeck.

1566 Fireball Jungle

1968, Americana, 96 minutes, Color. Director: José Priete (Joseph Prieto). Producer: G.B. Roberts. Screenplay: Harry Whittington. Photography: Clifford Poland.

Cast: John Russell, Lon Chaney, Jr., Randy Kirby, Alan Mixon, Chuck Daniel, Nancy Donohue, Vicki Nunis.

Kirby, whose brother was killed by thug Mixon, races at a Florida track under an alias in the hopes of implicating the killer in some sort of crime. Mixon has been hired by Russell to help him gain control of a number of tracks.

Chaney portrays a junk yard owner who is forced to fence a stolen car and who winds up being set afire by the baddies.

1567 The First Auto

1927, Warner Brothers, 6,767 feet. Director: Roy Del Ruth. Scenario: Anthony Coldewey. Story: Darryl Francis Zanuck. Photography: David Abel.

Cast: Barney Oldfield, Patsy Ruth Miller, Charles Emmett Mack, Russell Simpson, Paul Kruger, Frank Campeau, Douglas Gerrard.

A man who loves horses and detests the new horseless carriages fiddles with a racing car without knowing that his son is planning to use it in a race.

1568 Five the Hard Way

1969, Crown International, 82 minutes, Color. Director: Gus

Trikonis. Producer: Ross Hagen. Screenplay: Tony Houston. Story: Larry Billman. Photography: Jon Hall. Editor: Pat Somerset.

Cast: Ross Hagen, Diane McBain, Michael Pataki, Claire Polan, Richard Merrifield, Edward Parrish, Michael Graham.

Murder and rape take center stage in a low-grade actioner about the motorcycle racing circuit.

1569 The Flaw

1955, British, Cybex, 61 minutes. Director: Terence Fisher. Screenplay: Brandon Fleming.

Cast: John Bentley, Donald Houston, Rona Anderson, Tonia Berne, Doris Yorke, J. Trevor Davies, Cecilia Cavendish.

An auto racer's scheme to murder his wife is discovered by an attorney.

1570 For Pete's Sake!

1966, World-Wide, 90 minutes, Color. Director-Screenplay: James F. Collier. Photography: Richard Batcheller. Editor: Eugene Pendleton.

Cast: Billy Graham, Robert Sampson, Pippa Scott, Johnny Jensen, Al Freeman, Jr., Sam Groom, John Milford.

A family is terrorized by a motorcycle gang on their way back from a Billy Graham Crusade which has changed their lives. The father of the family accepts a challenge to race over mountain trails.

1571 Funny Car Summer

1973, Ambassador, 86 minutes, Color. Director: Ron Phillips. Producers: Ron Phillips, John Brooks. Concept: Alex Phillips. Photography: José Mignone. Editor: Lloyd Nelson.

A summer in the life of racer Jim Dunn as he travels around the country competing in drag races with his unusual rear engine car.

There's also a segment on kids' bike racing.

1572 Genevieve

1953, British, Universal-International, 86 minutes. Director-Producer: Henry Cornelius. Screenplay: William Rose. Photography: Christopher Challis. Editor: Clive Donner.

Cast: John Gregson, Dinah Sheridan, Kenneth More, Kay Kendall, Geoffrey Kern, Harold Siddons, Joyce Grenfell, Arthur Wontner.

Vintage automobiles are the real stars in a pleasant comedy about the rivalry between two couples in the annual London-Brighton rally for antique cars.

1573 Gentlemen of Nerve (aka **Some Nerve, Charlie at the Races**)

1914, Keystone, 1 reel. Director-Scenario: Charlie Chaplin.

Cast: Charlie Chaplin, Mabel Normand, Chester Conklin, Mack Swain, Phyllis Allen, Charley Chase, Slim Summerville.

Conklin takes Mabel to the auto races while Chaplin and Swain sneak in—although Swain got stuck on the way in. The four create a big ruckus in the stands.

1574 Grand Prix

1934, British, Columbia, 71 minutes. Director-Screenplay: St. John L. Clowes. Producer: S. Stock.

Cast: Milton Rosmer, Peter Gawthorne, John Stuart, Jillian Sande, Wilson Coleman, Lawrence Anderson.

When one of two racing car partners is killed testing a new kind of vehicle, it's up to the other's son to prove its value and win the hand of the beautiful maiden as well as the big race.

1575 Grand Prix

1966, Metro Goldwyn Mayer, 179 minutes, Color. Cinerama. Director: John Frankenheimer. Producer: Edward Lewis. Screenplay: Robert Alan Arthur. Photography: Lionel Linde.

Cast: James Garner, Eva

Marie Saint, Yves Montand, Toshiro Mifune, Brian Bedford, Jessica Walter, Antonio Sabato, Francoise Hardy, Adolfo Celi, Claude Dauphin, Genevieve Page.

Winner of Oscars for Best Sound and Best Sound Effects, **Grand Prix** follows the lives of four racing drivers as they compete in the nine-race World Championship of Drivers in Europe.

During a race in Monaco, Garner causes injuries to another driver and agrees to race for Japanese industrialist Mifune. Montand, in the meantime, skids on a Belgian track and kills two youngsters, while off the track there are a number of love affairs going on.

1576 Grandview U.S.A.

1984, Warner Brothers, Color. Director: Randal Kleiser. Producers: William Warren Blaylock, Peter W. Rea. Screenplay: Ken Hixon.

Cast: Jamie Lee Curtis, C. Thomas Howell, Patrick Swayze, Jennifer Jason Leigh, Troy Donahue.

A small-town Illinois boy wants to study dolphins in Florida instead of staying in the Midwest as his parents wish. When he starts making love to his girl friend in his father's car, the vehicle slides into the mud, and the two seek help at a demolition derby run by Curtis.

Curtis and the lad strike up a relationship after the boy thwarts a plot by his dad to force her off the property so a golf course can be built. Their relationship hurts the derby's ace driver, who has long loved Curtis and whose no-good wife is constantly cheating on him.

The youth (Howell) joins the derby but eventually has a reconciliation with his family, as, in true Hollywood fashion, all the loose ends are tied up.

1577 Greased Lightning

1919, Paramount, 5 reels. Director: Jerome Stern (some sources list it as Storm). Presented by: Thomas Ince. Screenplay: Julian Josephson. Photography: Chester Lyons.

Cast: Charles Ray, Wanda Hawley, Robert McKim, Willis Marks, Bert Woodruff, John P. Lockney, Otto Horfman.

A youth turns an old car into a racer, but can't convince a banker he's worthy of his daughter's hand until he uses the vehicle to track down a bank robber.

1578 Greased Lightning

1977, Warner Brothers, 96 minutes, Color. Director: Michael Schultz. Producer: Hannah Weinstein. Screenplay: Kenneth Vose, Lawrence DuKose. Photography: George Bouillet.

Cast: Richard Pryor, Beau Bridges, Pam Grier, Cleavon Little, Vincent Gardenia, Richie Havens, Julian Bond, Earl Hindman, Minnie Gentry, Lucy Saroyan, Noble Willingham.

The first black stock car champion, Wendell Scott, had a hard time rising to the top as this biography shows, spanning 25 years from his release from the army after World War II.

Besides the normal pressures of trying to win, Scott has to battle prejudice as he attempts to break the color barrier. He's befriended by Bridges, another driver.

Bridges would later help a woman break the stock car barrier in **Heart Like a Wheel.**

Greased Lightning culminates in Scott's victory in a 1971 championship race.

1579 The Great Race

1965, Warner Brothers, 150-180 minutes, Color. Director: Blake Edwards. Producer: Martin Jurow. Screenplay: Arthur Ross. Story: Edwards, Ross. Photography: Russell Harlan.

Cast: Tony Curtis, Jack Lemmon, Natalie Wood, Peter

Falk, Keenan Wynn, Arthur O'Connell, Vivian Vance, Dorothy Provine, Larry Storch, Ross Martin, Denver Pyle.

A 1908 New York to Paris auto race is the setting for wild comedy as the villainous Prof. Fate (Lemmon) matches wits and skill with his chief opponent, The Great Leslie (Curtis).

After most of the other cars are booby-trapped by Fate, Wood's car breaks down, and she's picked up by Curtis.

One sequence has them drifting across the ice to get from Alaska to Russia.

The film won an Oscar for Best Sound Effects. Most of the prints released to theaters were 150-157 minutes.

1580 The Green Helmet

1961, British, Metro Goldwyn Mayer, 88 minutes. Director: Michael Forlong. Producer: Charles Vetter. Screenplay: Jon Cleary. Photography: Geoffrey Faithfull. Editor: Frank Clarke.

Cast: Bill Travers, Ed Begley, Sidney James, Nancy Walters, Ursula Jeans, Megs Jenkins, Sean Kelly, Tuttle Lemkow, Gordon Tanner, Ferdy Mayne, Peter Collingwood.

A number of top racing drivers appear as themselves as a veteran driver finds his courage sapped by a number of recent crashes.

He's under pressure to retire not only by his girl friend but by his younger brother who wants to race but can't until his sibling retires.

Set in Italy, France and Florida, the older brother is hired by a man who wants to promote his tires.

1581 Gumball Rally

1976, Warner Brothers, 106 minutes, Color. Director-Producer: Chuck Bail. Screenplay: Leon Capetano. Story: Capetano, Bail.

Cast: Michael Sarrazin, Norman Burton, Gary Busey, John Durren, Susan Flannery, Harvey Jason, Tim McIntire, Joanne Nail, Raul Julia.

Another comedy about an illegal cross-country auto race, along the lines of **Cannonball** and **Cannonball Run**, finds Sarrazin and McIntire the main rivals in a drive from Manhattan to Long Beach, California.

Their mutual foe is cop Burton who wants to halt the illegal race.

1582 Heart Like a Wheel

1983, 20th Century-Fox, 113 minutes, Color. Director: Jonathan Kaplan. Producer: Charles Roven. Screenplay: Ken Friedman. Photography: Tak Fujimoto. Editor: O. Nicholas Brown.

Cast: Bonnie Bedelia, Beau Bridges, Lee Rossi, Hoyt Axton, Bill McKinney, Anthony Edwards, Dean-Paul Martin, Paul Bartel.

The struggle of three-time National Hot Rod Association champ Shirley "Cha Cha" Muldowney to break the sex barrier is told.

Married to a Schenectady, N.Y. mechanic and the mother of a son, she gets the racing bug and wants to turn pro.

When she has difficulty getting other drivers to sign the required papers for her to qualify, she's helped out by Connie Kalitta (Bridges); and as her career begins to soar, she separates from her husband who can't take the idea of her being a pro.

Although the film was generally well-received by critics, 20th Century-Fox took a long time in releasing it.

1583 Hearts and Sparks

1916, Keystone/Triangle.

Cast: Hank Mann, Bobbie Vernon, Nick Cogley, Billie Bennett, Tom Kennedy, Joe Lee.

Hiss the villain who holds the mortgage and demands the fair maiden marry him or else. Cheer the handsome hero as he invents a new kind of sparkplug to try in the big race.

Hiss the villain again as he tries all kinds of dirty tricks to stop our hero. We think you know how it ends.

1584 Heights of Danger

1953, British, ABPC, 60 minutes. Director: Peter Bradford. Producer: Howard Thomas. Screenplay: Betty Davies. Photography: Reg W. Cavender. Editor: Alex Milner-Gardner.

Cast: Basil Appleby, Sebastian Cabot, Freda Bamford, Wilfred Downing, Christopher Cabot, Richard Goolden, Jack Melford, Roger Snowden.

Not released in the United States until 1962, this action programmer finds a garage owner competing in an Alpine auto race for the cash he needs for his business to survive.

He must put up with a number of sabotage attempts engineered by a man who's out to buy him out.

1585 Hell on Wheels

1967, Crown International, 96 minutes, Color. Director: Will Zens. Producer: Robert Patrick. Screenplay: Wesley Cox. Photography: Leif Rise.

Cast: Marty Robbins, John Ashley, Gigi Perreau, Robert Dornan, Connie Smith, Robert Foulk, Frank Geistle.

Country music star Robbins stars as a racer with two brothers: One is a mechanic jealous of his brother's fame, and the other is a revenuer.

The mechanic winds up driving against his brother and getting involved with some moonshiners.

1586 Herbie Goes Bananas

1980, Buena Vista, 100 minutes, Color. Director: Vincent McEveety. Producer: Ron Miller.

Screenplay: Don Tait, based on characters created by Gordon Buford. Photography: Frank Phillips. Editor: Gordon D. Brenner.

Cast: Cloris Leachman, Charles Martin Smith, Joaquin Garay, III, John Vernon, Stephan W. Burns, Elyssa Davalos, Harvey Korman, Richard Jaeckel, Alex Rocco.

The fourth and last in the "Love Bug" series about that lovable racing Volkswagen finds Smith and Burns driving Herbie to a Brazilian road race (never shown).

They become involved with a band of smugglers, a Mexican orphan and a bullfight.

1587 Herbie Goes to Monte Carlo

1977, Buena Vista, 105 minutes, Color. Director: Vincent McEveety. Producer: Ron Miller. Screenplay: Arthur Alsberg, Don Nelson, based on characters created by Gordon Buford. Photography: Leonard J. South. Editor: Cotton Warburton.

Cast: Dean Jones, Don Knotts, Julie Sommars, Jacques Marin, Roy Kinnear, Bernard Fox, Eric Braeden, Xavier Saint Macary, Francois Laland.

Herbie the Love Bug is reunited with his former owner Jones and is entered in the Paris-Monte Carlo rally. Meanwhile, some thieves drop a gem stolen from a museum in Herbie's gas tank.

En route, the Volkswagen falls in love with a Lancia named Giselle and driven by Sommars, who's out to prove she's as good a driver as any of the men.

Knotts is Herbie's loony mechanic.

1588 Herbie Rides Again

1974, Buena Vista, 88 minutes, Color. Director: Robert Stevenson. Producer: Bill Walsh. Screenplay: Walsh. Photography: Frank Phillips. Editor: Cotton Warburton.

Cast: Helen Hayes, Ken Berry, Stefanie Powers, Keenan Wynn, Huntz Hall, Ivon Barry, Dan Tobin, Vito Scotti.

There's no auto racing involved in this first sequel to **The Love Bug** as Hayes refuses to sell her property to unscrupulous Wynn, who wants to build the world's tallest building on the site.

1589 High Gear

1933, Goldsmith, 65 minutes. Director: Leigh Jason. Story: Rex Taylor, Leigh Jason, Charles Saxton. Photography: Edward Kill.

Cast: James Murray, Joan Marsh, Jackie Searl, Eddie Lambert, Theodor Von Eltz, Ann Brody, Mike Donlin, Lee Moran.

High Gear (Murray) feels responsible for the death of his racing partner in a race, so he helps raise the man's crippled child while also romancing a girl reporter.

1590 High Speed

1932, Columbia, 60 minutes. Director: D. Ross Lederman. Story: Harold Shumate.

Cast: Buck Jones, Loretta Sayers, Wallace MacDonald, Mickey McClure, Ed La Saint, William Walling, Ward Bond, Pat O'Malley.

Cowboy star Jones this time is a cop who fights off the villains in police car chases and on the racetrack as he battles a crime syndicate.

During a race, one of the villains tries to drive him off the track by locking wheels with him.

1591 Hips, Hips, Hooray

1934, RKO Radio Pictures, 68 minutes. Director: Mark Sandrich. Story, Music, Lyrics: Harry Ruby, Bert Kalmar. Photography: David Abel.

Cast: Bert Wheeler, Robert Woolsey, Ruth Etting, Thelma Todd, Dorothy Lee, George Meeker, James Burtis, Matt Briggs, Spencer Charters.

Wheeler and Woolsey are lipstick salesmen who meet a beauty shop owner and become involved in a crazy cross-country automobile race and some stolen bonds.

During the race, the car does some ski jumps and floats over other cars with the help of helium in the tires.

1592 Hot Rod

1950, Monogram, 61 minutes. Director: Lewis D. Collins. Producer: Jerry Thomas. Screenplay: Dan Ullman. Photography: Gilbert Warrenton. Editor: Rose Livingston.

Cast: James Lydon, Art Baker, Gil Stratton, Jr., Gloria Winters, Myron Healy, Jack Blodgett, Jean Dean, Dennis Moore, William Vincent.

Lydon, who formerly played in the Henry Aldrich comedy series, portrays the son of a judge who tries to prove the need for a supervised track where kids can race their cars safely instead of on the streets.

After a number of difficulties, the kids get their track when a stick-up man is chased down.

1593 Hot Rod Action

1969, Cinerama Releasing, 76 minutes, Color. Director-Producer-Writer: Gene McCabe. Photography: Villis Lapeniecks, Mario Tosi, William Zsigmond. Editor: Anthony M. Lanza.

Narrator: Keith Jackson.

Nearly every aspect of auto racing is covered in this documentary which features many of the top drivers, including Craig Breedlove.

1594 Hot Rod Gang (aka **Fury Unleashed**)

1958, American-International, 71 minutes. Director: Lew Landers. Producers: Lou Rusoff, Buddy Rogers. Screenplay: Rusoff. Photography: Floyd Crosby. Editor: Robert S. Eisen.

Cast: John Ashley, Jody Fair, Steve Drexel, Henry McCann, Maureen Arthur, Gloria Grant, Doodles Weaver, Russ Bender, Kay Wheeler, Lester Dorr, Dub Taylor.

The heir to a fortune must hide his love for hot rods from his two rich aunts. He secretly puts together a rock and roll group and a hot rod club and tries to raise money to build a car he wants to enter in a national meet.

1595 Hot Rod Girl

1956, American-International, 79 minutes. Director: Leslie Martinson. Producer: Norman Herman. Screenplay: John McGreevey. Photography: Sam Leavitt. Editor: Leon Barsha.

Cast: Chuck Connors, Lori Nelson, John Smith, Frank Gorshin, Roxanne Arlen, Carolyn Kearney, Ed Reider, Del Erickson, Fred Essler, Russ Thorson, Mark Andrews.

Cop Connors tries to put an end to street drag racing and such by having a drag strip for the kids.

He enlists the support of teenager Smith, but when a newcomer (Andrews) arrives and causes a whole mess of trouble, Connors' crusade is dealt a major setback.

1596 Hot Rod Hullabaloo

1966, Allied Artists, 81 minutes. Director: William T. Naud. Producers: Naud, Martin L. Low. Screenplay: Stanley Schneider. Photography: Thomas E. Spalding. Editor: Ed Frank Toth.

Cast: John Arnold, Arlen Dean Snyder, Kendra Kerr, Ron Cummins, Val Bisoglio, Marsha Mason, William Hunter.

A youth enters a demolition derby to raise money for college but must face the opposition of residents who are against it and a brutal rival who's already caused the death of another driver.

1597 How Isaacs Won the Cup

1906, British, Norwood, 200 feet. Director: Harold Horgh.

A Jewish man wins an auto race but is stripped and thrown into a river.

1598 Indianapolis Speedway

1939, Warner Brothers, 82 minutes. Director: Lloyd Bacon. Producer: Sid Hickox. Screenplay: Sig Herzig, Wally Klein. Story: Howard and William Hawks. Editor: William Holmes.

Cast: Pat O'Brien, John Payne, Ann Sheridan, Gale Page, Frank McHugh, Grace Stafford, Granville Bates, John Ridgely, Regis Toomey, John Harron, Ed McWade, William Davidson.

A remake of **The Crowd Roars** finds O'Brien in Cagney's role as a crack driver who tries to cure younger sibling Payne of his racing fever.

In trying to teach him a lesson, O'Brien causes the death of pal McHugh (who also got killed in the original) and winds up on skid row because of remorse.

As in the original, when the younger brother is injured in the big finale race, O'Brien takes his place behind the wheel.

1599 Jalopy

1953, Monogram, 62 minutes. Director: William Beaudine. Producer: Ben Schwalb. Screenplay: Tim Ryan, Jack Crutcher. Photography: Harry Neumann. Editor: William Austin.

Cast: Leo Gorcey, Huntz Hall, Bernard Gorcey, Bob Lowry, Leon Belasco, Richard Benedict, Jane Easton, Murray Alper, David Condon, Tom Hanlon, Mona Knox.

Bowery Boys nonsense in which Hall accidentally discovers a formula which makes cars go faster and then must protect it from crooks.

In the big race, the Boys' car is raced backwards.

1600 Johnny Dark

1954, Universal-International, 85 minutes, Color. Director: George Sherman. Producer: William Alland. Screenplay: Franklin Coen. Photography: Carl Guthrie. Editor: Edward Curtis.

Cast: Tony Curtis, Piper Laurie, Don Taylor, Paul Kelly, Ilka Chase, Sidney Blackmer, Ruth Hampton, Russell Johnson, Joseph Sawyer, Scatman Crothers, Pierre Watkin.

Curtis is an auto plant engineer who winds up stealing the car he's designed to prove its worth in a border-to-border race from Canada to Mexico.

It was remade ten years later as **The Lively Set.**

1601 Jump (aka **Fury on Wheels**)

1971, Cannon, 97 minutes, Color. Director: Joe Manduke. Producer: Christopher C. Dewey. Screenplay: Richard Wheelwright. Photography: Greg Sander. Editor: George T. Norris.

Cast: Tom Ligon, Logan Ramsey, Collin Wilcox-Horne, Conrad Baine, Norman Rose, Lada Edmund, Jr.

Chet Jump (Ligon) is a tobacco farmer's son who tells his pappy "right now that Chevy's going to be our crop," as he goes out to hustle some drag races.

He joins the racing circuit, but financial difficulties force him to sign up with a sleazy used car salesman who runs his business like a football team and who sponsors a number of racing drivers in a way that they're never out of debt to him.

As a protest, Jump enters his Chevy in a demolition derby.

1602 Jumping Spot

1980, Japanese, Nikkatsu, 92 minutes, Color.

A young motocross racer decides to make a comeback after he's challenged by a rival.

1603 Kid Auto Races at Venice (aka **The Children's Automobile Race**)

1914, Keystone, 11 minutes. Director: Henry Lehrman. Producer: Mack Sennett. Photography: Frank D. Williams.

Cast: Charlie Chaplin, Billy Jacobs, Thelma Salter, Gordon Griffith, Charlotte Fitzpatrick, Henry P. Lehrman.

In only his second film for Keystone, Chaplin causes mass confusion during a kids' auto race.

It was during this film that Chaplin created his baggy pants image that would remain with him the rest of his career. He got the pants from Fatty Arbuckle, the bowler hat from Arbuckle's father-in-law and his moustache from Mack Swain.

1604 The Killers (aka **Johnny North**)

1964, Universal, 95 minutes, Color. Director-Producer: Don Siegel. Screenplay: Gene L. Coon, based on a story by Ernest Hemingway. Photography: Richard L. Rawlings. Editor: Richard Belding.

Cast: Lee Marvin, Angie Dickinson, John Cassavetes, Ronald Reagan, Clu Gulager, Claude Akins, Norman Fell, Virginia Christine, Don Haggerty, Seymour Cassel.

Originally planned for television but released to theaters instead, this is more well-known as a film in which Reagan played a villain than as a remake of the 1946 film which starred Burt Lancaster.

In the original film, Lancaster was an ex-boxer. In the remake, Cassavetes portrays Johnny North, a former racing car driver working as a mechanic, who's persuaded by Dickinson to drive the getaway car in a robbery.

It opens with two hired killers shooting a man and then trying to piece his life together in hopes of finding what happened to the money.

1605 King of the Mountain

1981, Universal, 90 minutes, Color. Director: Noel Nosseck. Producer: Jack Frost Sanders. Screenplay: H.R. Christian, inspired by the article "Thunder Road" by David Barry in **New West** Magazine. Photography: Donald Peterman. Editor: William Steinkamp.

Cast: Harry Hamlin, Joseph Bottoms, Deborah Van Valkenburg, Richard Cox, Dennis Hopper, Dan Haggerty, Seymour Cassel, Ashley Cox, Lillian Muller.

A garage mechanic (Hamlin), a musician (Bottoms) and a record producer (Richard Cox) all have one thing in common: They love to race. More a mood piece than an actioner, it features Hopper as a former top racer.

1606 Knightriders

1981, United Film Distribution Co., 145 minutes, Color. Director-Screenplay: George A. Romero. Producer: Richard P. Rubinstein. Photography: Michael Gornick. Editors: Romero, Pasquale Buba.

Cast: Ed Harris, Gary Lahti, Tom Savini, Amy Ingersoll, Patricia Tallman, Christine Forrest, Warner Shook, Brother Blue.

The director of **Night of the Living Dead** tried something different here, and whether it can be called a sports film is up to interpretation, but for the sake of thoroughness, we are including it.

An itinerant troupe of modern-day knights who are devoted to the principles of chivalry joust on their motorcycles.

Trouble enters in the form of modern-day greed which lures some of the jousters from the troupe.

1607 The Last American Hero (aka **Hard Driver**)

1973, 20th Century-Fox, 95 minutes, Color. Director: Lamont Johnson. Producers: William Roberts, John Cutts. Screenplay: Roberts, based on articles by Tom Wolfe. Photography: George Silano. Editor: Robbe Roberts.

Cast: Jeff Bridges, Gary Busey, Valerie Perrine, Geraldine Fitzgerald, Ned Beatty, Art Lund, Ed Lauter, William Smith, II, Gregory Walcott, Tom Ligon, Ernie Orsatti.

Based on the life of racer Junior Johnson (here called Junior Jackson and played by Bridges), the moonshining youth enrages local authorities with his driving ability, and they bust the still of his father (Lund) in retaliation, sending the elder Jackson to prison.

To pay for his father's attorney and to buy him some prison privileges, the younger Jackson starts racing professionally at the track of penny-pinching promoter Beatty.

Jackson's wild racing style gets him thrown off the track, and with the help of a girl he lands a spot racing in the big time, where he must learn to discipline himself to be a top racer.

One of the film's most poignant moments is when Jackson brings his dad one of the racing trophies he's won, after prison authorities give him permission to present it.

1608 The Last Chase

1981, Crown International, 101 minutes, Color. Director-Producer: Martyn Burke. Screenplay: Burke, C.R. O'Christopher, Taylor Sutherland. Photography: Paul Van Der Linden. Editor: Steve Weslake.

Cast: Lee Majors, Chris Makepeace, Burgess Meredith, Alexandria Stewart, George Touliatos, Ben Gordon, Diane D'Aguila.

In the not-too-distant future, Majors is a racing car driver who loses his nerve after he's in an accident in which two other drivers are killed. During a world-wide oil shortage, all cars are junked and become illegal, but Majors manages to hide his Porsche.

Thousands die of a mysterious illness, including Majors' wife and child. When, 20 years later, he hears of Air Free, California, he takes his car out of hiding and with the help of a computer-genius youth (Makepeace), sets off on a cross-country trek to reach it.

As Majors' ride becomes a symbol of liberty, the government orders aging jet pilot Meredith out to destroy him, and the two play a game of cat and mouse.

1609 The Last Meeting

1952, Italian, Lux, 92 minutes. Director: Gianni Franciolina.

Photography: Anchise Brizzi. Editor: Adriana Novelli.

Cast: Alida Valli, Amedeo Nazzari, Jean Pierre Aumont, Vittorio Sanipoli.

A married woman has a love affair with racing driver Aumont and eventually is forced into prostitution. Who should she meet in the bordello? That's right, her husband.

1610 Le Mans

1971, National General, 108 minutes, Color. Directors: Lee H. Katzin, John Sturges. Producer: Jack N. Reddish. Screenplay: Harry Kleiner. Photography: Robert B. Hauser, René Guissart, Jr. Editor: Donald W. Ernst.

Cast: Steve McQueen, Siegfried Rauch, Elga Andersen, Ronald Leigh-Hunt.

The fine opening sequence shows an early morning in the south of France as the site of the big race slowly awakens in anticipation of the event.

Driving through the countryside prior to the race, driver McQueen visits the spot where he was seriously injured in the race a year earlier. He also sees the widow of the man who was killed in the same crash.

The two, awkward at first, begin to talk to each other and work up a friendship.

A number of pro drivers are featured in the film which has a lot of exciting racing footage and a number of fiery crashes.

1611 The Leather Boys

1964, British, Allied Artists, 105-108 minutes. Director: Sidney J. Furie. Screenplay: Gillian Freeman. Photography: Gerald Gibbs. Editor: Reginald Beck.

Cast: Rita Tushingham, Colin Campbell, Dudley Sutton, Gladys Henson, Avice Landon, Lockwood West, Betty Marsden, James Chase, Martin Mathews, Johnny Briggs.

A young married couple have their problems but get together again during a motorcycle race to Scotland. New problems arise when the young husband finds his wife with another man, and a motorcycle club friend, who turns out to be a homosexual, invites the husband to take a trip with him.

1612 Lickety Split

1929, Educational, 2 reels. Director-Screenplay: Norman Taurog.

Cast: Lige Conley, Estelle Bradley, Jack Lloyd, Glen Cavender.

Here's something different: An auto polo comedy.

Lige is the assistant manager of an ice plant who goofs and causes the melting of a lot of ice. When he opens the door, he's swept away by the water into the midst of an auto polo game.

He joins in and finds his rival for the love of the plant owner's daughter is in the game, so he has an extra incentive.

1613 Little Fauss and Big Halsy

1970, Paramount, 97-100 minutes, Color. Director: Sidney J. Furie. Producer: Albert S. Ruddy. Photography: Ralph Woolsey. Editor: Argyle Nelson, Jr.

Cast: Robert Redford, Michael J. Pollard, Noah Beery, Lauren Hutton, Lucille Benson, Ray Ballard, Linda Gaye Scott, Ben Archibeck, Shara St. John.

A likable motorcycle racing schnook named Fauss (Pollard) strikes up a friendship with an absolutely good-for-nothing con man racer named Halsy (Redford).

Halsy takes advantage of Fauss at every opportunity, and after he's barred from the racing circuit gets Fauss to agree to race under Halsy's name.

The friendship begins to go sour with the arrival of a beautiful woman who opts for Halsy's good looks despite Fauss' sincere attentions.

Fauss breaks his leg during a race and returns home to live

with his parents but re-enters the racing circuit after Halsy has gotten the girl pregnant, and the two former friends race against each other.

1614 The Lively Set

1964, Universal, 95 minutes, Color. Director: Jack Arnold. Producer: William Alland. Screenplay: Mel Goldberg, William Word. Photography: Carl Guthrie. Editor: Archie Marshek.

Cast: James Darren, Pamela Tiffin, Doug McClure, Joanie Sommers, Marilyn Maxwell, Charles Drake, Peter Mann, Carole Wells, Frances Robinson, Greg Morris.

A remake of **Johnny Dark** casts Darren as an army veteran who designs cars and becomes a top racer. He's fired by Mann after one of his cars is wrecked, because Darren never gave it a wind tunnel test.

Undaunted, Darren builds a new car which he enters in the Tri-State Endurance Test.

1615 Love at the Wheel

1921, British, Butcher, 5,500 feet. Director: Bannister Merwin. Producer-Story: H.B. Parkinson. Scenario: Frank Miller.

Cast: Victor Humfries, Pauline Johnson, Leslie Steward, Annette Benson, May Price, A. Harding Steerman.

A man builds his own car after he's fired as a foreman at an auto plant and enters it in the big race.

1616 The Love Bug

1968, Buena Vista, 106 minutes, Color. Director: Robert Stevenson. Producer: Bill Walsh. Screenplay: Walsh, Don Dagradi. Story: Gordon Buford. Photography: Edward Colman.

Cast: Dean Jones, Michele Lee, David Tomlinson, Buddy Hackett, Joe Flynn, Benson Fong, Joe E. Ross, Iris Adrian.

One of the Disney studio's top non-cartoon hits (it inspired three sequels) is a comedy about a Volkswagen named Herbie, with a mind of its own, who adopts a losing racing car driver (Jones) who has shown kindness to it.

Jones had stopped villain Tomlinson from mistreating it.

Jones suddenly starts winning races behind Herbie as Tomlinson comes up with all kinds of nasty schemes, including getting the car drunk.

1617 The Love Race

1931, British, Pathe, 81 minutes. Director: Lupino Lane, Pat Morton. Producer: Stanley Lupino. Screenplay: Edwin Greenwood, based on a play by Stanley Lupino.

Cast: Stanley Lupino, Dorothy Boyd, Jack Hobbs, Dorothy Bartlam, Frank Perfitt, Wallace Arthur, Artie Ash, Florence Vie, Doris Rogers.

The bungling son of an automobile bigwig gets into all kinds of hot water with his fiancée and must prove his mettle by winning the big auto race against his rival for the gal's affections, after a number of comic complications.

1618 Lucky Devil

1925, Paramount, 5,935 feet. Director: Frank Tuttle. Scenario: Townsend Martin. Story: Byron Morgan. Photography: Alvin Wyckoff.

Cast: Richard Dix, Esther Ralston, Edna May Oliver, Tom Findley, Charles Sellon, Gunboat Smith, Joseph Burke, Eddie James.

A department store employee wins a racing car in a raffle, but loses all his money on a trip out west.

For the love of a girl, he fights a boxer to gain the entrance fee for an auto race at the county fair, but must race with the sheriff at his side because the car has been attached for non-payment of a bill.

1619 Mabel at the Wheel (aka **His Daredevil Queen**)

1914, Keystone, 2 reels. Directors: Mack Sennett, Mabel Normand.

Cast: Mabel Normand, Charlie Chaplin, Harry McCoy, Chester Conklin, Mack Sennett.

Chaplin is the villain in this one as he abducts McCoy, his rival for Mabel's hand, just before the Vanderbilt Cup Race. Mabel takes Harry's place and manages to win the race, despite a number of dirty tricks by Chaplin.

Normand was the film's original director but couldn't get along with Chaplin, who threatened to quit, so Sennett took over the directorial reins himself.

1620 Mabel's Busy Day

1914, Keystone, 844 feet. Producer: Mack Sennett.

Cast: Charlie Chaplin, Mabel Normand, Chester Conklin, Harry McCoy, Slim Summerville.

Mabel is losing money on her hot dog stand at the auto races. When Charlie tries to console her, he starts eating the hot dogs, enraging her to the point where she chases him.

1621 A Man and a Woman

1966, French, Allied Artists, 102-110 minutes, Color. Director-Story-Photography: Claude Lelouche. Editors: Lelouche, G. Boisser.

Cast: Anouk Aimee, Jean-Louis Trintignant, Pierre Barouh, Valerie Lagrange, Simone Paris, Antoine Sire, Souad Amidou, Yane Barry, Paul Le Person, Gerard Sire.

Lelouche's romantic drama was a big international box office hit, and Francis Lai's music score proved so popular it's practically become a cliche.

It's a film about taking risks. A woman visiting her daughter at boarding school misses the last train and accepts a ride home from a man who is visiting his son.

She's the widow of a movie stunt man. He's a widower who also puts his life on the line as a racing car driver. His wife committed suicide when he was seriously injured in a crash at the track.

The widow and widower begin a love relationship. Are they willing to take a chance on history repeating itself and form a permanent relationship?

1622 Maniacs on Wheels

1971, Cinemation Industries, 86 minutes, Color. Director: James Reed.

Cast: Brad Harris, Olinka Berova, Graham Hill.

Harris vies with Hill for the world auto racing championship; but when his partner is injured, he has to accept a cycle racer who has a bad reputation.

The newcomer not only challenges the track record but makes a play for the veteran's girl friend as well. Although he's supposed to let the ace win, the upstart decides to race to win after the veteran forces another driver to race, and the man is maimed in a crash.

The newcomer is fired from the team but hooks on with a rival firm.

There were no other credits either on the print we screened or on the promotional material for the movie.

1623 The Married Flapper

1922, Universal, 4,662 feet. Director: Stuart Paton. Scenario: Doris Schroeder. Story: Bernard Hyman. Photography: Jackson J. Rose.

Cast: Marie Prevost, Kenneth Harlan, Philo McCullough, Frank Kingsley, Lucille Rickson, Kathleen O'Connor, William Quinn, Hazel Keener, Burton Wilson.

A married man becomes a racing car driver after the family gets into financial trouble. His wife is carrying on an affair with another man, and when the husband finds out, he is injured in a fight.

To prove she loves her husband, the woman takes her husband's place during the auto race.

1624 Married Too Young

1961, Headliner, 80 minutes.

Cast: Harold Lloyd, Jr.

The "great" Edward Woods, whose grade Z-minus productions such as **Plan Nine from Outer Space** have won him a cult following, had his hand in this melodrama of a young racing driver who has all kinds of difficulties when he does as the title says.

1625 Mind Over Motor

1923, Principal Pictures, 5 reels. Director-Producer: Ward Lascelle. Scenario: H. Landers Jackson, based on a **Saturday Evening Post** story by Mary Roberts Rinehart.

Cast: Trixie Friganza, Ralph Graves, Clara Horton, Lucy Handforth, Caroline Rankin, Grace Gordon, Pietro Sosso, George Guyton, Larry Steers.

A woman innocently becomes the backer of a fixed auto race and gets into a car herself to drive to victory.

1626 Money for Speed

1933, British, United Artists, 72 minutes. Director: S. Bernard Vorhaus. Screenplay: Vera Allinson, Lionel Hale, Monica Ewer. Photography: Eric Cross.

Cast: John Loder, Ida Lupino, Cyril McLaglen, Moore Marriott, Marie Ault, John Hoskins, Cyclone Davis.

Two motorcycle racers are, guess what, in love with the same girl, and the hero is warned off the track after a race in which the other is injured, but he eventually wins the girl.

1627 Motor Competition

1905, British, Gaumont, 300 feet. Director: Alf Collins.

An early motor racing comedy.

1628 Motor Mad

1928, Educational, 2 reels. Director-Screenplay: N. Taurog.

Cast: Lige Conley, Jack Lloyd, Ruth Hiatt, Otto Fries.

A bungling bellhop accidentally wins a motorcycle hill climbing event and is entered in a race.

1629 Motorcycle Gang

1957, American-International, 78 minutes. Director: Edward L. Cahn. Producer: Alex Gordon. Screenplay: Lou Rusoff. Photography: Frederick E. West. Editor: Richard C. Meyer.

Cast: Steve Terrell, John Ashley, Anne Neyland, Carl Switzer, Raymond Hatton, Russ Bender, Jean Moorhead, Scott Peters.

A member of a legal motorcycle racing club (Terrell) is goaded into an illegal race by a jailbird (Ashley) who was involved in a hit-and-run death.

1630 Motoring Around the World

1908. No credits available.

Cars in a New York to Paris auto race encounter all kinds of difficulties.

One is captured by Indians and later sinks into the sea where it's swallowed by a whale which carries it to shore.

1631 Munster, Go Home!

1966, Universal, 90-96 minutes, Color. Director: Earl Bellamy. Producers: Joe Connelly, Bob Mosher. Screenplay: George Tibbles, Joe Connelly, Bob Mosher. Photography: Benjamin H. Kline. Editor: Bud S. Isaacs.

Cast: Fred Gwynne, Yvonne De Carlo, Al Lewis, Butch Patrick, Debbie Watson, Terry-Thomas, Hermione Gingold, Robert Pine, John Carradine, Bernard Fox.

Based on the TV comedy series, the Munster family goes to England to claim an estate they've inherited and become involved with counterfeiters, rivals for the inheritance and an auto race.

Herman Munster (Gwynne), the closest thing to Frankenstein, enters a fixed race.

1632 Naked Autumn

1963, French, United Motion Picture Organization, 98-103 minutes. Director: Francois Leterrier. Producer: Jean Thuillier. Screenplay: Roger Vailland, Leterrier. Photography: Jean Badal. Editor: Leonide Azar.

Cast: Simone Signoret, Reginald Kernan, Alexandra Stewart, Marcel Pagliero, Serge Rousseau.

A racing car driver and his wife retire to the country. He starts writing his memoirs, and she starts gambling and drinking.

They both befriend a younger woman, but when the man receives a new offer to race, he leaves both behind.

1633 National Championship Drag Racing

1966, Box Office International, 114 minutes.

A documentary about just what it says.

1634 National Class

1979, Yugoslavian, Center Film Productions, 90 minutes, Color. Director-Screenplay: Goran Markovic. Photography: Ziuko Zalar.

Cast: Dragan Nikolic, Bogdan Diklic, Gorica Popovic, Danilo Stojkovic, Olivera Markovic, Aleksandar Bercek.

A lazy youth has only two things on his mind: Girls and winning a big drag race in his Fiat.

1635 No Limit

1935, British, ABFD, 80 minutes. Director: Monty Banks. Producer: Basil Dean. Screenplay: Tom Geraughty, Fred Thompson. Story: Walter Greenwood. Photography: Robert G. Martin.

Cast: George Formby, Florence Desmond, Beatrix Fielden-Kaye, Peter Gawthorne, Alf Goddard, Florence Gregson, Evelyn Roberts.

A bungler builds his own motorcycle and enters it in a dirt track race on the Isle of Man. Noteworthy as the first big studio film for comic Formby, it was a big hit in its time.

He breaks the track record when the brakes on his homemade cycle fail and must overcome a bribery plot during the finals.

1636 The Notorious Gentleman (aka **The Rake's Progress**)

1945, Universal, 121 minutes. Director: Sidney Gilliat. Screenplay-Producers: Gilliat, Frank Launder. Story: Val Valentine. Photography: Wilkie Cooper, Jack Asher.

Cast: Rex Harrison, Lilli Palmer, Godfrey Tearle, Griffith Jones, Margaret Johnston, Guy Middleton, Jean Kent, Marie Lohr, Garry Marsh, David Horne.

Harrison is a totally carefree cad who squanders money and cares little about people until he becomes an auto racing driver and enters a race in Europe.

When Hitler seals the borders, the race ends, and Harrison meets a Jewish woman who's desperate to get out and winds up changing his life.

1637 On Any Sunday

1971, Cinema V, 80 minutes, Color. Director-Producer-Writer: Bruce Brown. Photography: Bob Bagley, Don Shoemaker, Bruce Brown, Allan Seymour, Gordon Brettelle, Bob Collins, Dan Wright, Richard Carrillo, Nelson Tyler, Mark Zavad, James Odom, Mark Brelsford. Editor: Don Shoemaker.

Narrator: Bruce Brown.

Steve McQueen and Malcolm Smith are among many top motorcycle drivers featured in this **Endless Summer**-type documentary of the cycle world.

A total of 150 hours of film was shot on all aspects of motorcycling.

1638 On Any Sunday II

1981, International Film Marketing/Arista, 90 minutes, Color. Directors: Ed Forsyth, Don Shoemaker. Producers: Shoemaker, Roger Riddle. Photography: Henning Schellerup, Tom Harvey, H. Allan Seymour, II. Editors: Ed Forsyth, Patrick Crawford.

Narrator: Larry Huffman.

More footage of the world's top motorcycle racers, including Kenny Roberts, Bob Hannah, Bruce Penhall and Brad Lackey.

1639 Once a Jolly Swagman (aka **Maniacs on Wheels**)

1949, British, GFD-Rank, 76 (U.S. version) -100 (British) minutes. Director: Jack Lee. Producer: Ian Dalrymple. Screenplay: William Rose, Jack Lee, based on a novel by Montagu Slater. Photography: H.E. Fowle, L. Cave-Chinn. Editor: Jack Harris.

Cast: Dirk Bogarde, Bonar Colleano, Bill Owen, Cyril Cusack, Patric Doonan, Thora Hird, James Hayter, Moira Lister, Stuart Linsell, Dudley Jones.

Bill Fox (Bogarde) rises from a factory hand to a top motorcycle racer but success causes him to get a swelled head.

He becomes involved with a rich girl but marries the sister of a fellow rider who had an accident. Fox is blacklisted for advocating a trade union for the race drivers and undergoes a change of personality during World War II.

1640 One By One

1974, Leavell-Brunswick, 100 minutes, Color. Director: Claude DuBoc. Producer: Pete Leavell. Editors: Jean Kargayan.

Narrator: Stacy Keach.

The 1973 Grand Prix season is the focus of this documentary which has one grisly fact that sets it apart from the others. Two of the four featured drivers—Peter Revson and Francois Cevert—were killed between the time of filming and its release. The other two drivers are Jackie Stewart and Mike Hailwood.

1641 The Pace that Thrills

1925, First National, 6,911 feet. Director: Webster Campbell. Story: Byron Morgan. Photography: T.D. McCord. Editor: John Krafft.

Cast: Ben Lyon, Mary Astor, Charles Beyer, Tully Marshall, Wheeler Oakman, Thomas Holding, Evelyn Walsh Hall.

The son of a woman convicted of murder is determined to clear her name and is branded a coward when he won't take any chances with his own life.

He enters an automobile race to prove otherwise.

1642 The Pace That Thrills

1952, RKO Radio Pictures, 63 minutes. Director: Leon Barsha. Producer: Lewis J. Rachmil. Screenplay: DeVallon Scott, Robert Lee Johnson. Photography: Frank Redman. Editor: Samuel E. Beetley.

Cast: Bill Williams, Steve Flagg, Carla Balenda, Cleo Moore, Robert Armstrong, Frank McHugh, Diana Garrett, John Hamilton, John Mallory.

Another love triangle, this time between a motorcycle racer and a cycle designer and a woman writer.

Williams plays a heel who redeems himself in the end by helping his rival win the race on an experimental bike.

1643 Pit Stop (aka **The Winner**)

1969, Goldstone, 92 minutes, Color. Director-Screenplay-Editor: Jack Hill. Producer: Lee Strosnider. Photography: Austin McKinney.

Cast: Brian Donlevy, Richard Davalos, Ellen McRae, Sid Haig, Beverly Washburn, George Washburn.

Unscrupulous driver Davalos causes a local racing hero to crash and starts dating his ex-girl friend.

1644 Portrait of an Assassin

1950, French, SEUF, 90 minutes. Director: Bernard Rolland. Screenplay: Henri Decoin, Marcel Rivet. Photography: Roger Hubert. Editor: Germaine Artus.

Cast: Pierre Brasseur, Erich von Stroheim, Maria Montez, Arletty, Dallo, Jules Berry.

Montez is a ruthless woman who's already caused one of her lovers (von Stroheim) to be crippled. Now, she's trying to get a married carnival daredevil motorcyclist to do a dangerous double loop for her.

Montez's dangerous road leads to murder.

1645 The Race

1916, Paramount, 5 reels. Scenario: Hector Turnbull, Clinton Stagg.

Cast: Robert Bradbury, Victor Moore, William Dale, Anita King, Mrs. Louis McCord, Ernest Joy, Horace B. Carpenter.

The son of an automobile manufacturer is disowned because of his carefree lifestyle and goes to work as a chauffeur.

Falling in love with a lady chauffeur, he becomes involved in a transcontinental auto race in which the girl is his rival.

Although he needs the prize money to get out of debt, the girl also needs the money badly, so the hero is torn on whether to throw the race.

1646 Race for a Kiss

1914, British, Hepworth, 225 feet. Director: Lewin Fitzhamon.

Cast: Lewin Fitzhamon, Dolly Dupone.

A jockey puts his horse in a race against an automobile with the driver of the latter being arrested for speeding.

1647 Race for Life (aka **Mark of Dust, Mask of Doubt**)

1955, British, Lippert, 68 minutes. Director: Terence Fisher. Producer: Michael Carreras. Screenplay: Richard Landau, based on a novel by Jon Manchup White. Photography: Jimmy Harvey. Editor: Bill Lenney.

Cast: Richard Conte, Mari Aldon, George Coulouris, Peter Illing, Alec Mango, Meredith Edwards, Jimmy Copeland, Jeremy Hawk, Richard Marner, Edwin Richfield, Tim Turner.

Conte's a former American racing champ who hooks up with an Italian team after World War II and races against the wishes of his wife.

1648 The Racers

1955, 20th Century-Fox, 112 minutes, Color. Director: Henry Hathaway. Producer: Julian Blaustein. Screenplay: Charles Kaufman, based on a novel by Hans Ruesch. Photography: Joe MacDonald. Editor: James B. Clark.

Cast: Kirk Douglas, Bella Darvi, Cesar Romero, Lee J. Cobb, Katy Jurado, Charles Goldner, John Hudson, George Dolenz, Agnes Laury, John Wengraf, Richard Allan.

The European locations enhance this racing tale of an ambitious racing driver (Douglas) whose desire for success lets nothing stand in his way until he sees the error of his ways.

1649 The Racing Fool

1927, Rayart, 4,956 feet. Director: Harry J. Brown. Scenario: George W. Pyper. Photography: Ben White.

Cast: Reed Howes, Ruth Dwyer, Ernest Hilliard, William Franey, James Bradbury, Sr., Myles McCarthy.

The son of an automobile manufacturer winds up racing for his father's rival when he discovers that his rival for a girl's love is plotting to throw the race.

1650 Racing for Life

1924, CBC Film Sales, 4,954 feet. Director: Henry MacRae. Screenplay: Wilfred Lucas. Photography: Allan Thompson.

Cast: William Fairbanks, Eve Novak, Philo McCullough, Wilfred Lucas, Ralph De Palma, Lydia Knott.

The boy friend of an auto manufacturer's daughter agrees to drive in a race the older man needs to win to stay in business but is kidnapped by his own crooked brother.

1651 Racing Hearts

1923, Paramount, 5,691 feet. Director: Paul Powell. Scenario: Will M. Ritchey. Story: Byron Morgan. Photography: Bert Baldridge.

Cast: Agnes Ayres, Richard Dix, Theodore Roberts, Robert Cain, Warren Rogers, J. Farrell MacDonald, Edwin J. Brady, Fred J. Butler, Robert Brower, Kalla Pasha.

The daughter of an automobile manufacturer who refuses to advertise builds a racing car while dad's away. When she learns her father's rival has bribed a driver to throw the race, she jumps into the car herself.

1652 A Racing Romeo

1927, Film Booking Offices of America, 5,992 feet. Director: Sam Wood. Screenplay: Byron Morgan. Photography: Charles G. Clarke.

Cast: Red Grange, Jobyna Ralston, Trixie Friganza, Walter Hiers, Ben Hendricks, Jr., Warren Rogers, Ashton Dearholt, Jerry Zier.

A garage owner (Grange) loses the annual town auto race, and more bad luck follows when his fiancée breaks a mirror.

The comic romantic complications continue until the hero enters another race and this time wins it.

1653 Racing Strain

1933, Maxim, 58 minutes. Director: Jerome Stern.

Cast: Wallace Reid, Jr., Dickie Moore, Paul Fix, Eddie Phillips, Otto Yama, J. Frank Glendon, Phyllis Harrington, Mae Bush, J. Farrell MacDonald.

A teenager overcomes his fear of racing cars after he sees his father killed in a crash and competes against veteran drivers.

1654 Racing Youth

1932, Universal, 66 minutes. Director: Vin Moore. Story: Earl Snell. Photography: George Robinson.

Cast: Frank Albertson, June Clyde, Louise Fazenda, Slim Summerville, Arthur Stuart Hall, Forrest Stanley, Eddie Phillips, Otis Harlan.

An auto designer comes to the rescue of a beautiful woman who's inherited an auto manufacturing company despite the machinations of a villainous manager.

The company's survival hinges on a big race.

1655 Rally

1970, Finnish, Color. Director: Risto Jarva.

Auto racing is deglamorized in this story of a rally driver, his wife and a mechanic. The racer marries the heir to a sausage fortune, but she cheats on him and he is permanently crippled in an accident.

1656 Red Hot Tires (aka **Racing Luck**)

1935, Warner Brothers, 56 minutes. Director: D. Ross Lederman. Screenplay: Tristram Tupper. Photography: Warren Lynch.

Cast: Lyle Talbot, Mary Astor, Roscoe Karns, Frankie Darro, Gavin Gordon.

The plot is laid on thick in a low budget actioner that features a lot of stock racing footage.

Gordon tries to get rid of his rival (Talbot) for a girl in a track accident, but he's killed himself, and Talbot winds up going to prison.

The girl (Astor) comes up with evidence clearing Talbot,

but he's already escaped and racing under an alias in South America. She tracks him down, gets him on a plane and to the track after the race has started, but he wins anyway.

As if that wasn't enough, guess who's at the track watching? The judge who sentenced him in the first place.

1657 Red Line 7000

1965, Paramount, 110 minutes, Color. Director-Producer-Story: Howard Hawks. Screenplay: George Kirgo. Photography: Milton Krasner. Editors: Stuart Gilmore, Bill Brame.

Cast: James Caan, Laura Devon, Gail Hire, Charlene Holt, John Robert Crawford, Marianna Hill, James Ward, Norman Alden, George Takei, Carol Connors, Idell James.

There's more spinning around the track than plot as it seems that everyone in the film is having a romantic relationship with more than one person.

After Caan's racing driver pal is killed in a crash, his bereaved girl friend believes she's a jinx because he was the third man she loved who died.

She becomes a partner in a night spot owned by a racing widow. A racer who won championships in Europe joins the circuit and falls for her, but she's afraid to get involved with him.

In the meantime, the driver drops his French girl friend, who starts a relationship with Caan, who's jealous of her former relationship with the other driver and tries to kill him on the track.

If you're still following this, bear in mind that there are even more plot complications squeezed in between numerous racing scenes.

1658 The Rejuvenation of Aunt Mary

1927, Producers Distributing Corp., 5,844 feet. Director: Erle C. Kenton. Story: Anne Warner. Photography: Barney McGill.

Cast: Mary Robson, Harrison Ford, Phyllis Haver, Franklin Pangborn, Robert Edeson, Arthur Hoyt, Betty Brown.

Dear old Aunt Mary (Robson) believes that one of her nephews (Jack) is studying to become a doctor, while in reality he is working on a motor for a racing car.

She becomes reunited with her childhood sweetheart, who's now a judge, and winds up as the mechanic for her nephew during the race.

1659 The Road Demon

1921, Fox, 5 reels. Director-Screenplay: Lynn Reynolds. Photography: Frank Good, Ben Kline.

Cast: Tom Mix, Claire Anderson, Charles K. French, George Hernandez, Lloyd Bacon, Sid Jordan, Charles Arling, Harold Goodwin, Billy Elmer.

A cowboy (Mix) trades his horse for an old car which he turns into a racer. With a big contract for his girl friend's father at stake, he enters it in a big race.

1660 Road Demon

1938, 20th Century-Fox, 65-70 minutes. Director: Otto Brower. Producer: Jerry Hoffman. Screenplay: Robert Ellis, Helen Logan. Photography: Edward Snyder. Editor: Jack Murray.

Cast: Henry Arthur, Tom Beck, Joan Valerie, Henry Armetta, Bill 'Bojangles' Robinson, Jonathan Hale, Murray Alper, Edward Marr, Lon Chaney, Jr., Eleanor Virzie.

Stock racing footage is used as Beck plays a man who races to clear the name of his father, who was killed by racketeers during a race. The villains made it appear as if his father was drunk during the race when he crashed.

1661 Roar of the Crowd

1953, Allied Artists, 70 minutes, Color. Director: William Beaudine. Producer: Richard

Heermance. Screenplay: Charles R. Marion. Story: Marion, Robert Abel. Photography: Harry Neumann. Editor: William Austin.

Cast: Howard Duff, Helen Stanley, Dave Willock, Louise Arthur, Minor Watson, Harry Shannon, Don Haggerty, Edna Holland, Ray Walker, Paul Bryar.

Duff promises wife Stanley he'll quit racing once he tries his hand in the Indianapolis 500, but he's crippled in a crash.

Trying his hand at other jobs, he still yearns to be back on the track, so his wife helps him save enough money for a racing car.

He gets into the Indy race only to find his leg prevents him from doing well.

In a break with the usual tradition of sports movie women, the wife tells him "Never mind, we'll win it next year."

1662 Roaring Road

1919, Paramount, 5 reels. Director: James Cruze. Scenario: Marion Fairfax, based on stories by Byron Morgan in the **Saturday Evening Post.**

Cast: Wallace Reid, Ann Little, Theodore Roberts, Guy Oliver, C.H. Geldart.

One of the popular Reid racing movies in which he plays a salesman for auto manufacturer J.D. "The Bear" Ward (Roberts). His two main passions in life are racing cars and romancing the boss's daughter, in interchanging order.

The climax is a race from Los Angeles to San Francisco between a car and a train.

1663 Roaring Road

1926, Bud Barsky Productions. Director: Paul Hurst.

Cast: Kenneth McDonald, Jane Thomas.

A young man puts together a racing car that combines the best features of cars made by rival manufacturers and enters it in a cross-country race.

1664 Round the Bend

1966, British, Border, 30 minutes. Director-Producer: O. Negus-Fancey. Story: Barry Cryer.

Cast: Barry Cryer, Bernard Bresslaw.

The hero becomes a stock car racer after he fails his driving test.

1665 Safari 3000

1982, UA/MGM, 92 minutes, Color. Director: Harry Hurwitz. Producers: Arthur Gardner, Jules V. Levy. Screenplay: Michael Harreschou. Story: Gardner, Levy, Harreschou. Photography: Adam Greenberg. Editor: Samuel E. Beetley.

Cast: David Carradine, Stockard Channing, Christopher Lee, Hamilton Camp, Ian Yule, Mary Ann Becold, Peter J. Elliott, Cocky Two Bull, Ben Maringa, James White.

A total of 92 vehicles start out on a 3,000 kilometer race through the roughest African terrain. Of those, six finish after going through jungles, rivers and an attack by 2,000 Zulus.

1666 Sahara

1983, UA/MGM, 104 minutes, Color. Director: Andrew V. McLaglen. Producer: Menahem Golan, Yoram Globus. Screenplay: James R. Silke. Photography: David Gurfinkel.

Cast: Brooke Shields, Lambert Wilson, Horst Buchholz, John Rhys-Davies, Ronald Lacey, John Mills, Steve Forrest.

Filmed in the Negev Desert, the story was inspired by the temporary disappearance of English Prime Minister Thatcher's son during a car rally in the Sahara.

It's set in 1927. Shields is the heiress to an automobile company and promises dying father Forrest she'll win a tough endurance test in the car he designed.

Donning a moustache, she enters the race as a man, with Buchholz, the company's arch-rival, also entered. She is captured by an Arab (Rhys-Davies) and rescued by a sheik (Wilson) and captured again, but still manages the win the race.

1667 7 Second Love Affair

1966, Robert Abel, 52 minutes, Color.

Drag racer Rick Stewart, mechanic Gene Adams and financier Jack Wayne are shown perfecting the vehicle they hope will set a new quarter-mile record.

Although the car explodes at the finish line, it does manage to set the record, which was broken again eight weeks later by another driver.

1668 Short Circuits

1981, French, Films Moliere, 95 minutes, Color. Director: Patrick Grandperret. Screenplay: Grandperret, Gerald Garnier, Nico Papatakis. Photography: Jacques Loiseleu, Bernard Lutic. Editors: Claude Reznick, Dominique Galieni.

Cast: Gerald Garnier, Pierre Trapet, Dominique Bernard, Christian Boucher, Jacques Bolles, Jolivet.

The manager of a motorcycle racing driver becomes involved in a burglary in order to raise cash to enter him in a big race.

1669 Sidecar Racers

1977, Australian, Universal, 100 minutes, Color. Director: Earl Bellamy. Producer: Richard Irving. Screenplay: Jon Cleary. Photography: Paul Onorato. Racing Sequences: Everett Creech.

Cast: Ben Murphy, Wendy Hughes, John Clayton, Peter Graves, John Mellion, John Derum, Peter Gwynne, Serge Lazareff, Paul Bertram, Patrick Ward.

A former Olympics swimmer for the U.S. team is bumming around Australia. He's also an expert driver and because of his sharp sense of balance, he's persuaded to become a sidecar partner to a motorcycle racer who has a reputation for recklessness and whose last partner was killed in an accident.

The swimmer learns the ropes and falls for the racer's girl, causing a conflict between the two men.

1670 Sidewinder One

1977, Avco-Embassy, 97 minutes, Color. Director: Earl Bellamy. Producer: Elmo Williams. Screenplay: Thomas McMahon, Nancy Voyles Crawford. Photography: Dennis Dalzell.

Cast: Marjoe Gortner, Michael Parks, Susan Howard, Alex Cord, Charlotte Rae, Barry Livingston, Bill Vint.

Snobbish Howard takes over a motocross troupe after her manufacturer brother (Cord) dies. With the help of Gortner, romance blooms between her and Parks.

1671 Silver Dream Racer

1980, British, Rank, 111 minutes, Color. Director-Screenplay: David Wickes. Producer: Rene Dupont. Photography: Paul Beeson. Editor: Peter Hollywood.

Cast: David Essex, Beau Bridges, Cristina Raines, Clarke Peters, Diane Keen, Lee Montague, Sheila White.

When his brother is killed, Essex gets his new-style motorcycle and is unbeatable on it. However, he faces the usual financial difficulties and faces loss of the bike if he loses the next race. His girl friend leaves, and he's got to handle dirty tricks by rival Bridges.

1672 Six Pack

1982, 20th Century-Fox, 110 minutes, Color. Director: Daniel Petrie. Producer: Michael Trikilis. Screenplay: Mike Marvin. Photography: Mario Tosi. Editor: Rita Roland.

Cast: Kenny Rogers, Diane Lane, Erin Gray, Barry Corbin, Terry Kiser, Bob Hannah, Tom Abernathy, Robbie Fleming, Anthony Michael Hall, Robby Still, Benji Wilhoite.

When a bunch of kids vandalizes his racing car, Rogers chases them and their vehicle winds up in the river. He rescues them and discovers they're being used by a crooked sheriff to steal parts.

Rogers is returning to racing after a two-year absence due to a crash caused by his former mechanic who is now an ace racing driver and his antagonist.

A love-hate relationship between Rogers and the kids forms, and they become his pit crew.

Beaten and dumped in a ditch by his rival prior to the Atlanta 500 race, he gets to the track and discovers the kids being taken away by the crooked sheriff, and he gives up a possible win to get them back.

1673 Skid Proof

1923, Fox, 5,565 feet. Director: Scott Dunlap. Scenario: Harvey Gates. Photography: Don Short.

Cast: Charles Jones, Laura Anson, Fred Eric, Jacqueline Gadsden, Peggy Shaw, Earl Metcalf, Claude Peyton, Harry Tracey.

A driver loses a race because of a shot from an airplane, but is hired as a movie actor. After saving a pretty girl from a villain, he gets the chance to race again.

1674 Smash Palace

1982, New Zealand, Atlantic, 95 minutes, Color. Director-Producer: Roger Donaldson. Screenplay: Donaldson, Peter Hansard, Bruno Lawrence. Photography: Graeme Cowley. Editor: Mike Horton.

Cast: Bruno Lawrence, Anna Jemison, Greer Robson, Keith Aberdein, Des Kelly.

A racing driver flips out because of marital problems and ends up in a violent confrontation with police.

1675 Smashing Through

1928, British, Gaumont, 7,098 feet. Director: W.P. Kellino. Producers: Maurice Elvey, V. Gareth Gundrey. Screenplay: L'Estrange Fawcett. Story: William Lees, John Hunter.

Cast: John Stuart, Alf Goddard, Eve Gray, Charles Ashton, Mike Johnson, Julie Suedo, Hayford Hibbs.

The inventor of a new kind of supercharger for a racing car falls into the clutches of that ever-present vamp.

1676 Smash-Up Alley: The Petty Story

1972, 83 minutes, Color. Director: Edward J. Lasko.

Cast: Richard Petty, Darren McGavin, Kathie Browne, Noah Beery, Jr., Pierre Jalbert, L.Q. Jones.

The careers of racing drivers Richard Petty, who portrays himself, and his dad, played by McGavin, are dramatized.

1677 Soap-Box Derby

1957, British, Children's Film Foundation, 64 minutes. Director-Screenplay: Darcy Conyers. Producer: Anthony Gilkison. Photography: Douglas Ransom.

Cast: Roy Townshend, Michael Crawford, Keith Davis, Alan Coleshill, Carla Challenor, Denis Shaw, Mark Daly.

It's the Battersea Bats vs. the Victoria Victors in the big soap-box derby between two teams of London urchins. The villainous Victors steal the Bats' new car and blame the car's inventor.

The lad must clear his name and find the car before the big race. Need we say who wins?

1678 Soiled

1924, Truart, 6,800 feet. Director: Fred Windemere. Producer: Phil Goldstone. Scenario: J.F. Natteford, based on a story by Jack Boyle. Photography: Bert Baldridge.

Cast: Kenneth Harlan, Vivian Martin, Mildred Harris, Johnny Walker, Maude George, Alec B. Francis, Robert Cain.

A racing car driver writes a check to pay off his girl friend's debt even though he doesn't have enough money in the bank.

Counting on the prize money from a big race to make the check good, he instead loses the race. The holder of the girl's IOU then makes advances to the girl as the hero tries to scrape up the money.

1679 Speed

1931, Educational, 2 reels. Director: Mack Sennett.

Cast: Andy Clyde, Marjorie Beebe, Alberta Vaughn, Frank Eastman, Walter Weems, Cyril Chadwick, Marion Sayers.

A comedy short featuring a race between a car and an airplane.

1680 Speed

1936, Metro Goldwyn Mayer, 70 minutes. Director: Edward L. Marin. Producer: Lucien Hubbard. Screenplay: Michael Fessler. Photography: Lester White.

Cast: James Stewart, Wendy Barrie, Una Merkel, Weldon Heyburn, Ted Healy, Ralph Morgan, Patricia Wilder, Robert Livingston, Walter Kingsford.

Stewart portrays a mechanic who comes up with a new idea that he hopes will win him a fortune at the Indianapolis Speedway.

1681 The Speed Classic

1928, First Division, 4,700 feet. Director: Bruce Mitchell. Story: Arthur Hoerl. Photography: Max Dupont, William Underhill. Editor: Bertha A. Montaigen.

Cast: Rex Lease, Mitchell Lewis, Mildred Harris, James Mason, Garry O'Dell, Otis Harlan, Helen Jerome Eddy.

A wealthy youth's fiancée breaks off the engagement when he can't be convinced to withdraw his entry in the Speed Classic against pro drivers.

He winds up in a Mexican jail through the efforts of a rival driver, but his sweetheart finds out and gets him out in time for the race and to get even with the guy who framed him.

1682 Speed Crazed

1927, Rayart, 5,241 feet. Director: Duke Worne. Scenario: Grover Jones. Story: Suzanne Avery. Photography: King Grey.

Cast: Billy Sullivan, Andree Tourneur, Joseph W. Girard, Harry Maynard, Albert J. Smith.

Some crooks kidnap the hero and force him to drive the getaway car in a holdup. He's arrested but escapes and goes to another town where he becomes a racing driver.

The same criminal who kidnapped the hero before does it again to prevent the car's owner from winning, but Our Hero escapes in time to get to the track.

1683 Speed Crazy

1959, Allied Artists, 75 minutes. Director: William Hole, Jr. Producer: Richard Bernstein. Screenplay: Bernstein, George Waters. Photography: Ernest Haller. Editor: Irving Berlin.

Cast: Brett Halsey, Yvonne Lime, Charles Wilcox, Slick Slavin, Jacqueline Ravell, Baynes Barron, Regina Gleason, Keith Byron, Charlotte Fletcher.

A no-goodnik murders a gas station attendant during a holdup and escapes in a hot rod. He becomes a mechanic in another town, where he wins a lot of races but makes a lot of enemies before the cops catch up to him.

1684 Speed Devils

1935, Syndicate, 56 minutes. Director: Joseph Henaberry.

Cast: Paul Kelly, Marguerite Churchill.

When racing car driver Kelly is in a smashup, his doctor advises him to give up racing, so he opens up a garage only to find crooked politicians trying to force their way into the business.

Garry O'Dell and Rex Lease share a lighter moment in 1928's The Speed Classic. (The Museum of Modern Art/Film Stills Archive.)

1685 Speed Fever

1978, Italian, Racing Pictures, 108 minutes, Color. Directors: Mario Morra, Oscar Orero. Producer: Alessandro Fracassi. Photography: Ottavio Fabbri.

Among the racing drivers featured in this documentary are Craig Breedlove, Niki Laura, James Hunt, Mario Andretti, Emerson Fittipaldi and Carlos Reutmann. The film's emphasis is on survival and features several crashes.

1686 Speed King

1923, Phil Goldstone, 5 reels. Director: Grover Jones. Photography: Arthur Todd.

Cast: Richard Talmadge, Virginia Warwick, Mark Fenton, Harry Van Meter.

A motorcycle racer (Talmadge) goes to a kingdom called Mandavia for a race and is hired by a villain to impersonate the king, who has been imprisoned in part of a plot by a neighboring kingdom to take over the country. The plot is foiled by the hero, who falls in love with the princess (Warwick) and is knighted for his efforts.

1687 The Speed Limit

1926, Lumas Film Corp., 5,675 feet. Director: Frank O'Connor. Story: James J. Tynan.

Cast: Raymond McKee, Ethel Shannon, Bruce Gordon, George Chapman, James Conley, Edward W. Borman.

Rivals for the love of a girl take turns playing tricks on each other until the young inventor of a new kind of tire is framed for auto theft by the other man.

He gets out of jail in time for the race and proves the value of his new tires.

1688 Speed Lovers

1968, Jemco Pictures, 102 minutes, Color. Director-Producer-Screenplay: William McGaha. Photography: Joe Shelton. Editors: John Fitzstephens, David Moscovitz, William Freda.

Cast: Fred Lorenzen, William McGaha, Peggy O'Hara, David Marcus, Carol Street, Glenda Brunson.

Stock car racer Lorenzen plays himself in this story of a young mechanic's son who wants to emulate Lorenzen.

1689 Speed Mad

1924, Columbia, 4,442 feet. Director: Jay Marchant. Story: Dorothy Howell. Photography: George Meehan. Editor: Charles J. Hunt.

Cast: William Fairbanks, Edith Roberts, Lloyd Whitlock, Melbourne MacDowell, John Fox, Jr., Florence Lee, Charles K. French.

A carefree youth who loves racing his car on back roads leaves home after an argument with his father and enters a race with a $5,000 prize.

A villainous broker who holds the mortgage on property owned by Our Hero's girl friend's father kidnaps him and ties him up in a freight car; but as you might expect, if he didn't get to the track on time, there wouldn't be much of a film.

1690 Speed Maniac

1919, Fox, 5 reels.

Director: E.J. LeSainte. Screenplay: Denison Clift. Story: H.H. Van Loan.

Cast: Tom Mix, Eva Novak, Charles K. French, Hayward Mack, L.C. Shumway, Helen Wright, Jack Curtis, George Stone, George H. Hackathorn.

Mix gets plenty of chances to show off his fistic skills, his horsemanship and his auto racing ability in this actioner.

1691 The Speed Merchants

1974, Color. Producer: Michael Keyser.

Another documentary about auto racing, featuring such drivers as Mario Andretti, Jacky Ickx and Brian Redman.

1692 Speed to Spare

1937, Columbia, 60 minutes. Director: Lambert Hillyer. Screenplay: Bert Granet, Hillyer. Photography: Benjamin Kline.

Cast: Charles Quigley, Dorothy Wilson, Eddie Nugent, Patricia Farr, Gene Morgan, John Gallaudet, Jack Gardner.

How's this for a coincidence? Two brothers who were separated at birth each become racing drivers unknown to each other and love the same girl.

The rivalry becomes so intense one brother tries to kill the other during a race and instead causes the death of another driver.

1693 Speed to Spare

1948, Paramount, 57 minutes. Director: William Berke. Screenplay: Milton Raison. Photography: Ellis W. Carter. Editor: Monty Pearce.

Cast: Richard Arlen, Jean Rogers, Richard Travis, Pat Phelan, Nanette Parks, Roscoe Karns, Ian McDonald, Paul Harvey.

A racing driver quits to join the trucking business and finds new dangers with runaway trucks, explosives and the like.

1694 The Speeding Venus

1926, Producers Distributing Corp., 5,560 feet. Director: Robert Thornby. Adaptation: Finis Fox, based on a story by Welford Beaton. Photography: George Benoit.

Cast: Priscilla Dean, Robert Frazer, Dale Fuller, Johnny Fox, Ray Ripley, Charles Sellon.

A woman participates in a Detroit-to-Los Angeles auto race to help her boy friend get a half-interest in a manufacturing firm. Naturally, there's a villain who tries to prevent the win.

1695 Speedway

1929, Metro Goldwyn Mayer, 6,962-7,075 feet. Director: Harry Beaumont. Adaptation: Byron Morgan, Alfred Block, Ann Price. Photography: Henry Sharp. Editor: George Hively.

Cast: William Haines, Anita Page, Karl Dane, John Miljan, Polly Morgan.

A race car driver deserts his racing stepfather during the Indianapolis 500, but they have a reconciliation before the final fadeout.

1696 Speedway

1968, Metro Goldwyn Mayer, 90-95 minutes, Color. Director: Norman Taurog. Producer: Douglas Laurence. Screenplay: Phillip Shuken. Photography: Joseph Ruttenberg. Editor: Richard Farrell.

Cast: Elvis Presley, Nancy Sinatra, Bill Bixby, Gale Gordon, William Schallert, Virginia Meyerink, Ross Hagen, Carl Ballantine, Poncie Ponce.

Presley's a racing car driver with lots of financial problems and a beautiful IRS agent (Sinatra) on his tail. He gives a large portion of his winnings to the poor father of some little girls, while his manager (Bixby) loses a lot on horses.

A crisis sets in when Presley's auto is damaged in an accident, and he's got to raise enough money to enter it in the big race.

Racing sequences were filmed at the Charlotte Speedway in North Carolina.

1697 Spinout

1966, Metro Goldwyn Mayer, 93 minutes, Color. Director: Norman Taurog. Producer: Joe Pasternak. Screenplay: Theodore J. Flicker, George Kirgo. Photography: Daniel L. Fapp. Editor: Rita Roland.

Cast: Elvis Presley, Shelley Fabares, Diane McBain, Deborah Walley, Dodie Marshall, Jack Mullaney, Will Hutchins, Warren Berlinger, Carl Betz, Una Merkel.

Three women vie for the hand of confirmed bachelor Presley, who heads a singing group and also races autos. He enters his vehicle in the Santa Fe Road Race. The usual mixture of music and girls in a typical Presley film.

1698 Sporting Youth

1924, Universal, 6,712 feet. Director: Harry Pollard. Scenario: Harvey Thew. Story: Byron Morgan. Photography: Clyde De Vinna.

Cast: Reginald Denny, Laura La Plante, Hallam Cooley, Frederick Vroon, Lucille Ward, Leo White, Henry Barrows, Malcolm Denny, Rolfe Sedan, L.J. O'Connor.

A chauffeur who's deeply in debt dreams of becoming a great racing driver. His wish comes true when he's sent on an errand and is mistaken for a famous driver.

He's aided by the daughter of a rich automobile manufacturer he falls in love with.

1699 The Steel Arena

1973, L-T Films, 96 minutes, Color. Director-Screenplay: Mark L. Lester. Producers: Lester, Peter S. Traynor. Photography: John A. Merrill. Editor: Dave Peoples.

Cast: Dusty Russell, Gene Drew, Buddy Love, Dutch Schnitzer, Bruce Mackey, Laura Brooks.

True-life racing driver Russell stars in a super-low-budget story of a man who becomes a star in a demolition derby.

He joins an auto thrill show, where he incurs the jealousy of rival driver Mackey, who tries to kill him. Russell survives the attempt but tries an extremely risky stunt.

1700 Stock Car

1955, British, Butcher, 68 minutes. Director: Wolf Rilla. Producer: A.R. Rawlinson. Screenplay: Rawlinson, Victor Lyndon. Photography: Geoffrey Faithfull.

Cast: Paul Carpenter, Rona Anderson, Susan Shaw, Henry Fowler, Robert Rietty, Paul Whitsun Jones, Sabrina.

An American driver in England romances a lady garage owner and enters his car in a race. He's also got to battle some crooks.

1701 Stop Me Before I Kill! (aka **The Treatment, The Full Treatment)**

1961, British, Hammer-Columbia, 93-110 minutes. Director-Producer: Val Guest. Screenplay: Guest, Ronald Scott Thorn. Photography: Gilbert Taylor. Editor: Bill Lenny.

Cast: Ronald Lewis, Claude Dauphin, Diane Cilento, Francoise Rosay, Bernard Braden, Katya Douglas, George Merritt.

Newly-wed racing driver Lewis is injured in a crash, and then tries to strangle his wife every time they make love.

A psychiatrist who wants the woman for himself uses drugs to convince the driver he's a psychopath.

1702 Straightaway

1934, Columbia, 58 minutes. Director: Otto Brower. Screenplay: Lambert Hillyer. Photography: Dan Clark. Editor: Otto Mayer.

Cast: Tim McCoy, Sue Carol.

Cowboy star McCoy stars in a low budget actioner set in Indianapolis, involving crooks who try to blackmail the brother of a racing driver.

1703 Stroker Ace

1983, Universal, 96 minutes, Color. Director: Hal Needham. Producer: Hank Moonjean. Screenplay: Needham, Hugh Wilson. Photography: Nick McLean. Editors: Carl Kress, William Gordean.

Cast: Burt Reynolds, Ned Beatty, Jim Nabors, Loni Anderson, Parker Stevenson, Bubba Smith.

There are lots of crashes and gag driving in a typical Needham comedy featuring Reynolds as a stock car driver who's forced by circumstances to become a promo man for chicken king Beatty.

In one sequence, he has to drive in full chicken costume, including the feet. Nabors portrays his trusty mechanic.

1704 Super Speed

1925, Rayart, 5,227 feet. Director: Albert Rogell. Producer: Harry J. Brown. Story: J.W. Grey, Henry Roberts Symonds.

Cast: Reed Howes, Mildred Harris, Charles Clary, Sheldon Lewis, Martin Turner, George Williams.

A wealthy youth who drives a milk truck falls in love with a girl whose father is deeply in debt to a crook who's planning to steal a new kind of supercharger for a racing car.

The hero (Howes) enters the race using the new invention, but surprise, surprise, he's kidnapped by the villain's henchmen. Naturally, he escapes in time to get in the race.

1705 Superbug (aka **Super Wheels, Superbug, The Craziest Car in the World**)

1975, Swiss-German, Allied Artists, 83-90 minutes, Color. Director: Rudolf Zehetgruber. Producer: Konstantin W. Nowak. Screenplay: Gregor W. Nazzani. Photography: Rudiger Meichsner.

Cast: Robert Mark, Salvatore Borges, Kathrin Oginski, Walter Giller, Walter Roderer, Ruth Recklin, Evelin Kraft, Ullrick Beiger, Peter Staub, Gerhard Frickhofer.

Any resemblance between **The Love Bug** and **Superbug** is totally more than coincidental.

A talking car named DuDu, which also can fly like a helicopter, is entered in a marathon race across the Alps to help raise funds for an orphanage.

Besides the usual assortment of villains doing their dirty tricks on the road, the two nuns who run the orphanage also enter the race, using a two-fronted car, à la the push-me-pull-you from **Doctor Dolittle,** which can be driven in either direction.

There was a sequel, **The Return of Superbug,** but no racing was involved in that one. In fact, the "intelligent" part of the car was removed early in the sequel and walked around the rest of that film as a kind of talking giant spider.

1706 Superbug, the Wild One

1977, German, 90 minutes, Color.

Cast: Richard Lynn.

The talking Volkswagen this time is involved in a car rally across Africa.

1707 Superspeed

1935, Columbia, 55 minutes. Director: Lambert Hillyer. Screenplay: Harold Shumate. Photography: Benjamin Kline.

Cast: Norman Foster, Mary Carlisle, Florence Rice, Charley Grapewin, Arthur Hohl, Robert Middlemass, George McKay.

Lots of sports are mixed in this tale of a football star who also attempts to perfect a new racing car device. He's got to overcome sabotage from a rival car factory and decide between two women who are after his affections.

Besides auto racing, there are motorboat racing scenes.

1708 Take It to the Limit

1980, Variety International, 95 minutes, Color. Director-Producer: Peter Starr. Writers: Charles Michael Lorre, Starr. Photography: Michael Chevalier, Jeremy Lepard, Mark Zavad. Editor: John Bryant.

Narrator: Alan Oppenheimer.

Among the top motorcycle racers who tell how they hit the top are Barry Sheene, Russ Collins, Steve Baker, Scott Autrey, Mike Hallwood and Kenny Roberts.

1709 Teen Age Thunder

1957, Howco, 78 minutes. Director: Paul Helmick. Producer: Jacques Marquette. Screenplay: Rudy Makoul. Photography: Marquette. Editor: Irving Schoenberg.

Cast: Charles Courtney, Melinda Byron, Robert Fuller, Tyler McVey, Paul Bryar, Helen Heigh, Gilbert Perkins.

A youth who works at a service station secretly builds a hot rod for a big race because his father is against the idea.

The station's owner, who needs money to help his polio-stricken son, aids him.

1710 10 Laps to Go

1938, States Rights Release, 67 minutes. Director: Elmer Clifton. Producer: Fanchan Royer. Story: William F. Bleecher. Adaptation: Charles R. Condon. Photography: Arthur Martinelli. Editor: Edward Schroeder.

Cast: Rex Lease, Muriel Evans, Duncan Renaldo, Tom Moore, Charles Delaney, Marie Prevost, Yakima Canutt, Edward Davis.

A racer loses his nerve after he's forced over a wall and crashes. He also finds himself accused of dirty deeds but tracks down the villain (Renaldo) and takes over the wheel of his car with ten laps to go.

1711 Those Daring Young Men in Their Jaunty Jalopies (aka **Monte Carlo or Bust!**)

1969, Paramount, 122 minutes, Color. Director-Producer: Ken Annakin. Screenplay: Annakin, Jack Davies. Photography: Gabor Pogany. Editor: Peter Taylor.

Cast: Tony Curtis, Susan Hampshire, Terry-Thomas, Eric Sykes, Gert Frobe, Peter Schmidt, Peter Cook, Dudley Moore, Bourvil.

An attempt to cash in on the comedy success of **Those Magnificent Men in Their Flying Machines** concerns a 1500-mile Monte Carlo Rally across Europe in the 1920's.

Terry-Thomas and Curtis each own a half share in an auto factory, Curtis getting his half from his father, who won it in a poker game.

There are the usual dirty tricks played by the contestants with the finale of the race being down a winding mountain road.

1712 Thunder Alley

1967, American International, 88-90 minutes, Color. Director: Richard Rush. Producer: Burt Topper. Screenplay: Sy Salkowitz. Photography: Monroe Askins. Editors: Ronald Sinclair, Kenneth Crane.

Cast: Annette Funicello, Fabian, Diane McBain, Warren Berlinger, Jan Murray, Stanley Adams, Maureen Arthur, Michael T. Mikler, Kip King, Sandy Reed, Michael Bell.

A driver, who's plagued by blackouts caused by his guilt over an accident involving his brother, is suspended when he causes the death of another driver.

He goes to work for an auto thrill show and helps train another driver for racing. They become teammates in a 500-mile race.

1713 Thunder in Carolina

1960, Howco, 92 minutes. Director: Paul Helmick. Producer: J. Francis White. Screenplay: Alexander Richards.

Cast: Rory Calhoun, John Gentry, Connie Hines, Alan Hale, Ed McGrath, Troyanne Ross, Trippie Wisecup.

Calhoun is a moonshiner-turned-racing driver who retires after injuring his leg in a crash. He teaches all he knows to garage owner Gentry, much to his regret. Race sequences were filmed at the Southern 500.

1714 Thunder in Dixie (aka **Thundering Wheels**)

1965, MPI, 76 minutes. Director-Producer: William T. Naud. Screenplay: George Baxt. Photography: Thomas E. Spalding.

Cast: Harry Millard, Judy Lewis, Nancy Berg, Mike Bradford, Richard Petty, Ted Erwin, Richard Kuss.

Set at the Dixie 400 race in Atlanta, Millard and Bradford portray former racing partners who are now bitter enemies.

Bradford blames Millard for the death of his girl friend and tries to kill him on the track but winds up being injured himself.

1715 Time Out for Love (aka **Les Grandes Personnes**)

1963, French-Italian, Zenith International, 91-96 minutes.

Director: Jean Valere. Producers: Bertrand Javal, Yvon Guezel. Screenplay: Valere, Roger Nimier. Photography: Raoul Coutard. Editor: Leonide Azar.

Cast: Jean Seberg, Maurice Ronet, Micheline Presle, Francoise Prevost, Annibale Ninchi, Fernando Bruno.

Racing driver Ronet juggles romances with three different women as he hopes to save his business by winning the big race.

1716 Timerider

1983, Jensen-Farley, 93 minutes, Color. Director: William Dear. Producer: Harry Gittes. Screenplay: Dear, Michael Nesmith. Photography: Larry Pizer. Editors: Suzanne Pettit, Kim Secrist, R.J. Kizer.

Cast: Fred Ward, Belinda Baver, Peter Coyote, Ed Lauter, Richard Masur, Tracey Walter, L.Q. Jones.

A motorcycle racer strays off course during a desert race and winds up in the path of a time experiment. He's transported through a time warp into the Old West where he meets a beautiful woman and tangles with a whole gang of outlaws.

He scares one old geezer to death by appearing on his motorcycle. Scientists, in the meantime, try to find him to bring him back to the 20th century.

1717 Tiny Lund: Hard Charger

1969, Marathon, 89 minutes, Color. Photography: Charles Hartman. Editor: Victor Kanefsky.

Independent stock car driver Lund is the focus of this documentary as he's shown competing against teams of factory-sponsored drivers.

1718 To Please a Lady

1950, Metro Goldwyn Mayer, 90 minutes. Director-Producer: Clarence Brown. Screenplay: Barre Lyndon, Marge Decker. Photography: Harold Rosson. Editor: Robert J. Kern.

Cast: Clark Gable, Barbara Stanwyck, Adolphe Menjou, Will Geer, Ted Husing, Roland Winters, Frank Jenks, Emory Parnell.

Racer Gable and journalist Stanwyck carry an on-again, off-again romance which finds her getting him banned from midget car racing after she believes his ruthlessness caused another driver's death.

Gable turns to stunt driving and gets a full-size car to race at Indianapolis. He wins Stanwyck's love in the racing finale by proving he's not reckless.

1719 Today Is for the Championship

1980, Breakthrough Racing, 110 minutes, Color. Director-Producer: Dan Weisburg. Photography: Peter Smokler. Editor: James Oliver.

Werner Erhard, the founder of est, applies his philosophy to race car driving.

1720 Too Much Speed

1921, Paramount, 4,629 feet. Director: Frank Urson. Scenario: Byron Morgan. Photography: Charles E. Schoenbaum.

Cast: Wallace Reid, Agnes Ayres, Theodore Roberts, Jack Richardson, Lucien Littlefield, Jack Herbert, Guy Oliver, Henry Johnson.

Another of the popular Wallace Reid racing comedies. Here, he retires from racing at the urging of his auto manufacturing prospective father-in-law but accepts a challenge from a rival firm's driver to race.

After the prospective father-in-law calls the wedding off, the young lovers elope and are chased. Reid buys a car with his own money and enters it in a race. He wins a big contract for his future father-in-law's company, and all is forgiven.

1721 Track of Thunder

1967, United Artists, 83 minutes, Color. Director: Joe Kane. Producer: E. Stanley Williamson. Screenplay: Maurice J. Hill. Photography: Alan Stensvold. Editor: Verna Fields.

Cast: Tommy Kirk, Ray Stricklyn, H.M. Wynant, Brenda Benet, Faith Domergue, Majel Barrett, Chet Stratton, James Dobson.

A gambling syndicate's front man at the racetrack uses the newspapers to promote a feud between drivers Kirk and Stricklyn, childhood friends who both love the same girl.

As the stories spread, the rivalry between the two men becomes real and more intense, and the crowds at the track grow as well.

1722 Two-Lane Blacktop

1972, Universal, 102 minutes, Color. Director: Monte Hellman. Producer: Michael S. Laughlin. Screenplay: Rudolph Wurlitzer, Will Cory.

Cast: James Taylor, Warren Oates, Laurie Bird, Dennis Wilson, Harry Dean Stanton, Alan Vint, Bill Keller, Rudolph Wurlitzer, Jaclyn Hellman.

Racer Taylor and mechanic Wilson travel around the American West looking for drag races to enter.

They meet former test pilot Oates who's out looking for adventure and agree to a cross-country race to Washington, D.C. with their cars the stakes.

1723 Very Confidential

1927, Fox, 5,620 feet. Director: James Tinling. Scenario: Randall H. Faye. Story: James Kevin McGuinness, Randall H. Faye. Photography: Joseph August.

Cast: Madge Bellamy, Patrick

Cunning, Mary Duncan, Joseph Cawthorn, Carl von Haartmann, Marjorie Beebe.

A fashion model impersonates a famous sportswoman during a summer in Alaska in the hopes of snaring a man she loves. To carry the impersonation through, she enters an auto race through the mountains.

1724 Viva Knievel!

1977, Warner Brothers, 104-106 minutes, Color. Director: Gordon Douglas. Producer: Stan Hough. Screenplay: Antonio Santillan, Norman Katkov. Photography: Fred Jackman.

Cast: Evel Knievel, Lauren Hutton, Gene Kelly, Red Buttons, Leslie Nielson, Marjoe Gortner, Frank Gifford, Cameron Mitchell, Dabney Coleman, Albert Salmi.

The daredevil stunt driver plays himself as evil Nielson and rival rider Gortner plot to kill Knievel and load a duplicate of the driver's truck with cocaine.

Knievel, in the meantime, romances Hutton, a photographer assigned to photograph his spectacular jumps, and tries to straighten out his drunken mechanic (Kelly).

1725 Viva Las Vegas

1964, Metro Goldwyn Mayer, 86 minutes, Color. Director: George Sidney. Producers: Sidney, Jack Cummings. Screenplay: Sally Benson. Photography: Joseph Biroc.

Cast: Elvis Presley, Ann-Margret, Cesare Danova, William Demarest, Nicky Blair, Jack Carter, Robert B. Williams, Bob Nash, Eddie Quillan, Roy Engel, Ford Dunhill.

When Elvis defeats Danova in a race, he turns down an offer to drive for him and plans to race his own car in the Las Vegas Grand Prix. Their rivalry is enhanced when they both fall for Ann-Margret.

Elvis' crisis occurs when he loses the money he needs for the entry fee and has to take a job as a waiter.

1726 Wall of Death (aka **There Is Another Sun**)

1951, British, Butcher-Realart, 95 minutes. Director: Lewis Gilbert. Producer: Ernest G. Roy. Screenplay: Guy Morgan. Story: James Raisin.

Cast: Maxwell Reed, Susan Shaw, Lawrence Harvey, Hermione Baddeley, Leslie Dwyer, Meredith Edward, Robert Adair, Earl Cameron.

A Wall of Death motorcycle rider for a carnival and a boxer team up to rob their boss.

1727 Weekend of a Champion

1972, British, MGM-EMI, 90 minutes, Color. Director: Frank Simon. Producer: Roman Polanski. Photography: Bill Byrne. Editor: Derek York.

Famed racer Jackie Stewart is profiled during a weekend at the Monte Carlo race as he makes preparations, relaxes and competes.

1728 Weekend Warriors

1966, Champion Film Productions, 90 minutes, Color. Producers: Leonard Mishkind, Jim Dempsey, Sol Gordon, Albert B. Lefton.

Gordon Collett, Connie Kalitta, Bill Jenkins and Don Garlits are among the drag racers featured in this look at the 1964 summer nationals at Indianapolis and the 1965 winter nationals at Phoenix, Arizona.

1729 What's Your Hurry?

1920, Paramount, 5 reels. Director: Sam Wood. Story: Byron Morgan.

Cast: Wallace Reid, Lois Wilson, Charles Ogle, Clarence Burton, Ernest Butterworth.

Reid this time is a racer in love with the daughter of a truck manufacturer who makes him publicity manager.

He comes to the rescue of thousands of residents when he

rushes dynamite through nearly impassable roads to prevent flooding from a dam burst.

1730 The Widow

1955, Italian-French Distributing Corp. of America, 89 minutes.

Directors: Patricia Roc, Massimo Serrato, Akim Tamiroff, Maria Ferrero.

Cast: Patricia Roc.

Roc falls in love with race car driver Serrato, but he's got a crush on Ferrero instead.

1731 The Wild Racers

1968, American-International, 79 minutes, Color. Director: Daniel Haller. Producer: Joel Rapp. Screenplay: Max House. Photography: Nestor Almendros, Daniel Lambre. Second Unit Photography: Francis Ford Coppola. Editor: Verna Fields.

Cast: Fabian, Mimsy Farmer, Alan Haufroct, Judy Cornwell, David Landers, Warwick Sims, Talia Coppola.

Fabian is the teammate of a star European racer who's supposed to support the ace's lead during races. Instead, he blows out his car and also makes a play for the man's woman.

He learns his lesson, however, and gets his shot at the glory when the star is injured.

1732 Winning

1969, Universal, 123 minutes, Color.

Director: James Goldstone. Producer: John Foreman. Screenplay: Howard Rodman. Photography: Richard Moore. Editors: Edward A. Biery, Richard C. Meyer.

Cast: Paul Newman, Joanne Woodward, Robert Wagner, Richard Thomas, David Sheiner, Clu Gulager, Barry Ford, Robert Quarry, Bobby Unser, Tony Hulman.

A 17-car smashup is the highlight of the big race in this story of a racer (Newman) who leaves his wife after finding her in bed with rival Wagner.

He romances divorcee Woodward, who has a teenage son, but his relationship with her is anything but smooth.

1733 The Young Racers

1963, American-International, 82 minutes, Color. Director-Producer: Roger Corman. Screenplay: R. Wright Campbell. Photography: Floyd Crosby. Editor: Ronald Sinclair.

Cast: Mark Damon, William Campbell, Luane Anders, Robert Campbell, Patrick Magee, John McLaren, Milo Quesada, Anthony Marsh, Marie Versini, Beatric Altariba.

Driver-turned-writer Damon sets out to write an expose of a racer (William Campbell) who's as ruthless with his women as he is on the racetrack.

When Campbell makes a play for Damon's girl friend, the two rivals become involved in a grudge race.

Winter Sports

It's not our intention in this chapter to review every film which has a skiing sequence, such as the numerous beach party-type films of the 1960's or the many German mountain films of the late 1920's to early 1930's.

Similarly we're not going to include every skiing documentary by the prolific Warren Miller, but only those which have gone into general release.

Some of the films we feel worth mentioning, however, are **Body and Soul** (1927 version), **Ski Fever** and the sequences in **The Spy Who Loved Me** and **On Her Majesty's Secret Service,** the latter two being James Bond action films.

1734 Champion of Pontresina

1934, German, Terra, 85 minutes. Director: Herbert Selpin. Story: Hans Richter. Photography: Sepp Allgejer.

Cast: Sepp Rist, Walter Rilla, Vivigenz Eockstedt, Abi Ghibo.

A ski team's training regimen suffers when the ace starts romancing an American girl.

1735 Downhill Racer

1969, Paramount, 101 minutes, Color. Director: Michael Ritchie. Producer: Richard Gregson. Screenplay: James Salter, based on a novel by Oakley Hall. Photography: Brian Probyn. Editor: Richard C. Harris.

Cast: Robert Redford, Gene Hackman, Camilla Sparv, Joe Jay Jalbert, Kenneth Kirk, Dabney Coleman, Jim McMullan, Christian Doermer, Oren Stevens, Karl Michael Vogler.

Some of the most exciting skiing scenes captured on film highlight the tale of two skiers (Redford, Kirk) who are called to the U.S. team when one of its top performers is injured.

When Redford wins a big race, he and the top U.S. racer (McMullan) begin a rivalry that ends when the latter breaks his leg, and Redford is the last American hope in the Winter Olympics.

1736 Fascinating Youth

1926, Paramount, 6,882 feet. Director: Sam Wood. Scenario: Paul Schofield. Story: Byron Morgan. Photography: Leo Tover.

Cast: Charles Rogers, Ivy Harris, Jack Luden, Walter Goss, Claud Buchanan, Mona Palma, Thelma Todd.

The son of a hotel owner is promised he can marry the girl of his choice if he can revive business at a mountain resort.

When a number of movie stars (appearing as themselves) turn down the offer to appear at the hotel, some of the hero's friends disguise themselves as the stars, but his girl friend saves the day by showing up with some real actors.

The hero also sponsors an ice boat race to rev up business and winds up in the race against a champion.

1737 Hot Dog ... The Movie

1983, United Artists/MGM, 96 minutes, Color. Director: Peter Markle. Producer: Edward S. Feldman. Screenplay: Mike Marvin. Photography: Paul G. Ryan. Editor: Stephen Rivkin.

Cast: David Naughton, Patrick Houser, Tracy N. Smith, John Patrick Reger, Frank Koppola, James Saito, Shannon Tweed, George Theobald, Marc Vance, Erik Watson, Lynn Wieland.

Animal House-type humor is the key to this comedy set in Squaw Valley about a youth (Houser) who competes against world class skiers in the World Free-Style Championship.

He incurs the wrath of the top Austrian skier, and the two take turns playing dirty tricks on each other and wooing the same girl.

The final competition, which is akin to dancing on skis, features a lot of dazzling footage.

1738 It Ain't Easy

1972, Dandelion, 90 minutes, Color. Director: Maury Hurley. Producer: Richard A. Diercks. Screenplay: Mary Olson. Photography: Ron Eveslage. Editor: Walter Goins.

Cast: Lance Henricksen, Barra Grant, Bill Moor, Granville Van Dusen, Joseph Maher, Pierrino Mascarino.

A man returns to his Minnesota backwoods home to find that trapping is no longer a worthwhile business so he becomes a snowmobile racer.

He becomes the prime suspect when his girl friend and a drug smuggler are both found murdered.

1739 Last of the Ski Bums

1969, U-M Film Distributors, 86 minutes, Color. Director-Producer-Writer-Photography-Narrator: Dick Barrymore.

Cast: Ron Funk, Mike Zuetell, Ed Ricks, Jean-Claude Killy, Heini Messner, Gerhard Neaning, Bernard Orcel, Guy Perillat, Pepi Stiegler, Robert Didier, Desire LaCroix.

Three guys ski in the Alps and watch a lot of the greats in action and then gamble in Monte Carlo until they run out of money. Then, it's back for more skiing.

1740 Love on Skis

1933, British, British Lion, 65 minutes. Director: L. Vadja.

Cast: Bill and Buster, Joan Austin, Ralph Rogan, Jack Lester.

The romantic comedy plot is little more than an excuse to show lots of skiing and ice skating action at St. Moritz.

1741 The Man Who Skied Down Everest (aka **Everest Symphony**)

1971, Ishihan International, 100 minutes, Color. Director: Isso Zenlya. Photography: Mitsuji Kanau.

Skier Yuichiro Miura sets out to scale Mount Everest in the Himalayas and ski down it. The documentary contains more action than many fiction films as they hit many obstacles during the trek, and six members of the expedition are killed.

1742 The Other Side of the Mountain

1975, Universal, 101-103 minutes. Director: Larry Peerce. Producer: Edward S. Feldman. Screenplay: David Seltzer, based on the book **A Long Way Up** by E.G. Valens. Photography: David M. Walsh. Editor: Eve Newman.

Cast: Marilyn Hassett, Beau Bridges, Belinda J. Montgomery, Nan Martin, William Bryant, Dabney Coleman, Bill Vint, Hampton Fancher, William Roerick, Dori Brenner.

Here's the story of skier Jill Kinmont who was considered a cinch to land an Olympics berth in 1956 until she was seriously injured in a race in Utah.

Her struggle to make something of her life after the crippling injury is the main focus of the film.

1743 The Other Side of the Mountain—Part II

1978, Universal, 105 minutes, Color. Director: Larry Peerce. Producer: Edward S. Feldman. Screenplay: Douglas Day Stewart. Photography: Ric Waite. Editors: Eve Newman, Walter Hannemann.

Cast: Marilyn Hassett, Timothy Bottoms, Nan Martin, Belinda J. Montgomery, Gretchen Corbett, William Bryant, James A. Bottoms.

Hassett once again portrays crippled skier Kinmont who becomes a teacher in Los Angeles and tries to find romance.

1744 The Ski Bum

1971, Avco-Embassy, 94 minutes, Color. Director: Bruce Clark. Producer: David R. Dawdy. Screenplay: Marc Siegler.

Cast: Zalman King, Charlotte Rampling.

One of the best things that ever happened to Peter O'Toole's career was when he didn't star in this as originally scheduled. A costly bomb that almost no one saw, it bears practically no resemblance to the Romain Gary novel of the same name.

It concerns the relationship of a hostile ski lodge instructor with a hostess who's cheating on hubby.

1745 Ski Champ

1962, W. German, Comet Productions, 87 minutes, Color. Director: Hans Grimm. Producer: Georg Richter. Screenplay: Franz Geiger, based on a novel by Kurt Marx. Photography: Klaus von Rautenfeld and Ernst Kalinke. Editor: Anneliese Schonnebeck.

Cast: Tony Sailer, Oliver Grimm, Maria Perschy, Dietmar Schenherr, Waltrant Haas, Carla Hagen, Heinrich Gretler.

Lots of spectacular stunt skiing highlights this light tale with music about a number of top skiers assembling at an Alpine hotel for a major international competition.

The hero is torn between career and romance and is blamed when a rival is injured during a test run. The extremely thin plot takes a total back seat to the action.

1746 Ski Champs

1951, William H. Brown, 76 minutes, Color. Director-Photography: Dick Durrance.

Narrators: Lowell Thomas, Tor Toland.

A championship international ski meet at Aspen, Colorado draws such celebrities as Dagmar Rom, Zeno Colo, Christian Pravda, Georges Schneider, Celina Seghi, Stein Erickson and Paula Kahn. Their preparations for the meet are shown as well as the competition itself.

1747 Ski Country

1984, Island Alive, Inc., 92 minutes, Color. Director-Producer-Writer: Warren Miller. Photography: Don Brolin.

Billed as the "ultimate downhill adventure film," this documentary is an **Endless Summer** on skis as it explores the world's top ski slopes.

Miller is the undisputed king of ski documentaries with well over 30 to his credit, averaging one feature per year.

1748 Ski on the Wild Side

1967, Sigma III, 104 minutes, Color. Director-Producer: Warren Miller. Photography: Miller, Don Brolin, Red Attin.

Narrator: Miller.

Many of the world's top skiers are featured in competition in California, Colorado, Vermont, Wyoming, France, the Soviet Union, Yugoslavia, New Zealand and Japan.

1749 Ski Patrol

1940, Universal, 64 minutes. Director: Lew Landers. Producer:

Warren Douglas. Screenplay: Paul Huston. Photography: Milton Krasner. Editor: Ed Curtis.

Cast: Luli Deste, Philip Dorn, Samuel S. Hinds, Stanley Fields, Edward Norris, Hardie Albright, Kathryn Adams, John Qualen, John Arledge, John Ellis, Reed Hadley.

During the 1936 Olympics, a Russian takes first place in skiing and a Finn second, and they declare that war is a thing of the past.

Just a few years later, members of the Finnish skiing team are among the defenders of a mountain being invaded by the Russians.

1750 Slalom

1936, Austrian, George Kraska-World, 67 minutes. Director: Max Obai. Producer: H.H. Sokal. Screenplay: Dr. Arnold Fanck. Photography: Hans Schneeberger, Richard Angst, Heinrich Goertner.

Cast: Guzzi Lantschner, Walter Rimi, Hella Hartwich.

To prove she's as good as any man at winter sports, a girl beats her boy friend at nearly every kind of event, including skiing, bobsledding and ice skating.

In one scene, the actors ski along railroad tracks as they're pulled by a train.

1751 Snow Job (aka **The Ski Raiders**)

1972, Warner Brothers, 90 minutes, Color. Director: George Englund. Producer: Edward L. Rissien. Screenplay: Ken Kolb, Jeffrey Bloom. Editor: Gary Griffin.

Cast: Jean-Claude Killy, Vittorio De Sica, Daniele Gaubert, Cliff Potts, Lelio Cuttazzi.

A famous skier (Killy) who has romantic problems joins in a bank heist, with Killy getting plenty of opportunities to display his skills in front of the camera.

1752 Snowball Express

1972, Buena Vista, 90 minutes, Color. Director: Norman Tokar. Producer: Ron Miller. Screenplay: Don Tait, Jim Park, Arnold Margolin. Photography: Frank Phillips. Editor: Robert Stefford.

Cast: Dean Jones, Nancy Olson, Harry Morgan, Keenan Wynn, Johnny Whitaker, Kathleen Cody, Dick Van Patten.

When an insurance man inherits a broken-down ski lodge, he's got to thwart a scheming banker who wants it for himself in a typical 1970's Disney comedy.

Beside several ski sequences, there's a snowmobile race.

1753 Song of Norway

1955, British, E.J. Fancey, 32 minutes. Director: MacLean Rogers.

Cast: Eric Micklewood, Adrienne Scott, Vanda Godsell, Graham Stark, Andrew Timothy.

A hotel receptionist enters herself in a ski race.

1754 Storms Over Mont Blanc

1931, German, 96 minutes. Director-Screenplay: Dr. Arnold Fanck. Photography: Hans Schneeberger, Richard Angst, Sepp Aligeier.

Cast: Leni Riefenstahl, Sepp Rist, Ernest Udet, Friedrich Kayssler, Matthia Wieman.

A ski contest highlights this mountain film that's typical of many produced by the Germans during this era. Riefenstahl would go on to become Nazi Germany's top filmmaker, directing **Olympia** (see Olympics chapter) and **Triumph of the Will.**

1755 They Met on Skis

1939, French, C.L. Import, 75 minutes. Director-Producer: Henri Sokal. Photography: Otto Heller, Adrien Porchet, Albert Bernitz.

Cast: Wissia Dina, Henri Presles, Charpin, Assia, Max Dearly.

France's top winter athletes appear in a romance story about the rivalry between two Alpine innkeepers.

1756 12 Girls and One Man

1959, Austrian, UFA, 92 minutes, Color. Director: Hans Quest. Screenplay: Kurt Nachmann, Helmut Andica. Photography: Hannes Staudinger. Editor: Dr. Herbert Gruber.

Cast: Toni Sailer, Margit Nvenka, Gunther Phillip, Joe Stoecki.

A dozen girls who are taking a ski trip meet Olympics champ Sailer.

1757 Winter Carnival

1939, United Artists, 91 minutes. Director: Charles F. Riesner. Producer: Walter Wanger. Screenplay: Lester Cole. Story: Budd Schulberg. Photography: Merrit Gerstad. Editor: Dorothy Spencer.

Cast: Ann Sheridan, Richard Carlson, Helen Parrish, James Corner, Robert Armstrong, Alan Baldwin, Joan Brodel, Marsha Hunt.

Music and comedy mix as a Dartmouth skiing champ vies with a European nobleman, who's a ski wizard himself, for the love of a girl.

1758 Winter Wonderland

1947, Republic, 71 minutes. Director: Bernard Vorhaus. Producer: Walter Colmes, Henry Sokal. Screenplay: Peter Goldbaum, David Chandler, Arthur Marx, Gertrude Purcell. Photography: John Alton. Editor: Robert Jahns.

Cast: Lynne Roberts, Charles Drake, Roman Bahnsen, Eric Blore, Mary Eleanor Donahue, Renee Godfrey, Janet Warren, Harry Tyler.

A ski instructor and a farmer's daughter find romance, with a big ski race the main hope for the gal to get out of trouble.

Wrestling

Despite the enormous amount of show business atmosphere connected with the sport, wrestling films have somehow never managed to catch on in the United States despite a constant trickle of films from the silent era on.

Flesh in 1932 and **Deception** in 1933 were both well-made exposés of racketeering in the wrestling world; but instead of inspiring more films, the genre seemed to stagnate until the late 1940's and early 1950's when the likes of **Alias the Champ, Body Hold, Mr. Universe** and others started appearing.

The constant popularity of the sport insures the continuation of the trickle, but the wrestling film will apparently never achieve the popularity of the boxing film. The exception may be in Mexico, which in the 1960's produced films with wrestlers as heroes literally by the dozen. The low budget productions usually featured a masked wrestling hero such as Santo (in American versions called Samson) or Neutron battling against mad scientists or some superhuman villain.

As few were ever released in the United States, we're only including some of those in our listings. Other films worthy of mention are the Wheeler and Woolsey comedy **On Again, Off Again,** the silent **Men Who Forget** and the Amos 'n' Andy cartoon, **The Rasslin' Match.**

1759 Abbott and Costello in the Foreign Legion

1950, Universal-International, 79 minutes. Director: Charles Lamont. Producer: Robert Arthur. Screenplay: John Grant, Martin Ragaway, Leonard Stern. Story: D.D. Beauchamp. Photography: George Robinson. Editor: Frank Gross.

Cast: Bud Abbott, Lou Costello, Patricia Medina, Walter Slezak, Douglas Dumbrille, Leon Belasco, Marc Lawrence, Wee Willie Davis, Tor Johnson, Sam Menacker, Jack Raymond.

When an Algerian wrestler returns home, Abbott and Costello go after him to try to get him to come back to the United States.

They're tricked into joining the Foreign Legion and help smash a sinister plot in the usual madcap Abbott and Costello manner. They also find their wrestler.

1760 Alias the Champ

1949, Republic, 60 minutes. Director: George Blair. Producer: Stephen Auer. Screenplay: Albert De Mond. Photography: John MacBurnie. Editor: Harold Minter.

Cast: Gorgeous George, Robert Rockwell, Barbara Fuller, Audrey Long, Jim Nolan, Sammy Menacher, Joseph Crehan, Bomber Kulkovich, Super Swedish Angel, Mike Ruby, Jim Lennon, Billy Varga, Bobby Mamogoff, George Temple, Jack Sockeye McDonald.

Gorgeous George in all his glory steals the show as a wrestler who won't go along with the mob when it tries to muscle in on the game.

In retaliation, they frame him by poisoning an opponent who dies in a match against George.

It's up to wrestling administrator Rockwell to help clear George, while at the same time romancing a female manager (Long). Many of wrestling's top names appear as themselves.

1761 . . . All the Marbles (TV Title: **The California Dolls**)

1981, Metro Goldwyn Mayer, 113 minutes, Color. Director: Robert Aldrich. Producer: William Aldrich. Screenplay: Mel Frohman. Photography: Joseph Biroc. Editors: Irving C. Rosenblum, Richard Lane.

Cast: Peter Falk, Vicki Frederick, Laurene Landon, Tracy Reed, Burt Young, Bryant King, Claudette Nevins, Richard Jaeckel, John Hancock, Lenny Montana, Joe Greene, Mike Mazurki.

The California Dolls are a lady tag team managed by cheapskate Falk and playing in second rate arenas. When they're short-changed by mobster Young, Falk retaliates by smashing his new car.

When engagements are hard to find, the girls, after much protest, agree to a mud wrestling match at a carnival, during which they drag the promoter into the mud with them.

After a lot of conniving, Falk manages to get them a match against the champion Toledo Tigers in their home town. They win but are beaten in a rematch in Chicago.

With the world championship bout set between the two tag teams, Falk engineers some of the biggest hype and pomp since Elizabeth Taylor in **Cleopatra** only to find that Young has ordered the referee to stack the deck against the Dolls.

1762 Aria for an Athlete

1980, Polish, Film Polski, 108 minutes, Color. Director-Screenplay: Filip Bajon. Photography: Jerzy Zielinski.

Cast: Krysztof Majchrzak, Pola Raska, Roman Wilhelmi, Bogusz Bilewski, Wojciech Pszoniak.

Set at the turn of the century, the life of the "world's strongest man," wrestler Wladyslaw Goralewicz, is dramatized.

As a youth, he joins a travelling circus but is fired when he wins a wrestling match he was supposed to lose. He goes on to fame as the top wrestler of his time.

He engages in a bitter rivalry with two wrestling brothers who fight dirty; and when one is killed in a match, Goralewicz's career ends.

1763 Beloved Brute

1924, Vitagraph, 6,719 feet. Director-Producer: J. Stuart Blackton. Photography: L.W. O'Connell, Ernest Smith.

Cast: Victor McLaglen, William Russell, Marguerite De La Motte, Wilfred North, Ernie Adams.

A wrestler heeds Horace Greeley's advice and heads west with a girl, ever mindful of his father's prediction that he'll be defeated in the ring by his long-lost brother.

The wrestler travels from town to town taking on challengers for no-holds-barred matches until who should get into the ring with him but his brother.

1764 Below the Belt

1980, Atlantic Leasing, 98 minutes, Color. Director: Robert Fowler. Producers: Fowler, Joseph Miller. Photography: Alan Metzger, Misha Suslov.

Cast: Regina Baff, Mildred Burke, Jane O'Brien, Shirley Stoler, Dolph Sweet, John C. Becher, James Gammon, Annie McGreevey, Billie Mahoney, Ric Mancini, Titi Paris.

Filmed mostly in 1974 and held on the shelf for a long time after its completion, this look at the world of women's wrestling was suggested by the novel **Smithereens** by Rosalyn Drewler.

Waitress Rosa Rubinsky (Baff) attempts to rise to wrestling stardom as Rosa Carlo, the Mexican Spitfire.

She trains with true-life champ Mildred Burke for a match against behemoth Terrible Tommy (O'Brien).

1765 The Big Show-Off

1945, Republic, 69 minutes. Director: Howard Bretherton. Producer: Sydney M. Williams. Screenplay: Leslie Vadnay, Richard Weil. Photography: Jack Greenhalgh.

Cast: Arthur Lake, Dale Evans, Lionel Stander, George Meeker, Paul Hurst, Marjorie Manners, Sammy Stein, Louis Adlon, Dan Toby.

To impress a girl, a nightclub pianist tells her he's the masked wrestler.

1766 Blonde Pickup

1955, Globe Roadshows. Director: Robert C. Dertano. Producer: George Weiss.

Cast: Timothy Farrell, Clare Mortensen, Rita Martinez, Peaches Page.

A senate commission and hit men both get on the tail of gym owner Farrell who promotes crooked lady wrestling matches and tampers with horses.

1767 Blood and Guts

1978, Canadian, Ambassador, 92 minutes, Color. Director: Paul Lynch. Producer: Peter O'Brien. Screenplay: Joseph McBride, William Gray, John Hunter. Photography: Mark Irwin. Editor: William Gray.

Cast: William Smith, Micheline Lanctot, Henry Bockman, Brian Patrick Clarke, John McFadyen, Ken James.

Smith and Clarke, members of a travelling wrestling troupe playing before small town crowds, become bitter rivals when they fall in love with the same girl.

1768 Body Hold

1949, Columbia, 63 minutes. Director: Seymour Friedman. Producer: Rudolph C. Flothow. Screenplay: George Bricker. Editor: James Sweeney.

Cast: Willard Parker, Lola Albright, Hillary Brooke, Allen Jenkins, Roy Roberts, Gordon Jones, Sammy Menacher, Frank Sully, John Dehner, Billy Varga, Henry Kulky, Ed "Strangler" Lewis.

Wrestling champ Jones is ordered crippled in the ring when he demands a better deal from his promoter. Looking for a new champ, along comes plumber Parker on a repair job.

He's built up into a top wrestler; but when he, too, becomes disillusioned, he's in line for the same rough treatment as his predecessor.

1769 Came the Brawn

1938, Metro Goldwyn Mayer, 10 minutes. Director: Gordon Douglas. Producer-Screenplay: Hal Roach. Photography: Art Lloyd. Editor: William Ziegler.

Our Gang's Alfalfa believes the Masked Marvel he's going to wrestle is Waldo, but tough guy Butch is a last-minute sub. Porky and Buckwheat come to the rescue by pulling Butch's clothes off so that he's too embarrassed to continue.

1770 Deception

1933, Columbia, 70 minutes. Director: Lew Seiler. Screenplay: Harold Tarshis. Story: Nat Pendleton. Photography: Chet Lyons.

Cast: Leo Carrillo, Dickie Moore, Nat Pendleton, Thelma Todd, Barbara Weeks, Frank Sheridan, Henry Armetta, Hans Steinke.

An expose of the wrestling racket features Pendleton as an ex-grid player who takes to the mat and is built up for publicity purposes through a series of mixed matches. Because of jealousy over a girl, his manager turns on him.

He's defeated by the champ, but he starts working harder and makes a comeback in a rematch against Steinke.

Pendleton, the author of **Deception**, was a former Olympic wrestler.

1771 Doctor of Doom

1965, Mexican, K. Gordon Murray, 77 minutes. Director: René Cardona. Producer: William Calderon Stell. Screenplay: Alfredo Salazar. Photography: Enrique Wallace. Editor: Jorge Bustos.

Cast: Lorena Velazques, Roberto Canedo, Armando Silvestre, Chucho Salinas, Elizabeth Campbell, Jorge Mondragon, Sonia Infante, Matha "Guera" Solis, Irma Rodriguez.

Lovers of camp will have a field day with this Mexican "horror" film about a mad doctor who puts a gorilla's brain into the head of a lady wrestler.

Two of her wrestling friends, The Golden Rubi and Gloria Venus, come to the rescue, defeating the doctor and his gorilla.

1772 Fight for Your Lady

1937, RKO Radio Pictures, 67 minutes. Director: Ben Stoloff. Producer: Albert Lewis. Adaptation: Ernest Pagano, Harry Segall, Harold Kusell. Photography: Jack MacKenzie. Editor: George Krone.

Cast: John Boles, Jack Oakie, Ida Lupino, Margot Grahame, Gordon Jones, Erik Rhodes, Billy Gilbert, Paul Guilfoyle.

Jilted singer Boles teams up with wrestling promoter Oakie.

1773 The Fighters

1982, Congo, ONACI, BP, 90 minutes, Color. Director-Screenplay-Photography: Jean Michel Tchissoukou. Editors: Felix Yiloukoulou, Marie-Christian Rougerre.

Cast: Albertine Ngalou, Nzikov, Joseph Kengue, Baranger Dubois.

A form of wrestling in the Congo known only as "fighting" is the focus of this love story between a wrestler and a girl whose parents don't like the guy.

"Fighting is sport, not aggression" the referee reminds the wrestlers before a match as he warns them not to try to hurt each other. When the hero loses a big match at a village festival, he tries to kill himself, but his girl friend comes to the rescue.

1774 The Fighting Doctor

1926, Hercules, 4,900 feet. Director: Robert North Bradbury. Screenplay: Grover Jones.

Cast: Frank Merrill.

A doctor incurs the wrath of a jealous suitor while on a house call to care for a crippled boy and the owner of a gymnasium convinces them to fight it out on the wrestling mat.

The rival, who is also a swindler, gets the hero into a match with a pro and kidnaps the girl during the match. After winning the match, the hero pursues the villain in a car and then a speedboat.

1775 Flesh

1932, Metro Goldwyn Mayer, 95 minutes. Director: John Ford. Story: Edmund Goulding. Photography: Arthur Edeson.

Cast: Wallace Beery, Karen Morley, Ricardo Cortez, Jean Hersholt, John Miljan, Vince Barnett, Herman Bing, Edward Brophy, Greta Meyer.

Polikaj (Beery) rises from a beer garden waiter to German wrestling champ and comes to the United States. He falls under the influence of a mobster (Cortez) and a faithless woman and winds up winning a wrestling title he was supposed to lose.

He marries the mobster's moll, thinking the crook is her brother and never dreaming the baby isn't his own. When the woman leaves him and he sees Cortez striking her, Polikaj strangles him.

1776 Grips, Grunts and Groans

1937, Columbia, 2 reels. Director: Preston Black.

It's typical Three Stooges madness as Curly takes the place of a wrestler who runs out.

1777 Handle with Care

1935, British, Radio, 55 minutes. Director: Redd Davis. Producer: George King, Randall Faye. Screenplay: Faye. Photography: Geoffrey Faithfull.

Cast: Molly Lamont, Jack Hobbs, James Finlayson, Henry Victor, Vera Bogetti, Margaret Yarde.

A pair of ex-crooks get mixed up with spies and a wacky wrestling match in which one of them takes a special pill to gain strength.

1778 Hercules in New York

1970, RAF Industries, 90 minutes, Color. Director: Arthur A. Seidelman. Producer-Screenplay: Aubrey Wisberg. Photography: Leo Lebowitz. Editor: Donald P. Finamore.

Cast: Arnold Strong, Arnold Stang, Deborah Loomis, James Karen, Ernest Graves, Tammy McDonald, Taina Elg, Michael Lipton, Mark Tendler, Dennis Tinesino.

A bored Hercules is banished to Earth and becomes a pro wrestler, befriending weakling Stang. He's also robbed of his strength; and in the film's most memorable scene, rides a chariot down Broadway.

Atlas and Samson come to his aid when the going gets tough.

1779 Here Come the Co-Eds

1945, Universal, 79 minutes. Director: Jean Yarbrough. Producer: John Grant. Screenplay: Grant, Arthur T. Horman. Story: Edmund L. Hartmann. Photography: George Robinson.

Cast: Bud Abbott, Lou Costello, Peggy Ryan, Martha O'Driscoll, Jane Vincent, Lon Chaney, Jr., Bill Stern, Pierre Watkin, Joe Kirk, Richard Lane.

Abbott and Costello are caretakers at a snooty girls' school which is in deep mortgage trouble. Among the film's better sequences is the restaurant scene in which an oyster in Costello's soup keeps on spitting at him. There's also a fund-raising basketball game.

It's the wrestling scene which earns it a listing here, however, as Costello is talked into meeting the Masked Marvel, not knowing it's his bitter enemy Chaney.

Even before the match begins, Costello takes a beating as the referee declares "no eye gouging" and proceeds to illustrate what he means by gouging Costello's eyes. Each time the ref mentions a no-no, he demonstrates it on poor Lou.

1780 Invasion of the Zombies

1961, Mexican, Azteca. Director-Screenplay: Benito Alzraki. Producer: Fernando Oses.

The masked wrestler Santo takes on an entire army of zombies created by a mad scientist in another outrageously campy Mexican film.

1781 Micki and Maude

1984, Columbia, 117 minutes, Color. Director: Blake Edwards. Producer: Tony Adams. Screenplay: Jonathan Reynolds. Photography: Harry Stradling. Editor: Ralph E. Winters.

Cast: Dudley Moore, Amy Irving, Ann Reinking, Richard Mulligan, George Gaynes, Wallace Shawn, John Pleshette, H.B. Haggerty, Lu Leonard, Priscilla Pointer.

Rob (Moore) is married to Micki (Reinking), a lawyer who's too busy with her career to give him a child. When he learns his mistress Maude (Irving) is pregnant, he marries her also. Reinking then tells him she's pregnant too.

Helping to make life from there on miserable for the hapless man with two pregnant wives is Maude's father, a professional wrestler (Haggerty).

Among the real-life pro wrestlers making guest appearances in the comedy are Jack "Wildman" Armstrong, Andre the Giant, Big John Studd, Chief Jay Strongbow and Madman O'Rourke.

1782 Mr. Universe

1951, United Artists-Eagle Lion, 89 minutes. Director-Producer: Joseph Lerner. Screenplay: Searle Kramer. Photography: Gerald Hirschfeld. Editor: Geraldine Lerner.

Cast: Vince Edwards, Jack Carson, Janis Paige, Bert Lahr, Robert Alda, Maxie Rosenbloom, Joyce Matthews, Harry Landers, Donald Novis, Murray Rothenberg, Dennis James.

Con man Jeff Clayton (Carson) talks physical culture contest winner Tommy Tomkins (Edwards) into becoming a wrestler.

The comedy's theme is the innocent in the den of wolves as Tomkins believes the sport is honest, not knowing that the wrestlers rehearse the fixed matches beforehand.

Tomkins rises to the top, honestly he thinks, by defeating such opponents as Ivan the Terrible, the Missing Link and Newton the Teuton as even Clayton doesn't level with him.

1783 My Breakfast with Blassie

1983, Artist Endeavors International, 60 minutes. Directors-Producers: Johnny Legend, Linda Lautrec.

Cast: Andy Kaufman, Freddie Blassie, Lynn Elaine, Laura Burdick, Linda Burdick, Linda Hirsch, Bob Zmuda.

In a takeoff on the popular **My Dinner with Andre**, comedian Kaufman has breakfast with wrestling manager Blassie at a fast food place in Los Angeles. Blassie tells tales of his days as a wrestler, particularly the biting he's famous for.

1784 Neutron Against the Death Robots

1961, Mexican, Commonwealth United. Director-Screenplay: Frederico Curiel. Producer: Luis Garcia de Leon.

Cast: Wolf Ruvinskis.

One of numerous Mexican wrestling films featuring the masked hero Neutron finds him battling robots, a bomb and an evil brain.

Among the numerous other Neutron film adventures are **Neutron, The Black Mask** (1960), a three-part serial (Chapter One: **The Black Mask**, Chapter Two: **Caronte Triumphs**, Chapter Three: **The Diabolical Invention**); **Neutron vs. Doctor Caronte** (1960), another serial (Chapter One: **Neutron vs. Doctor Caronte**, Chapter Two: **The Treatment of Doctor Caronte**, Chapter Three: **Face to Face**), **The Robots of Death** (1960); **Neutron vs. The Sadistic Criminal** (1964) and **Neutron vs. The Karate Assassins** (1964); still another three-parter (Chapter One: **Neutron vs. The Karate Assassins**, Chapter Two: **The Crime Organization**, Chapter Three: **The Treason**).

1785 Night and the City

1950, 20th Century-Fox, 101 minutes. Director: Jules Dassin. Producer: Samuel G. Engel. Screenplay: Jo Eisinger, based on a novel by Gerald Kersh.

Cast: Richard Widmark, Gene Tierney, Googie Withers, Hugh Marlowe, Francis L. Sullivan, Herbert Lom, Stanley Zbysko, Mike Mazurki, Charles Farrell, Ada Reeve.

A heel (Widmark) tries his hand at the wrestling racket in London by promoting aging ex-champ Zbysko. He runs afoul of gangster Lom for his efforts.

The film's highlight is a dandy wrestling match between Zbysko and Mazurki which is one of the best ever put on screen.

1786 Night of the Bloody Apes

1970, Mexican, Jerand Films, 84 minutes, Color. Director: Rene Cardona. Producer: Guillermo Calderon Stell. Screenplay: Cardona and Rene Cardona, Jr. Photography: Paul Martinez Solares. Editor: Jorge Bustos.

Cast: Jose Flores Moreno,

Carlos Lopez Moctezuma, Norma Lazareno, Agustin M. Solares, Armando Silvestre, Javier Rizo, Noelia Noel.

A beautiful red-clad masked lady wrestler loses her nerve in the ring after she puts an opponent into a coma, but her boy friend snaps her out of it.

Meanwhile, a surgeon transplants a gorilla's heart into the body of his dying son who turns into a murderous ape man who relishes tearing off the clothes of beautiful women.

The horrified surgeon tries to correct his mistake by replacing the gorilla's heart with that of the comatose wrestler, but instead of growing big breasts the ape man goes on another murder rampage.

Unlike many similar Mexican wrestling-horror films, at least the lady wrestler-heroine doesn't battle the beast in the ring.

1787 No Holds Barred

1952, Monogram, 65 minutes. Director: William Beaudine. Producer: Jerry Thomas. Screenplay: Tim Ryan, Jack Crutcher, Bert Lawrence. Photography: Ernest Miller. Editor: William Austin.

Cast: Leo Gorcey, Huntz Hall, Marjorie Reynolds, Bernard Gorcey, Leonard Penn, Henry Kulky, Tim Ryan, John Indrisano, Mike Ruby.

The Bowery Boys enter the wrestling world when they discover that Satch (Hall) is immune to pain--in different parts of his body at different times. There are almost always racketeers to battle in Bowery Boys comedies, and this is no exception with the old kidnapping angle thrown in.

In the finale match, Satch's rear end is immune to pain, so he fights mostly with that.

1788 Nouvelles Luttes Extravagantes

1900, French, Star Films, 150 feet. Director: George Méliès.

A trick film by film pioneer Méliès features a wrestler who's dismembered but becomes whole again and a battle between a fat wrestler and a skinny one. The fat wrestler squashes the other one and rolls him up, but the skinny wrestler is restored to normal and explodes the fat one.

1789 On Demande Une Brute

1934, French. Directors: Charles Barrois, Rene Clement. Screenplay: Jacques Tati, Alfred Savvy.

Cast: Jacques Tati.

French comedian Tati portrays a wrestler in this short.

1790 The One and Only

1977, Paramount, 98 minutes, Color. Director: Carl Reiner. Producers: Steve Gordon, David V. Picker. Screenplay: Gordon. Photography: Victor J. Kemper. Editor: Bud Molin.

Cast: Henry Winkler, Kim Darby, Gene Saks, William Daniels, Polly Holliday, Harold Gould, Herve Villechaize, Brandon Cruz.

Kooky egomaniac Winkler tries to make the big time as a wrestler under Saks' tutelage, but he also sets his sights on winning Darby's love.

1791 Paradise Alley

1978, Universal, 107 minutes, Color. Director-Screenplay: Sylvester Stallone. Producers: John F. Roach, Ronald A. Suppa. Photography: Laszlo Kovacs. Editor: Eve Newman.

Cast: Sylvester Stallone, Kevin Conway, Anne Archer, Joe Spinell, Armand Assante, Lee Canalito, Aimee Eccles, Terry Funk, Joyce Ingalls, Frank McRae.

In 1940's Hell's Kitchen, three brothers try to work their way up via the wrestling world and come up against hood Conway.

Stallone is the con man of the group, while Assante is the crippled war vet who manages ice man Canalito. The finale match for big money pits them against Conway's wrestler, the vicious Frankie the Thumper (Funk).

1792 Pindown Girl

1951, Arena Productions, 80 minutes.

"See intimate secrets of gorgeous girl wrestlers with the naked eye of the camera" blared the ads for this seldom-seen movie which also featured "the strange love life of a wrestling gal."

1793 The Pride of the Force

1933, British, Wardour, 74 minutes. Director-Producer: Norman Lee. Screenplay: Lee, Syd Courtenay, Arthur Woods. Photography: Claude Friese-Greene.

Cast: Leslie Fuller, Nan Bates, Faith Bennett, Alf Goddard, Hal Gordon, Ben Welden, Frank Perfitt, Pat Aherne, King Curtis.

Comic Fuller plays twins in this one. When his brother quits the police force to become a wrestler for a circus, a slow-witted farmer takes his place on the force and becomes a hero.

1794 Roped In

1928, Educational, 2 reels. Director: Charles Lamont.

Cast: Al St. John, Robert Graves, Bull Montana.

St. John is an author on wrestling who winds up in a grudge match against Bull Montana after he antagonizes him on a train trip in this comedy short.

1795 Samson in the Wax Museum

1963, Mexican, American-International, 90 minutes. Director: Alfonso Corona Blake. Producer: Alberto Lopez. Screenplay: Fernando Galiana, Julio Porter.

Cast: Santo, Claudio Brook.

During the early 1960's, spurred by the success of **Hercules** and **Hercules Unchained,** there was a spate of foreign-made spectaculars featuring legendary muscle men such as Atlas and Samson.

Apparently trying to cash in on the fad, the film distributor took some Mexican wrestling films featuring a masked hero called "Santo" and changed the name to Samson.

In this one, Santo or Samson defeats another mad scientist who's turning people into exhibits for his wax museum.

1796 Samson vs. the Vampire Women

1961, Mexican, American-International, 89 minutes. Director-Screenplay: Alfonso Corona Blake. Producer: Luis Garcia DeLeon.

Cast: Santo, Lorena Welazquez.

Another Santo/Samson adventure in which he battles two vampire women inside the wrestling ring and thwarts their plans to turn men into slaves. Good fun if you like camp.

Santo also appeared in these film adventures, among others: 1952—**The Silver Mask.** 1961—**Santo vs. the Diabolical Brain** (Chapter One: **Santo vs. The Diabolical Brain;** Chapter Two: **Town Without Law;** Chapter Three: **The Final Fight).** 1961—**Santo vs. the Crime King** (Chapter One: **Santo vs. the Crime King;** Chapter Two: **The Mafia;** Chapter Three: **Deaths in the Frontier).** 1961—**Santo in the Hotel of Death** (Chapter One: **Santo in the Hotel of Death;** Chapter Two: **The Secret Tunnel;** Chapter Three: **The Treasure of Death).** 1961—**Santo vs. the Monsters.** 1963—**Santo vs. the Strangler** (Chapter One: **Santo vs. the Strangler;** Chapter Two: **The Black Panther;** Chapter Three: **The Ghost of the Theater).** 1963—**Santo vs. the Spirit** (Chapter One: **Santo vs. the Spirit;** Chapter Two: **The Violator of Corpses;** Chapter 3: **Fatal Ambush).** 1966—**Santo of the Silver Mask vs. The Invasion of the Martians.** 1966—**Santo of the Silver Mask vs. the Villains of the Ring.** 1968—**Santo vs. the Blue Demon in Atlantis.** 1968—**Santo and the Blue Demon vs. the Mon-**

sters. 1969—**Santo and the Vengeance of the Vampire Women.** 1971—**Santo and the Daughter of Frankenstein.** 1971—**Santo vs. the Living Atom.** 1971—**Santo vs. the Royal Eagle.** 1972—**Santo vs. Dracula and the Wolfman.** 1973—**Santo and the Blue Demon vs. Dr. Frankenstein** (The Blue Demon is another wrestling hero who had his own film series, but these films have never been released in the United States). 1974—**Santo Mantequilla en la V. Llorona.** 1974—**Santo vs. Dr. Death.**

1797 Silent Witness

1962, Emerson, 70 minutes. Director-Producer: Ken Kennedy. Screenplay: Frank Jessy. Photography: Richard Cunha. Editor: Herbert L. Strock.

Cast: George Kennedy, Tris Coffin, Marjorie Reynolds, Andrea Lane, Billy Shanley, Dick Haynes.

Kennedy portrays a wrestler who accidentally kills a nightclub performer and who tracks down the newsboy who witnessed it.

The climax finds Kennedy grabbing the boy on a roller coaster at a closed Denver amusement park but then having a heart attack.

1798 Sit Tight

1931, Warner Brothers, 77 minutes. Director: Lloyd Bacon. Story: Rex Taylor.

Cast: Joe E. Brown, Winnie Lightner, Claudia Dell, Paul Gregory, Lotti Loder, Hobart Bosworth, Frank Hagney, Snitz Edwards.

Brown, who helps out at Lightner's health resort, gets into a big mess because of his mouth, as usual, bragging that he's a top wrestler called Jo Jo the Tiger.

With the help of a cigar butt applied at the right place at the right time, Brown is spurred to victory in the ring.

1799 Superargo

1968, Italian-Spanish, Columbia, 83 minutes, Color. Director: Paul Maxwell. Producer: Oliver Wells. Screenplay: Richard Lovelace. Photography: Geoffrey Packett. Editor: Andy Maivel.

Cast: Ken Wood, Guy Madison, Liz Barrett, Diana Loris, Harold Sambiel, Thomas Blank, Dennis McCloud.

This may sound like another Mexican wrestling adventure, but it's European. No matter, it's still camp with the production values only slightly higher than its Mexican counterparts.

A masked mystic wrestler named Superargo, who levitates himself when the going gets rough, battles a mad scientist who's creating an entire army of zombies composed of top athletes from all over the world he's kidnapped.

1800 Superargo vs. Diabolicus

1968, Italian-Spanish, Columbia, 88 minutes, Color. Director: Nick Nostro. Producer: Ottavio Poggi. Screenplay: Jesus Jaime Balcazar. Story: Mino Giarda. Photography: Francisco Marin. Editor: Teresa Alcocer.

Cast: Ken Wood, Gerard Tichy, Loredana Nusciak, Monica Randal, Francisco Castillo Escalona, Emilio Messina, Valentino Macchi, Geoffrey Copleston.

When Superargo's wrestling career is interrupted when he kills a man in the ring, he's hired as a secret agent to defeat Diabolicus, who's manufacturing artificial gold.

1801 El Superflaco (aka **Chiquito Pero Picoso)**

1967, Mexican, Alfa Films, 90 minutes. Director: Miguel M. Delgado. Producer: Fidel Pizarro. Screenplay: Gunther Gerszo, Carlos Orellana. Photography: José Ortiz Ramos.

Cast: Evangelina Elizondo, Alfonso Pompin Iglesias, Wolf Ruvinskis, Daniel Chino Herrera, Jose Jasso.

A runt is injected with hormones which make him a super wrestler; but just as he's supposed to meet the champ, the effects wear off in this minor comedy.

The wrestling champ is portrayed by Ruvinskis, better known for his portrayal of the masked wrestling hero in the **Neutron** series.

1802 Swing Your Lady

1938, Warner Brothers, 79 minutes. Director: Ray Enright. Producer: Sam Bischoff. Screenplay: Joseph Schrank, Maurice Leo, based on a play by Kenyon Nicholson and Charles Robinson. Photography: Arthur Edeson.

Cast: Humphrey Bogart, Nat Pendleton, Louise Fazenda, Penny Singleton, Frank McHugh, Allen Jenkins, Ronald Reagan, Leon Frank, Daniel Boone Savage.

A lady blacksmith agrees to wrestle with a male wrestler for a $100 purse in a match promoted by Bogie. When the pro wrestler (Pendleton) falls in love with her, she's replaced in the ring by her boy friend with the stipulation that the winner of the match gets to marry her.

1803 Take Down

1979, Buena Vista, 107 minutes, Color. Director-Producer: Keith Merrill. Screenplay: Merrill, Eric Hendershot. Photography: Reed Smoot. Editor: Richard Fetterman.

Cast: Edward Herrmann, Kathleen Lloyd, Lorenzo Lamas, Maureen McCormick, Nick Beavvy, Stephen Furst, Kevin Hooks, Vincent Roberts, Darryl Peterson.

The usual stuff about an English teacher who takes over a horrible high school wrestling team and turns it around, with the help of Lamas and another team member, who responds only to music.

It received very limited distribution.

1804 Tell It to Sweeney

1927, Paramount, 6,006 feet. Director: Gregory LaCava. Producer: B.P. Schulberg. Screenplay: Percy Heath. Photography: H. Kinley Martin.

Cast: Chester Conklin, George Bancroft, Jack Luden, Doris Hill, Franklin Bond, William H. Tooker.

The son of a railroad president is challenged to a wrestling match by his bully rival (Bancroft) for a girl's love.

1805 There Lived a Wrestler

1983, Indian, Thundathil, 120 minutes, Color. Director-Screenplay-Editor: P. Padmarajan. Producer: R. Suresh.

Cast: Rasheed, Nedumudi Venu, Jayanthy, K.G. Devaki Amma, Ashok.

A wrestler is taken in by villagers who hope to clean up by placing bets on him. The wrestler, however, becomes unhappy with his lot and wants to leave.

1806 The Touchables

1968, British, 20th Century Fox, 94-97 minutes. Director-Original Idea: Robert Freeman. Producer: John Bryan. Screenplay: Ian La Frenais. Photography: Alan Pudney. Editor: Richard Bryan.

Cast: David Anthony, Judy Huxtable, Esther Anderson, Marilyn Rickard, Kathy Simmonds, Ricki Starr, James Villiers, Harry Baird, Michael Chow, Joan Bakewell.

Four girls kidnap a rock star at a wrestling match and tie him up in their own private "pleasure dome," where they proceed to take turns making love to him.

Meanwhile, a villainous black wrestler named Lillywhite lusts after the singer himself and sends his henchmen to track him down, but the good guy wrestlers come to the rescue and battle it out.

1807 Trouble Brewing

1939, British, Associated British, 87 minutes. Director: Anthony Kimmins. Producer: Jack Kitchin. Screenplay: Kimmins,

Angus MacPhail, Michael Hogan. Photography: Ronald Neame.

Cast: George Formby, Garry Marsh, Googie Withers, Gus Mc-Naughton, Joss Ambler, Ronald Shiner, Tiger Tasker.

Battling Tiger Tasker in the wrestling ring is just one of the many wacky adventures encountered by Formby, who portrays a newspaper printer who tries to track down those responsible for a counterfeit horse race ticket.

1808 Vision Quest

1984, Warner Brothers, Color. Director: Harold Becker. Producers: Peter Guber, Jon Peters. Screenplay: Darryl Ponicsan, based on the novel by Terry Davis. Photography: Owen Roizman. Editor: Maury Winetrobe.

Cast: Matthew Modine, Linda Fiorentino, Michael Schoeffling, Ronny Cox, Charles Hallahan, Harold Sylvester, J.C. Quinn, Daphne Zuniga, James Gammon, Robert Blossom.

On his 18th birthday, a high school wrestler sets his sights on winning the state of Washington's high school wrestling title, a college scholarship and the girl of his dreams.

His unyielding determination wins over his tough coach. It was filmed in Spokane.

1809 The Wrestler (aka **The Maim Event**)

1974, Entertainment Ventures, 95 minutes, Color. Director: Jim Westman. Producer: W. R. Frank. Screenplay: Eugene Gump. Photography: Gil Hubbs. Editor: Neal Chastain.

Cast: Billy Robinson, Ed Asner, Elaine Giftos, Verne Gagne, Sarah Miller, Harold Sakata, Sam Menacher.

Honest promoter Asner battles the mob as wrestler Robinson is out to take away Gagne's crown. Among the big name wrestlers appearing as themselves—and proving to be one big happy family outside the ring—are Dusty Rhodes, The Crusher, Hardboiled Haggerty, Dick Murdoch, The Bruiser, Lord James Blears and Superstar Billy Graham.

1810 The Wrestler's Wife

1907, Pathe, 360 feet.

No further information available.

1811 Wrestling Burlesque

1903, British, 37 feet.

A wrestling fan takes on an imaginary opponent.

1812 The Wrestling Queen

1975, Harnell, Color. Producer: Wayne Wellons. Photography: John Sammons.

Among the featured professional wrestlers appearing are Vivian Vachon, "Cowboy" Bill Watts, Mad Dog Vachon, Grizzly Smith, Marie "Fifi" Laverne, Danny Hodge, Jean "The Giant" Ferre, Butcher Vachon.

1813 Wrestling Women vs. the Aztec Mummy

1964, Mexican, American-International, 88 minutes. Director: Rene Cardona. Producer: Guillermo Calderon Stell. Screenplay: Abel Salazar.

Cast: Lorena Velazquez, Armando Silvestre.

It's good woman wrestlers vs. evil woman wrestlers with a mummy thrown in for good measure.

Other Sports

During the course of our research, we came across a number of films which simply couldn't be categorized in one of the other chapters.

We would have liked to have included bowling films in a separate chapter, but there haven't been enough of them to warrant it.

Rather than dismissing many worthy films with a brief mention, we felt the best way was to put them all together in a chapter of their own.

1814 The Baltimore Bullet

1980, Avco-Embassy, 103 minutes, Color. Director: Robert Ellis Miller. Producer: John F. Brascia. Screenplay: Brascia, Robert Vincent O'Neill. Photography: James A. Crabe. Editor: Jerry Brady.

Cast: James Coburn, Omar Sharif, Bruce Boxleitner, Renee Blakely, Jack O'Halloran, Calvin Lockhart, Michael Learner, Jeff Temkin, Willie Mosconi.

This lighthearted clone of **The Hustler** features Coburn as an aging pool hustler, with Boxleitner as his partner and Sharif their quarry.

Nick Casey (Coburn) is considered the world's greatest pool player who's aching for another shot at the Deacon (Sharif), the only man ever to beat him.

High-rolling Deacon has just been released from prison and agrees to play Casey if the latter can raise $20,000. The Deacon is confident of victory because he claims Casey chokes whenever high stakes are involved.

Eleven of the world's top pool players appear as themselves.

1815 Dreamer

1979, 20th Century-Fox, 93 minutes, Color. Director: Noel Nosseck. Producer: Michael Lobell. Screenplay: James Procter, Larry Bischof. Photography: Bruce Surtees. Editor: Fred Chulack.

Cast: Tim Matheson, Susan Blakely, Jack Warden, Richard B. Shull, Barbara Stuart, Owen Bush, Marya Small, Matt Clark, John Crawford, Pedro Gonzalez-Gonzalez.

A Midwest boy rises from an unknown to challenge Dick Weber as national bowling champion. When the boy's coach (Warden) dies, he leaves him a special ball to use in the big games. Warden's philosophy to the young bowler (Matheson) was "you don't beat a person, you beat the pins."

The film's credits are a treat, showing old-time bowlers in action.

1816 Goofy

Walt Disney's cartoon character Goofy appeared in a long-running series of sports cartoons in the 1940's. 1944's **How to Play Football** was nominated for an Academy Award. The basketball cartoon **Double Dribble** featured players who all looked like Goofy and who had the names of the members of Disney's staff.

The series includes: 1941—**The Art of Skiing**; 1942—**How to Play Baseball**; 1942—**Olympic Champ**; 1942—**How to Swim**; 1944—**How to Play Golf**; 1944—**How to Play Football**; 1945—**Hockey Homicide**; 1946—**Double Dribble**; 1949—**Goofy Gymnastics**; 1949—**Tennis Racquet.**

1817 The Hustler

1961, 20th Century-Fox,

135 minutes. Director-Producer: Robert Rossen. Screenplay: Rossen, Sidney Carroll, based on a novel by Walter Tevis. Photography: Gene Shuftan. Editor: Dede Allen.

Cast: Paul Newman, Jackie Gleason, Piper Laurie, George C. Scott, Myron McCormick, Willie Mosconi, Vincent Gardenia, Jake LaMotta, Michael Constantine, Murray Hamilton.

The tale of Eddie Felson (Paul Newman) who challenged the pool room king Minnesota Fats (Gleason) won Academy Awards for best black and white art direction and best black and white cinematography. It also earned nominations for Newman as best actor, Laurie as best actress and for best picture.

Pool hustler Felson comes to New York to challenge champ Fats, and in a grueling 36-hour match ultimately loses to the champ.

Broke, he meets up with a crippled woman and starts hustling again, but he finally challenges the wrong person and winds up with broken fingers.

After linking up with hood Scott, he challenges Fats to a rematch.

1818 Kidder and KO

1918, Pathe. Screenplay: John W. Grey.

Cast: Bryant Washburn, Harry Dunkinson, Wadsworth Harris, Gertrude Selby.

The son of a canned fish bigwig is good only for winning billiard championships. Dad gets fed up with him and, handing him $50, tells him he'll get no more money until he turns that into $1,000 he earned by himself.

Like so many other silent film heroes, he heads west to make his fortune.

1819 Moonshine Bowling

1983, Canadian, National Film Board of Canada, 88 minutes, Color. Director: Andre Forcier. Producers: Bernard Lalonde, Louis Laverdiere. Screenplay: Forcier, Jacques Marcotte, Michele Pratt, Guy L'Ecuyer, Michel Cote, Bernard Lalonde. Photography: Francois Gill, Andre Gagnon.

Cast: Guy L'Ecuyer, Michel Cote, Robert Gravel, Lucie Miville, Gaston Lepage, Michel Gagnon.

A bowling comedy set in Quebec, this troubled production was completed in 1979 but took four years to edit and release. It concerns the large number of weird characters who frequent the Moonshine Bowling Alley, including one of its employees, a former bowling star who attempts to make a comeback during a tournament.

1820 The Negro in Sports

1950, Chesterfield Cigarettes, 10 minutes. Director: William Trent, Jr. Producer: E.M. Glucksman.

Jesse Owens and Bill Lund narrate a rare movie glimpse at the top black athletes of the era.

1821 Sportorama

1963, Paramount, 64 minutes, Color.

Six **Sports Illustrated** short films are strung together into a single feature. They are: **Boats A-Poppin', A Sport Is Born, King of the Keys, Speedway, The Big A** and **Ten Pin Tour.**

1822 Sports Immortals

1939, 20th Century-Fox, 11 minutes.

Among the sports stars featured are Red Grange, Helen Wills Moody, Susanne Lenglen, Barney Oldfield, Grover Cleveland Alexander, Babe Ruth, Knute Rockne, Sonja Henie, Man O'War, Jack Dempsey, Bobby Jones, Gertrude Ederle and Paavo Nurmi.

1823 Sports in Moggyland

1912, British, Diamond, 340 feet.

A group of wooden toys holds a sports festival.

1824 Sports in Toyland

1914, British, Excel, 310 feet. Director: Stuart Kinder.

Some more toys flex their athletic muscles.

1825 The Tragedy of Youth

1928, Tiffany-Stahl, 6,361 feet. Director: George Archainbaud. Story: Albert Shelby LeVino. Photography: Faxon Dean. Editor: Robert J. Kern.

Cast: Patsy Ruth Miller, Warner Baxter, William Collier, Jr., Claire McDowell, Harvey Clarke, Margaret Quimby, Billie Bennett, Stepin Fetchit.

When her husband neglects her for his bowling, a newlywed begins an extramarital love affair.

1826 What Makes Lizzy Dizzy?

1942, Columbia, 2 reels. Director: Jules White.

Cast: Harry Langdon, Elsie Ames, Dorothy Appleby, Monty Collins, Bud Jamison, Lorin Raker, Kathryn Sabichi, Kay Vallon.

Comedy short featuring Langdon and friends in a bowling tournament.

1827 Women in Sports

1982, Altana, 28 minutes, Color. Producer: Dan Klugherz. Editor: Joan Kuehl.

Using a blend of footage from newsreels, kinetoscopes, old Hollywood movies, advertising stills and art reproductions, the history of women in sports is traced from ancient Greece to the present, including their acceptance in Little League baseball and their participation in the New York City Marathon.

Athletes in Films

Almost from the beginning of the motion picture industry, filmmakers realized the box office potential of casting athletes in the movies.

From 1910 on, the names of well-known athletes began appearing with increasing regularity. Baseball players Hal Chase, Frank (Home Run) Baker and Turkey Mike Donlin and racing car driver Barney Oldfield are just a few of the many athletes who turned their sights to the film industry. That started a trend which has continued up to the present day with such big-name athletes as O.J. Simpson, Jim Brown, Muhammad Ali and Bernie Casey to name just a few.

We have not attempted to list every single athlete who has had a minor role in a film or who has had cameo roles. As with the main film listings, it was sometimes difficult where to draw the line. Our choices may sometimes seem a bit arbitrary, but we believe we have included every athlete who has gone on to either a major role or has made repeated appearances on the screen. In some cases we have included actors who became athletes after their film careers already had begun, such as Vince Van Patten and Harry (Peanuts) Lowrey.

It's now necessary to define just who qualifies as an actor-athlete for the purpose of this book. We have included only professional athletes, Olympians, collegiate All-Americans and certain other specialists like Arnold Schwarzenegger and Evel Knievel. In the case of baseball, we have only included major leaguers and not minor leaguers, such as Kurt Russell, who played in the Los Angeles Dodgers system, or semi-pro players like Joe E. Brown. Otherwise, this would be a volume approaching the size of Webster's Dictionary.

There are a number of athletes we feel deserve passing mention, if not a separate listing, for their film careers. These athletes appeared in minor roles or in cameos, and we don't feel they can genuinely be considered actors. This includes boxing champions Joe Frazier (**Ali the Man, Ali the Fighter,** 1975; **Rocky,** 1976); Sonny Liston (**Head,** 1968); Carlos Palomino (**Dance of the Dwarfs**); Tony Zale (**The Golden Gloves Story,** 1950); Gus Lesnevich (**Requiem for a Heavyweight,** 1962) and Gene Fullmer **The Devil's Brigade,** 1968); and fighters Steve Belloise (**Requiem for a Heavyweight,** 1962); Tami Mauriello (**On the Waterfront,** 1954); Chico Vejar (**The Midnight Story** and **World in My Corner,** 1956); Joe Jeannette (**Square Joe,** 1921), Eddie Mustafa Muhammad (**Raging Bull,** 1980); and John W. "Bull" Young (**One Round O'Brien Comes Back,** 1913). Young's acting career ended prematurely when he died of a broken neck after being knocked out by future world heavyweight champion Jess Willard on August 22, 1913.

Also, National Football Leaguers Deacon Jones, Clancy Williams, Cookie Gilchrist and Tody Smith (**Black Gunn,** 1972); Johnny Unitas (**Gus,** 1976); Ernie Nevers (**Spirit of Stanford,** 1942); Ray Nitschke (**Head,** 1968; **The Longest Yard,** 1974); Norm Van Brocklin (**The Long Gray Line,** 1955); Ernie Wheelwright (**The Longest Yard,** 1974); Roger Brown (**Paper Lion,** 1968); Ed "Too Tall" Jones and Lyle Alzado (**The Double McGuffin,** 1979) and Paul Hornung (**The Devil's Brigade,** 1968) and former Yale University football coach Herman Hickman (**The All-American,** 1953).

Also, baseball's Leo Durocher (**Main Street to Broadway,** 1953); Bill Dickey (**The Pride of the Yankees,** 1942; **The Stratton Story,** 1949); Mark Koenig (**The Pride of the Yankees,** 1942; **The Babe Ruth Story,** 1948); Whitey Ford and Ralph Houk (**Safe at Home,** 1962); Charley Lau (**Max Dugan Returns,** 1983); Yogi Berra (**A Touch of Mink,** 1962); Vida Blue (**Black Gunn,** 1972); Tommy Lasorda (**Americathon,** 1979); Bill Veeck (**The Kid from Cleveland,** 1949); Babe Pinelli (**The Kid from Left Field,** 1953); Chief Bender, Jack Coombs and Rube Oldring (**The Baseball Bug,** 1911); Frank Chance (**Peerless Leader,** 1913); John McGraw (**The Universal Boy,** 1914; **Right Off the Bat,** 1915); Bob Meusel (**Slide, Kelly, Slide,** 1927; **The Pride of the Yankees,** 1942) and Jimmy Dykes, Merv Shea and Gene Bearden (**The Stratton Story,** 1949).

Also, tennis's Bjorn Borg (**Racquet,** 1979); hockey's Max Bentley (**Paperback Hero,** 1973) and Derek Sanderson (**Face-Off,** 1971); wrestlers Verne Gagne (**The Wrestler,** 1974); Hulk Hogan (**Rocky III,** 1982) and Ox Baker (**Escape from New York,** 1981); golfer Walter Hagen; German Olympic skier Hannes Schneider (**Peak of Fate,** 1925); 1968 Olympic decathlon gold medal winner Bill Toomey (**The World's Greatest Athlete,** 1973) and basketball All-American Hank Luisetti (**Campus Confessions,** 1938).

Then there were golfing greats John Farrell and Bobby Jones, who made golf shorts, and William Demarest, who had a short-lived boxing career as "Battling McGovern" before going on to make more than 100 motion pictures.

Racing driver Parnelli Jones appeared in **Checkered Flag or Crash** (1966) and **Dirt** (1979) while racing driver Fred Lorenzen had a role in **Speed Lovers** (1968) and Dusty Russell was in **The Steel Arena** (1973).

1828 Kareem Abdul-Jabbar

The 7-foot-2 Jabbar is the NBA's all-time leading scorer, surpassing former NBA great-turned actor Wilt Chamberlain during the 1983-84 season. A practicing Moslem, Kareem changed his name from Lew Alcindor in 1971. The native of New York City led the University of California at Los Angeles to three consecutive National Collegiate Athletic Association titles (1967-69) and was the tournament's most valuable player all three times before going on to join the Milwaukee Bucks of the NBA. He was Rookie-of-the-Year in 1969-70 and won six NBA MVP Awards (1971-72-74-76-77-79). He was traded to the Los Angeles Lakers after the 1974-75 season. Jabbar helped Milwaukee win the NBA title in 1970-71 and led the Lakers to championships in both 1979-80 and 1981-82.

Films include: 1979--**Game of Death; The Fish That Saved Pittsburgh;** 1980--**Airplane.**

1829 Frankie Albert

Frankie Albert was a rarity in professional football—a left-handed quarterback and a very good one at that. The Stanford University All-American joined the San Francisco 49ers in the fledgling All American Football Conference in 1946 and remained with the club for seven years, the last three in the established National Football League. During his four seasons in the AAFC, Albert guided the 49ers to a 38-14-2 mark, a .731 winning percentage. Each year, however, San Francisco finished second to the powerful Cleveland Browns in the Western Division each year. When the AAFC folded after four years of action, Albert and San Francisco, along with Cleveland and Baltimore, moved into the NFL. Albert completed 316 passes, connecting

Kareem Abdul-Jabbar.

on 52.4 percent, for 3,847 yards and 27 touchdowns in his three NFL seasons. He also handled the punting duties for the 49ers and averaged 44.3 yards per kick, second best in the NFL, in 1951. Albert coached San Francisco in 1956-57-58 and had a 19-16-1 record. He portrayed himself in the 1942 Columbia picture **Spirit of Stanford.**

Films include: 1942—**Spirit of Stanford.**

1830 Muhammad Ali

Muhammad Ali was the only boxer ever to win the world heavyweight championship three different times, taking the title from Sonny Liston, George Foreman and Leon Spinks. Ali, born Cassius Clay in Louisville, Kentucky, knocked out Liston in eight rounds on February 25, 1964, in Miami Beach, Florida; Foreman in eight rounds on October 30, 1974, in Kinshasa, Zaire, and decisioned Spinks in 15 rounds on September 15, 1978, in New Orleans, Louisiana. Three of his greatest fights were against Joe Frazier with Ali winning two, including "The Thrilla in Manila." He successfully defended his title against the likes of Liston, Floyd Patterson, George Chuvalo, Ernie Terrell, Ken Norton, Earnie Shavers and Jimmy Young. He retired after being stopped by Larry Holmes in a bid for a fourth world heavyweight crown in 1980. The former Olympic gold medal winner finished his pro career with a 57-4 record. On June 25, 1976, Ali fought a 15-round exhibition match against sumo wrestler Antonio Inoki in Tokyo. One of the most flamboyant, charismatic and colorful fighters ever to step into the ring, Ali always had rhymes for his opponents and described his fighting style as "Float like a butterfly, sting like a bee." Ali portrayed himself in the 1977 film **The Greatest.**

Films include: 1962—**Requiem for a Heavyweight;** 1969—**Float Like a Butterfly, Sting Like a Bee** (documentary); 1970—**A.K.A. Cassius Clay** (documentary), **The Super Fight** (documentary); 1972—**Baddest Daddy in the Whole World** (documentary), **Money Talks, Black Rodeo;** 1975—**Ali the Man, Ali the Fighter** (documentary); 1977—**The Greatest;** 1981—**Body and Soul.**

1831 Vijay Amritraj

Vijay, which means victory in Hindi, was ranked among the top 20 tennis players in the world until injuries slowed down his game in the late 1970's. He was a mainstay of the Indian Davis Cup team during the 70's and led India to the Davis Cup final in 1974; but his government and the Indian Tennis Federation declined to play South Africa in the final because of that country's apartheid policy. In both 1973 and 1974, the smooth-stroking Vijay reached the quarter-finals of the United States Open and in 1973 was a quarter-finalist at Wimbledon. He reached the semi-finals in Wimbledon doubles in 1976 and won the World Championship Tennis doubles title in 1977 with Dick Stockton. Vijay played World Team Tennis for the San Diego Friars in 1975 and the Los Angeles Strings in 1976 and when they won in 1978. The native of Madras, India, is now an American citizen.

Films include: 1979—**Players;** 1983—**Octopussy.**

1832 Art Aragon

Art Aragon, "The California Golden Boy," was an outstanding lightweight fighter who lost a 15-round decision to champion James Carter for the world title on August 14, 1953, in Los Angeles, California. Three months earlier, Aragon earned a shot at the crown by outpointing Carter in a 10-round non-title bout in Los Angeles. Carter, the first man to hold the same world championship three times, decisioned Aragon in a third meeting, a non-title

Muhammad Ali.

bout on May 3, 1956 in Los Angeles. Aragon also won a ten-round decision over Lauro Salas in Los Angeles on March 4, 1952, just two months before Salas won the world championship.

Films include: 1951—**To Hell and Back;** 1952—**The Ring;** 1953—**Off Limits;** 1956—**World in My Corner;** 1972—**Fat City.**

1833 Henry Armstrong

Pound for pound, Henry Armstrong was one of the greatest fighters ever to enter the boxing ring. The native of Columbia, Mississippi, was the only fighter to hold three world championships simultaneously, reigning as featherweight, lightweight and welterweight king. He kayoed Petey Sarron to win the featherweight title on October 29, 1937; decisioned Barney Ross to capture the welterweight crown on May 31, 1938, and outpointed Lou Ambers to take the lightweight championship on August 17, 1938. He relinquished his featherweight title near the end of 1938, lost his lightweight crown to Ambers in 1939 and successfully defended his welterweight championship 19 straight times before losing a 15-round decision to Fritzie Zivic on October 4, 1940. Armstrong battled middleweight king Ceferino Garcia to a 10-round draw on March 1, 1940, in an attempt to win a fourth different world championship. Armstrong, who was born Henry Jackson and fought early in his career as Melody Jackson, was ordained a Baptist minister in 1951. He posted a 143-22-8 record during his 15-year career and was elected to the Boxing Hall of Fame in 1954.

Films include: 1939—**Keep Punching;** 1941—**The Pittsburgh Kid;** 1946—**Joe Palooka, Champ.**

1834 Buddy Baer

The 250-pound younger brother of former world heavyweight champion Max Baer, Buddy was a fine fighter in his own right. Born Jacob Henry Baer, he twice fought Joe Louis for the title. The Brown Bomber won both bouts, winning on a disqualification in the seventh round on May 23, 1941 in Washington, D.C., and on a first round knockout on January 9, 1942, at New York's Madison Square Garden.

Films include: 1937—**Transatlantic Trouble** (aka **Take It from Me**); 1949—**Africa Screams;** 1951—**Quo Vadis, Two Tickets to Broadway;** 1952—**The Big Sky, Jack and the Beanstalk, Flame of Araby;** 1953—**Dream Wife, Fair Wind to Java;** 1954—**Jubilee Trail;** 1955—**Slightly Scarlet;** 1957—**Hell Canyon** (aka **Hell Canyon Outlaws**); 1958—**Once Upon a Horse, Giant from the Unknown;** 1961—**Snow White and the Three Stooges;** 1962—**The Bashful Elephant;** 1966—**Ride Beyond Vengeance.**

1835 Max Baer

Max Baer was one of the most popular fighters ever to enter the square ring. At the height of his popularity in the early 1930's, he starred opposite Myrna Loy in the 1933 film **The Prizefighter and the Lady.** A year later, on June 14, 1934, he won the world heavyweight championship by knocking out Primo Carnera in 11 rounds in New York City. He lost his title a year later when James J. Braddock won a 15-round decision. Baer fought the likes of Joe Louis, Max Schmeling, King Levinsky, Tommy Farr, Tony Galento, Tommy Loughran and Lou Nova during a 65-13 career that earned him election into the Boxing Hall of Fame in 1968. After his boxing days, he resumed his movie career. He was formerly married to actress Dorothy Dunbar. A brother, Buddy, also appeared in films while a son, Max, Jr., starred in **The Beverly Hillbillies.** Baer died in a Hollywood, California, hotel in 1959.

Films include: 1933—**The Prizefighter and the Lady;** 1938—**Fisticuffs** (short); 1940—**Two Mugs from Brooklyn;** 1942—**The Navy Comes Through;** 1943—**Ladies Day, Buckskin Frontier;** 1944—**The Iron Road;** 1949—**Africa Screams, Bride for Sale;** 1950—**Riding High;** 1951—**Skipalong Rosenbloom;** 1956—**The Harder They Fall;** 1957—**Utah Blaine;** 1958—**Once Upon a Horse, Over She Goes.**

1836 Home Run Baker

He hit just 93 career homers—minuscule compared to the totals of modern players--but in the dead ball era, a fantastic feat. John Franklin Baker hit .307 during his 13-year major league career (seven with the Philadelphia A's and six with the New York Yankees) and appeared in six World Series with a lifetime .363 average. It was in the 1911 World Series that the native of Trappe, Maryland, earned his nickname "Home Run" by hitting homers against the legendary Christy Mathewson and Rube Marquard of the New York Giants in separate games to help the A's win the championship. He hit .375 with five runs-batted-in and seven runs scored in six series games. Baker, who along with Stuffy McInnis, Jack Barry and Eddie Collins formed Connie Mack's "$100,000 infield" with the A's, led the American League in home runs four consecutive years (1911-14). He was inducted into the Baseball Hall of Fame in 1955. Baker died in 1963.

Films include: 1913—**The Shortstop's Double;** 1914—**Home Run Baker's Double.**

1837 Lem Barney

Lem Barney ranks as one of the finest defensive backs in National Football League history. The talented cornerback, drafted in the second round by the Detroit Lions out of Jackson State, earned NFL Rookie-of-the-Year honors in 1967 after intercepting ten passes for 232 yards and three touchdowns. During his brilliant 11-year career with the Lions, he earned All-Pro recognition and played in numerous pro bowl games. He registered more than 4,000 total return yards during his career and ranks among the NFL's leading pass interceptors with 56 interceptions for 1,077 yards and seven TDs.

Films include: 1968—**The Paper Lion;** 1974—**The Black Six.**

1838 Bo Belinsky

The fun-loving playboy from New York City broke into the major leagues in 1962 and was an instant success on the field with the Los Angeles Angels and off the field with starlets of Hollywood. The handsome six feet two southpaw pitched a no-hitter over Baltimore on May 5, 1962, en route to an 11-12 campaign that included three shutouts and 145 strikeouts. He allowed just 149 hits in 187 innings to rank third in the American League in fewest hits allowed per nine innings. He fell to 2-9 the following year and wound up being suspended by the Angels during the 1964 season when he posted a 9-8 record and a 2.86 earned run average. He then spent five uneventful seasons in the majors, pitching for Philadelphia, Houston, Pittsburgh and Cincinnati, and his once bright career ended with a lifetime 28-51 mark.

Films include: 1967—**C'mon, Let's Live a Little.**

1839 Bruce Bennett

Herman Brix was an outstanding athlete at the University of Washington and a silver medal Olympic shot putter long before Columbia Pictures changed his name to Bruce Bennett. Brix, a native of Tacoma, Washington, finished second to record-setting John Kuck of the United States in the 1928 Olympic Games at Amsterdam,

Holland. Both Kuck and Brix surpassed the previous Olympic shot put record in the competition. Thanks to actor Douglas Fairbanks, Sr., and director Sam Wood, Brix subsequently turned to Hollywood for a career. He was still using his given name in 1935 when he made **The New Adventures of Tarzan.** By 1939, however, Columbia Pictures changed his name to Bruce Bennett.

Films include: 1931--**Touchdown;** 1934--**Student Tour;** 1935--**The New Adventures of Tarzan;** 1936--**A Million to One;** 1937--**Two Minutes to Play, Million Dollar Racket, Danger Patrol, Amateur Crook, Shadow of Chinatown** (serial); 1938--**Tarzan and the Green Goddess, The Lone Ranger** (serial); **Hawk of the Wilderness** (serial), **Flying Fists;** 1939--**My Son Is Guilty;** 1940--**Blazing Six Shooters, The Man with Nine Lives, The Secret Seven, Before I Hang;** 1941--**The Phantom Submarine, The Officer and the Lady;** 1942--**Atlantic Convoy, Sabotage Squad;** 1943--**The More the Merrier, Sahara;** 1945--**Mildred Pierce, Danger Signal;** 1946--**A Stolen Life;** 1947--**The Man I Love, Nora Prentiss, Cheyenne, Dark Passage;** 1948--**The Treasure of Sierra Madre, Silver River, To the Victor;** 1949--**The Younger Brothers, Task Force;** 1950--**Mystery Street, The Second Face;** 1951--**The Great Missouri Raid, The Last Outpost, Angels in the Outfield;** 1952--**Sudden Fear;** 1955--**Strategic Air Command;** 1956--**Love Me Tender, Bottom of the Bottle;** 1957--**Three Violent People;** 1958--**Flaming Frontier;** 1959--**The Alligator People;** 1961--**The Fiend of Dope Island;** 1962--**The Outsider.**

1840 John Beradino

John Berardino (he dropped the second "r" after his baseball career) spent 11 years in the major leagues as an infielder with the St. Louis Browns (1939-42, 46-47, 51), the Cleveland Indians (1948-49, 52) and the Pittsburgh Pirates (1950, 52). In 1940, he hit 31 doubles, 16 homers and drove home 85 runs while leading American League shortstops in total chances per game with the Browns. A year later, he batted .271 with 30 doubles and 89 RBIs. He spent the next three years in military service before returning to St. Louis in 1946. In 1948, the native of Los Angeles, California, was a utility infielder for the World Champion Cleveland Indians. For many years he has been a star on the television soap opera **General Hospital.**

Films include: 1949--**Kid from Cleveland;** 1953--**Kid from Left Field;** 1956--**Behind the High Wall, The Killer Is Loose;** 1958--**The Naked and the Dead, Wild Heritage, The World Was His Jury;** 1960--**Seven Thieves;** 1962--**The Scarface Mob.**

1841 Doc Blanchard

Felix (Doc) Blanchard, "Mr. Inside" on three powerhouse West Point teams, was a three-time all-American and the 1945 Heisman Trophy winner as collegiate football's outstanding player. The six foot, 205 pounder gained 1,908 yards and scored 38 touchdowns in his three seasons with the Black Knights. The pulverizing fullback ran the 100 yards in ten seconds flat and teamed with "Mr. Outside," Glenn Davis, to make Army one of the most awesome teams in college football. After graduation, he made the military service his career and retired as a colonel. Blanchard and Davis portrayed themselves in **The Spirit of West Point,** a movie about the two Army gridiron greats.

Films include: 1947--**The Spirit of West Point.**

1842 Joe Bonomo

Joe Bonomo was a body builder, amateur wrestler and a professional football player who went on to earn the title "Hercules of the

Top: John Beradino. Bottom, L–R: Doc Blanchard, Army coach Red Blaik, and Glenn Davis.

the Screen." While making movies, Bonomo also did some pro wrestling on the side under the name of Joe Atlas. He had over 100 matches before retiring from the sport and never lost. Born in the Coney Island section of Brooklyn, New York, on Christmas Day, 1901, he starred in six sports in high school and went on to play with the Hiltons, Coney Island's first professional football team. In 1921, he entered an amateur wrestling tournament in New York City, but lost for the championship to future Olympian Nat Pendleton, later of motion picture fame. Bonomo was a frequent visitor to the famous Bothner's Gym in New York, America's wrestling headquarters, and he learned from the likes of such professionals as Jim Londos, Ed (Strangler) Lewis and Bull Montana, who also turned to a career in the movies. In 1921, he won the "Modern Apollo" contest in New York City, the forerunner of the Mr. America competitions, and with it began a career in the cinema that saw him become one of Hollywood's top-ranked serial stars and stuntmen. He made his debut as a stuntman--although he thought he was one of the regular actors--in the 1921 film **A Light in the Dark** starring Hope Hampton and subsequently appeared in the original **Hunchback of Notre Dame** (1923) with Lon Chaney. As an actor, he portrayed pirates, gypsies, adagio dancers, doormen, policemen, sailors, cowboys. You name it, and Bonomo played it. He was a Tiger-man in the 1932 film **Island of Lost Souls** and a gorilla in the 1932 movie **Murders in the Rue Morgue.** He made hundreds of films with thousands of stunt sequences in serials, two-reelers and features. He starred in the 1925 series **The Great Circus Mystery** which was the first of its kind to play top first run theaters. Bonomo also appeared in the 1929 series **Phantoms of the North** which added recorded music to film at theaters in an attempt to present it as a "sound" movie. His film career declined when the sound era came in because he had extreme difficulty memorizing his lines. Bonomo, who also turned to vaudeville, eventually returned to his family's Turkish Taffy business and subsequently became a successful businessman. He died in 1978.

Films include: 1921--**A Light in the Dark, Hurricane Hutch** (serial); 1923--**Beasts of Paradise** (serial), **The Eagles Talons** (serial), **The Hunchback of Notre Dame;** 1924--**Wolves of the North** (serial), **The Iron Man** (serial), **The College Cowboy** (serial); 1925--**The Great Circus Mystery** (serial), **Perils of the Wild** (aka **Swiss Family Robinson**) (serial); 1927--**Heroes of the Wild** (serial), **The Golden Stallion** (serial); 1928--**The Chinatown Mystery** (serial); 1929--**Phantoms of the North** (serial), **Noah's Ark;** 1931--**The Vanishing Legion** (serial), **Phantom of the West** (serial); 1932--**Island of Lost Souls, Murders in the Rue Morgue, The Last Frontier** (serial), **The Lost Special** (serial), **The Sign of the Cross, As You Desire Me;** 1934--**Cleopatra.**

1843 Terry Bradshaw

Terry Bradshaw quarterbacked the Pittsburgh Steelers to an unprecedented four Super Bowl victories and was named the postseason classic's most valuable player twice. The six feet three Bradshaw, selected out of Louisiana Tech in the first round of the 1970 National Football League draft, guided the Steelers to ten playoff appearances during his 14-year career. He led Pittsburgh to successive Super Bowl victories in 1975 (over Minnesota) and 1976 (over Dallas) and again in 1979 (over Dallas) and 1980 (over Los Angeles). Bradshaw tossed a record four touchdown passes in Super Bowl XIII ('79) and com-

Terry Bradshaw.

pleted 14 passes for 309 yards and two TDs in Super Bowl XIV ('80) to earn back-to-back MVP awards. He set career Super Bowl records for most TD passes (nine) and most passing yards (932). Bradshaw retired after the 1983 season. He has made numerous television commercials.

Films include: 1978--**Hooper;** 1980--**Smokey and the Bandit II;** 1981--**Cannonball Run.**

1844 Don Bragg

Don Bragg set an Olympic record when he won a gold medal in the pole vault event at the 1960 Games in Rome, Italy. Following his triumph, the muscular Bragg appeared as Tarzan in the film **Tarzan and the Jewels of Opar.** The movie, however, was blocked by a suit over copyright and never released.

1845 Mark Breland

Film careers often beckon Olympic heroes, but for 1984 gold medal boxer Mark Breland was a professional actor before the Games in Los Angeles, California. Breland, who won the Olympic gold in the welterweight class, portrayed the first black cadet at a South Carolina military academy in the movie **Lords of Discipline.** The six feet three Breland was discovered when a freelance casting director saw his picture in a newspaper magazine story about amateur boxing. He was undefeated in his international boxing career and was a three-time world champion at 147 pounds.

Films include: 1983--**Lords of Discipline.**

1846 Jim Brown

Paul Brown, the legendary football coach of the Cleveland Browns, had a simple game plan: Just hand the ball to Jim Brown and get out of his way. In nine years with the Browns, big "No. 32" led the National Football League in rushing eight times and twice was named the league's most valuable player. He scored a record 126 touchdowns and gained a record 12,312 yards. He averaged 5.2 yards per carry. In short, he was the best the game had ever seen. Brown was born on St. Simon Island, off the Georgia coast but was raised in Manhasset, Long Island. He went on to become an All-American in both football and lacrosse at Syracuse University. In 1957, he was named the NFL's Rookie of the Year and was the league's MVP in 1958 and 1965. He played in nine straight pro bowls and set the standards for others to try to attain. In 1966, Brown walked away from football and turned his attention toward acting. He was inducted into the Pro Football Hall of Fame in 1971. Brown was the first bonafide black male "sex symbol" of the American cinema.

Films include: 1964--**Rio Conchos, Kenner;** 1967--**Dirty Dozen;** 1968--**Riot, Dark of the Sun, The Split, Ice Station Zebra;** 1969--**100 Rifles;** 1970--**Tick Tick Tick, El Condor, The Grasshopper;** 1972--**Slaughter, Black Gunn;** 1973--**Slaughter's Big Rip-Off, I Escaped from Devil's Island, The Slams;** 1974--**Three the Hard Way;** 1975--**Take a Hard Ride;** 1976--**Do They Cry in America?;** 1977--**Kid Vengeance;** 1978--**Fingers.**

1847 Johnny Mack Brown

Johnny Mack Brown, one of the early Western heroes of the movies, was the Frank Merriwell of the 1926 Rose Bowl game. Brown, a standout halfback for the University of Alabama, led a third quarter surge that carried the Crimson Tide to a stunning 20-19 upset victory over the University of Washington on that memorable New Year's Day. Brown scored two touchdowns, including one on a 59-yard pass, as Alabama registered 20 third quarter points to overcome a 12-0 halftime Washington lead. His gridiron exploits eventually earned him induction into the College Football Hall of Fame. The native of Dothan, Alabama, who earned All-American recognition at Alabama, turned his back on a professional football career and headed for Hollywood. He died in Woodland Hills, California, in 1975.

Films include: 1927—**The Bugle Call, Fair Co-Ed**; 1928—**Soft Living, Square Crooks, Annapolis, Our Dancing Daughters, Lady of Chance, Divine Woman, The Play Girl**; 1929—**The Single Standard, Woman of Affairs, Coquette, The Valiant, Jazz Heaven**; 1930—**Billy the Kid, Undertow, Hurricane, Montana Moon**; 1931—**The Great Meadow, The Secret Six, The Last Flight, Lasca of the Rio Grande, Laughing Sinners**; 1932—**Flames, The Vanishing Frontier, Malay Nights, 70,000 Witnesses**; 1933—**Son of a Sailor, Saturday's Millions, Female, Hollywood on Parade, Fighting with Kit Carson** (serial); 1934—**Three on a Honeymoon, It Ain't No Sin, Marrying Widows, Belle of the Nineties, Cross Streets, Against the Law**; 1935—**St. Louis Woman, Courageous Avenger, The Rustlers of Red Dog, The Right to Live**; 1936—**The Desert Phantom, Lawless Land, Rouge of the Range**; 1937—**Wells Fargo, Bar Z Bad Man, Guns in the Dark, A Lawman Is Born, Boothill Brigade, Wild West Days** (serial); 1938—**Born to the West, Flaming Frontiers** (serial); 1939—**Desperate Trails, Oklahoma Frontier, The Oregon Trail** (serial); 1940—**Bad Man from Red Butte, Chip of the Flying U, West of Carson City, Riders of Pasco Basin, Son of Roaring Dan, Ragtime Cowboy Joe, Law and Order, Pony Post**; 1941—**Bury Me Not on the Lone Prairie, The Man from Montana, The Masked Rider, Law of the Range**; 1942—**Ride 'Em Cowboy, The Silver Bullet, Stagecoach Buckaroo, The Old Chisholm Trail, Deep in the Heart of Texas, Arizona Cyclone, Fighting Bill Fargo, The Boss of Hangtown, Little Joe the Wrangler**; 1943—**The Texas Kid, The Ghost Rider, The Stranger from Pecos, Tenting Tonight on the Old Camp Ground, Cheyenne Roundup, Lone Star Trail**; 1944—**Range Law, West of the Rio Grande, Land of the Outlaws, Raiders of the Border, Law of the Valley, Partners of the Trail**; 1945—**Gun Smoke; The Navajo Trail, Flame of the West**; 1946—**Under Arizona Skies, Trigger Fingers, Drifting Along, The Haunted Mine, Gentleman from Texas, Shadows on the Range, Raiders of the South**; 1947—**Land of the Lawless, Valley of Fear, Trailing Danger, Code of the Saddle, Flashing Guns**; 1948—**Frontier Agent, Triggerman, Overland Trails**; 1949—**The Fighting Ranger, Stampede, Western Renegades, Law of the West, West of El Dorado, Range Justice**; 1950—**Over the Border, West of Wyoming, Short Grass, Six Gun Mesa, Outlaw Gold, Law of the Panhandle**; 1951—**The Man from Sonora, Oklahoma Outlaws, Blazing Bullets, Montana Desperado, Texas Lawmen**; 1952—**Texas City, Dead Man's Trail, Man from the Black Hills**; 1953—**Canyon Ambush**; 1965—**The Bounty Killer, Requiem for a Gunfighter**; 1966—**Apache Uprising.**

1848 Tim Brown

Tim Brown was one of the National Football League's great all-purpose backs during his 10-year career. The Ball State University product joined Green Bay in 1959 but was released after two games. He went on to star with the Philadelphia Eagles from 1960 through 1967, playing on their 1960 NFL championship team. He then played one season with Baltimore before retiring after their Super Bowl III loss to the New York Jets. In 1962, he broke the NFL record for combined net yardage (2,306 yards). The following season, he surpassed his own NFL mark with 2,428 yards. He is eighth on the all-time NFL combined yardage list with 12,684 yards (3,862 rushing, 3,399 receiving, 4,781 kickoff returns, 639 punt returns and three fumble returns). In 1961, he returned a kickoff 105 yards for a touchdown against Cleveland, tying the NFL mark for the second longest kickoff return. In 1966, he returned five kickoffs for 247 yards, including a record two TDs on runs of 93 and 90 yards, against Dallas. Brown tied another NFL record when he returned a missed field goal 99 yards for a TD against St. Louis in 1962. The native of Richmond, Indiana, born Thomas Allen Brown, began his acting career in the 1969 film **M*A*S*H.** In addition to movies, he has appeared in numerous television shows and commercials.

Films include: 1969—**M*A*S*H;** 1972—**A Place Called Today, Black Gunn;** 1973—**Sweet Sugar, Inside Straight, Girls Are for Loving, Bonnie's Kids;** 1975—**Nashville, Stud Brown,** (aka **Dynamite Kid**); 1976—**Gus, Do They Cry in America?;** 1977—**Zebra Force.**

1849 Dick Butkus

Dick Butkus used his tremendous competitiveness and great strength to wreak havoc on his opponents during his nine-year career (1965-73) with the Chicago Bears of the National Football League. The two-time All-American at the University of Illinois was selected by the Bears in the first round of the 1965 draft and went on to play in eight straight pro bowls. The great middle linebacker intercepted 22 passes and recovered 25 opponents' fumbles during his career which was cut short by a serious knee injury. The six feet three, 245 pounder was an All-NFL selection seven times. Butkus made several popular television beer commercials with another former NFL star, Bubba Smith, that led to a TV series, **Blue Thunder,** and movies for both men.

Films include: 1976—**Gus;** 1984—**Johnny Dangerously.**

1850 Tony Canzoneri

The five feet four, 135 pounder from Slidell, Louisiana, was one of the greatest lightweight boxers of all time. He was the featherweight, junior welterweight and twice the lightweight champion of the world. He won his first pro title on February 10, 1928, when he decisioned Benny Bass for the featherweight crown in New York City. He went on to knock out Al Singer in one round on November 14, 1930, in New York City to win the world lightweight championship and captured the junior welterweight title six months later with a third round kayo of Jackie (Kid) Berg in Chicago. Tony lost the lightweight crown in 1933 to Barney Ross but regained it with a 15-round decision over Lou Ambers in New York City on May 10, 1935. He had 18 championship fights during a brilliant career that saw him win 138 bouts. Canzoneri was elected to the Boxing Hall of Fame in 1956. He died in 1959 in New York City.

Films include: 1933—**Mr. Broadway;** 1949—**Ringside.**

1851 Primo Carnera

"The Ambling Alp" from the town of Sequals, just outside of Venice, Italy, took the American public by storm in the early 1930's with his awesome reputation as a superman following early round knockouts over either aging or hopelessly overmatched opponents. On February 10, 1933, Primo knocked out Ernie Schaaf in the 13th round at New York's Madison Square Garden as the crowd yelled "fake." Three days later, Schaaf died as the result of that KO punch, silencing the cries of "fix." On June 29, 1933, the six feet five and three-fourths, 260 pounder won the heavyweight championship by knocking out Jack Sharkey in the sixth round at Long Island, New York. He successfully defended his crown by whipping Paolino Uzcudun in Rome and Tommy Loughran in Miami, Florida. But on June 14, 1934, Max Baer floored Carnera ten times before the fight was stopped in the 11th round with Baer the new champion. Ironically, Baer and Carnera appeared together in the 1933 movie **The Prizefighter and the Lady.** He retired from the ring in 1946 and turned to pro wrestling, touring the U.S., Europe, Australia and South Africa. He put together an 88-14 record during his boxing career with 68 knockouts. He died in Italy in 1967. In 1956, actor Humphrey Bogart starred in the film **The Harder They Fall,** loosely based on the life of Carnera. Mike Lane played the role of the mammoth boxer.

Films include: 1931--**The Bigger They Are** (short); 1933--**The Prizefighter and the Lady;** 1949--**The Iron Crown;** 1954--**Prince Valiant, Casanova's Big Night;** 1960--**Hercules Unchained.**

1852 Georges Carpentier

The popular Frenchman was part of boxing's first "Million Dollar" gate when he fought Jack Dempsey for the heavyweight championship on July 2, 1921, at Boyle's Thirty Acres in Jersey City, New Jersey. Dempsey received $300,000 for the fight. Carpentier, who was stopped in four rounds, got $200,000 as 80,183 spectators paid $1,789,238 to see the fight. The 175 pounder from Lens, France, known as "The Orchid Man," won the welterweight championship of France on June 15, 1911, with a 16-round kayo of R. Eutache and the European welterweight title four months later with a ten-round knock out over Young Joseph in London, England. In his first American fight, he knocked out Battling Levinsky in four rounds to win the world's light heavyweight championship on October 12, 1920, in Jersey City. During World War I, he served in the French Army as a lieutenant in the Aviation Corps. He had an 85-15-5 record fighting in every weight class from flyweight through heavyweight. He was elected to the Boxing Hall of Fame in 1964. He died in 1975.

Films include: 1912--**The Romance of Carpentier;** 1913--**Carpentier vs. Bombadier Wells Fight;** 1920--**The Wonder Man, Le Match Criqui-Ledoux;** 1922--**A Gypsy Cavalier** (aka **My Lady April);** 1928--**La Symphonie Pathetique;** 1929--**The Show of Shows;** 1930--**Hold Everything, Georges Carpentier in Naughty but Nice** (short); 1934--**Toboggan.**

Other French films: **The Adventures of a Champion, The Treasure of Keriolet.**

1853 Bernie Casey

The product of Bowling Green University spent eight outstanding seasons in the National Football League as a premier pass receiver for the San Francisco 49ers (1961-66) and Los Angeles Rams (1967-68). He caught 50 or more passes five times during his eight years, four times with the 49ers (1962-64-65-66) and once with the Rams (1967). His pass catching heroics helped Los Angeles to an 11-1 record and the Coastal Conference title in 1967. He is fourth on the San Francisco all-time career list in pass receiving with 277 receptions for 4,008 yards and 27 touchdowns. In 1964, he caught 58 passes for 808 yards; and on November 13, 1966, Casey grabbed 12 passes for 225 yards in a game against the Chicago Bears.

Films include: 1969--**Sons of the Magnificent Seven;** 1970--**Tick Tick Tick;** 1972--**Black Gunn, Boxcar Bertha, Hit Man;** 1973--**Cleopatra Jones, Maurie** (aka **Big Mo);** 1975--**Cornbread, Earl and Me;** 1977--**Brothers;** 1979--**The**

Watts Monster; 1980--**Sharkey's Machine;** 1983--**Never Say Never Again;** 1984--**Revenge of the Nerds.**

1854 Wilt Chamberlain

Wilt the Stilt was the greatest offensive player in basketball history. On March 2, 1962, the seven feet one center scored an incredible 100 points against the New York Knicks and finished the 1962-63 campaign with an unbelievable 4,029 points in 80 games for a 50.4 average. The awesome and powerful Chamberlain led the National Basketball Association in scoring for seven straight seasons and in rebounds five times with a record 55 in one game. He was selected the league's most valuable player four times and was a perennial all-league and All-Star team choice. His all-time scoring mark of 31,419 career points was broken by Kareem Abdul-Jabbar during the 1983-84 season, but he still holds the NBA career records for scoring average (30.1) and rebounds (23,924). In 1968, Los Angeles Lakers owner Jack Kent Cooke paid Chamberlain a reported $3 million for five seasons, making Wilt at the time the highest-paid pro athlete in history. The Philadelphia, Pennsylvania, product spent two years at the University of Kansas and then played a season with the Harlem Globetrotters before joining the old Philadelphia Warriors of the NBA. He also played with San Francisco and the Philadelphia 76ers.

Films include: 1984--**Conan the Destroyer.**

1855 Randall (Tex) Cobb

Randy (Tex) Cobb was one of the few fighters to go the distance in a title fight with Larry Holmes as he dropped a 15-round decision for the World Boxing Council championship on November 26, 1982, at the Houston Astrodome. The former Abilene Christian University football player also fought heavyweight contender Earnie Shavers. The 234-pound boxer won 20 of his first 22 fights, including 18 by knockouts, before his title match with Holmes. He flattened his first seven opponents in less than three rounds. In addition to his boxing career, Cobb was proficient in the sport of kick-boxing, an art he displayed during a scene in the 1983 film **Uncommon Valor.**

Films include: 1979—**The Champ;** 1983—**Uncommon Valor.**

1856 Billy Conn

"The Pittsburgh Kid" came within a whisker of upsetting a bigger and heavier Joe Louis for the world heavyweight championship on June 18, 1941. Conn, who gave up his world light heavyweight crown to compete as a heavyweight, was way ahead on points as the two fighters squared away in the 13th round at New York's Yankee Stadium. As Conn, who was boxing circles around Louis, moved in for the kill, the Brown Bomber caught him with an uppercut, and Billy went down for the count, just seconds before the end of the round. After the war, the two were rematched again with Louis putting Conn away in the eighth round at Yankee Stadium on June 19, 1946. Years later, Conn asked Louis why he didn't let him borrow the crown for six months. "Billy," Louis remarked, "you HAD that title for 12 rounds." He retired from the ring after fighting a six-round exhibition with Louis in Chicago on December 10, 1948, with a 63-10 career record. He decisioned Melio Bettina in 15 rounds to win the light heavyweight crown on September 25, 1939. He fought the likes of Fritzie Zivic, Fred Apostoli, Gus Lesnevich, Bob Pastor, Henry Cooper and Tony Zale, among others, and was elected to the Boxing Hall of Fame in 1965.

Films include: 1941—**The Pittsburgh Kid.**

1857 Chuck Connors

His real name is Kevin Joseph Connors, and he played major league baseball with the Brooklyn Dodgers and Chicago Cubs and pro basketball with the Boston Celtics.

The Brooklyn, New York, native attended Seton Hall University in South Orange, N.J., before embarking on a professional baseball and basketball career. He played with the Celtics during the 1946-47 season and briefly during the 1947-48 campaign. The six feet five first baseman made his big league debut with the Dodgers in 1949 but found Gil Hodges holding forth at first base. He was subsequently traded to the Cubs and was the starting first sacker at Chicago in 1951. He called it quits after the '51 season and switched to acting. He began playing in bit roles and in "B" movies until he became famous as television's "Rifleman."

Films include: 1952—**Pat and Mike;** 1953—**South Sea Woman;** 1954—**Human Jungle;** 1955—**Target Zero, Three Stripes in the Sun, Good Morning Miss Dove;** 1956—**Hold Back the Night, Hot Rod Girl, Walk the Dark Street;** 1957—**Tomahawk Trail, Death in Small Doses, Designing Woman, Hired Hand;** 1958—**Big Country;** 1962—**Geronimo;** 1963—**Flipper, Move Over Darling;** 1965—**Synanon;** 1966—**Ride Beyond Vengeance;** 1970—**Captain Nemo and the Underwater City;** 1971—**The Deserter, Support Your Local Gunfighter;** 1972—**Mad Bomber, Proud and the Damned, Embassy;** 1973—**The Police Connection, Soylent Green;** 1974—**99 44/100% Dead;** 1975—**Pancho Villa;** 1979—**Tourist Trap;** 1982—**Airplane II: The Sequel.**

1858 James J. Corbett

Gentleman Jim Corbett was the second world heavyweight champion under the Marquis of Queensberry Rules, knocking out "The Boston Strong Boy" John L. Sullivan in the 21st round in New Orleans, Louisiana, on September 7, 1882. The legendary lawman Bat Masterson was the timekeeper. He retired in 1895, but returned to the ring and lost title bouts to Jim Jeffries in New York on May 11, 1900, and in San Francisco on August 14, 1903. He was elected to the Boxing Hall of Fame in 1954. Corbett, who appeared on the stage and in vaudeville, fought Peter Courtney in the first boxing film produced by Thomas Edison in 1894 in Orange, N.J. He was divorced from actress Olive Lake. Corbett died in 1933 in Bayside, New York. In 1942, a film critic called Corbett "the greatest athlete-entertainer of them all." Errol Flynn portrayed him in the 1942 film **Gentleman Jim.**

Films include: 1894—**Corbett and Courtney** fight film; 1913—**The Man from the Golden West;** 1915—**The Lady and the Burglars;** 1919—**The Midnight Man** (serial); 1920—**The Prince of Avenue A;** 1922—**The Beauty Shop;** 1924—**Broadway After Dark;** 1929—**Happy Days, James J. Corbett and Neil O'Brien** (short); 1930—**At the Round Table** (short); 1942—**Gentleman Jim** (film clips); 1968—**The Legendary Champions** (documentary).

1859 Buster Crabbe

Buster Crabbe, swimming hero of the 1932 Olympics, was a hero to countless youngsters during the 1930's and 1940's when he starred as Tarzan, Flash Gordon, Buck Rogers and other derring-do characters. Crabbe, who styled himself as "King of the Serials," was perhaps the most celebrated of cliff-hanger serial heroes, escaping fictional death on the screen virtually every Saturday afternoon for decades. Clarence Lindon Crabbe was born in Oakland,

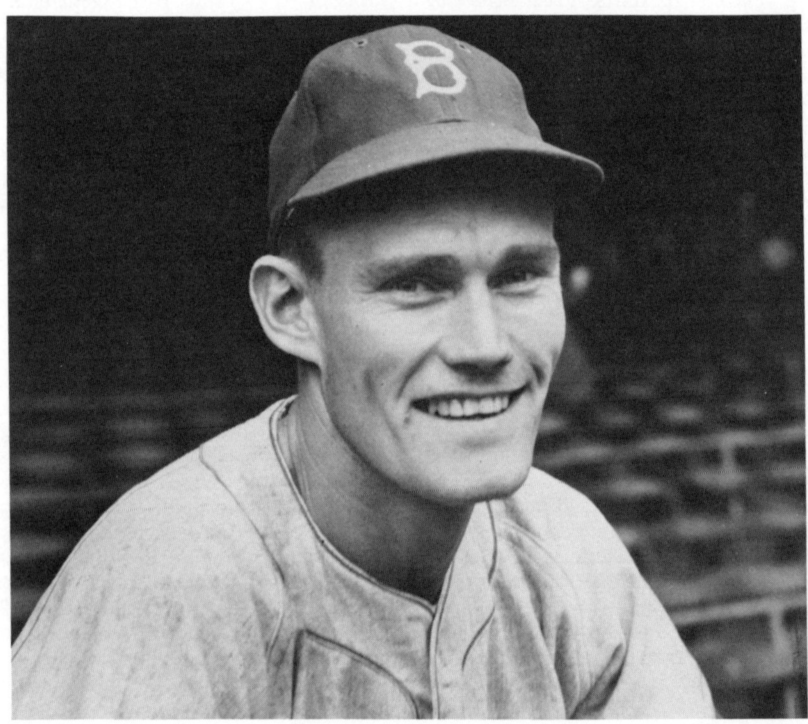

Timothy Brown, top, Chuck Connors, bottom.

California, but grew up in Hawaii where he developed into an outstanding swimmer and a 16-letterman in high school. Later, at the University of Hawaii, he won the light heavyweight boxing championship. After coming up emptyhanded in the 1928 Olympics in Amsterdam, Holland, Crabbe won a gold medal in the 400 meter freestyle event in record time in the 1932 Olympics in Los Angeles, California. During his competitive swimming career, he had broken five world records and held more than 50 world and national swimming championships. He died in 1983.

Films include: 1930—**Good News**; 1932—**The Most Dangerous Game, That's My Boy**; 1933—**King of the Jungle, Man of the Forest, Tarzan, the Fearless** (serial); **To the Last Man, The Sweetheart of Sigma Chi; The Thundering Herd**; 1934—**Search for Beauty, You're Telling Me, Badge of Honor, We're Rich Again, She Had to Choose, The Oil Raider**; 1935—**Hold 'em Yale, The Wanderer of the Wasteland, Nevada**; 1936—**Drift Fence, Desert Gold, Arizona Raiders, Flash Gordon** (serial), **Rose Bowl, Lady, Be Careful, Arizona Mahoney**; 1937—**Murder Goes to College, King of Gamblers, Forlorn River, Sophie Lang Goes West, Thrill of a Lifetime, Daughter of Shanghai**; 1938—**Flash Gordon's Trip to Mars** (serial), **Red Barry, Tip-off Girls, Hunted Men, Illegal Traffic**; 1939—**Buck Rogers** (serial), **Unmarried, Million Dollar Legs, Colorado Sunset, Call a Messenger**; 1940—**Flash Gordon Conquers the Universe** (serial), **Sailor's Lady**; 1941—**Jungle Man, Billy the Kid Wanted, Billy the Kid's Roundup**; 1942—**Billy the Kid Trapped, Billy the Kid's Smoking Guns, Law and Order, Jungle Siren, Wildcat, Mysterious Rider, Sheriff of Sage Valley, Queen of Broadway**; 1943—**The Kid Rides Again, Fugitive of the Plains, The Renegade, Western Cyclone, Cattle Stampede, Blazing Frontier, Devil Riders, The Drifter**; 1944—**Thundering Gunslingers, Nabonga, Frontier Outlaws, Valley of Vengeance, The Contender, Fuzzy Settles Down, Rustler's Hideout, Wild Horse Phantom, Oath of Vengeance**; 1945—**Gangster's Den, His Brother's Ghost, Shadows of Death, Border Badmen, Stagecoach Outlaws, Fighting Bill Carson, Lightning Raiders, Prairie Rustlers**; 1946—**Gentlemen with Guns, Ghost of Hidden Valley, Terrors on Horseback, Overland Raiders, Outlaws of the Plains, Swamp Fire, Prairie Badmen**; 1947—**The Last of the Redmen, The Sea Hound**; 1948—**Caged Fury**; 1950—**Captive Girl; Pirates of the High Seas** (serial); 1952—**King of the Congo**; 1956—**Gun Brothers**; 1957—**The Lawless Eighties**; 1958—**Badman's Country**; 1960—**Gunfighters of Abilene**; 1965—**The Bounty Killer**; 1971—**The Comeback Trail** (unreleased); 1980—**Swim Team.**

1860 Glenn Davis

"Mr. Outside" of the famed Davis-Blanchard duo, he ranks as one of the most versatile players in college football history. Davis scored 59 touchdowns in his storied career at Army and gained an amazing 4,129 yards from rushing and passing. He holds the major college record for most yards gained per play in one season—11.7; and, as a two-way performer, averaged 58 minutes a game. No major collegian ever approached his remarkable career average of almost one TD every nine plays. In 1946, Davis won the coveted Heisman Trophy as college football's outstanding player after finishing runnerup the previous two years. He served in the army until 1950, when he resigned his commission to join the Los Angeles Rams of the National Football League. Injuries cut his career short, but he still managed to help the Rams to the 1951 NFL championship. Davis and Blanchard played themselves in **The Spirit of West Point,** a film about the two West Point football heroes. He was formerly married to actress Terry Moore.

Films include: 1947—**The Spirit of West Point.**

1861 Wee Willie Davis

Former six-time National Wrestling Alliance champion Lou Thesz calls Davis one of professional wrestling's outstanding competitors during the 1930's. The mammoth grappler toured Australia and throughout the United States and Canada, meeting the leading wrestlers of his day. In the movies, he'll be best remembered for his role as Abdullah in **Abbott and Costello in the Foreign Legion.**

Films include: 1950—**Abbott and Costello in the Foreign Legion;** 1952—**Son of Paleface, Sound Off;** 1955—**To Catch a Thief.**

1862 Man Mountain Dean

Frank S. Leavitt became one of professional wrestling's great personalities of the 1930's as Man Mountain Dean. The super-heavyweight and National Wrestling Alliance champion Jim Londos tangled before a record crowd of 39,000 in Los Angeles, California, in 1934. The popular wrestler doubled for actor Charles Laughton in the 1933 movie **Private Life of Henry VIII.** He died in Norcross, Georgia, in 1953.

Films include: 1933—**Private Life of Henry VIII;** 1935—**Reckless, We're in the Money;** 1937—**Three Legionaires, Big City;** 1938—**The Gladiator;** 1960—**Surprise Package.**

1863 Jack Dempsey

The "Manassa Mauler" was one of the hardest punching fighters ever to step into the boxing ring. He won the world heavyweight title when champion Jess Willard failed to answer the bell for the fourth round on July 4, 1919, in Toledo, Ohio. Dempsey successfully defended his crown against Billy Miske, Bill Brennan, Georges Carpentier, Tommy Gibbons and Luis Firpo before losing the title to Gene Tunney on a decision on September 23, 1926. He lost the controversial "long count" rematch with Tunney 10 months later. Dempsey's July 2, 1921, title bout with Carpentier at Boyle's Thirty Acres in Jersey City, New Jersey, was boxing's first million dollar gate. The 190 pounder, who started fighting in 1914 as Kid Blackie, ended his career with a 60-7-6 record and was elected to the Boxing Hall of Fame in 1954. He eventually became a boxing and wrestling referee and a New York City restauranteur. He died in 1983. During the silent serial era, it was popular to feature athletes in the role of the heroes and Pathe starred Dempsey in the 1920 serial **Daredevil Jack.**

Films include: 1920—**Daredevil Jack** (serial); 1932—**Dempsey Returns** (documentary); 1933—**The Prizefighter and the Lady;** 1936—**The Idol of Millions** (documentary); 1953—**Off Limits;** 1962—**Requiem for a Heavyweight.**

1864 Babe Didrikson

Mildred Ella Didrikson Zaharias, known to her legion of fans simply as "Babe," was perhaps the greatest all-around woman athlete in history. A softball, basketball and track and field star, the native of Port Arthur, Texas, won gold medals in the javelin and 80-meter hurdles and the silver medal in the high jump at the 1932 Olympics in Los Angeles, California. She actually broke the world record for high jumping, but the judges disqualified her for using the "Texas Roll," denied her the record and a third gold medal, giving her a second place finish. She turned professional shortly after the Olympics, found virtually no competition, and turned to golf. She captured the United States Women's Amateur golf title in 1946 and the British Women's Amateur championship

Jack Dempsey.

in 1947 before going on to become the foremost women's professional golfer. The champion of champions died in 1956. She was married to professional wrestler George Zaharias. Susan Clark portrayed Babe in a 1975 television film version of her life story.

Films include: 1952—**Pat and Mike.**

1865 Mike Donlin

Mike Donlin still managed to hit .333 over a 12-year major league career that was sprinkled with a suspension, a broken leg, a holdout and a voluntary retirement. The five feet nine lefty-hitting outfielder, nicknamed Turkey Mike, broke in with the St. Louis Cardinals in 1899 and played with the Baltimore Orioles, Cincinnati Reds, New York Giants, Boston Braves and Pittsburgh Pirates. He hit .351 with the Reds in 1903 before being dealt to John McGraw's Giants a year later. In 1905, Donlin batted a career high .356 with 216 hits and a league-leading 124 runs scored as he helped the Giants win the National League pennant. He topped all hitters in the World Series with a .316 mark as New York won the championship in five games over the Philadelphia A's. He batted over .300 ten times during his dozen years in the big leagues. Donlin died in Hollywood, California, in 1933.

Films include: 1915—**Right Off the Bat;** 1923—**Woman Proof, Railroaded, The Unknown Purple;** 1924—**Oh, Doctor; Flaming Barriers, Hit and Run, The Trouble Shooter;** 1925—**Raffles, The Unnamed Woman, Fifth Avenue Models;** 1926—**The Sea Beast, Ella Cinders, Her Second Chance, The Fighting Marine** (serial and feature); 1927—**The General; Slide, Kelly, Slide;** 1928—**Riley the Cop, Warming Up, Beggars of Life;** 1929—**Thunderbolt, Below the Deadline, Noisy Neighbors;** 1930—**Born Reckless, Hot Curves;** 1931—**Arrowsmith,**

Iron Man, The Tip Off; 1932--**Air Hostess, High Gear.**

1866 Carl Eller

The perennial All-Pro defensive end helped the Minnesota Vikings to four Super Bowl appearances during his outstanding National Football League career. The six feet six, 250 pounder was selected on the first round of the 1964 draft out of the University of Minnesota where he earned All-American honors. Eller won the George Halas award in 1971 as the NFL's best defensive player. His speed and ferocious hitting caused six opponents' fumbles in 1974.

Films include: 1974--**The Black Six.**

1867 Julius Erving

His spectacular dunks and crowd-pleasing play earned Julius Erving acclaim as the most exciting player in basketball history. Nicknamed Dr. J, the six feet six native of Roosevelt, New York, was the National Basketball Association's most valuable player in 1980-81 and was selected as the MVP in both the 1977 and 1983 NBA all-star games. In addition, he won two MVP awards in the old American Basketball Association plus three ABA scoring titles. He played five years in the ABA, two with the Virginia Squires and three with the New York Nets before being traded to the Philadelphia 76ers in 1976. He averaged 26.9 points per game on 2,100 points for the 76ers in 1979-80 and 31.9 ppg on 2,268 points with the Squires in 1972-73, both career highs for the former University of Massachusetts product.

Films include: 1979--**The Fish That Saved Pittsburgh.**

1868 Lou Ferrigno

The inspiring athlete and body builder developed a sizeable following for his role in the popular television series **The Incredible Hulk.** But, prior to the hit series, the six feet five Ferrigno was already well known for his athletic and body building prowess. He was named Mr. Teenage America, Mr. America and Mr. International and won two consecutive Mr. Universe titles.

Films include: 1977--**Pumping Iron;** 1983--**Hercules.**

1869 Terry Funk

The 238 pounder from Amarillo, Texas, is a former National Wrestling Alliance champion, winning the title on December 10, 1975, by defeating Jack Brisco in Miami Beach, Florida. He lost the NWA crown to Harley Race on February 6, 1977, in Toronto. Terry made his film debut as Frankie the Thumper in **Paradise Alley.**

Films include: 1978--**Paradise Alley.**

1870 Roman Gabriel

The former North Carolina State All-American and the National Football League's most valuable player in 1969 passed for 29,444 yards and 201 touchdowns during his 17-year career in the NFL. The six feet four, 225-pound quarterback was a first round draft choice of Los Angeles in 1962 and spent 11 seasons with the Rams, establishing virtually all L.A. season and career passing marks. He was traded to Philadelphia in 1973 and was named the NFL's "Comeback Player of the Year" when he led the league in pass attempts, completions and yardage, and threw 23 TD passes for the Eagles. Roman completed 2,366 career pases, seventh best in NFL history, and his 29,444 yards passing is ninth in league annals. The four-time pro bowl participant had just 3.31 percent of his passes intercepted (149 of 4,498 attempts), the lowest figure in NFL history.

Films include: 1968--**Skidoo;** 1969--**The Undefeated.**

Julius Erving.

1871 Tony Galento

Two-ton Tony Galento, the saloon keeper from East Orange, New Jersey, was a roughhouse slugger during his boxing career who came within a whisker of knocking out heavyweight champion Joe Louis in a title bout. On June 28, 1939, Louis came off the canvas to kayo Galento in the fourth round and retain his crown in New York City. Galento fought many prominent fighters, knocking out leading heavyweight contenders Nathan Mann, Al Ettore and Natie Brown (twice) and losing to Max Baer and Arturo Godoy. He subsequently turned to pro wrestling after tangling with an octopus, boxing a kangaroo, touring with a 550-pound bear and riding a bronco.

Films include: 1954--**On the Waterfront;** 1956--**The Best Things in Life Are Free;** 1958--**Wind Across the Everglades.**

1872 Lou Gehrig

Henry Louis Gehrig, the most durable player in baseball history, was a legend before he left the sport even though he spent the majority of his career in the shadow of Babe Ruth. The native of New York City, nicknamed the Iron Horse because of his durability and great strength, played 2,130 consecutive games with the New York Yankees, considered by many as baseball's most untouchable record. Gehrig's streak began on June 1, 1925, as a pinch-hitter (the next day he replaced an ailing Wally Pipp at first base) and continued until May 2, 1939, when he removed himself from the starting lineup. While the product of Columbia University never possessed the crowd-pleasing ability of Ruth, his batting feats were legendary. Five times he hit more than 40 homers, 13 straight years he drove home over 100 runs, eight times he had 200 or more hits and for 12 consecutive years he batted .300 or better. He was the American League's most valuable player in both 1927 and 1936 and batted .361 in seven World Series. A month after he took himself out of the Yankee lineup, Gehrig entered the Mayo Clinic for tests, which revealed that he had the rare disease amyotrophic lateral sclerosis--known today as "Gehrig's Disease." Doctors gave him two years to live. On July 4, 1939, the Yankees honored him at a moving ceremony at Yankee Stadium; and that summer he was voted into Baseball's Hall of Fame. The captain of the Yankees died on June 2, 1941. Gary Cooper portrayed Gehrig in the film **Pride of the Yankees.**

Films include: 1938--**Rawhide;** 1942--**The Ninth Inning.**

1873 Gorgeous George

George Wagner was an expert, tough, but very ordinary, professional wrestler in the 1940's when the native of Seward, Nebraska, decided to change his style. He set his hair, dyed it blond, hired a valet to spray incense and perfume around the ring and became Gorgeous George--pro wrestling's number one box office attraction. Performing the Gorgeous George kiss, he would gallantly take a lady's hand and bend down to touch his lips to it, but instead he would turn his wrist and kiss the back of his own hand. Gorgeous George, who played the role so long and so ardently that he actually came to believe he was what he pretended to be, was reportedly pro wrestling's first millionaire. Loved by women and detested by men, he traveled throughout the world as wrestling's greatest attraction during the 1940's and 50's. Despite his great wealth, when Gorgeous George died in 1963 at the age of 48, his friends and family had to take a collection to pay for his funeral.

Films include: 1949--**Alias the Champ.**

Lou Gehrig.

1874 Frank Gifford

Frank Gifford has been a familiar sight as a pro football announcer on network television, was a four-time All-Pro during the halcyon days in New York Giants history. An All-American halfback at the University of Southern California, Gifford was the Giant's top draft pick in 1952 and went on to become the National Football League's Player of the Year in 1956, a seven-time pro bowl participant and a member of five Eastern Conference championship teams and one NFL championship team. The Santa Monica, California, native, who played halfback, flanker and defensive back during his 12-year career (1952-60, 62-64), gained 9,753 combined yards, including 3,609 yards rushing. The 195 pounder broke into the sportscasting business in 1961 when he sat out the season with a serious head injury suffered the previous year. He ended his retirement the following season and played three more years with the Giants. Gifford, who was enshrined into the Pro Football Hall of Fame in 1977, scored 484 points and caught 367 passes during his outstanding career.

Films include: 1953--**The All American;** 1968--**Paper Lion;** 1973--**The World's Greatest Athlete;** 1976--**Two Minute Warning;** 1977--**Viva Knievel.**

1875 Althea Gibson

Althea Gibson, who learned her skills on the streets of Harlem, was the "Jackie Robinson of tennis." She was the first black player to win the coveted Wimbledon crown (July 1957), the first to represent the United States in the Wightman Cup Matches and the first to capture the National Women's Grass Court Championship (August 1957). She first came into national prominence in 1950 when she became the first of her race to play in the National Championships at Forest Hills, New York, and narrowly missed upsetting the then Wimbledon champion A. Louise Brough. Althea was the women's singles champion of the black American Tennis Association from 1947 through 1957 and was mixed doubles champion in 1948-50 and 1952-55. She was named to the International Tennis Hall of Fame in 1971 and to the Women's Sports Hall of Fame in 1980.

Films include: 1959--**The Horse Soldiers.**

1876 Red Grange

The "Galloping Ghost" from the University of Illinois was a three-time collegiate All-American who went on to help establish the professional National Football League. Number 77 joined the Chicago Bears on Thanksgiving Day, 1925, and his magic name produced the first huge pro football crowds on a 17-game barnstorming tour. Some 70,000 people watched Grange and the Bears play the New York Giants at the Polo Grounds during the tour. The following year, Grange and his manager, C.C. Pyle, founded the rival American Football League after a salary dispute with the Bears. The AFL folded after one season, and Grange and his New York Yankees joined the NFL in 1927. A year later, he left football and became an entertainer. In 1929, Grange returned to the NFL and played with the Bears until he retired after the 1934 season. During his high school (Wheaton, Illinois), college and pro career, Grange rushed for 33,820 yards and scored 2,566 points. At Illinois, he once scored five touchdowns (four in the first 12 minutes) and passed for a sixth against Michigan. He scored on runs of 95, 65, 54, 48 and 15 yards. He was a four-time All-NFL halfback and was a charter member of both the College and Pro Football halls of fame. Grange was reportedly paid $300,000 to star

Gorgeous George.

in the 1926 silent film **One Minute to Play.**

Films include: 1926--**One Minute to Play;** 1927--**A Racing Romeo;** 1931--**The Galloping Ghost** (serial).

1877 Rocky Graziano

More than three decades after Rocky Graziano hung up his boxing gloves, the former world middleweight champion is still one of the most popular athletic personalities in the country. Graziano, born Rocco Barbella, fought his way out of a tough neighborhood in New York City's Little Italy to win the middleweight title by knocking out Tony Zale in the sixth round on July 16, 1947, in Chicago, Illinois. It was the second of three classic bloodbaths with Zale for the world championship. Graziano, who lost two of the battles with Zale, was stopped by Sugar Ray Robinson in a bid to win back the crown on April 16, 1952. He fought the likes of Billy Arnold, Freddie Cochrane (twice), Marty Servo, Charley Fusari, Tony Janiro (three times) and Johnny Greco en route to a 67-10-6 career ring record. He was elected to the Boxing Hall of Fame in 1971. Rocky's second career began in 1956 when he starred with Martha Raye in a hit national network television series. He later appeared in movies and is in constant demand for TV commercials. Paul Newman portrayed him in the 1956 film **Somebody Up There Likes Me.**

Films include: 1957--**Mister Rock and Roll;** 1958--**Country Music Holiday;** 1960--**Teenage Millionaire;** 1967--**Tony Rome.**

1878 Joe Greene

Mean Joe Greene's supreme physical assets made him one of the premier defensive tackles in the National Football League during his 14-year career with the Pittsburgh Steelers (1969-82). The Steeler dominance of the 1970's began when they selected Greene on the first round of the 1969 draft, and he went on to bulwark the defensive unit known as the "Steel Curtain." His exceptional leadership qualities and outstanding playing ability helped Pittsburgh win four Super Bowls (1975-76-79-80). The perennial All-Pro was named the NFL's defensive Rookie of the Year in 1969 and was the league's most valuable defensive player in 1972. At North Texas State, he was a unanimous choice as the country's top defensive lineman in 1968. Greene and five other NFLers, Gene Washington, Carl Eller, Lem Barney, Mercury Morris, and Willie Lanier appeared in the film **The Black Six** as Vietnam veterans who form a motorcycle gang and are determined to stay at peace until one of the vet's brothers is killed by a white gang plotting to get the six. He also starred in a popular soda commercial for television.

Films include: 1974--**The Black Six;** 1975--**Lady Cocoa;** 1980--**Smokey and the Bandit II;** 1981--**All the Marbles.**

1879 Rosey Grier

The mammoth defensive tackle was a member of the famous "Fearsome Foursome" of the New York Giants that helped defeat the Chicago Bears, 47-7, for the National Football League championship in 1956. Grier joined the Giants out of Penn State in 1955 and teamed with Andy Robustelli, Dick Modzelewski and Jim Katcavage to form an awesome defensive front four for the NFL club. He went on to help the Giants win Eastern Conference titles in 1958 (losing the NFL crown in sudden death to Baltimore), 1959, 1961 and 1962 before being dealt to the Los Angeles Rams in 1963. In 1956, he was named All-Pro. Grier retired after the 1966 campaign.

Films include: 1972--**Skyjacked,**

Rocky Graziano.

The Thing with Two Heads; 1975--**Timber Tramps;** 1979--**The Glove;** 1980--**The Gong Show Movie.**

1880 H.B. Haggerty

Haggerty, a noted heavy in dozens of films and television shows, played professional football with the Detroit Lions and Green Bay Packers and was a professional wrestler before turning to an acting career. He once held the United States Heavyweight Wrestling Championship crown.

Films include: 1969--**A Dream of Kings, Paint Your Wagon;** 1975--**Framed;** 1977--**Black Fist; Final Chapter--Walking Tall;** 1979--**Buck Rogers in the 25th Century;** 1980--**The Big Brawl;** 1984--**Micki and Maude.**

1881 Mickey Hargitay

Mickey Hargitay was a world-renowned body builder and the former husband of the late actress Jayne Mansfield.

Films include: 1967--**Spree, Bloody Pit of Horror;** 1973--**Lady Frankenstein.**

1882 Tom Harmon

Number 98, Harmon of Michigan, won the coveted Heisman Trophy in 1940 as the outstanding performer in collegiate football. During his three-year career with the Wolverines, he scored 33 touchdowns, kicked two field goals and 33 points after touchdowns for 237 points, and tossed 16 TD passes. He gained 3,438 yards rushing and passing, and played almost every minute of his three seasons. He spent four years as a pilot during World War II, earning a Silver Star, and subsequently played briefly with the Los Angeles Rams of the National Football League. Harmon's eventual career in broadcasting is even more outstanding than his gridiron accomplishments. He has reported live on major sporting events from the Olympics to the Rose Bowl. Harmon, who is married to actress Elyse Knox, portrayed himself in the 1941 film **Harmon of Michigan** and appeared in a number of other motion pictures.

Films include: 1941--**Harmon of Michigan;** 1946--**Gentleman Joe Palooka;** 1946--**The Sweetheart of Sigma Chi;** 1947--**The Spirit of West Point;** 1948--**Triple Threat;** 1951--**That's My Boy;** 1952--**The Rose Bowl Story, Pat and Mike;** 1953--**The Caddy, Off Limits, The All-American;** 1955--**An Annapolis Story;** 1975--**Return to Campus.**

1883 Len Harvey

Len Harvey fought unsuccessfully for both the world middleweight and light heavyweight championships during his pro boxing career. Middleweight king Marcel Thil won a 15-round decision over Harvey to retain the title in London, England, on July 4, 1932, and champion John Henry Lewis retained his light heavy crown with a 15-round decision over Harvey in London on November 9, 1936. On June 20, 1942, Freddie Mills won the British Empire light heavyweight title by flattening Harvey in two rounds in London.

Films include: 1933--**The Bermondsey Kid;** 1935--**Excuse My Glove.**

1884 Chester Hayes

Lou Thesz, former six-time National Wrestling Alliance champion, described Hayes as a "very able, very good wrestler" during the 1930's and 40's who went on to train chimps for the movies.

1885 Carol Heiss

Carol Heiss was one of four women figure skaters from the United States to win Olympic gold medals during a two-decade period at the Winter Games. Heiss captured her gold in 1960 at Squaw Valley, California, following Tenley Albright's gold in 1956 and preceding Peggy Fleming (1968) and Dorothy Hamill (1976). She won the world championship in 1956 and held

Rosey Grier.

the title through 1960, longer than anyone but Sonja Heine. She was national champion 1957-60 and North American champion in 1957 and 1959. At the 1960 Olympics, the native of New York City recited the athlete's oath.

Films include: 1961—**Snow White and the Three Stooges.**

1886 Sonja Henie

For over two decades, the name of Sonja Henie shone brightly in lights all over the world. The three-time Olympic figure skating champion grossed millions with her winning smile and sense of showmanship as she skated in the movies and ice shows. The native of Oslo, Norway, began skating at the age of eight and won her first figure skating title, the Norwegian national championship, at 14. Then in 1928, 1932 and 1936, she won gold medals and set world figure skating marks in three consecutive Winter Olympics. She also won ten straight world championships. With no new worlds to conquer in figure skating, she turned professional, toured with an ice show, and set out for Hollywood and a successful movie career. The blue-eyed blond combined her radiant personality with the beauty and precision of her figure skating to become one of the leading stars at 20th

Century-Fox in the late 1930's. Her films were typically romantic vehicles with thin stories surrounding her skating numbers. Some of her co-stars included Tyrone Power and Don Ameche. She died in 1969.

Films include: 1927--**Svy Dager for Elisabeth** (Norweigan); 1936--**One in a Million;** 1937--**Thin Ice;** 1938--**Happy Landing, My Lucky Star;** 1939--**Second Fiddle, Everything Happens at Night;** 1941--**Sun Valley Serenade;** 1942--**Iceland;** 1943--**Wintertime;** 1945--**It's a Pleasure;** 1948--**Countess of Monte Cristo;** 1958--**Hello London** (aka **London Calling**).

1887 Mike Henry

Mike Henry went from being a linebacker in the National Football League to playing Tarzan in the movies. The University of Southern California standout played three seasons with the Pittsburgh Steelers (1959-61) and three with the Los Angeles Rams (1962-64) before turning to an acting career. In addition to his Tarzan movies, he appeared in the popular film **Smokey and the Bandit** and its sequels.

Films include: 1967--**Tarzan and the Great River, Tarzan and the Valley of Gold;** 1968--**Tarzan and the Jungle Boy, The Green Berets, More Dead Than Alive;** 1969--**Number One;** 1970--**Rio Lobo;** 1972--**Skyjacked;** 1973--**Soylent Green;** 1974--**The Longest Yard;** 1975--**Adios Amigo;** 1977--**Smokey and the Bandit;** 1980--**Smokey and the Bandit II;** 1983--**Smokey and the Bandit III.**

1888 Elroy Hirsch

"Crazylegs" Hirsch mixed sprinter speed with halfback elusiveness to be named the all-time National Football League flanker in 1969. A year earlier, he was enshrined in the Pro Football Hall of Fame. The talented six feet two, 190 pounder, who played at both Wisconsin and Michigan, led the College All-Stars to an upset victory over the NFL's Los Angeles Rams in 1946 and then joined the Chicago Rockets of the fledgling All-America Football Conference. In 1949, Hirsch put on the uniform of the Rams and became the key part of L.A.'s revolutionary "three-end" offense. In 1951, he led the NFL in both scoring (102 points) and receiving (66 receptions for 1,495 yards) with ten of his 17 TD catches long-distance bombs. Hirsch scored a TD in 11 straight games over the 1950-51 seasons. He retired after the 1957 season with 387 career receptions for 7,209 yards, 60 TDs and 405 points scored. The native of Wausau, Wisconsin, portrayed himself in the Republic Pictures film **Crazylegs, All American.**

Films include: 1953--**Crazylegs, All American;** 1955--**Unchained;** 1957--**Zero Hour.**

1889 Eleanor Holm

Swimming star Eleanor Holm was the queen of her time and one of the greatest of all time. The native of Brooklyn, New York, participated in the 1928 Olympic Games in Amsterdam at the age of 14, won a gold medal in the 1932 Games in Los Angeles and was dropped from the 1936 U.S. Olympic team after breaking training rules. She was banned from the Berlin Games because she drank champagne during a party although no one accused her of being drunk. During the 1932 Olympics, she set a record in winning the 100-meter backstroke and overall in her career captured 12 national Amateur Athletic Union championships. Eleanor was named one of the Wampus Baby Stars of 1932, along with Ginger Rogers and Mary Carlisle and later starred as Jane in the 1938 film **Tarzan's Revenge.** Impresario Billy Rose (her husband) starred Eleanor in his aquacade at the 1939 World's Fair in New

Elroy Hirsch.

York City. She was elected to the International Swimming Hall of Fame in 1966.

Films include: 1938--**Tarzan's Revenge.**

1890 John Indrisano

Johnny Indrisano, a native of Boston, Massachusetts, was a talented welterweight boxer who, besides appearing as an actor in many motion pictures, served as a technical advisor for a number of films, including **Somebody Up There Likes Me.** He won ten-round decisions over champions Joe Dundee in 1927 and Jackie Fields in 1932 in non-title bouts. He also fought former welterweight and middleweight champion Lou Brouillard three times (winning twice) and won a ten-round decision over future middleweight king Vince Dundee. He was found hung to death in San Fernando Valley, California, in 1968.

Films include: 1935--**The Winning Ticket, She Gets Her Man, Two Fisted;** 1936--**Laughing Irish Eyes;** 1937--**Every Day's a Holiday;** 1941--**Ringside Maisie;** 1944--**Lost in a Harem;** 1945--**Live Wires, Johnny Angel, Duffy's Tavern, The Naughty Nineties;** 1946--**The Kid from Brooklyn, Criminal Court, Crack-Up, Mr. Hex;** 1947--**Killer McCoy, Christmas Eve, A Palooka Named Joe, Body and Soul;** 1948--**In This Corner, Lulu Belle, Trouble Makers, The Numbers Racket, Knock on Any Door, The Accused, Bodyguard, Fighting Fools, Fighting Mad** (aka **Joe Palooka in Fighting Mad**); 1949--**Bride for Sale, Tension, Shadow on the Wall, Joe Palooka in the Counterpunch, The Lady Gambles;** 1950--**The Yellow Cab Man;** 1951--**Pier 23, Callaway Went Thataway;** 1952--**Glory Alley, No Holds Barred;** 1953--**Shane;** 1956--**The Cruel Tower;** 1957--**Chicago Confidential;** 1958--**Hot Spell;** 1959--**Some Like It Hot, Career;** 1960--**The Purple Gang, Ocean's Eleven;** 1961--**Blueprint for Robbery;** 1962--**A Swingin' Affair** (aka **Rebel in the Ring**), **Who's Got the Action?** 1963--**Hud, Four for Texas, Under the Yum Yum Tree;** 1964--**Where Love Has Gone, The Best Man, A House Is Not a Home;** 1965--**The Human Duplicator;** 1967--**The Ambushers, Barefoot in the Park;** 1968--**The Legend of Lylah Clare.**

1891 James J. Jeffries

Nicknamed the Boilermaker, the native of Carroll, Ohio, won the world heavyweight championship by knocking out Bob Fitzsimmons in 11 rounds at New York's Coney Island on June 9, 1899. It was only his 13th professional fight. The six feet two and a half, 220 pounder successfully defended his title by beating Tom Sharkey on points in 25 rounds, knocked out James J. Corbett in 23 rounds, stopped Gus Ruhlin in five rounds, kayoed Fitzsimmons in eight rounds in a return match, upended Corbett in ten rounds and flattened Jack Munroe in two rounds. Lack of opponents forced him to retire undefeated in March 1905. On July 4, 1910, he came out of retirement in an effort to regain the world title but was knocked out in 15 rounds by champion Jack Johnson in Reno, Nevada. He went on to appear in motion pictures for three decades. Jeffries was elected to the Boxing Hall of Fame in 1954. He died in Burbank, California, in 1953.

Films include: 1924--**Jeffries, Jr.** (short); **Kid Speed** (short); 1926--**Prince of Broadway;** 1927--**One Round Hogan;** 1928--**Beau Broadway;** 1932--**Midnight Patrol, They Never Come Back, The Fighting Gentleman;** 1933--**The Prizefighter and the Lady;** 1937--**The Big City;** 1940--**Barnyard Follies;** 1941--**Mr. Celebrity;** 1968--**The Legendary Champions** (documentary).

1892 Bruce Jenner

Bruce Jenner, who shattered

Olympic and world records in the 1976 decathlon, has become a motion picture and television actor since winning the gold medal in Montreal, Canada. He registered a record 8,618 points in the grueling decathlon competition at the 1976 Games.

Films include: 1980--**Can't Stop the Music.**

1893 Ingemar Johansson

The colorful Swede was the undefeated European heavyweight champion when he surprised Floyd Patterson by knocking out the world champ in three rounds to win the title at New York's Yankee Stadium on June 26, 1959. Virtually a year later, Patterson regained his crown by knocking out Johansson in five rounds in Gothenburg, Sweden, and retained the title when he flattened Johansson in six rounds on March 13, 1961, in Miami Beach, Florida. He retired in 1963 to enter business, ending his pro career with a 26-6 record. Prior to turning professional, he represented Sweden in the 1952 Olympics in Helsinki, Finland. He lost on a disqualification to Ed Sanders of the U.S. in the second round of the heavyweight final.

Films include: 1959--**All the Young Men;** 1960--**48 Hours to Live** (aka **Man in the Middle**).

1894 Jack Johnson

Jack Johnson, the first black to win the world heavyweight championship, was the controversial athlete of his time. "The Galveston Giant" won the title when he stopped Tommy Burns in the 14th round in Sydney, Australia, on December 26, 1909, and lost it in Havana, Cuba, on April 5, 1915, when Jess Willard knocked him out in the 26th round of a scheduled 45-round bout. For the last three years of his reign, he lived in self-exile in Europe. He inspired a number of early boxing films based on the black versus white theme. Born John Arthur Johnson in Galveston, Texas, he retired in 1928 with a 79-8-12 career mark. On November 27, 1945, at the age of 67, he fought three one-minute rounds against both Joe Jeannette and John Ballcourt in an exhibition match in New York. He was elected to the Boxing Hall of Fame in 1954. Johnson was killed in an auto accident in Raleigh, North Carolina, in 1946.

Films include: 1921--**For His Mother's Sake, As the World Rolls On;** 1922--**Black Thunderbolt;** 1932--**Madison Square Garden;** 1970--**Jack Johnson** (documentary).

1895 John Lester Johnson

John Lester Johnson was a talented fighter in the early 1900's who gained prominence by battling Jack Dempsey to a ten-round no decision. Johnson faced the future world heavyweight champion on July 14, 1916, in New York City and reportedly broke Dempsey's ribs in the fight. Johnson made his acting debut in the 1921 film **Square Joe** in which he and another fighter, Joe Jeannette, portrayed boxers in a story about black life.

Films include: 1921--**Square Joe;** 1923--**Flames of Wrath;** 1937--**Bargain with Bullets;** 1938--**Tarzan's Revenge;** 1961--**Professor Creeps.**

1896 Rafer Johnson

Rafer Johnson probably turned in the most dramatic decathlon victory in the history of the Olympic Games when he edged C.K. Yang to win the gold medal in the 1960 Games at Rome, Italy. At the end of nine events, Johnson held an edge of 67 points over the Formosan. It was Johnson's ability in the field events that had balanced Yang's track and jumping prowess. Yang, who like Johnson trained at the University of California at Los Angeles, needed to outrun Johnson by ten seconds or more in the final event--the 1,500--to win the decathlon. Yang beat Johnson to the tape but by only 1.2 seconds, and Rafer had the gold medal. Four years earlier, Johnson won a silver medal at the Olympic Games in Melbourne, Australia, when he finished second to Milt Campbell of the United States in the decathlon. Johnson was at Robert F. Kennedy's side when the presidential candidate was assassinated in 1968.

Films include: 1961--**The Pirates of Tortuga, The Sins of Rachel Cade, The Fiercest Heart;** 1962--**Wild in the Country; The Lion;** 1965--**Billie, None but the Brave;** 1967--**Tarzan and the Great River;** 1968--**Tarzan and the Jungle Boy;** 1970--**The Games, The Last Grenade, Soul Soldier.**

1897 Tor Johnson

Born Tor Johansson in Sweden, he turned to the movies as a second career after a successful stint in professional wrestling in the 1930's. He died in San Fernando, California, in 1971.

Films include: 1935--**The Man on the Flying Trapeze;** 1943--**Swing Out the Blues;** 1944--**The Canterville Ghost, Lost in a Harem, The Ghost Chasers;** 1945--**Sudan;** 1947--**Road to Rio;** 1948--**State of the Union, Behind Locked Doors;** 1949--**Alias the Champ;** 1950--**Abbott and Costello in the Foreign Legion, The Reformer and the Redhead;** 1951--**The Lemon Drop Kid, Dear Brat;** 1952--**The San Francisco Story;** 1953--**Houdini;** 1956--**The Black Sheep, Bride of the Monster, Carousel, Plan 9 from Outer Space;** 1957--**The Unearthly, Journey to Freedom;** 1959--**Night of the Ghouls** (aka **Revenge of the Dead;** 1961--**The Beast of Yucca Flats.**

1898 Duke P. Kahanamoku

The Hawaiian swimming star was another of the many Olympic heroes who subsequently enjoyed a career in the movies. The native of Honolulu set Olympic records in winning the 100 meters freestyle event, first in 1912 at Stockholm, Sweden, and again in 1920 at Antwerp, Belgium. The two-time gold medal winner took a silver medal in the 1924 games at Paris, France, at the age of 34 when he finished second to Johnny Weissmuller, who went on to a career as a movie Tarzan. In addition to making films, Duke also served as sheriff of Honolulu. He died in 1968.

Films include: 1925--**Adventure, Lord Jim;** 1926--**Old Ironsides;** 1927--**Isle of Sunken Gold;** 1928--**Woman Wise;** 1929--**The Rescue;** 1930--**Girl of the Port; Isle of Escape;** 1949--**Wake of the Red Witch;** 1955--**Mr. Roberts;** 1968--**I Sailed to Tahiti with an All Girl Crew.**

1899 Joe Kapp

The six feet three product of the University of California spent eight seasons (1959-66) in the Canadian Football League before joining the Minnesota Vikings of the National Football League. He quarterbacked the Vikings to their first NFL championship in 1969 and into Super Bowl IV. Kapp played two seasons with Calgary and six with Vancouver of the CFL. In 1962, he completed 197 passes for 3,279 yards and 28 touchdowns with Vancouver. He joined Minnesota in 1967, and with his brash, opportunistic style, led the Vikings to the NFL title in 1969 with playoffs victories over Los Angeles and Cleveland. Kansas City of the American Football League, however, stopped the Vikings, 21-7, to win the Super Bowl in 1970. Kapp tied an NFL record in 1969 when he threw seven TDs against Baltimore and set club marks with 28 completions for 449 yards in the same game. He was the NFL's most valuable player in 1969. The following year he joined the Boston Patriots after a contract dispute with

Minnesota. In 1982, he was named head football coach at his alma mater, California.

Films include: 1973--**The World's Greatest Athlete;** 1974--**The Longest Yard;** 1976--**Two Minute Warning;** 1977--**Semi-Tough, The Choirboys.**

1900 Alex Karras

Alex was one of the most agile pursuers of quarterbacks in the National Football League during his playing days with the Detroit Lions. The University of Iowa standout joined the Lions in 1958 and went on to earn All-Pro honors as a defensive tackle in 1960-61-62-65. The six feet two, 225 pounder was a master at using his hands and arms to fight his way past would-be blockers. His brothers, Lou and Ted, also played in the NFL, the former with Washington and the latter with Pittsburgh, Chicago, Detroit and Los Angeles. Alex, who also was a professional wrestler, went on to a successful career in television and motion pictures after retiring from the NFL.

Films include: 1968--**Paper Lion;** 1974--**Blazing Saddles;** 1974--**Win, Place and Steal;** 1975--**The Great Lester Boggs;** 1980--**When Time Ran Out;** 1981--**Nobody's Perfekt;** 1982--**Victor, Victoria; Porky's;** 1984--**Against All Odds.**

1901 Annette Kellerman

Australia's "Million Dollar Mermaid," crippled by polio shortly after birth and forced to wear large steel braces, overcame her handicap and went on to thrill crowds with her sensational aquacades and became the first woman to attempt to swim the English Channel. A champion swimmer and diver, she performed at theaters in Melbourne and London. Her act, which included staying under water for 2½ minutes and wearing a one-piece bathing suit, was the first successfully presented aquacade on stage. While touring the United States in 1907, she was arrested in Boston for wearing the then-shocking one-piece bathing suit on a beach. In 1909, Annette attempted several times to swim the English Channel, once getting three-quarters across before giving up. During her seven world tours, she astounded onlookers from Buenos Aires to Shanghai by making a 75-foot dive into a 40-ton glass tank of water. In 1953, Esther Williams starred in the musical film **Million Dollar Mermaid,** the life story of Annette Kellerman, and it was a box office hit. "The Diving Venus" as she was also known, died in 1975 in Southport, Australia.

Films include: 1909--**Miss Annette Kellerman, Fancy Swimming and Diving Displays;** 1914--**Neptune's Daughter;** 1916--**Isle of Love, A Daughter of the Gods;** 1917--**The Honor System;** 1918--**Queen of the Sea;** 1920--**The Art of Diving, What Women Love;** 1924--**Venus of the South Seas.**

1902 Jean Claude Killy

Frenchman Jean Claude Killy swept all three men's alpine skiing events in the 1968 Winter Olympics at Grenoble in the French Alps. He is only the second men's skier to triple in the Winter Olympics, winning gold medals in the downhill, giant slalom and slalom. Toni Sailer, the first men's skier to sweep all three events (1956 Winter Olympics in Cortina d'Ampezzo), also became a movie actor.

Films include: 1967--**Ski on the Wild Side;** 1969--**Last of the Ski Bums;** 1972--**Snow Job.**

1903 Bernard King

One of the premier power forwards in the National Basketball Association, Bernard King stepped off the campus of the University of Tennessee after his junior year to be named to the NBA's All-Rookie team with the New Jersey Nets in 1977-78. At Tennessee, he was an All-American in 1976

Alex Karras.

and a three-time Southeast Conference all-star. As a rookie with the Nets, he averaged 24.2 points per game. He played with Utah and Golden State before being traded to the New York Knickerbockers in 1982. In his first season with Golden State, he became the first-ever winner of the NBA Comeback Player of the Year award. During the 1983-84 season with the Knicks, the six feet seven native of Brooklyn, New York, registered back-to-back 50-point games, tying a career high mark set against Philadelphia in 1981.

Films include: 1979--**Fast Break.**

1904 Joe Klecko

Joe Klecko, one of the outstanding defensive linemen in the National Football League, passed up college for two years to be a trucker.

The six feet three, 269 pounder joined the New York Jets in 1977 after earning All-American and All-East recognition at Temple University. In 1981, he was a consensus All-Pro and made his first Pro Bowl appearance after leading the NFL and setting a club record with $20\frac{1}{2}$ quarterback sacks. A knee injury sidelined the Chester, Pennsylvania, native for most of the 1982 season, but he came back in 1983 to be selected

Bernard King.

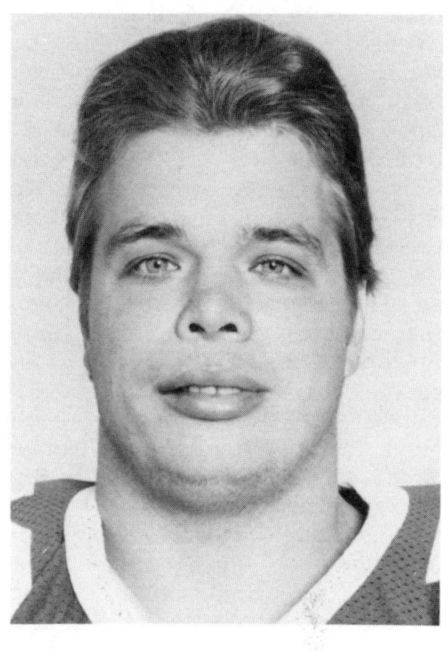

Joe Klecko.

to the Pro Bowl for the second time and earned All-Pro second team and All-American Football Conference honors. Klecko, a two-time ECAC club heavyweight boxing champion at Temple, once sparred with former world champ Joe Frazier in Philadelphia.

Films include: 1980--**Smokey and the Bandit II**; 1981--**The Cannonball Run.**

1905 Evel Knievel

Evel Knievel is America's most spectacular motorcycle performer. From the start of his daredevil career--jumping his bike over crates of rattlesnakes--Knievel has thrilled millions with his dangerous exploits. Among his hair-raising jumps was his leap over 50 cars at the Los Angeles Coliseum, his jump over the fountains at Caesar's Palace in Las Vegas and his death-defying skycycle jump into the Snake River Canyon. Born Bobby Knievel in Butte, Montana, Knievel participated in semi-pro football and ice hockey, participated in rodeos and entered ski-jumping contests before becoming a professional motorcyclist. During his extraordinary career, the colorful Knievel has broken some 100 bones in his body. George Hamilton portrayed him in the 1971 film **Evel Knievel.**

Films include: 1977--**Viva Knievel.**

1906 Henry Kulky

During the 1930's and 1940's, Kulky, known in professional wrestling as "Bomber Kulkavich," was an outstanding junior heavyweight, according to National Wrestling Alliance legend Lou Thesz. The native of Hastings-on-the-Hudson, New York, gave up the mat game and turned to the movie screen in 1947. He died in Oceanside, California, in 1965.

Films include: 1947--**A Likely Story**; 1948--**Call Northside 777**; 1949--**Tarzan's Magic Fountain, Bandits of El Dorado**; 1950--**Body**

Hold, South Sea Sinner, Wabash Avenue, Jiggs and Maggie Out West; 1951--**The Guy Who Came Back, Love Nest, Chinatown Chump** (short), **Fixed Bayonets, The Kid from Amarillo;** 1952--**Gobs and Gals, My Wife's Best Friend, Red Skies of Montana, What Price Glory?; The World in His Arms, No Holds Barred;** 1953--**The Charge at Feather River, Down Among the Sheltering Palms, The 5,000 Fingers of Dr. T, The Glory Brigade, Target Hong Kong, The Robe;** 1954--**Abbott and Costello Meet the Keystone Kops, Fireman, Save My Child; Hell and High Water; The Steel Cage, Tobor the Great, Yukon Vengeance, A Star Is Born;** 1955--**Illegal, New York Confidential, Prince of Players;** 1957--**Sierra Stranger;** 1959--**Up Periscope, Gunfight at Dodge City;** 1960--**Guns of the Timberland;** 1964--**A Global Affair.**

1907 Jake LaMotta

Robert DeNiro's 1980 Academy Award-winning performance as Jake LaMotta in **Raging Bull** revived interest in the former world middleweight champion. The hard-punching native of the Bronx, New York, who fought Sugar Ray Robinson six times during his 106-fight career, stopped Marcel Cerdan at Briggs Stadium, Detroit, Michigan, on June 16, 1949, to win the title. The Frenchman was unable to come out for the 10th round because of an injured shoulder. LaMotta successfully defended his crown in bouts against Tiberio Mitri and Laurent Dauthuille in 1950 before losing the championship on February 14, 1951, when Robinson knocked him out in the 13th round in Chicago, Illinois. LaMotta, who lost all but one of his fights with Robinson, battled such top fighters as Fritzie Zivic (four times), Tommy Bell (three times), Robert Villemain (twice), Tony Janiro and Billy Fox during his 13-year 83-19-4 career.

Films include: 1961--**Rebellion in Cuba, The Hustler.**

1908 Mike Lane

Another one of the many professional wrestlers who turned to acting after a mat career. The giant-like Lane, a prominent grappler in the 1940's, played the role of Toro Moreno in the film **The Harder They Fall,** loosely based on the life of former heavyweight boxing champion Primo Carnera.

Films include: 1956--**The Harder They Fall;** 1957--**Hell Canyon** (aka **Hell Canyon Outlaws);** 1958--**Frankenstein—1970;** 1960--**Who Was That Lady?;** 1961--**Valley of the Dragons.**

1909 Willie Lanier

The six feet one, 245 pounder was considered one of pro football's best middle linebackers during his National Football League career with the Kansas City Chiefs. In 1968, the former two-time small college All-American at Morgan State intercepted four passes for 120 yards, including a 75-yard touchdown run. In 1975, Lanier intercepted five aerials for 105 yards. The agile linebacker, who was named to numerous All-Pro teams, was selected defensive most valuable player of the 1971 Pro Bowl game.

Films include: 1974--**The Black Six.**

1910 Roland La Starza

The "Bronx Butcher Boy" was one of the leading heavyweights of the early 1950's. He fought Rocky Marciano twice, losing a ten-round decision in a non-title bout on March 24, 1950, and suffering a TKO In 11 rounds for the world heavyweight championship on September 24, 1953, at the Polo Grounds in New York City.

Films include: 1967--**Point Blank;** 1973--**The Outfit.**

1911 Canada Lee

Canada Lee was a standout welterweight fighter during the 1920's and early 30's who went on to win stage and screen acclaim. Lee fought four men, Vince Dundee, Jack Britton, Tommy Freeman (twice) and Lou Brouillard, who either had been champions or would go on to become champions. Within a two-week period in 1928, he battled future middleweight king Dundee to a ten-round draw in New York City and dropped a ten-round decision to former welterweight champ Britton in Boston, Massachusetts. As a boy, Lee studied the violin but deserted musical circles to become a professional jockey. For two years, he raced at Jamaica, Aqueduct, Belmont and on the Canadian circuit. He quit the saddle when he became overweight and eventually tried his hand at boxing. After winning numerous amateur titles in New York, he turned professional in 1927. He retired from the ring in 1933, because of an injury which left him blind in one eye and turned to band leading. He also went on to become a screen, stage, radio and television actor. He starred in the Broadway play **Native Son** and had a featured role in the box office movie hit **Lifeboat.** Born Leonard L. Canegata, although his name was also listed as Lionel Canagata, he died in 1952, at the age of 45, of a heart attack in his native New York City.

Films include: 1939--**Keep Punching;** 1944--**Lifeboat;** 1947--**Body and Soul, The Roosevelt Story** (narrator); 1949--**Lost Boundaries;** 1952--**The Beloved Country.**

1912 Meadowlark Lemon

Meadowlark Lemon was the Clown Prince of basketball during his flamboyant career with the Harlem Globetrotters. The six feet two North Carolina native joined the world famous basketball magicians in 1954, and was their foremost attraction for nearly three decades. The comedy star of the Globetrotters was also an outstanding scorer with a patented hook shot, many times bringing capacity crowds to their feet with his half court accuracy. His continuous, high-pitched chattering with all his teammates, opponents, officials and fans was an integral part of the Globetrotters' success. The Harlem Globetrotters, the ambassadors of goodwill, have spread the gospel of basketball in nearly 100 foreign countries and during that period, Meadowlark Lemon was truly the Clown Prince of basketball. He was caricatured in a children's television cartoon series about the Globetrotters in the 1970's.

Films include: 1979--**The Fish That Saved Pittsburgh.**

1913 Benny Leonard

Benny Leonard retired as the undefeated world lightweight champion on January 15, 1925, some seven-and-a-half years after he won the title by knocking out Freddie Welsh in the ninth round in New York City. Leonard, the longest reigning lightweight king in history, made a comeback as a welterweight in 1931. He called it quits after Jimmy McLarnin knocked him out on October 7, 1932. During his tenure as lightweight king, Leonard attempted to win the world welterweight crown from Jack Britton but lost on a foul in the 13th round in New York City on June 26, 1922. Leonard, born Benjamin Leiner in New York, registered an 89-5-1 record with 115 no decisions during his 16-year career. He was elected to the Boxing Hall of Fame in 1955. In 1943, he became a referee on the staff of the New York State Athletic Commission. Leonard died in 1947 in New York City. During the height of his boxing

Joe Louis (right) matches fists with Jersey Joe Walcott.

popularity, Leonard made a series of two-reel boxing shorts, including **Jazz Bout, Hitting Hard** and **Breaking In.**

1914 Ed "Strangler" Lewis

Born Robert H. Friedrich, he went on to become one of professional wrestling's great names of the 1920's and 30's as Ed "Strangler" Lewis. He held the National Wrestling Alliance title five times, first winning the championship in 1920 over Joe Stecher. He last held the crown in 1932 when he defeated Dick Shikat in Long Island City, New York. He split two championship matches with Stanislaus Zbyszko, another mat great who became a movie actor. He died in 1966.

Films include: 1943--**Nasty Nuisance.** 1950--**Body Hold.**

1915 Joe Louis

Long after Joe Louis hung up his boxing gloves, he remained one of the country's most popular and beloved figures. The Brown Bomber, who began fighting in 1934, retired as undefeated world heavyweight champion on March 1, 1949, after defending his title a record 25 times. Louis, born Joe Louis Barrow in Lafayette, Alabama, but raised in Detroit, Michigan, moved into the heavyweight picture in 1935 with quick knockouts over former champions Primo Carnera, King Levinsky and Max Baer. On June 19, 1936, however, Max Schmeling put a temporary stop to Louis' road to a title fight with a 12-round knockout in New York City. Louis finally got his chance at the crown and kayoed James J. Braddock in eight rounds to win the championship in Chicago, Illinois, on June 22, 1937. After three title defenses, Louis was matched against Schmeling in a 1938 fight billed as a battle between democracy and fascism--Louis the symbol of America against Schmeling, the symbol of Hitler's Nazi Germany--and the champ flattened Schmeling in just over two minutes of the first round at New York's Yankee Stadium. On January 9, 1942, he knocked out Buddy Baer in one round and donated his title purse to the Naval Relief Fund; and just two months later, he kayoed Abe Simon in six rounds and again donated his title purse, this time to the Army Relief Fund. He went on to serve four years in the army, returning to the ring on June 19, 1946 to stop Billy Conn to retain his title. He retired undefeated less than three years later and began a series of exhibition bouts. But, because of tax problems with the Internal Revenue Service caused by poor financial advice, he returned to the ring. On September 27, 1950, he lost a 15-round decision to champion Ezzard Charles. It was only Louis' second career setback. On October 26, 1951, however, America wept as Rocky Marciano finally ended the Brown Bomber's brilliant career with an eight-round knockout in New York. In 1954, with a 68-3 record, he was elected to the Boxing Hall of Fame. His battles in the ring were as legendary as his problems with the IRS. He tried everything, including wrestling, to pay back the taxes he owed the government; and finally in 1970, the IRS and Louis came to an agreement. Louis will be remembered for many great things. One was the speech he made to the Navy Relief Society in 1942 when he said, "I'm only doing what any red-blood American would do. We gonna do our part, and we will win, because we are on God's side." Joe Louis was a great champion and a true American hero. He died in 1983, and was buried in Arlington National Cemetery under a special executive decree of President Reagan. Coley Wallace portrayed him in the 1953 film **The Joe Louis Story.**

Harry Lowrey.

Films include: 1938--**Spirit of Youth;** 1943--**Sergeant Joe Louis on Tour;** 1946--**Joe Palooka, Champ;** 1947--**The Fight Never Ends;** 1955--**The Square Jungle;** 1970--**The Phynx.**

1916 Peanuts Lowrey

Harry "Peanuts" Lowrey was an actor well before he became a professional baseball player. In fact, he became an actor some 14 years before he reached the major leagues with the Chicago Cubs in 1942. Lowrey, who lived next door to the Hal Roach movie lot in Culver City, California, appeared in 14 **Our Gang** comedy shorts in 1926 and 1927. He eventually turned to professional baseball and played 13 seasons in the majors with the Cubs, Cincinnati Reds, St. Louis Cardinals and Philadelphia Phillies, finishing with a .273 lifetime batting average. In 1945, Lowrey hit .283 and had a career high 89 runs batted in to help the Cubs win the National League pennant. The five feet eight outfielder batted .310 in the '45 World Series against the Detroit Tigers. He appeared in the 1946 All-Star Game and had one of only three National League hits. Lowrey hit .303 with the Cardinals in 1951 and led National League pinch-hitters in pinch hits in both 1952 and 1953. He coached for many years in the majors with the Phillies, San Francisco Giants, Montreal Expos, Cubs and California Angels. Lowrey appeared in the 1952 film **The Winning Team.** His movie credits list the spelling of his last name as Lowry.

Films include: 1926--**Uncle Tom's Uncle, Thundering Fleas, Shivering Spooks, The Fourth Alarm, War Feathers;** 1927--**Seeing the World, Telling Whoppers, Bring Home the Turkey, Ten Years Old, Love My Dog, Tired Business Men, Baby Brother, Chicken Feed, Olympic Games;** 1952--**The Winning Team.**

1917 Charles "Kid" McCoy

The "Corkscrew Kid," born Norman Selby, was a natural middleweight but fought men in the light heavy and heavyweight divisions. On March 1, 1896, he knocked out Tommy Ryan in 15 rounds to win the welterweight crown at Masbeth, Long Island. He outgrew the welterweight class, vacated the title and went into the higher weight divisions. On April 22, 1903, McCoy and Jack Root met in Detroit, Michigan, for the newly established light heavyweight championship with Root winning the title in a ten-round bout. The five feet eleven, 160 pounder from Rush County, Indiana, fought James J. Corbett, Joe Choynski (three times), Tom Sharkey, Peter Maher and Kid Carter among others during a fantastic 81-6-9 career that included 35 knockouts. He fought exhibitions from 1916 through 1918 and again in 1922 at the age of 49. McCoy committed suicide at his home in Detroit in 1940. He was elected to the Boxing Hall of Fame in 1957.

Films include: 1919--**Broken Blossoms** (aka **Yellow Man and the Girl**); 1921--**Bucking the Line, To a Finish, Straight from the Shoulder;** 1922--**Arabia, Oathbound;** 1923--**April Showers;** 1930--**The Painted Angel;** 1931--**Loose Ankles.**

1918 Victor McLaglen

Victor McLaglen, a star of British and Hollywood silent and sound films who won an Academy Award for his role in the 1935 movie **The Informer,** once fought Jack Johnson for the world heavyweight championship. The native of Tunbridge Wells, England, was a prizefighter in Canada and was matched against Johnson in the champion's first title defense after winning the crown from Tommy Burns. On March 10, 1909, the 22-year-old McLaglen, billed as a "great white hope" to win the crown from the famed black fighter, was unable to lift the title from Johnson as the six-round bout ended in no decision in Vancouver, British Columbia. McLaglen, who was usually cast as a big, barbarous, but soft-hearted man of action, died in 1959.

Films include: 1920--**The Call of the Road;** 1921--**Corinthian Jack, The Prey of the Dragon, Carnival, The Sport of Kings;** 1922--**The Glorious Adventure, A Romance of Old Bagdad, Little Brother of God, A Sailor Tramp, The Crimson Circle;** 1923--**The Romany, Heartstrings; M'Lord of the White Road, In the Blood;** 1924--**The Beloved Brute, The Boatswain's Mate, Women and Diamonds** (aka **It Happened in Africa** or **Conscripts of Misfortune**), **The Gay Corinthian, The Passionate Adventure;** 1925--**The Hunted Woman, Percy, The Fighting Heart, The Unholy Three, Winds of Chance;** 1926--**Beau Geste, What Price Glory, Men of Steel, The Isle of Retribution;** 1927--**Loves of Carmen;** 1928--**Mother Machree, A Girl in Every Port, Hangman's House, The River Pirate;** 1929--**Captain Lash, Strong Boy, King of the Khyber Rifles, The Cock Eyed World, The Black Watch, Sez You-Sez Me, Hot for Paris;** 1930--**Happy Days, On the Level, A Devil with Women, Wings of Adventures;** 1931--**Not Exactly Gentlemen, Dishonored, Women of All**

Nations, Wicked, Annabelle's Affairs; 1932--**Guilty as Hell, Devil's Lottery, While Paris Sleeps, The Slippery Pearls** (short), **The Gay Caballero, Rackety Rax;** 1933--**Hot Pepper, Laughing at Life, Dick Turpin;** 1934--**No More Women, Murder at the Vanities, The Lost Patrol, Wharf Angel, The Captain Hates the Sea;** 1935--**The Informer, Under Pressure, Professional Soldier, Great Hotel Murder;** 1936--**Mary of Scotland, The Magnificent Brute, Under Two Flags, Klondike Annie;** 1937--**Nancy Steele Is Missing, This Is My Affair, Wee Willie Winkie, Sea Devils;** 1938--**We're Going to Be Rich, Battle of Broadway, The Devil's Party;** 1939--**Captain Fury, Ex-Champ, Let Freedom Ring; Gunga Din, Pacific Liner, Black Watch, Rio, Full Confession;** 1940--**Diamond Frontier, The Big Guy, South of Pago Pago;** 1941--**Broadway Limited;** 1942--**China Girl, Call Out the Marines, Powder Town;** 1943--**Forever and a Day;** 1944--**Tampico, Roger Touhy—Gangster, The Princess and the Pirate;** 1945--**Rough, Tough and Ready, Love, Honor and Goodbye;** 1946--**Whistle Stop;** 1947--**Foxes of Harrow; Michigan Kid, Calendar Girl;** 1948--**Fort Apache;** 1949--**She Wore a Yellow Ribbon;** 1950--**Rio Grande;** 1952--**The Quiet Man;** 1953--**Fair Wind to Java;** 1954--**Prince Valiant, Trouble in the Glen;** 1955--**Many Rivers to Cross, Lady Godiva, Bengazi, City of Shadows;** 1956--**Around the World in 80 Days;** 1957--**The Abductors;** 1959--**Sea Fury.**

1919 Jimmy McLarnin

"Baby Face" Jimmy McLarnin had three memorable fights with Barney Ross for the world welterweight championship during his outstanding 14-year ring career. McLarnin won the title when he knocked out Young Corbett in the first round on October 29, 1933, in Los Angeles, California, but lost it a year later when Ross scored a 15-round decision in New York. The native of Belfast, Ireland, retained the title when he outpointed Ross in 15 rounds four months later in New York City. McLarnin, however, lost the crown for the second time to Ross in another 15-round decision on May 28, 1935, again in New York City. He retired in 1936 with a 63-11-3 career mark fighting such outstanding opponents as Sammy Mandell for the world lightweight title, Al Singer, Young Jack Thompson, Lou Brouillard, Benny Leonard, Lou Ambers and Tony Canzoneri (twice).

Films include: 1937--**The Big City;** 1946--**Joe Palooka, Champ.**

1920 Mickey Mantle

Mickey Mantle succeeded Babe Ruth, Lou Gehrig and Joe DiMaggio as the New York Yankee superstar that helped continue the team's dynasty in baseball. Named after his father's favorite player, Mickey Cochrane, the native of Spavinaw, Oklahoma, joined the Yankees as a 19-year-old rightfielder, playing adjacent to the legendary DiMaggio in 1951. Despite suffering from osteomyelitis throughout his career, Mantle played 18 years, won the most valuable player award three times (1956-57-62), hit 536 career homers and won the triple crown (homers, batting and runs batted in) in 1956. He hit .300 or better five straight years and ten times overall with a career high .365 in 1957. The switch-hitter belted 54 homers in 1961 and 52 round-trippers in 1956. Mickey, who moved to center field after DiMaggio retired, was one of the greatest power hitters in the history of the game, hitting tape measure shots from either side of the plate that left fans in awe. His longest homer was measured at 565 feet in Washington in 1953. The Yankees captured 12 pennants

Mickey Mantle.

and seven world championships during his 18 years. He was elected to the Baseball Hall of Fame in his first year of eligibility (1974), only the seventh player to achieve that distinction.

Films include: 1962--**Safe at Home, That Touch of Mink.**

1921 Rocky Marciano

The Brockton (Mass.) Blockbuster, born Rocco Francis Marchegiano, retired as undefeated world heavyweight champion on April 27, 1956. He had 49 fights in a career that began in 1947 and knocked out 43 of his opponents. He won the title by flattening champion Jersey Joe Walcott in 13 rounds in Philadelphia, Pennsylvania, on September 23, 1952, and then kayoed Walcott in one round in Chicago in his first title defense. He went on to successfully defend his championship against Roland LaStarza, Ezzard Charles (twice), Don Cockell and Archie Moore. His impressive list of knockout victims include Joe Louis, Rex Layne, Lee Savold, Harry Matthews and Freddie Beshore. During his high school days, he was considered an excellent baseball prospect. He was elected to the Boxing Hall of Fame in 1959. He made his movie debut in the Jerry Lewis feature **The Delicate Delinquent** in 1957. On August 31, 1969, the day before his 46th birthday, he was killed in an airplane crash in Iowa.

Films include: 1957--**The Delicate Delinquent;** 1960--**College Confidential;** 1970--**The Super Fight** (documentary).

1922 Roger Maris

Roger Maris electrified the baseball world in 1961 when the New York Yankee slugger surpassed the legendary Babe Ruth's single season home run mark of 60 by belting 61. Maris was one of the most feared power hitters in baseball in the early 1960's, earning back-to-back Most Valuable Player awards in 1960 and 1961. In that record-smashing 61 in '61 season, Maris was named the Major League's Player of the Year by **The Sporting News,** Male Athlete of the Year by the Associated Press, Man of the Year by **Sport** Magazine, Sportsman of the Year by **Sports Illustrated** and won the coveted Hickok Belt as the Top Professional Athlete of 1961. In the five consecutive seasons that the Yankees won the American League flag (1960-64), Maris averaged 36.4 homers a year. Roger, who also played with Cleveland, Kansas City and St. Louis during a 12-year career, hit 275 lifetime homers and appeared in seven World Series. He died December 14, 1985.

Films include: 1962--**Safe at Home, That Touch of Mink.**

1923 Mil Mascaras

The man with a thousand masks is considered one of the most popular wrestlers in the world. He is never seen without one of his masks, not even when acting in motion pictures. For more than two decades, the 240 pounder from Mexico City has electrified his fans with his great repertoire of aerial kicks and maneuvers. He was introduced to professional wrestling in 1960 in Mexico City while training for the Olympics and subsequently came to Los Angeles where he quickly built up a West Coast following. He went on to win the Americas Heavyweight Championship as well as the Americas Tag Team Championship and the Texas Tag Team Championship. His film career has been as successful as his mat career. One of Mexico's leading movie stars, he has appeared in films distributed in the United States through Columbia Pictures, always wearing his mask as the hero chases the bad guys and rescues the heroine.

Films include: **Mil Mascaras, Los Canallas, Enigma De Muerte.**

Rocky Marciano.

1924 Christy Mathewson

Christy Mathewson attended Bucknell University where he was elected class president, was a member of two literary societies and the glee club, not the perfect background for a professional baseball player at the turn of the century. Mathewson, however, was also a pretty good baseball player and left Bucknell in 1899 to sign a pro baseball contract. By the end of the 1900 season, he was with the New York Giants and began a major league pitching career that lasted 17 years. Nick-named Big Six, probably due to his height (six feet one and a half), Matty went on to post a lifetime 367-186 record with a 2.13 earned run average, 2,502 strikeouts and 77 shutouts. He won 20 or more games 13 times, on three occasions getting over 30 victories. Utilizing his famous "fadeaway" pitch (now known as the screwball), Matty helped hurl the Giants into four World Series. The righthander pitched two no-hitters during his career and also won three games in the 1905 World Series. In 1918, while managing the Cincinnati Reds, he entered the army and inhaled poison gas while in action overseas. He died in 1925 in Saranac Lake, New York. In 1936, Matty, along with Babe Ruth, Ty Cobb, Honus Wagner and Walter Johnson, was in the first group of baseball greats elected to the Hall of Fame.

Films include: 1914--**Love and Baseball.**

1925 Bob Mathias

Bob Mathias was the first athlete in Olympic history to win successive gold medals in the decathlon competition. In 1948, as a 17-year-old California schoolboy, he won his first gold medal at London, England, and repeated the feat four years later at Helsinki, Finland. Unlike some other Olympic gold medal winners, Mathias did not become a movie Tarzan but did enjoy a brief motion picture career before going on to be elected to Congress. He portrayed himself in the film **The Bob Mathias Story.**

Films include: 1954--**The Bob Mathias Story;** 1958--**China Doll;** 1961--**The Minotaur;** 1962--**It Happened in Athens.**

1926 John Matuszak

John Matuszak was a big, mobile, aggressive defensive line-man during his ten-year career in the National Football League. The six feet eight, 275 pounder helped the Oakland Raiders win two Super Bowls, the first over Minnesota in 1977 and the second over Philadelphia in 1981. The victory over the Vikings in Super Bowl XI was Oakland's first NFL championship while the triumph over the Eagles in Super Bowl XV enabled the Raiders to become the first wild card team to win the post-season classic. The rugged Matuszak began his pro career with the Houston Oilers after being the first selection in the entire 1973 draft and went on to be named to the NFL All-Rookie team. The following year, the native of Oak Creek, Wisconsin, jumped to the Houston Texans of the World Football League, but a court ruling returned him to the Oilers. He was traded to the Kansas City Chiefs in the middle of the 1974 season and remained with them through the 1975 campaign. He joined Oakland as a free agent in 1976 after spend-ing the pre-season with Washington and played with the Raiders until he retired after the 1982 season. The former Tampa University All-American recovered a fumble for a touchdown in 1975 while playing for the Chiefs.

Films include: 1979--**North Dallas Forty;** 1981--**Caveman;** 1984--**The Ice Pirates.**

1927 Mike Mazurki

Mike Mazurki, who has been

Roger Maris.

typecast as a villain for most of his movie career, was an outstanding wrestler during a professional career that saw him compete in more than 4,000 matches. He wrestled such greats as Ed "Strangler" Lewis, Jim Browning, Jim Londos, Gus Sonnenberg, Joe Savoldi and Lou Thesz and was popular in Japan where he varied free style wrestling with sumo, judo and karate. For a number of years he refereed championship wrestling matches. He is president of "The Cauliflower Alley Club," an association of former sports professionals, wrestlers and boxers, in Hollywood. The former four-letterman at Manhattan College in New York City was working as an auditor for a Wall Street firm and simultaneously studying law at Fordham University, when he was lured to pro basketball, football and then into wrestling. While wrestling in Los Angeles, Mazurki was seen and signed by director Josef von Sternberg to portray the Chinese coolie wrestler in the 1941 film **Shanghai Gesture.**

Films include: 1940--**Two Mugs from Brooklyn;** 1941--**Shanghai Gesture;** 1943--**Behind the Rising Sun;** 1944--**Murder My Sweet;** 1945--**The Spanish Main, Dakota, Dick Tracy;** 1947--**Sinbad the Sailor, Nightmare Alley, Unconquered;** 1948--**I Walk Alone, Relentless;** 1949--**Abandoned Woman, Come to the Stable, The Devil's Henchman, Neptune's Daughter, Rope of Sand, Samson and Delilah;** 1950--**Night and the City, Dark City, He's a Cockeyed Wonder;** 1951--**Criminal Lawyer, My Favorite Spy, Pier 23, Ten Tall Men;** 1954--**The Egyptian;** 1955--**Davey Crockett, King of the Wild Frontier; New Orleans Uncensored, Kismet, Blood Alley;** 1956--**Around the World in 80 Days, Comanche;** 1957--**Hell Ship Mutiny, Man in the Vault;** 1958--**Man Who Died Twice, The Buccaneer;** 1959--**Some Like It Hot;** 1960--**The Facts of Life;** 1961--**Pocketful of Miracles, Double Trouble;** 1962--**Swingin' Along, Zotz!, Five Weeks in a Balloon;** 1963--**It's a Mad, Mad, Mad World, Four for Texas, Donovan's Reef;** 1964--**Cheyenne Autumn;** 1965--**Requiem for a Gunfighter;** 1966--**Seven Women;** 1967--**The Adventures of Bullwhip Griffin;** 1974--**Challenge to Be Free;** 1975--**The Wild McCullochs;** 1978--**The Magic of Lassie;** 1979--**Gas Pump Girls;** 1980--**Sam Marlowe, Private Eye** (aka **The Man with Bogart's Face**); 1981--**All the Marbles;** 1982--**Hey, Goodlooking;** 1984--**Doin' Time.**

1928 Freddie Mills

The popular English fighter won the British Empire Light Heavyweight title by knocking out Len Harvey in two rounds on June 20, 1942, in London. He was kayoed by world heavyweight champ Gus Lesnevich in ten rounds on May 14, 1946, in a title bout in London but came back to win the crown with a 15-round decision over Lesnevich two years later in London. He held the championship until January 24, 1950, when he was knocked out in ten rounds by Joey Maxim in London. He retired at the age of 30 with a career 73-17-6 mark that included 52 knockouts to enter television and movies. He later became a restaurateur. He died from a gunshot wound on July 25, 1965, in London.

Films include: 1952--**Emergency Call** (aka **The Hundred Hour Hunt**--U.S., 1953); 1958--**Kill Me Tomorrow;** 1960--**Carry on Constable;** 1961--**Carry on Regardless** (U.S., 1963); 1964--**Saturday Night Out.**

1929 Bull Montana

Bull Montana successfully combined careers in professional wrestling and motion pictures during the 1920's. The legendary champion Lou Thesz described Montana as one of the "really good wrestlers" of the Roaring

Twenties. Born Lugia Montagna in Vogliera, Italy, his acting career spanned four decades. He died in 1950 in Los Angeles, California.

Films include: 1919--**Victory, Brass Buttons, The Unpardonable Sin, Put Up Your Hands;** 1920--**Treasure Island, Go and Get It;** 1921--**The Four Horsemen of the Apocalypse, Crazy to Marry, The Foolish Age, One Wild Week;** 1922--**Gay and Devilish, The Three-Must-Get-There's, The Timber Queen** (serial); 1923--**Breaking Into Society, Hollywood, Held to Answer;** 1924--**Jealous Husbands, The Fire Patrol, Painted People;** 1925--**Bashful Buccaneer, Dick Turpin, The Gold Hunters, Manhattan Madness, Secrets of the Night, The Lost World;** 1926--**Vanishing Millions** (serial); **The Sky Rocket, The Son of the Sheik, Stop, Look and Listen;** 1928--**How to Handle Women, Good Morning Judge, Roped In;** 1929--**The Show of Shows, Tiger Rose;** 1935--**Palooka from Paducah** (short); 1937--**The Big City;** 1943--**Good Morning Judge.**

1930 Carlos Monzon

The native of Santa Fe, Argentina, is considered one of the greatest middleweights in the history of boxing. He posted an amazing 89-3-9 record with 61 knockouts during a 15-year career. Monzon held the world championship for nearly seven years, winning the title by knocking out Nino Benvenuti in 12 rounds in Rome, Italy, on November 7, 1970, and retiring on August 29, 1977, a month after his 14th straight successful title defense. He stopped Benvenuti in three rounds in a return match six months later in Monte Carlo in his initial title defense. He also defeated former welterweight and middleweight champ Emile Griffith in two title defenses. Prior to winning the world championship, Monzon won the Argentine middleweight title and the South American middleweight crown. He retired from boxing three weeks after his 35th birthday and began a full-time acting career.

Films include: 1973--**La Mary.**

1931 Archie Moore

Archie Moore held the world light heavyweight championship longer than any other fighter in history--nine years--and only when the ruling boxing organizations withdrew its recognition of him, did Moore lose the title. Moore, who started fighting in 1936, earned world-wide recognition by winning the championship from Joey Maxim on December 17, 1952. He successfully defended his crown nine times, beating off challenges from Maxim (twice), Harold Johnson, Bobo Olson, Yolande Pompey, Tony Anthony, Yvon Durelle (twice) and Giulio Rinaldi. On February 7, 1961, the National Boxing Association lifted Moore's title, but every other boxing board recognized him as the champ. In February 1962, however, New York withdrew its recognition and took away Moore's crown. During his championship reign, Moore twice fought for the world heavyweight title. On September 21, 1955, Rocky Marciano got up from a first-round knockdown and kayoed Moore in the ninth round; and on November 30, 1956, Floyd Patterson won the vacant crown by knocking out Moore in the fifth round. He retired in 1964 at the age of 49 and entered the movie and television field. Moore, who was born Archibald Lee Wright, had a 194-26-8 career record, including 141 knockouts.

Films include: 1960--**The Adventures of Huckleberry Finn;** 1963--**The Carpetbaggers;** 1966--**The Fortune Cookie;** 1973--**The Outfit.**

1932 Frank Moran

The Pittsburgh, Pennsylvania, native was one of the leading

heavyweight contenders in the world during his boxing days, twice fighting for the championship. On June 27, 1914, champion Jack Johnson retained his title with a 20-round win over Moran in Paris, France, with popular French fighter Georges Carpentier refereeing the bout. On March 25, 1916, Moran battled champion Jess Willard for ten rounds with no decision in a title fight in New York City. A law prevented decisions at the time; but if Moran had won by a knockout, he would have taken the crown from Willard. Other leading fighters he fought were Gunboat Smith (three times), Bombardier Billy Wells and Al Palzer. The six feet one and a half, 200 pounder posted a 34-11-2 record with 24 knockouts and 13 no decisions during a career that spanned from 1910 through 1922. He died in Hollywood, California, in 1967.

Films include: 1928--**Ships of the Night;** 1933--**Hooks and Jabs** (short), **Sailor's Luck, Gambling Ship;** 1934--**Three Chumps Ahead** (short), **No More Women, The World Moves On, By Your Leave;** 1936--**Mummy's Boys;** 1937--**Shall We Dance?** 1938--**Battle of Broadway;** 1939--**Captain Fury;** 1940--**The Great McGinty;** 1941--**Federal Fugitives, A Date with the Falcon, Sullivan's Troubles;** 1942--**Butch Minds the Baby, Sullivan's Travels, The Corpse Vanishes;** 1943--**Ghosts on the Loose;** 1944--**The Great Moment, Return of the Ape Man, Hail the Conquering Hero, The Miracle of Morgan's Creek;** 1945--**Yolanda and the Thief;** 1946--**Pardon My Past;** 1947--**Mad Wednesday;** 1948--**A Miracle Can Happen;** 1949--**The Lady Gambles.**

1933 Glenn Morris

Glenn Morris was acclaimed the "greatest athlete in the world" after he won the gold medal in the decathlon in the 1936 Olympics in Berlin, Germany. The product of Colorado A&M, who set a world record in the ten-event, two-day competition, went on to play professional football as an end with the Detroit Lions in the National Football League in 1940. He portrayed Tarzan in the 1938 film **Tarzan's Revenge** with another Olympic gold medal winner, swimmer Eleanor Holm, playing Jane. Morris died in Palo Alto, California, in 1974.

Films include: 1937--**Decathlon Champion** (short); 1938--**Tarzan's Revenge, Hold That Co-Ed.**

1934 Mercury Morris

Eugene "Mercury" Morris helped the Miami Dolphins to three Super Bowl appearances and two National Football League championships (1972 and 1973). The speedster from West Texas State gained 1,000 yards and scored 12 touchdowns as the Dolphins went through the 1972 campaign undefeated. The following season, Morris rushed for 954 yards, including a 197-yard game, and registered 10 TDs. In 1970, he had a career high 302 combined net yards in a game.

Films include: 1974--**The Black Six.**

1935 Joe Namath

Broadway Joe, the 1969 Super Bowl hero of the New York Jets, was one of the most flamboyant personalities of the 1960's and '70's. The native of Beaver Falls, Pennsylvania, came out of the University of Alabama to help give the young American Football League equality with the older and more established National Football League. Namath, whose quick wrists enabled him to complete 1,836 passes for 27,057 yards and 170 touchdowns during his 12-year career (1965-76) with the Jets, sparked New York to a stunning 16-7 upset victory over the Baltimore Colts in Super Bowl III as the Jets became the first AFL team to win the Super Bowl. Namath, who predicted the win over the Colts, was named the Most Valuable Player of the Super Bowl. He also was the AFL MVP, the Hickok Belt winner as the Pro Athlete of the Year and the George Halas Award winner as the Most Courageous Pro Player in 1969. Namath was named the Jets MVP in 1968, '69 and '74. He retired after playing the 1977 season with the Los Angeles Rams. Namath made his movie debut as a Marine in the 1970 film **Norwood** starring Glen Campbell. In addition to movies, he has appeared on the stage.

Films include: 1970--**Norwood, C.C. and Company;** 1971--**The Last Rebel;** 1979--**Avalanche Express.**

1936 Ken Norton

The native of San Diego, California, was recognized by the World Boxing Council (WBC) as the world heavyweight champion in 1978 when Leon Spinks declined to meet him for the title. That same year, he lost the crown in a 15-round split decision to Larry Holmes in Las Vegas, Nevada. Norton fought Muhammad Ali three times during his career, splitting a pair of 12-round decisions in non-title fights in 1973 and losing to Ali for the title in a 15-round decision in 1976, with Ali suffering a broken jaw. Norton also lost a championship fight with George Foreman in 1974.

Films include: 1975--**Mandingo;** 1976--**Drum.**

1937 Lou Nova

Lou may be the only person ever to fight for the world heavyweight championship and conduct a recital of his poetry in New York's famous Carnegie Hall. The Los Angeles, California, native won the U.S. and world amateur heavyweight boxing championship in 1935 and turned professional a year later. After winning 20 straight fights, he lost to "Slapsie" Maxie Rosenbloom on June 3, 1938. He bounced back to knock out four straight opponents and then demolished British champion Tommy Farr. On June 1, 1939, he entered the ring in New York City as a heavy underdog against former champ Max Baer but surprised everyone with an 11th round kayo victory. Lou knocked out Baer in a rematch on April 4, 1941, in New York City with the ex-champ calling it a career after the eighth round flattening. On September 21, 1941, Lou, the leading contender for the heavyweight title, was knocked out in six rounds by champion Joe Louis. Since hanging up his gloves in 1945, he has been a sports columnist, lecturer, standup comic, poet and actor. In 1956, he gave a recital of his poetry in Carnegie Hall.

Films include: 1946--**Joe Palooka, Champ;** 1949--**Cowboy and the Prizefighter;** 1950--**Where the Sidewalk Ends;** 1951--**Double Dynamite** (aka **It's Only Money**), **Half Angel;** 1953--**Clipped Wings;** 1954--**World for Ransom, Prince Valiant;** 1956--**The Leather Saint;** 1964--**What a Way to Go;** 1967--**Thoroughly Modern Millie;** 1968--**Blackbeard's Ghost.**

1938 Packy O'Gatty

Packy O'Gatty, who appeared in nearly 1,000 boxing exhibitions for wounded servicemen at different camps and hospitals during World War I, was the first man elected to the Boxing Historians Hall of Fame. O'Gatty, born Pasquale Agati in Cannitello, Italy, was a talented bantamweight (118 pounds) who once fought a three-round exhibition bout with heavyweight champion Jack Dempsey on March 9, 1922, in New York. He registered a 58-8-5 mark with 61 no decisions during his 14-year ring career. He retired after a three-round exhibition match with welterweight champion Jimmy McLarnin in July 1928 in Detroit, Michigan. O'Gatty, who also fought bantamweight champions

Ken Norton.

Kid Williams and Pete Herman, was elected to the Hall of Fame in 1963. He died in 1966 in New York City.

Films include: 1936--**Laughing Irish Eyes;** 1940--**East of the River;** 1958--**Missile Monster.**

1939 Barney Oldfield

Barney Oldfield, born Berna Eli near York Township, Fulton County, Ohio, was the first great race car driver, tearing up the roads in the early 1900's. In addition to being a race car driver and movie actor, he also was a circus performer. He died in 1946.

Films include: 1913--**Barney Oldfield's Race for a Life;** 1925--**The Speed Demon;** 1927--**The First Auto;** 1932--**Speed in the Gay 90's** (short).

1940 Merlin Olsen

A two-time All-American at Utah State, Merlin Olsen won the Outland Trophy as the nation's outstanding collegiate lineman in 1962. He was a first round draft choice of the Los Angeles Rams and starred for 15 years as a defensive tackle in the National Football League. He was named Defensive Rookie of the Year in 1962, most valuable lineman in 1973 and the NFL's Most Valuable Player in 1974. The perennial All-Pro was the recipient of the Vince Lombardi Dedication Trophy in 1976 and set an NFL record by being named to the Pro Bowl 14 straight years. He received the NFL Alumni Career Achievement Award in 1981. In 1980, Merlin became the youngest person named to the College Football Hall of Fame. While playing with the Rams, he prepared for his acting career by appearing in movies and on television. He starred on TV's top-rated series **Little House on the Prairie.**

Films include: 1969--**The Undefeated;** 1971--**One More Train to Rob;** 1975--**Mitchell.**

1941 Charles Paddock

The "World's Fastest Human" tag has always been applied to sprinters and Charles Paddock was the original "WFH" as he won a gold medal in the 100 meters at the 1920 Olympics in Antwerp, Belgium, in a record tying 10.8 seconds. He also won a silver medal that year for finishing second in the 200 meters. Four years later, he again won an Olympic silver medal in the 200 meters in Paris, France.

Films include: 1925--**Nine and Three-Fifths Seconds;** 1926--**The Campus Flirt;** 1927--**High School Hero, The College Hero;** 1928--**Olympic Hero.**

1942 Pele

They called him "The Black Pearl," and to the world of soccer Edson Arantes do Nascimento was simply known as Pele, the greatest player in the history of the international sport. The native of Tres Coracoes, Brazil, led his country to the World Cup championship in 1958 and again in 1970. The "King of Soccer" was lured out of retirement in 1975 by the Cosmos of the North American Soccer League, and he popularized a sport that had been considered "foreign" to North Americans and gave it instant major league status. He filled stadiums wherever he played during his three years (1975-77) with the Cosmos, thrilling fans with his quick feet and patented bicycle kick. He helped the Cosmos to the NASL championship in 1977, was named the league's most valuable player in 1976 and was a three-time first team all-star. He scored more than 1,200 goals during his long career, and his legend will live as long as there is a youngster kicking a soccer ball.

Films include: 1977--**Pele;** 1981--**Victory;** 1983--**A Minor Miracle.**

Pele.

1943 Nat Pendleton

A broken leg helped Nat Pendleton end one career and begin another. The native of Davenport, Iowa, entered professional wrestling in the 1920's after being an amateur champion and a U.S. Olympian. But, as wrestling great Lou Thesz recalled, "John Pesek broke Nat's leg in a match and that helped lead to his movie career." He appeared in countless films, beginning with roles requiring mat experience and gradually becoming a top character actor. He died in 1967 in San Diego, California.

Films include: 1924--**The Hoosier Schoolmaster;** 1926--**Let's Get Married;** 1929--**The Laughing Lady;** 1930--**Fair Warning, The Sea Wolf, Last of the Duanes, The Big Pond, Liliom;** 1931--**Secret Witness, Larceny Lane, Vigor of Youth, The Sea Beneath, The Star Witness, Mr. Lemon of Orange, Blonde Crazy, Spirit of Notre Dame, Pottsville Paluka, Cauliflower Alley, Manhattan Parade;** 1932--**Horse Feathers, You Said a Mouthful, The Sign of the Cross, Taxi;** 1933--**Deception, Whistling in the Dark, Baby Face, I'm No Angel, College Coach, Lady for a Day, Penthouse;** 1934--**Manhattan Melodrama, Lazy River, The Thin Man, Death on the Diamond, The Gay Blade, The Cat's Paw;** 1935--**Times Square Lady, Baby Face Harrigan, Here Comes the Band, Reckless, Murder in the Fleet, It's in the Air;** 1936--**The Great Ziegfield, The Garden Murder Case, Sworn Enemy, Trapped by Television;** 1937--**Under Cover of Night, Song of the City, Gangway, Life Begins in College;** 1938--**Fast Company, Swing Your Lady, Arsene Lupin Returns, The Shopworn Angel, The Crowd Roars, Young Dr. Kildare;** 1939--**The Marx Brothers at the Circus, Another Thin Man, On Borrowed Time, It's a Wonderful World;** 1940--**Northwest Passage, Dr. Kildare's Strange Case;** 1941--**Flight Command, Buck Privates, Top Sergeant Mulligan;** 1942--**Jail House Blues, Calling Dr. Gillespie;** 1945--**Rookies Come Home;** 1947--**Scared to Death, Buck Privates Come Home;** 1949--**Death Valley;** 1964--**Big Parade of Comedy** (documentary).

1944 Richard Petty

Richard Lee Petty is probably the best known name in international motorsports competition. He finished the 1983 season with a record 198 career victories, almost 100 victories more than his nearest competitor, and became the first driver to surpass $5 million in career winnings. In his 26 years of stock car competition, Petty has tasted victory at least once in all but four years. He won the National Association for Stock Car Auto Racing Winston Cup championship seven times (1964, 1967, 1971-72, 1974-75, 1979) and finished second six times. Petty won a record 27 races, including ten straight, in 1967 and in 1971 became NASCAR's first driving millionaire and was selected the American Driver of the Year. In 1979, Petty set a new record for single season earnings with $531,292. His father, Lee, was a three-time grand national champion and a son, Kyle, drives on the NASCAR circuit. Films include: 1965--**Thundering Dixie;** 1972--**Smash-Up Alley: The Petty Story.**

1945 Vera Ralston

Vera Hruba Ralston was one of the leading figure skating champions in her native Czechoslovakia in the 1930's and was Republic Studios' answer to Olympic figure skating queen turned movie actress, Sonja Henie.

Films include: 1942--**Ice Capades Review** (aka **Rhythm Hits the Ice**); 1944--**Lake Placid Serenade;** 1949--**The Fighting Kentuckian;** 1950--**Surrender;** 1951--**Belle Le Grand;** 1952--**Hood-**

Richard Petty.

lum Empire, The Wild Blue Yonder; 1953--**Fair Wind to Java, A Perilous Journey;** 1954--**Jubilee Trail, Timberjack;** 1956--**Accused of Murder;** 1957--**Gunfire at Indian Gap, Spoilers of the Forest;** 1958--**Man Who Died Twice, The Notorious Mr. Monks.**

1946 Bobby Riggs

An aging Bobby Riggs may have lost to Billie Jean King in the much ballyhooed "Battle of the Sexes" tennis match at the Houston Astrodome, but some four decades earlier he scored a rare triple victory by winning three championships at Wimbledon in the same year. In 1939, Riggs won the Wimbledon singles title and teamed with Elwood Cooke to win the doubles crown and with Alice Marble to take the mixed doubles championship. He also won the U.S. Outdoor tennis championship in 1939 and 1941 and teamed with Marble to win the U.S. Outdoor mixed doubles event in 1940. Riggs turned professional in 1942 and teamed with Don Budge to win the U.S. Professional doubles title. In 1946 and 1947, Riggs dominated the U.S. Professional championships, winning the singles title both years and teaming with Frank Kovacs, II, to take the double crown in 1946 and with Budge to win the doubles title in 1947. He came back to win the U.S. Professional singles championship in 1949.

Films include: 1979--**Racquet.**

1947 Paul Robeson

Paul Robeson was one of the most variously gifted men of this century. And, as penned in a **Sports Illustrated** article some years back, he was "also among the most embattled, his espousal of unpopular causes gradually obscuring his protean achievements . . . this son of a runaway slave can claim the distinction of having been cheered as an All-American and reviled as an un-American all within the same lifetime." The Princeton, New Jersey, native won a scholarship to Rutgers University and earned 12 varsity letters, four each in football, baseball and basketball. He was a football All-American in both 1917 and 1918 and, following Rutgers' 14-0 win over the celebrated Newport Naval Reserve team made up of college All-Americans in 1918, selector Walter Camp called Robeson "the greatest defensive end ever to trod the gridiron." He played three seasons of pro football with Akron, Hammond and Milwaukee in the American Professional Football Association (the forerunner of the National Football League) while attending Columbia University's law school. It was at that time that he was persuaded to take part in an amateur stage production at the Harlem YMCA. He did so well that after being admitted to the New York bar he decided not to practice law but to agree to Eugene O'Neill's personal request to star in his plays **All God's Chillun Got Wings** and **The Emperor Jones.** Robeson, who also began starring in films and giving singing recitals, quickly became one of the most accomplished performers of his day. He made the first of his several trips to the Soviet Union in 1934 and gradually became enchanted

Vera Ralston.

Paul Robeson.

with leftist ideology as a possible answer to discrimination against blacks in the United States. His championship of the common man caused much controversy. He died in 1976.

Films include: 1924--**Body and Soul**; 1929--**Borderline**; 1933--**Emperor Jones**; 1935--**Sanders of the River** (aka **Bosambo**); 1936--**Song of Freedom**, **Show Boat**; 1937--**Big Fella**, **King Solomon's Mines**, **Jericho** (aka **Dark Sands**); 1940--**Proud Valley**; 1942--**Native Land** (narrator), **Tales of Manhattan.**

1948 Jackie Robinson

Jack Roosevelt Robinson was an exciting and controversial player who made a great impact on the game of baseball when he became the first black player in the major leagues in the 20th century. Branch Rickey, president of the Brooklyn Dodgers, decided to challenge baseball's color barrier and signed Robinson after he played with the Kansas City Monarchs of the Negro American League in 1945. The native of Cairo, Georgia, led the International League in hitting with a .349 mark at Montreal in 1946 and was promoted to the Dodgers during spring training the following year. Robby, subjected to ugly racial insults, let his skills do the talking and won the Rookie of the Year award in 1947, helping the Dodgers win the National League pennant. In 1949, he was named the NL's most valuable player when he batted .342 with 203 hits, 124 runs batted in, 122 runs scored and 32 stolen bases. Robinson, who was a four-sport star at the University of California at Los Angeles, appeared in six World Series during his ten-year career and finished with a lifetime .311 batting average. He was elected to the Baseball Hall of Fame in 1962. Jackie portrayed himself in the film **The Jackie Robinson Story.** He died in 1972 in Stamford, Connecticut.

Films include: 1950--**The Jackie Robinson Story.**

1949 Sugar Ray Robinson

It's a general consensus of boxing experts that Sugar Ray Robinson, pound for pound, was the greatest fighter to enter the ring. He held the world welterweight and middleweight titles, was unsuccessful in a bid for the light heavyweight crown and retired as undefeated middleweight king on December 18, 1952, with a 13-year record of 130-3-2. Some two years later, Sugar Ray returned to the ring and continued to fight for 11 more years before retiring a second time at the age of 45. During his "second career," he won and lost the world middleweight championship three times. He knocked out Bobo Olson for the title, lost it to Gene Fullmer, regained it from Fullmer, lost it to Carmen Basilio, regained it from Basilio and lost it for the last time to Paul Pender. Robinson won the vacant welterweight championship by outpointing Tommy Bell on December 20, 1946, and then gave up the title after knocking out Jack LaMotta in 13 rounds to win the world middleweight crown on February 14, 1951. Champion Joey Maxim foiled Sugar Ray's attempt to win the light heavyweight title with a 14-round knockout on June 25, 1952. Robinson, born Walker Smith in Detroit, Michigan, fought such standouts as Sammy Angott (three times), Marty Servo (twice), Fritzie Zivic (twice), Henry Armstrong, LaMotta (six times), Kid Gavilan (twice), Steve Belloise, Charley Fusari, Randy Turpin (twice), Rocky Graziano and Joey Giardello during his two-and-a-half decades in the ring. His final record read 174-19-6, and in 1967 he was elected to the Boxing Hall of Fame. In 1968, Sugar Ray began a career as an actor.

Films include: 1968--**The Detective, Paper Lion, Candy;** 1977--**Telefon.**

1950 Knute Rockne

The legend of Knute Rockne lives decades after his untimely death in 1931 in an airplane crash while he was on his way to California to make some movies. As a player at Notre Dame, Rockne had a major role in making the forward pass what it is today and later as a coach at his alma mater, he revolutionized the sport. In 1913, Rockne, an end, and quarterback Gus Dorais stunned a powerful Army team and popularized the forward pass by displaying an aerial attack that gave the Fighting Irish a 35-14 victory. As a coach, he guided Notre Dame to 13 straight winning seasons, five undefeated campaigns and 20 consecutive wins en route to a 105-12-5 career mark (1918-30). He instituted a "motion backfield" that became so successful at Notre Dame that it was outlawed in the 1920's. And, on top of all his achievements, his locker room speeches were as legendary as the man himself. Pat O'Brien portrayed the College Football Hall of Fame coach in the 1940 film **Knute Rockne.** In 1929 and 1930, Rockne hosted a series of short films on football for Universal Pictures.

1951 Slapsie Maxie Rosenbloom

Rosenbloom, nicknamed "Slapsie Maxie" by sportswriter Damon Runyon for his unorthodox slapping style in the ring, was one of the great light heavyweight fighters in history. He fought 289 bouts during a 17-year career, winning all but 35 fights. On June 25, 1930, Maxie won the light heavyweight title by decisively outpointing Jimmy Slattery in 15 rounds at Buffalo, N.Y., and defeated him again in a 15-round decision in Brooklyn, New York, on August 5, 1931. He held the crown for more than four years, successfully defending the title eight times, before Bob Olin won the championship with a 15-round decision in New York on November 16, 1934. During his brilliant career, he battled the likes of John Henry Lewis (four times), James J. Braddock (twice), Mickey Walker (twice), Young Stribling, Lou Nova, Bob Pastor and King Levinsky among others. He was elected to the Boxing Hall of Fame in 1972 and to the Jewish Sports Hall of Fame. During his long and successful Hollywood career, he typically portrayed punch-drunk characters. He died in Los Angeles, California, in 1976.

Films include: 1933--**Mr. Broadway;** 1936--**Muss 'Em Up, Kelly the Second;** 1937--**Nothing Sacred, The Big City;** 1938--**The Kid Comes Back, Mr. Moto's Gamble, Gangs of New York, The Amazing Dr. Clitterhouse, Submarine Patrol;** 1939--**Women in the Wind, The Kid from Kokomo, Each Dawn I Die, 20,000 Men a Year;** 1940--**Passport to Alcatraz;** 1941--**Ringside Maisie, Louisiana Purchase;** 1942--**To the Shores of Tripoli, The Boogie Man Will Get You;** 1944--**Swing Fever, Irish Eyes Are Smiling;** 1945--**Men in Her Diary;** 1948--**Hazard;** 1951--**Skipalong Rosenbloom, Mr. Universe;** 1955--**Abbott and Costello Meet the Keystone Kops;** 1956--**Hollywood or Bust;** 1959--**The Beat Generation;** 1966--**Don't Worry We'll Think of a Title.**

1952 Barney Ross

Barnet Rosofsky, a native of New York City, started boxing as an amateur in 1926 and won the Golden Gloves and Inter-City titles in 1929 before turning professional. He captured the lightweight and junior welterweight championships by beating Tony Canzoneri in ten rounds at Chicago, Illinois, on June 23, 1933. He eventually vacated the lightweight throne, having outgrown the class, and won the world welterweight championship by outpointing Jimmy McLarnin in 15 rounds on May 28, 1934. McLarnin regained the title four months later, but Ross took it back on May 28, 1935, at the Polo Grounds in New York City with a 15-round decision. Some three years later, Henry Armstrong took the crown in 15 rounds, bringing to an end Ross' 74-4-3 ring career. In 1942, the former champion joined the U.S. Marines and was wounded at Guadalcanal. He was elected to the Boxing Hall of Fame in 1956. Ross died in Chicago, Illinois, in 1967. Cameron Mitchell portrayed Ross in the 1957 film **Monkey on My Back.**

Films include: 1962--**Requiem for a Heavyweight;** 1965--**The Doctor and the Playgirl.**

1953 Tim Rossovich

Tim Rossovich was the number one draft choice of the National Football League's Philadelphia Eagles in 1968 after helping the University of Southern California to the national championship. The six feet four, 250-pound defensive end was the leader of the USC line that stopped Indiana as the Trojans won the Rose Bowl, 14-3. He earned All-American honors and was co-captain of the team. Rossovich, using balance, agility and quickness to harass opposing quarterbacks, was selected to the Pro Bowl in 1969, his second season in the NFL. A year later he led the Eagles defense with 174 combined tackles (85 initial hits, 89 assists) despite playing all season with an injured ankle. He also played with the Houston Oilers.

Films include: 1979--**The Main Event;** 1980--**The Long Riders;** 1981--**Looker, Cheech & Chong's Nice Dreams;** 1982--**Night Shift, Trick or Treats.**

1954 Werner Roth

Werner, an outstanding defender during his eight-year career in the North American Soccer League, was named to the Cosmos' All-Decade Team (1971-80). When

Werner Roth.

he retired in 1979, he was the Cosmos record-holder for total games played, regular season games and minutes. He helped the Cosmos win the NASL championship three times (1972, '77, '78) and was the team's most valuable player in 1974. Roth was a NASL All-Star in 1975.

The steady, defensive-minded center back was also captain of the Cosmos. In addition to the NASL team, he was a former member and captain of the United States National Team. Born in Yugoslavia, he was naturalized as a U.S. citizen in 1968. He holds a degree in architecture and interior design from Pratt Institute in Brooklyn, New York, and served as National Soccer Director of Special Olympics.

Films include: 1979--**Manny's Orphans** (aka **Kick**); 1981--**Victory.**

1955 Babe Ruth

George Herman Ruth is, without a doubt, the most famous figure in American sports history. The Babe and legend went together. A product of a Baltimore, Maryland, reform school, he was beloved by children and had a deep affection for them. Long after he left the game, he was still a box-office attraction; and his name lives on today in the Babe Ruth leagues throughout the country. With his mighty swing, Babe Ruth changed the complexion of the game from a succession of base hits to the long ball. After establishing himself as one of the American League's premier pitchers with the Boston Red Sox (1915-19), he was sold to the New York Yankees on December 26, 1919, and went on to bring renewed respectability to a sport devastated at the time by the Black Sox scandal. During his 15 years with the Yankees (1920-34), he hit 659 of his 714 career homers. He led the AL in homers 11 times, runs batted in six times, walks 11 times, runs scored eight times, slugging 12 times and hit over .300 14 times, finishing with a lifetime .342 mark. Ruth retired in 1935 and toured Japan and Europe and became an international celebrity. His name and face were recognized around the world. In 1936, he was one of the first five players ever elected to the Baseball Hall of Fame. He died on August 16, 1948, in New York City and thousands passed his body as it lay in state in the lobby of Yankee Stadium--The House That Ruth Built. Actor William Bendix portrayed the Babe in the 1948 film **The Babe Ruth Story.** In the early 1930's, Universal Pictures produced a series of shorts featuring the great Yankee slugger.

Films include: 1920--**Headin' Home;** 1927--**Babe Comes Home;** 1928--**Speedy;** 1937--**Home Run on the Keys** (musical short); 1942--**Pride of the Yankees, The Ninth Inning.**

1956 Toni Sailer

As a 20-year-old, the talented Austrian became the first skier to sweep all three men's alpine skiing events as he won gold medals in the downhill, giant slalom and slalom events in the 1956 Winter Olympics at Cortina d'Ampezzo. He went on to become a European movie actor and one of the youngsters who thrilled to his screen efforts was Jean Claude Killy, who repeated in these same events a dozen years later at Grenoble in the French Alps and also became an actor.

Films include: 1959--**12 Girls and One Man;** 1962--**Ski Champ.**

1957 Harold Sakata

Harold Sakata is best known for his role as Oddjob in the James Bond film **Goldfinger;** but during the 1940's and '50's, he was an outstanding professional wrestler. The legendary National Wrestling Alliance champion Lou Thesz described Sakata as a "weightlifter

Babe Ruth.

turned heavyweight wrestler who competed throughout the United States, Canada and Japan."

Films include: 1964--**Goldfinger; 1970--The Phynx; 1974--The Wrestler** (aka **The Maim Event**); 1975--**Impulse;** 1980--**Freeze Bomb.**

1958 Max Schmeling

Maximillian Adolph Otto Siegfried Schmeling is the only German to become the world heavyweight boxing champion. The native of Brandenburg won the crown vacated by Gene Tunney from Jack Sharkey on a fourth round foul at New York's Yankee Stadium on June 12, 1930. He returned home to Germany where Adolf Hitler cited him as a perfect example of the Aryan superman. On July 3, 1931, Schmeling made a successful title defense when he scored a 15-round technical knockout over Young Stribling at Cleveland's Municipal Stadium. He lost his title in a disputed 15-round decision to Sharkey on June 21, 1932, in Long Island, New York. Almost four years later, Schmeling stunned the boxing world when he knocked out Joe Louis in one round in one of the game's biggest upsets. On June 22, 1938, after Louis won the crown from James Braddock, Schmeling and Louis were rematched, but the German's attempt to regain the title resulted in a humiliating first round knockout as the champ took him out in a little over two minutes. He returned to Germany and eventually was drafted into the army and assigned to a paratroop outfit. He was wounded during the battle of Crete. In 1947, he returned to the ring after an absence of eight years and had five more fights before retiring late in 1948 with a 56-10-4 career mark. He was elected to the Boxing Hall of Fame in 1970.

Films include: 1936--**Knock-Out.**

1959 Arnold Schwarzenegger

He began lifting weights as a teen in Austria; and by the time he was an adult, Arnold Schwarzenegger had won Mr. Olympia six times, Mr. Universe five times and was named Mr. World once. The six feet two, 235 pounder measures 22 inches around the arms, 57 inches around the chest and has 28½-inch thighs. He made his movie debut in the 1977 documentary **Pumping Iron** and film producers liked his potential, and he shortly began acting in feature movies.

Films include: 1977--**Pumping Iron;** 1978--**Stay Hungry;** 1979--**The Villain;** 1982--**Conan the Barbarian;** 1984--**Conan the Destroyer, The Terminator.**

1960 Tom Sharkey

A member of the Boxing Hall of Fame, he fought John L. Sullivan, James J. Corbett twice and Bob Fitzsimmons twice in non-title fights and lost in 25 rounds to James Jeffries for the world heavyweight championship during a brilliant career around the turn of the century. He had matches with Sullivan, Corbett and Fitzsimmons during a six-month period in 1896, battling Corbett to a four-round draw in San Francisco, fighting a three-round no decision with Sullivan in New York and winning on a foul over Fitzsimmons in eight rounds in San Francisco. In rematches, the native of Dundalk, Ireland, won on a foul in nine rounds over Corbett in New York City in 1898 and was kayoed by Fitzsimmons in two rounds in Coney Island, New York, in 1900. His greatest fights, however, were against Jeffries. On May 6, 1898, Jeffries, then a promising heavyweight contender, defeated Sharkey in 20 rounds in San Francisco. When Jeffries kayoed Fitzsimmons for the title in 1899, he made his first championship defense against Sharkey. The result, however, was the same as Jeffries retained his crown with a hard-fought 25-round victory at Coney Island. Sharkey, who was elected to the Boxing Hall of Fame in 1959, posted a 40-6-5 career record that included 37 knockouts. After retiring from the ring, he subsequently moved to California and teamed with Jeffries in vaudeville and personal appearance tours. He died in San Francisco in 1953.

Films include: 1928--**Good Morning Judge;** 1932--**Madison Square Garden.**

1961 Al Silvani

Al Silvani is a veteran boxing trainer who has served as a technical adviser for countless motion pictures pertaining to boxing and appeared in all three **Rocky** films. The native New Yorker helped train more than a dozen world titleholders, including Rocky Graziano, Jake LaMotta, Floyd Patterson and Alexis Arguello. He not only worked with Graziano and LaMotta but helped train the actors who portrayed them in the movies--Paul Newman and Robert DeNiro. He trained actor Clint Eastwood for fight scenes in the film **Paint Your Wagon,** Elvis Presley for **Kid Galahad** and taught Sylvester Stallone to look like a club fighter with the heart of a champ in the **Rocky** series.

Films include: 1976--**Rocky;** 1977--**Bobby Deerfield;** 1979--**Rocky II;** 1982--**Rocky III.**

1962 Abe Simon

The mammoth Simon was among the leading heavyweights in the late 1930's and early 1940's. The six feet four, 255-pound native of Richmond Hill, New York, ended his eight-year ring career on March 27, 1942, when he was knocked out in six rounds by champion Joe Louis for the world title in New York's Madison Square Garden. It was Simon's second shot at Louis' crown with the Brown Bomber scoring a technical knockout in the 13th round on March 21, 1941, in Detroit's Olympia Arena. Simon finished with a 38-10-1 record, facing the likes of Jersey Joe Walcott, Lou Nova and Buddy Baer in addition to his two battles with Louis. He died in 1969 in Queens, New York.

Films include: 1954--**On the Waterfront;** 1958--**Never Love a Stranger.**

1963 O.J. Simpson

They called him "Juice," and, to say the least, he was very sweet on the gridiron. During his two seasons at the University of Southern California, O.J. piled up a monumental record, gaining 3,187 yards, scoring 34 touchdowns and winning the Heisman Trophy as the country's outstanding collegiate football player in 1968. He went on to become a legendary rusher in the National Football League, playing with the Buffalo Bills (1969-77) and the San Francisco 49ers (1978-79). In 1973, Simpson set an all-time rushing record and became the first player to reach 2,000 yards in a single season when he gained 2,003 yards. Four times he led the NFL in rushing, six times he rushed for more than 200 yards and overall in his career he gained 11,236 yards. In 1973, he rushed for 100 or more yards in 11 games and accomplished the feat 42 times during his career. In 1976, O.J. ran for a record 273 yards against the Detroit Lions.

Films include: 1974--**The Klansman, The Towering Inferno;** 1975--**Killer Force;** 1977--**The Cassandra Crossing;** 1979--**Firepower.**

1964 Bruce Smith

The great University of Minnesota halfback won the Heisman Trophy in 1941 as the country's finest collegiate football player. He was the catalyst of three of Minnesota's greatest teams, sparking

O.J. Simpson.

the Gophers to undefeated national championships in both 1940 and 1941. He was captain of the team and a 1941 All-American. Smith, one of the fastest players in the Big 10 Conference although weighing well over 200 pounds, was selected the best college player in the 1941 All-Star game at Chicago, Illinois. He portrayed himself in the 1942 film **Smith of Minnesota.** He died in 1967.

Films include: 1942--**Smith of Minnesota.**

1965 Bubba Smith

The six feet seven, 265 pounder established himself as one of the National Football League's outstanding defensive ends after the Baltimore Colts made him their first selection in the 1967 draft. The former Michigan State All-American used his great size and speed to help the Colts defeat the Dallas Cowboys in the 1971 Super Bowl. An outstanding pass rusher, Bubba was an All-Pro selection in 1970 and 1971. He missed the entire 1972 season due to an injury and was traded to the Oakland Raiders in 1973. Smith went on to a movie career after making several popular television beer commercials with another NFL great, Dick Butkus. A brother, Tody, also an NFL performer, appeared in the film **Black Gunn.**

Films include: 1983--**Stroker Ace, Police Academy.**

1966 Gunboat Smith

Edward J. "Gunboat" Smith was a journeyman fighter who battled such ring greats as Jack Dempsey (twice), Jess Willard, Georges Carpentier, Jack Dillon (three times) and Battling Levinsky (five times) in non-title bouts during his career. He won a 20-round decision over future light heavyweight champ Levinsky on January 27, 1915, in New Orleans, Louisiana, and dropped 20-round decisions to future heavyweight champ Willard in San Francisco, California, on May 20, 1913, and former light heavyweight king Dillon on February 16, 1917, in New Orleans. He also had four no decisions against Levinsky and lost on a foul to Carpentier.

Films include: 1925--**The Fear Fighter, The Shock Punch;** 1927--**We're All Gamblers.**

1967 Freddie Steele

Freddie Steele won the National Boxing Association middleweight championship in 1936 and successfully defended his crown five times during his two-year title reign. The native of Tacoma, Washington, outpointed Babe Risko on July 11, 1936, to win the NBA crown in Seattle, Washington. He went on to beat back challenges from Gorilla Jones, Risko, Frankie Battaglia, Ken Overlin and Carmen Barth before losing his championship when Al Hostak stopped him in the first round on July 26, 1938. During his ten-year boxing career, he took on such past and future champions as Ceferino Garcia (twice), Fred Apostoli (twice), Vince Dundee, Gus Lesnevich and Solly Krieger on his way to an 84-5-5 record. He died in Aberdeen, Washington, in 1984. He had a major role in the 1945 film **The Story of G.I. Joe.**

Films include: 1945--**The Story of G.I. Joe.**

1968 Sandor Szabo

A popular wrestler in the National Wrestling Alliance, he won the championship on June 5, 1941, when he defeated former football hero Bronko Nagurski in St. Louis, Missouri. His reign lasted until February 19, 1942, when Bill Longson defeated him in St. Louis. Among his film credits was the role of Paul Maxey in the 20th Century-Fox movie **Dreamboat** starring Clifton Webb and Ginger Rogers. He died in 1966.

Films include: 1936--**Once**

in a Blue Moon; 1943--**Mission to Moscow;** 1952--**Dreamboat;** 1955--**Hell's Island.**

1969 Professor Toru Tanaka

Professor Toru Tanaka was an outstanding professional wrestler who teamed with Mr. Fuji to win the World Wrestling Federation tag-team championship in the 1970's. He also held the Texas wrestling championship as well as the All-Asia and Hawaiian wrestling titles during his mat career.

Films include: 1981--**An Eye for An Eye;** 1983--**Revenge of the Ninja.**

1970 Joe Theismann

Quarterback Joe Theismann was the National Football League's most valuable player in 1983 after completing 276 passes for 3,714 yards and 29 touchdowns. For the second straight year, "Hollywood Joe" had led his Washington Redskins into the Super Bowl and was the toast of pro football. Yet, 13 years earlier, Theismann opted to bypass the NFL and the Miami Dolphins, who made him a fourth-round draft pick out of Notre Dame in 1971, and play with the Toronto Argonauts in the Canadian Football League. After three CFL seasons, in which he passed for 6,093 yards and 40 TDs, and rushed for 1,054 yards, Theismann joined the Redskins in 1974 after Washington obtained his NFL rights from Miami. He became the regular quarterback in 1978 and through his 10 NFL seasons has passed for more than 20,000 yards and 128 TDs. He also is the only Redskin quarterback to ever run for over 1,000 yards in a career. The South River, New Jersey, native, who was runner-up in the Heisman Trophy balloting to Jim Plunkett in 1970 after setting numerous passing marks at Notre Dame, hit 15 of 23 passes for 143 yards and two TD's, including the game clincher in the final two minutes, to lead Washington past Miami in Super Bowl XVII (1983). A year later, he completed 16 passes for 243 yards, but the Redskins lost Super Bowl XVIII to the Raiders. In addition to his film work, Theismann has been a guest on numerous television talk shows and has appeared in TV commercials and prime-time series.

Films include: 1980--**Sam Marlowe, Private Eye** (aka **The Man with Bogart's Face**); 1984--**Cannonball Run II.**

1971 Jim Thorpe

Jim Thorpe was selected the top American athlete of the first half of the 20th century. The King of Sweden called him the "greatest athlete in the world" after he won gold medals in both the pentathlon and decathlon in the 1912 Olympics. Yet the career of the Sac and Fox Indian from Oklahoma is a narrative of triumph and tragedy. Shortly after winning the medals in Stockholm, it was revealed that Thorpe played two seasons of professional baseball in the Eastern Carolina League, and the Amateur Athletic Union subsequently removed his name from the Olympic records and awarded his gold medals to the second place finishers in both events. Thorpe, who brought great football and track glory to the Carlisle Indian School in Pennsylvania, was finished as an amateur and signed a contract with John McGraw's New York Giants. Thorpe, however, was not a success in baseball, hitting .252 in 289 major league games over a seven-year period with the Giants, Cincinnati Reds and Boston Braves. While baseball gave Thorpe a seasonal occupation, it was his return to football that brought him to great athletic acclaim once again. In 1915, he became the first big-name athlete to play pro football, signing with the pre-National Football League Canton Bulldogs. In addition to Canton, Thorpe played for the Cleveland Indians, Oorang Indians, Toledo Maroons, Rock Island Independents, New York Giants and Chicago Cardinals during his 13-year career. He was named "The Legend" on the all-time NFL team and in 1963 was enshrined as a charter member of the Pro Football Hall of Fame. Drinking, ill health and financial problems continued to plague him until he died in Lomita, California, in 1953, virtually a forgotten man. Only after his death did the public once again realize how truly great an athlete Thorpe was during the early part of the 20th century. Some seven decades after his ecstasy and agony of the 1912 Olympics, Thorpe's gold medals were returned to his family. He appeared in a number of motion pictures, mostly as an extra, including his unbilled virtual cameo appearance in the 1949 James Cagney classic **White Heat.** Burt Lancaster portrayed him in the 1951 film **Jim Thorpe, All American.**

Films include: 1931--**Battling with Buffalo Bill, Touchdown;** 1932--**White Eagle; My Pal, the King; Airmail, Hold 'Em Jail;** 1933--**Wild Horse Mesa;** 1935--**Code of the Mounted, Behold My Wife, The Red Rider, Wanderer of the Wasteland, Rustlers of Red Gap** (serial), **She, Fighting Youth;** 1936--**Sutter's Gold, Wildcat Trooper, Treachery Rides the Range, Hill Tillies** (short); 1937--**The Big City;** 1940--**Henry Goes to Arizona, Arizona Frontier, Prairie Schooners;** 1944--**Outlaw Trail;** 1949--**White Heat;** 1950--**Wagonmaster.**

1972 Jose Torres

When Jose Torres knocked out Willie Pastrano to win the world light heavyweight championship, he captured the gold that had eluded him nine years earlier in the 1956 Olympics. Torres, who turned pro in 1958, won a silver medal when he lost a decision to Hungary's Laszlo Papp for the Olympic light middleweight title. Torres gained a shot at the world light heavyweight crown after knocking out former middleweight champ Bobo Olson in one round in New York on November 27, 1964. Some four months later, Torres earned his gold when he kayoed Pastrano in nine rounds in New York City to win the world title. He successfully defended his crown against Wayne Thornton, Eddie Cotton and Chic Calderwood before losing it to Dick Tiger in a 15-round decision on December 16, 1966. He retired in 1969 with a 41-3-1 career record. In 1984, he was appointed New York State Athletic Commissioner.

Films include: 1968--**Wild 90, Beyond the Law, The Big Gundown;** 1969--**Death Rides a Horse;** 1970--**The Five Man Army;** 1982--**The Last Fight.**

1973 Gene Tunney

James Joseph "Gene" Tunney, the "Fighting Marine," won both the American light heavyweight and world heavyweight championships during a 14-year career that saw him post a 56-1-1 record. His lone setback occurred on May 23, 1922, when Harry Greb won the American light heavyweight title with a 15-round decision in New York City. Tunney, who won the crown from Battling Levinsky on January 13, 1922, regained the championship with a 15-round decision on February 23, 1923, and retained it with another decision over Greb some ten months later. He subsequently relinquished the crown and entered the heavyweight ranks. On September 23, 1926, he scored a unanimous ten-round decision over Jack Dempsey in Philadelphia to win the heavyweight title. A year later, 104,943 people crowded into Chicago's Soldiers Field to watch the rematch and saw Tunney retain his crown with a ten-round decision. The bout was marked by the controversial "long count" where Dempsey floored Tunney, but the count did not start until the ex-champ went to a neutral corner. Tunney got to his feet before the count of ten and went on to win the fight. He retired as the undefeated heavyweight king after knocking out Tom Heeney in 11 rounds on July 26, 1928. During World War II, he was chief recreation officer in the U.S. Navy. The New York City native was elected to the Boxing Hall of Fame in 1955. He died in 1978 in Greenwich, Connecticut. In 1926, Pathé Pictures paid Tunney $24,000 plus 25 percent of the gross receipts to star in the serial **The Fighting Marine.**

Films include: 1926--**The Fighting Marine** (serial).

1974 Vince Van Patten

Vince Van Patten is one of the very few actors who became a professional athlete **after** he started his acting career. Son of veteran actor Dick Van Patten, Vince made his acting debut when he was nine. By the time he was 20, he was already playing professional tennis. The native of Brooklyn, New York, won a few small pro tournaments in 1977 and 1978; but the turning point of his tennis career came at Maui, Hawaii, in 1978 when he was a wild card and pushed veteran pro Raul Ramirez to three tough sets in the first round. Enthused by his showing, Van Patten completed the film **Yesterday** and then joined the World Tennis Championship pro tour in early 1979. He won the satellite event in Green Bay, Wisconsin, in 1979 and reached the semi-finals of the Paris Indoor Championships.

Films include: 1973--**Charley and the Angel;** 1979--**Yesterday, Rock 'n Roll High School;** 1980--**Survival Run;** 1981--**Hell Night.**

1975 Leon Wagner

"Daddy Wags" was one of the American League's premier power hitters in the 1960's. The left-handed slugger hit 211 career homers and belted 23 or more roundtrippers a year from 1961 through 1966, with a high of 37 in 1962. He played with San Francisco, St. Louis, the Los Angeles Angels, Cleveland and the Chicago White Sox during his 12-year career and finished with a lifetime .272 average. Wagner drove home 107 runs with the Angels in 1962 and 100 with the Indians in 1964. The native of Chattanooga, Tennessee, was one of the first outfielders to catch fly balls with one hand and was always known as a flashy dresser. In addition to motion pictures, he has appeared in television commercials and a segment of **The Man from Uncle.**

Films include: 1974--**A Woman Under the Influence;** 1976--**Bingo Long Travelling All-Stars and Motor Kings.**

1976 Jersey Joe Walcott

Jersey Joe Walcott became the oldest fighter ever to win the world heavyweight championship when he knocked out Ezzard Charles in seven rounds on March 7, 1951, at the age of 37. Born Arnold Raymond Cream in Merchantville, New Jersey, Walcott began boxing in 1930 and retired in 1953 after Rocky Marciano knocked him out for the second straight time. Walcott fought Joe Louis twice for the title, losing a split decision in their first meeting on December 5, 1947, and battled Charles four times in championship bouts, winning twice. He also met such fighters as Joe Baski, Jimmy Bivins, Lee Oma, Abe Simon, Joey Maxim (three times) and Al Ettore en route to a 49-17-1 career record and a place in the Boxing Hall of Fame (1969). After retiring, he became a referee and for years served as the New Jersey State Athletic Commissioner.

Films include: 1956--**The Harder They Fall.**

1977 Coley Wallace

Coley Wallace never enjoyed the same success in professional boxing that he attained as an amateur when he was only one of three fighters to beat future world heavyweight champion Rocky Marciano. He fought for several years in the heavyweight division, facing among others former heavyweight king Ezzard Charles, who knocked him out in ten rounds in San Francisco, California, on December 16, 1953. Wallace portrayed Joe Louis in the 1953 film **The Joe Louis Story.**

Films include: 1953--**The Joe Louis Story.**

1978 Michael Warren

Michael Warren was a three-year basketball standout at the University of California at Los Angeles who teamed with Lew Alcindor (Kareem Abdul-Jabbar) to lead the Bruins to three consecutive National Collegiate Athletic Association championships (1967-69). He was named to the NCAA All-Tournament team in 1967 and scored 17 points for UCLA in the title game against Dayton. The Bruins were 88-2 during the talented guard's varsity career. After his initial movies, he landed a starring role in the award-winning television series **Hill Street Blues.**

Films include: 1971--**Drive, He Said;** 1972--**Butterflies Are Free;** 1973--**Cleopatra Jones;** 1976--**Norman . . . Is That You?;** 1979--**Fast Break.**

1979 Gene Washington

Gene Washington ended his ten-year National Football League career in 1978 as one of the greatest wide receivers in the history of the San Francisco 49ers. He began his collegiate football career at Stanford as a quarterback but was shifted to receiver in his sophomore year after suffering a shoulder injury. He went on to lead the Pacific Eight Conference in pass receiving as a junior and was named All-Conference. Selected on the first round by the 49ers in 1969, he went on to earn All-Pro honors as one of the NFL's most dangerous deep threats. In 1970, he caught 53 passes for 1,100 yards and 12 touchdowns. Washington, who played in numerous Pro Bowl games, set San Francisco records for most touchdowns in a season (12) and most yards gained receiving in a career (6,664). He scored 59 TDs.

Films include: 1972--**Black Gunn;** 1974--**The Black Six;** 1975--**Lady Cocoa.**

1980 Kenny Washington

The talented Washington was an outstanding running back for the University of California at Los Angeles (UCLA). He went on to play with the Los Angeles Rams in the National Football League from 1946 through 1948. On November 2, 1947, he electrified the crowd when he ran 92 yards for a touchdown against the Chicago Cardinals--the longest run from scrimmage that season and against a team that went on to win the NFL title. He died in 1971 in Los Angeles.

Films include: 1940--**While Thousands Cheer;** 1947--**The Foxes of Harrow;** 1948--**Rogue's Regiment;** 1949--**Easy Living, Rope of Sand, Pinky;** 1950--**The Jackie Robinson Story;** 1969--**Changes;** 1970--**Tarzan's Deadly Silence.**

1981 Bob Waterfield

Bob Waterfield was one of the greatest quarterbacks in National Football League history. His statistics speak for themselves. As a rookie in the NFL in 1945, he was named the league's most valuable player as he led the Cleveland Rams to the NFL championship. The Elmira, New York, native passed for two TDs and kicked an extra point to key the Rams past Washington, 15-14, in the title game. The University of California at Los Angeles (UCLA) product went on to earn All-NFL honors three times and twice led the league in passing. His career marks include 11,849 yards and 90 touchdowns passing, 573 points on 13 TDs, 315 PATs and 60 field goals and a lifetime 42.4-yard punting average. He once had a punt of 86 yards (October 5, 1947 vs. Green Bay). During his first four years with the Rams (the franchise switched to Los Angeles from Cleveland in 1946), he also played defensive back and intercepted 20 passes. The six feet two, 200 pounder played for the Rams from 1945 through 1952. He was enshrined in the Football Hall of Fame in 1965. Waterfield was formerly married to actress Jane Russell. He died in 1983.

Films include: 1948--**Triple Threat;** 1951--**Jungle Manhunt;** 1953--**Crazylegs, All American.**

1982 Carl Weathers

The world knows him as Apollo Creed, but football fans on the west coast and in Canada knew him first as an outstanding player at Long Beach City College, San Diego State and with the Oakland Raiders and British Columbia Lions. The six feet two, 204-pound native of New Orleans, Louisiana, played professionally in the National Football League as a linebacker with Oakland in 1970 and 1971 and then spent three years with the B.C. Lions in the Canadian Football League. During the off-season with the Lions, he completed his Theatre Arts Degree at San Francisco State and by 1974 began pursuing his lifelong desire to be an actor. He established himself as an actor in the role of Apollo Creed in the Academy Award-winning film **Rocky** and two hit box office sequels, **Rocky II** and **Rocky III.**

Films include: 1975--**Bucktown, Friday Foster;** 1976--**Rocky;** 1977--**Semi-Tough, Close Encounters of the Third Kind;** 1979--**Rocky II, Force Ten from Navarone;** 1981--**Death Hunt;** 1982--**Rocky III.**

1983 Johnny Weissmuller

Johnny Weissmuller, the best-known and most popular of the numerous Tarzan actors, won five swimming gold medals in the 1924 and 1928 Olympic Games. In fact, the native of Windber, Pennsylvania, won an astounding 67 world and 52 national titles. During his undefeated career, he smashed 174 individual marks, helped break 21 relay records and held every freestyle record from 100 yards to the half mile. In 1950, he was named the greatest swimmer of the past half century by world sportswriters. Yet, Weissmuller had to overcome childhood polio before rising to prominence as a world-class swimmer. "My doctor said I should take up some sort of exercise to build myself up," he once recalled. "I got into a swimming pool at the YMCA and liked it, and I found I had a natural flair for it." Weissmuller developed into a six feet three, 200 pounder and was discovered by novelist Cyril Hume, who was writing a screenplay for a film of an Edgar Rice Burroughs Tarzan story.

He was eventually offered the role without even a screen test by director William S. Van Dyke and producer Bernard Hyman. He went on to appear in a dozen Tarzan films before moving to Columbia in the late 40's where he starred in the Jungle Jim series. He also had the title role in the Jungle Jim television series. he died in 1984 in Acapulco, Mexico.

Films include: 1929--**Glorifying the American Girl;** 1932--**Tarzan the Ape Man;** 1934--**Tarzan and His Mate;** 1936--**Tarzan Escapes;** 1939--**Tarzan Finds a Son;** 1941--**Tarzan's Secret Treasure;** 1942--

Tarzan's New York Adventure; 1943--**Tarzan Triumphs, Stage Door Canteen, Tarzan's Desert Mystery;** 1945--**Tarzan and the Amazons;** 1946--**Tarzan and the Leopard Woman, Swamp Fire;** 1947--**Tarzan and the Huntress;** 1948--**Tarzan and the Mermaids, Jungle Jim;** 1949--**The Lost Tribe;** 1950--**Captive Girl, Mark of the Gorilla, Pygmy Island;** 1951--**Fury of the Congo, Jungle Manhunt;** 1952--**Jungle Jim in the Forbidden Island, Voodoo Tiger;** 1953--**Savage Mutiny, Valley of the Headhunters, Killer Ape;** 1954--**Jungle Man-Eaters, Cannibal Attack;** 1955--**Jungle Moon Men, Devil Goddess;** 1970--**The Phynx.**

1984 Bombardier Bill Wells

A native of London, England, he posted a 37-12 record with 33 knockouts during his professional boxing career that spanned from 1910 through 1925. He won the British heavyweight title by kayoing Ian Hague in six rounds in London on April 24, 1911. Wells lost fights to popular French boxer Georges Carpentier on June 1 and December 8, 1913. The six feet three fighter won the All-India championship in 1909. He will be remembered as the person who sounded the gong in Rank Films productions as their trademark. He died in 1967 in London.

Films include: 1913--**Carpentier vs. Bombardier Wells Fight, Willie vs. Bombardier Wells;** 1916--**Kent, the Fighting Man;** 1918--**The Great Game** (aka **The Straight Game**); 1919--**Silver Lining;** 1926--**Game Chicken;** 1927--**The Ring;** 1936--**Excuse My Glove, Melody of My Heart;** 1937--**Mark Up, Concerning Mr. Martin.**

1985 Roy White

The Los Angeles, California, native is one of the all-time New York Yankee favorites. The onetime outfielder, who subsequently served the Yankees in the front office and as a coach, ranks among the top 20 Yankees in career hits, doubles, homers, runs batted in, runs scored, stolen bases and games played. He first joined the Bronx Bombers in 1965 and remained with them for 15 years, finishing with a lifetime .271 batting average and 1,803 hits. He was a standout during the lean years and as the Yankees were rebuilding and developing into American League pennant winners in '76, '77 and '78 and World Champions in '77 and '78. He was the only Yankee outfielder to ever field 1.000 for a season. The talented switch-hitter went on to play three years with the Yorimuri Giants of Toyko in Japan's Central League when his playing days with the Yankees ended after the 1979 season.

Films include: 1973--**No Place to Hide** (aka **Rebel**); 1976--**The Premonition.**

1986 Esther Williams

Esther Williams won the 100-meter freestyle national championship in 1939 with a 1:09 effort, swimming for the Los Angeles Athletic Club and, a year later, was ready for the 1940 Olympics. World War II, however, interrupted the Olympic Games. Olympic swimming hero Johnny Weissmuller subsequently selected her to appear opposite him in the 1940 San Francisco World's Fair Aquacade. She went on to appear in numerous MGM movies, doing much to popularize synchronized swimming. In 1966, she was elected to the International Swimming Hall of Fame.

Films include: 1942--**Andy Hardy's Double Life;** 1943--**A Guy Named Joe;** 1944--**Bathing Beauty;** 1945--**Thrill of a Romance, Easy to Wed;** 1946--**This Time for Keeps;** 1947--**Fiesta;** 1948--**On an Island with You;** 1949--**Take Me Out to the Ball Game, Neptune's Daughter;** 1950--**Pagan Love Song;** 1951--**Duchess of Idaho;** 1952--**Texas Carnival, Shirts Ahoy;** 1953--**Million**

Dollar Mermaid, Dangerous When Wet; 1954--**Easy to Love, Jupiter's Darling;** 1956--**The Unguarded Moment;** 1961--**The Big Show.**

1987 Jess Willard

The six feet six and a quarter, 250-pound Pottawatomie County, Kansas, giant won the world heavyweight title when he knocked out champion Jack Johnson in the 26th round of a scheduled 45-round bout in Havana, Cuba, on April 5, 1915. On July 4, 1919, he defended his crown against Jack Dempsey at Bay View Park Arena in the shores of Maumee Bay on Toledo, Ohio. The scheduled 12-round bout ended abruptly when Willard called a halt during the intermission between the third and fourth rounds, and Dempsey was awarded a third round knockout and the championship. Willard received $100,000 for the title defense while the Manassa Mauler received $27,500. Willard registered a 24-6-1 career record with 20 knockouts and five no decisions. He died in Los Angeles, California, in 1968.

Films include: 1915--**Heart Punch;** 1919--**The Challenge of Chance;** 1933--**The Prizefighter and the Lady;** 1968--**The Legendary Champions** (documentary).

1988 Keith Wilkes

In the ten seasons that Jamaal Wilkes, formerly Jackson Keith Wilkes, has played in the National Basketball Association (1974-84), he has helped his team make the post-season playoffs ten times, win the Western Division title five times and the NBA championship three times. He was a first round selection of the Golden State Warriors in 1974 after earning All-American recognition and helping the University of California at Los Angeles win the National Collegiate Athletic Association championships in 1972 and 1973. He was named the NBA Rookie of the Year in 1975. He has scored 14,222 points (18.4 points per game) through his first ten seasons and played in three NBA All-Star Games. He scored a career high 1,827 points (22.6 ppg) in 1980-81, the second of three straight seasons that he registered 20 or more points a game. Wilkes played three seasons with the Warriors and the last seven with the Los Angeles Lakers, helping Golden State to the NBA title in 1974-75 and Los Angeles to NBA championships in 1979-80 and 1981-82. In 1975, he starred as Cornbread in the film **Cornbread, Earl and Me.**

Films include: 1975--**Cornbread, Earl and Me.**

1989 Fred Williamson

The Northwestern product, nicknamed "The Hammer" for the forceful way he stopped pass receivers, was one of the outstanding defensive backs in the old American Football League with both the Oakland Raiders and the Kansas City Chiefs. After breaking in with the Pittsburgh Steelers of the National Football League in 1960, Williamson played four seasons with the Raiders and three with the Chiefs. In 1962, he set an Oakland record when he intercepted a pass against San Diego and returned it 91 yards. He played with Kansas City in Super Bowl I against the Green Bay Packers in 1967.

Films include: 1969--**M*A*S*H;** 1970--**Tell Me That You Love Me, Julie Moon;** 1972--**Hammer, The Legend of Nigger Charley;** 1973--**Black Caesar, Hell Up in Harlem, The Soul of Nigger Charley, That Man Bolt, Three the Hard Way;** 1974--**Three Tough Guys, Black Eye;** 1975--**Bucktown, Boss Nigger, Take a Hard Ride, Adios Amigos;** 1977--**Mr. Mean;** 1980--**Fist of Fear Touch of Death;** 1981--**Counterfeit Commandos;** 1982--**One Down Two to Go, The Last Fight;** 1983--**1990 Bronx Warriors;** 1984--**Vigilante.**

Jamaal Wilkes.

1990 Stanislaus Zbyszko

The native of Poland was one of wrestling's great names of the Roaring 20's, twice winning the National Wrestling Alliance championship. He first won the title in 1922 when he defeated Ed "Strangler" Lewis in New York, only to lose it in a rematch with Lewis later that year in Wichita, Kansas. He regained the NWA crown in 1925 by dethroning champion Wayne Munn in Philadelphia but lost it the same year to Joe Stecher in St. Louis. He died in 1967 in St. Joseph, Missouri.

Films include: 1932--**Madison Square Garden;** 1950--**Night and the City.**

Actors' Portrayals

This section deals with actors who portrayed athletes in movies. Not included are athletes appearing as themselves; they are dealt with sufficiently in the Athletes in Films chapter. The only exception is athletes who not only portrayed themselves, but who also had actors portray them in other films (e.g., Joe Louis). Documentary films are not included here.

The release date of the film is followed by the name of the actor portraying the athlete and the film's title.

1991 Harold Abrahams

Abrahams won a gold medal in the 100 meters at the 1924 Olympics in Paris, France.

1981--Ben Cross--**Chariots of Fire.**

1992 Grover Cleveland Alexander

The Hall of Fame pitcher won 373 games during a 20-year career in the major leagues with the Philadelphia Phillies, Chicago Cubs and St. Louis Cardinals.

1952--Ronald Reagan--**The Winning Team.**

1993 Muhammad Ali

Ali is the only fighter ever to win the world heavyweight championship three different times. He dominated the boxing profession during the 1960's and 1970's.

1977--Phillip MacAllister (Ali as a boy)--**The Greatest;** himself (as an adult)--**The Greatest.** 1980--himself--**Body and Soul.**

1994 Luke Appling

The Hall of Famer is the only shortstop who ever led the American League in batting twice, winning the title in 1936 with a .388 average and in 1943 with a .328 average.

1949--Dean White--**The Stratton Story.**

1995 Doc Blanchard

Blanchard was a three-time All-American at West Point and the 1945 Heisman Trophy winner as college football's outstanding player.

1947--Rudy Wissler (Blanchard as a boy)--**The Spirit of West Point;** himself (as an adult)--**The Spirit of West Point.**

1996 Frank Cavanaugh

The Iron Major was a World War I military hero who had an outstanding football coaching career at Boston College (1919-26, 50 wins, 14 losses) and Fordham (1927-34, 34 wins, 14 losses). 1943--Pat O'Brien--**The Iron Major.**

1997 Bob Champion

This courageous jockey triumphed over cancer and rode his horse to victory in Britain's 1981 Grand National.

1984--John Hurth--**Champions.**

1998 Jim Corbett

Corbett knocked out John L. Sullivan to become the second world heavyweight champion under the Marquis of Queensberry Rules.

1942--Errol Flynn--**Gentleman Jim.**

1999 Joe Cronin

Cronin was a Baseball Hall

of Famer who served as player-manager, nonplaying manager, general manager and president of the American League.

1957--Bart Burns--**Fear Strikes Out.**

2000 Dizzy Dean

He won 30 games for the St. Louis Cardinals in 1934 and 28 a year later. An injury shortened the Hall of Fame pitcher's career.

1952--Dan Dailey--**The Pride of St. Louis.**

2001 Paul Dean

The other half of the famous Dean brothers pitching duo for the St. Louis Cardinals, he hurled a no-hitter against Brooklyn in 1934.

1952--Richard Crenna--**The Pride of St. Louis.**

2002 Angelo Dundee

A veteran boxing trainer, Dundee handled Muhammad Ali's successful career.

1977--Ernest Borgnine--**The Greatest.**

2003 Frank Frisch

A Hall of Fame second sacker for John McGraw's New York Giants and later with the St. Louis Cardinals, Frisch eventually became the manager of the great St. Louis Gashouse Gang.

1952--Stuart Randall--**The Pride of St. Louis.**

2004 Lou Gehrig

The New York Yankees first baseman played in more consecutive games (2,130) than any other major leaguer in history. He died two years after a crippling illness took him out of the lineup. The Hall of Famer had a lifetime .340 batting average.

1942--Gary Cooper--**Pride of the Yankees.**

2005 George Gipp

Gipp was an All-American running back for Knute Rockne at Notre Dame. He died of an illness during his senior year. Rockne echoed "Win one for the Gipper" during a locker room speech at the halftime of a football game against Army.

1940--Ronald Reagan--**Knute Rockne, All American.**

2006 Miki Gorman

After emigrating to the United States from her native Japan, she became one of the nation's top female marathon runners.

1981--Yoko Shimada--**My Champion.**

2007 Rocky Graziano

He fought his way out of a tough New York City neighborhood to win the world middleweight championship by knocking out Tony Zale.

1956--Terry Rangno (Rocky as a boy)--**Somebody Up There Likes Me;** Paul Newman (as an adult)--**Somebody Up There Likes Me.**

2008 Ben Hogan

A member of golfing's Hall of Fame, he won PGA crowns in both 1946 and 1948 and was named PGA Player of the Year in 1948, 1950, 1951 and 1953. He won the U.S. Open in 1948, 1950, 1951 and 1953.

1951--Glenn Ford--**Follow the Sun.**

2009 Rogers Hornsby

The Hall of Famer is the greatest right-handed hitter in the history of baseball. He batted over .400 three times, including a high of .424 in 1924, and had a lifetime .358 average.

1952--Frank Lovejoy--**The Winning Team.**

2010 Miller Huggins

He earned his spot in the Hall of Fame as a manager, guiding the New York Yankees to three world championships and six American League pennants in 12 seasons.

1942--Ernie Adams--**Pride of the Yankees.** 1948--Fred Lightner--**The Babe Ruth Story.**

2011 Inman Jackson

This great Chicago high school basketball star joined the Harlem Globetrotters a year after they were founded and remained a part of their organization for more than four decades. He was credited with being the first to put showmanship into the Globetrotters game.

1954--Sidney Poitier--**Go Man Go.**

2012 Jack Johnson

He was the first black to win the world heavyweight boxing championship and was the most controversial athlete of his time.

1970--James Earl Jones (as Jack Jefferson)--**The Great White Hope.**

2013 Junior Johnson

Johnson was one of the nation's top racing drivers.

1973--Jeff Bridges (as Junior Johnson)--**Hard Driver** (aka **The Last American Hero**).

2014 Jill Kilmont

Considered a cinch to make the U.S. Olympics team, she was paralyzed in a skiing accident in Utah in 1956.

1975--Marilyn Hassett--**The Other Side of the Mountain;** 1978--Marilyn Hassett--**The Other Side of the Mountain II.**

2015 Evel Knievel

This daredevil has thrilled millions with his dangerous exploits as America's most spectacular motorcycle performer.

1971--George Hamilton--**Evel Knievel.** 1977--himself--**Viva Knievel.**

2016 Jake LaMotta

LaMotta was a hard-punching fighter who won the world heavyweight championship in 1949 and fought Sugar Ray Robinson six times during a 13-year boxing career.

1980--Robert DeNiro--**Raging Bull.**

2017 Eric Liddell

Liddell finished first in the 400 meters to win a gold medal at the 1924 Olympics in Paris, France.

1981--Ian Charleson--**Chariots of Fire.**

2018 Sonny Liston

Liston won the world heavyweight championship by knocking out Floyd Patterson in 1962 and lost it to Cassius Clay, later known as Muhammad Ali, in 1964.

1977--Roger Mosley--**The Greatest.**

2019 Joe Louis

The Brown Bomber was one of America's most popular boxers who retired as undefeated world heavyweight champion after defending his title a record 25 times.

1947--himself--**The Fight Never Ends.** 1953--Coley Wallace--**The Joe Louis Story.**

2020 Joe McCarthy

Marse Joe was one of the greatest managers in baseball history. He won nine pennants and seven world championships during his 24 years as a manager, five with the Chicago Cubs, 16 with the New York Yankees and three with the Boston Red Sox. The Hall of Famer had a .614 winning percentage.

1942--Harry Harvey--**The Pride of the Yankees;** 1952--Hugh Sanders--**The Winning Team.**

2021 Marty Maher

For decades he served as the varsity trainer for the athletes at the United States Military Academy at West Point.

1955--Tyrone Power--**The Long Gray Line.**

2022 Christy Mathewson

Big Six won 367 games during his 17-year career in the majors, all but one with the New York Giants. The Hall of Famer won more than 30 games on three occasions.

1914--himself--**Love and Base Ball.** 1942--Fay Thomas--**Pride of the Yankees.**

2023 Billy Mills

His blazing finish in the 10,000 meters with less than one and a half seconds dividing the three medalists earned the U.S. runner a gold medal at the 1964 Olympics in Tokyo, Japan.

1983--Robby Benson--**Running Brave.**

2024 Shirley Muldowney

"Cha Cha" had to overcome a number of sex barriers to become the first woman drag racing champion. She was a three-time National Hot Rod Association champ.

1983--Bonnie Bedelia--**Heart Like a Wheel.**

2025 Jimmy Piersall

The talented but troubled outfielder played with five different teams during his 15-year career. He hit a career high .322 with Cleveland in 1961 and had a lifetime .272 batting average.

1957--Peter J. Votrian (Jimmy as a boy)--**Fear Strikes Out;** Anthony Perkins (as an adult)--**Fear Strikes Out.**

2026 Wally Pipp

Regular first baseman for the New York Yankees, Pipp will be remembered for getting sick and therefore allowing Lou Gehrig to take over his position. Twice he led the American League in homers.

1942--George McDonald--**Pride of the Yankees.**

2027 Branch Rickey

Rickey's greatest contribution to baseball was to challenge baseball's color barrier and sign Jackie Robinson for the the Brooklyn Dodgers.

1950--Minor Watson--**The Jackie Robinson Story.**

2028 Oscar Robertson

Many consider the Big O the greatest guard in National Basketball Association history. The Hall of Famer scored 26,710 career points.

1973--Jitu Cumbuka--**Maurie** (aka **Big Mo**).

2029 Jackie Robinson

The first black player in the majors in the 20th century was an exciting and controversial player who made a great impact on the game. The Hall of Famer went on to spark Brooklyn to six National League pennants during his ten-year career.

1950--Howard Louis MacNeely (Jackie as a boy)--**The Jackie Robinson Story;** himself--**The Jackie Robinson Story.**

2030 Knute Rockne

The legendary Notre Dame football great is credited with revolutionizing the sport, both as a player and later as a coach at his alma mater.

1929--J. Farrell MacDonald--**The Spirit of Notre Dame.** 1940--Johnny Sheffield (Knute at age 7)--**Knute Rockne, All American;** Pat O'Brien (as an adult)--**Knute Rockne, All American.** 1955--James Sears--**The Long Gray Line.**

2031 Barney Ross

Ross won the lightweight, junior welterweight and welterweight boxing crowns during his Hall of Fame fighting career. Lost only four times in 81 bouts.

1957--Cameron Mitchell--**Monkey on My Back.**

2032 Col. Jacob Ruppert

The brewery magnate was the owner of the New York Yankees during the Babe Ruth-Lou Gehrig dynasty years.

1948--Matt Briggs--**The Babe Ruth Story.**

2033 Babe Ruth

The Sultan of Swat is the most famous figure in American sports history. The legend of the baseball great lives throughout the world.

1927--himself--**Speedy.** 1942--himself--**Pride of the Yankees.** 1948--Bobby Ellis (Babe as a boy)--**The Babe Ruth Story;** William Bendix (as an adult)--**The Babe Ruth Story.**

2034 Abe Saperstein

Saperstein is the founder and owner of the Harlem Globetrotters, the world famous basketball magicians.

1951--Thomas Gomez--**The Harlem Globetrotters.** 1954--Dane Clark--**Go Man Go.**

2035 Max Schmeling

The only German to become the world heavyweight champion. His second fight against Joe Louis was ballyhooed as a battle between Germany's fascism and America's democracy.

1953--Buddy Thorpe--**The Joe Louis Story.**

2036 Wendell Scott

He became the first black stock car champion after breaking down the racial barrier.

1977--Richard Pryor--**Greased Lightning.**

2037 Maurice Stokes

The National Basketball Association star was stricken at the height of his outstanding career with the Cincinnati Royals. He was Rookie of the Year in 1955-56 and a three-time second team All-NBA pick.

1973--Bernie Casey--**Maurie** (aka **Big Mo).**

2038 Monte Stratton

It was this Chicago White Sox pitcher's comeback from the amputation of his right leg that inspired baseball fans across the country more than a generation ago.

1949--James Stewart--**The Stratton Story.**

2039 John L. Sullivan

The Boston Strong Boy was the first world heavyweight champion under the Marquis of Queensberry Rules and the last bare knuckle champion.

1933--George Walsh--**The Bowery.** 1936--John Kelly--**Gentleman from Louisiana.** 1942--Ward Bond--**Gentleman Jim;** John Kelley--**My Gal Sal;** 1945--Greg McClure--**The Great John L.**

2040 Jim Thorpe

This Sac and Fox Indian, whose life is a narrative of triumph and tragedy, was selected America's top athlete of the first half of the 20th century.

1951--Burt Lancaster--**Jim Thorpe, All American.**

2041 Jack Twyman

The Basketball Hall of Famer scored 15,840 points during his 11-year National Basketball Association career. But, more importantly, he was the guardian for his stricken Cincinnati teammate Maurice Stokes.

1973--Bo Swenson--**Maurie** (aka **Big Mo).**

2042 Tony Zale

His three middleweight championship bouts with Rocky Graziano were classic bloodbaths. He won two of the three before losing his title to Marcel Cerdan.

1956--Courtland Shepard--**Somebody Up There Likes Me.**

Selected Bibliography

In researching this book, we have tried whenever possible to use the most primary sources--the films themselves. Particularly in the case of older films, this is sometimes impossible as prints of these movies often no longer exist. We also obtained much information from people involved in the makings of the films. Many of these sources are listed in the acknowledgments.

We next sought out original studio material on the films but found that they, like many of the existing research materials, contain discrepancies and aren't 100 percent reliable as to accuracy.

In the 20th Century-Fox presskit for **Oxford Blues**, for example, it's stated the finale race is between Oxford and Cambridge, when anyone who saw the film knows Harvard is the opponent. It also states that it's an eight-man race while in reality it's a two-man boat race.

In addition, some of the anecdotes in the pressnotes on certain films must be taken with a grain of salt as they might be tales told by a publicist, signifying nothing.

The newspapers, magazines, books and other publications listed below are just a fraction of the research materials we found helpful and which the reader might want to look up for further research.

We'd like to take this opportunity to thank all those persons who lent us materials and films; in particular, one television station which prefers to remain anonymous which publicly aired certain films at our request.

Also, because a large portion of this book is devoted to baseball and the people at the National Baseball Hall of Fame and Museum in Cooperstown, New York, were so cheerfully helpful to us, we are donating a copy to them for their permanent collection.

An Actor Guide to the Talkies, 1949-1964 By Richard Bertrand Dimmitt; The Scarecrow Press, 1967

An Actor Guide to the Talkies, 1965-1974 By Andrew A. Aros; The Scarecrow Press, 1977

The American Film Institute Catalog of Motion Pictures: Feature Films, 1961-1970; R.R. Bowker Co., 1976

The American Film Institute Catalog of Motion Pictures Produced in the United States: Feature Films 1921-1930, R.R. Bowker Co; 1971

The Baseball Encyclopedia; The Macmillan Co., 1969

Baseball's Hall of Fame By Robert Smith; Bantam Books, 1973

Big U: Universal in the Silent Days By I.G. Edmonds; A.S. Barnes & Co., 1977

The Big V By Anthony Slide; Scarecrow Press, 1976

Bound and Gagged By Kalton C. Lahue; Castle Books, 1968

Box Office Magazine

The British Film Catalogue, 1895-1970 By Denis Gifford; McGraw Hill Book Co., 1973

Le Cinema Francais, 1890-1962 By Georges Sadoul; Flammarion Books, 1962

Circulating Film Library Catalog: Museum of Modern Art
Continued Next Week By Kalton C. Lahue; University of Oklahoma Press, 1969
Cosmos, 1979, Media Guide (N.Y. Cosmos soccer team)
The Disney Films By Leonard Maltin; Crown Publishing, 1973
Dreams for Sale: The Rise and Fall of the Triangle Film Corporation By Kalton C. Lahue; A.S. Barnes & Co., 1971
Ealing Studios By Charles Barr; The Overlook Press, 1980
The Encyclopedia of Sports By Frank G. Menke; A.S. Barnes & Co., 1953
Famous People on Film By Carol A. Emmens; The Scarecrow Press, 1977
Film Daily, particularly its yearbooks, from 1924 up
The Film Encyclopedia By Ephraim Katz; Crowell Publishers, 1979
The Filmgoers Companion By Leslie Halliwell; Hill and Wang, 1970
Film-Index, 1929 By Einar Lauritzen and Gunnar Lundquist; Tryckeri and Tidningsaktiebolaget, 1973
The Films of Robert Rossen By Alan Casty; Museum of Modern Art, 1969
The Films of Sherlock Holmes By Chris Steinbrunner and Norman Michaels; Citadel Press, 1978
The Films of Twentieth Century-Fox By Tony Thomas and Aubrey Solomon, Citadel Press, 1979
Finnish Cinema By Peter Cowie; A.S. Barnes & Co.; 1976
Forever Ealing By George Perry; Pavilion Books, 1981
47th Annual Heisman Trophy Memorial Award Ceremonies Program; Downtown Athletic Club Journal, 1981
Frame By Frame: A Black Filmography By Phyllis R. Klotman, Indiana University Press, 1979
French Cinema Since 1946, Volumes I and II By Roy Armes; A.S. Barnes & Co., 1976
The Great Movie Series By James Robert Parish; A.S. Barnes & Co., 1971
A Guide to World Championship Tennis and Media Information By Tod Humphries, WCT, 1980
Guinness Book of Olympic Records By Norris McWhirter; Bantam Books, 1979
Hail, Columbia By Rochelle Larkin; Arlington House, 1975
Harold Lloyd: The King of Daredevil Comedy By Adam Reilly; Collier Books, 1977
Hemingway and Film By Gene D. Phillips; Frederick Ungar Publishing Co., 1980
Holmes of the Movies By David Stuart Davies; Bramhall House, 1978
The House of Horror: The Complete Story of Hammer Films, Edited by Allen Eyles, Robert Atkinson and Nicholas Fry; Lorrimer Publishing Ltd., 1981
Index to Motion Pictures Reviewed by Variety, 1907-1980, By Max Joseph Alvarez; Scarecrow Press, 1982
International Film Guide—various years; A.S. Barnes & Co.
The Jersey Journal
Kubrick: Inside a Film Artist's Maze By Thomas Allen Nelson; Indiana University Press, 1982
Leni Riefenstahl: The Fallen Film Goddess By Glenn B. Infield; Thomas Y. Crowell Co., 1976
Le Livre D'Or du Cinema, 1983-1984, By Michel Lebrun; Solar 1983
Los Angeles Lakers, 1983-1984, Press Guide
Los Angeles Times
Make It Again, Sam: A Survey of Movie Remakes By Michael B. Druxman; A.S. Barnes & Co., 1975
Marvelous Melies By Paul Hammond; Gordon Fraser, 1974

Mexican Cinema: Reflections of a Society, 1896-1980, By Carl J. Mora; University of California Press, 1982
Modern Screen--various issues
The Most Important Art: Soviet and Eastern European Film After 1945 By Mira Liehm and Antonin J. Liehm; University of California Press, 1977
Motion Picture and Television--various issues
Motion Picture Daily
Motion Picture Herald
Motion Pictures from the Library of Congress Paper Print Collection, 1894-1912, By Kemp R. Niver; University of California Press, 1967
Movie Life--various issues
Movie Mirror--various issues
Movie Stars Parade--various issues
Movie Story--various issues
Movieland--various issues
Movies from the Mansion: A History of Pinewood Studios By George Perry; Elm Tree Books, 1982
Movies on TV By Steven H. Schuer; Bantam Books, various editions
Moving Picture Stories
NASCAR Official Record Book and Press Guide, 1984
National Film Archives Catalog, The British Film Institute, 1966
National Football League Encyclopedia By Roger Treat; 1966
National Football League Record Manual, 1983, Dell Distributing
Newark Star-Ledger
New York Times
Our Gang: The Life and Times of the Little Rascals By Leonard Matin and Richard W. Bann; Crown Publishing Inc., 1977
Philadelphia Eagles 1977 Media Guide
Photoplay--various issues
Republic Studios: Between Poverty Row and the Majors By Richard Maurice Hurst; Scarecrow Press, 1979
The Ring 1980 Record Book; The Ring Publishing Corp., 1980
Ronald Reagan: The Hollywood Years By Tony Thomas; Citadel Press, 1980
Saturday Afternoon at the Bijou By David Zinman; Arlington House, 1973
Screen--various issues
Screen Guide--various issues
Screen Romances--various issues
Screen Stories--various issues
Screen World By John Willis; Crown Publishing Inc., various editions
Screenland--various issues
Selected Short Subjects By Leonard Maltin; Da Capo, 1972
The Sporting News NBA Guide; The Sporting News Publishing Co., 1984
The Sporting News NBA Register; The Sporting News Publishing Co., 1984
The Strongman By Joe Bonomo; Bonomo Studios Inc., 1978
Tarzan of the Movies By Gabe Essoe; Citadel Press, 1968
The Triangle--various issues
To Be Continued By Ken Weiss and Ed Goodgold; Bonanza Books, 1972
TV Movies By Leonard Maltin; Signet Books, various editions
Ty Cobb By John D. McCallum; Praeger Publishers, 1975
Universal Pictures By Michael G. Fitzgerald; Arlington House, 1977
The Vanishing Legion: A History of Mascot Pictures, 1927-1935, by Jon Tuska; McFarland & Co. Inc., 1982
Variety
Washington Post
Washington Redskins 1984 Press Guide

Whatever Became Of . . . ? By Richard Lamparski; Ace Books, various editions

Whatever Happened to Gorgeous George? By Joe Jares; Prentice-Hall, 1974

Who Was Who on Screen, Second Edition By Evelyn Mack Truitt; R.R. Bowker Co., 1977

General Index

Entry numbers in *italics* refer to the biographies in the Athletes in Films chapter. **Boldface** entries refer to page numbers in the chapter introductions. All other numbers refer to the entry numbers for specific films.

Title Index

We have included here all films mentioned in this book, including their alternate titles, except those mentioned in the Athletes in Films chapter so as to keep this index exclusively for sports and sports-related films.

Entry numbers in **boldface** refer to the page numbers in the chapter introductions. All other numbers refer to entry numbers.